DISPENSATIONALISM
tomorrow & beyond
a theological collection in honor of Charles C. Ryrie

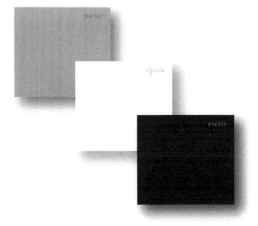

David E. Olander
S. Jeff Heslop
Gary E. Gilley
John A. Tucker
John C. Whitcomb
Jerry Hullinger
Kevin D. Zuber
Robert L. Thomas
Christopher Cone
Paul N. Benware
David Criswell
John F. Hart
Charles H. Ray
Michael Stallard
Ron J. Bigalke Jr
Arnold G. Fruchtenbaum
&
Charles C. Ryrie

Christopher Cone, General Editor

Dispensationalism Tomorrow & Beyond:
A Theological Collection in Honor of Charles C. Ryrie
©2008 Christopher Cone

Published by Tyndale Seminary Press
Ft. Worth, TX

ISBN – 0-9814791-0-3
ISBN13 – 978-0-9814791-0-1

All Scripture quotations, except those noted otherwise are from the New American Standard Bible, ©1960,1962,1963,1968,1971,1972,1973,1975, and 1977 by the Lockman Foundation.

"Dispensationalism, then, claims to be a help in supplying the answer to the need for Biblical distinction, in offering a satisfying philosophy of history, and in employing a consistently normal principle of interpretation. These are basic areas in proper understanding of the Bible. If dispensationalism has the answers, then it is the most helpful tool in Biblical interpretation. If not, it ought to be discarded as worthless."

- Charles C. Ryrie
Dispensationalism Today, 1965, page 21

Table of Contents

Preface

Lewis Sperry Chafer once described a spiritual Christian as "an exhorter both by precept and example".[1] Such an exhorter, though, is a rare commodity. Thus it is a true privilege and a blessing to encounter one who demonstrates maturity in these areas. And while we of course esteem no man as bearing the perfection that is belonging only to our Lord, we are encouraged to be examples (1 Tim 4:12; Titus 2:7) and even to imitate those who are exemplary (1 Thes. 2:14;1 Cor. 11:1).

Charles C. Ryrie is one such example.

With his 1957 article (which is reprinted here as Chapter 1) on *The Necessity of Dispensationalism* (and numerous subsequent works) Dr. Ryrie has been (and continues to be) tremendously influential in the grounding of dispensational theology in at least several very important ways: (1) by attending to vital matters of definition and realizing the importance of precision and clarification to ensure no misunderstanding, (2) by defining and emphasizing the threefold *sine qua non* of distinction between Israel and the church, literal interpretation, and doxological purpose, (3) by avoiding the temptation to 'specialize' in any particular area of the Bible and instead recognizing (and teaching) that the whole counsel of God requires the attention of every Bible student (and teacher), and (4) recognizing the value of balance – he says, "There is nothing more devastating to the practice of spiritual living than an imbalance."[2] Note his characteristic emphasis on spiritual living. These theological contributions are paramount, and are vitally connected, as they should be, with living the right kind of life.

For many years Dr. Ryrie has demonstrated in his writing and teaching an unshakable commitment to the word of God, always approaching the Biblical text with a marked humility and respect for God's revelation, handling it faithfully and honestly. In an arena where believers so often cut one another down as if at war with each other, Dr. Ryrie has illustrated for us how to contend for the faith without being contentious. His attitude is epitomized in a plea to the readers of his 1965 publication, *Dispensationalism Today*:

---

[1] Lewis Sperry Chafer, *He That Is Spiritual* (Grand Rapids, MI: Zondervan, 1967), Original Author's Preface.

[2] Charles C. Ryrie, Balancing the Christian Life (Chicago, IL: Moody Press, 1969), 9.

> Every Christian has a right to his convictions about Biblical truth, but as long as we are in earthly bodies, none of us can be infallible. No one in any age has all the truth – not the apostolic fathers, nor the Reformers, nor dispensationalists, nor nondispensationalists. Nevertheless, we should hold with conviction the truth as we believe God has given us the understanding of it. False humility (which is often manifest these days in "broadmindedness" and "rethinking") does not evince due credit to the teaching ministry of the Holy Spirit. A cocksure attitude, on the other hand, does not give credence to the limitations and fallibility of the human mind. The balance between these extremes is well expressed in Paul's words: "Speaking the truth in love" (Eph. 4;15).[3]

This call to speak the truth in love is of course universal for all believers, and is perhaps especially appropriate for all who would seek to teach, write, or otherwise communicate Biblical doctrine. Should there be any doubt as to how to fulfill this call, Dr. Ryrie's writings serve as a tremendous primer.

If these contributions were not significant enough, there are the scores of Bible students and teachers personally impacted by Dr. Ryrie – every contributor to this book has been profoundly touched by Dr. Ryrie and his ministry, and the writers here speak for many more when we collectively voice our appreciation for him.

So, dear Dr. Ryrie, thank you so much for your service to our Lord, for teaching God's word with such clarity, for being so generous with your time and fellowship, for being such an encouragement, for being an exhorter both by precept and example. We love you, and hope you will enjoy this tiny morsel of the fruit of your labors. Additionally, we hope that the writings presented here will reflect a positive assertion of dispensational theology and an unabashed yet loving interaction with controversies which are at present so impacting it. We hope to, as you have exhorted us and provided example, speak the truth in love.

Christopher Cone

---

[3] Charles C. Ryrie, *Dispensationalism Today* (Chicago, IL: Moody Press, 1965), 206-207.

Contributors

Charles C. Ryrie, Th.D, Ph.D, Litt.D
Former President & Distinguished Professor of Theology,
Philadelphia College of the Bible
Professor Emeritus, Dallas Theological Seminary
Author of many books, including:
> *The Ryrie Study Bible*
> *Dispensationalism Today*
> *Dispensationalism*
> *Basic Theology*
> *Balancing the Christian Life*
> *So Great Salvation*

David E. Olander, Th.D, Ph.D
Professor of Biblical Languages and Theology, Tyndale Theological Seminary

Arnold Fruchtenbaum, Ph.D
Founder, Ariel Ministries
Author of many books, including:
> *Israelology: The Missing Link in Systematic Theology*
> *The Footsteps of the Messiah*
> *The Messianic Jewish Epistles*
> *Judges and Ruth*
> *Messianic Christology*
> *Hebrew Christianity: Its Theology, History, and Philosophy*

S. Jeff Heslop, Th.D
Dean, Tyndale Theological Seminary Learning Center, Mason, OH.

John C. Whitcomb, Th.D
President, John Whitcomb Ministries, Inc.
Founder, Christian Workman School of Theology
Author:
> *The Genesis Flood (Co-Author)*
> *The World That Perished: An Introduction to Biblical Catastrophism*
> *The Early Earth: An Introduction to Biblical Creationism*
> *The Bible and Astronomy*
> *Our Created Moon (Co-Author)*

Jerry Hullinger, Th.D
Professor, Pensacola Bible College

Kevin D. Zuber, Ph.D
Professor of Theology, Moody Bible Institute

Robert L. Thomas, Th.D
Professor of New Testament, Master's Seminary
Author/Editor of many books, including :
>   *Evangelical Hermeneutics: The New Versus the Old*
>   *A Harmony of the Gospels (Co-Editor)*
>   *Revelation 1-7: An Exegetical Commentary*
>   *Revelation 8-22: An Exegetical Commentary*
>   *New American Standard Exhaustive Concordance (General Editor)*

Christopher Cone, Th.D, Ph.D
President
Professor of Bible & Theology, Tyndale Theological Seminary
Author:
>   *The Promises of God: A Bible Survey*
>   *Prolegomena: Introductory Notes on Bible Study & Theological Method*

Paul N. Benware, Th.D
Professor, School of Biblical Studies, Philadelphia Biblical University
Author:
>   *Survey of the Old Testament*
>   *Survey of the New Testament*
>   *Understanding End Times Prophecy*
>   *Leaders in the Making*
>   *The Gospel of Luke*
>   *Ambassadors of Armstrongism*
>   *Commentary on Daniel*

John F. Hart, Th.D
Professor of Bible, Moody Bible Institute

David Criswell, Th.D
Editor-in- Chief, *The Evangelical Standard.*
Author:
>   *Controversies in Revelation: A Comparative Analysis of Premillennial*
>   *Interpretation*
>   *Controversies in the Prophets: Isaiah through Malachi*

Charles H. Ray, Th.D
Dean of Online Studies
Professor of Bible & Theology, Tyndale Theological Seminary

Ron J. Bigalke Jr., Ph.D
Dean, Tyndale Theological Seminary Learning Center, Savannah, GA.
Associate Editor, *Journal of Dispensational Theology*
Director, Eternal Ministries, Inc.
Author:
> *Progressive Dispensationalism*
> *Revelation Hoofbeats*
> *The Genesis Factor: Myths and Realities*
> *One World: Economy, Government, & Religion in the Last Days*

John Adams Tucker, D.Min
Ph.D Candidate, Tyndale Theological Seminary

Michael Stallard, Ph.D
Professor of Systematic Theology
Director, Ph.D Studies, Baptist Bible Seminary, Clarks Summit, PA
Author:
> *The Early Twentieth Century Dispensationalism of Arno C. Gaebelein*

Gary E. Gilley, Th.D
Pastor, Southern View Chapel, Springfield, IL.
Author:
> *I Just Wanted More Land*
> *This Little Church Went to Market*
> *This Little Church Stayed Home*
> *Is That You Lord?*

"The essence of dispensationalism, then, is the distinction between Israel and the church. This grows out of the dispensationalist's consistent employment of normal or plain interpretation, and it reflects an understanding of the basic purpose of God in all His dealings with mankind as that of glorifying Himself through salvation and other purposes as well."

- Charles C. Ryrie

Dispensationalism Today, 1965, page 47

1

The Necessity of Dispensationalism[1]
Charles C. Ryrie

One of the evident features of the history of Christian doctrine is the fact that the church generally focused its discussions on one area of theology at a time. In our own day the area is eschatology, and discussions of eschatology are being heard in all groups. In conservative circles these discussions are raising questions in another field—dispensationalism. This is not to say that the liberals are unaware of the growing prominence being given to dispensationalism, but it is to affirm that evangelicals are having to give their attention increasingly to the dispensational question. This is shown by John Wick Bowman's pronouncement that the Scofield Bible because of its dispensational teaching "represents perhaps the most dangerous heresy currently to be found within Christian circles" ("The Bible and Modern Religions. II. Dispensationalism," *Interpretation*, 10:172, April, 1956).

Recent and current interest in eschatology is only one of the reasons for the increased interest in dispensationalism. One ventures to predict that if current discussions concerning the rapture question continue, posttribulationists will be forced to do more than just reiterate the usual arguments against pretribulationism, for they will of necessity have to reckon with the entire dispensational approach to the Scriptures. They will be forced to deal with that which they recognize—namely, that pretribulationism is "an essential element" in dispensationalism (George E. Ladd, *The Blessed Hope*, p. 37).

In addition, the rise of ultradispensationalism has focused increased attention on the whole question. The proponents of this view have propagated it widely and in doing so have accomplished at least two things. They have added to their own numbers, and they have done those of us who consider ourselves true dispensationalists the service of causing us to present more detail concerning our position in order that we may distinguish it from their teaching.

Too, those who embrace covenant theology have contributed and doubtless will continue to contribute to the discussion of dispensationalism. The many individuals and groups which follow the covenant theology

---

[1] Reprinted with permission from Charles C. Ryrie, The Necessity of Dispensationalism, in *Bibliotheca Sacra*, Vol. 114, No. 455, July 1957.

tradition will surely not stand by if discussions of the dispensational question increase in the coming days, and by that very participation the whole matter will be brought into more prominence. Therefore, because of the increasing interest in eschatology and especially in pretribulationism, because of the aggressiveness of the ultradispensationalists, and because of the ever-present protagonists of covenant theology, one can scarcely agree with the idea that "the trend today is away from dispensationalism—away from the Scofield notes..." ("Is Evangelical Theology Changing?" *Christian Life*, 17:18, March, 1956).

This article is not an answer to anybody. Neither is it a redefining of the dispensational position, for the author does not feel it needs redefining—the able exponents of this and past generations have ably defined it. Rather, it is an attempt to state a basic approach to the concept of dispensationalism, for it is felt that if the features which make up this approach are basic enough, then the concept to which they lead will have to be deemed necessary or at least be given considered attention.

The Necessity of Biblical Distinctions

Though the statement is bold, it may be stated without fear of controversy that there is no interpreter of the Bible who does not recognize the need for certain basic distinctions in the Scriptures. The theological liberal, no matter how much he speaks of the Judaistic background of Christianity, recognizes that Christianity is nevertheless a different thing from Judaism. There may be few or many features of Judaism which in his mind carry over into Christianity, but still the message of Jesus was something new. Therefore, the material of the Old Testament is distinguished from that of the New.

The covenant theologian for all his opposition to dispensationalism also makes certain rather important distinctions. In fairness, it must be said that his dispensational distinctions are viewed as related to the unifying and underlying covenant of grace. Nevertheless, within his concept of this covenant he does make some very basic distinctions. Berkhof will serve as an example (*Systematic Theology*, pp. 293-301). After rejecting the usual dispensational scheme of Biblical distinctions, he enumerates his own scheme of dispensations or administrations, reducing the number to two—the Old Testament dispensation and the New Testament dispensation. However, within the Old Testament dispensation Berkhof lists four subdivisions which, although he terms them "stages in the revelation of the covenant of grace," are distinguishable enough to be listed. In reality, then, he finds these four plus the one New Testament dispensation or five periods of differing administrations of God. Thus the covenant theologian finds Biblical distinctions a necessary part of his theology.

The dispensationalist finds his answer to the need for distinctions in his dispensational scheme. The word *dispensation* (oikonomia) is a Scriptural term and is found in Luke 16:2–4; 1 Corinthians 9:17; Ephesians 1:10; 3:2, 9 ; Colossians 1:25; and 1 Timothy 1:4. It simply means an administration or arrangement. Now the dispensationalist uses the word theologically as a title for the distinctive administrations of God throughout the entire Bible. For instance, under Moses God administered the world in a distinctive way; therefore, he calls that *administration* (not *period* necessarily) the Mosaic dispensation. To say that it is not valid to use the word this way because the Bible never uses it in specific connection with certain of the dispensationalists' dispensations is of no consequence. Do we not use the word *atonement* of the work of Christ on the cross even though it is never used that way in the Bible? Certainly freedom must be granted to use a term theologically which may not be used in that way Biblically as long as the theological use is not un-Biblical.

Thus it is clear that all interpreters feel the need for distinctions. Obviously this does not prove that the dispensationalists' distinctions are the correct ones, but it demonstrates that the concept of the necessity of distinctions is very basic to the proper interpretation of the Scriptures, and it shows that in a certain sense every Christian is a dispensationalist. Chafer correctly observed that "any person is a dispensationalist who trusts the blood of Christ rather than bringing an animal sacrifice" and "any person is a dispensationalist who observes the first day of the week rather than the seventh" (Lewis Sperry Chafer, *Dispensationalism*, p. 9). Therefore, dispensationalism is based on a valid and basic approach to the Scriptures in the necessity for Biblical distinctions.

The Necessity of a Philosophy of History

The Scriptures per se are not a philosophy of history but they contain one. It is true that the Bible deals with ideas, but with ideas that are interpretations of historical events. This interpretation of the meaning of historical events is the task of theology, and it is a task that is not without its problems. The chief problem is that both covenant and dispensational theology claim to represent the true philosophy of history as contained in the Scriptures. The problem is further complicated by the fact that if a philosophy of history is defined as "a systematic interpretation of universal history in accordance with a principle by which historical events and successions are unified and directed toward ultimate meaning" (Karl Lowith, *Meaning in History*, p. 1), then in a certain sense both systems of theology meet the basic requirements of the definition. However, the way in which the two systems meet these requirements proves that dispensationalism alone is the valid system. Notice that the definition centers in three things: (1) the recognition of "historical events and successions" or a proper concept of the progress of revelation; (2) the unifying principle; and (3) the ultimate goal of history. Let us examine both systems in relation to these three features.

Concerning the goal of history, dispensationalists find it in the establishment of the millennial kingdom on earth while the covenant theologian regards it as the eternal state. This is not to say that dispensationalists minimize the glory of the eternal state, but it is to insist that the display of the glory of the God who is sovereign in human history must be seen in the present heavens and earth as well as in the new heavens and earth. This view of the realization of the goal of history within time is both optimistic and in accord with the requirements of the definition. The covenant view, which sees the course of history continuing the present struggle between good and evil until terminated by the beginning of eternity, obviously does not have any goal within temporal history and is therefore pessimistic. McClain points up this contrast very clearly when he says of the covenant theology: "According to this view, both good and evil continue in their development side by side through human history. Then will come catastrophe and the crisis of divine judgment, not for the purpose of setting up of a divine kingdom in history, but after the close of history…. Thus history becomes the preparatory 'vestibule' of eternity…. It is a narrow corridor, cramped and dark, a kind of 'waiting room,' leading nowhere *within* the historical process, but only fit to be abandoned at last for an ideal existence on another plane. Such a view of history seems unduly pessimistic, in the light of Biblical revelation" (Alva J. McClain, "A Premillennial Philosophy of History," *Bibliotheca Sacra*, 113:113–14, April-June, 1956). Thus in relation to goal in a proper philosophy of history only dispensationalism with its consummating dispensation of the millennium offers a satisfactory system.

A second requirement of a philosophy of history is a proper unifying principle. In covenant theology the principle is the covenant of grace. This is the covenant which it is alleged the Lord made with man after the fall in which He offered salvation through Jesus Christ. In short, the covenant of grace is God's plan of salvation, and therefore the unifying principle of covenant theology is soteriological. In dispensationalism the principle is theological or perhaps better eschatological, for the differing dispensations reveal the glory of God as He shows off His character in the differing stewardships culminating in history with the millennial glory. If the goal of history is the earthly millennium, and if the glory of God will be manifested then in the personal presence of Christ in a way hitherto unknown, then the unifying principle of dispensationalism may be said to be eschatological (if viewed from the goal toward which we are moving) or theological (if viewed from the self-revelation of God in every dispensation). Although the dispensationalist's principle is much broader and therefore less confining, it must be admitted that this alone does not prove it is the more valid one. We must also consider the third part of our definition of a philosophy of history.

Only dispensationalism does justice to the proper concept of the progress of revelation. Covenant theology does include in its system different modes of administration of the covenant of grace and, although these modes would give an appearance of an idea of progressiveness in revelation, in practice there is extreme rigidity in covenant theology. James Orr, himself a covenant theologian, criticizes the covenant system along this very line: "...it failed to seize the true idea of development, and by an artificial system of typology, and allegorizing interpretation, sought to read back practically the whole of the New Testament into the Old. But its most obvious defect was that, in using the idea of the Covenant as an exhaustive category, and attempting to force into it the whole material of theology, it created an artificial scheme which could only repel minds desirous of simple and natural notions" (James Orr, *The Progress of Dogma*,p. 303). Covenant theology, then, because of the rigidity of its unifying principle of the covenant of grace can never show within its system proper progress of revelation.

Dispensationalism, on the other hand, can and does give proper place to the idea of development. Under the various administrations of God different revelation was given to man, and that revelation was increasingly progressive in the scope of its content. Though similarities are present in various dispensations, they are part of a true development and not a result of employing the unifying principle of the covenant of grace. The particular manifestations of the will of God in each dispensation are given their full yet distinctive place in the progress of the revelation of God throughout the ages. Only dispensationalism can cause historical events and successions to be seen in their own light and not to be reflected in the artificial light of an overall covenant.

Therefore, a correct philosophy of history with its requirements of a proper goal, a proper unifying principle, and a proper concept of progress is best satisfied by the dispensational system. Like the approach of Biblical distinctions, the approach through the proper concept of the philosophy of history leads to dispensationalism.

The Necessity of Consistent Hermeneutics

On the problem of valid hermeneutical principles much has been written. In relation to the present discussion, the question relates to literal or allegorical interpretation, for if literalism is the valid hermeneutical principle then that is an approach to the Scriptures which if consistently applied can only lead to dispensational theology.

It is not within the scope of this article to rediscuss the entire matter of allegorical and literal interpretation. It must suffice to show that only dispensationalism consistently employs the principles of literal interpretation. Covenant theologians are well known for their stand on allegorical interpretation especially as it relates to the prophetic Word, and they are equally well known for their amillennialism which is only the natural outcome of allegorizing. Premillennialists who are not dispensationalists also have to depart from literal interpretation at certain points in their eschatology. For example, Ladd in order to add support to his posttribulational view is forced to regard the 144,000 of Revelation 7 as referring not to literal Israel but to spiritual Israel or the church (*op. cit.*, p. 126). Further, he cannot abide the dispensationalist's idea of the Jewish character of Matthew's Gospel (*ibid.*, pp. 133-34), but he nowhere explains, for instance, how he can interpret in any literal way our Lord's words of commission to the twelve recorded in Matthew 10:5–10. Anyone who attempts to interpret literally this commission which forbade the disciples to go to the Gentiles and the commission which commands the same group to go to the Gentiles (Matt 28:19–20) either gives up in confusion or resorts to spiritualizing one of the passages or recognizes a dispensational distinction. If literal interpretation is the only valid hermeneutical principle and if it is consistently applied it will cause one to be a dispensationalist. As basic as one believes literal interpretation to be, to that extent he will of necessity become a dispensationalist.

The Necessity of Proper Definition

The usually quoted definition of a dispensation is the one that appears in the notes of the *Scofield Reference Bible*: "A dispensation is a period of time during which man is tested in respect to obedience to some *specific* revelation of the will of God" (p. 5). The usual criticism leveled against this definition is that it is not true to the meaning of oikonomia since it says nothing about a stewardship and emphasizes the period of time aspect. The criticism may be somewhat valid, for a dispensation is primarily a stewardship, administration, or arrangement and not a period of time. Age and dispensation are not synonymous in meaning even though they may exactly coincide in history. A dispensation is basically the arrangement involved, not the time involved; therefore, a proper definition must emphasize this.

In addition, it is obvious that dispensationalists teach that at least certain features of certain dispensations overlap. Perhaps that idea would more accurately be expressed by saying that each dispensation builds on the preceding ones. Obviously, that means that similar or even the same principles which obtained during former ones are sometimes included in the succeeding one. If a dispensation is an arrangement or economy, then some details of the various arrangements will be the same. Thus, dispensations supersede each other in the sense of building on each other in line with the idea of progress of revelation and the philosophy of history which climaxes in an ultimate goal in time. Therefore, the ideas of dispensations ending, superseding, building, progressing, and having similar and different features must also be included in the definition.

In the light of the foregoing discussion, is it possible to formulate a proper definition of a dispensation? We suggest this one. A dispensation is a distinguishable economy in the outworking of God's purpose. If one were describing a dispensation, he would include other things such as the ideas of testing, failure, and judgment, but we are seeking a definition, not a description. The definition proposed, though brief and perhaps open to the criticism of oversimplification, seems sufficiently inclusive. In this theological use of the word *economy* the emphasis is put on the Biblical meaning of the word. Economy also suggests the fact that certain features of some dispensations may be similar. Although socialistic and capitalistic economies are quite different in their basic concepts, nevertheless similar functions of the economy are performed in both systems. Likewise, in the different economies of God's running of the affairs of this world certain features will be similar. However, the word *distinguishable* in the definition points out the fact that there are some features which pertain particularly to each dispensation and which mark it off as a different economy. The particular features will distinguish, though the distinguishable dispensation will not be dissimilar in all its particulars. Finally, the phrase *the outworking of God's purpose* in the definition reminds us that the viewpoint in dispensationalism is God's. These are economies instituted and brought to their purposeful conclusion by God. The distinguishable feature is put there by God, and the purpose is God's.

Using this definition in light of the above explanation, let us apply it first to the usual dispensational scheme and second to the problem of ultradispensationalism. It is not difficult to justify most of the usual seven dispensations on the basis of this definition. If one is a premillennialist, then the distinguishable economy of God in the millennium during which Christ is visibly present is easily recognized. This present dispensation whose principal, not exclusive, characteristic is grace also is easily justified by the definition. The same is apparent with the Mosaic dispensation of the law, and the point need not be labored. It is the time between the beginning of creation to the giving of the law that gives rise in some minds to the question of the validity of all the dispensations which are said to belong to that period. However, before the fall of man the arrangement was certainly distinguishably different from that after the fall. Already we have accounted for five dispensations: innocence, whatever name should be given to that which obtained after the fall and to the time of Moses, the law, grace, and the millennial kingdom. The very fact that it is difficult to find a suitable name to cover the entire economy from the fall to Moses ought to make one examine carefully the validity of trying to view that entire period as having only one dispensation operating during it. It should be apparent that up to the time of Abraham God's administration concerned all nations, whereas with Abraham He began to single out one nation, and in the singling out He made a very distinctive covenant with Abraham. Therefore, the distinguishable characteristic of God's dealing with Abraham in promise seems sufficient to delineate the dispensation of promise. The only question that remains is whether or not the dispensations of conscience and government are valid. Suppose there is only one dispensation during this period, what will it be called? If there are two, what are the distinguishing features that justify two?

The problem is complicated by the fact that the revelation of Scripture covering this long period is very brief, but from what is revealed we must seek an answer. It seems to this writer that there is sufficient warrant in God's new arrangement for human government in the time of Noah to distinguish a dispensation at that time (cf. Gen 9:6 with 4:15). If this be agreed with, then there are seven dispensations, and one must admit that the more one studies in the light of a basic definition the conclusion is that there are seven dispensations. It seems to be somewhat fashionable these days to avoid this conclusion or at least to minimize the earlier dispensations, but if one has a consistently workable definition and if one applies it throughout all history, then it seems hard not to conclude that there are seven.

But what of the ultradispensationalists who insist on dividing the present economy of grace? Is something distinguishably different being done since Paul that was not done from Pentecost to Paul? (It matters little for purposes of this discussion whether the ultradispensationalists' dispensation of grace or of the church begins in Acts 9, 13 , or 28 . The point is that a separate dispensation is made of the Jewish church and of the Pauline church.) What the ultradispensationalist fails to recognize is that the distinguishableness of a dispensation is related to what God is doing, not to what He reveals at the time. It is certainly true that within the scope of any dispensation there is progressive revelation, and in the present one it is obvious that not all of what God was going to do was revealed on the Day of Pentecost. These are economies of God, not of man, and we determine the limits of a dispensation not by what any one person within that dispensation understood but by what we may understand now from the completed revelation of the Word. Actually we today are in a better position to understand than the writers of the New Testament themselves. Ultradispensationalists fail to recognize the difference between the progress of doctrine as it was during the time of revelation and the representation of it in the writings of the Scripture. On this point Bernard has well observed that "there would be a difference between the actual course of some important enterprise—say of a military campaign, for instance—and the abbreviated narrative, the selected documents, and the well-considered arrangement, by which its conductor might make the plan and execution of it clear to others. In such a case the man who read would have a more perfect understanding of the mind of the actor and the author than the man who saw; he would have the whole course of things mapped out for him on the true principles of order" Thomas Dehany Bernard, *The Progress of Doctrine in the New Testament*, p. 35). The distinguishable feature of this economy is the formation of the church which is His body. This is the work of God; therefore, the question which decides the beginning of this dispensation is, When did God begin to do this? not, When did man understand it? Only by consulting the completed revelation can we understand that God began to do this work on the Day of Pentecost (Acts 1:5; 11:15–16 {Acts 11}; 1 Cor 12:13; Col 1:18), and therefore whether Peter and the others understood it then does not determine the beginning of the dispensation. The distinguishable feature of this dispensation is the formation of the church, and since that began at Pentecost there has been only one economy since that day. The ultradispensationalist can offer only the distinguishing feature of a Jewish church as over against a Gentile church which is the body of Christ, but such a distinction has no validity since there are Jews in today's

Gentile church and since the baptism of the Spirit first occurred at Pentecost. Thus the same economy has been operative since the Day of Pentecost.

We have tried to show in this brief discussion the validity of dispensational theology. It is based on the valid necessity for Biblical distinctions, it alone most fully satisfies a proper philosophy of history, only dispensationalism provides the key to consistent literalism, and properly defined it becomes the only valid system of Biblical interpretation.

"Consciously or unconsciously everyone operates on the basis of some presuppositions. The atheist who says there is no god has to believe that basic presupposition. And believing it, he then views the world. The agnostic not only affirms we cannot know but must believe that as basic to his entire outlook on the world and life. If we can know about the true God then his whole system is smashed. The theist believes there is a God. He mounts confirmatory evidence to support that belief, but basically he believes."

- Charles C. Ryrie
Basic Theology, 1982, page 16

2

Four Pillars of Dispensationalism[1]

Christopher Cone

Introduction

Admittedly and without apology, this approach begins with circular reasoning. Specifically, it begins with the defining circle of self-authenticating truths upon which the system is (and will be) developed. While this might cause some to discount the approach, it must be realized at the outset that at issue here is not one option beginning with circular reasoning as opposed to another option which does not. Any approach to worldview necessarily begins with an application of circular reasoning. That is, a worldview must by very definition begin with its own self-authenticating pronouncements of truth. Whether or not the pronouncements of the defining circle are valid is the question to consider, not whether such pronouncements are in fact made. The Biblical worldview claims exclusivity in its validity, never presenting an apologetic for its own validity, but rather assuming it as necessary and foundational truth. The positive assertions that the fear of the Lord is the beginning of knowledge (Prov. 1:7) and wisdom (Prov. 9:10) provide the epistemological base for any effective theological method. In this *presuppositional dispensational* approach, the Solomonic epistemology will be adhered to.

Pillar I: The Existence of the Biblical God

Definition

As first principal, the God of Scripture exists. Not merely as *a* deity, but as the One who has divinely disclosed Himself through means in which His exclusivity is decisively pronounced. If there is any other existent deity, then He cannot be one (at least not an honest one), for He consistently claims uniqueness in bearing this attribute (i.e., Deut 4:35; Is. 45:5; Joel 2:27; Rev. 22:13, etc.). He exists exclusively as the Truth in contradistinction to any and every other proposed foundational or fundamental truth.

He is holy, holy, holy. This is the most emphasized descriptive of God in Scripture (Is. 6:3; Rev. 4:8). The triplicate emphasis acknowledges the

---

[1] Reprinted with permission from Christopher Cone, Presuppositional Dispensationalism, in The Conservative Theological Journal, Vol. 10. No. 29, May/June 2006.

superlative nature of the holiness of God, and also seems to emphasize the perfections of the Trinity, identifying the holiness of the Three.

The holiness of God is not a singular attribute, but rather a descriptive of all that God is, in His character and His working. As it is the only descriptive used of Him three times consecutively in both Hebrew and Greek, and as such provides evidence of the centrality of holiness as God's self concept as His own superlative description of Himself[2]. We thus understand that by very nature God is infinitely and utterly incomprehensible (Is. 55:8-9).

Explanation
To begin the task of proving or demonstrating the existence of God, it must necessarily be assumed that there is (or needs be) an objective ground of empirical or rational neutrality whereby there abides a framework of characteristics or rules to which God must Himself submit in order to provide verification of His own existence. If there exists such a ground, then the author of that ground (who would be by necessity superior to God) or even the ground itself must then be the true deity, with God as subservient and bound to it. If such a mythical scenario were to exist, then His existence would be summarily dismissed. Hence the effort to prove God's existence proves faulty in motivation (there exists no epistemological reason to seek proof of the existence of God besides that of the primal desire to deny it) and in methodology (there exist no tools for accomplishing this task, and if the task is commenced it must utilize improper and inadequate tools). It is not insignificant that the Biblical writers provided no apologetic for the existence of God; rather His existence is stated, assumed, and necessary throughout the Biblical revelation as the reality-defining circle of foundational truth (Gen. 1:1; Ps. 14:1 etc.).

Therefore, the task here lies not in the realm of proving, demonstrating, or even defending His existence empirically or rationally, but rather in beginning with *the* Beginning: building upon the presupposition of His existence as the foundational and defining truth of reality. Belief in His existence is warranted due to His own self-authentication (in general,

---

[2] Dabney succinctly sums up the centrality of His holiness to any accurate description of Him: "Holiness, therefore, is to be regarded, not as a distinct attribute, but as the resultant of all God's moral attributes together. And as His justice, goodness, and truth are all predicated of Him as a Being of intellect and will, and would be wholly irrelevant to anything unintelligent and involuntary, so His holiness implies a reference to the same attributes. His moral attributes are the special crown; His intelligence and will are the brow that wears it. His holiness is the collective and consummate glory of His nature as an infinite, morally pure, active, and intelligent Spirit." [RL Dabney, *Systematic Theology*, (Pennsylvania: Banner of Truth Trust, 1985) 272-273].

special, and personal [in Christ] revelation), and the knowledge of His existence is inescapable.[3]

It (His existence) is the necessarily foundational truth of the defined epistemology (Biblical theism, per Prov. 1:7; 9:10), and as such is the necessary element of preunderstanding for further examination of the system.

In short: If the positive assertion of the existence of the Biblical God is an untrue assertion, then there could be no grounds for the legitimacy of the Biblically theistic system (or any system for that matter, for what would *any* absolute be based upon?[4]), but if the legitimacy of the system as a whole be logically warranted then belief in His existence likewise must be warranted, and therefore must be altogether acknowledged. Thus, belief in His existence is required as the basis for all human predication. If He exists, then He is the definer of epistemology. If He does not, then there can be no absolute definition of anything, let alone a coherent approach to epistemology. Van Til represents this truth cogently:

> All of the theistic arguments should really be taken together and reduced to the one argument of the possibility of human predication. Intelligent predication about anything with respect to nature or with respect to man were impossible unless God existed as the ultimate reference point of it all.[5]

How then to escape the charge of methodological fideism?

This approach *does not* advocate faith[6] as the sole or final source of dependence in the ascertaining of truth. Rather it simply finds its epistemological base defined in Scripture (i.e., the divine definition in Prov. 1:7; 9:10; and the human response in Rom. 1:18-21, etc.) and submits itself consistently to that definition, just as any epistemology must be founded upon principals of definition which must be maintained consistently

---

[3] Van Til communicates this skillfully: "Everything in the created universe therefore displays the fact that it is controlled by God, that it is what it is by virtue of the place that it occupies in the plan of God. The objective evidence for the existence of God and of the comprehensive governance of the world by God is therefore so plain that he who runs may read. Men cannot get away from this evidence. They see it round about them. They see it within them. Their own constitution so clearly evinces the facts of God's creation of them and control over them that there is no man who can possibly escape observing it. If he is self-conscious at all he is also God-conscious. No matter how men may try they cannot hide from themselves the fact of their own createdness. Whether men engage in inductive study with respect to the facts of nature about them or engage in analysis of their own self-consciousness they are always face to face with God their maker." [Cornelius Van Til, *The Defense of the Faith* (Philadelphia: Presbyterian & Reformed, 1955), 195].

[4] see Smith's denial of God based on his argument against the necessity of first cause [George Smith, *Atheism: The Case Against God* (Amherst, NY: Promotheus Books, 1989), 223-225].

[5] Van Til, *Introduction to Systematic Theology* (Philadelphia: Presbyterian & Reformed, 1974), 102.

[6] besides that of the necessary defining circle of faith as is required by any system.

throughout its application (again, a defining circle is found here, just as will necessarily be in any approach to epistemology).

The foundationalist approach that a proposition must be either fundamental to knowledge or based on evidence in order to be rationally justifiable[7] will generally conclude that the existence of God does not fit qualifications[8] as foundational truth, and therefore must be demonstrated by evidence. However, if the Biblical God exists, then He has defined that which is fundamental to knowledge – precisely His own reality, and thus the first pillar is not a fideistic pillar, but an epistemologically presuppositional pillar. Accusations of fideism here are unjustified.

Van Til has been criticized for developing a theology rather than an apologetic, and with this assessment I partially agree: The presuppositional apologetic (perhaps best stated by Van Til) is an epistemological beginning to theological method. It never presumes to make a defense of the existence of God. The Biblical mandate of *apologia* is in context of the believer's hope (1 Pet. 3:15) with specific reference to the gospel (Php. 1:7 & 16), but never in reference to the existence of Yahweh, God.

Importance to the Dispensational System

The existence of the Biblical God is the foundational truth whereby reality is measured. Any legitimate attempt at human predication and interpretation of the universe must be founded upon this premise, and as a result, the myth of an empirical neutral ground becomes apparent. Any theological method which depends on a non-existent empirical or rational neutrality is ultimately flawed at the base and thus wholly unfit for the epistemological task of theological development[9].

The logical necessity of belief in the existence of the Biblical God as the starting point for theological method is demanded by Kuyper as he identified faith in the existence of the object to be investigated as the *conditio sine qua non* of investigation.[10] One would not begin any course of study without a basic understanding of certain ground rules from presupposition. Without the positive assertion of the existence of the Biblical

---

[7] James Beckwith, "Philosophy and Belief in God: The Resurgence of Theism in Philosophical Circles", Masters Seminary Journal 2, (Spring 1991), 61-77.

[8] "Foundationalism is the view that a belief is a rational belief only if it is related in appropriate ways to a set of presuppositions which constitute the foundations of what we believe. It assumes, from the outset, that belief in God is not among these foundational propositions." [D.Z. Phillips, *Faith After Foundationalism* (London: Routledge, 1988), 3].

[9] Historically, dispensationalism, while not positively asserting the neutral middle ground, has seemingly done little to positively deny it. As a result, the system faces increasing epistemological challenges, particularly related to hermeneutic theory.

[10] Abraham Kuyper, *Principles of Sacred Theology* (Grand Rapids: Baker Book, 1980), 48.

God as the primal foundational truth, what are the basic ground rules in theological method? And who determines them? An approach so subjective as to operate from any other starting point than that of God's reality would hardly be efficacious for producing a legitimate result.

Pillar II: Divine & Authoritative Self-Disclosure

Definition
God has divinely and authoritatively disclosed Himself, for the purpose of His own glorification[11], via creation of and action in history (*general revelation*), by communication through language (*special revelation*), and by sent representation (*personal revelation*).

Explanation
God continuously makes Himself known[12] in *general (natural) revelation* (Acts 14:14-17) divinely by [1] the initial creative work itself (Is. 40), [2] by other marvelous divine activities using that which has been created (Ex. 15:1-21), and [3] within the creation itself (Ps. 19:1-6; Rom. 1:20).

Solomonic epistemology recognizes God's self-disclosure in this manner and the resultant imprint on the hearts of men: "He has made everything appropriate in its time. He has also set eternity in their heart, yet so that man will not find out the work which God has done from beginning even to end." (Ecc. 3:11). Pauline epistemology also recognizes the function of general revelation as resulting in the universal understanding of God's invisible attributes, His eternal power and divine nature (Rom. 1:18-20[13]).

With these divinely inspired epistemological descriptives Calvin agrees, citing man's innate sense of deity as stemming from an act of *implanting* on the part of God:

> There is within the human mind, and indeed by natural instinct, an awareness of divinity. This we take to be beyond controversy. To prevent anyone from taking

---

[11] Here is present the 3rd element of Ryrie's *sine qua non* of dispensationalism, namely that the underlying purpose of God in all of His creation is the glory of God [Charles Ryrie, *Dispensationalism Today* (Chicago: Moody, 1965), 46]. This is in full agreement with the Biblical record as evidenced in: Ps. 19:1; 21:5; 97:6; 106:47; 115:1; Is. 6:3; 43:7; 49:3; Jer. 33:9; Hab. 2:14; Jn. 17:1; 2 Cor. 4:15; 8:19; Eph. 1:6, 12, 14; Php. 1:11; 2:11; Rev. 4:11; 5:12-13; 15:4.
This is the doxological center: *The glorification of God as the understood purpose for all things.*

[12] B.B. Warfield, *The Works of Benjamin Warfield, Vol I: Revelation & Inspiration*, (Grand Rapids, MI: Baker, 2003), 5.

[13] For a thorough handling of the ramifications of Rom. 1:18-21 in presuppositional thought see David L. Turner, "Cornelius Van Til and Romans 1:18-21, A Study in the Epistemology of Presuppositional Apologetics" in Grace Theological Journal, Vol 2 *GTJ* 2:1 (Spr 81): 45—81.

refuge in the pretense of ignorance, God has implanted in all men a certain understanding of His divine majesty.[14]

Van Til also acknowledges the efficacy of general revelation to the end that natural man knows that he is the creature of God, knows that he is responsible to God, and knows that he should live to the glory of God.[15]

One accomplishment then of general revelation is man's inescapable awareness of God, as impressed upon him by God[16], resulting in man's awareness of man's responsibility to God. Yet despite the profundity and efficacy of general revelation, it possesses intrinsic limitation in that it is sufficient to provide only enough revelation of God to present every man without excuse (Rom. 1:20). It is intentionally incomplete and ineffective[17] for the task of presenting the content necessary for application of grace resulting in regeneration. This is no inherent flaw, but rather a designed feature facilitating the need for and provision of further revelation, thus representing the first processive step in the execution of God's methodology for self-disclosure.

Following *general revelation*, God also has revealed Himself (in non-continuous fashion[18]), in many portions and in many ways (Heb. 1:1), through men moved by the Holy Spirit who spoke from God (2 Pet. 1:21), in *special revelation* by the cumulative progress of God-breathed[19] (2 Tim. 3:16) Scripture. This Scripture is inerrant (as the word of truth, 2 Tim. 2:15) in its original text and as such is necessarily authoritative for all aspects of life[20].

God's chosen vehicle for this authoritative special revelation was language. God used language to communicate with Himself before man was created. He blessed creation (Gen. 1:22), thereby using language to reveal Himself to creation. He gave imperatives (1:24, etc.), and finally He communicated with man. Human language does not have human origin, but rather originates with God, and for His purposes. The whole earth spoke His language (11:1) until He confused the language (11:9). This basic argument for the origin of language is central to the issue of authority, relating to

---

[14] John Calvin, *Institutes* (Philadelphia: Westminster, 1940), 43.

[15] Van Til, *The Defense of the Faith*, 111.

[16] W.G.T. Shedd, *Dogmatic Theology, Vol. 1* (Nashville, Thomas Nelson, 1980), 63.

[17] Warfield, *The Works of Benjamin Warfield, Vol I: Revelation & Inspiration*, 7.

[18] *non-continuous* here meaning that at a certain point (that point identified in 1 Cor. 13:10, in this writer's estimation), His special revelation was complete, and that beyond that point He has not added to it or altered it, nor presently does He add to it or alter it, nor will He ever add to it or alter it.

[19] It is vital here to understand clear definition: that the writings themselves were inspired, not the writers, rather the human authors were moved of God and spoke from the Holy Spirit, despite Turretin's assertion to the contrary.

[20] For further definition, see the nineteen articles of *The Chicago Statement on Biblical Inerrancy (1978)*, with which this writer agrees.

human origin, and ultimately to the authority of the revelation itself.[21] Due to the divine origin of human language, Lockhart's axiom stands: Language is a reliable medium of communication[22].

Insofar as God used language to communicate Himself to man it is evident that He intended His revelation to be cognitively understood by those to whom it was directed. The means of special revelation by way of language varied (as expressed in Heb. 1:1), but included theophanies, dreams and visions, direct interaction, miracles and signs, and prophets.[23] In each methodological approach, inarguably God sufficiently made Himself understood in the cognitive sense.

Special revelation functions as furthering the glorification of God, particularly in communication of the reconciliatory plan with stated impact of restoring the soul, and bringing wisdom, joy, and enlightenment (Ps. 19:7-8), and more precisely directed as [1] giving the unregenerate man wisdom leading to salvation (2 Tim. 3:15), and [2] giving the regenerate man adequacy and equipping for every good work (2 Tim 3:17). In short, God's revelation of this type makes possible the *gnosis* necessary for positional relationship with Him – the knowing unto salvation[24], and provides the hortatory means whereby one can properly walk in a manner worthy of that positional relationship. The Old and New Testaments together provide the *special revelation* of God to the sinner, without which a true ethical interpretation of life is an impossible proposition.[25]

If the central purpose of *special revelation* is the glory of God, and the central theme of God within it is the reconciliatory plan, then the central Character is Jesus Christ. Thus, at the base *special revelation* points to God's *personal revelation* (Jn. 5:39) in His Son, Jesus Christ (Jn. 1:18; He. 1:1). The Christ, as the *personal revelation* of God, is both representative (Col. 1:13-18; Heb. 1:3) in that He represents God *as* God (being very God) to man, and hortatory (Jn. 1:18), in that He teaches the means of rightful positional

---

[21] Terry says: "The origin of human speech has been a fruitful theme of speculation and controversy. One's theory on the subject is likely to be governed by his theory of the origin of man. If we adopt the theory of evolution according to which man has been gradually developed, by some process of natural selection, from lower forms of animal life, we will very naturally conclude that language is a human invention, constructed by slow degrees to meet the necessities and conditions of life. If, on the other hand, we hold that man was first introduced on earth by a miraculous creation and was made at the beginning a perfect specimen of his kind, we will very naturally conclude that the beginnings of human language were of supernatural origin." [Milton Terry, *Biblical Hermeneutics* (Grand Rapids: Zondervan, 1976), 69].

[22] Clinton Lockhart, *Principles of Interpretation* (Delight, AR: Gospel Light, 1915), 20.

[23] Rene Pache, *The Inspiration & Authority of Scripture*, (Salem, WI: Sheffield, 1992), 20-22.

[24] John Calvin, *Institutes* 1:6:1.

[25] Cornelius Van Til, *Christian Theistic Ethics* (Philadelphia: Presbyterian & Reformed, 1974), 15.

relationship with God — namely belief *in* Him. He is therefore both the Revealed and the self-disclosing Revealer.

As self-disclosing, God naturally speaks with absolute authority. Therefore the Bible does not appeal to human reason in order to justify what it says. It comes to the human being with absolute authority.[26] It bears the mark of truthful self-authentication "as white and black things do of their color, or sweet and bitter things do of their taste"[27]. As authoritative, all elements of His revelation require human response, and man is held accountable for his response.

Importance to the Dispensational System
Of particular importance here is the characterization of God's revelation as *authoritative*. The mere presupposition of propositional revelation is necessitated by the first pillar. It is the *worthiness* of revelation that is at issue in the second pillar.

In all forms of revelation, that which God has communicated of Himself is done so effectively and accomplishing with certainty the result which He desires.

As authoritative, God's *special revelation* (as that which is profitable for teaching, reproof, correction, and training in righteousness) demands human submission, and is never subject to any authority on the interpreter's part (2 Pet. 1:20-21).

Pillar III: Incapacity of Man to Comprehend Revelation
Definition
Once man has a proper perspective and understanding of the reality of and the essentially communicated identity of God, he can begin to have a proper understanding of himself[28]. As man is a reflection of his Creator, he can not successfully grasp his own nature without having first ascertained that of his Creator, thus the understanding of natural man's incapacity to comprehend (to willfully receive as truth) even while cognitively understanding God's revelation must come after the first pillar recognition of the Biblical God, which of course presumes the necessity of and authority of Scripture, the foundation of the second pillar.

How then does man respond to divine revelation? How *can* he respond to divine revelation?

---

[26] Cornelius Van Til, *A Christian Theory of Knowledge* (Philipsburg, NJ: Presbyterian & Reformed, 1969), 15.
[27] John Calvin, *Institutes* 1:7:2.
[28] John Calvin, *Institutes* 1:1:2.

First, man has understood God's general revelation in the cognitive sense (Rom. 1:18-23). There is no doubt here that man's failure is not one of lacking understanding of the character of God, rather it is lacking the proper response to submission to Him *as* God, The cognitive fundamental of His existence has been resisted by the fallen human mind, and has been replaced by worship of the creation itself, the failure here not being a lack of understanding, but a lack of fearing Him *as* God, and thus man possesses ultimately an innate inability to arrive at wisdom.

Second, man has understood God's special revelation through Scripture in the cognitive sense. As revealed using the tools of language, Scripture is grammatically understood by the unbeliever (although with remarkably increasing difficulty), yet the unbeliever understands the self authenticated truths to be foolishness (1 Co. 2:14) and thus fails to respond positively[29], ultimately rejecting the claims of Scripture.

Third, man has understood God's personal revelation in Christ Jesus in the cognitive sense. Every man has been enlightened by the incarnation of Christ (Jn. 1:9) – Christ has explained the Father, and while understood cognitively[30], He is not received, for darkness is preferred by humanity over the light He provides (Jn. 3:19). Why then does man, while understanding cognitively the revelations of God, consistently fail to grasp them in the personal sense without His divine aid?

The Noetic Effects of Sin
The death promised in Gen. 2:17 was a result of disobedience to the command not to eat of the tree of the *knowledge* of good and evil. The epistemology of the human race was changed at the moment Adam ate, accompanied by the spiritual death – the separation of man from fellowship with God. This change in the mind was certainly not for the better, despite Satan's promise that the offenders would be like God, knowing good and evil. Satan was half right – as humanity from that point forward would indeed know evil, yet would be fully incapable of grasping good. Roughly 1500 years after Adam's sin, God described the thoughts of the human heart as 'only evil continually' (Gen. 6:5). Later, God characterizes the human heart as more deceitful above all else and desperately sick (Jer. 17:9). The Satanic promise of *knowing good* proved to be a deception - the following of which left humanity without the capacity to rightly think and appraise reality. The

---

[29] although there are varying levels of understanding with varying usages/misusages (Neh. 8:8; Mt. 21:45; Lk. 20:19; Php. 1:15-17; 1 Ti. 1:6-7; 2 Tim. 3:5-7; Jam. 1:22; Jude 4).
[30] note that His opponents clearly understood His claims, yet failed to acknowledge them as truth (Jn. 5:18,39-40; 8:57-59).

spiritually dead man was no longer able (as the pre-fall Adam surely seemed to be, Gen. 2:16, 19) to understand, appraise, or respond positively to God's revelation (1 Cor. 2:14). Although creation pours forth truth and revelation of God (Ps. 19), that truth, being understood and clearly seen in natural revelation (Rom. 1:19), has been suppressed (Rom. 1:18) by the human mind.

The noetic effects of sin result in more than simply the lack of ability to appraise spiritual things (1 Cor. 2:14-16), there is, in the human mind, a bent to suppress and reject the truth of God, as men love the darkness rather than light (Jn. 3:19). As a result, God has given the ungodly over to a depraved mind (Rom. 1:28), and further, the minds of the perishing are blinded by Satan (2 Cor. 4:3-4), continuing the contrast between the natural mind and the regenerated mind (Jam. 3:13-18). The freedom of neutrality that Satan seemed to offer was nothing of the sort; rather it proved to be bondage to faulty thinking, as none are disposed to fear God (Rom. 3:18), and since the fear of the Lord is the beginning of knowledge (Prov. 1:7), there are none who can claim a right epistemology without the intervening of God. The supplementing of human reason with divine revelation is not effective for bringing about the positional knowledge[31] of God. Rather, as Van Til notes, the fundamental conclusions of the fallen mind (as suppressing the truth of God) must be reversed.[32]

This is why the four pillars (the fourth yet to be identified), if hypothesized by the unbeliever, will not and cannot translate of their own accord to saving faith. The right hypothesizing of the four prerequisites by the unbeliever can only allow perhaps a mere glimpse of the unity and beauty of God's revelation, and therefore the unbeliever's need to receive it, and therefore an awareness of his need of Divine assistance in doing so. Van Til explains that the only way to see is to first believe:

> [T]his God cannot be proved to exist by any other method than the indirect one of presupposition. No proof for this God and for the truth of His revelation in Scripture can be offered by an appeal to anything in human experience that has not itself received its light of the sun for the purposes of seeing by turning to the darkness of a cave.[33]

So how then does the incapable natural man believe in order to see? How then does God communicate in special revelation His truth to the human mind? For who can rightly appraise His revelation? His ways are higher, yet

---

[31] *ginosko* as defining eternal life in Jn 17:3 in contradistinction to the *ginosko* of Rom. 1:21.

[32] Van Til, *An Introduction to Systematic Theology* , 15-16.

[33] Van Til, *The Defense of the Faith*, 109.

His word accomplishes what He desires, namely the revelation of Himself to those who are lower, despite their inherent limitations (Is. 55:8-9). How then does He overcome the effects of sin?

The Drawing Work of the Father
Based on His choosing (Rom. 9:15-16), the Father draws to Himself those whom He wishes (Jn. 6:44). None can come of personal volition, and even if any could, they would not, for there is none who seeks after Him (Rom. 3:12-18). He has chosen those whom He will draw, even before the foundations of the world (Eph. 1:4-6), and His drawing work is efficacious, ultimately resulting in the glorification of those whom He has chosen (Rom. 8:30). His drawing work seems best to be equated with His calling work (Gal. 1:4-6, 15), and refers to His active involvement in bringing man to Himself, creating in man the ability to respond positively to His revelation. Also note Mt. 16:15-17 – the truth regarding Jesus Christ is revealed by the Father – He is the Logos, the Word, the very Idea of God (Jn. 1:1-5) and Jesus Christ reveals the Father.

The Revealing Work of Christ
By virtue of His relationship with the Father, only Christ can adequately explain or reveal Him (Jn. 1:18). There is no other who possesses this divine relation (as only begotten God), and there is therefore no other to whom humanity can look for the explanation of God's character. Christ claimed to be the only access to the Father (Jn. 14:6). His revelation of the Father is both representative (as the very image of God, Col. 1:15; as the exact representation, Heb. 1:3), and hortatory (in teaching about the character of the Father, Jn. 16:12; 17:4-8). As the revelation of the Father, Christ is the primary topic of special revelation (Lk. 24:27, 45; Jn. 5:39). Without His revealing work, man would have no enlightenment (Jn. 1:9), no explanation of the Father (1:18).

The Illuminating Work of the Holy Spirit
The Spirit guides into all truth (Jn. 16:7-11, 13). He is given to the believer so that[34] the believer will have comprehension[35] of that given by God (1 Cor. 2:12). Chafer emphasizes on this point that "...in so far as He opens the understanding to the Scriptures, He unveils that which He has originated"[36].

---

[34] note the *hina* purpose clause of 1 Cor. 2:12.
[35] *eidomen* rather than *ginoskomen*, highlighting accurate *cognitive* rather than *experiential* understanding, reversing enslavement to the noetic effects of sin, providing the believer with the mind of Christ (1 Cor. 2:12-16).
[36] L S Chafer, *Systematic Theology, Vol 6* (Grand Rapids: Kregel, 1993), 37.

By virtue of the anointing of the Holy Spirit, which every believer possesses, He is the Divine Teacher of the believer (1 Jn. 2:27). Without Him the individual is simply 'worldly-minded (Ju. 19). Without His convicting work (Jn. 16:8) and divine enablement (1 Co. 12:3) the individual would be fully incapable to respond with repentance leading to the knowledge of the truth (2 Tim. 2:25).

Importance
John Whitcomb adroitly points out a significant flaw in certain apologetic approaches, saying,

> it must be admitted that Christians have too often been guilty of building systems of apologetics on *other foundations than the one set forth in Scripture*.[emphasis mine] Instead of giving the impression that men are eagerly waiting for proof that Christianity is true, the Bible exposes men's hearts as sealed shut against any and all finite pressures for conversion.[37]

Whitcomb's characterization is also applicable to theological method. If the apologetic foundations are flawed, then by virtue of the apologetic relation to theological method, the theological foundations are equally flawed.
Both methodologies – apologetic and theological – must find their base, form, and function in Scripture.

Man's incapacity can not be overcome by noetic achievement. The great chasm between man and God can only be bridged by the hand of God through His work both allowing and enabling man to respond in faith. Yet, as He revealed Himself with the tools of language, He does not work in counteraction to the basic principles of language (i.e., hermeneutic principles). Therefore, there is dual responsibility borne in developing proper apologetic and theological method: (1) God's part: He must reveal Himself to and illuminate those whom He has chosen to know Him (positionally), and (2) the believer's part: the believer must be (a.) dependant upon God's divine guidance and (b.) diligent to rightly utilize the tools of language in order to understand His revelation.

Pillar IV: Utilization of a Consistent Hermeneutic
Definition
Due to the fixity of special revelation (1 Cor. 12:10; Heb. 2:2-4), the use of language as the chosen vehicle, and the intrinsic authority of Scripture, the

---

[37] John C. Whitcomb, Contemporary Apologetics and Christian Faith, Part I, Biblioethica Sacra: 134,104

utilization of a consistent hermeneutic approach to Scripture is demanded.[38] Ryrie offers three evidences for the legitimacy of a consistent literal hermeneutic: (1) Biblical – based on the clearly literal fulfillments of prophesy historically fulfilled, (2) Philosophical – based on the purpose of language as given by God to communicate with man, and (3) Logical – based on the need for objective interpretation and the absence of objectivity which parallels the absence of a consistent literal hermeneutic.[39] Paul Tan likewise identifies the consistent use of the literal hermeneutic is good hermeneutics.[40] It is maintained here that not only is a consistent application of hermeneutic method *good* (as Ryrie and Tan suggest), but it is additionally both *possible*[41] and *necessary*.

Definition

The hermeneutic principles utilized must honor the authoritative revelation of God as such, and therefore cannot enthrone the interpreter, but must instead acknowledge the enthronement of the Revealer.

The task of the interpreter is that of rightly dividing the word of truth (2 Tim. 2:15). The interpreter is not a collaborator in the recording of the word of truth, and thus possesses no authority to eisegete his own understandings into the text or to modify in any way the words and meanings given by the Author.

If this be so, then an acknowledgment must be made of the hierarchy within the dual authorship of Scripture. Men were moved by the

---

[38] a significant point of departure in progressive dispensational thought is evident in disagreement with this assertion of need for a fixed hermeneutic: Blaising argues: ""Given the nature of biblical literature and a history of practicing historical-grammatical exegesis, hermeneutical developments are inevitable, including distinctions of various levels of hermeneutical certainty and the exploration and testing of multiple hermeneutical options. It is the actual practice of historical-grammatical exegesis by dispensational scholars that is proving this fixed-interpretation view of dispensationalism inadequate" [Craig Blaising, Developing Dispensationalism Part 2: Development of Dispensationalism by Contemporary Dispensationalists Bibliothica Sacra 145:579 (Jul 88) p. 258]. It seems to be upon this ground that Blaising (along with Bock) refer later to the complementary hermeneutic as a refinement of literal interpretation [Blaising & Bock, *Progressive Dispensationalism* (Grand Rapids: Baker Books, 1993), 52]. Blaising again suggests that although there have been many dispensational works which directly or indirectly imply a fixed or confessional method of interpreting Scripture, no "scholarly advocate of dispensationalism" has specifically made the claim as to the legitimacy of such. [Craig Blaising, Developing Dispensationalism Part 2: Development of Dispensationalism by Contemporary Dispensationalists *Bibliotheca Sacra* 145:579 (Jul 88) p. 256].

[39] Charles Ryrie, *Dispensationalism Today* (Chicago: Moody Press, 1965), 88-89.

[40] Paul Tan, *The Interpretation of Prophecy* (Dallas: Bible Communications, 1974), 21.

[41] Some, like coventalist John Gerstner, have suggested that it is impossible to maintain a consistently literal hermeneutic, particularly in approaching Biblical prophecy, and that dispensationalists in practice are inconsistent in their hermeneutic approach. [e.g., John Gerstner, *Wrongly Dividing The Word Of Truth* (Morgan, PA: Sole Deo Gloria, 2000), 93, 96, & 110]. While these accusations can be readily dealt with, they are valuable still in that they provide the interpreter pause and a reminder to avoid interpretive carelessness.

Spirit to write, but their words were God's words (2 Pet. 1:20-21). Undoubtedly, the words of Scripture themselves were inspired (2 Tim. 3:16), and not the men God used to pen them. It is therefore the interpreter's task to submit to the authority of the Revealer, and thus to accept, as they stand, the Scriptures' assertions as truth.

Proportionate to the level of authority the interpreter allows himself, there are three hermeneutic methodologies that bear consideration. The three approaches will here be referred to as accommodation, partial-accommodation, and non-accommodation.

The accommodation hermeneutic encompasses any hermeneutic methodology which fully accommodates the authority of the interpreter over revelation. In particular, full accommodation is characterized by one of two assertions (or both): [1] language is of human origin, and does not provide a vehicle conducive to absolute understanding of propositional revelation, and therefore the hermeneutic process, like human language, is subject to advancement and must evolve, and [2] the writings of Scripture are not themselves propositional revelation, but rather contain some degree of revelation, and it is the interpreter who must determine what is revelation, what is not, and must likewise delineate meaning either by experiential interpretation (enthroning the heart of the interpreter) or by rational interpretation (enthroning the mind of the interpreter). The accommodation hermeneutic can be consistently applied, yet, clearly it causes the second pillar to crumble. Therefore, in this approach the accommodation hermeneutic is not a viable option.

The mediating approach is the partial-accommodation hermeneutic, which uses a sometimes literal approach, but in practical application at other times elevates the authority of the interpreter either by (in extreme cases) outright distaste for conclusions arrived at through literal methodology, or indirectly and unintentionally by (in moderate cases) seeking to alleviate seeming discrepancy by methodology that lends itself more toward reliance on a deductive, eisegetical approach.

To differing degrees, and with differing motivation, each variant of the partial-accommodation hermeneutic wanders from the literal historical-grammatical system. Alexandrian allegorism, multilayer hermeneutic[42], phenomenological hermeneutic[43], double-revelation[44] ramifications, genre

---

[42] e.g., Origen's literal, moral, spiritual; Clement's natural, moral, mystical, prophetical; Middle Ages fourfold: literal, moral, allegorical, anagogical; Swedenburg's natural, spiritual, celestial; etc.

[43] as utilized by Calvin in his commentary on Genesis, particularly in 1:6 as he refers indirectly to the literal hermeneutic here as lacking 'common sense' and that Scripture here only deals with the 'visible appearance of the world' and that no truths pertaining to astronomy are therein presented.

override, and canonical process/ complementary [45] are a few notable nuances of partial-accommodation hermeneutical method. Each of these approaches to some degree or another enthrones the interpreter in issues where clarity of interpretation is seemingly difficult, and thus results (often unintentionally) in an unwarranted collaboration of interpreter with writer in the revelatory process. This type of collaboration violates the Author's divine right of singular authority over His revelation. Partial-accommodation approaches are inconsistent both in method and in practical submission to divine revelatory authority due to varying levels of interpreter authority. Partial-accommodation violates the fourth pillar (due to inconsistency) and sometimes crushes the second (due to occasional enthroning of the interpreter); therefore it is not a viable option.

The non-accommodation hermeneutic makes no room for the enthroning of the interpreter. Rather it squarely and consistently requires in theory the submission of the interpreter to the authoritative revelation and requires in practice an inductive and exegetical application, pulling out of the text the fixed and singular meaning placed there by the Divine Author. Only the literal grammatical historical method consistently acknowledges fixity, singularity, and authority of revelation. The non-accommodation approach is the only one of the three options that does not infringe upon the second pillar, and therefore (in this approach) it is the only viable option.

Importance

The conclusions of the literal method are soundly dispensational-premillennial. Even opponents of dispensational conclusions readily admit them as necessary results of the literal methodology. Berkhof argues against the literal method in such cases of difference only because its conclusions are "entirely untenable"[46] in his estimation. He further states that literalism results in "all kinds of absurdities"[47], based upon conclusions (with straw-men added) he cares not to accept. Gerstner admits that "on points where we differ, there is a tendency for the dispensationalists to be literalistic where the non-dispensationalist tends to interpret the Bible figuratively".[48] The literal approach is less concerned with conclusions and more concerned with a hermeneutic method that submits to the revelatory authority, yet the

---

[44] as identified and critiqued by John C. Whitcomb, Jr. in Biblical Inspiration and the Double-Revelation Theory, *Grace Theological Journal*, Vol. 4:1, (Winter, 1963).

[45] with some variations by Childs, Bock & Blaising, Saucy, et al; the characterization as a partial-accomodation approach is explained in footnote under the results of a literal-grammatical approach.

[46] Louis Berkhof, *Systematic Theology* (Grand Rapids, MI: Eerdmans, 1941), 712.

[47] Ibid., 713.

[48] Gerstner, *Wrongly Dividing the Word of Truth*, 93.

conclusions of the literal approach are distinctly idiosyncratic. Ryrie emphasizes the relation between the methodology and the conclusions:

> if literalism is the valid hermeneutical principle then that is an approach to the Scriptures which if consistently applied can only lead to dispensational theology...only dispensationalism consistently employs the principles of literal interpretation.[49]

It is from within the framework of conclusions of a non-accommodation approach that Ryrie's *sine qua non*[50] emerges, not as a set of theological presuppositions, but as characteristic results.

Four results of a literal grammatical-historical approach are particularly notable:

1. Consistent and practical submission in the interpretive process to the divine authority, inerrancy, and infallibility of Scripture.

As a result of respectful consideration of the self authenticating nature of special revelation, the approach to Scripture is exegetical rather than eisegetical, and is primarily inductive (beginning with the text to find the theology) rather than primarily deductive (beginning with the theology in order to determine the text). Here the interpreter avoids the error of enthroning himself as authoritative over God's revelation.

2. A recognition of the cumulative nature of revelation, applied in the interpretation of the New Testament in light of the Old Testament (and not vice versa)[51].

Stallard identifies this as a paramount principle in his four steps[52] of theological method, rightly prioritizing the OT vs. the NT, simply as a product

---

[49] Charles Ryrie, The Necessity of Dispensationalism, Biblioethica Sacra 114:455 (Jul 57).

[50] 1. distinction between Israel and the church, 2. literal hermeneutic, and 3. doxological purpose of God (Ryrie, *Dispensationalism Today*, 44-47).

[51] at this point progressive dispensationalism is seen to utilize a partial-accommodation hermeneutic, as Blaising, Bock, Saucy, *et al* demonstrate in practice a re-definition of cumulative revelation and suggest that the resultant complementary hermeneutic is actually a refinement of the literal hermeneutic, when in fact, it is simply a different hermeutic method entirely [see Robert Saucy, *The Case For Progressive Dispensationalism* (Grand Rapids: Zondervan, 1993), 20-29 & 70-71; Blaising & Bock, *Progressive Dispensationalism* (Grand Rapids: Baker Books, 1993), 100-105; Harold Bateman IV, *Three Central Issues in Contemporary Dispensationalism* (Grand Rapids: Kregel, 1999), 89-94].

[52] Stallard's four principles adapted as follows:
1. recognition of one's preunderstanding.
2. formulation of Biblical theology of the Old Testament from a literal grammatical historical interpretation of the Old Testament.
3. formulation of Biblical theology of the New Testament from a literal grammatical historical interpretation of the New Testament.
4. production of systematic theology by harmonizing input from 2 and 3.

of cumulative revelation. Ryrie declared this recognition "an imperative"[53] without which will be raised "unresolvable contradictions"[54].

Notice Christ's approach to handling OT revelation in His appearance to the two on the road to Emmaus: "And beginning with Moses and with all the prophets, He explained to them the things concerning Himself in all the Scriptures" (Lk. 24:27). His listeners later described His process as "explaining the Scriptures" (24:32). Christ makes reference to this order within Scripture on other occasions as well, and His characterizations are not simply acknowledgments of the commonly held structure of the OT revelation. It is significant that in order to explain the Scriptures, Christ Himself started at the beginning.

If the NT is postulated by the OT, as Kuyper suggests[55], by logical conclusion the NT must be interpreted on the basis of the revelation given in the OT. While there is inconsistency regarding the acknowledgment of the cumulative nature of revelation among those of non-literal persuasion[56], there can be none for those holding to a literal hermeneutic.

3. Awareness of the doxological center

Even as Christ is the central Character in special revelation (Jn. 5:39), His primary purpose is doxological and not redemptive (Jn. 17:4; 1 Pet. 4:11)[57]. The redemptive plan is a means to the accomplishment of God's revealed purpose: specifically, His own glorification[58]. The doxological purpose extends further than the Westminster assertion[59] regarding the chief end of man. It is God's self proclaimed purpose in all of (human) history.

4. Recognition of the complete distinction between Israel and the church

To Israel belong the covenants (specifically Land, Davidic, and New Covenants as fulfillment of the Abrahamic) which ensure a future of restoration and literal fulfillment for Israel. The church is entirely distinct

---

[adapted from Mike Stallard, *Literal Hermeneutics, Theological Method, and the Essence of Dispensationalism*]

[53] Charles Ryrie, *Basic Theology* (Wheaton, Victor Books, 1986), 114.

[54] Ibid.

[55] Abraham Kuyper, *Principles of Sacred Theology* (Grand Rapids, Baker Book House, 1980), 461

[56] e.g., see Berkhof's practical struggle with this issue [Louis Berkhof, *Systematic Theology* (Grand Rapids, Eerdmans, 1941), 715].

[57] the non-dispensationalist generally argues that the redemptive center provides continuity/ unity within Scripture, and emphasizes only one people of God, and thus provides a significant evidence against the distinction between Israel and the church [e.g., O.T. Allis, *Prophecy & The Church* (Philipsburg, NJ: Presbyterian & Reformed, 1945), 17-18.

[58] Ps. 86:9, 12; Ezek. 39:13; Jn. 17:3-4; Rom. 11:36, 12:1-2; 1 Co. 6:20, 10:31; Eph. 2:8-10; 1 Tim. 1:5; 1 Pet. 4:11; Is. 6:3 & Rev. 4:11, etc.

[59] Man's chief end is to glorify God, and to enjoy him forever. [Shorter Catechism, 1].

from national Israel, yet benefits (in fulfillment of Gen 12:3c, etc.) from blessings promised to Abraham through his descendants. Specifically, the church benefits from the New Covenant promise to Israel regarding forgiveness of sin (Jer. 31:34).[60]

A.C. Gaebelein recognized that both Jew and Gentile would participate in the Kingdom Age, but *not as one body*[61], yet the mystery is revealed (Eph. 2:11-3:6) that in the current age exists a body (the body of Christ) — distinct from national Israel, made up of both Jew and Gentile. God's purpose in and for the two distinct groups are made evident in Romans 9-11, and in that same context the distinction between the two groups can readily be seen. Chafer highlights the distinction, identifying twenty-four specific differences between Israel and the church.[62] The distinction is really at the heart of Ryrie's *sine qua non* (strategically identified as the first element), and until only recently[63] has been a universally agreed upon principle in dispensational thought. It must be noted that this principle of distinction is not a theological presupposition, but rather an inevitable result of the consistent application of the literal grammatical-historical hermeneutic brings about this conclusion, a fact that non-dispensationalists readily admit[64].

Conclusion

These four pillars, with their associated results provide an essential framework for presuppositional dispensationalism, an attempt to build theological method upon the proper foundational elements (i.e., a Biblical epistemology, recognizing the existence and authority of the Divine Revealer), and to further develop and positively assert dispensational conclusions as those arising naturally from the natural, plain-sense reading of Scripture. The purpose in view here is not to move toward a mediating

---

[60] this element of blessing as bestowed on the church is highlighted in Eph. 2:11-3:6, and 1 Jn. 2:25), and does not (1) replace the church with Israel, (2) include the church in any other aspects of the New Covenant, or (3) invalidate or alter in any way the covenant promises made to Israel.

[61] A.C. Gaebelein, *The Annotated Bible: Romans-Ephesians* (NY: Our Hope), 252.

[62] Chafer, *Systematic Theology, Vol 6*, 47-53.

[63] the advent of progressive dispensationalism has brought a blurring of the lines between Israel and the church, epitomized by Saucy's assertion that "there is a mediating position between non-dispensationalism and traditional dispensationalism...and it denies a radical discontinuity between the present church age and the messianic kingdom promises." [Saucy, *The Case for Progressive Dispensationalism*, 20], and identified in Lanier Burns' characterization that "The difference between traditional and progressive dispensationalists is the extent to which Old Testament covenants are realized (in other words, fulfilled) in the church age." [Bateman, Three Central Issues in Contemporary Dispensationalism, 290].

[64] see Berkhof, Systematic Theology, 712; A.H. Strong, *Systematic Theology* (Philadelphia: Judson Press, 1947), 1011; O.T. Allis, Prophecy & The Church, 54; etc..

position, nor is it to justify any particular system, but rather to approach God's word with necessary humility and to unashamedly stand firm on the assertions made therein. This approach seeks to provide an apologetic synthesis within the theological method – the Biblically theistic worldview must be the stated basis of the theological framework. We must begin at the beginning, by casting off the shackles of atheistic modes of thought which so presently invade our theological (and apologetic) method, and build the base from a Biblical epistemology. This approach seeks to provide a cohesive, consistent framework of approach to Biblical revelation, one which can deal cogently with historical and contemporary issues, proposing Biblical solutions using consistent hermeneutical methodology. And finally this approach seeks to encourage revitalization and renewed passion for the value of God's word as that which is entirely profitable for teaching, for reproof, for correction, for training in righteousness – as the *sole standard* of thought and conduct for the believer.

"When we ask someone to believe in the Lord Jesus Christ, we are asking something very difficult. For one reason, we are asking the person to believe in Someone he or she has never seen. Someone who lived in the very distant past. Someone who has no living eyewitness who can vouch for His character and the truth of His words. Someone whose biography was written very long ago and by those who were His friends."

- Charles C. Ryrie
So Great Salvation, 1989, page 117

3

Priorities in Presenting the Faith

John C. Whitcomb

My personal experience with Christian apologetics began in February, 1943, when I was a student at Princeton University. It had not been my privilege to be raised in a Christian home nor to attend a Bible-teaching church. But God, in His grace, used a couple of Christian students at the university to invite me time and time again to attend a weekly Bible class being taught by a Princeton alumnus and former missionary to India.

The Gospel message was graciously presented, and after several months of such teaching, I surrendered to the claims and the authority of the Lord Jesus Christ. As far as I could tell there were no other Christians in the student hall where I stayed at that time, but I had made several good friends, one of whom was a sophisticated intellectual from a wealthy home. I was convinced that the conversion of such a man could bring great changes in the student hall, so one day I invited him to attend our Bible class. My hopes were high, because I was prepared to convince him that no one else could match this Bible teacher who had led me to the Lord. The conversation, as I recall over the years, proceeded as follows: 'Harry, here is a teacher who can really make the message of the Bible clear and convincing. Why not come with me on Sunday afternoon and see for yourself?'

'The Bible?' he replied. 'Why should I take time to study a religious book that is already nearly two thousand years out of date? You know yourself that there isn't a single science professor here at Princeton who takes the Bible seriously on the origin of the world. The idea of creation by divine fiat is no longer held by intelligent people. I really have no interest in the Bible.'

Stung by this flat rejection of God's Word on the basis of a scientific consensus, I retreated to my Christian friends. Were there any publications of a scholarly nature, I asked, that could help my friend see the weaknesses of evolutionism and thus the possibility of supernatural creation? Except for a few small booklets, nothing came to hand; but armed with these I approached Harry again. He was surprisingly gracious. 'Thanks for going to all the trouble of collecting these booklets for me. I really didn't know that anyone who takes Genesis literally could write a book. I'll tell you what I'll do. Some day, if I ever have the time, I'll look into it.'

That was it. It was a polite but final brush-off.

I was deeply dismayed at this and similar failures to convert my friends to Christianity, and discussed the problem with my Bible teacher. 'What's wrong with me? Is it my personality, or do I need more time to collect better arguments?' Instead of lecturing his new disciple on the intricacies of biblical apologetics, he very wisely invited me to join him in a brief visitation to one of the other dormitories where a new student had five months earlier somewhat rashly filled in a survey card indicating his interest in attending our Bible study class.

As the door swung open in response to our knock, pipe smoke poured into the hallway. 'I'm John Whitcomb and this is the Bible teacher of the Princeton Evangelical Fellowship. Is Tom Smith here?' A trampling of feet and the crash of a table lamp were heard as various figures fled in terror, leaving our victim to fend for himself against unwanted intruders.

'The Princeton Evangelical Fellowship? Oh yes, I guess I did sign a card last fall; but I'm not interested in the Bible anymore. I used to think it was true, but five months of study here has been enough to convince me it is full of errors.'

'I'm fascinated to hear you say that,' my teacher quietly commented. 'Tell me, what particular errors did you discover in the Bible that convinced you it is not true?' This was unexpected. Was a firm rebuff not sufficient to end this uncomfortable conversation? Surely the general consensus of this great university was sufficient to silence anyone who still believed the Bible to be true? Tom thought for a moment and answered, 'Jonah and the whale! There's your proof. No educated person today could believe for one moment that a whale could have swallowed a man and then spit him out on the shore alive three days later!'

Here was the crisis for me. How could we handle this direct challenge to the historicity of the book of *Jonah*? Perhaps we could find in the university library some books on whales that would demonstrate their ability to swallow men alive. Perhaps we could even find historical evidence of men who had actually survived such an ordeal. That would convince him that the book of *Jonah* is as infallible as the rest of the Bible! Providentially, it was my teacher who answered him first. 'Tom, I'm frankly very thankful that it is the book of *Jonah* you seem to be struggling with. There is no more fascinating book in the Old Testament then *Jonah*. Some day, if we have time, I would like to discuss with you the entire message of that book, which was alluded to by Christ Himself for a very important reason. In the meantime, however, would you mind if I explained to you why I have come to believe that the Bible is the Word of God and therefore true in all its parts?' Impressed with the irresistible graciousness and confidence of this man who seemed to know from personal experience the God of Whom he spoke, Tom gave his cautious consent.

'Tom, I felt the way you do about God's Word when I was a student here thirty years ago. I thought I had all the answers I needed concerning life. But I was wrong. In His infinite love, God reached down to me in my deep personal need and showed me through the familiar words of His matchless Book that my root problem was sin, deliberate alienation from God Himself.' What he heard was not a scientific, historical, or philosophical, defense of Christianity, but a Gospel-saturated testimony directed prayerfully to his heart. As I recall the conversation, Tom did raise some questions about Christianity and the Bible. The questions were not totally ignored, but the answers were always amplified by new perspectives on the Gospel and appeals for surrender to Christ. It was this approach that ultimately led to a proud university student acknowledging the lordship of Christ in his life.

All of this forced me to take a new look at some basic factors of Christian apologetics that I had seriously neglected. I have come to believe that my initial ignorance concerning these biblical principles also characterizes many frustrated and fruitless Christian workers today. My problem was basically two-fold. I had underestimated the depth of man's rebellion against God, and I was unaware of the absolutely crucial part which the Word of God must have, through the convicting and illuminating work of the Holy Spirit, in bringing sinful men to Christ. In our efforts to make the Bible and Christianity attractive and acceptable to men, we find ourselves immediately confronted with two stupendous obstacles: man's fallen nature and the Satanic forces which surround him. Though these facts should come as no great surprise to one who is even superficially acquainted with Christianity, it is astonishing to me how few of the better known evangelical works on Christian apologetics today give them serious consideration.

One is almost led to believe when reading such books that what we *really* need to win intellectuals to Christ (in addition to the Gospel) is an arsenal of carefully developed arguments against various false religious and philosophical systems. We also seem to need an impressive array of evidences from, say, archaeology and history, that the Bible and Christianity are true.[1] But if we are to be truly honest with the biblical perspectives on this question, we must admit that we have too often been guilty of building

---

[1] For example, John Warwick Montgomery boldly asserts: 'Non-Christian positions must be destroyed factually and the Christian religion established factually. Any lesser procedure is the abrogation of apologetic responsibility to a fallen world.' (*Once upon An A priori*, in *Jerusalem and Athens*, edited by E R Geehan [Nutley, NJ: Presbyterian and Reformed Publishing Co, 1971], 388).

our systems of apologetics upon other foundations than the one set forth in Scripture. Instead of giving us the impression that men are eagerly waiting for proof that Christianity is true, we find the Bible exposing men's hearts as sealed shut against any and all merely human intellectual pressures for conversion.

The basic problem of the non-Christian is not merely academic and intellectual, it is moral and spiritual. The Bible indicates that *all* unbelievers (including so-called honest doubters) are enemies of God, under divine judgment because of their deliberate distortion of all reality to fit into their own spiritual frame of reference. There is not the slightest desire in the natural man to seek Him, find Him, and acknowledge Him for Who He is – 'The wicked, through the pride of his countenance, will not seek after God: God is not in all his thoughts' (*Psalm 10:4*)[2]. On another occasion, the Holy Spirit informs us by the pen of David that – 'The Lord looked down from heaven upon the children of men, to see if there were any that did understand, and seek God' (*Psalm 14:2*). But what did He see? 'They are all gone aside, they are all together filthy: there is none that doeth good, no, not one' *(quoted in Romans 3:10-12).*

Not only does the unbeliever not seek and practice truth, he consistently suppresses whatever truth he does receive: 'For the wrath of God is revealed from heaven against all ungodliness and unrighteousness of men, who hold [*suppress*] the truth in unrighteousness... they are without excuse' (*Romans 1:18-20*). In fact, the Scriptures make it clear that fallen men, so far from being open to arguments about God's claims upon them, are in a state of enmity against Him, because 'the carnal mind is enmity against God: for it is not subject to the law of God, neither indeed can be' (*Romans 8:7*).

Christian apologetics has been traditionally concerned with giving rational answers to the challenges of unbelievers concerning God's special revelation in Scripture. But what kind of minds are we appealing to? To what extent have sin and spiritual rebellion against God affected man's rational capacities? Ponder these statements: 'And you hath he quickened, who were dead in trespasses and sins; wherein in time past ye walked according to the course of this world...fulfilling the desires of the flesh and of the mind; and were by nature the children of wrath, even as others'(*Ephesians 2:1-3*). 'Walk not as other Gentiles walk, in the vanity of their mind, having their understanding darkened, being alienated from the life of God through the ignorance that is in them, because of the blindness of their hearts' (*Ephesians 4:17-18*).

---

[2] All Scripture quotations in this chapter are from the King James Version.

But is the human 'mind' not capable of detaching itself from the so-called 'heart' and drawing its own conclusions about God independently of the downward direction of our fallen nature? The answer is – no. Mark our Lord's explanation of the unbreakable relationship between the mind and the heart – 'Out of the heart proceed evil thoughts' (*Matthew 15:19; cf. Mark 7:21*). The Scriptures offer us no hope of bringing about a fundamental change in a man's thinking about God apart from a profound change in his 'heart', the moral and spiritual center of his personal being.

In addition to the obstacle of the human 'heart-mind' being in utter opposition to the truth of God, there is the obstacle of Satan, 'the god of this world', and his demonic forces. This leads me to realize that when I speak to an unbeliever about Christ, I am not really speaking to one person but to two or more persons, all but one of whom is invisible.

The apostle Paul spoke of this fact several times. He explained that – 'we wrestle not against flesh and blood, but against principalities, against powers, against the rulers of the darkness of this world, against spiritual wickedness in high places' (*Ephesians 6:12*). He knew that Christians formerly 'walked....according to the prince of the power of the air, the spirit that now worketh in the children of disobedience.' (*Ephesians 2:2*). He recognized that – 'if our gospel be hid, it is hid to them that are lost: in whom the god of this world hath blinded the minds of them which believe not, lest the light of the glorious gospel of God, should shine unto them' (*2 Corinthians 4:3-4*). In the parable of the sower, our Lord also spoke of this obstacle to the reception of His Word when he identified the birds that devoured the seed – 'When anyone heareth the word of the kingdom, and understandeth it not, then cometh the wicked one, and catcheth away that which was sown in his heart. This is he which received seed by the way side' (*Matthew 13:19*).

A system of Christian apologetics that underestimates the power of Satan in the minds of unbelievers may not exactly be guilty of reviling angelic majesties as Jude warns us, but by ignoring the extent of Satan's power, it is unable to follow Michael's example and to say effectively: 'The Lord rebuke thee' (*Jude 9*). What we desperately need today is an apologetic with power. If the Biblical picture of man's enmity against God and control by Satan is correct, then how can Christians ever persuade men to turn from sin and Satan to the true and living God? The biblical answer, of course, is that they cannot. The Scriptures do not say that it is difficult for the unbeliever to accept spiritual truth. They say that is it impossible. 'The natural man receiveth not the things of the Spirit of God: for they are foolishness unto him: neither can he know them, because they are spiritually discerned' (*1 Corinthians 2:14*). When our Lord once made a similar pronouncement concerning an entire segment of society, 'his disciples... were exceedingly amazed, saying, Who then can be saved?' His answer provides for us the key to all truly effective Christian apologetics today: 'With men this is impossible; but with God all things are possible' (*Matthew 19:25-26*).It seems quite obvious, then, that God never intended that Christians should win the lost through purely philosophical and academic arguments, or even that they should by this means remove the mental obstacles within unbelievers so that the Word of God might penetrate their hearts. If this had been God's plan, the vast majority of Christians throughout history would have been automatically disqualified from effective witness, for they would have been unable to meet highly educated unbelievers on their own level in intellectual debate. 'For ye see your calling, brethren, how that not many wise men after the flesh, not many mighty, not many noble, are called: but God hath chosen the foolish things of the world to confound the wise... that no flesh should glory in his presence' (*1 Corinthians 1:26-29*).

The Biblical method of winning men to Christ (including the intellectuals of our day) is to lovingly, patiently and prayerfully present the true Gospel 'according to the scriptures' (*1 Corinthians 15:3-4*) from the context of a godly life (*1 Thessalonians 1:5; 2:3-12*). Only the 'quick, and powerful' Word of God can penetrate the unbeliever's shield of defense and pierce into his heart (*Hebrews 4:12*), and thus only God may receive the glory for the genuine conversion of sinful men. Once converted by God's Holy Spirit, a man for the first time in his life enjoys the proper perspective and frame of reference for analyzing his intellectual problems concerning Christian doctrines, even if he never finds the complete answers this side of Heaven.

Paul's own conversion is an instructive illustration of this divine dynamic. Instead of presenting a list of questions to the Lord Jesus when he was overwhelmed by His presence on the Damascus road, Saul of Tarsus simply cried out, 'What shall I do, Lord?' (*Acts 22:10*). With his spiritual blindness removed by God – 'straightway he preached Christ in the synagogues, that He is the Son of God' (*Acts 9:20*). He 'was not disobedient unto the heavenly vision' (*Acts 26:19*) even though it must have required years for him to rethink everything that he had previously learned about the Scriptures in the light of this transforming new revelation. The book of *Acts* contains numerous examples of such proclamations of God's revealed message, resulting in conviction of sin by the Holy Spirit and genuine conversion (*Acts 2:36-38; 8:34-36; 10:42-48; 16:31-34*).

Another important New Testament example of this approach to Christian apologetics may be found in Paul's admonition to the Corinthian church to turn from worldly wisdom and from an unwarranted glorying in certain sign-gifts in order that they might give themselves to the clear proclamation of God's Word. He said: 'But if all prophesy, and there come in one that believeth not, or one unlearned, he is convinced of all, he is judged of all: and thus are the secrets of his heart made manifest; and so falling down on his face he will worship God, and report that God is in you of a truth' (*1 Corinthians 14:24-25*).[3] It is perfectly obvious from this remarkable passage that neither human wisdom nor empirical signs were an adequate substitute for the clear proclamation of God's Word. However, if the Christian communicator constantly appeals to God's Word in order to establish its truth in the mind of the unbeliever, is he not guilty of reasoning in a circle? If the unbeliever refuses to accept the Scriptures as divinely inspired, should not the communicator temporarily abandon the Bible until he has demonstrated its truth independently by appealing to the vast array of archaeological, historical, scientific, and other facts that tend to confirm its claims? The answer to this question is – no. If Christianity is merely *one* circle of truth to be conditioned and defined by *other* circles of truth, then it is not true at all, because the Scriptures boldly and consistently claim to be God's eternal, all-inclusive, unique, final, and absolutely authoritative Word. This is the crucial foundation of true Christian apologetics.

When the Christian appeals to God's Word he is appealing to the *only* ultimate circle of truth concerning God and spiritual realities. This circle is so vast and profound that it includes everything that exists, both within and beyond the universe, both visible and invisible – including the unbeliever himself and the very 'god of this world' who blinds him! To turn off the light of God's Word, as it were, in order to establish first a 'common ground' with the unbeliever is thus to abandon truth in order to grope together with an unregenerate mind in the darkness that characterizes this world-system apart from God. Revealed truth is self authenticating and self-vindicating, like light. Peter stated - 'Ye do well that ye take heed [*to the Word of God*], as unto a light that shineth in a dark place, until the day dawn' (*2 Peter 1:19*).

Imagine a man lost within the deep recesses of the dark underground cavern in utter despair of ever finding his way out. If a friend had a general idea of his location, how could he best come to his rescue? Should he rush into the cave, careless of his pathway, and sit with him in darkness, sharing with him the common ground of being lost? Would it not

---

[3]It is quite wrong to say – 'If a man has a prejudice against the Gospel it is the function of apologetics and evidences to remove that prejudice... Apologetics and Christian evidences cut down these objections to enable the Gospel once again to directly confront the consciousness of a man' (*Protestant Christian Evidences* [Chicago: Moody Press, 1953], pp15-16).

be much wiser to take along a powerful flashlight, marking his path as he enters the cavern so that he could retrace his steps to the safety of the world above? However, suppose that the lost man, in his utter despair, refused to believe that his friend had a flashlight and that there was a way out? Should the would-be rescuer sit there in darkness and argue with him concerning the size, make, power, and previous performance of his flashlight? Since the lost man still has the capacity to recognize light when he sees it, should not his friend immediately end the debate by *inviting him to look at the light* as he switches on the flashlight?

Man's amazing capacity to hear and to see in the physical realm did not come about by chance. 'The hearing ear and the seeing eye, the Lord hath made both of them' (*Proverbs 20:12*). Neither is man's capacity to recognize God's truth a product of chance. Every human being has this capacity and will be judged by the Creator on the basis of his use of it. John tells us that Christ is 'the true Light, which lighteth every man that cometh into the world' (*John 1:9*). Thus, man has an innate knowledge of his Creator. 'That which may be known of God is manifest in them; for God has shewed it unto them' (*Romans 1:19*). When a man is therefore confronted with Christ, the Light of the world, it is no help to him to accommodate him when he demands another light first. When a Christian apologist turns off the light of his Lord and begins groping to find light from the general consensus of scientific opinion, he has entered into a spiritual cavern from which there is no escape. What he must do is to keep the heart and mind of his unbelieving friend exposed to God's Word in one way or another, all the time praying that the Spirit of God might bring conviction of sin and a willingness to trust the Savior. If he does not respond to God's infallible Word, which is His *special* revelation, what assurance do we gain from the Bible that He will respond to the witness of *general* revelation, such as the various theistic proofs for God's personal existence and historical evidences for the truth of Christianity?

The Christian who adopts such a Bible-centered method must, however, prepare himself for intense criticism, even from fellow Christians. To subordinate rationalistic argumentation to the supremacy of Scripture is to cut across the grain of all our natural inclinations and invite the accusation of obscurantism. 'After all,' we are being told on every side, 'with so many false religions, cults, and philosophies in the world today, is it not the right and responsibility of an intelligent person to investigate carefully the validity of Christianity in comparison with other possible alternatives before making a final decision?' Again, the answer is – 'no'. Christianity is not simply one of the several available religious truth systems. Nor is our Lord Jesus Christ just one of several saviors we may investigate at our leisure and on our own terms. Furthermore, our intelligent investigator is far from being neutral and unbiased in spiritual matters. He can not sit in judgment with complete objectivity as one religion after another passes in view, waiting to find one that is logically coherent, historically and scientifically factual, and personally satisfying before adopting it as his own. Quite to the contrary, men are active enemies of the one true God of revelation and redemption, in whose image and likeness we have all been created, and in Whom 'we live and move, and have our being' (*Acts 17:28*). While it is true that the divine image has been marred through the Fall, it is nevertheless very much intact (*Genesis 9:6; 1 Corinthians 11:7; James 3:9*). It is precisely because man does bear God's image that he inwardly *knows Who* this God is. That is why he runs away from God and His Word and hides his face from Him, (*cf. Genesis 3:10; Isaiah 53:3*). That is why he also hinders or suppresses the truth in unrighteousness (*Romans 1:18*) and 'hateth the light, neither cometh to the light' (*John 3:20*). Sinful men cannot innocently claim that God is an unknown entity to them-'Because that, when they knew God, they glorified him not as God neither were thankful; but became vain in their imaginations, and their foolish heart was darkened' (*Romans 1:21*). These are the reasons why sinful men actually have no right to demand 'proper credentials' when the Creator says to them: 'Repent! Believe My Word! Obey Me – NOW!' When the Holy Spirit says to the human heart, 'Believe on the Lord Jesus Christ,' it is potential suicide to procrastinate, investigate or debate. 'Behold, now is the day of salvation' (*2 Corinthians 6:2*). 'God...now commandeth all men every where to repent' (*Acts 17:30*). God may graciously prolong the appeal, but sinful man cannot presume upon this!

Let us look at the matter from a different perspective. If an unregenerate man actually did have the right to demand full intellectual satisfaction concerning the claims of God's Word before accepting them, he would be the greatest of fools for settling for anything less than a complete demonstration. But in order to have such a demonstration he would have to examine carefully *all* the pertinent facts and *every* possible alternative before receiving Christ as his Lord. Of course, he would die long before he could arrive at the place where he could make a decision on this basis. Such an approach to Christian apologetics is not only unbiblical but it leads to logical absurdities! To give an unbeliever the impression that he has a right to demand answers to all the rational problems relating to the Bible and Christianity before he repents of his sin and turns to Christ for forgiveness, is to set him up on a pedestal of intellectual and spiritual pride from which he will *never* descend. What can such endless debates actually accomplish in preparing such a person for 'the day when God shall judge the secrets of men by Jesus Christ according to my gospel' (*Romans 2:16*)?

What can be said for such rationalistic apologetics when God has commissioned us to present 'all the counsel of God' (*cf. Matthew 28:18-20; Acts 20:27; 2 Timothy 2:2; 4:2*)? And how do we respond to Paul's admonition to Timothy – 'be gentle unto all men, apt to teach [i.e.: *to teach revealed truth*], patient, in meekness instructing [*i.e.: with Scripture*] those that oppose themselves; if God peradventure will give them repentance to the acknowledging of the truth; and that they may recover themselves out of the snare of the devil' (*2 Timothy 2:24-26*)? If the New Testament is our infallible guide in such matters, we must conclude that the Christian who will be most effectively used by God in winning people to Christ is not the one who knows the most about secular philosophy, psychology, history, archaeology, or natural science (important though these disciplines may be in their proper place in developing a comprehensive Christian world-and-life view). It will be the Christian who knows most about God's Word, and who humbly seeks God's daily strength and wisdom in obeying it. The best Christian apologist is the best student Scripture, who, to use the Bible's own terms to describe him, is 'a workman that needeth not to be ashamed,' because he is 'rightly dividing the word of truth' (*2 Timothy 2:15*). He will be a man like Apollos – 'mighty in the scriptures...instructed in the way of the Lord... [*who*] spake and taught diligently the things of the Lord,' and thus by God's Word 'he mightily convinced' unbelievers (*Acts 18:24-28*).

The writer finds himself in complete agreement with those who insist that Christianity is supremely rational. This is not because the Christian understands everything that God has revealed, for even the apostle Paul refused to make such a claim (*Romans 11:33; I Corinthians 13:9; see also 2 Peter 3:16*). The reason why one must insist on the essential rationality of Christianity is because of the nature of God Himself. His thoughts have been communicated to us effectively and in truth. The Bible is perspicuous (*1 John 2:20, 27*). However, man's finiteness will prevent him from knowing God exhaustively. The Gospel may be foolish 'to them that perish' (*1 Corinthians 1:18*), but it is *not* intrinsically foolish; it is perfect and infinite wisdom (*1 Corinthians 1:20-29*). Thus, the Christian message is *ultimately rational*. But this is very far from saying that the Christian message can be communicated *rationalistically* to lost men.

The apostle Peter, by the Spirit of God, commanded each believer to 'be ready always to give an answer [Gk: *apologian*] to every man that asketh you a reason of the hope that is in you' (*1 Peter 3:15*). Does this mean that the Christian must go outside the sphere of revelational truth to provide intellectual and academic justification for his faith in God's Word to the unbeliever? Could Peter himself have fulfilled such a command in view of his very limited background? Would the apostle Paul, who was widely known for his great learning (*Acts 26:24; cf: 22:3*), have indulged in such pursuits for the philosophically-minded Corinthians in view of his avowed determination 'not to know any thing among you, save Jesus Christ and him crucified...that your faith should not stand in the wisdom of men, but in the power of God' (*1 Corinthians 2:2 and 5*)? Hardly so. One therefore suspects from the very outset that the very popular semi-rationalistic interpretation of *1 Peter 3:15* is misguided.[4] This suspicion is confirmed by an examination of the immediate context of the passage. Peter was writing to persecuted Christians who were being terrorized by their pagan neighbors. They were commanded, however, not to sink into despair, but to recognize their truly 'blessed' situation (*cf. Matthew 5:10; James 5:11*). Furthermore, they were neither to fear nor to be troubled (*1 Peter 3:14; cf. Isaiah 8:12*). But why should they adopt such an attitude? Was it because they knew they could out-maneuver their enemies in intellectual debate? Definitely not! Early Christians did not include 'many wise men according to the flesh' among their number (*1 Corinthians 1:26*). Their confidence was really based upon their spiritual resources in Christ the Lord, Whom they were to *sanctify* in their hearts. Furthermore, the words that follow Peter's command to 'be ready always to give an answer' are highly significant. This defense is to be made with 'meekness and fear' (*cf. Colossians 4:6*) and with 'a good conscience; that ... they may be ashamed that falsely accuse your good conversation in Christ.' Note carefully that these conditions have nothing to do with rationalistic debate, for a basic assumption underlying such debate is that a correct answer is effective regardless of the presence or absence of meekness, reverence or godliness in the one giving the answer. But in a spiritual witness to the truth of God, these factors are absolutely vital.

It is clear from this passage, then, that no spiritually effective answers can be given to unregenerate people by Christians concerning the hope that is in them until they have learned to *sanctify the Lord God* in their own hearts. But what does that really mean? The term *sanctify* in this context presupposes that Christians are themselves sanctified or holy – set apart for God. In the immediate context, then, Peter is saying that the

---

[4] Whereas pure rationalism in apologetics would claim that unbelievers can be argued directly into the kingdom, semi-rationalism claims that – 'The purpose of apologetics is always merely to clear away the intellectual obstructions so that the Scriptures and the Holy Spirit may do their work' (Edward John Carnell, '*How Every Christian Can Defend His Faith*,' in *Moody Monthly*, February, 1950.) .

believer must confess his inability to convert men by mere human reasonings, and recognize God's unique and sovereign ability to do the converting. He must learn to pray that the God Who knows the hearts of all men and Who knows how to penetrate those hearts with His own Word will present His Word, by His Spirit, to the hearers, and be glorified by the results.

During the 1944 Ardennes campaign in Belgium, better known as the Battle of the Bulge, the writer served as a 'fire direction computer' in a US field artillery battalion. It was his job to sit with two other men in a basement behind the front lines and to telephone directions to the artillerymen who handled the twelve 105mm guns. The really dangerous job was entrusted to the forward observer, usually a lieutenant. He had to position himself in a high place near enough to the front lines to see enemy tanks approaching. When the tanks came into view, a potential crisis emerged. He could either panic or he could follow strict instructions. If he panicked and fled to the rear, the tanks would proceed unchallenged, and the battle might be lost, including the forward observer. Or, he might rush toward the tanks and start firing on them himself. That would also prove disastrous to him, and to his military unit. There was, however, a third alternative. That would be to 'sanctify' the field artillery in his heart! In other words, he could follow instructions and phone the 'fire direction center,' giving them the number, size, location and apparent speed and direction of movement of the enemy tanks, confessing thereby his inability to handle them in his own strength, and the ability of the field artillery to do the job which he could not do. It hardly seems necessary to explain that once the artillery had located these tanks, they were in desperate danger. As dozens of armour-piercing shells whistled over the head of the forward observer and penetrated the tanks one by one, exploding inside, *he was giving his greatest apologetic to the challenge that confronted him.*

As God's 'forward observers' in Satan's world of demons and fallen men, Christians must learn to call upon their Lord. No other system has ever really worked nor ever shall. What, then, is the 'answer' that each of us must be prepared to give to everyone who asks us to give an account for the hope that is in us? The answer must be basically God's Word, not our own word. God's thoughts are vastly higher than our thoughts (*Isaiah 55:*9), and His words penetrate far deeper into men's hearts than our words. In every sincere soul-winning effort, the believer soon discovers that his own words are dead, inactive and dull. But – 'the Word of God is quick, and powerful, and sharper than any two-edged sword, piercing even to the dividing asunder of soul and spirit, and of the joints and marrow, and is a discerner of the thoughts and intents of the heart' (*Hebrews 4:12*).

It was Christ the Lord Who set the apologetic example for all believers when He thrice defeated Satan with accurate, appropriate quotations from the Word of God, and with the formula – 'It is written' (*Matthew 4:1-11*). In His great confrontation with unbelieving Pharisees in *John 8:12-59*, our Lord appealed constantly to *basic spiritual realities*, such as the witness of His Father (*John 8:14, 26, 28, 29, 38, 42, 49, 54*), rather than to sign-miracles. It is noteworthy that 'as he spake these words, many believed on him' (*v30*).

Do modern Christians sometimes feel that they have, because of archaeological, historical, scientific, and other discoveries that shed light on the Scriptures, *a superior apologetic*, to that of our Lord and His apostles, and of the early church? If so, they have not really sanctified the Lord God in their hearts and their answers to lost men can bring neither conviction nor conversion in the biblical sense of those terms. God's work must be done in God's way if it is to receive God's approval (*cf. 1 Corinthians 3:10-15*).

"For the Christian, theology must be built on the Bible. We recognize it is Scripture that gives us the doctrines of our faith. It does this not only by providing clear proof texts, but also by giving clear principles, and by offering the data from which we can make deductions or inductions on logical conclusions. But the basis of all our theology, however derived, must be the Scripture."

- Charles C. Ryrie

Basic Theology, 1982, page 525

4

Basic Distinctives of Dispensational Systematic Theology
Charles H. Ray

When we hear the word "dispensationalism," the first branch of systematic theology that comes to mind is eschatology. Ecclesiology soon follows. Beyond that, we don't generally see much of a connection. Actually, dispensationalism touches every major branch of systematic theology to one degree or another. The purpose of this chapter is to demonstrate the significance of this pervasive influence, and, by contrast, the perverting influence of amillennialism and postmillennialism.[1]

Christology

Dispensationalism has little disagreement with amillennialism and postmillennialism in the area of Christology. All hold to the full deity of Christ and the full humanity of Christ, for example. Differences surface in the matter of Jesus' role as the Davidic King.

The normal understanding of passages such as Luke 1:32 is that Jesus will sit on a literal throne in Jerusalem someday: "He will be great, and will be called the Son of the Most High; and the Lord God will give Him the throne of His father David." Amillennialists don't see it that way.

Amillennialist Loius Berkhof spends several pages in his *Systematic Theology* speaking about the Kingdom of Christ (406-411), but says nothing about the Davidic Covenant except its eternality.[2] "But though He was permitted to rule as Mediator even before His incarnation, He did not publicly and formally assume His throne and inaugurate His spiritual kingdom until the time of His ascension and elevation at the right hand of God, Acts 2:29-36; Phil. 2:5-11."[3] Thus, Berkhof believes Jesus is now on David's throne.

Postmillennialist Charles Hodge agrees and states that the

> Jews were not disappointed in the general impression made on their minds by the predictions relating to the Messiah. It was only in the explanation of details that

---

[1] Most of this article is based on John Walvoord's *The Millennial Kingdom* (Findlay, OH: Dunham Pub. Co., 1959; repr. Zondervan, 1983).

[2] Louis Berkhof, *Systematic Theology* (Carlisle, PA: Banner of Truth, 1958, 1998).

[3] Ibid., 410.

they failed. The Messiah was a king; He did sit upon the throne of David, but not in the way in which they expected ...[4]

Pneumatology

Dispensationalism, postmillennialism, and amillennialism do not share the same understanding of the work of the Holy Spirit. Dispensationalists believe the Church began when the Spirit began His baptizing ministry in Acts 2, as Chafer says,

> There could be no Church on earth until the advent of the Holy Spirit; for the most basic and fundamental reality respecting the Church is that she is a temple for the habitation of God through the Spirit. She is regenerated, baptized, and sealed by the Spirit.[5]

Amillennialists acknowledge this aspect of the Spirit's ministry but do not view it as particularly significant. I searched through Hodge and Berkhof on this issue and found almost nothing. Hodge mentions the baptism of the Spirit but does not associate it with the Church. The index of Berkhof's work does not list the baptism of the Spirit. Both camps seem to teach that the work of the Holy Spirit is essentially the same in the Old and New Testaments. Some non-dispensationalists associate the baptism of the Holy Spirit with the beginning of the New Testament Church, but nevertheless label it "spiritual Israel", as Bruce does here:

> The baptism of the Spirit, or baptism with the Spirit, is thus the work of the risen Christ. By this act he brought his church into being. The church - the people of God in New Testament times - is continuous with the people of God in Old Testament times ...[6]

Angelology

Amillennialists cannot agree among themselves as to the state of Satan and his demons. They seem to teach that evil angels are bound but can still have some influence on humans, like a dog chained to a tree. Yet this explanation doesn't harmonize well with the biblical data. Berkhof writes that demons "are even now chained to hell and pits of darkness ... II Pet. 2:4; Jude 6."[7] The flaw here is that 2 Peter 2:4 and Jude 6 do not refer to *all* demons. The bound evil spirits mentioned by Peter and Jude are a certain group of

---

[4] Charles Hodge, *Systematic Theology* (Logos version), 3:791.

[5] Lewis Sperry Chafer, *Systematic Theology* (Dallas: Dallas Seminary Press, 1947-48; repr. Kregel, 1993), 4:45.

[6] F. F. Bruce, *Jesus: Past, Present, and Future* (Downers Grove, IL: IVP, 1979), 45.

[7] Berkhof, 149.

demons, probably the ones discussed in Genesis 6 since both authors (Peter and Jude) talk about other stories from Genesis in the next few verses.

Hodge, on the other hand, allows more freedom for demons than does Berkhof. He writes that

> evil spirits ... are represented as being exceedingly numerous, as everywhere efficient, as having access to our world, and as operating in nature and in the minds of men.[8]

Amillennialists give conflicting assessments because they are not sure what to do with Revelation 20:2, "And he laid hold of the dragon, the serpent of old, who is the devil and Satan, and bound him for a thousand years." Amillennialists believe that the Millennium is the Church Age, and thus since the Millennium has already started, Satan is already chained. As noted above, that conclusion contradicts numerous passages which speak of the activity of Satan and his demons. Peter wrote, "Be of sober spirit, be on the alert. Your adversary, the devil, prowls about like a roaring lion, seeking someone to devour" (1 Pet. 5:8). Dispensationalists offer a simpler explanation. Satan isn't bound because the Millennium hasn't started yet.

Soteriology

Covenant theology holds to two or three theological covenants: a covenant of works (between God and Adam), a covenant of grace (between God and the elect - some say all of fallen humanity), and possibly a covenant of redemption (among the Members of the Godhead). Yet none of these are discussed implicitly in the Bible. Concerning the covenant of works, Hodge admits that it "does not rest upon any express declaration of the Scriptures."[9]

Likewise the Covenant system contends that the salvation of humans is the overriding theme of the entire Bible[10], and draws support for this notion by claiming that (1) the covenant of grace is mentioned in various passages from Genesis to Revelation, and (2) the Biblical covenants (Abrahamic, Davidic, New, *etc.*) are progressive revelations of the covenant of grace. Note Berkhof's comment in this regard:

---

[8] Hodge, 1:644.

[9] Ibid., 2:117.

[10] If this is true, then covenant theologians have a very difficult time explaining how angels fit into God's grand plan.

> The covenant of grace, as it is revealed in the New Testament, is essentially the same as that which governed the relation of Old Testament believers to God.[11]

Covenant theology seeks to prove the point by claiming that particular passages contain "covenant terminology," especially something on the order of "I will be your God, and you will be My people" (Gen. 17:7; Jer. 31:33; 2 Cor. 6:16; 1 Pet. 2:9, 10).

Dispensationalism acknowledges the consistency of God's plan of salvation (it always has been and always will be by grace through faith), but would disagree with the covenant theologian in seeing every phase (or dispensation) as having soteriological significance. In this regard, two covenants chiefly stand out — the Noahic and the Mosaic. In the Noahic Covenant, God promised He would never again flood the world as He had just done (Gen. 9:9-11). The Mosaic (or Sinaitic) Covenant focused on a way of life. Neither one has a direct bearing on soteriology.

Finally, dispensationalism asserts that the overriding theme of the Bible is God's glory, which includes the salvation of man but is not limited to it.[12] Other aspects of the Lord's creation and work that bring Him glory are (1) the good angels who praise Him, and (2) the final judgment on fallen angels and unbelieving people.

Ecclesiology

This section will be discussed in four parts: the origin of the Church, the members of the Church, the Church and Israel, and the Church and the Kingdom.

The Origin of the Church.

Non-premillennialists cannot agree among themselves as to how and when the Church started. Berkhof agrees with the Belgic Confession: "This Church has been from the beginning of the world..."[13] However, he also believes that the "establishment of the covenant with Abraham marked the beginning of an institutional Church."[14]

Wayne Grudem, an historic (or covenant) premillennialist, contradicts himself in this matter, too. He gives this simple definition: "The church is the community of all believers for all time."[15] In other words, the Church began

---

[11] Berkhof, 299, 300.

[12] This is not to say covenant theologians ignore the glory of God. Berkhof (272) wrote that the common aim of the Covenant of Works and the Covenant of Grace is to glorify God.

[13] Berkhof, 571.

[14] Ibid., 295.

[15] Wayne Grudem, *Systematic Theology* (Grand Rapids: Zondervan, 1994), 853.

with Adam. But later on when he writes about the Spirit giving spiritual gifts at Pentecost, he says that "happened in the early church."[16] How could the activities of Acts 2 be described as taking place in the early years of the Church if the early years of the Church were actually in Genesis?

Dispensationalists have good reasons for believing that the Church did not commence until the pouring out of the Holy Spirit as detailed in Acts 2. This baptizing ministry of the Spirit was unknown until then (cf. 1 Cor. 12:13).

Nowhere in the Old Testament is the Church mentioned. This is supported by the fact that Paul classified the Church as a mystery:

> If indeed you have heard of the stewardship of God's grace which was given to me for you; that by revelation there was made known to me the mystery, as I wrote before in brief. And by referring to this, when you read you can understand my insight into the mystery of Christ, which in other generations *was not made known* to the sons of men, as it has now been revealed to His holy apostles and prophets in the Spirit; to be specific, that the Gentiles are fellow heirs and fellow members of the body, and fellow partakers of the promise in Christ Jesus through the gospel, of which I was made a minister, according to the gift of God's grace which was given to me according to the working of His power.
>
> To me, the very least of all saints, this grace was given, to preach to the Gentiles the unfathomable riches of Christ, and to bring to light what is the administration of the mystery which for ages has been *hidden in God*, who created all things; in order that the manifold wisdom of God might now be made known through the church to the rulers and the authorities in the heavenly places. (Eph. 3:2-10; emphasis added)

Whatever this mystery is, it was completely unknown before the time of Paul. He writes that it was "hidden in God" and "in other generations was not made known to the sons of men." The mystery, it turns out, is that the Jews and Gentiles are "fellow heirs," "fellow members," and "fellow partakers." These terms mean that Gentiles are equal participants with the Jews in the favoritism shown to them by Yahweh.

The word "fellow" is significant here. It comes from a translation of the Greek prefix *sun-*, found in the front of all three words used in this verse. It's not that the Gentiles are second-class heirs, members, and partakers. They can now experience the exact same privileges that the Jews experience.

Amillennialists argue that "the body" of which the Gentiles are members was a body that existed previously. The Gentiles were merely added to it. But that is not how Paul explained it. He equates this body with the "one *new* man" (Eph. 2:15; emphasis added). So this body (which is the Church of course) is not old, it only recently came into being.[17]

---

[16] Ibid., 1018.

[17] Amillennialists also look to the word ekklesia to fortify their contention that the Church was present in the Old Testament. They point to Acts 7:38 where Stephen talks about "the church in the wilderness"

Jesus' words in Matthew 16:18 are another indication the Church did not exist in Old Testament times. Christ said: "I will build [future tense] My church." It would seem odd to speak of the Church in the future tense if it were already under construction. Peter noted that the pouring out of the Holy Spirit happened "at the beginning" (Acts 11:15). The beginning of what? The Church! A number of verses suggest the Church could not have come into being until the death, resurrection, and ascension of Christ. Acts 20:28 is one example. In this farewell address to the Ephesian elders, Paul states that they should "shepherd the church of God which He purchased with His own blood." That is, the Lord did not obtain the Church (so to speak) until His crucifixion. A number of other passages in Ephesians are crucial to our understanding of the beginning of the Church. In chapter 1 Paul reveals that only *after* the Father raised the Son did He make "Him as head over all things to the church" (Eph. 1:19-22). Ephesians 2:20 makes it plain that the foundation of the Church consists of Jesus and the apostles. A foundation is laid at the *beginning* of a project. Ephesians 4:8-12 declares that the body of Christ could not be built up until Jesus provided spiritual gifts, and that couldn't happen until Christ ascended to the Father's right hand.

The Members of the Church.

Covenant theology generally supports the practice of infant baptism. This observance came about as a result of the belief that just as circumcision was the sign of the Old Covenant, so baptism is the sign of the New Covenant. Furthermore, since all male Jewish infants eight days old were circumcised, it stands to reason that children born to believing parents should be placed in the "covenant community" of the Church. Some of Berkhof's statements, though, are at best confusing and at worst contradictory. He asserts that baptism "is intended only for properly qualified rational beings, namely, for believers and their children."[18] By "children" I assume he is including infants – but are babies rational beings? And what does he mean by "qualified"?
Berkhof later admits: "Now it is perfectly true that the Bible points to faith as a prerequisite for baptism, Mark 16:16; Acts 10:44-48; 16:14, 15, 31, 34."[19] But on the same page just a few lines down he claims the Bible "nowhere lays down the rule that an active faith is absolutely essential for the reception of baptism."

(only the KJV, RV, and RSV use "church" in this verse). But Stephen is not using ekklesia in the technical sense of "church" but in the general sense of "assembly." Amillennialists also point out that ekklesia is used in the LXX to identify a gathering of God's people. However, ekklesia did not have the meaning "church" in 200 BC.

[18] Berkhof, 631.

[19] Ibid., 637.

The primary proof-text is Col. 2:11, 12: "and in Him you were also circumcised with a circumcision made without hands, in the removal of the body of the flesh by the circumcision of Christ; having been buried with Him in baptism, in which you were also raised up with Him through faith in the working of God, who raised Him from the dead."

Much could be said in response to this connection between circumcision and baptism but only a few remarks will be given. Circumcision and baptism are too distinct from each other to consider them related. Infants were eligible for the rite of circumcision because of physical birth. People are eligible for baptism because of a spiritual birth. Infants are not mentally capable of understanding what is going on. Candidates for baptism must have exercised faith in Christ. Circumcision was an external sign that this *male* baby is a Jew. Baptism is an external symbol for something that has already happened internally. It seems clear from the New Testament that only those who acknowledge that they are sinners and trust Christ for their salvation are entitled to baptism.

The Church and Israel.

The relationship between the Church and Israel is perhaps the key issue that distinguishes dispensationlism from other forms of millennialism. Fruchtenbaum summarizes the viewpoints nicely:

> Covenant Premillennialism believes in both a national salvation and a national restoration of Israel. Postmillennialism believes in a national salvation, but not a national restoration of Israel. Amillennialism rejects both.[20]

One can see from Fruchtenbaum's comment that this issue is rather complex. That those in a certain camp sometimes disagree among themselves further complicates things. Let's take covenant premillennialism to provide an example of what happens when the line between Israel and the Church is blurred: covenant premillennialism appears to teach that the Church has replaced Israel for now, but there will be a distinction between them during the Millennial Kingdom.[21] Like all debates concerning theology or the Bible, this one boils down to hermeneutics. Covenant premillennialist George Ladd declares that the New Testament should be used to *reinterpret* some passages in the Old Testament:

---

[20] Arnold G. Fruchtenbaum, *Israelology: The Missing Link in Systematic Theology* (Tustin, CA: Ariel Ministries, 1996), 314.

[21] Most of this section is based on Fruchtenbaum's *Israelology*.

Paul's use of the Old Testament is not so much to seek a one-to-one equating of prophecy and fulfillment as to place the new redemptive events squarely in the stream of Old Testament redemptive history. This leads him to find in the Old Testament meanings that do not readily appear in the quotations in their Old Testament setting. Thus he can apply to the church quotations that in the Old Testament refer only to Israel (Rom. 9:25-26; cf. Hos. 2:23; 1:10). This cannot be labeled a manipulation or misuse of the Old Testament. ...Jesus... is the Messiah foretold in the Old Testament, and that the people of the Messiah are the true people of God, continuous with the Israel of the Old Testament. The church is in fact the true Israel of God.

Therefore the Old Testament must be read in the light of its fulfillment in Christ with the illumination of the Holy Spirit...the Spirit enables the believer to understand from the Old Testament the meaning of the redemptive event wrought in history in Jesus Christ. The new understanding of the Old Testament is controlled by the event of Jesus Christ.[22]

LaSor contends that there is only one distinction between Israel and the Church, and that has to do with chronology:

There is a sense in which the church is *not* Israel. Most obvious, of course, is the simple chronological fact that the church exists this side of Calvary, and Israel in the Old Testament was on the other side, before Calvary was a historical event.[23]

Notice he has to specify that it was the Israel of the *Old* Testament, as opposed to the Israel of the *New* Testament. LaSor then pursues two lines of evidence to prove that the Church is indeed Israel: (1) the similarities between the two entities, and (2) some passages which supposedly demonstrate that the Church is (for now at least) Israel. Some of the similarities he sees are that both are a people called out of the nations by God, both were redeemed by God's work of redemption, both were given the Law (to Israel on stone, and to the Church in our hearts), both are called a kingdom of priests, both have Jesus as their Messiah, and both look forward to a day when the Son of David will reign in righteousness.[24] None of these factors are of any consequence because similarity does not mean identity. The passages LaSor utilizes to buttress his thesis are the same ones used by virtually all covenant theologians – Rom. 9:4-8, Gal. 6:15, 16, and Eph. 2:11-19. Romans 9:4-8 reads,

...who are Israelites, to whom belongs the adoption as sons and the glory and the covenants and the giving of the Law and the temple service and the promises, whose are the fathers, and from whom is the Christ according to the flesh, who is

---

[22] George E. Ladd, *A Theology of the New Testament* (Grand Rapids: Eerdmans, 2002, rev. ed.), 433, 434.

[23] William S. LaSor, *Israel: A Biblical View* (Grand Rapids: Eerdmans, 1976), 85. Emphasis in original.

[24] Ibid., 94, 95.

over all, God blessed forever. Amen. But it is not as though the word of God has failed. For they are not all Israel who are descended from Israel; neither are they all children because they are Abraham's descendants, but: "through Isaac your descendants will be named." That is, it is not the children of the flesh who are children of God, but the children of the promise are regarded as descendants.

LaSor is correct in recognizing that Paul is speaking here of two groups, namely, physical Israel and spiritual Israel. Yet LaSor goes beyond the evidence and concludes Paul is equating spiritual Israel with the Church. Notice the context: in the next several verses of Romans 9 Paul writes about people and events from the *Old* Testament. Moo concludes the second use of "Israel" in verse 6 does not refer to the Church because

> (1) Verses 1-5 establish the parameters within which Paul's language of Israel in Rom. 9-11 must be interpreted, and these verses focus on ethnic Israel. Throughout these chapters, Paul carefully distinguishes between Israel and the Jews on the one hand and the Gentiles on the other. Only where clear contextual pointers are present can the ethnic focus of Israel be abandoned. (2) Paul explains v. 6b in vv. 7-13 with examples of God's selection of his people from *within* ethnic Israel. (3) Verses 27-29, which, as we have seen, relate closely to vv. 6-13, feature OT quotations that focus on the idea of the remnant — again, a group existing within ethnic Israel. The "true Israel" in v. 6b, therefore, denotes a smaller, spiritual body *within* ethnic Israel rather than a spiritual entity that overlaps with ethnic Israel. Paul is not saying "it is not *only* those who are of Israel that are Israel," but "it is not *all* those who are of Israel that are Israel."[25]

Galatians 6:15, 16 reads,

> For neither is circumcision anything, nor uncircumcision, but a new creation. And those who will walk by this rule, peace and mercy be upon them, and upon the Israel of God.

Non-dispensationalists make much of the phrase "the Israel of God," claiming it is another name for the Church. Fruchtenbaum explains:

> ...like all Covenant Theologians, [LaSor] ignores that there are two groups mentioned in the passage: the *them* and the *Israel of God*. As has been shown before, there is no textual or contextual reason to depart from the primary meaning of kai, which means "and," or to resort to a secondary meaning of "even." The *them* refers to the Gentile believers to and of whom Paul had been writing throughout the epistle. The *Israel of God* refers to Jewish believers specifically and not to the Church at large. There is no exegetical reason to make the Israel here a reference to the Church.[26]

---

[25] Douglas J. Moo, *The Epistle to the Romans* (Grand Rapids: Eerdmans, 1996; NICOT), 574. Emphasis in original.

[26] Fruchtenbaum, 252. Italics in original.

Dispensationalist Earl Radmacher adds,

> Whether the *kai* is taken as a simple copulative joining two different groups or whether the "Israel of God" is singled out from the total group (which interpretation seems more likely) it nevertheless distinguishes between Jewish believers and Gentile believers in the church. Thus, the grammar alone presents a strong argument for the distinction. There are other arguments, however, which add great strength to this interpretation. The context of Galatians is favorable to the idea of singling out the true Jews for special mention. The apostle's argument is with the Judaizers... After attacking these Jews, who would be considered Israel after the flesh, it is perfectly logical for Paul, when extending his blessing, to recognize those Jews who had left this legalism and were following the rule of the new creation, the *ekklesia*. Thus, he clarified to the Gentiles that he was not attacking Jews as such, and, likewise, he expressed his love for his "brethren according to the flesh." Surely, if the New Testament wanted to equate the *ekklesia* and Israel, it would have done so plainly, and in many places, for the term *Israel* is used frequently throughout.[27]

Scholars of every stripe agree that the vast majority of occurrences of "Israel" in the New Testament refer to ethnic Israel, yet some want to make an exception for Galatians 6:16 with no compelling reason for doing so.

A third passage covenant theologians emphasize in equating Israel and the Church is Ephesians 2:11-19:

> Therefore remember that formerly you, the Gentiles in the flesh, who are called "Uncircumcision " by the so-called "Circumcision," which is performed in the flesh by human hands -- remember that you were at that time separate from Christ, excluded from the commonwealth of Israel, and strangers to the covenants of promise, having no hope and without God in the world. But now in Christ Jesus you who formerly were far off have been brought near by the blood of Christ. For He Himself is our peace, who made both groups into one and broke down the barrier of the dividing wall, by abolishing in His flesh the enmity, which is the Law of commandments contained in ordinances, so that in Himself He might make the two into one new man, thus establishing peace, and might reconcile them both in one body to God through the cross, by it having put to death the enmity. AND HE CAME AND PREACHED PEACE TO YOU WHO WERE FAR AWAY, AND PEACE TO THOSE WHO WERE NEAR; for through Him we both have our access in one Spirit to the Father. So then you are no longer strangers and aliens, but you are fellow citizens with the saints, and are of God's household.

In the following quote from amillennialist Robert Reymond, note that he (1) mentions the similarity between Israel and the Church, and (2) stresses the soteriological nature of the Church:

---

[27] Earl D. Radmacher, *The Nature of the Church* (Hayesville, NC: Schoettle Publishing, 1996), 184, 185. Italics in original.

And Gentiles who come into this *ekklesia,* as Paul would later declare, "have been brought near" to the "commonwealth...of Israel" and Israel's "covenants of promise" (Eph. 2:12-13), and...with elect Jews are God's "new man" (Eph. 2:14-16). Jesus' *ekklesia* then is the true New Testament "assembly of the Lord" and thus the continuing expression of that spiritual "Israel" within Old Testament national Israel of which Paul speaks (Rom. 9:6). That is to say, just as there was a true spiritual "Israel" within Old Testament national Israel, so also Jesus' *ekklesia,* as the Israel of God exists within professing Christendom. And just as Old Testament Israel was God's national theocratic kingdom, so also Jesus' *ekklesia* is God's soteric theocratic kingdom with Messiah as its sovereign and its members responsible to obey their Sovereign's every command (Matt. 28:20).[28]

But this passage does not state that Gentiles are now within the covenants of Israel, for the Church (the "one new man," v. 15) never was a party to the covenants. No passage of Holy Writ mentions a covenant between God and the Church.

After explaining that there is no difference between the two Greek words for "new" (kaino and neo),[29] Hoehner gives the natural interpretation of Ephesians 2:

In the present context kaino is used to show that Christ has created a whole new person entirely different from the two former persons, namely, Jews and Gentiles. It is not that Gentiles become Jews as Gentile proselytes did in pre-NT times nor that Jews become Gentiles, but both become "one new person" or "one new humanity," a third entity. ...The new corporate person, who is called "one body"...in verse 16, refers to the church. ...This coincides with Paul's admonition not to offend three groups of people: the Jews, the Greeks/Gentiles, and the church of God (1 Cor 10:32). The Jews and the Greeks/Gentiles are presented as unconverted and the church is that which is composed of Jewish and Gentile believers. They are not Jews or Gentiles but a body of Christians who make up the church.[30]

Even Barth admits,

Correspondingly, when in Eph 2:15 Christ is called creator and creates a person, then the term "one new man" must mean a person distinct from Christ. No other person can be meant than the "bride of Christ." While this bride is never explicitly named the New Eve, she is identified as the church in 5:23-32 (cf. II Cor 11:2) or as the people or property of God in 1:14.[31]

---

[28] Robert L. Reymond, *A New Systematic Theology of the Christian Faith* (Nashville: Thomas Nelson, 1998, 2nd ed., revised and updated), 824, 825.

[29] A previous generation of scholars held these two words were not synonyms, but that they are used in Ephesians 4:24 and Colossians 3:10 interchangeably suggests they are synonymous.

[30] Harold W. Hoehner, *Ephesians* (Grand Rapids: Baker, 2002), 378-380.

[31] Markus Barth, *Ephesians 1-3* (New York: Doubleday, 1974), 309.

Finally, it should be noted that the definition amillennialists have for the Church conflicts with their position as to when it started. Amillennialist Bruce Milne defines the Church as the "total people of God spread through all the ages, the total company of the elect."[32] I assume that "all the ages" would go back at least as far as Abraham, and maybe even to Adam. It is no surprise, then, that Berkhof believes that at the time of the exodus it was the Church that was coming out of Egypt. He writes that "the whole nation constituted the Church."[33] The problem is most of those people were not believers as shown by the fact that they were eager to make a golden calf! Israel and the Church are completely distinct entities.

The Church and the Kingdom.

Amillennialists and postmillennialists perceive very little difference between the Church and the Kingdom, and since they believe the Church is the "new" (or "true") Israel, the Church, the Kingdom, and Israel are essentially the same. One reason Berkhof puts forth to demonstrate the intimate relationship between the Church and the Kingdom has to do with the fact that Christ is the head of the Church. He claims that the word head "as applied to Christ, is in some cases practically equivalent to 'King.'"[34] He cites these passages: 1 Corinthians 11:3; Ephesians 1:22, and 5:23. If we were to apply Berkhof's reasoning to the other parts of 1 Corinthians 11:3 and Ephesians 5:23, the result would be nonsense. Do we want to set up the husband as "king" over his wife?

Too, amillennarians have no adequate explanation for the Kingdom promises to Israel found in the Old Testament. Most of them hold to one of two methods. The first method is to spiritualize those promises. They are either being fulfilled in the Church, or will be fulfilled in heaven. Calvin proposed this view in his *Institutes*, saying

> The ground of controversy is this: our opponents hold that the land of Canaan was considered by the Israelites as supreme and final happiness, and now, since Christ was manifested, typifies to us the heavenly inheritance; whereas we maintain that, in the earthly possession which the Israelites enjoyed, they beheld, as in a mirror, the future inheritance which they believed to be reserved for them in heaven.[35]

One promise in the Hebrew Scriptures is that Israel will be regathered. The Lord declared to Ezekiel (37:21): "Behold, I will take the sons of Israel from

---

[32] Bruce Milne, *Know the Truth* (Downers Grove, IL: IVP, 1998, rev. ed.), 265.
[33] Berkhof, 570.
[34] Ibid., 406.
[35] John Calvin, *Institutes of the Christian Religion* (Logos version), II, xi, 1.

among the nations where they have gone, and I will gather them from every side and bring them into their own land." Keil and Delitzsch believe this passage

> is not to be taken literally, but symbolically or typically, and that we are not to expect it to be literally fulfilled. We are forced to this conclusion by the fact that, through the coming of Christ, and the kingdom of heaven which began with Him, the idea of the people of God has been so expanded, that henceforth not the lineal descendants of Abraham, or the Jewish nation merely, but the church of confessors of Jesus Christ, gathered together out of Israel and the Gentiles, has become the people of God, and the economy of the Old Testament has ceased to constitute the divinely appointed from of the church of God.[36]

A second method to get around the Kingdom promises is to assert that they were conditional and thus Israel has forfeited them by her disobedience. The short answer to that is simply to ask, how many of us deserve our salvation? Amillennialist R. V. G. Tasker is stark in his comments on Matthew 21:35-43:

> Because of this rejection of Jesus the Messiah, which came as the climax of a long series of rejections of the prophets God had sent to it (35, 36), the old Israel as such would forfeit the right to receive the blessings appertaining to the kingdom of God. These blessings would in consequence be made available to a less exclusive people of God which would contain men of all races and nations (43); and the murderers of God's Son would themselves be destroyed (41).[37]

Postmillennialists utilize many of the same anti-Semitic arguments. Boettner speaks for many postmillennialists when he postulates

> In or about the spring of the year 30 A.D., the mass of those who then called themselves Israelites ceased to be such...having forfeited their citizenship in the commonwealth of Israel by refusing to accept the Messiah.[38]

Here is Hodge's opinion:

> The literal interpretation of the Old Testament prophecies relating to the restoration of Israel and the future kingdom of Christ, cannot by possibility be carried out ...[39]

In comparing and contrasting amillennialism and postmillennialism, Walvoord writes,

---

[36] C. F. Keil and Franz Delitzsch, *Commentary on the Old Testament* (E-sword version).

[37] R. V. G. Tasker, *The Gospel According to St. Matthew* (Grand Rapids: Eerdmans, 1961; TNTC), 204.

[38] Loraine Boettner, *The Millennium* (Philadelphia: The Presbyterian and Reformed Pub. Co., 1964), 318.

[39] Hodge, 3:809.

Some amillenarians such as Prof. William Hendricksen and some conservative postmillenarians such as Charles Hodge hold that Israel's promises of blessings will be fulfilled to those of Israel in the flesh who come to Christ and become part of the Christian church. The promises are to be fulfilled, then, to Israel, but to Israel in the church. Hodge takes this as a final triumph of the gospel and even envisions some regathering of Israel for this purpose. Under both of these forms of interpretation, no post-advent kingdom is required to fulfill Israel's promises. All will be fulfilled in the present age.

It is clear, however, to all that many of the promises cannot be literally applied to present earth conditions. Two expedients are followed by the amillenarian and postmillenarian interpretation. Some promises are cancelled as having been conditional in the first place. Others are spiritualized to fit the pattern of the present age. This interpretation is based upon a somewhat contradictory set of principles. One view is that the promises to Israel were never intended to be taken literally and hence are rightly spiritualized to fit the church. The other is that they were literal enough, but cancelled because of Israel's sin. The concept of Israel prevailing among amillenarians and postmillenarians is therefore confused and inherently contradictory. There does not seem to be any norm or central consistency except in their denial of a political and national future for Israel after the second advent. What unity exists in their system rests upon this denial.[40]

Once all of the factors are considered, it is quite reasonable to conclude that the Scriptures as teaching that the Kingdom promises to Israel still apply, and will be fulfilled during the 1000-year Millennial reign of Christ on earth.

In this section on ecclesiology, we have examined the origin of the Church, the members of the Church, the Church and Israel, and the Church and the Kingdom. The consistent use of a literal hermeneutic leads to the conclusion that the Church began in Acts 2, that the Members are those who have trusted Christ as their Savior, that the Church and Israel are two distinct entities, and that the Church has not taken over the Kingdom promises to Israel.

Eschatology

Certainly the greatest disparity among dispensationalism, amillennialism, and postmillennialism resides in the realm of eschatology. Dispensationalism stands alone in its emphasis of a consistently literal hermeneutic. Amillennialists and postmillennialists believe Jesus will literally return,[41] yet, because the way their theological system functions, they are forced to spiritualize His 1000-year Kingdom and the Tribulation. Anthony Hoekema tries to clarify the amillennialist position, saying,

---

[40] John F. Walvoord, "Millennial Series: Part 11: The Theological Context of Premillennialism" (*BibSac* 108:431): 278, 279.

[41] Except for full preterists.

The term *amillennialism* is not a happy one. It suggests that amillennialists either do not believe in any millennium or that they simply ignore the first six verses of Revelation 20, which speak of a millennial reign. Neither of these two statements is true. ...it is true that amillennialists do not believe in a literal thousand-year earthly reign which will follow the return of Christ ...amillennialists believe that the millennium of Revelation 20 is not exclusively future but is now in process of realization.[42]

Hoekema clearly believes Christ's Kingdom has already started. One reason offered for this conclusion is Revelation 20 does not follow Revelation 19 chronologically. "Rather, Revelation 20:1 takes us back once again to the beginning of the New Testament era."[43] Furthermore, it is assumed that Christ took the Davidic throne at His ascension. In regard to Revelation 20:4-6, Hoekema writes,

There is no indication in these verses that John is describing an earthly millennial reign. The scene, as we saw, is set in heaven. Nothing is said in verses 4-6 about the earth, about Palestine as the center of this reign or about the Jews. The thousand-year reign of Revelation 20:4 is a reign with Christ in heaven of the souls of believers who have died.[44]

What is likewise strange about non-dispensational beliefs is that the Tribulation is also happening during this age. Apparently both amillennialists and postmillennialists advocate this doctrine.[45] Concerning Matthew 24:21, Hoekema claims,

There is no indication in Jesus' words that the great tribulation which he predicts will be restricted to the Jews, and that Gentile Christians, or the church in distinction from the Jews, will not have to go through it. This view, commonly taught by dispensationalists, has no basis in Scripture. For if tribulation, as we have just seen, is to be suffered by Christians throughout this entire age, what reason is there for restricting the final tribulation to the Jews? What reason is there for restricting the elect for whose sake the days of that final tribulation will be shortened (Matt. 24:22) to the elect among the Jews?[46]

Yet a key (and unanswered) question here is: how could the Kingdom and the Tribulation possibly be cotemporaneous?

---

[42] Anthony A. Hoekema, "Amillennialism" in *The Meaning of the Millennium* ed. by Robert G. Clouse (Downers Grove, IL: IVP, 1977), 155, 156.

[43] Ibid., 160.

[44] Ibid., 169.

[45] It is quite difficult to ascertain what amillennialists and post-millennialists believe about the Tribulation because they write so little about it.

[46] Anthony A. Hoekema, *The Bible and the Future* (Grand Rapids: Eerdmans, 1982), 151.

Postmillennialists hold to many of the same views. They teach that the Church Age will eventually become the Kingdom. Boettner summarizes this belief.

> Postmillennialism is that view of the last things which holds that the kingdom of God is now being extended in the world through the preaching of the gospel and the saving work of the Holy Spirit in the hearts of individuals, that the world eventually is to be Christianized and that the return of Christ is to occur at the close of a long period of righteousness and peace commonly called the millennium. It should be added that on postmillennial principles the Second Coming of Christ will be followed immediately by the general resurrection, the general judgment, and the introduction of heaven and hell in their fullness.[47]

Later he writes,

> The postmillennialist looks for a golden age that will not be essentially different from our own so far as the basic facts of life are concerned. This age gradually merges into the millennial age as an increasing proportion of the world's inhabitants are converted to Christianity. Marriage and the home will continue, and new members will enter the human race through the natural process of birth, as at present. Sin will not be eliminated but will be reduced to a minimum as the moral and spiritual environment of the earth becomes predominantly Christian.[48]

Hodge talks about the tribulation taking place just before the Second Coming, but says nothing about it being seven years in duration:

> The Scriptures, then, as they have been generally understood in the Church, teach that before the Second Advent, there is to be the ingathering of the heathen; that the Gospel must be preached to all nations; and also that there is to be a national conversion of the Jews; but it is not to be inferred from this that either all the heathen or all the Jews are to become true Christians. In many cases the conversion may be merely nominal. … enough [will] remain unchanged in heart to be the germ of that persecuting power which shall bring about those days of tribulation which the Bible seems to teach are to immediately precede the coming of the Lord.[49]

Both amillennialists and postmillennialists have little to say about the Tribulation such as that mentioned in Daniel 9 and 12, Matthew 24, Revelation 7, and other places. Again, this silence is explained by the fact that non-premillennialists are not sure what to do with it.

The postmillennialist in particular, with his optimistic outlook on life, has a difficult time inserting it into his scheme.

---

[47] Loraine Boettner, "Postmillennialism" in *The Meaning of the Millennium*, 117.

[48] Ibid., 120-121.

[49] Hodge, 3:811.

Dispensationalists contend that the Millennial Kingdom and the Tribulation cannot and should not be so readily allegorized and overlooked. No good reason has ever been presented as to why Revelation 20 should not be taken literally. How strange that John would write "thousand years" several times in the first few verses if that expression were to be taken in some non-literal manner. He could have used the indefinite phrase "a long time" just as he used "a short time" in verse 3. Too, take a close look at Acts 1:5-8, one of Jesus' post-resurrection appearances:

> "...for John baptized with water, but you will be baptized with the Holy Spirit not many days from now." So when they had come together, they were asking Him, saying, "Lord, is it at this time You are restoring the kingdom to Israel?" He said to them, "It is not for you to know times or epochs which the Father has fixed by His own authority; but you will receive power when the Holy Spirit has come upon you..."

This would have been the perfect opportunity for Christ to inaugurate His Kingdom, but He didn't. In fact, He contrasts the baptizing work of the Holy Spirit with the coming of the Kingdom in a very clear manner ("but," *alla*).

Similarly, the Scriptures are not that enigmatic about the Tribulation. It is mentioned in numerous Old and New Testament passages (Is. 26:20, 21; 34:2-8; Jer. 30:5-9; Dan. 12:1; Joel 1:15; 2:1, 2; Mt. 24; 2 Thess. 2; and most of Revelation). One of the most powerful descriptions of the Tribulation is given in 2 Thessalonians 2:1-4:

> Now we request you, brethren, with regard to the coming of our Lord Jesus Christ and our gathering together to Him, that you not be quickly shaken from your composure or be disturbed either by a spirit or a message or a letter as if from us, to the effect that the day of the Lord has come. Let no one in any way deceive you, for it will not come unless the apostasy comes first, and the man of lawlessness is revealed, the son of destruction, who opposes and exalts himself above every so-called god or object of worship, so that he takes his seat in the temple of God, displaying himself as being God.

The Bible is about as clear on the subject of the duration of the Tribulation as it is on the subject of its future existence. (The more significant passages here are Dan. 7:25, 9:27, 12:7; Rev. 12:6, 14.) Daniel 9:26, 27 announces that "the prince who is to come...will make a firm covenant with the many for one week." The simplest way to understand this "week" is to interpret it as a seven-year period.[50] No other unit of time (day, week, *etc.*) makes good sense here.

---

[50] See Charles H. Ray, "Daniel 9:24-27, Part I" in *The Conservative Theological Journal* August 2001, Vol. 5, No. 15, 168-178.

Bibliology

Hermeneutics is *the* issue for any debate of a biblical or theological nature. A person's principles of interpretation are the cornerstone for how the rest of his belief system works itself out. Any addition to a plain or normal hermeneutic (such as progressive dispensationalism's complementary hermeneutic), or any inconsistency (such as the switch to the spiritualizing method of the non-premillennialist) can result in nothing but error. The Bible student who sets aside the literal hermeneutic also sets aside all the norms, standards, and controls for understanding the Sacred Text properly. Then what is the direct connection to Bibliology? Walvoord answers that it has to do with the reliability of the Bible:

> While amillennialism can hardly be blamed for destructive higher criticism which has undermined faith in the Bible, it can be said that it had no defense against it as far as its method and attitude are concerned. After all, if Scripture which teaches something contrary to a preconceived theory can be altered by spiritualizing it, of what importance is the concept of inerrancy?[51]

Boettner criticizes the literal method because, like most non-premillennialists, he doesn't seem to understand it:

> Premillennialists often materialize and literalize the prophecies to such an extent that they keep them on an earthly level and miss their true and deeper meaning.[52]

The Lord did not reveal His Word to us in the form of a puzzle. He communicated using normal human language. That being the case, we should approach the Scriptures with that principle in mind.

Conclusion

The average pew-sitter has very little concern as to whether he is an amillennialist, dispensationalist, or postmillennialist. He can't comprehend what the fuss is all about. What he needs to be told is a Christian's method of interpretation is what the fuss is all about, and choosing the right method is very important, and thus one's hermeneutic impacts virtually every branch of systematic theology, and is ultimately responsible for key distinctions between dispensational and non-dispensational theological systems.

---

[51] Walvoord, 73.
[52] Boettner, *The Meaning of the Millennium*, 137.

"If God is the originator of language and if the chief purpose of originating it was to convey His message to humanity, then it must follow that he, being all-wise and all-loving, originated sufficient language to convey all that was in His heart to tell mankind. Furthermore, it must also follow that He would use language and expect people to understand it in its literal, normal, and plain sense."

- Charles C. Ryrie

Dispensationalism, 1995, page 81

5

The Importance of the Biblical Languages
David E. Olander

> *Every word of God is tested; He is a shield to those who take refuge in Him. Do not add to His words Lest He reprove you, and you be proved a liar.* (Proverbs 30:5-6)

God Chose Specific Languages with Which He Posited His Word

God has graciously given man His inerrant Word in written form. It was not without eternal and infinite wisdom God chose the time, manner, and specific languages He would use to record His Word. He even chose precise linguistics, tenses, grammar, forms, meanings, and cultural differences with known dialects of the languages in which to place His exact words. He chose Hebrew (also Aramaic) and Greek as His primary languages to communicate with all men. God gave His Word using approximately 40 different authors over almost 2000 years in precisely two languages, Hebrew and Greek. All this is by infinite design and it is far more than something incidental or that which any man could do. This involves an infinite mind with exact purpose resulting in complete perfection and flawless preservation. Nothing else is inspired except God's complete inerrant Word in the original languages.

This ultimate design by the Designer eliminates any kind of conspiracy or deception for this would not be possible especially with such a vast amount of data over the decades, centuries, and now several millennia. There is no religion or faith on the planet that comes close to having such massive documentation especially copies of the original texts. Other faiths are limited to one or two writers with almost no verification, manuscripts, or documentation. Other faiths really have nothing compared to what God has allowed to be preserved concerning His Word. In addition, it is amazing that when there arose great controversy or debate about various text in any of the Word, certain manuscripts were found which documented any know discrepancy with precise accuracy and consistency. Through the ages, every charge against the Word of God has been adequately explained. Yet man refuses to acknowledge that God has spoken.

God has given His perfectly inerrant Word in such a way that only God alone could have accomplished this task. Man is accountable for understanding the magnitude of this gracious gift of His supernatural revelation. There is nothing comparable to His Word except the living Word alone, the Lord Jesus Christ. Every diligent student of the Word of God recognizes and observes this magnificent truth. All this is nothing short of miraculous that is the very fact that God has given and perfectly preserved His written revelation. He has given a great treasure and an extraordinary eternal gift, the gift of His written Word.

The written Word points directly to the living eternal Word, His Son. The eternal Son always pointed directly to the written Word for it spoke of Him (Luke 24:26-27; John 5:39). God gave His Word in a manner and language that was not enigmatic, cryptic, or mysterious, but in a way, all can understand. While there may be things in His Word hidden because of spiritual blindness, God gave His Word in a manner for all to know. He posited it in known languages for the nations of the world to listen and respond. Therefore, man is fully culpable for understanding what God has revealed. Blessed is the one who has great honor and respect for the Word of God (Is. 62:2). The reformers were quite aware of all this and their plea was always to go 'back to the sources':

> In proportion then as we value the gospel, let us zealously hold to the languages. For it was not without purpose that God caused his Scriptures to be set down in these two languages alone--the Old Testament in Hebrew, the New in Greek. Now if God did not despise them but chose them above all others for his word, then we too ought to honor them above all others (Martin Luther).[1]

In the Institutes, Calvin noted how perfectly and completely God preserved the Law and the Prophets in Hebrew in spite of religion and the people:

> The Hebrew language lay not only unesteemed, but almost unknown; and to be sure, if God had not been pleased to care for their religion, it would have perished completely... And through whom did God preserve for us the doctrine of salvation embraced in the Law and the Prophets, that Christ in his own time might be made manifest.[2]

---

[1] Martin Luther, An excerpt from: *"To the Councilmen of All Cities in Germany That They Establish and Maintain Christian Schools,* 1524.

[2] "The miracle appeared not only in that God delivered the Tables of his covenant from the bloody edicts of Antiochus, but also in that the Jewish people, ground down and wasted by such manifold misfortunes, were soon almost exterminated, yet the writings remained safe and intact. The Hebrew language lay not only unesteemed, but almost unknown; and to be sure, if God had not been pleased to care for their religion, it would have perished completely. For after the Jews were brought back from exile, how much they departed from the true use of the mother tongue appears from the prophets of that age, a fact with noting because from this comparison one more clearly perceives the antiquity of the Law and the Prophets. And through whom did God preserve for us the doctrine of salvation embraced in the Law and the Prophets, that Christ in his own time might be made manifest." John Calvin, *Institutes of the Christian Religion* (Philadelphia: Westminster Press, 1960), 1:1:8:10, 90.

Calvin wrote quite intensely on the particular miracle of the preservation of Scripture in the original languages in the Institutes. The fact the reformers were going back to the sources (copies of the originals – sola scriptura) meant they knew and believed how well His Word was preserved in spite of years of opposition and destruction of documents, books, and manuscripts. Reformers did not have to rely on translations such as the LXX, Latin, etc. While historical works and other traditions even translations may confirm and identify a particular explanation or interpretations such as translations do today, they are still not copies of the Text from the original languages. They fall very short of the original. Calvin comments:

> Since Antiochus (they say) ordered all books to be burned (1 Macc. 1:56-57), where did the copies that we now have come from?... For it is well known that directly after the persecutions had ceased, the books were extant, and were acknowledged without controversy by all the godly, who were brought up on their doctrine and knew them intimately. But even though all wicked men, as if conspiring together, have so shamelessly insulted the Jews, no one has ever dared charge them with substituting false books. For whatever, in their opinion, the Jewish religion may be, they confess Moses to be its author... let us rather ponder here how much care the Lord has taken to preserve his Word, when, contrary to everybody's expectation, he snatched it away from a most cruel and savage tyrant, as from a raging fire... Who does not recognize as a remarkable and wonderful work of God the fact that those sacred monuments, which the wicked has persuaded themselves had utterly perished, soon returned and took their former place once more, and even with enhanced dignity? For the Greek translation followed, which published them abroad throughout the world.[3]

The fact that His Word is so perfectly preserved in Hebrew and Greek should be an extraordinary testimony or witness for anyone who questions the Word of God. The Word is as perfectly preserved as is His created, chosen, and elect nation of Israel, the Jews. All this should also be an incentive for any teacher or student of the Word to have the greatest respect for His inerrant Word. The fact that God has preserved His Word so perfectly in the original would mean He wants His people to at least know that and esteem exactly what He has done. Man is fully accountable for all He has revealed and has no excuse.

Believers are challenged to get into God's infinite and eternal truth – to get into His Word that He posited in the exact languages, structure, form, words He wanted man to know. This is the Infinite communing directly with the finite. This is the Creator of the universe communing directly with the creature. This is a loving Father speaking directly to His children. He gave

---

[3] John Calvin, *Institutes of the Christ Religion* (Philadelphia: Westminster Press, 1960), 1:1:8:10, 89-90.

man His perfect and inerrant Word flawlessly preserved in the original languages. There is no single greater miracle than this today on the planet.

God Has Communicated with Man Primarily Through One Nation and One Language

The Scriptures are God's inerrant, plenary, and primary revelation to man. God chose to use certain men and primarily one nation through whom He revealed Himself and His purpose. He personally created and elected Israel (Is. 43:1-15; Rom. 9), and gave this nation precedence over all other nations (Deut. 7:6-9; 14:2). His purpose was primarily doxological displaying within this nation His personal presence, glory, and His Word (Ex. 25:8; 29:45-46; 1 Kings 6:13; 2 Chron. 6:6; 12:13; Ezek. 43:7, 9). Israel was to be a light to the nations as God chose to dwell among His people, Israel (Ex. 25:8; 29:45-46). He will do this in His future covenanted kingdom (Jer. 31:33; Zech. 2:10), and eternally as His earthly kingdom will be transferred to the eternal state after He subdues all enemies (1 Cor. 15:24-28; Rev. 21:5, 22-23). This is one reason the Lord said to pray for His coming kingdom (Mt. 6:10). Without the completed inerrant Text revealing a chosen nation, a chosen land, a chosen king and kingdom, and chosen languages through which to reveal His plan and purpose, man is left nothing but idle speculation.

God chose one nation with one language to communicate His Word. If there were other nations with multiple languages, it would be impossible to put any of this together. It would make no sense or just nonsense. Nations come and go, and also languages, but Israel is preserved by God forever (Jer. 31:35-37). Paul spoke entirely of the nation Israel, the Jews, in Romans 9, 10, and 11. Some say Israel past, present, and future respectively. These were Israelites by definition, and he used the word 'Israelites' just to make sure everyone knew that forever He meant *the* Jews, no substitutions and no replacement. "Who are Israelites, to whom belongs the adoption as sons and the glory and the covenants and the giving of the Law and the temple service and the promises" (Rom. 9:4). Some say God gave the Arabs oil, but to Israel He gave His Word. Which one would you have? God manifest Himself primarily to the nation Israel. Israel was the keeper of the Word and all the promises. All eternal and unconditional covenants of promise were made exclusively with Israel and can only be fulfilled in and through Israel. It is very interesting to look at one of these promises that is most significant and is applicable to *all* the nations of the world.

This one promise is justification by faith alone. This was God's promise to justify or declare righteous all (all peoples, all nations, etc.) who believe in Him. "And the Scripture, foreseeing that God would justify the

Gentiles by faith, preached the gospel beforehand to Abraham, saying, "All the nations shall be blessed in you" (Gal. 3:8).[4] Salvation by grace, or justification by faith alone, is a major doctrine yet it is rooted completely in the Abrahamic covenant. This is a direct reference to one of the promises made to Abraham in Gen. 12:1-3 recorded in one language. This is also a great theological link to the Old Testament Text proving a direct connection between the Hebrew OT and the Greek NT. Note also in Gal. 3:8 what Scripture says God says. They are equal. Therefore, justification by faith alone to all the nations was promised in the original Abrahamic covenant. Scripture presents a covenant of grace and here it is recorded eternally in Hebrew in the original Abrahamic covenant. No one need look further for some implied covenant of grace which simply does not exist. Everyone is saved or justified the same way as Abraham, the believer (Gal. 3:9).[5]

The fact that God gave the Word in Hebrew in the Old Testament (Greek in the New Testament) limits what is in the Text. The original language restricts and confines what is in the Text. This is most essential to comprehend and appreciate. One cannot add any word(s)- let alone whole covenants - that are simply not in Scripture. To do so reads far too much into what He has inerrantly given and preserved. It is amazing what He has preserved or sealed, as many more might believe in covenants and other teachings that simply do not exist. God has communicated with all mankind primarily through one nation using Hebrew and Greek. Anything more than this is adding to the Word of God and anything less than this takes away from the Word of God.

---

[4] "And the <u>Scripture, foreseeing</u> that God would justify the Gentiles by faith, <u>preached</u> the gospel beforehand to Abraham, saying, "All the nations shall be blessed in you" (Galatians 3:8,). προϊδοῦσα δὲ ἡ γραφὴ ὅτι ἐκ πίστεως <u>δικαιοῖ</u> τὰ ἔθνη ὁ θεός, <u>προευηγγελίσατο</u> τῷ Ἀβραὰμ ὅτι ἐνευλογηθήσονται ἐν σοὶ πάντα τὰ ἔθνη (Galatians 3:8). Note some of the intricacies here. The Scripture foreseeing (προϊδοῦσα) that ... preached (προευηγγελίσατο)... It is interesting that the Scriptures themselves heralded this great truth of justification by faith. All this is by Scripture of itself; the idea here is very much sola scriptura. Note also the word for justify (δικαιοῖ). This is a pres. act. indic. from δικαιόω. This is saying that He was continually justifying the nations by faith alone from the giving of the covenant itself. Some ask how God justified in the OT. Here is it and the languages truly confirm it. One's theology might not, but the Text does!.

[5] "Even so Abraham believed God, and it was reckoned to him as righteousness. Therefore, be sure that it is those who are of faith who are sons of Abraham. And the Scripture, foreseeing that God would justify the Gentiles by faith, preached the gospel beforehand to Abraham, saying, "All the nations shall be blessed in you." So then those who are of faith are blessed with Abraham, the believer" (Galatians 3:6-9). True believers are children of Abraham but this does not make one an Israelite, a Jew, or Israel. When one believes as Abraham, one does not change nationality. Abraham technically was not Jewish. He had other children who were/are not Israel or Jews by definition. Scripture is quite clear on all this especially in the languages.

The Reformers Knew to go Back to the Original Languages

Calvin, Luther, and other major Reformers knew His Word had been perfectly preserved through years of devastation. They had to move away from all translations as primary sources such as the Latin and even the LXX. Nothing could take the place of the original Greek and Hebrew and they seemed to understand this exceptionally well. They knew what they had to do and they certainly did go back to the sources. This has to be the greatest move and achievement of the Reformers. Luther comments on this exact issue:

> Truly, if there were no other benefit connected with the languages, this should be enough to delight and inspire us, namely, that they are so fine and noble a gift of God, with which he is now so rightly visiting and blessing us Germans above all other lands. We do not see many instances where the devil has allowed them to flourish by means of the universities and monasteries; indeed, these have always raged against languages and are even now raging. For the devil smelled a rat, and perceived that if the languages were revived a hole would be knocked in his kingdom which he could not easily stop up again. Since he found he could not prevent their revival, he now aims to keep them on such slender rations that they will of themselves decline and pass away. They are not a welcome guest in his house, so he plans to offer them such meager entertainment that they will not prolong their stay. Very few of us my dear sirs see through this evil design of the devil. Therefore, my beloved Germans, let us get our eyes open, thank God for this precious treasure, and guard it well, lest the devil vent his spite and it be taken away from us again.[6]

Luther would not be very popular in most churches today. How many truly understand a real subtle work of the enemy. Perhaps the Laodicea mentality (Rev. 3:14-22) was not only apathetic and lukewarm toward things of Christ, but actually having a stagnant and indifferent attitude toward every jot and tittle of His Word. That so few seem to truly understand this may a significant cause of apostasy – there is minimal commitment (especially) to solid doctrine, and ambivalence toward His inerrant Word (especially the details).

It is not uncommon in this time to see schools and seminaries move away from the flagships of languages and exegesis – and even delete them all but completely. Exegesis or real interpretation can really *only* be done from the original languages, not from translations. How many realize and see through the evil design of the enemy particularly to move the reader from the original Text. Pastor/Teachers often say 'I just don't have the time.' Believers, especially pastor/teachers should be as close to the Greek and

---

[6] Martin Luther, An excerpt from: *"To the Councilmen of All Cities in Germany That They Establish and Maintain Christian Schools*, 1524.

Hebrew as the Reformers – if not closer, for language study is at present made so much easier by the numerous resources available today -there are more resources, better access to copies of the originals, greater documentation of the originals, many more manuscripts, and classic works made accessible in almost every language. There are things in the media that make some of these works completely accessible. There is really no excuse for any of the above except a determined departure from the Word of God in the original languages.

During the Reformation, there was the belief that the true and accurate gospel of Jesus Christ was completely at stake. This concerned especially a departure from the original languages. They actually go hand in hand. These words of Luther to his fellow citizens still ring true:

> Therefore, my beloved Germans, let us get our eyes open, thank God for this precious treasure, and guard it well, lest the devil vent his spite and it be taken away from us again. Although the gospel came and still comes to us through the Holy Spirit alone, we cannot deny that it came through the medium of languages, was spread abroad by that means, and must be preserved by the same means. For just when God wanted to spread the gospel throughout the world by means of the apostles he gave the tongues for that purpose... Formerly no one knew why God had the languages revived, but now for the first time we see that it was done for the sake of the gospel, which he intended to bring to light and use in exposing and destroying the kingdom of Antichrist... And let us be sure of this: we will not long preserve the gospel without the languages. The languages are the sheath in which this sword of the Spirit is contained.[7]

The gospel is recorded and preserved eternally and inerrantly in God's Word, for the gospel is truly the Word of God. If the original languages of God's Word were not preserved or respected as such, then what is the source for the gospel of Jesus Christ? Which book, translation, church, religion, faith, etc., is the infinitely inerrant source? Are any of these *the* absolute inerrant source(s) that cannot err? It cannot be a translation or any translation for no translation is inerrant. No manuscript is inerrant except for the originals in the original languages. We have many copies of the original manuscripts. They are the source(s), for these are our copies of the originals.

> And let us be sure of this: we will no longer preserve the gospel without the languages... Hence, it is inevitable that unless the languages remain, the gospel must perish... Experience too has proven this and still gives evidence of it. For as soon as the languages declined to the vanishing point, after the apostolic age, the

---

[7] Ibid.

gospel and faith Christianity itself declined more and more until under the pope they disappeared entirely.[8]

The reformers moved back to the source of faith and the source for the faith. How can one know absolute truth exists especially concerning God? How can anyone know and believe God has given eternal life to those who believe Him? This is only known through and by the Word of God. How does one know all the facts concerning Christ especially that He is the eternal Son of God? Where did they get their information? How does one know He has been raised from the dead? Where does faith rest? The answer is very simple and given many times in Scripture, 'it has been written'. "Many other signs therefore Jesus also performed in the presence of the disciples, which are not written in this book; but these have been written (ταῦτα δὲ γέγραπται) that you may believe that Jesus is the Christ, the Son of God; and that believing you may have life in His name" (John 20:30-31).[9]   John tells the reader the exact purpose why 'these things' were written or recorded. These things have been recorded in order that you might believe Jesus is the Christ, the Son of God. One must believe Jesus is the eternal Son of God (Who He is and what He did). One who believes has eternal life. Faith rests completely on what has been written. Take away the Word of God or alter these words in any way and faith no longer remains. These things were recorded precisely and inerrantly that one might believe. One demonstrates his faith, trust, belief in God by taking Him at His Word. Calvin understood this perfectly in defining faith.

> Faith rests upon God's Word... first, we must be reminded that there is a permanent relationship between faith and the Word. He could not separate one from the other any more than we could separate the rays from the sun from which the come. For this reason, God exclaims in the book of Isaiah: 'Here me and your soul shall live' (Isa. 55:3)...Therefore if faith turns away even in the slightest degree from this goal toward which it should aim, it does not keep its own nature, but becomes uncertain credulity and vague error of mind. The same Word is the basis whereby faith is supported and sustained; if it turns away from the Word it falls. Therefore, take away the Word and no faith will then remain.[10]

---

[8] Ibid.

[9] Πολλὰ μὲν οὖν καὶ ἄλλα σημεῖα ἐποίησεν ὁ Ἰησοῦς ἐνώπιον τῶν μαθητῶν [αὐτοῦ], **ἃ οὐκ ἔστιν γεγραμμένα** ἐν τῷ βιβλίῳ τούτῳ· **ταῦτα δὲ γέγραπται** ἵνα πιστεύ[ς]ητε ὅτι Ἰησοῦς ἐστιν ὁ χριστὸς ὁ υἱὸς τοῦ θεοῦ, καὶ ἵνα πιστεύοντες ζωὴν ἔχητε ἐν τῷ ὀνόματι αὐτοῦ." (John 20:30-31). Notice the perfect participle construction of 'it is written.' The fact 'it is written' mean one can believe for faith rests only in the Word of God.

[10] John Calvin, *Institutes of the Christian Religion* (Philadelphia: Westminster Press, 1960), 1:3:2:6, 548-549

When there is a move away from the original languages, there is a move away from the very root of the true faith, especially the gospel of Jesus Christ. "These things I have written to you who believe in the name of the Son of God, in order that you may know that you have eternal life" (1 John 5:13).[11] Take away the words or alter the word of John, i.e. 'these things I have written', and no one would be able to believe that Jesus is the Messiah, the Son of God. "And John shows this same wellspring of faith in these words: 'These things have been written that you may believe' (John 20:31)."[12]

Did you notice there was a problem on the road to Emmaus in Luke 24? They did not recognize the resurrected Christ (Luke 24:16). The question is why. "And He said to them, O foolish men and slow of heart to believe in all that the prophets have spoken" (Luke 24:25). He wanted them to believe all God's Word *first* for it spoke of Him (Luke 24:27). Their faith must rest on the very Word of God. This is very comparable to the rich man and Lazarus (Luke 16:19-31). They both died with Lazarus going to the place of blessing and the rich man to Hades. The rich man in his torment said "I beg you, Father, that you send him (*Lazarus*) to my father's house for I have five brothers that he may warn them, lest they also come to this place of torment" (Luke 16:27-28). The rich man believed that if someone went back from the dead, they (his five brothers) would believe. There was only one possible response. Even if someone went (comes) back from the dead no one will believe. They must believe the Word of God first (Luke 16:30-31).

Faith rests entirely on the Word of God. Faith does not rest on any men, church, creed, signs, miracles, wonders, gifts, healings, tongues, experiences, etc. For all these are not flawless and were always to be tested with the completely inerrant Word of God (Deut. 13:1-4; 18:20-22; 1 Cor. 12:3; 1 John 4:1-4 and many other passages). Why go to the inferior when God has supplied the infinite, eternal, and flawless.

Christianity appears to be moving right along today full of life and very user friendly. There seems to be no sense of urgency by anyone about any of these crucial issues. One would think that history would tell us something. Yet the adage seems to hold that man learns from history that he learns nothing from history. The reformers did not really develop anything new; they just got back to the truth or the source which is God's truth. They revived truth/s from which the church had long departed. All

---

[11] Ταῦτα ἔγραψα ὑμῖν ἵνα εἰδῆτε ὅτι ζωὴν ἔχετε αἰώνιον, τοῖς πιστεύουσιν εἰς τὸ ὄνομα τοῦ υἱοῦ τοῦ θεοῦ" (1 John 5:13). Note the word order especially on 'these things, I have written.' There is no doubt John is putting complete emphasis on 'what has been written.'

[12] Calvin, 548.

they really did was revive truth that had already existed, and they could not have done this without getting back to the Word in the original languages. Sola Scriptura was the cry to get back to the autographa. The reformers knew they had to get back to the original languages in which the truth of the gospel of Jesus Christ was inerrantly preserved. If this had not happened, there would have been no true reformation.

The Language Connection between the Old and New Testaments

There are those who seem to identify a certain disconnect or discontinuity between the Old and New testaments. Some argue changes were made in the Word from the languages themselves especially from Old Testament Hebrew to the New Testament Greek (koine). They want a unity but not what Scripture presents. Somehow, they believe there is a departure from God's intended plan especially with Israel or His original plan. However, have things changed at all from His original and eternal oath-bound covenanted promises with Israel? Have thing changed in God's overall program, plan, and purpose from the Old Testament Hebrew text to the New Testament Greek text? This is not possible for God does not change, even His plan/s (Mal. 3:6).

One observation that is germane to the argument is that the New Testament gospels are part of the Old Testament (under the old covenant, the Law) though they are in Greek. There is no disjunctive in any sense, or any type of a division or separation. In fact, it is quite the opposite and proves a direct connection.

Up to Christ's death on the cross, the law (Mosaic Law) was in effect and He observed the law perfectly. Therefore all four gospels are directly connected or linked with Mosaic Law (the Hebrew Old Testament), and most observe this. The new covenant (Jer. 31:31-34; Heb. 8:8-12) did not go into effect until the death of Christ (Heb. 10:10-18, esp. 17). The fact that the new covenant is in effect does today not mean it is fulfilled or is being fulfilled. This is not possible, for the house of Israel and the house of Judah literally (Jer. 31:31-34) can only fulfill this covenant literally. The Scriptures are very clear, and preserved perfectly in Hebrew, that His new covenant is made exclusively with the house of Israel and the house of Judah (Jer. 31:31). This was never an expression for any other group or people (church) other than the nation Israel, the Jews.[13] He is the One Who has set and chosen the

---

[13] The Lord most likely preserved it this way so that not one else could lay claim to a fulfillment except His covenant people, Israel, the Jews. To overlook this or bypass it is nothing more than willful rejection of what is in the Text. The Text is perfectly clear. The epistle to the Hebrews does nothing more than support this completely.

times, peoples, and limits on all these things, and He has recorded all this in His Word in His own infinite way in Hebrew and Greek. This shows how the Old Testament Hebrew Scriptures connect to the New Testament Greek. Just a cursory look at this issue only proves even more how He preserved His Word with not one discontinuity between the testaments.

There is another issue that might be raised at this time concerning His words from the cross, "It is finished!" (John 19:30). "When Jesus therefore had received the sour wine, He said, "It is finished!" (τετέλεσται) And He bowed His head, and gave up His spirit" (John 19:30).[14] Note the context of the verse coming just after 19:28. "After this, Jesus, knowing that all things had already been accomplished (πάντα τετέλεσται) in order that the Scripture might be fulfilled, (τελειωθῇ ἡ γραφή) said, "I am thirsty." (John 19:28).[15] Contextually the reference to 'it is finished' is completely and entirely referenced with the Scriptures (OT). This is a vital link for any understanding of these specific words especially of Christ from the cross. It is most interesting to note that the same root word in these verses is being used for finished, accomplished, and fulfilled.[16] They are all directly related to the Old Testament Hebrew precisely especially Psalm 69:21. It is impossible to say there is no direct connection between the Old Testament Hebrew and the Greek New Testament. They fit together flawlessly, and this was only by infinite and eternal design.

One of the most obvious connections between the OT Hebrew and NT Greek is that the Hebrew Text was translated into Greek. The LXX translation became one of the vehicles for God's Word at that time. The LXX, the oldest of the several translations of the Hebrew Scripture, gave rise to the Old Latin and Syriac versions among others. Just as we have many translations today, they had their translations in their day. The LXX not only smoothed out some of the original Hebrew, it allowed His Word to go into the then known world.[17] Yet everything is perfectly preserved and nothing has changed especially His plan and determined purpose which He had covenanted with His chosen people, Israel, the Jews. Connecting both the Old and New Testaments in Greek really proves a unity of design and purpose. Certain reformers seemed to have observed this issue.

---

[14] ὅτε οὖν ἔλαβεν τὸ ὄξος [ὁ] Ἰησοῦς εἶπεν· **τετέλεσται**, καὶ κλίνας τὴν κεφαλὴν παρέδωκεν τὸ πνεῦμα (John 19:30).

[15] Μετὰ τοῦτο εἰδὼς ὁ Ἰησοῦς ὅτι ἤδη **πάντα τετέλεσται**, ἵνα **τελειωθῇ ἡ γραφή**, λέγει· διψῶ."

[16] τελέω ...1. bring to an end, finish, complete something...Pass. be brought to an end, be finished, completed ...2. carry out, accomplish, perform, fulfill, keep τι something. ... Gal 5:16. ὡς ἐτέλεσαν πάντα τὰ περὶ αὐτοῦ γεγραμμένα when they had carried out everything that was written (in the Scriptures) concerning him (BADG, 810).

[17] Calvin, 90.

The plan of God concerning His Word appears to be:

> OLD TESTAMENT HEBREW SCRIPTURES (OT)　　(inspired)
> LXX GREEK SEPTUAGINT (LXX)　　(not inspired)
> GREEK NEW TESTAMENT (GNT)　　(inspired)

There is no disconnect here. One text appears to give rise to the next. The fact that GNT quotes the LXX so often makes certain this was the main source or Text used at that time. While not the original or inspired text, the LXX connects both the Old Testament Hebrew and New Testament Greek in many ways.

So why is the New Testament in Greek? This is exactly how God planned to posit His inerrant Word. The answer is usually given that the primary Gentile population was Greek speaking from the Hellenistic Empire. However, the major and oldest translation linked directly to the OT Hebrew language and linguistics was the Greek LXX. A more difficult question is why did the Jews adopt the Greek version (LXX)?

> Why did the Jews make the Greek version of their Scriptures which we call the Septuagint (LXX)? The reason given by the Letter of Aristeas, that the king of Egypt and his official librarian wanted a complete collections in Greek of the books of all peoples, seems insufficient. Nor does cultural interest of Greek-speaking Jews explain the project. The language of the LXX does not have the literary quality to be expected in a version prompted by cultural interest. Probably the basic reason was that Jews in Egypt (and elsewhere in the Dispersion) had come increasingly to use Greek in business and social contacts, and hence a translation of the Scriptures into the language they knew best. An added incentive may have been the desire to have an effective tool for mission work among Greek-speaking Gentiles.[18]

The Greek LXX became a vital link between the Hebrew of the Old Testament and the Greek of the New Testament. The percentage of quotes from the LXX to the Greek NT is extremely high. Several of the reformers noticed this yet it must be kept in mind they (the reformers) were not dealing with myriads of translations. They knew they must go back to the original sources (Hebrew and Greek) quite independent of other languages especially Latin. While they did not divorce themselves from Latin, it was not the major text. What this really does is take the Hebrew Text and connect it perfectly to the Greek NT. A peculiar linguistic link flows between the two testaments. No man or conspiracy could have possibly have planned or done this for no conspiracy is planned over thousands of years with about 40

---

[18] Floyd V. Filson, *The Biblical Archaeologist*, Vol. 9, No. 2 (May, 1946): 34.

different authors with two distinct languages. This was not possible for anyone especially connecting OT Hebrew to the NT Greek. Who would have ever thought of such a thing, yet here it is. This proves not only infinite brilliance but also an infinite mind and plan.

The Original Languages Prove Certain Stability

While very few things in life stay constant, one thing that does change or evolve continually is language. Languages come and go. They are extant then dead, and languages always change. Meanings of words also change very much through the years, decades, and even the centuries. What a particular word meant several years ago may not have the same connotation today. Every year or so major dictionaries add more words and meanings. The new Oxford English Dictionary (OED) reported adding some 2,700 new entries. Even basic grammar that was taught years ago is not identically the same today. This is just English and this is just one language. English is also a very recent language in the history of man and developing (depends who you ask). Americans have never been accused of speaking good or proper English. Modern Greek is definitely not biblical Greek, and older German is not modern German. This can be said of every language.

However, the original biblical languages of Greek and Hebrew force everyone, every nation, every culture, every new generation, to look back and examine the original language and meaning. These languages cannot change for God has already posited His Word in these languages. This involves using the extant copies, and studying the historicity of the grammar, the culture of the time, and the etymology of the words themselves among many other things. This is the historical grammatical interpretation. This is like a hedge or a built in boundary condition such as required for all true analytical computations from geometry to complex variables in advanced calculus. One must have a basic definition for a word to mean anything, and then context will determine its most relevant definition and function. Yet if the original languages were changing or evolving or had changed in any manner, then it would be all but impossible to determine any essential meaning required for proper definition and finally a true primary interpretation of the Text.

The original languages also present certain stability with emphasis on writing style of the time and the writing styles of the biblical writers themselves. While this might present definite challenges, the biblical language enthusiast knows this cannot change. God has thus preserved and built in a certain stability with His Word so that no one can alter any jot or tittle of His very words. The Word is complete and unchanged, unchanging, and immutable as He is, for it is literally His absolute Word. This would and should encourage the diligent bible student to purse His truth in a deeper and more realistic way in the original languages.

While not demeaning translations, they are still translations. The true bible teacher or student should understand unmistakably that God has posited His Word in such a way as to preserve it eternally (Ps. 119:89). If this were not so, how could this be God's eternal inerrant Word? Translations will make it readable, but they are not the original. What He has declared has been determined solely and exclusively by Him in eternity, so we have His actual eternal Word in unchangeable words, entity, and design. All else can and will change but His Word cannot possibly change for He is immutable. He is also absolute and immutable in all that He says and does right down to every detail, jot, and tittle. It is not possible for any part of any letter to change for He has established His Word with complete certainty. What He has posited by His own being or perfections requires absolute perfection, completeness, inerrancy, and immutability. His Word has a built-in eternal fixity and completeness. Translations can and do change meaning and variations attached to the meanings. Nevertheless, His Word as given in the original languages is unvarying with perfect and absolute constancy and absolute divine authority and perfection.

For the reformers to move away from Latin in any manner was a huge issue, more of a death wish. The first printed bible, the Gutenberg Bible (1456) was the Latin Vulgate. Nevertheless, the reformers knew God gave His Word in Hebrew and Greek, not Latin or any translations. There was the common refrain 'back to the sources.' Luther a brilliant scholar in biblical languages used available Greek and Hebrew manuscripts for his German translation. Certain reformers wanted to the put the Word into the people's language/s. However, they knew enough to use what they had from the copies of the original Greek and Hebrew manuscripts. They knew perfectly well Greek and Hebrew was what He determined for His Word. This was a huge undertaking and the true *sola scriptura* as opposed to *prima scriptura*, the church, translations esp. Latin, and tradition.

Hebrew and Greek Preserve Singularity of Meaning in a Concise Manner

Verbal inspiration of Scripture means the Text is preserved in the original languages. Verbal inspiration extends only to the original autographs or autographa. While no translation is inspired, most try to reflect the meaning of the original. Yet this presents certain issues as inspiration extends not only to the words but also to the word order, tenses, articles, and many other associated issues. Inspiration extends even to the letters themselves or even parts of each letter or word (Mat. 5:18; Luke 16:17). One does not need be a Greek or Hebrew scholar, but certain knowledge of the biblical languages may solve many problems for the interpreter or allow one to feel more confident with his or her interpretation. The Biblicist does not just study theology. He must study His Word! A true theologian is above all else a student of the Word of God. He knows the original languages preserve the Text flawlessly in a concise and succinct way. He also knows he must use literal grammatical and historical interpretation from the original languages. Literal means the *normal* use of the language.

Translations reflect an intended meaning but not always of the original Text. This is not always done by accident and may mirror the theology of the translator or interpreter. It is sometimes difficult to give the Text an exact rendering in any other language or translation. Certain word order, word meaning, articles, tenses, moods, voice, participles, etc. are sometimes difficult to explain or bring into another language. Sometimes it is impossible to reflect the exact meaning of the Text in certain languages other than the original. This takes some time and explanation and translations cannot always replicate this. Even parallel versions of five or ten translations are often not able to reflect the simplest of explanations one may obtain from the original languages.

The original languages offer a more precise meaning than the translations and there are many examples of this exact issue in both the Hebrew Old Testament and the Greek New Testament. The following examples are from both.

Examples from the Hebrew Old Testament
Old Testament Construction and Grammar
For instance, how is it possible to reflect or explain an octaval acrostic[19] such as Psalm 119 in any other language or translation? There is much more in

---

[19] Each group of eight verses begins with the successive letter of the Hebrew alphabet. The Hebrew alphabet has 22 letters, therefore Psalm 119 has 176 verses. This is just one example in the Hebrew Scriptures.

this Psalm, especially the word order, and very special words used repeatedly with radiant sophistication and beauty. Only Hebrew in the original can reflect the genius of the Hebrew poetry and wisdom literature. It is impossible to bring the magnificence of complexity writers have woven into any language especially that which is in the genius of Hebrew. In Psalm 119, 'the Psalmist uses ten different words for the law or the Word of God, every verse except verses 90, 112, and 132 mentioning at least one of these terms: *law* (i.e., instruction or revelation), *testimonies* (or precepts), *ways, precepts* (or orders), *statutes* (or decrees), *commandments, judgments* (or ordinances), *word, path, word* (the last "word" meaning promise or utterances as in vs. 11.'[20] The Psalmist is proclaiming all he needs is the Word of God. Hebrew adds great depth and meaning.

There is always the enduring debate of literal creationism and a literal twenty-four hour day at creation. Hebrew grammar and construction can certainly help with an understanding of this particular issue. "And God called the light day, and the darkness He called night. And there was evening and there was morning, one day" (Genesis 1:5). Note that on the first day, there was light and darkness as God created the light on the first day. There were no luminaries yet to separate or sustain night and day, or evening and morning. Yet it is clear this is one day. The Hebrew construction for one day is used about ten times in Hebrew and does not have the meaning of more than a twenty four hour day (Gen. 1:5; 27:45; 33:13; Num. 11:19; 1 Sam. 9:15; 27:1; Ezr. 10:17; Isa. 9:13; Jon. 3:4; Zech. 14:7). While this may not settle the issue, it certainly adds great weight for those who hold to literal grammatical historical interpretation.

Old Testament Word Meaning

"Thou hast dealt well with Thy servant, O Lord, according to Thy word. Teach me good discernment and knowledge, For I believe in Thy commandments" (Psalm 119:65-66). The Psalmist asks the Lord to teach him good 'discernment.'[21] The word in Hebrew has the root meaning of taste or perceive. This word can also be used as a figure such as judgment, discretion, or discernment. It also has the meaning of decision or decree in Aramaic. Calvin has as his translation from the original language 'teach me goodness of taste and knowledge.' "As the verb טָעַם *taam*, signifies *to taste*, the noun which is derived from it properly denotes *taste*. It is, however,

---

[20] Charles C. Ryrie, *The Ryrie Study Bible* (Chicago: Moody Press, 1978), 911.

[21] טַעַם taste, judgment — 1. *taste* of manna; in syrup of mallow; of Moab under fig. of wine. 2. fig. *judgment, discretion, discernment*. 3. (late Aramaism) *decision, decree*. Brown, F., Driver, S. R., & Briggs, C. A., *Brown-Driver-Briggs Hebrew and English Lexicon of The Old Testament*. Boston: Houghton, Mifflin & Co, 1907, reprinted 1981, 381.

applied to the mind. David, there is no doubt, prays that knowledge, accompanied with sound discretion and judgment, might be imparted to him... As it was by the guidance of the Holy Spirit that he became thus inclined to obedience, he pleads that another gift may be bestowed upon him, the gift of a sound taste and good understanding."[22] Note that Calvin was very detailed about using the original language. There is unfounded criticism he did not do this, but these are nothing but inaccurate statements. "Calvin's students were expected to know Hebrew, Greek, and Latin. Calvin taught in Latin on the original texts of the bible written in Hebrew and Greek. He did extensive word studies, literary work, and he dealt with all manner of biblical Hebrew syntax. Quite aware of Hebrew idiom in the original, he often compared it with idiomatic expressions from both Greek and Latin. He frequently based his interpretation of biblical passages solely on points of Hebrew and Greek grammars."[23]

Going to the original(s) can help us get a better understanding or concept of what He has spoken and has actually revealed to be preserved forever. This is impossible from any translation. Calvin went to the sources using the original languages as literally as possible, and he fully dealt with all the linguistics involved with the language. He dealt with meanings, word order, grammar, and specific nuances of meanings within the language. The reformers were able to do some remarkable work mainly because they knew quite well to get back to the original languages.

---

[22] "After having confessed that the had found, by experience, the faithfulness of God to his promises, David here adds a request similar to what is contained in the 64th verse, namely, that he may grow in right understanding; although the phraseology is somewhat different; for instead of *thy statutes*, as in that verse, he here uses *goodness of taste and knowledge*. As the verb טעם *taam*, signifies *to taste*, the noun which is derived from it properly denotes *taste*. It is, however, applied to the mind. David, there is no doubt, prays that knowledge, accompanied with sound discretion and judgment, might be imparted to him. Those who read, disjunctively, goodness and taste, mar the whole sentence. It is, however, necessary, in order to our arriving at the full meaning, that the latter clause should be added. He asserts that he believed God's commandments, in other words, that he cheerfully embraced whatever is prescribed in the law; and thus he describes himself as docile and obedient. As it was by the guidance of the Holy Spirit that he became thus inclined to obedience, he pleads that another gift may be bestowed upon him, the gift of a sound taste and good understanding. Whence we learn, that these two things,-- right affection and good understanding – are indispensably necessary to the due regulation of the life. The prophet already believed God's commandments; but his veneration for the law, proceeding from a holy zeal, led him to desire conformity to it, and made him afraid, and not without cause, of inconsiderately going astray. Let us then learn, that after God has framed our hearts to the obedience of his law, we must, at the same time, ask wisdom from him by which to regulate our zeal." John Calvin, *Commentary on the Book of Psalms* (Grand Rapids: Baker Book House, 1989), Vol. 6, 450. Note that Calvin was very detailed about using the original language. There is unfounded criticism he did not do this, but these are nothing but inaccurate statements.

[23] John D. Currid, *Calvin and the Biblical Languages* (Glasgow: Bell & Bain, 2006), 49.

Psalm 23 is perhaps the best-known and beloved Psalm in the world. "The Lord is my shepherd, I shall not want[24]" (Psalm 23:1). There is possibly not one person who does not know this psalm, something about it, or just heard it. The basic meaning of the word for 'want' in Hebrew has the root meaning of lack, need, be lacking, or decrease. The Psalmist, David, is yielding up his heart to the Lord saying that because I know You (the great and only Jehovah) as my Shepherd, I shall never ever be lacking or in need of anything. As long as I have You as my Shepherd I won't ever be in need, be lacking, I will never decrease, I will never want. The Psalmist could easily say this for he has Jehovah personally as his Shepherd and Guide. While David faced complete loss and even death, he knew His Shepherd would never fail him. He knows that even in the deepest valleys, He is there watching and guiding. He knew that he could never be separated from the true Shepherd. That would not be possible even in death. He knows the great Shepherd is there with Him guiding, leading, supplying, and fulfilling every need even in deepest anguish. David had been there and he could say this with his whole heart. While many believers have been in desperate need and great despair even unto death, the one who has Jehovah as his or her Shepherd shall never want. "For I know whatever befall me, Jesus doeth all things well."[25] Psalm 23 has comforted multitudes for literally thousands of years.

A powerful example of word meaning from the Hebrew is in Is. 53:10. "But the Lord was pleased To crush Him, putting Him to grief; If He would render Himself as a **guilt offering**, He will see His offspring, He will prolong His days, And the good pleasure of the Lord will prosper in His hand" (Isaiah 53:10, NASB). "Yet it pleased the LORD to bruise him; he hath put him to grief: when thou shalt make his soul **an offering for sin**, he shall see his seed, he shall prolong his days, and the pleasure of the LORD shall prosper in his hand" (KJV). The word for 'offering' in Is. 53:10 is אָשָׁם (asham) a guilt offering.[26] There were basically five offering in the Mosaic or Levitical system (under law). All the offerings were types of the true offering, the

---

[24] חָסֵר lack, need, be lacking, decrease ... חִסֵּר *cause to lack* or *fail, diminish* (act.) ... Aramaic חֲסַר, ... *want, lack*, ... 1. lack: ... *thou hast not lacked anything* ... *diminish, decrease*, of waters ... Pi. *cause to lack*, ... Hiph...*cause to be lacking, fail,* ...חָסֵר adj. needy, lacking, in want of— Brown, F., Driver, S. R., & Briggs, C. A., *Brown-Driver-Briggs Hebrew and English Lexicon of The Old Testament* (Boston: Houghton, Mifflin & Co, 1907, reprinted 1981), 341.

[25] Fanny Crosby, *All the Way My Savior Leads Me.* (from many Christian hymnals). "For such is God, Our God forever and ever; He will guide us until death" (Psalm 48:14). He is our Guide even unto death for He has been there.

[26] אָשָׁם ... offence, guilt... 1. *offence, trespass, fault* ψ 68:22 (*guiltiness* RV). 2. *guilt* ... 3. *compensation*, לְהָשִׁיב הָאָשָׁם אֵלָיו *to whom to return the compensation* (or satisfaction for injury)... This offering seems to have been confined to offences against God or man that could be estimated and so covered by compensation. The ordinary trespass-offering was a ram, together with restitution and a penalty of a fifth of its value. Brown, Driver, Briggs, 79.

body and blood of Christ. What makes this interesting in Is. 53:10, is that He is called explicitly the אָשָׁם (asham) or guilt offering. To the Jewish nation, this would be extraordinarily significant. There is no way any other person or people could be the אָשָׁם . Only by using Hebrew is one able to get closer to the significance of this particular offering. The translations really do not reflect the depths of this word.

Examples from the Greek New Testament
The Article

> Nothing is more indigenous to the Greek language than its use of the article... When we begin to find the article used with phrases, clauses, and entire sentences, we are, so to speak, swamped in Greek.[27]

Here are three major translations. "I tell you that He will bring about justice for them speedily. However, when the Son of Man comes, will He find faith on the earth?" (Luke 18:8, NASB). "I tell you that he will avenge them speedily. Nevertheless when the Son of man cometh, shall he find faith on the earth?" (KJV). "I tell you, he will see that they get justice, and quickly. However, when the Son of Man comes, will he find faith on the earth?" (NIV). Yet the Greek text has an article before faith so the rendering would be 'the faith.' Of at least eight translations or more, not one had the article. While this may not seem that significant, to those who are truly into the Word in detail, this is quite significant. The rendering would be 'will He find the faith on the earth.' This would indicate 'the faith' as an embodiment of truth rather than just faith in general. Just this one article would affect meaning in context exegetically especially eschatologically.

There are so many examples in Scripture but there are several very interesting ones in the book of Acts. "These all with one mind were continually devoting themselves to prayer, along with the women, and Mary the mother of Jesus, and with His brothers" (Acts 1:14, NASB). "These all continued with one accord in prayer and supplication, with the women, and Mary the mother of Jesus and with his brethren" (KJV). "They all joined together constantly in prayer, along with the women and Mary the mother of Jesus, and with his brothers" (NIV). As all these seem the same with respect to the translations, yet the Greek New Testament (GNT) has literally 'the prayer.'[28] They were most likely praying a very specific prayer rather

---

[27] H. E. Dana and Julius R. Mantey (A *Manual Grammar of the Greek New Testament*. Toronto: The Macmillan Company, 1955), 135-138.

[28] οὗτοι πάντες ἦσαν προσκαρτεροῦντες ὁμοθυμαδὸν **τῇ προσευχῇ** σὺν γυναιξὶν καὶ Μαριὰμ τῇ μητρὶ τοῦ Ἰησοῦ καὶ τοῖς ἀδελφοῖς αὐτοῦ (Acts 1:14) . While this may not seem that significant, this adds a

than just praying. This would make sense, as their prayer or this prayer may have been very particularly the request for the coming Holy Spirit in His ministry. They certainly were expecting the coming of God the Holy Spirit Who had been promised to them (Acts 1:4-5). Therefore, this would not just be praying as some general prayer. This conclusion might be drawn from the context with certain translations, yet the singular article in context in the GNT most assuredly confirms the specificity of their request. Again, while this may not seem to be very significant, the weight of such can affect basic understanding and interpretation dramatically especially in this section of Acts. What is interesting, not one of the translations reflects this from the original.

Another interesting verse is Acts 20:21. "Solemnly testifying to both Jews and Greeks of repentance toward God and faith in our Lord Jesus Christ" (Acts 20:21). There are many who teach repentance and faith as two completely separate acts. One must repent and then believe. They claim these words or acts are unrelated and are not connected biblically. While these words are not identical in meaning, they can be and are used synonymously throughout the New Testament. They insist repentance and faith are always used separately, although John never used the word repent in relation to saving faith. This is very significant. Acts 20:21 has one Greek article joining repentance and faith in this one verse. The two words are inseparable. They can and are used synonymously. One must be honest with the Text. "Repentance focuses on changing one's mind about his former conception of God and disbelief in God and Christ; while faith in Christ, of course, focuses on receiving Him as personal Savior."[29] One article can make a great different.

Peter's use of the Joel prophecy has one article that is not always viewed properly. "But this is what was spoken of through the prophet Joel" (Acts 2:16, NASB). "But this is that which was spoken by the prophet Joel" (KJV). "No, this is what was spoken by the prophet Joel" (NIV). "But this is what was spoken by the prophet Joel" (NKJV). "No, this is what was spoken through the prophet Joel" (NRSV). "But this is what was spoken by the prophet Joel" (Acts 2:16). These translations are about the same quoting Joel 2:28-32. Peter was simply using the Joel prophecy to instruct the people that these Galileans (eleven plus Peter, Acts 2:7, 11, 14) were speaking of the mighty deeds of God in known dialects were not drunk (Acts 2:15). This was

---

somewhat different dimension on what was happening in Acts 2. No matter what the exact meaning, Luke is most likely drawing attention to the prayer not just 'praying.' Articulation most often signifies identity, anarthrous is normally a quality. Therefore, something appears to be significant with this prayer.

[29] Charles C. Ryrie, *So Great a Salvation* (Victor Books, 1989), 98.

a work of God the Holy Spirit, and this should have been no surprise to those hearing.

Peter was not trying to specify any fulfillment in prophecy. The GNT (Greek New Testament) supports this perfectly: 'but (ἀλλὰ) this is (τοῦτό ἐστιν) that spoken (τὸ εἰρημένον) by (through) the prophet Joel (διὰ τοῦ προφήτου Ἰωήλ). Peter was not saying 'this is *that*'[30] making what they were hearing or seeing identical or equivalent as given in the Joel prophecy. The Greek construction used here does not support this. He did not say this is that, like that, similar to that, or was he making some comparison. Peter was not quoting these verses as a fulfillment in any manner. This was not possible for the Joel prophecy will only be fulfilled in the Day of the Lord (Joel 2:1-27). The context of these verses in Joel will bear this out. The GNT is very clear as to the grammar for this is nothing more than a perfect participle with articulation i.e. 'this is that spoken or that which was spoken.'[31] What is interesting is that the Greek with its use of the article used here actually supports this interpretation.

"And that we may be delivered from perverse and evil men; for not all have **faith** (2 Thessalonians 3:2, NAS); "And that we may be delivered from unreasonable and wicked men: for all *men* have not **faith**" (KJV); "And pray that we may be delivered from wicked and evil men, for not everyone has **faith**" (NIV); "and that we may be delivered from unreasonable and wicked men; for not all have **faith**" (NKJ); "and that we may be rescued from wicked and evil people; for not all have **faith**" (NRS); "and that we may be delivered from wicked and evil men; for not all have **faith**" (RSV), etc., etc. All the translations with this verse are very consistent. The GNT reveals there is an article before the word faith.[32] Just this one article suggests a very different take on these verses. Paul was encouraging the Thessalonians to pray for him that the Word may progress even in times of great persecution (2 Thes. 3:1). He asked prayer specifically for deliverance from evil men for not all men have 'the faith' (2 Thes. 3:2). Paul did not request prayer for those who were unfaithful or lacking faith as the translations may suggest.

---

[30] (Acts 1:16) Some suggest that this passage means 'this is that' in a literal sense as some fulfillment. There are other constructions in Greek that might be used in relation to supporting something that is equal, equivalent, or in apposition. This is not the construction used in this verse. And there are no variants indicated.

[31] ἀλλὰ τοῦτό ἐστιν τὸ εἰρημένον διὰ τοῦ προφήτου Ἰωήλ (Acts 2:16). This is <u>τοῦτό ἐστιν</u> that spoken <u>τὸ εἰρημένον</u> There is really not much more than that and fully supported by the GNT. Peter was stressing the fact that these men were not drunk (Acts 2:14-15) ἀλλὰ but (strong adversative) then quoting the Joel prophecy would cause them to realize this was truly a work of the Holy Spirit. This was not something which man could do even if drunk. This was a true work of the God and this should not surprise them.

[32] "καὶ ἵνα ῥυσθῶμεν ἀπὸ τῶν ἀτόπων καὶ πονηρῶν ἀνθρώπων· οὐ γὰρ πάντων ἡ πίστις" (2 Thessalonians 3:2, NA27) .

The reference here to 'the faith' would be better understood as the embodiment of the truth "once delivered' (Jude 1:3). This is very specific and the translations and many commentaries do not seem to grasp the significance here.

Many similar passages such as these give us a fuller or deeper meaning just by noting the article. "Fight the good fight of faith; take hold of the eternal life to which you were called, and you made the good confession in the presence of many witnesses" (1 Timothy 6:12). The word faith has an article before it. Very few translations have reflected the article. So the translation might be better rendered as 'fight the good fight of <u>the</u> faith.'[33] This actually makes more sense than just a general sense of faith. To fight for 'faith' in essence is quite pejorative. By observing the GNT and noting the article may save much time getting closer to a better understanding and interpretation at just a glance. What may be a waste of time to some may be a great time saver and give the bible teacher a greater confidence with the Text. Many bible teachers just compare the translations. Would it not be a consideration for getting back to the original languages?

One does not have to be fluent in biblical Greek or Hebrew. However, when dealing with certain passages such as some of those presented, the languages add certain nuances that nothing else would accomplish. Just read the many translations and commentaries. Many times, there are no solid interpretations or conclusions for many difficult passages. While Greek or Hebrew many not solve the problem, they often add greater insight or complexity that the Author might want us to know. Would not the Lord want us to do this anyway? Any exegete of the Word should do all possible in the languages to be as honest with the Text as possible. Many read much too much into the Scriptures. We are accountable for what is there, what He has provided with every jot and tittle. We are limited and accountable for exactly what He has given us. This is why we look to every word and its meaning in context especially in the original languages.

---

[33] ἀγωνίζου τὸν καλὸν ἀγῶνα <u>τῆς πίστεως</u>, ἐπιλαβοῦ τῆς αἰωνίου ζωῆς, εἰς ἣν ἐκλήθης καὶ ὡμολόγησας τὴν καλὴν ὁμολογίαν ἐνώπιον πολλῶν μαρτύρων (1 Timothy 6:12). "Fight the good fight of <u>the</u> faith; take hold of the eternal life to which you were called, and you made the good confession in the presence of many witnesses." This actually makes more sense than just a general sense of faith. To fight for 'faith' in essence is quite pejorative. Note also the cognate with the imperative. This really has great power in the original and lends itself for very specific battle lines.

New Testament Word Meaning

A very interesting example of word meaning from the original is in Rom. 6:7. "For he who has died is <u>freed</u> from sin" (Rom. 6:7, NASB). "For he that is dead is <u>freed</u> from sin" (KJV). "Because anyone who has died has been <u>freed</u> from sin" (NIV). Paul is making it very clear that the believer is positionally freed from sin in Christ Jesus. However, just reading the passage in context, the question might be raised just how free. Is one totally free from sin, never to be bothered by sin again? Some seem to think so. The real key is the meaning of the root word for 'freed' from Greek. Is it from the word δικαιόω[34] (dikaio). This word means to show justice, do justice to someone, or justify, vindicate, and treat as just or righteous. "Paul, who has influenced later writers, uses the word almost exclusively of God's judgment... especially of men δικαιοῦσθαι *be acquitted, be pronounced and treated as righteous* and thereby become δίκαιος, receive the divine gift of δικαιοσύνη, as a theological technical term *be justified ... make free* or *pure ... be set free, made pure* ἀπό *from* .... ὁ ἀποθανὼν δεδικαίωται ἀπὸ τ. ἁμαρτίας *the one who died is freed from sin* Ro 6:7."[35] This word is primarily a forensic or legal term used to declare or pronounce someone 'free' in that he or she is acquitted and treated as right or righteous. Right or righteous in this case is being right with God. Unredeemed men are not right with God. They are unrighteous and condemned eternally. What all men need is the gift of righteousness (Rom. 5:18).[36] His righteousness applied to the believer's account is the only reason Paul can say 'for he who has died is freed from sin.' Believers are declared 'free' from the guilt of sin because of Who He is and what He did. It is by His righteousness that one is declared right or righteous with God. Jesus is the eternal Son of God (Mat. 16:13-20; 1 John 5:20) become flesh Who died for our sin. He was buried and was raised on the third day according to the Scriptures (1 Cor. 15:1-4). He who believes the

---

[34] "ὁ γὰρ ἀποθανὼν δεδικαίωται ἀπὸ τῆς ἁμαρτίας" (Romans 6:7). The key with this verse is simply the meaning of δεδικαίωται freed. δικαιόω ...1. *show justice, do justice* τινά *to someone* ...2. *justify, vindicate, treat as just* ...3. Paul, who has influenced later writers, uses the word almost exclusively of God's judgment. esp. a. of men δικαιοῦσθαι *be acquitted, be pronounced and treated as righteous* and thereby become δίκαιος, receive the divine gift of δικαιοσύνη, as a theological t.t *be justified* ...c. δικαιόω *make free* or *pure* (Ps 72:13) and pass. δικαιοῦμαι *be set free, made pure* ἀπό *from* .... ὁ ἀποθανὼν δεδικαίωται ἀπὸ τ. ἁμαρτίας *the one who died is freed from. sin* Ro 6:7 ... Arndt, W., Gingrich, F. W., Danker, F. W., & Bauer, W., *A Greek-English lexicon of the New Testament and other early Christian* (Chicago: University of Chicago Press, 1979), 197.

[35] Arndt, W., Gingrich, F. W., Danker, F. W., & Bauer, W., *A Greek-English lexicon of the New Testament and other early Christian* (Chicago: University of Chicago Press, 1979), 197

[36] "For if by the transgression of the one, death reigned through the one, much more those who **receive** the abundance of grace and of **the gift of righteousness** will reign in life through the One, Jesus Christ" (Romans 5:17). One hears very little of the gift of righteousness today, yet this righteousness flows from His cross and this is actually what saves any man (Rom. 1:16-17). My hope is built on nothing less....

gospel is freed from sin. He shall be free indeed!

Another interesting area is word meaning in the various translations. "And when this sound occurred, the multitude came together, and were bewildered, because they were each one hearing them speak in his own language... And how is it that we each hear them in our own language to which we were born?" (Acts 2:6, 8). Most all translations are consistent here and use the word "language". The word "language" is not that bad, but the actual word should be dialect.[37] This is quite significant as this is more than just a language. It is regional and localized and often can be more sophisticated or difficult. This is why the response was "And they were amazed and marveled, saying, "Why, are not all these who are speaking Galileans?" (Acts 2:7). Literally, they were hearing the twelve speaking in their (the hearers) own dialects. How can these twelve Galileans (Acts 2:14) literally speak in these known dialects of the hearers? These Galileans were from Galilee and they had their own way of speaking there or their own dialect. The miracle was not in the hearing as some may suggest. These were known languages with more than eighteen cultural or tribal groups represented with different languages and linguistical variants known only in certain locations or regions (Acts 2:8-11)[38]. The question is how can this be? The question is how these twelve can know our exact dialect/s in which we were born. This is not possible as an act of man. This could not be learned overnight. The word "dialect" certainly adds more to the Text. While we do not want to read more into the Text than what is there, we certainly want to know exactly what is there in the very words. This can only be done from the original language.

Matthew 3:2 presents a very distinct command. "Repent, for the kingdom of heaven is at hand" (Matthew 3:2). A.T. Robertson made this

---

[37] γενομένης δὲ τῆς φωνῆς ταύτης συνῆλθεν τὸ πλῆθος καὶ συνεχύθη, ὅτι ἤκουον εἷς ἕκαστος **τῇ ἰδίᾳ διαλέκτῳ** λαλούντων αὐτῶν. ἐξίσταντο δὲ καὶ ἐθαύμαζον λέγοντες· οὐχ ἰδοὺ ἅπαντες οὗτοί εἰσιν οἱ λαλοῦντες Γαλιλαῖοι; καὶ πῶς ἡμεῖς ἀκούομεν ἕκαστος **τῇ ἰδίᾳ διαλέκτῳ** ἡμῶν ἐν ᾗ ἐγεννήθημεν (Acts 2:6-8, NA27) **διάλεκτος**... language of a nation or a region **γλῶσσα**... tongue...a. literally... as an organ of speech... Mk 7:33, 35;...b. fig., of forked flames Ac 2:3 ...2. language ... πᾶσα γ, every language=every person, regardless of the language he speaks Ro 14:11; Phil 2:11... Note the nuance of **διάλεκτος** being a recognized language of a region or country as opposed to language in general. This is why the response was: "And they were amazed and marveled, saying, "Why, are not all these who are speaking Galileans? "And how is it that we each hear them in our own language (**διάλεκτος**) to which we were born?" (Acts 2:7-8). The dialektos was very localized or regional, and they knew the twelve were Galileans (2:7). How were these Galileans able to speak in the known dialects of the hearers? The Text is quite clear with all this. This may not be perfect, but it surely makes a great deal of sense.

[38] "And how is it that we each hear them in our own language (τῇ ἰδίᾳ διαλέκτῳ ἡμῶν) to which we were born? (ἐν ᾗ ἐγεννήθημεν).. "Parthians and Medes and Elamites, and residents of Mesopotamia, Judea and Cappadocia, Pontus and Asia, Phrygia and Pamphylia, Egypt and the districts of Libya around Cyrene, and visitors from Rome, both Jews and proselytes, Cretans and Arabs—we hear them in our own tongues speaking of the mighty deeds of God" (Acts 2:8-11).

comment. "Repent (*metanoeite*); Broadus used to say that this is the worst translation in the New Testament. The trouble is that the English word 'repent' means 'to be sorry again' from the Latin *repoenitet* (impersonal). John did not call on the people to be sorry, but to change (think afterwards) their mental attitudes (*metanoeite*) and conduct. The Vulgate has it 'do penance' and Wycliff has followed that. The Old Syriac has it better: 'Turn ye.' The French (Geneva) has it 'Amendez vous.'[39] This very important word has the idea or primary meaning of changing one's mind. The English word for 'repent' does not carry the same value. The focus is usually on the Latin, the French, or some translation for meaning. Here is just one more example of why it is so important to do some work in the languages.

What did Mary actually say in her response to Gabriel? (Luke 1:37). When Mary was told about the coming child (Luke 1:26-36), she responded "For nothing will be impossible with God" (Luke 1:37, NASB) "For with God nothing shall be impossible" (KJV). "For nothing is impossible with God" (NIV). While these are all very acceptable translations, in the GNT is πᾶν ῥῆμα (every word) is part of Mary's response "ὅτι οὐκ ἀδυνατήσει παρὰ τοῦ θεοῦ (will not be impossible with God) πᾶν ῥῆμα" (Luke 1:37, NA27). While this does not fundamentally change the meaning, it reveals a more exact connotation to her response. This might be expressed, 'for nothing (πᾶν ῥῆμα in all He has declared, all spoken referring to the whole matter revealed) will be impossible with God.' The word which He has just revealed would be performed literally and Mary by faith expressed this in her response. Again, while these translations are quite adequate, the GNT renders a more literal gradation or nuance. Many times this verse appears to quoted out of context. The GNT forces one to stay with all the many details of the original language.

New Testament Tense
Greek tenses can also give us a better understanding of the text. For instance, blasphemy of the Holy Spirit was the accusation that Christ was doing miracles by the power of Satan or was demon possessed (Mat. 9:34; 12:22-32; Mark 3:28-30; Luke 11:15; John 7:20). The leaders went too far in their accusations against Him, and they had to have an explanation for His miracles. Most all the tenses in Greek in these verses are in the present or imperfect, which indicates continuous or durative action. They were not just making an accusation or two, 'They were (continually) saying 'He (continually) has an unclean spirit' (Mark 3:30). 'The Pharisees were (continually) saying, He is (continually) casting out demons by the ruler of

---

[39] A. T. Robertson, *Word Picture in the New Testament, Matthew* (Nashville: Broadman Press, 1930), 24.

demons' (Mat. 9:34).   This makes it easier to comprehend His response (Mat. 12:25-32). Jesus used the present tenses Himself asking them how He could be continually doing this. This would not be possible. One might destroy one or two of his own feigning his true agenda, but how could He be continually doing this in the power of the enemy. The enemy would not be able to remain standing. The words here reflect how important the tenses can be and how important each word can be resulting in a more concise and accurate meaning.

New Testament Text
One example checking the manuscripts (copies) and the transmission of the Text is: "And when He had given thanks, He broke it, and said, "This is My body, which is for you; do this in remembrance of Me" (1 Corinthians 11:24, NASB). "And when he had given thanks, he broke it and said, "This is my body, which is for you; do this in remembrance of me" (NIV). "And when he had given thanks, he brake it, and said, Take, eat: this is my body, which is broken for you: this do in remembrance of me" (KJV). Was His body broken or any bones? Scripture reveals not one bone was broken (John 19:31-36). With a critical Text, it is very difficult to support the translation 'which is broken for you.' This appears to be added and not part of the original Text using internal and external evidences.

Even if one does not agree with some of the above, it is imperative to do fresh study of every Text especially from the original languages. This will help the student of the Word arrive at a more accurate and crisp meaning.   Many pastors, teachers, or students of the Word would do well to keep afresh their great respect how God posited His Word in the original languages. To play down the original languages in any respect is very foolish especially for a teacher of the Word of God.

What we have is exactly that God wants us to have. Most students of the Word must understand this. We have exactly what He intended, literally word for word, even jot for jot and tittle for tittle. There is no more and no less. This is very significant, as there can be no more revelation added in any sense. What we have in the original languages limits the overall Text. Once God completed the Text, there was no more. Anything additional is merely a copy of the original. This is very important to keep in focus as translations and other works will add to the Text. Unfortunately, this is normal and a trend throughout church history. The copies of the Text are just that, they are copies and not translations.

Translations are used primarily for reading and study smoothing out the original languages. As the original languages limit the Text, there should be great concern with the original Text and the transmission of the same. The primary concern is with transmissional issues not translations. Even if one accepts the Alexandrian, Western, TR, Byz, Majority (texts), etc. as the true text, this does not solve the issue for they are not inspired copies or compilations of inspired copies. Such users or devotees maybe inspired that way, but those copies or manuscripts are not. Manuscripts are still manuscripts unless the original. A manuscript by any other name is still a manuscript, it is a copy. The student of the Word is concerned with the transmission of the original Text in the manuscripts. The Hebrew of the Old Testament limits the Text. The Greek New Testament in the original language limits the Text. A. T. Robertson makes this comment about the Greek New Testament: "There is nothing like the Greek New Testament to rejuvenate the world, which came out of the Dark Ages with the Greek New Testament in its hand.... The Greek New Testament is the New Testament. All else is translation. Jesus speaks to us out of every page of the Greek. Many of his *ipissima verba*[40] are here preserved for us, for our Lord often speaks in Greek. To get these words of Jesus it is worth while to plow through any grammar and to keep on to the end."[41]

Importance of the Original Languages to Dispensationalism

All men are fully accountable for what God has revealed both naturally and supernaturally. God's Word is fully preserved and every jot and tittle of every word is God breathed (inspired) for it is heaven sent. These words are exactly what He has given. Every jot and tittle is what God has sent for us to know. It is His revelation of Himself to all men. It takes a certain discipline to fully appreciate what He has provided in the original Text of Hebrew and Greek. Since God cannot err, then God's Word by definition is inerrant.

The Enemy will do all in his power to keep one away from the true words of God, or distort the true words of God. His primary attack is on the Word and men of the Word. Any departure or variation from these God given words is considered accursed (Rev. 22:18-19). For instance in the garden he (the serpent) said, "Indeed, has God said, 'You shall not eat from any tree of the garden?" (Gen. 3:1); "And the serpent said to the woman, "You surely shall not die" (Gen. 3:4); He had the identical approach with the last Adam. "And the tempter came and said to Him, "If You are the Son of God" (Mt. 4:3); "and said to Him, "If You are the Son of God throw Yourself down; for it is written, 'He will give His angels charge concerning You'; and

---

[40] Lat. the very words.

[41] A. T. Robertson, *A Grammar of the Greek New Testament in the Light of Historical Research* (Nashville: Broadman Press, 1934), xix.

'On their hands they will bear You up, Lest You strike Your foot against a stone" (Mt. 4:6). Satan must do any and everything to corrupt God's perfect Word.

This is Satan's genuine ploy, corruption of His Word, and the reformers understood this well. If anything else is inerrant or inspired other than the autographa, then additional or variant revelation is inevitable. This is why signs, miracles, wonders, prophecy, even gifts of the Spirit, always were to be tested by His Word (Dt. 13:1-4; 18:20-22; 1 John 4:1-4). However, we have that which is more certain than anything else (2 Peter 1:19-21). We have the completed Word of God.

If the original Text were not held to as given by God in the original languages, then inerrancy would mean nothing. Any departure from what God has provided unerringly in the original languages of Hebrew and Greek would mean a departure from inerrancy. Certain methodology in hermeneutics such as not holding consistently to a literal rendering i.e. the normal use of the language in the original is a departure from the Text. To say that these words as given by God could mean most anything with no limit renders any language incomprehensible especially the Text as given in Hebrew and Greek. Any system of theology that does not hold to the absolute authority of the Word of God in the original languages using the normal use of the languages has departed from inerrancy.

Dispensationalism as a system of theology has always held to inerrancy using a consistent historical grammatical interpretation. Dispensationalism has a foundation of a consistent literal rendering from Scripture, i.e. literal interpretation meaning the normal use of the original languages and their grammar. While there are variations of interpretations within dispensationalism, they are at most minor. Most opponents assail the minor. Yet, there is consistent agreement among dispensationalists on inerrancy concerning His Word as the complete authority for all faith and practice. Very few systems of theology if any come close to this standard. Dispensationalism has never been accused of its consistently inerrant and literal exegesis of Scripture. Actually, it is quite the opposite. Dispensationalists are often accused of being exegetically too literal in their exegesis. It is hard to believe this is a problem, but for some it is divisive and untenable.[42]   Solid biblical exegesis is the flagship and mainstay of

---

[42] "The Premillennialism of the Present. In the second quarter of the nineteenth century a new form of Premillennialism was introduced under the influence of Darby, Kelley, Trotter, and their followers in England and America, a Premillennialism wedded to Dispensationalism. The new views were popularized in our country especially through the Scofield Bible, and are widely disseminated through the works of such men as Bullinger, F.W. Grant, … They really present a new philosophy of the history of redemption, in which Israel plays a leading role and the Church is but an interlude. Their guiding principle prompts

dispensational schools holding to inerrancy and using a consistent literal hermeneutic. If one holds to a consistent literal hermeneutic, the result will be a dispensational approach and interpretation of Scripture. Many admit to this, even the antagonists of dispensational theology.[43]

Concluding Thoughts

Why go to the original Greek and Hebrew? Why take so much time or why spend any effort using the languages? Look at all the translations there are today. There seems to be new ones arriving on the market all the time, even translations derived from other translations. Bible study and study of the Word at seminary or bible college/s normally means avoiding the original biblical languages and comparing all the translations. This is often a form of exegesis and interpretation. This is becoming a norm from some Bible schools or seminaries: "Does not require study of the biblical languages for graduation." There are no inerrant, inspired, perfectly authoritative, plenary, God-breathed, manuscripts (copies) or translations. Herein lies the problem. This is why there have been so many translations and there will be many more. No one language can make an exact rendering from another. There is nothing God-breathed or inspired but the Scriptures in the original languages. Why go to a translation when one can go to the complete, perfect, absolute, and unchangeable. Why not go to the source God has preserved perfectly and has given as a gift to man.

God means what He says and He says what He means (Gen. 3:1). God meant what He said in a very literal sense in the normal use of language. God gave language to be understood literally and not to deceive. What God has spoken was meant to be fully understood by the reader or hearer. God spoke plainly. No matter how much one may agree or disagree, the Greek New Testament *is* the New Testament. The Hebrew Old Testament *is* the Old Testament. All else are translations and the works of men.

---

them to divide the Bible into two books, the book of the Kingdom and the book of the Church. In reading their descriptions of God's dealings with men one is lost in a bewildering maze of covenants and dispensations, without an Ariadne thread to give safe guidance. Their divisive tendency also reveals itself in their eschatological program... Objections to Premillennialism... The theory is based on a literal interpretation of the prophetic delineations of the future of Israel and the Kingdom of God, which is entirely untenable... The New Testament certainly does not favor the literalism of Premillenarians. Moreover this literalism lands them in all kinds of absurdities, for it involves the future restoration of all the former historical conditions of Israel's life..." L. Berkhof, *Systematic Theology* (Grand Rapids: WM. B. Eerdmans Publishing Co., 1941, reprinted 1979), 710-713.

[43] "The theory is based on a literal interpretation of the prophetic delineations of the future of Israel and the Kingdom of God, which is entirely untenable." Berkof admits premillennial dispensationalism is based on a literal interpretation which he claims is 'untenable.' Ibid., 712-713.

"Most people know something of the doctrines they believe but little of the hermeneutics on which they have been built. Principles of interpretation are basic and preferably should be established before attempting to interpret the Word so that the results are not only correct interpretations but a right system of theology growing out of those interpretations."

- Charles C. Ryrie
Dispensationalism, 1995, page 79

6

The Principle of Single Meaning[1]
Robert L. Thomas

That a single passage has one meaning and one meaning only has been a long-established principle of biblical interpretation. Among evangelicals, recent violations of that principle have multiplied. Clark Pinnock insists that we add "future" meanings to the "historical" meaning of a text. Mikel Neumann has expanded the role of contextualization. Greg Beale and Grant Osborne advocate multiple meanings for several features in Revelation 11. Recent works on hermeneutics advocate multiple meanings for a single passage. Kenneth Gentry argues for preterist views on Revelation. Progressive dispensationalism promotes "complementary" hermeneutics. However, the single-meaning principle is of foundational importance in our understanding of God's communication with humankind, just as it has been since the creation of the human race. The entrance of sin in Genesis 3 brought confusion to our communication with God that has continued ever since.

Many years ago Milton S. Terry stated a basic hermeneutical principle that contemporary evangelicals have difficulty observing, the principle of single meaning: "A fundamental principle in grammatico-historical exposition is that the words and sentences can have but one significance in one and the same connection. The moment we neglect this principle we drift out upon a sea of uncertainty and conjecture.[2]

More recently, Bernard Ramm stated the same principle in different words: "But here we must remember the old adage: 'Interpretation is one; application is many.' This means that there is only one meaning to a passage of Scripture which is determined by careful study."[3] Summit II of the International Council on Biblical Inerrancy concurred with this principle: "We affirm that the meaning expressed in each biblical text is single, definite and

---

[1] Reprinted with permission from Robert L. Thomas, *Evangelical Hermeneutics: The New Versus the Old* (Grand Rapids, MI: Kregel, 2002)

[2] M. S. Terry, *Biblical Hermeneutics: A Treatise on the Interpretation of the Old and New Testaments* (1885; reprint, Grand Rapids: Zondervan, 1947), 205.

[2] B. Ramm, *Protestant Biblical Interpretation: A Textbook on Hermeneutics*, 3d rev. ed. (Grand Rapids: Baker, 1970), 113.

fixed. We deny that the recognition of this single meaning eliminates the variety of its application."[4]

Current Status of the Single-Meaning Principle

Almost anywhere one looks in evangelical dialogue and publications these days, one finds violations of the single-meaning principle. As a consequence, evangelicals have drifted out "upon a sea of uncertainty and conjecture," as Terry predicted about a hundred years ago.[5] The following discussion cites several examples to illustrate this sea of uncertainty and conjecture and then elaborates on the importance and background of the principle.

Clark Pinnock

In November of 1998 Clark Pinnock presented a paper entitled "Biblical Texts—Past and Future Meanings," before the Hermeneutics Study Group that met prior to the Annual Meeting of the Evangelical Theological Society. I was invited to respond to his paper—the paper that has since appeared in print.[6] His paper and article offered an alternative to "antiquarian hermeneutics"[7]—as he called them—otherwise known as grammatical-historical hermeneutics. I concluded in a response to his presentation that his approach was extremely close to "Aquarianism," as compared with the "antiquarianism" he opposed. Part of that response is reproduced in the following paragraphs.

Pinnock denied leanings toward New Age teaching, but the similarities between his hermeneutical approach and that of New Age teaching are undeniable. As the title of his paper suggests, he proposed the combining of future meanings with past meanings in interpreting Scripture. I addressed this proposal in one section of my response, which follows.

> Professor Pinnock is apparently unwilling to sever connections with past methods of hermeneutics as evidenced in these words: "While making use of literary and historical scholarship, we are not the prisoners of the textual past, but are privileged for the opportunity and accountable for listening for the Word of the Lord and

---

[4] Article VII, "Articles of Affirmation and Denial," adopted by the International Council on Biblical Inerrancy, 10-13 November 1982.

[5] W. C. Kaiser Jr. noted this same trend among evangelicals over twenty years ago when he said that the assigning of multiple meanings was part of the slippage of evangelical scholarship into "easy-going subjectivism" ("The Single Intent of Scripture," in *Evangelical Roots: A Tribute to Wilbur Smith*, ed. K. Kantzer [Nashville: Nelson, 1978], 123). He urged evangelicals "to begin a new 'hermeneutical reformation' to correct this type of growing malpractice" in exegetical procedures (ibid., 138). His warning has gone unheeded by many.

[6] C. Pinnock, "Biblical Texts—Past and Future Meanings," *Wesleyan Theological Journal* 34, no. 2 (fall 1999): 136-51.

[7] Ibid., 137-38.

watching for the fulfillment of God's promises which are still outstanding."[8] But he wants to combine the traditional method with the method that will yield the "new" and "fresh" meanings.

He seems unaware, however, that the moment he does that he has junked the traditional method. Traditional grammatical-historical hermeneutics place tight restrictions on what the text can yield by way of interpretation. Proposals such as Professor Pinnock's violate those restrictions so that his approach cannot fall into the category of "literary and historical scholarship."

One of the restrictions he violates is that which limits the meaning of the text to what it meant in its original setting. He exceeds that limitation in his statement, "Witnesses to the gospel cannot be content with past meanings in an antiquarian way."[9] That statement is contrary to the principle that according to traditional guidelines the past meanings are the substance of biblical interpretation.

He writes elsewhere, "The meaning of the Bible is not static and locked up in the past but is something living and active."[10] On the contrary, meaning is static and locked up in the past insofar as traditional hermeneutics are concerned.

He adds to this: "It [i.e., cruciality] means that we ask not only whether a given interpretation is true to the original meaning, but also whether it is pertinent to the present situation or an evasion of what matters now."[11] From these words it would appear that a given interpretation could be true to the original meaning and also an evasion of what matters now. In the latter case, presumably a traditional interpretation could be at odds with a new interpretation pertinent to the present situation. That too goes against the principles of traditional interpretation.

He evidences that he allows for truthfulness of conflicting interpretations of the same passage when he states, "Interpretation is an unfinished task and even the possibility that there may not be a single right answer for all Christians everywhere cannot be ruled out."[12] In such an instance the right brain has clearly gained the upper hand and the rationality of traditional interpretation crumbles into ashes.

Traditional hermeneutics limit each passage to one interpretation and one only. From that one interpretation may stem many applications that are "crucial" to contemporary situations, but to call those applications interpretations is a serious misnomer. The practice of assigning "future" meanings to the text cannot be combined with traditional hermeneutics without destroying the latter.

---

[8] Ibid., 138. My response took wording from Pinnock's original paper. His wordings cited here have been revised slightly to match those in the published article.

[9] Ibid.

[10] Ibid., 140. In speaking about "the event of Jesus Christ," the centerpiece of Scripture, Pinnock writes, "To read it properly, we have to go beyond the historical descriptions and consider the extension of the story into the present and future" (ibid., 139). "Going beyond" the historical descriptions necessitates assigning additional meanings to that event and to Scripture.

[11] Ibid., 137.

[12] Apparently Pinnock expunged this comment—found on page 8 of his paper—before publication, but he still maintains the viewpoint I represented in the cited statement. In his published piece he writes, "Different answers are given in the Bible to similar sorts of issues because the text itself has been contextualized in different ways. This leaves room *for us to decide* about future meanings and applications" (ibid., 143, emphasis added).

My response to Professor Pinnock apparently fell on deaf ears, because the version that appeared in print in 1999 did not differ substantially from what Pinnock read to the Hermeneutics Study Group in 1998. He appears to be oblivious to the single-meaning principle, hence the sea of uncertainty.

Mikel Neumann
At that same meeting in November of 1998 at which Pinnock spoke, missiologist Mikel Neumann of Western Baptist Theological Seminary, Portland, Oregon, presented "Contextualization: Application or Interpretation?" His point was that contextualization overshadows interpretation of the biblical text. This paper made such statements as: "Contextualization might be seen as an umbrella which covers interpretation and application" (8).[13] "Context is not merely an addendum called application" (4). "Contextualization begins with the interpreter's personality as a function of his or her culture and encompasses the process of interpretation and application" (3). He defended that approach by saying that "a hermeneutical approach that ignores either the culture of the interpreter of Scripture or the culture of the person to whom he or she desires to communicate, is an inadequate approach" (3-4).

I again quote from my statement of response:

> Neither the culture of the interpreter nor the culture of the person to whom the interpreter communicates has anything in the world to do with the meaning of the biblical text. The meaning of the biblical text is fixed and unchanging. This is not to say that the exegetical task is finished. It must ever be open to new insights as to a more refined understanding of what the Spirit meant when He inspired the writers to pen Scripture, but that refined understanding must come through a closer utilization of the rules of grammar and the facts of history surrounding the text in its original setting. It is not open to a redefined understanding stemming from a reading back into the text of some consideration either from the interpreter's culture or from that of the one to whom the interpreter communicates.

Through his insistence on making the cultural situation of the interpreter and that of the people to whom the interpreter communicates the message of the text an integral part of interpretation, Professor Neumann—unwittingly I believe—introduced meanings additional to the one meaning of the text as determined by its grammar and historical setting. More paddling around in the sea of uncertainty.

---

[13] Numbers in parenthesis cite page numbers in Neumann's unpublished paper.

Greg Beale and Grant Osborne

In November of 1999 I was invited back to the Hermeneutics Study Group to respond to Greg Beale and Grant Osborne and their handling of the apocalyptic genre in the book of Revelation. Both men described their hermeneutical approaches as eclectic. Osborne's eclecticism combined futurist, preterist, and idealist principles.[14] Beale's combination was idealist and futurist.[15] It is beside the point for the present discussion, but worth noticing that an eclectic system of hermeneutics allows an interpreter to choose whatever meaning suits his preunderstood theological system in any given passage. Eclecticism in hermeneutics leaves the interpreter free to vary his principles of interpretation from literal to allegorical and back to literal and so on, *ad infinitum*. His interpretation becomes simply a rehashing of his preunderstanding of what the passage should mean, and it repeats itself from passage to passage.

Of illustrative relevance here, however is Osborne's interpretation of "the great city" in Revelation 11:18. He assigns two and possibly three meanings to the expression. The city is Jerusalem, and it is Rome, and secondarily it is all cities that oppose God. Beale does essentially the same: Babylon = Rome = the ungodly world city. Perhaps Osborne's identification of the two witnesses of Revelation 11 is an even more flagrant violation of the single-meaning principle. He sees them both as two individuals of the future and as a corporate picture of the church. Yet the rapture of these two witnesses pictures only the rapture of the church, he says. One would ask, What happened to the two individuals?[16]

More waves from the sea of uncertainty.

Grant Osborne

In the panel discussion following the papers and responses at this November 1999 meeting, Osborne challenged my statement of response that a passage can have only a single meaning. Therefore I went to his volume *The Hermeneutical Spiral* to refresh my memory on his view of this principle and found that his book on hermeneutics differs from the time-honored grammatical-historical standard regarding single meaning. In his

---

[14] G. R. Osborne, "My Interpretive Approach" (paper presented to the Hermeneutics Study Group, November 1999), 1. Osborne's commentary on Revelation is forthcoming from Baker Book House.

[15] G. K. Beale, The Book of Revelation: A Commentary on the Greek Text (Grand Rapids: Eerdmans, 1999), 48-49.

[16] By following grammatical-historical principles, this writer identifies "the great city" as Jerusalem and the two witnesses as two individuals—probably Moses and Elijah—who will testify in Jerusalem during the future seventieth week of Daniel. See R. L. Thomas, *Revelation 8-22: An Exegetical Commentary* (Chicago: Moody, 1995), 87-89, 93-94.

hermeneutical volume, he advocates double meanings in cases of single words. He speaks of "deliberate ambiguity" on the part of authors of Scripture. He sites "the famous word-play on wind/spirit in Genesis 1:2" as "a fairly simple example" of this.[17] He also cites the Gospel of John as famous "for its widespread use of double meaning."[18] His examples include *anothen gennethenai*, "born from above/again" in John 3:3, 7; *hydor zon*, "living/flowing water" in 4:10-11; and *hypsotho*, "lifted up (to the cross/the Father)" in 12:32.[19] He portrays John as speaking in riddles by his frequent use of double meanings.

Yet in neither of these contexts does the biblical writer give even the slightest hint that he intends a double meaning. Such hermeneutical advice as this creates further turbulence on the sea of uncertainty.

Klein, Blomberg, and Hubbard

Among recent books on hermeneutics, Osborne's volume is not alone in fostering uncertainty. The work *Introduction to Biblical Interpretation* by William Klein, Craig Blomberg, and Robert Hubbard Jr. offers the same advice as Osborne. In their chapter on "The Goals of Interpretation," they entitle one section "An author may intend a text to convey multiple meanings or levels of meaning."[20] They cite Isaiah 7:14 as an example of intended double meaning, as being fulfilled in the immediate future (8:1-4) and in the distant future (Matt. 1:23).[21] They also cite John 3:3 and Jesus' use of *anothen* with its double entendre "again" and "from above" followed in its context by the use of *pneuma* with its double entendre of "wind" and "spirit."[22]

Examples of double meaning cited by Osborne and by Klein, Blomberg, and Hubbard are at best highly questionable and at worst outright error. Nothing in context justifies the conclusion that the authors or Jesus, the speaker, intended a double meaning in these passages. In isolated instances elsewhere, however, when a text has a double meaning, the context will always make that clear. One case that comes to mind is John 11:50 where Caiaphas, the high priest said, "You do not realize that it is better for you that one man die for the people than that the whole nation perish," as he addressed the Sanhedrin. In 11:51-52 John takes the words in

---

[17] G. R. Osborne, *The Hermeneutical Spiral: A Comprehensive Introduction to Biblical Interpretation* (Downers Grove, Ill.: InterVarsity, 1991), 88-89.

[18] Ibid., 89.

[19] Ibid.

[20] W. W. Klein, C. L. Blomberg, and R. L. Hubbard Jr., *Introduction to Biblical Interpretation* (Dallas: Word, 1993), 122 (emphasis Klein et al.).

[21] Ibid.

[22] Ibid., 123 n. 19.

a sense different from the way Caiaphas intended them. Caiaphas meant them to speak of Jesus' death being necessary to keep peace with the Romans, but John understood them to refer to Jesus' sacrificial death for the Jewish nation and for all people everywhere.

The context of John 11 makes the double entendre quite conspicuous. Wherever biblical authors use such a double entendre, the immediate context will always make that clear. But it is a violation of grammatical-historical principles to find double meanings in a context where no such indicators appear. No such signposts occur with the two witnesses in Revelation 11, Isaiah's prophecy of the virgin birth of the Messiah, Moses' use of "spirit" in Genesis 1, or with John's references to the new birth and his use of *pneuma* (John 3), to living water (John 4), and to Christ's being lifted up (John 12).

Gordon Fee
The confusion of application with interpretation violates the principle of one interpretation. The incorporation of application—or, as some call it, "contextualization"—into the hermeneutical process leads inevitably to multiple meanings for a single passage. Almost every recent work on hermeneutics advocates merging the two disciplines of interpretation and application, which were formerly quite distinct.[23] With that policy advocated, the transformation of some of the many applications into multiple interpretations is inescapable.[24]

This is a feature that distinguishes an egalitarian explanation of 1 Timothy 2:11-15 from a complementarian approach. For example, Fee writes, "My point is a simple one. It is hard to deny that *this* text prohibits women teaching men in the Ephesian church; but is the unique text in the New Testament, and as we have seen, its reason for being is not to correct the rest of the New Testament, but to correct a very *ad hoc* problem in Ephesus."[25]

---

[23] Cf. chapter 7 of this volume and B. A. Shealy, "Redrawing the Line Between Hermeneutics and Application," *The Master's Seminary Journal* 8, no. 1 (spring 1997): 89-91.

[24] Crapanzano notes that liberal theologians question the traditional distinction between interpretation and application. He seems to doubt such a distinction himself when he writes, "Although a case can always be made for non-figurative readings of Scripture, it is impossible to make such a case for application since it always depends upon a metaphorical link between text and (present-day) context." V. Crapanzano, *Serving the Word: Literalism in America from the Pulpit to the Bench* (New York: New Press, 2000), 118-19.

[25] G. D. Fee, "Issues in Evangelical Hermeneutics, Part III: The Great Watershed—Intentionality and Particularity/Eternality: 1 Timothy 2:8-15 as a Test Case," *Crux* 26 (December 1990): 36 (emphasis Fee's).

In applying 1 Timothy 2: 11-15 to modern situations, Fee, in essence, gives the text a new meaning that is exactly opposite to what even he admits to be Paul's meaning. As a result, the text has two meanings, one for the kind of conditions that existed at Ephesus and another for the conditions that existed elsewhere and exist today.

Fee's definition of hermeneutics coincides with his conclusion about multiple meanings, however. In a book he coauthored with Stuart, he says that the term *hermeneutics* encompasses the whole field of interpretation, including exegesis. However, he chooses to confine it to a "narrower sense of seeking the contemporary relevance of ancient texts."[26] In other words, for him, hermeneutics is simply present-day application of a biblical text.

No wonder Fee and Stuart, in their book on hermeneutics, include nothing about limiting interpretation to a single meaning. No wonder the stormy waves on the sea of uncertainty are rising higher and higher.

DeYoung and Hurty

James DeYoung and Sarah Hurty strongly advocate seeking a meaning beyond the grammatical-historical meaning of the text.[27] Since the New Testament writers found such a "deeper" meaning in their use of the Old Testament, they reason, we should follow their example.[28] They call the meaning derived from grammatical-historical interpretation the *existential meaning* of a passage, and the deeper meaning they call the *essential meaning*. They allow a single passage to have a number of essential meanings because the essential meaning of a word may differ from that of a sentence and its passage and its whole story.[29]

How do they limit the range of possible essential meanings? They apply a paradigm of reality that they call "the Kingdom Center"[30] They call this the central theme and worldview of the Bible. Yet that control seems to have no significant impact on their freedom to find whatever deeper meaning they choose. It does not restrain them from presenting an egalitarian view of women's role in the church.[31] In this case, their "deeper meaning" overrides the grammatical-historical meaning of the text.

---

[26] G. D. Fee and D. Stuart, *How to Read the Bible for All Its Worth*, 2d ed. (Grand Rapids: Zondervan, 1993), 25.

[27] J. DeYoung and S. Hurty, *Beyond the Obvious: Discover the Deeper Meaning of Scripture* (Gresham, Ore.: Vision House, 1995), 67-80.

[28] Ibid., 33-48, 225.

[29] Ibid., 230-31.

[30] Ibid., 83-98.

[31] Ibid., 280-87; cf. also D. McCartney, "The New Testament's Use of the Old Testament," in *Inerrancy and Hermeneutic*, ed. H. M. Conn (Grand Rapids: Baker, 1988), 103.

McCartney, Clayton, Klein, Blomberg, and Hubbard

The work by Dan McCartney and Charles Clayton, like that by Klein et al., suggests another route for placing some kind of control on these extra meanings that "go beyond" the grammatical historical. Klein et al. advocate a controlled reader-response approach to the text. The limit they place on the meanings beyond the historical is the consensus of the believing community.[32] McCartney and Clayton speak of typology or *sensus plenior*. They reason this way: "Since the New Testament writers do not cover everything in the Old Testament, we may expect large areas where the typology or *sensus plenior* has not been stated explicitly in the New Testament."[33] How do they propose to place a limit on these additional meanings of the Old Testament? Their solution also involves observing the manner of "the Holy Spirit's directing of the church."[34]

That type of limitation essentially leaves the meaning of Scripture "up for grabs." The believing community currently uses the Bible to support all sorts of teachings, everything from covenant theology to dispensationalism or somewhere between the two, from complementarianism to egalitarianism, from homosexuality to heterosexuality, from the openness of God to the complete sovereignty of God, from conditional immortality to unconditional eternal punishment for the lost. Ultimately, all these differences stem from someone allowing a given passage to have more than its grammatical-historical sense. The believing Christian community has no consensus that limits meaning beyond the grammatical-historical one. The absence of a consensus leaves the interpreter free to follow his or her own personal whims.

McCartney and Clayton go so far as to call the practice of limiting a passage to a single meaning "ridiculous from a general hermeneutical point of view" and "perverse from a theological one."[35] They are obviously disciples of neither Terry nor Ramm nor grammatical-historical principles. They make such statements in connection with their practice of reading New Testament meanings back into the Old Testament as additions to the grammatical-historical meaning of the Old Testament. That, of course, is the basis for the system of covenant theology when it allegorizes large portions of the Old Testament.

---

[32] Klein et al, *Introduction to Biblical Interpretation*, 139, 145.

[33] D. McCartney and C. Clayton, *Let the Reader Understand: A Guide to Interpreting and Applying the Bible* (Wheaton: Victor, 1994), 157.

[34] Ibid., 164.

[35] Ibid., 161.

Kenneth Gentry

The writings of theonomist Kenneth Gentry also illustrate the contemporary practice of finding multiple meanings in a single passage. When discussing the 144,000 of Revelation 7, he expresses the possibility that they may represent the church as a whole, including both Jews and Gentiles.[36] Yet just ten pages later he sees them definitely representing Christians of Jewish extraction.[37] He makes the latter identification because he needs something to tie the prophecy's fulfillment to the land of Judea as his theological system requires. The double meaning assigned to the same group apparently does not bother him.

He goes further in connection with the theme verse of Revelation. He identifies the "cloud coming"—as he calls it—of Christ of Revelation 1:7 with the Roman invasion of Judea in 67-70.[38] On the next page he says Christ's cloud coming was the Roman persecution of the church in 64-68. For him, the cloud coming mentioned in the Revelation's theme verse refers to two comings of Christ in the A.D. 60s. The verse has two meanings, and the waves of uncertainty are about to capsize the ship.

Bock, Blaising, and Pate

Another recent example of the identification of multiple meanings in a single passage comes in the methodology of progressive dispensationalism. That system allows for *complementary* additions in meaning that alter the original sense conveyed by a passage.[39] These later alterations are in view when Craig Blaising and Darrell Bock write, "There also is such a thing as complementary aspects of meaning, where an additional angle on the text reveals an additional element of its message or a fresh way of relating the parts of a text's message."[40] Bock admits at least in part that this amounts to a change of meaning: "Does the expansion of meaning entail a change of meaning? . . . This is an important question for those concerned about consistency within interpretation. The answer is both yes and no. On the one hand, to add to the revelation of a promise is to introduce 'change' to it through addition."[41]

---

[36] K. L. Gentry Jr., *Before Jerusalem Fell: Dating the Book of Revelation* (Tyler, Tex.: Institute for Christian Economics, 1989), 223-24.

[37] Ibid., 233.

[38] Ibid., 143.

[39] C. A. Blaising and D. L. Bock, "Dispensationalism, Israel and the Church: Assessment and Dialogue," in *Dispensationalism, Israel, and the Church: The Search for Definition*, ed. C. A. Blaising and D. L. Bock (Grand Rapids: Zondervan, 1992), 392-93.

[40] C. A. Blaising and D. L. Bock, *Progressive Dispensationalism* (Wheaton: Victor, 1993), 68.

[41] D. L. Bock, "Current Messianic Activity and Old Testament Davidic Promise: Dispensationalism, Hermeneutics, and New Testament Fulfillment," *Trinity Journal* 15 NS (1994): 71.

He goes on with an attempt to justify the "no" part of his answer by calling the change "revelatory progress."[42] Revelatory progress, however, has to do with later additional revelation on the same general subject through another writing, not—as he holds—additional meanings affixed to a single earlier passage.

Blaising and Bock illustrate their "multilayered" approach to hermeneutics by identifying Babylon in Revelation 17-18 in three different ways: as (1) Rome, (2) a rebuilt Babylon, and (3) other cities in "the sweep of history."[43] Progressive dispensationalist C. Marvin Pate further illustrates the multimeaning approach of that system when he joins preterists in adding Jerusalem of the past to the meanings assigned to Babylon.[44] His approach to Revelation is eclectic, combining elements of preterism and idealism with futurism.[45] He can agree with preterists, idealists, and futurists regarding the meaning of almost any passage in the book. His eclecticism leads him to ridiculous interpretations, such as having the second, third, and fifth seals predictive of wars that occurred long before Revelation was written.[46] Bock goes so far as to accuse the author of the present volume of holding to "a similar multiple setting view for some prophetic texts in a way that parallels" what Bock means by typology.[47] As evidence, he quotes a lengthy paragraph from my chapter in *Israel: The Land and the People*.[48] In that paragraph I point out how Paul in Acts 13:47 applies a portion of one of Isaiah's servant songs (Isa. 42:6) to himself and his ministry. Acknowledging my recognition that this is an additional meaning not gleaned from a grammatical-historical analysis of Isaiah 42:6, Bock cites my further statement: "The new meaning of the Old Testament prophecies applied to the church introduced by New Testament writers did not cancel out the original meaning and their promises to Israel. God will yet restore the nation of Abraham's physical descendants as He promised He would."[49] Then he immediately adds, "This

---

[42] Ibid.

[43] Blaising and Bock, *Progressive Dispensationalism*, 93-96. The "layered" approach approximates that of amillennialist Poythress who proposes four levels of communication in the symbolism of Revelation. V. S. Poythress, "Genre and Hermeneutics in Rev. 20:1-6," *JETS* 36 (1993): 41-43.

[44] C. M. Pate, "A Progressive Dispensational View of Revelation," in *Four Views on the Book of Revelation* (Grand Rapids: Zondervan, 1998), 160-61, 168-69. Pate actually allows for dating the book both early in the 60s and late in the 90s.

[45] Ibid., 145-46.

[46] Ibid., 151-57. Even with Pate's highly improbable early dating of the Revelation in the sixties, the predicted events preceded the prophecy that predicted them, which sequence is, of course, absurd.

[47] D. L. Bock, "Hermeneutics of Progressive Dispensationalism," in *Three Central Issues in Contemporary Dispensationalism: A Comparison of Traditional and Progressive Views*, ed. H. W. Bateman IV (Grand Rapids: Kregel, 1999), 107.

[48] Ibid., 107-8.

[49] Ibid., 108.

final statement is precisely what progressives say about how complementary meaning works."[50]

In order to cast me in a "complementary hermeneutical" role, however, Bock had to skip a paragraph between the lengthy paragraph he quoted and my summary statement about God's continuing purpose to fulfill Isaiah's prophecy to Israel. In the intervening paragraph that he chose to omit, I made several points that complementary hermeneutics would not tolerate. In the first sentence I stated that Paul's use of Isaiah 42:6 "was not a fulfillment of Isaiah's prophecy."[51] Complementary hermeneutics would say that it was a fulfillment. I also stated that this use of Isaiah "was an additional meaning furnished through the apostle to the Gentiles during the period of Israel's rejection."[52] In the same paragraph I said, "Any [OT texts] that they [NT writers] used relating to the new program and new people of God, the church, took on a different nature simply because Old Testament prophecy did not foresee the New Testament church."[53] No progressive dispensationalist advocating complementary hermeneutics would speak of the church being a new program and a new people in the sense that it was unforeseen in the Old Testament.

I cannot say whether or not Bock's omission of that paragraph was intentional, but the fact is he hopped right over the intervening paragraph so as to portray me in a certain way. His omission could have resulted from another characteristic of progressive dispensational hermeneutics, one that I have elsewhere called "hermeneutical hopscotch."[54] A player in hopscotch chooses the squares he wants to hop into and avoids stepping in others that would lose the game for him. Progressive dispensationalists tend to be selective in using passages to support their system of complementary hermeneutics. That may account for the exclusion of the paragraph discussed above.

Foundational Importance of the Single-Meaning Principle
The Standard
Compare the above approaches with the time-honored hermeneutics espoused by Terry and the importance they place on finding a single meaning when interpreting prophetic passages.

---

[50] Ibid.

[51] R. L. Thomas, "The Mission of Israel and the Messiah in the Plan of God," *Israel: The Land and the People*, ed. H. W. House (Grand Rapids: Kregel, 1998), 272.

[52] Ibid.

[53] Ibid.

[54] R. L. Thomas, "A Critique of Progressive Dispensational Hermeneutics," *When the Trumpet Sounds*, ed. Thomas Ice and Timothy Demy (Eugene, Ore.: Harvest House, 1995), 423.

The hermeneutical principles which we have now set forth necessarily exclude the doctrine that the prophecies of Scripture contain an occult or double sense. . . . We may readily admit that the Scriptures are capable of manifold practical *applications*; otherwise they would not be so useful for doctrine, correction, and instruction in righteousness (2 Tim. iii, 16). But the moment we admit the principle that portions of Scripture contain an occult or double sense we introduce an element of uncertainty in the sacred volume, and unsettle all scientific interpretation. "If the Scripture has more than one meaning," says Dr. Owen, "it has no meaning at all." "I hold," says Ryle, "that the words of Scripture were intended to have one definite sense, and that our first object should be to discover that sense, and adhere rigidly to it. . . . To say that words *do* mean a thing merely because they *can* be tortured into meaning it is a most dishonourable and dangerous way of handling Scripture."[55]

Terry adds,

We have already seen that the Bible has its riddles, enigmas, and dark sayings, but whenever they are given the context clearly advises us of the fact. To assume, in the absence of any hint, that we have an enigma, and in the face of explicit statements to the contrary, that any specific prophecy has a double sense, a primary and a secondary meaning, a near and a remote fulfillment, must necessarily introduce an element of uncertainty and confusion into biblical interpretation.[56]

Though Terry's use of his own principles in eschatology are at times suspect, his basic principles of hermeneutics make the most sense. Those principles are the substance of grammatical-historical interpretation. Interpret each statement in light of the principles of grammar and the facts of history. Take each statement in its plain sense if it matches common sense, and do not look for another sense.

Initial Departure from the Standard
That is the way God has communicated with humans from the beginning. His first words to man in Genesis 1:27-30 were,

And God created man in His own image, in the image of God He created him; male and female He created them. And God blessed them; and God said to them, "Be fruitful and multiply, and fill the earth, and subdue it; and rule over the fish of the sea and over the birds of the sky, and over every living thing that moves on the earth." Then God said, "Behold, I have given you every plant yielding seed that is on the surface of all the earth, and every tree which has fruit yielding seed; it shall be food for you; and to every beast of the earth and to every bird of the sky and to

---

[55] Terry, *Biblical Hermeneutics*, 493.

[56] Ibid., 495. In another place Terry adds, "Unless we find clear warrant for it in the word itself, we should never allow that any one passage or sentiment of divine revelation has more than one true import" (ibid., 162).

every thing that moves on the earth which has life, *I have given* every green plant for food"; and it was so. (NASB)

Scripture does not examine in detail the response to God's instructions, but apparently Adam understood them clearly, responded properly, and the human race was off to a great start.

But then God added to His communication. In Genesis 2:16b-17 He said, "From any tree of the garden you may eat freely; but from the tree of the knowledge of good and evil you shall not eat, for in the day that you eat from it you shall surely die" (NASB). Adam apparently understood this statement as God intended it, according to the grammar of His command and the historical situation of the tree of the knowledge of good and evil that stood in the Garden of Eden. In fact, He communicated it to Eve so well that Eve in 3:2b-3 was able to quote its essence to the serpent quite accurately: "From the fruit of the trees of the garden we may eat; but from the fruit of the tree which is in the middle of the garden, God has said, 'You shall not eat from it or touch it, lest you die'" (NASB). That was her answer to the serpent when he asked about God's prohibition against eating from trees in the Garden. Eve's hermeneutics were in great shape, as was God's communicative effectiveness. She worded her repetition of God's command slightly different from God's recorded message to Adam, but God probably repeated His original command to Adam in several different ways. Genesis has not preserved a record of every word He spoke to Adam.

Confusion entered the picture when the serpent suggested to Eve that God's plain statement had another meaning. He said, "You surely shall not die! For God knows that in the day you eat from it your eyes will be opened, and you will be like God, knowing good from evil" (Gen 3:4b-5 NASB). The serpent knew better than to suggest that God would lie in the perfect environment of the Garden of Eden. He simply suggested that Eve had misinterpreted God's statement, or by limiting her understanding to the plain sense of God's words, she had missed a second intended meaning. The serpent implied that she had missed God's double entendre or *sensus plenior*. The serpent's message to Eve was, "This is just God's way of telling you how to gain a knowledge of good and evil." The first human experience on the "sea of uncertainty" resulted when Eve and then Adam bought into the serpent's suggestion that God's statement was not limited to a single meaning. Such was the beginning of hermeneutical difficulties in understanding God's Word.

Departing Even Slightly from the Standard

Roy Zuck supports the principle of single meaning, but he treads on dangerous ground when, following Elliott Johnson, he adds related implications or "related submeanings."[57] To speak of a single meaning on one hand and of related submeanings on the other is contradictory. A passage either has one meaning or it has more than one. No middle ground exists between those two options.

Zuck uses Psalm 78:2 to illustrate related implications or related submeanings. The psalmist Asaph writes, "I will open my mouth in a parable" (NASB). Zuck limits the passage to one meaning, but says the passage has two referents, Asaph and Jesus who applied the words to Himself in Matthew 13:35.[58] Instead of saying the psalm has two referents, which in essence assigns two meanings to it, to say that the psalm's lone referent is Asaph, thereby limiting the psalm to one meaning, is preferable. Either Psalm 78:2 refers to Asaph or it refers to Jesus. It cannot refer to both. It is proper to say that it refers to Asaph and that Matthew 13:35 refers to Jesus. By itself, Psalm 78:2 cannot carry the weight of the latter referent.

In defending is double-referent view, Zuck apparently makes this same distinction, though he does not repudiate the double-referent terminology. He discusses Psalms 8, 16, and 22, noting that David wrote them about his own experiences, but that the New Testament applies them to Christ in a sense significantly different than that in which David used them.[59] His conclusions about these psalms and the New Testament use of them are accurate, but the psalms themselves cannot have more than one referent, hermeneutically speaking. Such would assign them more than one meaning. Neither the human author David nor the original readers of the psalms could have used the principles of grammar and the facts of history to come up with the additional referent or meaning that the New Testament assigns to the psalms. The source and authority for that additional meaning is the New Testament, not the Old Testament.

A discussion of how this single-meaning principle works out in the broader discussion of the New Testament use of the Old Testament will be a subject of chapter 9.

---

[57] Roy B. Zuck, *Basic Bible Interpretation* (Wheaton: Victor, 1991), 274; cf. E. E. Johnson, *Expository Hermeneutics: An Introduction* (Grand Rapids: Zondervan, 1990), 34.

[58] Ibid.

[59] Ibid., 275-77.

The Contemporary Drama

Evangelicals are drifting on the sea of uncertainty and conjecture because they neglect foundational principles of the grammatical-historical method of interpretation. They have become sophisticated in analyzing hermeneutical theory but seemingly have forgotten simple principles that exegetical giants of the past have taught and used. Evangelicals are currently reaping the harvest of confusion from this oversight.

For example, Daniel Wallace has provided a grammatical work entitled *Greek Grammar Beyond the Basics: An Exegetical Syntax of the New Testament*, a work that has a number of helpful features. In seeking to advance beyond the basics, however, Wallace has fallen into the same pit as have so many others by his neglect of the basics of hermeneutics. One of his glaring errors violates the principle of single meaning. In his consideration of a category he calls the "Plenary Genitive," he labors the point that a particular passage's construction may be at the same time both objective genitive and subjective genitive. In defense of this position he writes,

> One of the reasons that most New Testament grammarians have been reticent to accept this category [i.e., "Plenary Genitive"] is simply that most New Testament grammarians are Protestants. And the Protestant tradition of a singular meaning for a text (which, historically, was a reaction to the fourfold meaning employed in the Middle Ages) has been fundamental in their thinking. However, current biblical research recognizes that a given author may, at times, be *intentionally* ambiguous. The instances of double entendre, *sensus plenior* (conservatively defined), puns, and word-plays in the New Testament all contribute to this view. Significantly, two of the finest commentaries on the Gospel of John are by Roman Catholic scholars (Raymond Brown and Rudolf Schnackenburg): John's Gospel, more than any other book in the New Testament, involves double entendre. Tradition has to some degree prevented Protestants from seeing this.[60]

Instead of following traditional grammatical-historical interpretation and its insistence on limiting a passage to one meaning, Wallace consciously rejects the wisdom of past authorities so that he can keep in step with "current biblical research" and Roman Catholic scholars who advocate multiple meanings for the same passage. His volume could have been helpful, but this feature makes it extremely dangerous.

Someone needs to sound the alarm when evangelical leaders mislead the body of Christ. A mass evangelical exodus from this time-honored principle of interpreting Scripture is jeopardizing the church's access to the truths taught therein. Whether interpreters have forsaken the

---

[60] D. B. Wallace, *Greek Grammar Beyond the Basics* (Grand Rapids: Zondervan, 1996), 120 n. 134 (emphasis Wallace's).

principle intentionally or have subconsciously ignored it, the damage is the same. The only hope of escape from the pit into which so many have fallen is to reaffirm the principle of single meaning, along with the other hermeneutical principles that have served the believing community so well through the centuries.

Summary of "The Single-Meaning Principle"

Violator(s) of the Principle	Violation	Implications
Clark Pinnock	combine future meanings With past meanings	meaning of the Bible Is constantly changing
Mikel Neumann	context of the contemporary Interpreter and his audience Overshadows grammatical-historical interpretation	reading contemporary culture back into the biblical text
Beale and Osborne	"great city" in Revelation 11:8 identified as Jerusalem, Rome, Babylon, ungodly world city, all cities that oppose God	eclectic hermeneutics that switch from futurist to preterist to idealist
Grant Osborne	authors of scripture practiced deliberate ambiguity	finding double meaning where it was never intended
Klein, Blomberg, and Hubbard	authors may intend multiple meanings in a single passage	no contextual indicators to signal multiple meanings
Gordon Fee	contemporary application yields meaning different from grammatical-historical meaning	confusing contemporary application with interpretation
De-Young and Hurty	follow example of NT writers and find "deeper meanings" beyond the grammatical-historical meaning	"Kingdom center" control amounts to no control of essential meanings discovered
McCartney, Clayton, Klein, Blomberg, and Hubbard	controlled reader-response or sensus plenior approach to discover meanings; single-meaning principle "ridiculous"	evangelical believing community consensus amounts to no control at all
Kenneth Gentry	conflicting meanings for a single passage	meaning tailored to fit theological system at various points
Block, Blaising, and Pate	complementary hermeneutics that adds additional meanings to a passage as time goes on	selective use of passages that support and omission of passages that oppose
Danial Wallace	double entendre, sensus plenior (conservatively defined), puns, and wordplays, contribute to intentional ambiguity	single meaning eliminates possibility of intentional ambiguity

"Whether the world understands it or not, the Jews are God's chosen people. This is stated and restated in God's Word...Even in New Testament times, when the church had entered the picture, God reaffirmed that His choice of Israel had not been set aside."

- Charles C. Ryrie

The Final Countdown, 1982, page 44

7

The Role of Israel in Dispensational Theology
Arnold G. Fruchtenbaum

The issue of Israel is one of the major points of division in evangelical theology today. This is true both among Arminians and Calvinists. An evangelical theologian's view of Israel will determine whether he is a Covenant Theologian or a Dispensationalist. It will also determine what kind of Covenant Theologian he is: postmillennial, amillennial, or premillennial. The question of Israel is central for a proper Systematic Theology. Paul, in his epistle to the Romans, which contains the first Systematic Theology in Church history, expounds on Israel in the center of his epistle devoting three full chapters (9-11) out of sixteen to this topic. Yet, while there are many Systematic Theologies today which have systematized all areas of biblical truth, none thus far have developed an Israelology as part of their system.

Definition of Terms
Definition of key terms used in systematics will be helpful at this point:

Systematic Theology -a science which follows a humanly devised scheme or order of doctrinal development and which purports to incorporate into its system all the truth about God and His universe from any and every source. . . .

> . . . Systematic Theology may be defined as the collecting, scientifically arranging, comparing, exhibiting, and defending of all facts from any and every source concerning God and His works.[1]

Israelology - this term refers to a subdivision of Systematic Theology incorporating all theological doctrines concerning the people of Israel.

Israel - as used in this chapter, the term *Israel* is viewed theologically as referring to all descendants of Abraham, Isaac, and Jacob, also known as the Jews, the Jewish people, Israelites, Hebrews, etc.[2] The term is not limited to the present political and national state in the Middle East, which is merely a

---

[1] Lewis Sperry Chafer, *Systematic Theology*, 8 vols. (Dallas: Dallas Seminary Press, 1947), 1:5-6.
[2] Ibid., 7:205-206.

part of the whole; nor is it limited to those who adhere to the religion of Judaism only.

Hermeneutics -the science and art of Biblical interpretation[3]...Hermeneutics is the science that teaches us the principles, laws, and methods of interpretation.[4]

Dispensationalism - that system of theology which:

> ... views the world as a household run by God. In this household-world God is dispensing or administering its affairs according to His own will and in various stages of revelation in the process of time. These various stages mark off the distinguishably different economies in the outworking of His total purpose, and these economies are the dispensations.[5]

In this system there are usually, but not always, seven such dispensations.

Covenant Theology - that system of theology which "represents the whole of Scripture as being covered by covenants: (1) the covenant of works; and, (2) the covenant of grace."[6]

> Covenant theology, then, is a system of theology based upon the two covenants of works and of grace as governing categories for the understanding of the entire Bible.[7]

The Millennium or the Millennial Kingdom -

> The word *millennium* means *thousand years*. . . . this period of one thousand years is often identified with the many promises of the Old Testament of a coming kingdom of righteousness and peace on the earth in which the Jews would be leaders and in which all the nations would have great blessing both spiritual and economic.[8]

In this chapter the Millennium will also be referred to as the Messianic Kingdom.

---

[3] Bernard Ramm, *Protestant Biblical Interpretation* (Boston: W. A. Wilde Co., 1956), 1.
[4] Louis Berkhof, *Principles of Biblical Interpretation* (L. Berkhof, 1950; reprinted., Grand Rapids: Baker Book House, 1958), 11.
[5] Charles C. Ryrie, *Dispensationalism Today* (Chicago: Moody Press, 1965), 31.
[6] George N. M. Collins, "Covenant Theology," in *Baker's Dictionary of Theology* (Grand Rapids: Baker Book House, 1960), 144.
[7] Ryrie, *Dispensationalism Today*, 177.
[8] John F. Walvoord, *The Millennial Kingdom* (Grand Rapids: Dunham Publishing Co., 1959), 4.

Premillennialism - that system of theology "which holds the doctrine that the second coming of Christ precedes the millennium."[9] Premillennialism "is the teaching that Christ will reign on earth for one thousand years following His second advent. Premillennialism as a term derives its meaning from the belief that the second coming of Christ will be before this millennium and therefore pre-millennial."[10] All Dispensationalists are premillennial, whereas only a segment of Covenant Theologians are.

Postmillennialism - that system of theology which "teaches that the Second Coming of Christ will follow the thousand years of peace and righteousness."[11]

> . . . postmillennialism holds that the present age will end with a period of great spiritual blessing corresponding to the millennial promises accomplished through preaching the gospel. The whole world will be Christianized and brought to submission to the gospel *before* the return of Christ. The name is derived from the fact that in this theory Christ returns *after* the millennium (hence, *post* millennium).[12]

This view is held by a segment of Covenant Theologians.

Amillennialism – (or No-Millennium) that system of theology "which rejects the idea of any period of a thousand years either before or after the return of Christ."[13]

> This is the teaching that the only visible coming of Christ to this earth which the Church is to expect will be for judgment and will be followed by the final state. It is . . . a-millennial, because it rejects the doctrine . . . of a thousand years.[14]

The major segment of Covenant Theology today is amillennial.

The Significance and Importance of this Study

In one form or another, proponents of all systems of theology have wrestled with the question of Israel. All recognize the Jewish origins and roots of the Christian faith, and some kind of an official attitude towards the "People of the Book" has been displayed. In some, Israelology plays no vital role in their theology, whereas in others it is central.

---

[9] Charles L. Feinberg, *Premillennialism or Amillennialism?* (New York: American Board of Missions to the Jews, 1961), 1.

[10] Walvoord, *Millennial Kingdom*, 5.

[11] Charles C. Ryrie, *The Basis of the Premillennial Faith* (New York: Loizeaux Brothers, 1953), 13.

[12] Walvoord, *Millennial Kingdom*, 7.

[13] Feinberg, *Premill or Amill?*, 1.

[14] Oswald T. Allis, *Prophecy and the Church* (Oswald T. Allis, 1945; reprint ed., Nutley, NJ: Presbyterian & Reformed Publishing Co., 1974), 2.

Often it is the Israelology of a system that distinguishes one from another. Ryrie, a Dispensationalist, writes:

> What, then, is the *sine qua non* of dispensationalism? . . . A dispensationalist keeps Israel and the Church distinct. . . .This is probably the most basic theological test of whether or not a man is a dispensationalist, and it is undoubtedly the most practical and conclusive.[15]

A key factor, then, that distinguishes Dispensationalism from all other theologies is its Israelology. Chafer, another Dispensationalist, writes:

> Israel has never been the Church, is not the Church now, nor will she ever be the Church. A form of Covenant Theology which would thread all of Jehovah's purposes and undertakings upon His one attribute of grace could hardly avoid confusion of mind in matters related to His varied objectives. Covenant Theology, in consistency with its man-made premise, asserts its inventions respecting an Old Testament church, which, it is claimed, is an integral part of the New Testament Church and on the ground that, since God's grace is one unchanging attribute, its accomplishments must be the realization of one standardized ideal. The Covenant theory does retain Israel as such to the time of Christ's death. The Church is thought to be a spiritual remnant within Israel to whom all Old Testament blessings are granted and the nation as such is allowed to inherit the cursings.[16]

Again, it is Israelology that is the main distinguishing characteristic between Dispensationalism and Covenant Theology, the latter being subdivided into Premillennialism, Postmillennialism, and Amillennialism.

The degree of importance of Israelology to Dispensationalism is stated by Chafer:

> The Jewish nation is the center of all things related to the earth. . . . This great statement places Israel as the center of all divine purposes for the earth. Jehovah may chasten His people and even use the nations to that end, but invariably judgment falls on those who afflict Israel and simply because they do it maliciously nonetheless.[17]

Walvoord, another leading Dispensationalist, writes along the same vein:

> Unfortunately, the study of the future of Israel has been obscured by controversy in other areas of Biblical theology. Liberal or neo-orthodox theologians, who do not accept the infallibility of the Scriptures, tend to ignore what the Bible teaches about

---

[15] Ryrie, *Dispensationalism Today*, 44-45.
[16] Chafer, *Systematic Theology*, 4:311.
[17] Ibid., 4:313.

Israel. Among conservatives there is a radical division concerning the meaning of Biblical revelation in relation to Israel. Some contemporary amillenarians deny any future to Israel as such and consider the promises to Israel as being fulfilled in the church in the present age. Others believe that there will be a spiritual restoration of Israel, but tend to disregard the geographic and political aspects of Israel's promises.[18]

The fact that Israelology is what distinguishes Dispensationalism from Covenant Theology is not merely attested to by Dispensationalists, but it is also affirmed by Covenant Theologians. Allis, a Covenant Theologian of the amillennial school, writes:

> For in saying this he has placed his finger on the sore point in Dispensational teaching, the exaltation of the Jew *per se*. In their glorification of the Jew and the rosy future they assign to him, Dispensationalists vie with Zionists. The future belongs to the Jew![19]

Ladd, a Covenant Theologian from the premillennial school, writes:

> The concept that the Scriptures which refer to the Great Tribulation have to do only with Israel and not with the Church is an arbitrary method of interpreting the Word which, if carried out consistently, would make havoc of Biblical interpretation. We have found that dispensationalists themselves do not apply this method of "dividing the Word" in a consistent manner.[20]

Both Allis and Ladd criticize Dispensationalism over the issue of Israelology, yet Ladd wishes to distinguish his Covenant Premillennialism from Allis' Amillennialism. He does this by means of his own Israelology:

> There is therefore but one people of God. This is not to say that the Old Testament saints belonged to the Church and that we must speak of the Church in the Old Testament. . . . The Church properly speaking had its birthday on the day of Pentecost, for the Church is composed of all those who by one Spirit have been baptized into one body (I Cor. 12:13), and this baptizing work of the Spirit began on the day of Pentecost. While we must therefore speak of Israel and the Church, we must speak of only one people of God.[21]

All sides agree, then, that the factor of Israel is a distinguishing feature of the different theologies. Yet in spite of this admitted fact, Israelology as a separate

---

[18] John F. Walvoord, *Israel in Prophecy* (Grand Rapids: Zondervan Publishing House, 1962), 9.

[19] Allis, *Prophecy*, 219.

[20] George Eldon Ladd, *The Blessed Hope* (Grand Rapids: Wm. B. Eerdmans Publishing Co., 1956), 163.

[21] George Eldon Ladd, *The Gospel of the Kingdom* (Grand Rapids: Wm. B. Eerdmans Publishing Co., 1959), 117.

segment of Systematic Theology has never been systematized. This lack has been recognized by only one of the Systematic Theologies, that of Chafer:

> The works of Systematic Theology generally have recognized the redeemed people of this age, but only as a supposed sequence or continuation in the progress of the divine purpose in Israel. They refer to "the Old Testament Church" and to "the New Testament Church" as together constituting component parts of one divine project, thus failing to recognize those distinctions between Israel and the Church which, being so radical in character, serve to indicate the widest possible difference between them—difference in origin, difference in character and responsibility, and difference in destiny.[22]

Although Chafer points out the lack of most Systematic Theologies and has a great deal to say about the theology of Israel—more than all the others—he also fails to systematize the doctrine of Israel. His Israelology is scattered throughout his eight-volume *Systematic Theology*, and the index is of little help in this area. There is no separate section of "Israelology" in the one work where it was expected, yet Chafer is the most complete.

The Place of Israelology in Systematic Theology
The major divisions of Systematic Theology as given in logical sequence and found in most Systematic Theologies are as follows:

Bibliology - the doctrine of the Bible;
Theology Proper - the doctrine of God, the Trinity, the Father;
Christology - the doctrine of the Son;
Pneumatology - the doctrine of the Holy Spirit;
Angelology - the doctrine of angels;
Satanology - the doctrine of Satan;
Demonology - the doctrine of demons;
Anthropology - the doctrine of man;
Hamartiology - the doctrine of sin;
Soteriology - the doctrine of salvation;
Ecclesiology - the doctrine of the Church; and
Eschatology - the doctrine of last things.

These elements will be found in every work of Systematic Theology, and each element will be fully developed and systematized (though not always in the above order); but Israelology will be found missing as a major division. In all

---

[22] Chafer, *Systematic Theology*, 4:29-30.

Systematic Theologies, what exists of Israelology will only be partially developed. In Covenant Theology, the development will be minimal. In Dispensationalism, Israelology is only fully developed in its future aspect, not in its past and present aspects.

Logically, Israelology must come just prior to Ecclesiology and follow the same development. Both are a people of God but, historically, Israel precedes the Church. As Ecclesiology has been developed in its past, present, and future aspects, so must Israelology be. Only then will Systematic Theology be truly complete.[23]

Summary and Conclusions on the Israelology of Covenant Postmillennialism

The Israelology of Covenant Postmillennialism is based on Covenant Theology, and that very fact limits its development of a complete Israelology. The covenant of grace, upon which Covenant Theology is based, allows for only one people of God, and this one group is the Church. Hence, all Jews who have ever believed, regardless of what point in history, before or after Christ, are part of the Church. All Jews who now believe are part of the Church. All Jews who will believe in the future, including the time of the national salvation of Israel, will be part of the Church. In fact, the Church is "spiritual Israel."

Summary
Israel Past
The Church, being composed of all believers of all times, would have begun with Adam. With the call of Abraham and the development from him of a theocratic nation, the Church in its outward form became identified with the nation of Israel. The covenant God made with Abraham was an extension of the covenant of grace. The covenant of Sinai, containing the Law of Moses, was a rule of life for the Church and, as such, much of it still applies to the Church today. However, some things, like the Sabbath, require modifications and adjustments. From Moses until Christ the Church in its outward visible form was the nation of Israel, for Israel was the people of God, especially since most of the elect during this period were Jews.

Israel Present
The national relationship of Israel to the Church changed with the coming of Christ. When Israel rejected the Messiahship of Jesus, God in turn rejected Israel and cast them off. This rejection is not a total one, for there is a remnant

---

[23] For a more comprehensive handling of this central topic, please see Arnold Fruchtenbaum, *Israelology: The Missing Link in Systematic Theology*, (Tustin, CA: Ariel Ministries Press, 1989).

of Jews coming to saving faith. The Jews as a nation or people, however, have been cast off. Positionally they are still God's people, but experientially they are not, for they have been cast away from the place of blessing. The invisible Church now takes its outward form, not in any national identity such as Israel, but in the visible churches. The majority of the elect are no longer Jews but Gentiles because of the divine rejection and casting away. As for individual Jews today, they can become part of the Church by exercising faith; but there are no special privileges or obligations for the Jewish believer that are not also true for the Gentile believer. It was this very Jewish unbelief and God's rejection and casting away of the Jews that made possible a widespread propagation of the gospel among the Gentiles which should, in turn, provoke Jews to jealousy so that they too will believe. An effort in a special way should be made to evangelize the Jews. This should be consistently prayed for both as to their present salvation, but especially for the future salvation of the Jews as a nation. Jews should be respected, and anti-Semitism should be avoided and condemned.

Israel Future
The preaching of the gospel will have a steady growth, but at some point it will produce a massive revival among the Gentiles, resulting in the majority of the Gentiles being saved. This is the fullness of the Gentiles. When that fullness comes, a similar mass revival will occur among the Jews, resulting in the majority of the Jews being saved. In that way, all Israel will be saved. This will not result in a restoration of Israel to the land but in Israel's amalgamation into the Church. The fullness of the Gentiles and the saving of all Israel will result in a long period of peace and prosperity. It will last for a very long time, though not necessarily one thousand years. At the end of this long period will come a great apostasy and rebellion that will terminate with the second coming, a general resurrection, a general judgment, and the eternal state.

Conclusions
The Covenant Postmillennialist's acceptance of a national salvation of ethnic Israel allows for a greater development of Israelology than Covenant Amillennialism, but its denial of a literal restoration to the land results in a lesser development than Covenant Premillennialism or Dispensationalism. Its identification of Israel with the Church (less than the Covenant Amillennialist, but more than the Covenant Premillennialist) does not allow for a full-scale Israelology to develop to the extent that Dispensationalism does. The following are some specific areas.

Israel Past

Covenant Postmillennialism fails to adequately deal with three main subjects.

First, it fails to take into account all that was entailed in the Jewish covenants such as the Abrahamic, Sinaitic or Mosaic Land[24] Davidic and New Covenants. There is a tendency to mesh them all together as part of the outworking of the covenant of grace. Furthermore, there is a great emphasis on the spiritual facets and promises of these covenants, but a clear de-emphasis on its physical and material facets and promises. These covenants are not expounded on their own merit in the context in which they were given, but the tendency is to read New Testament truth back into the Old, assuming more knowledge than the Old Testament saint could have had.

Second, there is the issue of Israel's unique entity. Again, Covenant Theology does not allow for two peoples of God but only one. This one is the elect, it is the Church, and it is the spiritual Israel. Physical or ethnic Israel sometimes is this Church, but sometimes it is not. This view leads to the concept that not only was the way and the means of salvation always the same, but the content of faith was always the same. Here, too, a great deal of New Testament knowledge must be imputed to the Old Testament saint, which is not found in the Hebrew Scriptures. Too much at the center is the elect, and how Israel fits into all this is not as clear as it should be. The only-one-people concept puts the emphasis on the Church and not Israel, though clearly the Old Testament only speaks of Israel and not the Church. Covenant Postmillennialism, because of its Covenant Theology, simply refuses to recognize this. As a result, Israel as a distinct entity to whom both spiritual and physical privileges and promises belong fails to appear as such.

Third, there is the issue of the Law of Moses. This law is viewed as perpetual, and Postmillennialists insist that it did not terminate with the death of Christ. Yet it is obvious that many specific commandments can no longer be carried out. Some commandments are dismissed on the basis that they are ceremonial, and the death of Christ did terminate them. Others are dismissed on the basis of being connected with Israel as a theocratic state; since the Church is no longer connected with theocratic Israel, these commandments no longer apply. Still others are modified, such as the Sabbath being switched to Sunday. There is a failure to see the law as a unit or its purposes in relationship to Israel.

Israel Present

There are two failings of Covenant Postmillennialism in this area; however, not

---

[24] Also known as the Palestinian Covenant among many writers.

every individual Postmillennialist shares each failing, since they are not uniform in their thinking.

The first concerns the question, Does Israel now stand rejected by God? All agree that Israel has not been totally rejected, but there is confusion among them as to the nature of this rejection. Are the Jews no longer the chosen people in any sense? (Boettner) Is Israel still the chosen people but no longer in the place of blessing? (Murray) The failure here is to recognize what Paul said: that God has not cast away his people. The problem is not that God rejected Israel, but that Israel rejected the Messiahship of Jesus, which has led to the loss of blessing. The Covenant Postmillennialists have placed the rejection in the wrong place.

The second problem concerns the role of the Jewish believers today. Covenant Postmillennialism clearly sees the remnant as being part of ethnic Israel as well as part of the Church, but it never deals with the issue of its practical ramifications. Do Jewish believers have a right to continue as Jews and practice their Jewishness? Can a Jewish believer reach back to the Law of Moses to observe the Passover, as Hodge does to practice the Sabbath? There is no clear discussion in Covenant Postmillennialism on the role of the Jewish believers as part of the ethnic Israel or as part of the Church.

Israel Future
Covenant Postmillennialism differs little from Covenant Amillennialism and Covenant Premillennialism on the issues of Israel's past and present. Where the Postmillennialist's Israelology differs from that of his Covenant Theologian friends is in Israel's future—the Postmillennialist's belief in a national salvation of Israel separates him from Covenant Amillennialism. His rejection of a national restoration to the land separates him from Covenant Premillennialism. It is the latter that is the problem. It requires a great deal of spiritualization of unfulfilled prophecy (but not as much spiritualization as Amillennialism requires) to arrive at a denial of Israel's national restoration. The problem is one of partial allegorization. Because Covenant Postmillennialists believe in some type of Millennium with world peace and prosperity, they do see a degree of literal fulfillment well beyond that of the Amillennialist. However, it is not literal enough, so there is a denial of a national restoration of Israel during that Millennium. This requires a great deal of subjective allegorization of unfulfilled prophecy.

Too often, the tendency is to approach a prophetic passage with a covenant postmillennial bias and then interpret accordingly; so, the woman of Revelation 12 giving birth to the man-child represents the Church struggling to present Christ to the world. However, such an interpretation does not arise naturally from the text. The tendency is to ignore the Old Testament background and to proceed with a postmillennial interpretation which ignores the obvious and simple meaning of the text. Eschatological messages, such as Matthew 24, are interpreted as fulfilled in Jewish history while ignoring that same history. According to Matthew 24, what Israel will suffer in the period described by the passage will be the worst ever, both past and future (24:21). Covenant Postmillennialism insists this is a reference to A.D. 70. While that was certainly bad, it was hardly the worst when compared with subsequent persecutions, such as the Nazi Holocaust. Not only does Covenant Theology resort to allegorization of unfulfilled prophecy, it also ignores Jewish history.

Summary and Conclusions of the Israelology of Covenant Amillennialism

Cox gives a good summary of his Israelology as it relates to Israel and the Church:

> 1. God has always had but one spiritual people, represented by the remnant in every generation. 2. God's promises to Israel were conditional. 3. All earthly promises to Israel have been either fulfilled or invalidated through disobedience and unbelief. 4. Israel was a type of the church and was superseded by the church. 5. The church was prophesied in the Old Testament, *in Old Testament language*. 6. Christ was, and is, the only Hope of Israel. And Israelites (Jews) will be saved only if they accept him during *this* age. 7. The first advent of Christ completed Israel's redemption, and manifested the Israel of God (the church) referred to in Galatians 6:16. 8. Christ instituted a Jewish-Gentile church. 9. All unfulfilled spiritual promises to Israel are being fulfilled through the Christian church. 10. This does not represent a change in God's plan, but evidences progressive revelation.[25]

The Israelology of Covenant Amillennialism is based on Covenant Theology, which by its very nature limits the development of a complete Israelology. The covenant of grace, upon which Covenant Theology is based, allows for only one people of God, and this one people is the Church. Covenant Amillennialism has an even less developed Israelology than Covenant Postmillennialism because it uses the allegorical method of interpretation, especially in the area of Israel and prophecy, to a greater extent than Covenant Postmillennialism does. For both, the Church is the "spiritual Israel," and so for both, all Jews who have ever believed (before and after Christ), do believe, or will believe are part of the Church.

---

[25] Cox, *Biblical Studies*, 46-47.

Summary
Israel Past
Some from this school of theology believe that the covenant of grace began with Adam, while others believe it began with Abraham. Even the latter believe that the essence of the covenant of grace is already found in Genesis 3:15 in the Adamic context. From the time of its beginning, the covenant had a primary application only to the elect. Obviously, for the duration of the Old Testament, the vast majority of the elect were Jewish elect; but it is only to the elect that the promises of the covenant applied.

There were physical promises made by the prophets to the nation as a whole, but one of two things has happened concerning these physical promises. First, all the prophecies which were intended for a literal fulfillment have already been fulfilled with the return from the Assyrian and Babylonian captivities. All others have been cancelled because of Israel's unbelief. Now, only the spiritual promises have been left for fulfillment.

As for the covenants God made with Israel in the past, there is only one covenant, the covenant of grace. All the other covenants are considered as essentially the same and are, therefore, not to be viewed as separate covenants, but merely further revelations of the covenant of grace. All those facets of the one covenant of grace are related to the Church and not to Israel nationally, though during the Old Testament period the Church did move from a home phase, to an institutional phase. However, even this national phase concerned the elect of Israel and not national Israel as such. As for the Law of Moses, this was meant as a rule of life for the national Church. This law had elements which were permanent and elements which were temporary.

Israel Present
At the present time, there is no distinctive plan for Israel. National Israel today is not the people of God, it is not the chosen nation. It is the Church that is the people of God, the holy nation, and the chosen race. The Church is the spiritual Israel, the seed of Abraham, the heavenly Zion and Jerusalem, and the Olive Tree of Romans 11. It is the Kingdom of God.

God has not *cast away his people*, for there is an elect remnant from among the Jews that have, do, and will believe and become part of the Church. In fact, Jews will continue to believe in Christ right up to the Parousia or the second coming. This is happening contemporaneously with the *fullness of the Gentiles*. For this reason, Jewish evangelism must still be a mission of the Church. A few would even say that the Jews have a priority in this since the gospel is still *to the Jew first*. There are no remaining unfulfilled promises to the Jews. All promises are spiritual and are now being fulfilled in and through the Church.

Because Israel and the Church are the same, the history of Israel is now the history of the Church. With the New Testament phase of this history, the Church has separated from the national life of Israel and become an independent organization. Furthermore, baptism has now replaced circumcision as the sign of the covenant. Many of the commandments of the Law of Moses were terminated. All commandments which were purely national have been discarded since God is now through with Israel as a nation. Otherwise, the Law of Moses is still in effect. Now all distinctions between Jews and Gentiles have been erased and that forever. The Remnant of Israel is now to be viewed as being part of the Church, and not a   distinct entity within Israel.

Israel Future

It is here more than in Israel Past and Israel Present that the Covenant Amillennialists differ from the Covenant Postmillennialists. In the amillennial scheme, the present age (their Millennium) will terminate with the second coming,   which will be followed by the eternal state with no Millennium in between.

There will be no future national salvation of Israel. The expression *all Israel shall be saved* means only the sum total of all the elect, or of all Jewish remnants between Abraham and the Parousia. This happens at the same time as *the fullness of the Gentiles* and not subsequent to it. The *fullness of the Gentiles* and *all Israel shall be saved* terminate with the second coming. There will be no national salvation either preceding or following the second coming. Instead, the second coming will result in judgment for national Israel for their unbelief.

There will also be no future national restoration of Israel. Such prophecies are to be interpreted spiritually as a gathering into the Church, and the glorious future is that of the eternal state. The hope of Israel is salvation in the Church. The future of believing Israel is exactly the same as believing Gentiles: salvation and ultimate glorification through faith in Christ.

Conclusions

Covenant Amillennialism allows for the least development of Israelology when compared with the other two schools of Covenant Theology. Covenant Postmillennialism allows for further development because it does believe in a national salvation of Israel, which Amillennialism does not. Covenant Premillennialism can go even further, because it believes in a Millennium after the second coming, which Amillennialism does not. Because of its basis in Covenant Theology, it is limited in how much of an Israelology it can develop. For that reason, it shares many of the same weaknesses as Postmillennialism does and then some.

Israel Past

Covenant Amillennialism fails to adequately deal with three main subjects, the same three as with Covenant Postmillennialism. First, like Postmillennialism, it fails to take into account all that was entailed in the Jewish covenants. Whereas Postmillennialism de-emphasizes the physical and material facets and promises of the Jewish covenants, Amillennialism totally ignores and denies them. Second, like Postmillennialism, Amillennialism fails to see and recognize Israel's unique entity, and for the same reason claims there can only be one and not two peoples of God. Third, it shares the same failings as Postmillennialism on the issue of the Law of Moses.

Israel Present

There are two failings of Covenant Amillennialism in this area. First, Amillennialists all agree that God has not rejected Israel, but they limit this "Israel" to the elect or remnant Israel only. While Postmillennialists are split over the issue of whether the Jews are the chosen people, Amillennialists are not. They all agree that national Israel is not, but only the Church is. They have no place whatsoever left in their scheme for Israel today, and they see no theological significance to Jewish history in general or the State of Israel in particular. Second, while Postmillennialism sees the remnant of Israel as being part of both the Church and ethnic Israel, Amillennialism only affirms the former but not the latter. With rare exception, Amillennialists see no validity in Jewish believers practicing their Jewishness.

Israel Future

It is here that Covenant Amillennialism differs the most from its two sisters, Covenant Postmillennialism and Covenant Premillennialism. Its denial of a national salvation of Israel separates it from Covenant Postmillennialism and Premillennialism. Its rejection of a national restoration to the land separates it even further from Covenant Premillennialism. To arrive at their conclusion, they must resort to spiritualization and allegorization of unfulfilled prophecy to a greater degree than the other two schools. The conclusion is that the future of national Israel is one of judgment, but for the Church it is the glorious future of the eternal state.

Summary and Conclusions of the Israelology of Covenant Premillennialism

The Israelology of Covenant Premillennialism is based on Covenant Theology, which in turn limits the development of a complete Israelology. The covenant of grace, upon which Covenant Theology is based, allows for only one people of God, and this one people is the Church. However, the Premillennialism of Covenant Premillennialism allows for a far greater development of Israelology than either Covenant Postmillennialism or Covenant Amillennialism. It uses the allegorical method of interpretation in a much lesser degree than the other two schools of Covenant Theology. While it too believes the Church to be "spiritual Israel," it only affirms it for the present and the future. It is not so sure about Israel in the past.

Summary
Israel Past

Covenant Premillennialists are divided on the issue of the Church in the Old Testament. Some, like Buswell, follow the traditional covenantal viewpoint and assert that the Church existed in the Old Testament and the Church was the true Israel even then. Ladd and LaSor, however, see the Church as having its beginning in Acts two with LaSor strongly asserting that the Church is not the Israel of the Old Testament. Ladd insists that the Church was not foreseen in the Old Testament. What they all agree is that there is only one people of God. Buswell would say that the one people of God was always the Church. Ladd and LaSor would say that Israel was the people of God in the Old Testament, but the Church is the people of God in the New Testament. Most see the Old Testament as largely a history of Israel.

Buswell also follows the traditional covenantal viewpoint on the covenant of grace. This covenant was made with the Church. It is on this basis that Buswell defends the practice of infant baptism, insisting that infant baptism has replaced infant circumcision as the token of the covenant. On this same basis Buswell maintains that Sunday has replaced Saturday as the Sabbath. Ladd would probably largely follow Buswell's lead. LaSor, however, sees the Jewish facets of the Abrahamic Covenant more clearly.

As for the Law of Moses, this was the rule of life for a redeemed people. It was given to the people of God under the covenant of grace whether this people of God was Israel (Ladd, LaSor) or the Church (Buswell).

As for the Kingdom of God, Covenant Premillennialists do not equate it with the Church, but it was the Kingdom of God that created the Church.

Israel in the past was the people of God, the sons of the kingdom, the sons of the covenant, and the chosen people.

Israel Present

The turning point came with the coming of Jesus. Jesus offered to Israel the Kingdom of God; however, the kingdom that Jesus offered was not a literal earthly kingdom, but a spiritual kingdom, the kingdom of salvation. Israel rejected this kingdom, and when they did so, their status changed. They ceased to be the people of God, and now the Church is the people of God. It is the Church today that is the people of God, the holy nation, and the chosen race. The Church today is the spiritual Israel.

The Law of Moses is still in effect and the Church is under it. Obviously, the coming of Christ brought with it a number of changes, such as infant baptism replacing circumcision, and Sunday replacing Saturday as the Sabbath. The Law of Moses is still obligatory, but with many ramifications arrived at by a "true meaning" hermeneutic. It has "permanent validity," though some major modifications are required in light of Christ's coming; but the law has not been abolished for Christians.

Concerning the Israel of Romans 9-11, this passage speaks of two Israels. There is a literal Israel which is the national Israel that rejected the Messiah and lost its special privilege. There is also a spiritual Israel which is comprised of all Jewish and Gentile believers. This spiritual Israel is the Church. Today, the Church is the true Israel, and it is the chosen people, the people of God, the sons of the kingdom, and the sons of the covenant.

Concerning the Olive Tree, there is disagreement as to its meaning. One view is that it represents Abraham's faith (Buswell), while the other view is that it represents the one people of God (Ladd) which now is the Church. The Remnant of Israel is now to be viewed as part of the Church and not a distinct entity. The Church is the present form of the kingdom, for the kingdom was taken away from Israel and given to the Church. The Kingdom of God is active in the world today, but it is only active through the Church. The kingdom does not in any way relate to Israel today. There is only one Olive Tree, so there is only one people of God. Originally the Olive Tree people of old consisted of Israelites, but now it consists of believing Jews and Gentiles.

Concerning the New Covenant, this covenant was made with the Church. This view is based on the fact that the New Testament reinterprets the Old Testament. As a result, the New Covenant is the Church's and not Israel's.

God has not "cast away His people," however, and there is a remnant among the Jews today. Jews who become believers today become part of the

Church. The re-establishment of Israel as a nation is evidence that God has not cast away His people; however, this is as far as Covenant Premillennialists are willing to go to give any theological significance to the Jewish State. It is possible that the rebirth of Israel is part of God's purpose, but on this they are not sure. They are sure that not every promise made to Israel could be fulfilled by the Church, but the distinction between Israel and the Gentiles has ceased. Such a distinction was intended by God to be purely temporary.

Israel Future

Covenant Premillennialists can give this area its greatest development, well beyond Covenant Postmillennialists and Covenant Amillennialists, because of their belief in a future literal kingdom. There are, however, significant and sharp differences among them so that on the question of the Rapture or the Tribulation, they are divided into three major schools of thought: some are Pretribulationists; others are Midtribulationists; but the majority are Posttribulationists. Israelology is a major reason for this division.

While all of them believe in a national salvation and restoration of Israel, there is no consensus among them as to the basis for believing in this. They also lack a consensus as to how Jewish the Millennium will be. Covenant Premillennialism believes in both a national salvation and a national restoration of Israel. Postmillennialism believes in a national salvation, but not a national restoration of Israel. Amillennialism rejects both.

The lack of consensus is seen in a number of areas. One example is the interpretation of the 144,000 of Revelation seven. Buswell takes it literally in that it speaks of Jews and Jewish evangelism in the Tribulation. Ladd, however, interprets it allegorically as speaking of the Church and uses it as evidence of Posttribulationism. A second example concerns the nature of the Millennium. Buswell has no problem viewing it as a Jewish kingdom, since there is no other gospel than a Jewish gospel. Ladd, however, totally rejects the Jewish nature of the Millennium altogether. A third example is the basis for believing in a Millennium in the first place. Ladd sees no evidence at all for it in the Old Testament, and the only evidence is found in the New Testament, primarily Revelation 20. Buswell and LaSor, however, are not ready to dismiss the Old Testament evidence and do use Old Testament prophecy as a valid source for believing in a Millennium and in a restoration of Israel.

The Covenant Premillennialist who is also a Postribulationist believes that the Church will go through the Tribulation. The evidence is based on the fact that the Scriptures clearly teach that Israel will go through the Tribulation; and since they identify Israel with the Church, they conclude that the Church will go through the Tribulation.

Even these Covenant Premillennialists who do base their beliefs of a future restoration of Israel on Old Testament prophecies do not necessarily interpret all prophecy literally. For example, they reject a literal view of the Millennial Temple and sacrificial system of Ezekiel 40-48; however, they do believe in a national salvation of Israel, though this does not necessarily mean every individual Jew. It does mean, however, the vast majority of Jews. When Israel is saved as a nation, Israel will be assimilated into the Church.

Conclusions

The Covenant Premillennialist's acceptance of both a national salvation and a national restoration of Israel allows for the greater development of Israelology when compared with the other two schools of Covenant Theology, but it still falls short of Dispensationalism. Its identification of Israel with the Church, though less so than Postmillennialism or Amillennialism, does not allow for a full-scale Israelology to develop to the extent that Dispensationalism does. To some degree it shares some of the same weaknesses of Covenant Postmillennialism and Covenant Amillennialism. The following are some specific areas.

Israel Past

Covenant Premillennialism fails to adequately deal with the same three areas as the other two schools of Covenant Theology.

First, it too fails to take into account all that is entailed in the Jewish covenants. It is less guilty of this than the other two schools, since some Covenant Premillennialists do see these as Jewish covenants and admit that the Church is not found in the Old Testament. Others in the very same school do not. This lack of consensus on such a crucial question is a problem in itself. All of them still tend to allegorize some of the details of these covenants. Furthermore, the covenant of grace idea still plays a major role in their thinking and interpretation of Moses and the prophets.

Second, along with the other two schools, Covenant Premillennialism fails to see and recognize Israel's unique entity. Here too this school is less guilty of this than the other two schools, since it does recognize Israel's unique standing in the Old Testament; but they now insist that all this has been lost, taken away from Israel, and given to the Church. It also denies that there can be two peoples of God and believes that there is only one people of God. In the Old Testament it was Israel; now it is the Church, and so it will remain to all eternity. This, in turn, leads to the acceptance of some prophecies of Israel's future as being literal, but many others as not. Members of the same school disagree on which are literal and which are not. Still, the only-one-people concept puts the emphasis on the Church and not Israel. Somewhere along the line Israel as a distinct entity is assimilated into the Church and loses its own special calling.

Third, it shares all the same failings as the other two schools on the issue of the Law of Moses. In addition to using the same approach as the other two schools, Covenant Premillennialists have developed two unique hermeneutical principles to defend their position. The first is the "true meaning" principle used by Buswell, and the "reinterpretation of the Old Testament" principle used by Ladd. Clearly, they both fail to see the law as a unit or its purpose in relationship to Israel.

Israel Present

There are two failings of Covenant Premillennialism in this area:

First, while they affirm that God has not cast away His people, they also insist that Israel is no longer the people of God, for this is only true of the Church. There is no place in their scheme for Israel today. While they remain open to the possibility that the State of Israel may be part of God's prophetic program, they have very little to say about it theologically.

The second problem concerns the role of the Jewish believers today. They do see the Remnant of Israel as belonging to the Church but are unclear as to the remnant's position in relationship to Israel. For the most part, they view the remnant only in terms of the Church. They deny that the *Israel of God* is a Jewish remnant and insist it is the Church. They have nothing to say as to whether Jewish believers can continue practicing their Jewishness. There is no clear discussion in Covenant Premillennialism on the role of the Jewish believer as part of ethnic Israel or as part of the Church.

Israel Future

It is here that Covenant Premillennialism differs most from its two sisters in Covenant Theology. Its belief in a national salvation of Israel separates it from Covenant Amillennialism. Its belief in a national restoration of Israel separates it from Covenant Postmillennialism. However, its strong reluctance to base it on the prophecies of the Old Testament is very problematic. This requires a great deal of allegorizing of the prophecies of the Old Testament. Even Ladd admits at one point that his view of the Old Testament certainly sounds like Amillennialism. To base a theology of Israel's future only on Revelation 20 and a few scattered New Testament references leaves a lot to be desired. Ignoring such a wealth of Old Testament information leads to a shallow Eschatology in general, and a shallow Israelology in particular.

Summary and Conclusions of the Israelology of Dispensationalism

The Israelology of Dispensationalism is based on a literal intrpretation of Scripture and this, in turn, leads to making a consistent distinction between Israel and the Church. This allows for the greatest and most complete development of a systematic Israelology, far more so than any of the three schools of Covenant Theology. However, Dispensationalism has failed to actually do this, and dispensational writers simply integrate their Israelology into their Ecclesiology and their Eschatology. However, the subject of Israel and the key role it plays in Scripture is worthy of its own distinct place in Systematic Theology.

Summary

Israel Past

Israel as a nation was the object of a national election which put them in a place of privilege and blessing. This did not guarantee the salvation of every Jew, since salvation is a result of individual election. Those individually elected become believers and make up the Remnant of Israel. While the national election did not guarantee salvation, it did guarantee Israel's survival as a people.

Because of this national election, God entered into five covenants with Israel, four of which were unconditional and eternal, while one was conditional and temporary. The first covenant was the Abrahamic Covenant, which contained three key elements: a seed or a nation, a land, and blessings. The nation is the Jewish nation; the land is Canaan, or Palestine, or the Land of Israel; and the blessings were spiritual blessings which were also destined to extend to the Gentiles. The second covenant was the Mosaic Covenant, the only one which was conditional and temporary. It contained the Law of Moses, which was a rule of life for Israel, for the Old Testament saint, but it never was a way or means of salvation. It promised blessings for obedience and curses for disobedience. The third covenant is the Land Covenant which amplified the land aspect of the Abrahamic Covenant, promising a world-wide scattering and dispersion, followed by a world-wide regathering into the land. The fourth covenant is the Davidic Covenant, which amplified the seed aspect of the Abrahamic Covenant. When used as a collective singular, the *seed* refers to the Jewish nation. When it is used as an absolute singular, it refers to the Messiah. This covenant assures the continuance of the House of David, for the Messiah will come from him. Furthermore, it promised three eternal things: a house, a kingdom, and a throne. The eternity of the house, kingdom, and throne is guaranteed because the seed of David culminates in a descendant Who is Himself eternal. The fifth covenant is the New Covenant, which amplifies the blessing aspect of the Abrahamic Covenant, especially spiritual blessings. This covenant promised a national salvation of Israel. The covenant contained both physical and spiritual promises.

As for the Kingdom of God, Dispensationalists see two major facets of God's kingdom program.

The first facet is the Universal Kingdom or the Eternal Kingdom, which is God's rule over His creation by means of His sovereignty and providence. As the names imply, it is both universal (over all creation) and eternal (God's rule has no beginning or end).

The second facet is known as the Theocratic Kingdom or Mediatorial Kingdom, which is God's rule through human mediators. While a form of theocracy existed since Adam, it had a unique display with God's rule over Israel. The Theocratic Kingdom over Israel began with Moses and continued in its purely mediatorial form from Moses to Joshua, through the Judges, until Samuel. It then took a monarchial form from Saul to Zedekiah. The Theocratic Kingdom ended with the Babylonian destruction of Jerusalem. At that time, the Theocratic Kingdom in history ended and the Times of the Gentiles began. As the quality of the Theocratic Kingdom declined, the prophets spoke of a future facet of the kingdom program, the Messianic Kingdom, when God will exercise His rule through the Messiah.

Israel Present

When Jesus came, He offered to Israel the very kingdom which the prophets spoke of, the Messianic Kingdom, the earthly kingdom. In fulfillment of prophecy and the plan of God, Israel rejected the Messiah. As a result, the offer of the millennial form of the kingdom was rescinded, destined to be reoffered to a future Jewish generation, while the present generation was placed under a divine judgment that came in A.D. 70. In place of setting up the Messianic Kingdom following His death and resurrection, He instead returned to the Father. In place of the Messianic Kingdom, a different facet of God's kingdom program was inaugurated, which is the Mystery Kingdom. This is the way God's rule is manifested between the Jewish rejection of the Messiah and the Jewish acceptance of the Messiah. The Mystery Kingdom is not the Church, though the Church is included in that kingdom. The Mystery Kingdom is basically defined as "Christendom."

Christ also announced the formation of a new entity, distinct from Israel, through which the message of salvation is to go forth: the Church. The Church began in Acts two when the Holy Spirit began the work of Spirit baptism, and it is composed of all believers, Jews and Gentiles, from Acts two until the Rapture of the Church. The Church is not the new Israel or the spiritual Israel, but the *one new man*. She has not taken over Israel's covenants, blessings or promises, nor are God's promises to Israel being fulfilled in or through the Church. However, the Church is a *partaker* of Jewish spiritual blessings. The Jewish covenants contained both physical and spiritual promises. The physical promises were limited to the Jews, but the spiritual promises were to extend to the Gentiles. When the Church became a partaker, this was fulfilled and is still being fulfilled, but this does not make the Church Israel or the Kingdom of God.

As for Romans 9-11, the two Israels are not physical Israel and the Church, but physical Israel and spiritual Israel. Both Israels are composed of Jews only. Physical Israel includes all Jews, but spiritual Israel is only those Jews who believe. This is the same as the *Israel of God* of Galatians 6:16 and the Remnant of Israel. While the majority of the Jews have not believed, this does not mean that God has cast away His people. The truth is, the majority have always disbelieved while a minority, the remnant, believed. Today, also, there is a remnant according to the election of grace. Some believe that this remnant ceases to be part of the Commonwealth of Israel and becomes a member of the Church only, while others see Jewish believers to be in both groups. As for the Olive Tree, this is not the Church or Israel, but it is the place of blessing, rooted in the patriarchs and the Jewish covenants. The natural branches are Jews, and the wild olive branches are the Gentiles. Both groups have believers in the place of blessing. Today, Israel suffers under a judicial blindness, but this blindness is partial so that there is still a remnant. It is temporary until the fullness of the Gentiles comes in. Today, God is taking out from among the Gentiles a people for His name.

Israel Future

The fullness of the Gentiles comes when the set number of Gentiles God has ordained for the Church is complete, and then she is raptured. Because of the distinction that is maintained between Israel and the Church, Dispensationalists are pretribulationists.

Israel will undergo the seven years of Tribulation and is to be identified with the Woman of Revelation 12. Israel will suffer persecution during this period, and many will die; but one-third of the nation will survive. The 144,000 are a special class within Israel who will be used to proclaim the gospel world-wide, resulting in the salvation of myriads of Gentiles.

At some point in relationship to the second coming, Israel will experience a national salvation; for the blindness will be removed, and all Israel will be saved. Israel will also experience a national regathering and restoration back into the land and will have a prominent place above the Gentile nations in the Messianic Kingdom. Some, but not all, believe that Israel will undergo a special judgment in conjunction with the second coming to determine who will or who will not enter this kingdom. Others feel the Tribulation itself is the judgment upon Israel and so a separate judgment is not necessary.

In the Messianic Kingdom, which is to last a literal one thousand years, Israel will enjoy, receive, and fulfill all the promises and blessings of the four unconditional covenants. The saved nation will have her own distinct identity and will not be amalgamated into the Church. As for the Church, she will have a separate role in the kingdom as co-reigners with Christ.

Conclusions

Not bound to a covenant of grace, but only bound to the text of Scripture, Dispensationalism allows the Church to be the Church, but Israel is allowed to be Israel. Again, Dispensationalism, as a theological system, is the only one that has a basis for a full-fledged Israelology. Having failed to actually produce one has led to some confusion and inconsistency. The following are some specifics.

Israel Past

A major failing of Dispensationalism is a clear delineation between the physical and the spiritual blessings and promises of the Jewish covenants. This, in turn, has led to a failure to understand the Gentile role and participation in the spiritual blessings of the covenants. This is the root behind the view of some Dispensationalists that there are two new covenants instead of one. However, on the whole, this is Dispensationalism's second best developed area.

Israel Present

This is Dispensationalism's weakest area. This is the area where Dispensationalism's insistence on a distinction between Israel and the Church has not been consistently applied. Because they assume that God's program for Israel and God's program for the Church can never operate at the same time, some see no prophetic significance to Israel today, though the majority do. Even Dispensationalists sometimes state that Jews who believe cease to be Jews when they become part of the Church, though such a statement is inconsistent with the basic tenets of Dispensationalism. Another inconsistency includes recognition that the Sabbath no longer applies, but then insistence on a Sunday observance as mandatory.

Though very clear on the existence of a Jewish remnant today, as always, Dispensationalism shows a lack of consensus as to this remnant's relationship to the Body or Commonwealth of Israel. There is a clear failure to recognize that the remnant is always part of Israel and is not separated from it, and that it is possible to be part of the remnant and part of the Church at the same time. This, in turn, leads to confusion in other areas. For example, Dispensationalists insist that the Abrahamic Covenant is an eternal and unconditional covenant; and the token of the covenant is circumcision. This clearly implies that circumcision, while not mandatory for Gentiles, is mandatory for Jews. Yet even Dispensationalists cry "galatianism" when they hear of Jewish believers circumcising their sons ritually on the eighth day. Another example of confusion and inconsistency concerns the issue of Jewish Messianic congregations: Jewish-oriented churches that formulate a style of worship which is distinctively Jewish rather than Gentile. Yet, even some Dispensationalists claim that while all other nationalities can have ethnic churches, Jewish believers are forbidden to have Jewish ethnic churches. There is a lack of concern as to whether Jewish believers are permitted to be Jewish and practice their Jewishness.

Again, this area is Dispensationalism's greatest weakness and is the least developed area. On Jewish questions for the present, many Dispensationalists sound like Covenant Theologians!

Israel Future

This is Dispensationalism's most developed area of Israelology and what it is most noted for. As a result, to many, the word "Dispensationalism" conjures up the concept of prophecy rather than a system of theology. Here, too, there are weaknesses which Israelology could resolve, two in particular.

First, Dispensationalism is pretribulational, but has not always been clear as to *when* before the Tribulation the Rapture will occur. As a result, many have taught only on assumption that the Rapture will begin the Tribulation. However, this is not the case, and the Tribulation is a part of God's program for Israel and not the Church. The beginning of the Tribulation is somehow related to Israel, but most Dispensationalists have not been clear as to how it is related.

A second area of confusion is the relationship of Israel's national salvation to the second coming. There is a lack of understanding as to exactly what the basis or precondition to the second coming is. This, in turn, leads to a lack of concern as to whether that national salvation takes place before or after the second coming. This is also the reason there are questions raised about a special judgment of Israel to determine who is, and who is not, saved; yet Dispensationalism teaches that all Israel will be saved.

Only a separately developed Israelology that is not amalgamated into Ecclesiology and Eschatology can resolve these problems and answer these questions.

Conclusion

The three schools of Covenant Theology are based on the covenant of grace which, in turn, forces them to use an allegorical hermeneutic and, in turn, identify the Church as Israel. This limits the development of a full-scale Israelology. Not all three schools are equally guilty for they differ in the degree that they apply the allegorical hermeneutic and at what point Israel becomes the Church. Covenant Amillennialism has the least development of the three while Covenant Premillennialism has the most. Covenant Postmillennialism falls in between. However, all have shown themselves to be inadequate to provide a distinctive Israelology. Therefore, the search for a full-blown Israelology led to Dispensationalism.

Because only Dispensationalism makes a consistent distinction between Israel and the Church, and insists on a consistent use of literal or plain hermeneutics, only Dispensationalism allows for a fully developed Israelology as a separate division of Systematic Theology. However, it has failed to do so. The goal of our volume *Israelology: The Missing Link in Systematic Theology* was to present a fully developed Israelology: past, present, and future. In addition to these three major categories, additional categories were added for the sake of completeness. By and large, the material found under Israel Past and Future has always been a part of Dispensationalism, but has not always been systematized or, if so, not necessarily in this order. The material under Israel Present, for the most part, is the author's development. The final section on Other Relevant Topics is virtually exclusively the author's own development. The main purpose of this volume is to systematize Israelology. The secondary purpose is to discuss issues relevant to Israelology which have gone undeveloped in Dispensationalism for the above two reasons. For many Messianic Jews this is the most consistent theology since it allows the Bible to speak in a normal language and dispensational theology is the natural meaning of the biblical theology since it does not impose its theology on the Word, but it is a natural derivation of what the Bible teaches if simply taken literally, a fact even noted by some Covenant Theologians.

"Consider the dictionary definition of two words. The first is the word *develop*, which means "to set forth or make clear by degrees or in detail: expound." The second is the word *change*, which "implies making either an essential difference often amounting to a loss of original identity or a substitution of one thing for another." Hopefully, theology will *develop* in that sense of being made clearer. But theology may *change* either for the better or for the worse. If the substitution is more biblical, such change is desirable. If not, then it is not."

- Charles C. Ryrie
*Issues in Dispensationalism, 1994, page 15
(Willis & Master, eds.)*

8

Dispensational Definition & Division Revisited[1]

Christopher Cone

> ...an adequate definition of dispensationalism probably remains to be written. As soon as the suffixes are added to the word the subject is transferred immediately from Biblical to theological grounds. The recent literature on the subject has made it necessary to revise the theological definition...The current conception of the term in the popular mind is entirely inadequate.[2]

Despite their ring, these are not contemporary words. They are not banter akin to the present debate between classical and progressive dispensationalists. These words were penned in 1945 by Arnold Ehlert in a Dallas Theological Seminary doctoral dissertation approved by John Walvoord, and they reveal a dissatisfaction with traditional and contemporary definitions. This present discussion seeks to address certain inadequacies in definition and division.

Chronological Factors of Division: The Dispensations

Dispensation, from the Latin *dispensatio (management, administration[3])*, is the KJV translation of the Greek word *oikonomia* (e.g., 1 Cor. 9:17; Eph. 1:10; 3:2; Col 1:25) from which the English word *economy* gets its derivation. The Greek term is a compound which literally means *house-law*, and refers to stewardship, administration, or appropriation and management of resources. It is understood to be an arrangement, order, or plan.[4]

It is quite evident that there are such administrations in Scripture, and that the chronology of Scripture is marked with changes (sometimes slight) from one administration to another. Even those who oppose the

---

[1] From Christopher Cone, *Prolegomena: Introductory Notes on Bible Study & Theological Method* (Fort Worth, TX: Exegetica Publishing, 2007).
[2] Arnold Ehlert, "A Bibliography of Dispensationalism", Th.D Diss., Dallas Theological Seminary, November 1945, 33.
[3] D.P. Simpson, *Cassell's Latin Dictionary* (New York: MacMillan Publishing Co., 1959), 195.
[4] William F. Arndt & F. Wilbur Gingrich, *A Greek Lexicon of the New Testament and Other Early Christian Literature*, 4th Ed. (Chicago: The University of Chicago Press, 1957), 562.

theological system of dispensationalism recognize differing administrations within God's sovereign plan[5].

The Biblical writers clearly recognized that such distinctions exist. Note, for example, the various outlines/timelines within the Book of Daniel, Paul's use of terminology in the *oikonomia* passages, and also John's outline of Revelation [Rev. 1:19], which highlights a minimum of three such distinctions in his immediate context, etc.; and the second-generation church and beyond (including Justin Martyr, 110-165 AD; Irenaeus, 130-200 AD; Clement of Alexandria, 150-220 AD; Augustine, 354-430 AD, and others[6]), while certainly not recognizing the specific divisions we would speak of today, also observed chronological divisions in God's revealed plan. There has been much quality work revealing the historical recognition of these divisions, so the point is not belabored here, but John Calvin's acknowledgment of God's 'dispensing'[7] activity is worthy to be noted, as Calvin points out how elementary and how reasonable the concept of a dispensation really is, saying (among other things, in a discussion of dispensation and distinction between various Biblical economies),

> God ought not to be considered changeable merely because he accommodated diverse forms to different ages, as he knew would be expedient for each...Why then do we brand God with the mark of inconsistency, because he has with apt and fitting marks distinguished a diversity of times?[8]

Without perhaps too much ado it can be assumed that there is little question as to the existence/reality of dispensations[9], but rather the inquiry comes at the points of definition and division.

In recent years, definitions have been given more attention, and one definition has emerged to be, at present, perhaps most well known and commonly referenced: that of C.I. Scofield, who believed that a dispensation was

---

[5] Even the *covenant* system, holding to at least two basic divisions (law and grace) admits (at least) two distinct functional divisions in God's plan.

[6] For a more comprehensive list see Arnold Ehlert, "A Bibliography of Dispensationalism", Th.D Diss., Dallas Theological Seminary, November 1945, 10-29.

[7] John T. McNeill, ed., Ford Lewis Battles, trans., John Calvin, *Institutes of the Christian Religion*, Vol I (Philadelphia, PA: Westminster Press, 1940), 61.

[8] Ibid., 462.

[9] Ehlert has done a noble job of citing the historical evidence for such a statement; also Ryrie summarizes well some highlights in Wesley Willis and John Master, *Issues in Dispensationalism* (Chicago, IL: Moody Press, 1994), 15-27 and provides an excellent historical summary in Charles Ryrie, *Dispensationalism* (Chicago, IL: Moody Press, 1995), 61-77.

A period of time during which God deals in a particular way with man in respect to sin and to man's responsibility.[10]

With further demarcation he says,

These periods are marked off in Scripture by some change in God's method of dealing with mankind, or a portion of mankind, in respect of the two questions: of sin, and of man's responsibility. Each of the dispensations may be regarded as a new test of the natural man, and each ends in judgment, marking his utter failure in every dispensation.[11]

This specific characterization gives rise to Scofield's classic delineation of seven dispensations:

(1) Innocence - Gen. 1:3-3:6
(2) Conscience – Gen. 3:7-8:14
(3) Government – Gen. 8:15-11:9
(4) Promise – Gen. 11:10-Ex. 18:27
(5) Law – Ex. 19:1-Jn. 14:30
(6) Grace[12] – Acts 2:1 – Rev. 19:21
(7) Millennium – Rev. 20:1-5

In his definition, dispensations are limited in scope to periods of *time*, thus necessitating that they fit within the *chronological* framework of Genesis-Revelation (meaning from day one of creation week to the instituting of the new heavens and earth[13]). Therefore, those events taking place before and after the advent of time are not incorporated into his dispensational panorama. In addition – and perhaps more significantly, this definition has greater soteriological emphasis than doxological.

Note contemporary dependence on Scofield's definition, e.g., the following statement from Paul Enn's *Moody Handbook of Theology* (Chicago: 1989, p. 513): "Dispensationalism is a system of interpretation that seeks to establish a unity in the Scriptures **through its central focus on the grace of God** [emphasis mine]. Although dispensationalists recognize differing stewardships or dispensations **whereby man was put under a trust by the**

---

[10] C.I. Scofield, *Scofield Bible Correspondence Course*, Vol. I (Chicago: Moody Press, 1959), 46.

[11] C.I. Scofield, *Rightly Dividing the Word of Truth* (public domain), ch. 2.

[12] Although Scofield originally communicated his dispensational soteriology with some ambiguity (see Scofield Reference Bible, 1917,p. 1115), dispensationalists agree that salvation has always been by faith, with the content varying by dispensation.

[13] Ibid., 58.

Lord [emphasis mine], they teach that response to God's revelation in each dispensation is by faith (salvation is always by grace through faith). Dispensationalists arrive at their system of interpretation through two primary principles: (1) maintaining a consistently literal method of interpretation, and (2) maintaining a distinction between Israel and church." Note the emphasis on the redemptive plan and the focus on man. It is this writer's view that these particular emphases are inappropriate, and result in a less than ideal framework.

Because of these nuances, Scofield's definition (although we are tremendously indebted to and grateful for it) seems to be less than ideal, particularly in light of three notable Scriptural emphases:

(1) There are major events which take place before the commencing of time: including God's own existence, Self-relating (Jn. 17:24; Rom. 1:20; 16:26; 1 Tim. 1:17; 1 Pet. 1:20), goings forth (Mic. 5:2), and His choosing and predestinating work (Eph. 1:4-5; 3:11; 2 Tim. 1:9), etc.

(2) There is continuation of reality after the cessation of recorded time: including the future glorification of God and His continual sovereign rule (1 Tim. 6:16; 2 Pet. 1:11; 3:18), ongoing salvation and life of believers (Is. 45:17; Mt. 19:28; Jn. 3:15-16, 36; 5:24, 39; 6:40, 54; 17:3; 2 Cor. 4:17; Heb. 9:12; 1 Jn 2:25), and ongoing judgment and punishment of unbelievers (Mt. 18:8; 25:41, 46; Mk. 3:29; 2 Th. 1:9; Heb. 6:2).

(3) There is a weighty accent on the centrality of God's doxological plan, with the redemptive plan (to which Scofield here alludes, emphasizing man's sin and responsibility) subordinate to and fitting into the framework of the doxological (Ps. 86:9, 12; Ezek. 39:13; Jn. 17:3-5; Rom. 11:36, 12:1-2; 1 Co. 6:20, 10:31; Eph. 2:8-10; 1 Pet. 4:11; Is. 6:3 & Rev. 4:11). The centrality of God's doxological purpose is emphasized by Ryrie and included as the third element of his *sine qua non*, despite occasional suggestion by some that the doxological purpose is not germane to the dispensational viewpoint. In reality this element is *the most definitive result of a literal hermeneutic, and this writer would suggest therefore that it is the most necessary of the three elements*[14]. Scofield's definition of dispensations seems to fall short of recognizing this emphasis.

---

[14] Of course, the doxological purpose is derived through a literal reading of Scripture, and so it is also a resultant understanding from the consistent use of a literal hermeneutic, however, the centrality of the doxological purpose is clear nonetheless, and thus is placed as God's over-arching purpose in all things.

It is notable, in seeking a proper emphasis on this doctrine, that the major works of God revealed in Scripture *all* serve the doxological purpose (Ps. 86:9-10; Rev. 15:4); as a matter of fact, Scripture identifies no greater purpose for each of the following: God's Predestining & Calling Works (Eph. 1:5-12; 2 Pet. 1:3); The Ministry of Christ (Jn. 13:31-2; 17:1-5; 21:19; 2 Cor. 1:20; Heb. 13:21); Creation (Ps. 19; Is. 40; Rev. 4:11); The Keeping of His Word (Rom. 3:1-7; Salvation – Ps. 79:9; Rom. 15:7;16:25-27; Eph. 1:14; 1 Tim. 1:15-17; 2 Tim. 4:18; Jude 24-25); The Church (1 Cor. 10:31; 2 Cor. 4:15; Eph. 1:12; Phil. 1:11; 2 Th. 1:11-12; 1 Pet. 4:11,16); Fruitfulness of Believers (Jn. 15:8; 1 Cor. 10:31; The Kingdom – Phil. 2:11; 1 Thess. 2:12; Rev. 1:6); Sickness, Death, & Resurrection (1 Sam. 6:5; Lk. 17:11-18; Jn. 9:1-3; 11:4); Judgment (Rom. 3:7; Rev. 14:7); Deliverance of Israel (Is. 60:21; 61:3); The Fulfilling of Covenants & Summing up of All Things (Is. 25:1-3; 43:20; Lk. 2:14; Rom. 4:20; 15:8-9; 2 Cor. 1:20; 2 Pet. 1:3-4; Rev. 19:7).

While Chafer reckons the same number of dispensations as does by Scofield, perhaps a greater emphasis on the doxological purpose led Chafer to offer a more spacious perspective on the scope of the word. Chafer defines a dispensation as

> a period which is identified by its relation to some particular purpose of God – a purpose to be accomplished within that period.[15]

In Chafer's estimation, the focus of the dispensational construct is namely the particular purpose of God. This definition seems a more precise one in that it allows for a dispensational epicenter not so much relating to man and his redemption as much as to God and His doxological purpose, avoiding the error of the soteriological center and the mistake which Walvoord calls *the reductive error* – the use of one aspect of the whole as the determining element[16]. Ryrie's elaboration on the third element of his *sine qua non* begs for an even more refined definition of this strange unit of measure that is a dispensation. He says,

> To the dispensationalist the soteriological or saving program of God is not the only program but one of the means God is using in the total program of glorifying Himself. Scripture is not mancentered as though salvation were the main theme, but it is God-centered because His glory is the center. The Bible itself clearly teaches

---

Because of this emphasis it must be seen logically as the most essential element – or at the very least the most definitive result of a literal interpretation of Scripture.

[15] Lewis.Sperry Chafer, *Systematic Theology*, Vol I (Grand Rapids, MI: 1993), 40.

[16] Walvoord notes, in particular, that this is a mistake of covenant theology, in John Walvoord, *The Millennial Kingdom* (Grand Rapids, MI: Zondervan, 1959), 92.

that salvation, important and wonderful as it is, is not an end in itself but is rather a means to the end of glorifying God.[17]

Therefore perhaps a more refined definition, accounting for the doxological priority which Ryrie, Walvoord, and others have recognized would be as follows: *A dispensation is a particularly distinctive economy or administration in and by which God demonstrates or expresses His own glory.*

Dispensational Divisions

If then the definition which directly leads to the divisions is to be reconsidered, then perhaps the divisions themselves could be better expressed to accommodate the newly defined term. Historical dispensational delineations emphasizing either a primarily redemptive program[18] or a kingdom program[19] have come in all shapes and sizes, generally delineating anywhere from three (Gaebelain[20]), four (progressive dispensationalism[21]) five, seven (Scofield), sometimes up to eight dispensational divisions[22]. However, a synthetic overview accounting for God's doxological purpose seems to unveil no less than 12 dispensational divisions in Scripture. And while the number of dispensations may not be of tremendous significance (perhaps 3, 5, 7, or 8 *are* most appropriate numbers, after all), in this writer's estimation it does seem that the following 12 divisions most suitably represent the Biblical narrative in three specific ways: (1) the synthetic overview of Scripture based directly on the covenants and promises of God

---

[17] Charles Ryrie, *Dispensationalism Today* (Chicago, IL: Moody Press, 1969), 46.

[18] Including William Gouge (1575-1653); Pierre Poiret (1646-1719); John Edwards (1639-1716); Isaac Watts (1674-1748); Jonathan Edwards (1703-1758); John Fletcher (1729-1785); JN Darby (1800-1882); Robert Jamieson (1802-1880), A.R. Fausset (1821-1910), and David Brown (1803-1897) in their 6-volume commentary reference the term dispensation/dispensations well over 100 times, seeming to take a redemptive approach based on comments on Gen. 2:17, etc.; Charles Hodge (1797-1878); R.L. Dabney (1820-1898); J.R. Graves (1820-1893); George Pember (1837-1910); James Gray (1851-1935); C.I. Scofield (1843-1921); I.M. Haldeman (1845-1933); W. Graham Scroggie (1877-1958); L.S. Chafer (1871-1952); H.A. Ironside (1876-1951); etc.

[19] Adam Clarke's (1760/62-1832) and Richard Watson's (1781-1833) approaches have something of a kingdom overtone; John Cumming (1810-1881) places some focus on kingdom elements; Samuel Andrews (1817-1906) while based on a redemptive premise emphasizes gradual submission of mankind to the authority of God; G.B.M. Clouser highlights both redemptive and government elements; Clarence Larkin (1850-1924) has a kingdom emphasis; A.C. Gaebelain (1861-1942) and Alva McClain (1888-1968) both had strong kingdom emphases.

[20] See Michael C. Stallard, "The Theological Method of Arno C. Gaebelein", Ph.D Diss., Dallas Theological Seminary, 1992.

[21] Patriarchal (to Sinai), Mosaic (to Messiah's ascension), Ecclesial (to Messiah's return), Zionic (1.Millennial, 2. Eternal), from Craig A. Blaising and Darrell L. Bock, *Progressive Dispensationalism* (Grand Rapids, MI: Baker Books, 1993), 123.

[22] Blaising and Bock present an excellent chart of historical dispensational delineations in Craig A. Blaising and Darrell L. Bock, *Progressive Dispensationalism* (Grand Rapids, MI: Baker Books, 1993), 118-119.

fit very well within this framework; (2) each dispensation pre-announces (or at least logically necessitates) the coming of the next; and (3) this 12 division approach unites the kingdom and soteriological emphases cohesively *under* the doxological purpose as consistent with Ryrie's *sine qua non* and as a natural result of literal grammatical-historical interpretive approach.

Twelve Dispensations: The Unfolding Drama of Praise

(1) Planning
Eternity Past – Jn. 17:24; Acts 4:28; Eph. 1:4; 1 Pet. 1:20
Before the foundation of the world, in eternity past, God is. He related to Himself (Jn. 17:24), existing in aseity, lacking in no way, and being in essence and in character holy, holy, holy (Is. 6:3; Rev. 4:8). He had no intrinsic need for fellowship with any other being (yet uncreated) nor had He the need to create anything at all. Yet, before the foundation of the world, God made determination about specifically how and with whom He would glorify Himself, presenting His character later to His creation as a divine Self-expression. His predestining work provided the foundation of wisdom later to be revealed to His creation (1 Cor. 2:7), and set the stage for all that was to come (Acts 4:28), as all things would be in submission to the sovereign counsel of His will (Eph. 1:11). Included in His predestined plan some among His created beings would have unique relationship to Him (e.g., Eph. 1:5) by grace through faith (Hab. 2:4; Eph. 2:8-9). The revealed planning in eternity past demonstrated God to be sovereign, free to act, all-powerful, and worthy of worship by His creation.

Despite having at this point (in eternity past) no specific recorded announcement of the coming dispensation(s), logically the outworking of this planning stage is necessary.

(2) Prelude
Innocence of Man - Gen. 1:1-3:6
In accordance with His own plan He created the heavens and the earth and all they contain (Gen. 1-2). The apex of His creative work was man, created in His own image. He placed him in the Garden as a beneficiary of the doxological plan, and gave him but one imperative. The consequence for violating this one command was spiritual death (Gen. 2:17). Adam, for an undisclosed period of time, walked innocently and in fellowship with God. This era demonstrated (1) the perfection of God's creative working; (2) God's allowance of His creation to have fellowship with Him under specific and delineated terms, i.e., obedience – although it is clear even at this stage that

He would demonstrate man's inability to maintain obedience; and (3) by communicating and creating an alternative to willing human obedience (disobedience, Gen. 2:15), God demonstrated that His plan of the ages was far more complex than even the creative work revealed, that ultimately fellowship with Him could only be achieved by righteousness only He could provide – by grace through faith (which can be clearly as the dispensations unfold), and that His plan's culmination would be dependent wholly upon Himself, and not upon His finite creatures.

The imperative of Gen. 2:17 provides the backdrop for the following dispensation: either to be characterized by continued obedience or by dramatic disobedience. The command was given, and man would be tested. How he responded would define the mood of the next dispensation.

(3) Plight
Failure of Man – Gen. 3:6-6:7
Man's willing disobedience, calculated by God in His pre-creation planning, within a very short period of time transforms man - the apex of creation, made in the image of God - immediately into a depraved being, falling short of the glory of God and ultimately into nothing short of a fully evil and violently rebellious entity (Gen. 6:5) deserving of the fullness of God's wrath. This period demonstrates that no being would be able or allowed to approach the glory of God independent of the working of God, as man would have no ability to work his way into right standing with God, and evidences a gap between the holiness of the Sovereign Creator and the ungodliness and unworthiness of man unbridgeable by any other than God Himself. Veiled elements of the bridging of this gap are in view particularly with the veiled promise of redemption (3:15), the slaying of an animal to cover the first sinners (Gen. 3:21), and again with God's show of regard for Abel's animal sacrifice and disregard for Cain's offering of vegetation (4:4-5).

Gen. 6:3 pre-announces the next dispensation. Just as God would blot out man because of his wickedness (6:7), He would preserve the seed of man, allowing a lifespan of 120 years. Additionally, if one considered 6:8 as the conclusion to this dispensation, there would be further pre-announcement in the form of Noah's identification as finding favor in the eyes of the Lord.

(4) Preservation & Provision
Common Grace & Human Government – Gen. 6:8-11:9
In view of man's total and complete depravity, God would be rightly justified in the aggregate destruction of all mankind – specifically due to the conditional consequence of Gen. 2:17. But God limited Himself by His own word, as He had previously offered a veiled redemptive promise (3:15) which necessitated the survival and proliferation of man and woman. God therefore provided two elements for the protection of His promise, to His own glory: (1) the preservation of the seed of man through Noah and his family, by way of deliverance from the otherwise worldwide destruction of the flood; and (2) the provision of human government – the sovereignty of man over nature (Gen. 9:1-3) and over each other (9:5) - as a means whereby various controls would be in place to protect the life of mankind from both external threats (beasts of the field) and internal threats (the murderous sinfulness of man). This era additionally offered a tremendous contrast between the holiness of God and the depravity of man, as after the preservation and provision were accomplished, man still revolts against God, asserting his own method and will to achieve independence from God (Gen. 11:1-4). Such rebellious efforts, even still, are subject to God's sovereign control, Who thwarts man's attempts at independence (11:5-9), demonstrating once again that man's best efforts are worthless in achieving godliness.

(5) Promises Pronounced
Gen. 11:10-Ex. 18:27
Beginning with Abraham, God's soteriological and kingdom schematic is further unveiled. From this one man would arise a great nation (Gen. 12:2), possessing the definitive elements of a people, a land, and a kingdom – each element to be expanded and unveiled in future promises. This period traces the generations from Abraham, Isaac, Jacob and his twelve sons, to the birth of the Israelite nation as God extracts them, at just the right moment, from previously promised servitude in Egypt (Gen. 15:13-14). With this nation rapidly developing from Abraham's progeny God commences a grand work – both soteriological and kingdom oriented, yet focusing primarily on His character as the Covenant Keeping God – the One who rules and orchestrates to His own pleasure.

(6) Prerequisite Portrayed
The Broken Covenant: The Tutor – Ex. 19:1-Mal. 4:6 (Gal. 3:24-25)
Lest the people of God's choosing think that they have an inheritance of blessing apart from God's workings and unconditional promises, God initiates with Israel the conditional covenant through Moses – a covenant of obedience which if kept would result in the physical blessing of Israel in the land, and which if forsaken would result in a curse including the removal of Israel from the promised land (Deut. 28). Israel would be unable and even disallowed to fulfill this covenant (Deut. 31:16-21), characterizing this era as a graphic portrayal of man's incapacity to walk in accordance with God's holy demands, and effectively pointing to man's need for redemption which only Christ would be qualified to provide. The prerequisite to living under God's blessing and in His fellowship is a righteousness which only He can provide. During this era the holiness and righteousness of God is magnified, as the contrast between His character and that of man is accentuated.

Also of significance during this era is the expansion of the unconditionally promised elements of God's covenant with Abraham: (1) the land element from Gen. 15:18-21 is further delineated in Deut. 30; (2) the kingdom element, providing necessary leadership for a great nation, is clarified in 2 Sam. 7; and (3) the people element, without which the great nation would be devoid of any citizens, is unveiled in Jer. 31, providing a springboard to the fulfillment of the universal blessing element (Gen. 12:3) for all peoples.

(7) Promises Proffered
The Kingdom Offered – Mt. 1:1-12:45
The kingdom of God[23] refers to His universal & eternal rulership applied physically on earth in direct fulfillment of the covenant promises, particularly to Abraham (Gen. 12-17) and David (2 Sam. 7). Matthew (exclusively, as none of the other Gospel writers do) refers to the kingdom of heaven frequently, appealing to the Jewish mind via well understood terminology[24] and indicating that God's heavenly kingdom was poised to find an earthly home, fulfilling the promise to David. [Toussaint notably suggests these terms (kingdom of heaven and kingdom of God) as being used interchangeably[25] - this is a significant point in understanding the

---

[23] For an excellent discussion on the nature of the kingdom see Stanley Toussaint, *Behold the King* (Portland, OR: Multnomah Press, 1980), 19-20, 65-68, 171-173.
[24] George Peters, *The Theocratic Kingdom*, Vol I (Grand Rapids, MI: Kregel, 1972), 195.
[25] Stanley Toussaint, *Behold the King* (Portland, OR: Multnomah Press, 1980), 65-68.

identification and nature of the kingdom.] Peters recognizes the significance of this kingdom offer and its earthly scope:

> This kingdom is one pertaining to the earth. Before the creation of the world, it only existed in the determination or purpose of God but at creation the very foundation of the world was laid in preparation for it... 'From the foundation of the world' is indicative that God purposed this very earth, when founded, for this kingdom.[26]

It was a kingdom designed for the earth, and so promised to Abraham and David. The disciples rightly understood the kingdom offer as referencing the restoration of the Davidic kingdom and thus the hastening of the covenant fulfillments.

> It can be safely asserted...that it is a well-grounded belief that the Kingdom was something that they [the disciples] were acquainted with, and concerning which, as to its nature or meaning, they needed not, owing to its plain portrayal in the Old testament, and special instruction...nothing is alleged that they misapprehended the Kingdom of the prophets in its fundamental aspects...such supposed ignorance would reflect severely upon the covenants, prophecies, and preaching of the first preachers of 'the Gospel of the Kingdom'.[27]

Clearly then, Jesus' first public proclamation (Mt. 4:17) entailing the preliminary offer of this expected kingdom, was understood for what it truly was. This period of consideration was a unique time in Israel's history – an emphatically pivotal era (brief though it was), which if responded to positively would have certainly precipitated the fulfilling of the eschatological plan. Of course, in God's own predetermination and sovereignty, Israel's negative response to this offer had already been predicted (Is. 6:9-10). This temporary rejection would prove to be the opportunity God had designed to provide further fulfillment of the Gen. 12:3 universal blessing – in this case the specific element of blessing being God's righteousness being accessible through Christ by the gentiles as well as the Jews.

God's glory is demonstrated in this brief era through the outworking of His plan to (1) further refine and prepare the nation of Israel for promised future blessing, and (2) to pave the way for the unveiling of the mystery (later revealed in Rom. 11:25-36 & Eph. 2:11-3:12) – that God has provided a means whereby all mankind, both Jew and gentile, would have opportunity for salvation, by grace and through faith.

---

[26] Ibid, 35.
[27] Ibid, 183-184.

(8) Postponement & Propitiation
The Kingdom Postponed & New Covenant Ratified – Mt. 12:46-Acts 1:26
Immediately after Israel's prophesied (Is. 6:9-10, etc.) corporate rejection of Jesus as Messiah (and consequent rejection of the kingdom offer) begins an era of postponement which serves God's predetermined plan in a very significant way. Israel's covenant realizations are placed on hold while God provides the means for their ultimate fulfillment – namely the blood of Christ. Without the propitiatory work of Christ, as ratification of the New Covenant, there could be no fulfillment of the New Covenant, and thus all other covenant blessings would be rendered void as there could be no people to enjoy them into eternity since all men would otherwise stand eternally condemned. Therefore, this very brief period is pivotal in the execution of God's plan, as it provides the enablement to keep (literally and fully) the unconditional covenants of the Old Testament while also providing (in keeping with the universal blessing aspect of the Abrahamic Covenant, Gen. 12:3) an expansion of God's revealed focus to include the gentiles in the plan of eternal life.

This period is unique and set apart from the previous era, clearly delineated by Jesus' advancement of His mission and alteration of His teaching methods (beginning to teach the multitudes exclusively in parables, see Mt. 13). The most straightforward reading of Scripture demands an understanding that the Kingdom was postponed, and without this understanding the clarity of even Jesus' earthly ministry is compromised. Peters characterized this understanding as of significant import, saying

> The rejection of the postponement of the Kingdom, is a rejection of the only key that can unlock the singular and otherwise mysterious sayings of Jesus.[28]

This aspect of Jesus' earthly ministry seems at least to characterize this as a fully unique dispensation in the plan of God. Additionally, this era is distinct from the next particularly being defined by the ascension of Christ and the role of the Holy Spirit.

Ultimately God's glory is profoundly manifest in this short span as so many elements come together at this stage to bring continuity and cohesiveness to God's unfolding plan.

This era offers a unique characteristic in that all subsequent dispensations are pre-announced by Christ during this time: in Mt. 16:18 the Era of Participation (The Church Age), coupled with Jn. 14-16, describing the

---

[28] George Peters, *The Theocratic Kingdom*, Vol. I (Grand Rapids, MI: Kregel, 1978), 622-623.

coming role of the Holy Spirit during that time; in Mt. 24:1-28 the Era of Purification (The Tribulation Period); in Mt. 24:29-31 the Era of Promises Performed (The Kingdom Initiated); and in Lk. 18:29-30 and Jn. 6:40, 54 (in conjunction with His aggregate teaching on eternal life and eternal condemnation) the Postscript (Eternity Future) is certainly in view. Particularly in light of Christ's prophetic ministry during this time, these divisions seem quite natural.

(9) Participation
The Church Age - Acts 2:1- Rev. 3:22
Perhaps this era serves as the most surprising of the dispensations as its leading lady (the church) is nowhere to be found in Old Testament prophecy (despite allusions to an additional focus on the gentiles, as found in such passages as Gen. 12:3b; Deut. 32:20-21, 43; 2 Sam. 22:50; Ps. 18:49; 117:1; Is. 11:10; and later in Lk. 21:24, etc.). The church first appears by name in Mt. 16:18, is noticeably absent from earthly perspective in Rev. 4-19:10, and reappears (by strong implication and in correlation with Rev. 19:7-8) in Rev. 19:14. The scope of the church's blessing and focus is, during this age, in the heavenlies in Christ (Eph. 1:3).

Mystery aspects of the church include (1) the translation (rapture) of saints at the end of the church era (1 Cor. 15:51); (2) God's partial hardening of Israel (i.e., fostering the rejection of the kingdom offer, see Mt. 13:10-17, etc.) in order that the fullness of the gentiles might be fulfilled (Rom. 11:25); (3) God's subsequent self-revelation to all nations (Rom. 16:25-26); (4) the unity of Jew and gentile together in the body of Christ (i.e., the church, Eph. 2:11-3:12); (5) the relationship of Christ as husband to the church (Eph. 5:32); and (6) the indwelling of Christ via the Holy Spirit in the believer (Col. 1:27)

The inheritance of the church lies in the promise (singular, see Eph. 3:6; 2 Tim. 1:1; 1 Jn. 2:25, etc.), underscoring a significant area of distinction from Israel, whose inheritance is found in the covenants and promises (plural, see Rom. 15:8; Gal. 3:16; Eph. 2:12; Heb. 6:12; 7:6; 8:6; 11:17).

There are at least several key elements to be considered in this context which contribute significantly to the understanding of this dispensation, and those dealt with here are: (1) the new covenant and its relation or non-relation to the church, (2) the parenthesis problem, and (3) the illustration of the olive tree.

The New Covenant & the Church

Scripture contains by name eight direct (and other less direct but equally definite) references to the New Covenant: (1) Jer. 31:31 – here the New Covenant is identified as including at least the following specific elements: it is made directly with the houses of Israel and Judah (31:31); it is distinct from and unlike the Mosaic covenant (31:32); it is prophesied as still yet future (31:31); it is characterized by God at a future time writing His law on the hearts of the recipients (31:33); it signified a possession relationship between God and Israel/Judah (31:33); it resulted in universal knowledge of God within Israel/Judah (31:34); it entailed forgiveness of sin (31:34); and it included both physical and eternal restoration of Israel/Judah (31:27-28, 37-40). (2) Lk. 22:20 (Mt. 26:28; Mk. 14:24) – in this initiation of the New Covenant, the blood of Christ is pre-announced as the ratification of the New Covenant, which would be inaugurated with the coming of the kingdom (Lk. 22:18). (3) 1 Cor. 11:25 – Paul here recounts to the Corinthian church the initiation [Lord's Supper] of the New Covenant pointing to Christ's ratification [death and resurrection]. (4) 2 Cor. 3:6 (Rom. 11:25-32) – this passage delineates 'us' (the specific antecedent is identified in 1:19 as Paul, Silvanus, & Timothy) as servants (*diakonous*) of a *new covenant*. It is notable that while these servants of the New Covenant are *of* the church, there is no assertion or contextual indication that the New Covenant is made *with* the church. Rather it is most appropriate to understand that as ministers of the gospel, the apostles served to facilitate the New Covenant, just as the church serves as an instrument to move Israel to jealousy – thus hastening the inauguration of the Covenant. (5 & 6) Heb. 8:6-13 (7:22) – in describing the superiority of Christ's ministry, here the contrast is drawn between the Law (8:4) and the better covenant (8:6). The focus here is on Jesus and His superiority as exemplified by His role as Mediator of the New Covenant – the context of the Covenant here then is in relation to Him and not the church. He is the (immensely qualified) High Priest for the believer (8:1). Herein is the connection between the New Covenant and the church: the same Mediator of the New Covenant is the High Priest for the believer, and resultantly the believer is a beneficiary of certain elements of the New Covenant (e.g., forgiveness of sins and eternal life, Is. 55:5; Jer. 31:34; 1 Jn. 2:25) however, the bestowing of such benefits to the church is not connected to the New Covenant (since it was made only with Israel/Judah, Is. 55:1-11; 59:21; 61:8-9; Jer. 31:31; 32:37-42; 50:4-5; Ezek. 16:59-63; 34:22-31; 37:21-28) but rather to the Mediator who grants forgiveness, righteousness, and life based upon the choosing of God, to His glory. (7)

Heb. 9:15 – due to the death of the Mediator, the promise of the eternal inheritance can be received, for without eternal life, none of the eternal promises could be enjoyed. This premise magnifies the significance of the New Covenant, as it provided for the people element of the Abrahamic covenant. Without this element literally fulfilled, the Abrahamic covenant rings empty. (8) Heb. 12:24 (10:15-18, 29; 13:20) – this passage speaks to the efficacy of the blood of Christ, again emphasizing His identity as the Mediator of this better covenant. The significance of the New Covenant in each of the Hebrews passages lies in its relation to Christ, not to the church.

The Parenthesis Problem
O.T. Allis, recognizes that the basis of distinction between Israel and the church is indeed the literal interpretation of Old Testament prophecy, saying,

> The parenthesis view of the Church is the inevitable result of the doctrine that Old Testament prophecy must be fulfilled literally to Israel...[29]

Allis' mention of the parenthesis view references the understanding on the part of a number of dispensational theologians that the church is *parenthetical* – that it is an interruption of God's program with Israel. This understanding, while properly recognizing a distinction between Israel and the church, seems not to be an entirely accurate perspective. There is indeed clear distinction between Israel and the church, but the church represents not a *parenthesis* but rather simply *one stage or aspect* of God's redemptive program, serving as a cog in His doxological program. The application of the term *parenthesis* to the church implies a discontinuity in God's eternal plan, which in the view of this writer does not exist, and which seems to do injustice entirely to the doxological plan.

The Olive Tree
In Rom. 11:16-24 Paul presents the example of the olive tree, identifying (or at least alluding to) several key characters: The wild olive (the gentiles who are grafted in, 11:17); the branches (the Jews, 11:16); the root (the Messiah[30], 11:16-18; 15:12; Rev. 5:5 – *riza* as in the LXX Is. 11:10; 53:2). In

---

[29] O.T. Allis, *Prophecy and the Church* (Philipsburg, NJ: 1945), 54.

[30] Many see the root here as referencing Abraham or the covenants, but this seems unnatural, as (1) there is precedent for Christ as *the root* in prophecy – both contextually and grammatically, (2) there seems not to be precedent for Abraham or the covenants as *the root* in prophecy, and (3) although this is simply an illustration here, Christ as the root seems to more forcefully illustrate the point of the gentiles having

this picture Paul demonstrates that the gentiles have access to the Messiah (and consequently His salvation blessings) directly due to Israel's initial rejection of the Messiah. The gentiles, in this figure, are grafted not into Israel, nor to *all* the covenant promises, but to Christ Himself, reaping the profound benefit of His salvific work. It is here we see God's magnificent fulfillment of the seventh element of the Abrahamic Covenant (Gen 12:3b) – all the families of the earth blessed in Abraham - through Christ. Thus the mystery of the partial hardening is unveiled (11:25) as a predetermined element of God's grand plan: This remarkable and unexpected (although somewhat pre-announced) twist in His redemptive plan serves His doxological purpose, demonstrating His superlative wisdom – leaving Paul in wonderment at the thought (11:33-36).

This era of participation fills a limited timeframe, constituting the gap between Daniel's 69th and 70th week (Dan. 9:26-27), and the initial times of the gentiles (Lk. 21:24) leading to the fullness of the gentiles (Rom. 11:25) - elements which are consummated in the next dispensation.

(10) Purification
The Tribulation, Jacob's Trouble – Rev. 4:1-19:10 [Jer. 30:7]
Returning the focus on the nation of Israel and providing a continuation of the Daniel 9 timetable, this seven-year era will be inaugurated as a covenant is made with the many by the (Roman[31]) prince who is to come (Dan. 9:27). This covenant is broken at the midpoint (three and a half years), at which time the *great* tribulation (a period of more severe testing, see Mt. 24:15-22[32]) begins, culminating with the shaking of the heavens and the 2nd coming of the Messiah King (Mt. 24:29-30). This is the time of Jacob's distress (Jer. 30:7), preceding the restoration of the nation.

---

access to Christ due to the Jews' initial rejection of Him. (4) The gentiles were already promised blessing directly through the Abrahamic covenant, so the metaphor of grafting would seem unnecessary – the gentiles as blessed would be a natural result of the covenant, not a manufactured reality; whereas, to have a unity with Christ would seem to require grafting, (5) a grafting implies access to the full benefit of the root, whereas the gentiles do not enjoy all the blessing of the Abrahamic covenant, but certainly do enjoy the fullness of access to Christ.

[31] cf. Dan. 9:26 & 27.

[32] Walvoord agrees that the great tribulation takes place during the last 42 months of the tribulation, as he says, "The great tribulation, accordingly, is a specific period of time beginning with the abomination of desolation and closing with the second coming of Christ, in the light of Daniel's prophecies and confirmed by reference to forty-two months." [John Walvoord, Matthew: *Thy Kingdom Come* (Chicago, IL: Moody Press, 1974), 188]. It should be noted that neither Walvoord nor this writer seek to divide this seven year period into two disassociated parts (as Pentecost cautioned against [J. Dwight Pentecost, *Things to Come* (Grand Rapids, MI: Zondervan, 1958), 184]. Rather there is an exegetical distinction made between the two halves, yet both sections are a part of the tribulation period as evidenced by a comparison between Mt. 24:9 & 24:21.

God's glory is demonstrated during this period in at least three major ways: (1) His holiness is expressed as He faithfully judges (without any turning back) the nation for her failures (Jer. 30:24); (2) His protection of the nation, even as He watches over them "to pluck up, to break down, to overthrow, to destroy, and to bring disaster" (Jer. 31:28), provides a testament to His faithfulness and covenant keeping; (3) as a secondary purpose for this tribulation period, the wrath of the Lamb befalls the nations (Rev. 6:16-17), illustrating His worthiness as Judge and ultimately as King.

The period immediately following is preannounced in several key contexts, primarily (1) Jer. 31:27-34 – the time of judgment and refinement will be followed by a spiritual and physical restoration of the nation; and (2) Rev. 19-20 - The King will return triumphant with His redeemed, initiating the fulfillment of the Davidic promise of an eternal throne (2 Sam. 7).

(11) Promises Performed
The Kingdom Initiated – Rev. 19:11- 20:6

Major events unfolding during this period include: (1) the return of the King (Zech. 14:4), (2) the binding of Satan, (3) the inauguration of the promised Davidic Kingdom, (4) the release of Satan and corresponding final revolt – a revolt which sets the stage for God's final demonstration of His glory within the framework of revealed time: namely, the execution of His judgment.

(12) Postscript
Eternity Future – Rev. 20:7 – 22:21

Eternity future is inaugurated by the (1) great white throne judgment, (2) destruction of the old heaven and earth (Rev. 21:1). Although Chafer lists the destruction as taking place before the White Throne Judgment, note the like English phrases of the earth passing away (cf. Rev. 20:11 & Rev. 21:1), but this passing away is indicated by two different Greek terms (*ephugen* in 20:11 and *apelthan* in 21:1, the latter of which is anticipated in Mt. 5:18 with *parelthe* and Mt. 24:35 with *pareleusontai* – each from the same root, *erchomai*), implying two different actions or events, and (3) creation of the new heaven and earth, with the new Jerusalem described vividly, and God seen in all His glory, which shall be so magnificent as to eliminate the need for any external light:

> And there will no longer be any night; and they will not have need of the light of a lamp nor the light of the sun, because the Lord God will illumine them; and they will reign forever and ever. (Rev. 22:5)

Conclusion

While differing conclusions regarding the actual number of dispensations seem rather significant and certainly worthy of examination, it should be understood that as long as basic core elements (e.g., Ryrie's sine qua non, due to its accurate representation of Biblical emphases) are acknowledged, such acute divisions are not integral to the overall conclusions of dispensational theology. Such matters need be handled with cautious levels of dogmatism, as these divisions are not expressly revealed in the text of Scripture, but are rather derived deductively. Where there is minimal amount of revelation we must be exceedingly careful not to insert the maximum amount of commentary, Ryrie's comments here are worthy of attention:

> ...the difference of opinion as to number [of dispensations] is not due to a defect in the dispensational scheme but rather is due to lack of detailed revelation concerning the earliest periods of biblical history. We do not have preserved in the written record all that God may have said or revealed to man in those early periods...[33]

He identifies the calculation of dispensational divisions as a deductive[34] enterprise, underscoring the need for thoughtfulness and consideration, as the deductive process here can and does involve different premises.

The premise asserted here to have inestimable significance is God's doxological purpose. If indeed it bears as great a role as is revealed in Scripture - stemming in all actuality from God's worldview - then it necessarily must also be a *central tenet* in our thinking and in our walking. As a result of this focused attention, our systematic conclusions will reflect an increased estimation of Him, coupled with a decreased estimation of ourselves – developments requisite to a sound theology and a Biblical walk.

It may be argued, then, that this particular arrangement of divisions is lacking for one reason or another. It may also be argued that since the Bible does not directly identify any particular number of divisions that any codified enumeration is unwarranted. However, what is certain is the priority God places on His own purpose and His own glorification. This particular attempt at definition and enumeration is designed solely to respect that priority. Such singularly motivated attempts, this writer would hope, should

---

[33] Ryrie, *Dispensationalism*, 47.
[34] Ibid.

result in an overall understanding of the flow of Biblical history – past, present, and future – as contributing to this very course of direction.

> In Him we have redemption through His blood, the forgiveness of our trespasses, according to the riches of His grace which He lavished on us. In all wisdom and insight He made known to us the mystery of His will, according to His kind intention which He purposed in Him with a view to an administration suitable to the fullness of the times, *that is,* the summing up of all things in Christ, things in the heavens and things on the earth. In Him also we have obtained an inheritance, having been predestined according to His purpose who works all things after the counsel of His will, to the end that we who were the first to hope in Christ would be **to the praise of His glory**. (Eph. 1:7-12)

"If literal interpretation be the correct principle of interpretation, then it would seem to follow that it would be proper to expect it to apply to all the Scriptures. This, as we have tried to show, is the reason the matter of consistency in the application of plain interpretation is so important. The nonliteralist is the nondispensationalist, and the consistent literalist is a dispensationalist."

- Charles C. Ryrie

Dispensationalism Today, 1965, page 96

9

The New Testament Use of the Old Testament[1]
Robert L. Thomas

When interpreting the Old Testament and New Testament each in light of the single grammatical-historical meaning of each passage, two kinds of New Testament uses of the Old Testament surface, one in which the New Testament writer observes the grammatical-historical sense of the Old Testament passage and the other in which the New Testament writer goes beyond the grammatical-historical sense in using a passage. Inspired sensus plenior application (ISPA) designates the latter usage. Numerous passages illustrate each type of New Testament use of the Old Testament. The ISPA type of use does not grant contemporary interpreters a license to copy the method of New Testament writers, nor does it violate the principle of single meaning. The ISPA meaning of the Old Testament passage did not exist for humans until the time of the New Testament citation, being occasioned by Israel's rejection of her Messiah at His first advent. The ISPA approach approximates that advocated by John H. Walton more closely than other explanations of the New Testament use of the Old Testament. "Fulfillment" terminology in the New Testament is appropriate only for events that literally fulfill events predicted in the Old Testament.

Chapter 6 elaborated on the importance of finding the single meaning intended for each text. That discussion raised the issue of New Testament use of the Old Testament when the New Testament writer went beyond the grammatical-historical meaning of an Old Testament passage and assigned to it an additional meaning in connection with his New Testament context. This chapter will apply the principle of single meaning exactly to the New Testament use of the Old Testament.

That principle requires that every Old Testament passage must receive its own grammatical-historical interpretation, regardless of how a New Testament writer uses it. The Old Testament must not receive multiple meanings by being read through the eyes of the New Testament. When this

---

[1] Reprinted with permission from Robert L. Thomas, *Evangelical Hermeneutics: The New Versus the Old* (Grand Rapids, MI: Kregel, 2002)

principle is applied—i.e., when each Old Testament passage is limited to its single grammatical-historical meaning—the results are enlightening. One then discerns two kinds of uses of the Old Testament by New Testament writers. First, in some cases the New Testament writer abides by and applies the grammatical-historical sense of the passage. Second, sometimes the New Testament writer goes beyond the grammatical-historical meaning to assign a passage an additional meaning in connection with its New Testament context. In the former instance, a New Testament writer uses the Old Testament's literal sense. The latter quotations are a nonliteral use of the Old Testament. We may call this an "inspired *sensus plenior* application" (hereafter ISPA) of the Old Testament passage to a new situation.

Such a usage is inspired because, along with all Scripture, the New Testament in which it appears is inspired by God. It is *"sensus plenior"* in that it gives an additional or fuller sense than the passage had in its Old Testament setting. It is an application because it does not eradicate the literal meaning of the Old Testament passage but simply applies the Old Testament wording to a new setting.

Here we will sample only a few examples of these two types of usage, some from predictive prophecies of Christ's first coming and some from nonprophetic portions of the Old Testament.

Two Types of New Testament Treatments of Old Testament Prophesies

(1) Literal Use of the Old Testament in the New Testament
A number of Old Testament passages receive a literal treatment, that is, the New Testament records actual events or principles that satisfy the grammatical-historical sense of the Old Testament passage. Several examples illustrate this.

Matthew 1:23 with Isaiah 7:14
The Lord through Isaiah offered King Ahaz a sign in Isaiah 7:10-11, but Ahaz in feigned humility refused the offer (v. 12). Since Ahaz refused that sign, the Lord chose another, described in verse 14, the miraculous birth of a son to a virgin. The Hebrew word translated "virgin" refers to an unmarried woman (Gen. 24:43; Prov. 30:19; Song 1:3; 6:8), indicating that the birth of Isaiah's own son in Isaiah 8:3 could not have fulfilled this prophecy. Besides, birth of a son to Isaiah would hardly have satisfied the promise of a "sign" and the son's name of "Immanuel" in 7:14. Matthew noted the fulfillment of this prophecy in the birth of Israel's Messiah in Matthew 1:23 and applied the

name "Immanuel" (i.e., "God with us") from Isaiah 7:14 to Him. That was a literal fulfillment of Isaiah's Old Testament prophecy.

Acts 13:23 with Isaiah 11:1

Isaiah 11:1 predicts the coming of a shoot or rod from the stem of Jesse and a branch growing from Jesse's roots. The Babylonian captivity appears to have ended the Davidic dynasty in Israel, but life remained in the "stump" and "roots" of the Davidic line. Jesse was the father of David through whom the Messianic king was to come (Ruth 4:22; 1 Sam. 16:1, 12-13). Paul's sermon in Acts 13:23 notes the literal fulfillment of that prophecy through David, the son of Jesse, from whose offspring God would bring to Israel a Savior whose name was Jesus.

Matthew 21:42 with Isaiah 28:16 and Psalm 118:22

Old Testament references to "the chief corner stone" and "the stone which the builders rejected" found their literal fulfillment in the incarnation and death of Jesus Christ, according to Matthew 21:42 along with Mark 12:10; Luke 20:17; Acts 4:11; Romans 9:33; Ephesians 2:20; and 1 Peter 2:6-8. Christ provided the only sure refuge for Israel, who had made the mistake of relying on foreigners instead. At Jesus' first coming, Israel rejected Him, thereby stumbling in literal fulfillment of this prophecy.

Luke 3:4-6 with Isaiah 40:3-5

All four Gospels record the fulfillment of this prophecy of a voice crying in the wilderness in the preaching of John the Baptist. His was a prophetic exhortation to Israel to prepare for the revelation of the Lord's glory with the arrival of the Messiah. Luke 3:4-6 records the fullest account of the fulfillment. Matthew 3:3; Mark 1:3; and John 1:23 furnish briefer mentions of the same. The remnant of Israel was to remove obstacles from the coming Messiah's path by repenting of their sins. Both John the Baptist (Matt. 3:2) and Jesus (Matt. 4:17; Mark 1:15) reminded people of this necessity.

Matthew 3: 16-17 and 17:5 with Isaiah 42:1a

The personal Servant of the LORD spoken of in Isaiah 42:1a is Israel's Messiah, who was chosen (Luke 9:35) because the LORD delights in Him. In Matthew 13:16-17 (cf. Mark 1:10-11; Luke 3:22) at Christ's baptism and in Matthew 17:5 at His transfiguration, Matthew records the literal fulfillment of God's recognition of the Messiah as the one in whom He is pleased.

Matthew 26:67 and 27:26, 30 with Isaiah 50:6

Isaiah foresaw the cruel treatment of Jesus by the soldiers during and after His trial. Matthew records His being struck, slapped, scourged, and spat upon, as do Mark, Luke, and John also (cf. Mark 14:65; 15:19; Luke 22:63;John 18:22). The Old Testament anticipated that abusive treatment, and the New Testament recorded the prophecy's literal fulfillment.

John 12:37-38 with Isaiah 53:1

When he wrote, "Who has believed our report?" the prophet anticipated that Israel would not recognize her Messiah when He came. That expectation found literal fulfillment when Christ came. John 12:38 explicitly notes the fulfillment while John 1:9-11 implicitly does so by speaking of Christ's coming to His own people and His own people not welcoming Him.

Acts 8:32-33 with Isaiah 53:7-8

For the sake of the Ethiopian eunuch who was reading Isaiah 53, Philip identified Jesus as the one who fulfilled the prophecy of Isaiah about "a sheep that is silent before its shearers." Philip called the eunuch's attention to how Jesus, by remaining silent, was like "a lamb before its shearer." This fulfillment is literal again and serves as a good example to prove that Jesus fulfilled Old Testament prophecy and thus was the promised Messiah of Israel.

Matthew 26:63; 27:12, 14 with Isaiah 53:7

Isaiah prophesied that the Servant of the LORD would not open His mouth to protest His mistreatment. Matthew repeatedly notes that Jesus "kept silent," "made no answer," and "did not answer." Mark, Luke, John, and Peter emphasize the same point (Mark 14:61; 15:5; Luke 23:9; John 19:9; 1 Peter 2:23). Jesus fulfilled the prophecy literally.

John 1:29 with Isaiah 53:7

Isaiah refers to the Servant of the LORD as a lamb led to slaughter. The writer john quotes this recognition of Jesus as the Lamb of God who takes away the sin of the world (John 1:29). Peter refers to Him as an unblemished and spotless lamb (1 Peter 1:19). The writer John refers to Him again in a similar way when in a vision he saw a lamb standing as though slain (Rev. 5:6). Here is another New Testament recognition of literal fulfillment of Old Testament prophecy.

First Peter 2:22 with Isaiah 53:9
Isaiah wrote of the Servant's refraining from violence and from speaking deceitfully. In 1 Peter 2:22 Peter picks those details to show how Jesus fulfilled the predictions literally. He was innocent of all charges leveled against Him.

Luke 22:37 with Isaiah 53:12
Luke observes how Jesus was numbered with transgressors in literal fulfillment of the very same words recorded by Isaiah many centuries earlier.

Luke 4: 18-19 with Isaiah 61:1-2a
Luke quotes Jesus when He announced His own literal fulfillment of the prophecy about bringing good news to the afflicted. He offered promised kingdom blessings to his hometown of Nazareth in Israel, but that generation of Israelites rejected Him at His first coming, causing a postponement of the promised kingdom.

Matthew 21:5 with Isaiah 62:11; Zechariah 9:9
In describing Jesus' triumphal entry, Matthew connects the occasion with the literal fulfillment of the words of Isaiah and Zechariah to the daughter of Zion about her King coming to her riding on a donkey.

The Function of Literal Fulfillment
Fulfillments such as those listed above had great apologetic value in proving to Jewish readers of the Old Testament and others that Jesus was the promised Messiah. What Isaiah and other Old Testament prophets predicted would happen when the Messiah came happened in letter-perfect manner. The way Jesus met the criteria expected of Israel's Messiah was phenomenal, so much so that any clear-thinking person was bound to acknowledge that this was the one whom the Old Testament expected. The fulfillments were that precise.

(2) Nonliteral Uses of the Old Testament in the New Testament
The second type of New Testament citations of the Old Testament are inspired *sensus plenior* applications (ISPAs) of the Old Testament. In such uses, New Testament writers applied Old Testament texts to situations entirely different from what was envisioned in the corresponding Old Testament contexts. The New Testament writers disregarded the main thrust of grammatical-historical meaning of the Old Testament passages and

applied those passages in different ways to suit different points they were making. They usually maintained some connecting link in thought to the Old Testament passages, but the literal Old Testament meanings are absent from the quotation.

A number of passages where this is done illustrate ISPA usage.

Luke 20: 17-18 with Isaiah 8: 14-15
Isaiah's historical context refers the words to the stumbling and consequent captivity in Babylon of those who opposed Isaiah's message. Luke applies the same words to the stumbling of the generation of Israelites that rejected Jesus as Messiah and their consequent judgment. Paul and Peter do the same with Isaiah 8:14-15 (Rom. 9:32-33; 1 Peter 2:8). Note the change of reference. In the Old Testament instance the words referred to personal enemies of Isaiah and the temporal judgment inflicted on them; in the New Testament the generation of Israel that rejected Jesus at His first coming and eternal judgment against them are in view.

Hebrews 2:13a with Isaiah 8:17
For Isaiah, the words of hope spoke of the prophet's willingness to await the Lord's deliverance and His promised national salvation for the faithful remnant of Israel. The writer of Hebrews applies the words to Christ's trust and hope in God and His willingness to call them "brothers" who come from the same Father as He.

Hebrews 2:13b with Isaiah 8:18
The Isaiah passage speaks of Isaiah and his two sons. The writer of Hebrews applies the same words to Jesus, the Son of God, and His fellow human beings to show Jesus' human nature and full identification with the human race (Heb. 2:13b). In the New Testament sense, the reference is to Jesus instead of Isaiah and to humanity instead of Isaiah's two sons.

Matthew 4:12-16 with Isaiah 9:1-2
Isaiah's words speak of the gloom at the northern border of northeast Galilee when the Assyrian king invaded Israel, because that area was the first to suffer from the invasion as the Assyrians entered the land. The verses then speak of the coming of a great light by way of the transformation of that gloom at the end of Israel's captivity to foreign invaders, which will come at the second advent of Jesus Christ. In an ISPA of the words, Matthew 4:12-16 applies the two Isaianic verses to the time of Christ's first advent and

the honor received by Galilee when He launched His Galilean ministry in that territory. That, of course, is not a literal fulfillment of Isaiah's prophecy.

John 4:10, 14 with Isaiah 12:3
In Isaiah's context, the words anticipate the time Messiah will come to satisfy the physical thirst of the future generation of Israelites at the Messiah's second advent. The nation will enjoy the same provision then as the generation under Moses who had their physical thirst satisfied in the wilderness (cf. Exod. 17:1-7). According to John's gospel, Jesus applied the words to the woman of Samaria and her opportunity to receive "living water," a figurative reference to eternal life (John 4:10, 14). This is another ISPA of the Old Testament, this time by Jesus through the Gospel writer.

1 Corinthians 15:54 with Isaiah 25:8
The Isaiah context of 25:8 speaks of the time of Christ's future reign over the nations when God will "swallow up" death. He promises a time of prosperity for ethnic Israel. In 1 Corinthians, Paul applies the words to the future resurrection of those in Christ, the church, because of the resurrection of Christ Himself (15:54). Here is another nonliteral application of Old Testament prophecy.

1 Corinthians 14:21-22 with Isaiah 28: 11
The prophet foresees the Lord's prediction of subservience of the drunkards of Ephraim and Jerusalem to Assyrian taskmasters, who instruct them in a foreign language. This was God's punishment for not listening to His prophets speaking their own language. In his application of the same words, Paul refers to God's use of the miraculous gift of tongues as a credential to identify those who conveyed new revelation immediately following the first coming of Christ (1 Cor. 14:21-22). The meaning in Corinthians is quite different from that in Isaiah.

Matthew 11:5 with Isaiah 29:18 and 35:5
Isaiah speaks of the Day of the LORD, when the spiritual deafness and blindness of Israel will be replaced with spiritual hearing and eye-sight. These will come in conjunction with Israel's repentance at the future advent of her Messiah. In Matthew 11:5, Jesus applies the words in a nonliteral way to the physical healing of the deaf and blind that He accomplished during His earthly ministry at His first advent.

Hebrews 8:6, 10-12 with Isaiah 42:6
Isaiah promises that the Servant of the LORD will be a covenant, to the people and a light to the Gentiles in the day when Israel enters the benefits of her new covenant (see Jer. 31:31-34). That will happen when the Messiah returns and establishes Israel's kingdom on earth. Hebrews 8:6, 10-12 show that because of Israel's rejection of the Messiah at His first advent, the Servant extended the redemptive benefits of that new covenant to the church.

Matthew 11:5 and Luke 4: 18 with Isaiah 42:7
Isaiah promises that the servant of the LORD will open blind eyes and release Israel's prisoners from prison by giving them freedom in the future day of the LORD. Those will be days when spiritual eyes will be opened and spiritual freedom from physical captivity to their enemies will be achieved. Rather than referring the words who to His second coming and to spiritual enlightenment and literal freedom, however, Jesus in Matthew 11:5 and Luke 4:18 applied the words to acts of physical healing and the release of spiritual captives accomplished during His first advent.

Acts 13:47 with Isaiah 49:6
The Isaiah text contains God's promise that His Servant, the Messiah, will be a light to the Gentiles in providing salvation to the ends of the earth. That will happen during the future kingdom after His return. But in Acts 13:47 Paul uses the words in an entirely different manner. He applies them to his own ministry among the Gentiles during the present age, not to the LORD's servant during the future age of the kingdom. Here again is clearly a nonliteral application of the prophet's words.

Matthew 8:16-17 with Isaiah 53:4
Isaiah 53:4 promises that the Messiah Servant will bear Israel's spiritual griefs and carry their spiritual sorrows when He suffers on behalf of the nation. That was fulfilled in Jesus' death on the cross when He was wounded for their transgressions and bruised for their iniquities (cf. Isa. 53:5). Yet Matthew 8:16-17 applies the words to Jesus' healing power during His incarnation. This nonliteral application of the Old Testament is another meaning that God intended for Isaiah 53:4, but not a meaning whose authority lies in the Old Testament passage. The only way one knows this meaning is through the New Testament's insight into that additional meaning.

John 6:45 with Isaiah 54:13
Isaiah promises that all Israel's children will be taught by the LORD during the future kingdom when Christ is personally present to rule the earth. An authoritative application of the words, according to John 6:45, is to those with enough spiritual insight to come to Him during His first advent. Jesus made this application during His great discourse on the Bread of Life as He referred to those whom the Father draws to Him.

Romans 10:20 with Isaiah 65:1
Isaiah speaks of the unexpected turning of Gentiles to God during the time of Israel's blessing in her future kingdom, but Paul applies the verse to the church during the present age. Since the existence of such a body as the church was a mystery throughout the Old Testament, this must be an ISPA of the Isaiah passage. The principle of single meaning necessitates that the passage could not refer to both.[2]

Matthew 2: 15 with Hosea 11: 1
Sometimes the New Testament treats a nonprophetic Old Testament passage, such as Hosea 11:1, as though it predicted a New Testament occurrence. Hosea wrote about the historical exodus of the people of Israel from Egypt, but Matthew applies the same words to Jesus' departure from Egypt with His family after their flight to escape Herod the Great.[3] This furnishes another instance of ISPA.

Romans 3: 10b-18 with Psalms 5:9; 10:7; 14:1-3; 36:1; 53:1-3; 140:3; Proverbs 1:16; Ecclesiastes 7:20; Isaiah 59:7-8
Another example of a New Testament use of nonprophetic Old Testament passages comes by way of proof of the universal sinfulness of humanity in Romans 3:10b-18. None of the Old Testament passages cited here are used with the literal meaning of their original context.[4]

Clearly the New Testament sometimes applies Old Testament passages in a way that gives an additional dimension beyond their

---

[2] For a thorough discussion of the issues involved with these passages, see J. K. Brackett, "Paul's Use of the Old Testament in Romans 9-11" (Th.M. *thesis*, The Master's Seminary, Sun Valley, California, 1998), 83-113.

[3] See J. H. Walton, "Inspired Subjectivity and Hermeneutical Objectivity," *The Master's Seminary Journal* 13, no. 1 (spring 2002): 74-75, for further discussion of the relationship between these passages.

[4] For detailed discussion of these passages, see B. A. Shealy, "Paul's Use of the Old Testament in Romans 3:10-18: A Test Case for 'Inspired *Sensus Plenior* Application,'" (Th.M. *thesis*, The Master's Seminary, Sun Valley, California, 2002), 51-139.

grammatical-historical meaning. This does not cancel the grammatical-historical meaning of the Old Testament; it is simply an application of the Old Testament passage beyond its original meaning, the authority for which application is the New Testament passage. Such an application is an ISPA.

Questions Raised by ISPA-Type Citations

The ISPA of Old Testament passages by New Testament writers raises several questions. First, can today's interpreter imitate what New Testament writers did in assigning additional and different meanings in applying Old Testament passages? No, they cannot, because that would depart from grammatical-historical interpretation and violate the principle of single meaning. Current interpreters and preachers may apply the Old Testament passages to different situations, but their applications are not inspired, as are those of New Testament writers.

But someone will say, "Why can't we imitate the principles used in the New Testament writings? Don't we learn our hermeneutics from them?" The difference in qualifications is the answer. New Testament writers possessed the gift of apostleship and/or the gift of prophecy that enabled them to receive and transmit direct revelation from God. No contemporary interpreter possesses either of those gifts. Those gifts enabled the gifted ones to practice what is called "charismatic exegesis" of the Old Testament.[5] That practice entailed finding hidden or symbolic meanings that could be revealed through an interpreter possessing divine insight.[6] It was similar to the technique called *midrash pesher* that members of the Qumran community used,[7] but neither did the members of that community possess such gifts as apostleship and prophecy.

Another way of expressing the differences in qualifications is to point out that New Testament writers were directly inspired by God, but today's interpreters are not. That allowed New Testament authors prerogatives that readers of Scripture do not enjoy. Through direct revelation from God, they could assign applications based additional meanings to Old Testament passages. That rules out ISPA of Old Testament texts to new situations other than those applications that appear in the New Testament.

---

[5] D. E. Aune, *Prophecy in Early Christianity and the Ancient Mediteranean World* (Grand Rapids: Eerdmans, 1983), 252; and D. Hill, *New Testament Prophecy* (Atlanta: John Knox, 1979), 91.

[6] R. L. Thomas, *Revelation 1-7: An Exegetical Commentary* (Chicago: Moody, 1992), 26 n. 70; and idem, *Understanding Spiritual Gifts*, rev. ed. (Grand Rapids: Kregel, 1999), 33-34, 58-61, 133-72.

[7] Aune, *Prophecy in Early Christianity*, 252; and Hill, *New Testament Prophecy*, 91.

A second question relates to the principle of single meaning. Does not the New Testament's assigning of an application based on a second meaning to an Old Testament passage violate that principle? That the passage has two meanings is obvious, but only one of those meanings derives from grammatical-historical interpretation of the Old Testament itself. The other comes from a grammatical-historical analysis of the New Testament passage that cites it. The authority for the second meaning of the Old Testament passage is the New Testament, not the Old Testament. The Old Testament produces only the literal meaning. The *sensus plenior* meaning emerges only after an ISPA of the Old Testament wording to a new situation. The New Testament writers could assign such new meanings authoritatively because of the inspiration of what they wrote.

A third question is, "Did God know from the beginning that the Old Testament passage had two meanings?" Obviously He did, but until the New Testament citation of that passage, the second or *sensus plenior* meaning did not exist as far as humans were concerned. Since hermeneutics is a human discipline, gleaning that second sense is an impossibility in an examination of the Old Testament source of the citation. The additional meaning is therefore not a grammatical-historical interpretation of the Old Testament passage. The additional meaning is the fruit of grammatical-historical interpretation of the companion New Testament passage. The Old Testament passage has only one meaning.

Fourthly, someone might ask, "Why did the New Testament writers attach these *sensus plenior* meanings to Old Testament passages?" In almost every instance, if not every instance, the new meaning given to an Old Testament passage relates to Israel's rejection of her Messiah at His first advent and the consequent opening of the door to a new people, the Gentiles, for God to bless (see Rom. 9-11). The new people consisted of both Jews and Gentiles as fellow members of the body of Christ. That such a union would exist was unrevealed in the Old Testament, as Paul points out in Ephesians 3:1-7. New meanings through special divine revelation were necessary to give this new program a relationship with what God had been doing throughout the Old Testament period.

Comparisons with Other Approaches to Nonliteral Citations

Comparing the above method of handling the New Testament use of Old Testament passages—where the New Testament assigns, inspired *sensus plenior* applications—with other methods of handling companion passages will clarify what the explanation entails.

S. Lewis Johnson and J. I. Packer

J. I. Packer classifies the divine intent behind an Old Testament prophetic passage as "an extrapolation on the grammatico-historical plane, not a new projection onto the plane of allegory."[8] S. Lewis Johnson agrees.[9] ISPA agrees with them when they conclude that the New Testament finds a *sensus plenior* meaning in addition to the literal meaning of the Old Testament, but ISPA would emphasize that if that meaning is an extrapolation on that plane of the literal meaning, it exceeds the limits of grammatical-historical interpretation of the Old Testament. Though their method may not be classed as allegory, its handling of Old Testament passages is not through grammatical-historical means.

Johnson goes a step further and advocates that modern interpreters reproduce the exegetical method of the New Testament writers in their handling of the Old Testament.[10] That means going beyond the literal meaning of the Old Testament to discover *sensus plenior* meanings of Old Testament passages in addition to the ones divulged in the New Testament. That is another distinction between his approach and the ISPA approach that would emphasize the unique prerogative of New Testament writers to employ charismatic exegesis, and would insist that no one today possesses that prophetic gift.[11]

Elliott E. Johnson

Elliott E. Johnson resembles S. Lewis Johnson and Packer in finding two meanings, the divine author's meaning and the human author's meaning. He writes,

> The words of the text are both the words of God and the words of the human author. In some sense, then, the meaning of God and the human author is the same. In another sense, the meaning intended by God may well be richer than the meaning of which the human author was aware (1 Peter 1:10-11). The shared

---

[8] James I. Packer, "Biblical Authority, Hermeneutics, and Inerrancy," in *Jerusalem and Athens: Critical Discussion on the Theology and Apologetics of Cornelius Van Til*, ed. E. R. Geehan (Nutley, N.J.: Presbyterian and Reformed, 1971), 147-48.

[9] S. L. Johnson, *The Old Testament in the New: An Argument for Biblical Inspiration* (Grand Rapids: Zondervan, 1980), 50.

[10] Ibid., 93-94.

[11] J. DeYoung and S. Hurty disagree that the gift of prophecy ended in the early church and advocate that the gift, like all the other New Testament gifts, is available to all Christians today, enabling them to find meanings in Scripture that are deeper than the grammatical-historical meaning (*Beyond the Obvious* [Gresham, Ore.: Vision House, 1995], 136-38). Like S. L. Johnson, they believe that we should practice the hermeneutical methodology of the New Testament writers (ibid., 68-80).

meaning must be based on the words of the text. This meaning expressed may be conceived as a comprehensive or generic message.[12]

ISPA would differ with E. E. Johnson in his view that both divine and human meanings are discoverable in the Old Testament text and that it therefore has a generic message. That does not do justice to the principle of single meaning. I agree with him that the text has a stable meaning and is not changing with time under the influence of human reflection, as complementary hermeneutics insists. But that stable meaning is single and not generic or multi-faceted.

Bruce K. Waltke

Bruce K. Waltke in his canonical approach gives priority to New Testament revelation by asserting that the Old Testament is always to be read in light of the New Testament. He focuses on the divine intent of the Old Testament passage, even though the human author may not have comprehended the scope of what he was writing about. He agrees that "the text's intention became deeper and clearer as the parameters of the canon were expanded" and that "older texts in the canon underwent a correlative progressive perception of meaning as they became part of a growing canonical literature."[13] He rules out *sensus plenior* as a possible explanation, stating that the Old Testament writers wrote in ideal language. The unity between that ideal language and God's intention excludes the need to conclude that the New Testament writers through inspiration discovered a fuller sense in the Old Testament text. That fuller sense was always there, says Waltke.

Waltke's approach violates grammatical-historical principles that the meaning of a text is discoverable on the basis of the facts of the original historical setting and the principles of grammar. Literal interpretation does not postulate that the original readers were shut out from a text's meaning that could come to light only after centuries of waiting. Waltke by implication also violates the principle of single meaning when he implies that the author and original readers received one meaning and later recipients of the New Testament received another. For him, the multiple meanings included a literal fulfillment of Old Testament promises in the spiritual form

---

[12] E. E. Johnson, "A Traditional Dispensational Hermeneutic," in *Three Central Issues in Contemporary Dispensationalism*, ed. H. W. Bateman IV (Grand Rapids: Kregel, 1999), 67.

[13] B. K. Waltke, "A Canonical Process Approach to the Psalms," in *Tradition and Testament*, ed. J. S. Feinberg and P. D. Feinberg (Chicago: Moody, 1981), 7.

of the kingdom in the New Testament.[14] In reference to the Psalms, he explicitly rejects "the Antiochian principle of allowing but one historical meaning that may carry with it typical significance."[15]

Walter C. Kaiser Jr.

Walter C. Kaiser Jr.'s strong point is his insistence on authorial intent as determinative of a text's meaning. He rejects *sensus plenior* and limits unbridled attempts to find new meanings.[16] However, he fails to allow for the New Testament furnishing additional meanings for an Old Testament text. Rather he opts for attributing more to the Old Testament writers than is justifiable under grammatical-historical rules and for allowing that their promises were generic and had a series of fulfillments.[17] Though Kaiser claims that the series constitutes one idea, it is still a series. This, the idea of a series of meanings, violates the principle of single meaning.

He also contends that each human author was aware of all the stages of fulfillment, though not the time of fulfillment.[18] This assumption goes beyond what literal interpretive principles will justify. Some of Kaiser's exegetical practices in arriving at such a conclusion are severely strained. For example, he cites seven isolated words that David used in composing Psalm 40 to indicate David's awareness that his office and function served "as the current representative in a long series of fulfillments of the coming man of promise."[19] The seven words prove no such thing. Kaiser reads into the passage a preconceived meaning. This borders closely on use of the analogy of faith in the exegetical process that Kaiser himself so strongly opposes.[20]

Richard N. Longenecker and Douglas J. Moo

Richard N. Longenecker understands that New Testament writers who cited the Old Testament used methods of Jewish exegesis prevalent around New Testament times. He sees the discovery of the Dead Sea Scrolls as opening a new area of possibility for explaining how New Testament writers

---

[14] B. K. Waltke, "Is It Right to Read the New Testament into the Old?" *Christianity Today*, 2 September 1983, 77.

[15] Waltke, "Canonical Process Approach to the Psalms," 7.

[16] W. C. Kaiser Jr., "Legitimate Hermeneutics," in *Inerrancy*, ed. N. L. Geisler (Grand Rapids: Zondervan, 1979), 125-28; and idem, "The Single Intent of Scripture," in *Evangelical Roots: A Tribute to Wilbur Smith* (Nashville: Nelson, 1978), 137.

[17] W. C. KaiserJr., *The Uses of the Old Testament in the New* (Chicago: Moody, 1985), 67-68.

[18] E.g., ibid., 131-32.

[19] Ibid.

[20] Ibid., 69.

interpreted the Old Testament.[21] He classifies Jewish exegetical procedures under four headings: literal, *midrash, pesher,* and allegory.[22] He asks the question, "Is there a *sensus plenior* in the New Testament's use of the Old?" and answers that there is. He cites with approval a statement of Douglas J. Moo: "The question should rather be: Could God have intended a sense related to but more than that which the human author intended? I cannot see that the doctrine of inspiration demands that the answer to that question be negative."[23] Moo later adds, "It may be that some citations are best explained according to the traditional *sensus plenior* model: by direct, inspired apprehension, the New Testament authors perceive the meaning in a text put there by God but unknown to the human author. Even in this case, however, it is important to insist that this 'deeper meaning' is based on and compatible with the meaning intended by the human author."[24]

Longenecker then asks another question: "Can we reproduce the exegesis of the New Testament?" In rephrasing the question, he asks, "Are the exegetical methods that the New Testament writers used to arrive at their interpretations also either normative or exemplary for the interpretive practices of Christians today?" To this question he responds basically in the negative: "I do not think it my business to try to reproduce the exegetical procedures and practices of the New Testament writers, particularly when they engage in what I define as '*midrash,'* '*pesher,'* or 'allegorical' exegesis. Those practices often represent a culturally specific method or reflect a revelational stance or both—neither of which I can claim for myself"[25]

ISPA would concur with Longenecker and Moo regarding the presence of *sensus plenior* meanings attached to Old Testament passages by New Testament writers, and would agree with Longenecker in denying the prerogative to exercise the methodology of New Testament writers in today's exegesis. But ISPA would disagree with both of them when it strongly emphasizes the difference between the methods of Jewish hermeneutical practices such as at Qumran and those of the New Testament writers. The latter had the added guidance of the Holy Spirit, being in possession of revelational gifts of the Spirit that were unavailable to Jewish interpreters. In

---

[21] R. N. Longenecker, *Biblical Exegesis in the Apostolic Period*, 2d ed.
(Grand Rapids: Eerdmans, 1999), xxi-xxii.
[22] Ibid., xxv.
[23] Ibid., xxxiii-xxxiv; and D. J. Moo, "*The Problem of Sensus Plenior,*" in *Hermeneutics, Authority, and Canon*, ed. D. A. Carson and J. D. Woodbridge (Grand Rapids: Baker, 1995), 204.
[24] Ibid., 210.
[25] Longenecker, *Biblical Exegesis*, xxxviii.

this regard, the methods of the New Testament writers were absolutely unique and unrepeatable by present-day interpreters.

Darrell L. Bock

Darrell L. Bock formulates his method based on an eclectic approach that draws on elements of each of the methods described above.[26] Eclecticism in hermeneutics generally entails inconsistency because of following several approaches. He describes his view under four headings: dual authorship, language-referent, progress of revelation, and differing texts. Regarding dual authorship, he opts for a limited identification of the divine intent with the human author's intent. He states, "God could intend more than the human author did but never at the expense of the thrust of his wording."[27]

Bock's second heading, the language-referent, deals with where meaning resides. Is it at the level of sense—by which he refers to the definitions of words within a passage—or at the level of referents—by which he refers to the larger context of a passage's biblical theological context?[28] To this question Bock would answer both, not either/or. Next he deals with the progress of revelation. Under this third heading he discusses the impact of the history of Jesus' life and ministry on apostolic understanding of Scripture.[29] This approach has the events of the New Testament "refracting" or changing the church's understanding of the Old Testament by way of a deepened understanding.

Bock's fourth heading is differing texts by which he refers to places where New Testament writers altered the Hebrew text when they cited Old Testament passages. Here he suggests three possible explanations: distinguishing between textual (i.e., what Old Testament text was used) and conceptual (i.e., what point the text is making) forms of citations, changes in wording that are legitimate in light of an altered New Testament perspective, and changes because of a larger literary context.[30]

In his eclectic approach to the New Testament use of the Old Testament, Bock has inevitably violated grammatical-historical principles, since these were not his main concern in his survey of current methodologies. He has forsaken the quest for objectivity and inserted the

---

[26] D. L. Bock, "Part 1, Evangelicals and the Use of the Old Testament in the New," *BSac* 142, no. 567 (July 1985): 220.

[27] D. L. Bock, "Part 2, Evangelicals and the Use of the Old Testament in the New," *BSac* 142, no. 568 (October 1985): 309.

[28] Ibid., 309.

[29] Ibid., 311-14.

[30] Ibid., 314-15.

interpreter's preunderstanding as a major factor in interpretation.[31] He has substituted his "complementary" or multilayered reading of an Old Testament text that views a text's meaning from the standpoint of later events rather than limiting that meaning to the historical setting of the text's origin.[32] In the name of progress of revelation, he has refrained from limiting a passage to a single meaning in order to allow for later complementary additions in meaning, which of necessity alter the original sense conveyed by the passage.[33] He has advocated assigning meanings beyond those that grammatical-historical analysis will bear.[34] These deviations show what any eclectic approach to hermeneutics will yield.

John H. Walton
John H. Walton has made several important observations regarding the New Testament use of the Old Testament. One of his valid points is that objectivity in interpretation is an important goal, because a lack of objectivity is not so much a sacrifice of truth as it is a challenge to divine authority.[35] He laments the intrusion of the analogy of faith and its subjectivity when it glosses "a theological concept into a context where it has no ostensible role."[36] To allow such an intrusion is to lapse into subjectivity in interpretation.

In his discussion of typology Walton distinguishes two separate methods of interpretation, one by using hermeneutical guidelines that are objective in nature and the other by inspiration from God that is subjective in nature. He continues, "If you have inspiration, you do not need grammatical-historical hermeneutics. If you do not have inspiration, you must proceed by the acknowledged guidelines of hermeneutics. The credibility of any interpretation is based on the verifiability of either one's inspiration or one's hermeneutics."[37] Because no contemporary interpreter can claim inspiration, he concludes, "we cannot speak of reproducing the methods of the New Testament authors, for the subjectivity of their methods is not allowed to

---

[31] Cf. R. L. Thomas, "A Critique of Progressive Dispensational Hermeneutics," in *When the Trumpet Sounds,* ed. T. Ice and T. Demy (Eugene, Ore.: Harvest House, 1995), 417-18; see also chapter 13 of this volume.

[32] Cf. ibid., 419-20.

[33] Cf. ibid., 420-21.

[34] Cf. ibid., 422-23. Bock rejects principial-traditional hermeneutics, which is his name for grammatical-historical interpretation (cf. D. L. Bock, "Hermeneutics of Progressive Dispensationalism," *Three Central Issues in Contemporary Dispensationalism: A Comparison of Traditional and Progressive Views,* ed. H. W. Bateman IV [Grand Rapids: Kregel, 1999], 86, 97).

[35] Walton, "Inspired Subjectivity," 66-67.

[36] Ibid., 68. In this regard his opinion resembles that of Kaiser (Kaiser, *Uses of the Old Testament,* 69).

[37] Walton, "Inspired Subjectivity," 70.

those of us whose interpretation does not enjoy the affirmation of inspiration."[38]

In commenting on the citation of Hosea 11:1 in Matthew 2:15, Walton notes that the verse in the context of Hosea's prophecy has little connection with Matthew's use of it. Matthew is not interpreting the message of Hosea that was understood by Hosea and his audience through objective principles of grammatical-historical hermeneutics.[39] Even though Matthew associates fulfillment—using the verb *pleroo*—with Jesus' being brought by His parents from Egypt, Walton emphasizes that one cannot glean that from Hosea. That conclusion can come only from subjective association exercised through inspiration by the writer Matthew. Matthew does not interpret the message of Hosea; he identifies the fulfillment.[40]

Walton's comments stress a very important principle: On the basis of grammatical-historical interpretation, an Old Testament passage may have only one meaning, the meaning based on objective principles of literal interpretation. But on the basis of inspired subjectivity of a New Testament writer, it may also have an additional meaning, a meaning resting on the authority of the New Testament text, not on that of the Old Testament passage quoted.

ISPA agrees with Walton, except in his choice of terminology. It would use different ways of identifying the meaning of *pleroo* in such places as Matthew 2:15, as will be explained below.

William W. Klein, Craig L. Blomberg, and Robert L. Hubbard Jr.
William W. Klein, Craig L. Blomberg, and Robert L. Hubbard Jr. offer several options related to the New Testament use of the Old Testament:

- Biblical authors intended *only one sense* (meaning), and this historical sense—what the text would have meant at the time written to its original readers—remains the only legitimate object of exegesis. Whatever New Testament writers may have done with the Old Testament, we must limit our exegesis to the original historical sense of the text.
- Biblical writers intended to convey *multiple meanings* or levels of meanings in at least some of their writings. These texts have several meanings that readers may subsequently discover.
- Biblical authors intended only one sense, but that sense need not limit how later readers understand a text since perception always involves a creative interaction

---

[38] Ibid.; cf. also W. W. Klein, C. L. Blomberg, and R. L. Hubbard, *Introduction to Biblical Interpretation* (Dallas: Word, 1993), 125-32, and Longenecker, *Biblical Exegesis*, 193-98.
[39] Walton, "Inspired Subjectivity," 74.
[40] Ibid., 75.

between text and readers. Interpretation is a *"reader-response"* enterprise; so later readers—like the writers of the New Testament—may invent meaning never envisioned in the original context. Interpreters may do the same today.

- Biblical authors intended only one sense, but unknown to them the Holy Spirit encoded in the text additional and hidden meaning(s). When New Testament writers employed Old Testament texts, in places they were drawing out this fuller sense, the *sensus plenior*. Such a process may or may not be repeatable for modern interpreters.

- Biblical authors intended only one sense, though later readers may employ *creative exegetical techniques* to discover additional valid senses not intended by the original authors. Such techniques include midrash, pesher, or typology. There probably was some connection between original text and later sense, though the connection may appear arbitrary, if not undecipherable. The process mayor may not be repeatable today.[41]

Klein, Blomberg, and Hubbard eventually choose the last two options, noting that a fresh meaning need not be limited to the original sense.[42]

As has been observed, however, only the first option abides by guidelines of grammatical-historical interpretation. The principle of single meaning and the objectivity of sound hermeneutics requires the exclusion of additional meanings subjectively derived.

Appropriate Terminology

Some final considerations regarding "fulfillment" terminology seem to be in order. We repeat the words of Terry in this connection:

> We have already seen that the Bible has its riddles, enigmas, and dark sayings, but whenever they are given the context clearly advises us of the fact. To assume, in the absence of any hint, that we have an enigma, and in the face of explicit statements to the contrary, that any specific prophecy has a double sense, a primary and a secondary meaning, a near and a remote fulfilment, must necessarily introduce an element of uncertainty and confusion into biblical interpretation.[43]

Terry's elimination of the possibility of a near and a remote fulfillment is relevant at this point. ISPA concurs with his opinion of avoiding any more than one fulfillment, but probably for different reasons.

Most (if not all) English translations frequently render the Greek verb *pleroo* by the English word *fulfill.* In some instances this is unfortunate

---

[41] Klein et al., *Biblical Interpretation*, 131-32.
[42] Ibid., 145.
[43] Milton S. Terry, *Biblical Hermeneutics*, 2d ed. (Reprint; Grand Rap- ids: Zondervan, n.d.), 495.

because the two words do not cover the same semantic domain. In English, *fulfill,* when used in connection with Old Testament citations, carries the connotation of a historical occurrence of something promised or predicted. The Greek *pleroo,* however, covers more linguistic territory than that. Moo speaks to this point:

> *Pleroo* cannot be confined to so narrow a focus [as referring to fulfillment of an Old Testament prophecy]. . . . What needs to be emphasized, then, is that the use of *pleroo* in an introductory formula need not mean that the author regards the Old Testament text he quotes as a direct prophecy; and accusations that a New Testament author misuses the Old Testament by using *pleroo* to introduce nonprophetic texts are unfounded.[44]

The Greek verb carries other meanings in various contexts. One of those meanings is "complete." In the Matthew 2:15 citation of Hosea 11:1 Matthew uses it to indicate the completion of a *sensus plenior* meaning he finds in Hosea 11:1. The Hosea passage is not a prophecy and translating the word *fulfill* in this instance is misleading. Matthew's meaning is that in some sense the transport of Jesus by His parents from Egypt completed the deliverance of Israel from Egypt that had begun during the time of Moses.

In Mark 1:15 Jesus uses the same Greek verb to speak of the completion of a period of time prior to the drawing near of the kingdom of God. The English word *fulfill* would hardly communicate the correct idea in a case like that.

Such observations lead to the conclusion that it is unwise to use *fulfillment* terminology in connection with the Old Testament passages to which the New Testament assigns inspired *sensus plenior* applications. Frequently expositors and commentators have used such expressions as "initial fulfillment," "partial fulfillment," "near fulfillment," or something comparable to speak of Peter's use of Joel 2:28-32 in his Acts 2 sermon. That language gives the wrong impression because the Old Testament passage did not predict what happened on the Day of Pentecost. What happened on that day was an ISPA of Joel 2, whose authority was the Acts passage, not the Joel passage. The phenomena on the Day of Pentecost were in no sense a fulfillment of Joel's prophecy, a prophecy that pertained to the people of Israel, not to the church. The relevance of the happenings on that day were an ISPA of the Joel passage to an entirely different situation by Peter and Luke who recorded his words. It is misleading to call them in any sense a fulfillment of Joel.

---

[44] Moo, "Problem of *Sensus Plenior*," 191.

Fulfillment language is perfectly in order for Old Testament prophecies that literally fulfill what the Old Testament writers referred to, however. Such an instance is Matthew's reference to the virgin birth of Christ (Matt. 1:23) in fulfillment of Isaiah 7:14.

The Wrap-Up

Sometimes the New Testament interprets Old Testament prophecies in their literal sense, but other times it assigns an ISPA sense to them. That does not give license to the contemporary interpreter to imitate the hermeneutics of New Testament writers, because such a procedure would violate the grammatical-historical principle of single meaning. The New Testament writers could do it because of their status as writers of inspired Scripture.

When the New Testament writers made such applications, it did not violate that principle of single meaning, because the authority for the additional meaning was not the Old Testament source but the New Testament citation of that source. The Old Testament passage in itself continued to have only one meaning.

Of course, God from the beginning knew the Old Testament passage would eventually have that added meaning, but a literal interpretation of that passage did not yield that meaning. The grammatical-historical interpretation of the New Testament citation of that passage yields the additional meaning.

A suggested reason for the inspired *sensus plenior* applications of Old Testament passages in the New Testament is Israel's rejection of her Messiah at His first advent. One of the ramifications of that rejection was new revelation regarding Old Testament passages related to a body called the church, revelation that was not foreseen in or a part of the Old Testament.

Comparisons of this analysis of the New Testament's use of the Old Testament with other explanations revealed that none exactly coincides with the proposal here. The closest is that of John Walton in his article on "Inspired Subjectivity and Hermeneutical Objectivity." An observation resulting from the current proposal is that expositors and exegetes should refrain from using *fulfillment* terminology in cases where New Testament writers have made inspired *sensus plenior* applications of Old Testament passages to new situations.

Summary of "New Testament Use of the Old Testament"

Examples and Principles of Direct Fulfillment of Old Testament Prophesy	Examples and Principles of Inspired Sensus Plenior Application (ISPA) of Old Testament Passages
Examples: Matthew 1:23 with Isaiah 7:14; Acts 13:23 with Isaiah 11:1; Matthew 21:42 with Isaiah 28:16 and Psalm 118:22; Luke 3:4-6 with Isaiah 40:3-5; Matthew 3:16-17 and 17:5 with Isaiah 42:1a; Mathew 26:67 and 27:26, 30 with Isaiah 50:6; John 12:37-38 with Isaiah 53:1; Acts 8:32-33 with Isaiah 53:7-8; Matthew 26:63 and 27:12, 14 with Isaiah 53:7; John 1:29 with Isaiah 53:7; 1 Peter 2:22 with Isaiah 53:9; Luke 22:37 with Isaiah 53:12; Luke 4:18:19 with Isaiah 61:1-2a; Matthew 21:5 with Isaiah 62:11 and Zechariah 9:9	Examples: Luke 20:17-18 with Isaiah 8:14-15; Hebrews 2:13a with Isaiah 8:17; Hebrews 2:13b with 8:18; Matthew 4:12-16 with Isaiah 9:1-2; John 4:10, 14 with Isaiah 12:3; 1 Corinthians 15:54 with Isaiah 25:8; 1 Corinthians 14:21-22 with Isaiah 28:11; Matthew 11:5 with Isaiah 29:18 and 35:5; Hebrews 8:6, 10-12 with Isaiah 42:6; Matthew 11:5 and Luke 4:18 with Isaiah 42:7; Acts 13:47 with Isaiah 49:6; Matthew 8:16-17 with Isaiah 53:4; John 6:45 with Isaiah 54:13; Romans 10:20 with Isaiah 65:1; Matthew 2:15 with Hosea 11:1; Romans 3:10b-18 with Psalms 5:9; 10:17; 14:1-3; 36:1; 53:1-3; 140:3; Proverbs 1:16; Ecclesiastes 7:20; Isaiah 59:7-8
Principles: *Fulfillment* terminology appropriate only for New Testament passages that literally fulfill the single meaning of Old Testament prophesies	Principles: Limited to those with revelatory gifts *sensus plenior* based on New Testament authority *sensus plenior* unknowable until the New Testament *sensus plenior* caused by Israel's rejection

Summary of "New Testament Use of the Old Testament" cont.

NT Use of OT Advocates	Principles Advocated	ISPA Response
S. Lewis Johnson and J. I. Packer	• *sensus plenior* in addition to the literal meaning of the Old Testament • *sensus plenior* as extrapolation on the plane of literal meaning • modern interpreters reproduce exegetical methodology of the New Testament writers	• agrees • disagrees • disagrees
Elliot E. Johnson	• two meanings discoverable in the Old Testament • the text has a stable meaning unchanged with passing of time • stable meaning is generic or many-faceted	• disagrees • agrees • disagrees
Bruce K. Waltke	• Old Testament always read in light of New Testament • fuller sense of Old Testament texts always there, their changed intention deeper and clearer with canon's expansion • original writers and readers were shut out from the text's meaning	• disagrees • disagrees • disagrees
Walter C. Kaiser Jr.	• rejects New Testament assignment of *sensus plenior* meaning to Old Testament • rejects sensus plenior meanings discoverable by modern interpreters • generic meanings in Old Testament allow for several fulfillments of single passage • human author was aware of the series of fulfillments	• disagrees • agrees • disagrees • disagrees

Summary of "New Testament Use of the Old Testament" cont.

NT Use of OT Advocates	Principles Advocated	ISPA Response
Richard N. Longenecker and Douglas J. Moo	• sensus plenior meanings attached to Old Testament passages by New Testament writers • Methods of Jewish exegesis by New Testament writers produced sensus plenior meanings for Old Testament • contemporary interpreters can't produce New Testament methods of handling the Old Testament	• agrees • disagrees • agrees
Darrell L. Bock	• eclecticism drawing on other approaches • God sometimes intended more than the human author • New Testament events changing the way the church understood the Old Testament • interpreters preunderstanding a major factor in interpretation • complementary additions in meaning allowed	• disagrees • agrees • disagrees • disagrees • disagrees
John H. Walton	• objectivity in interpretation an important goal • intrusion of the analogy of faith not allowed • subjectivity allowable only with inspiration • contemporary interpreter cannot claim inspiration • Matthew 2:15 a *fulfillment* of Hosea 11:1 • objective interpretation determines only one meaning for Old Testament passages	• agrees • agrees • agrees • agrees • disagrees • agrees
William W. Klein, Craig L. Blomberg, and Robert L. Hubbard Jr.	• biblical authors intended only one meaning, but the Spirit encoded additional meanings for modern interpreters • biblical authors intended only one meaning, but modern interpreters may uncover additional senses	• disagrees • disagrees

"All doctrine is practical, and all practice must be based on sound doctrine. Doctrine that is not practical is not healthy doctrine, and practice that is not doctrinal is not rightly based."

- Charles C. Ryrie
Balancing the Christian Life, 1969, page 66

10

Do We Really Hold Scripture to be Sufficient?

John Adams Tucker

...and that from childhood you have known the sacred writings which are able to give you the wisdom that leads to salvation through faith which is in Christ Jesus. All Scripture is inspired by God and profitable for teaching, for reproof, for correction, for training in righteousness; so that the man of God may be adequate, equipped for every good work. (2ⁿᵈ Timothy 3:15-17, NASB)

Introduction

We serve a God who delights in His revelation, both that which is naturally revealed in His creation (Ps. 19:1-6), and that which is supernaturally revealed in His Word (Ps. 19:7-13). The headline verses of 2ⁿᵈ Timothy 3:15-17 clearly indicate that all Scripture, being inspired and therefore possessing divine authority, is both capable of teaching us what is right, and then correcting us when we err. Scripture is the source of wisdom for both positional and practical righteousness. These three verses, perhaps like no others, indicate in a very succinct way, the character and power of Scripture that first initiates the positional, once-for-all justification and then progresses into and explains the on-going, daily, practical life of sanctification. Through its equipping instruction, Scripture provides the basis for men to display and confirm God's righteous standards through their good works. Since Scripture accurately informs us of the wisdom that leads to salvation, since Scripture also accurately informs us of the teaching and correction that proficiently outfits and equips a Christian to successfully perform any task his Master might intend, we should not be surprised in the very least that Scripture is the most-favored target of the enemies of God.

The most effective attacks by Satan are always those that begin with questioning the very words, intentions and authority of whatever God says. It began in the Garden of Eden when Satan spoke through the serpent to Eve. In fact, the first-ever recorded conversation between any of God's created beings called into question the very words and intentions of the God Who created them, thereby undermining and disgracing His authority. Satan simply asked, "Indeed, has God said?" and it has all departed inexorably downhill from there. It will continue to do so until another conversation appears where "... many peoples will come and say, "Come, let us go up to the mountain of the LORD, To the house of the God of Jacob; That He may teach us concerning His ways, And that we may walk in His paths." For the law will go forth from Zion, And the word of the LORD from Jerusalem." (Isa. 2:3). *Maranatha, indeed!*

The Lord's Example: Victory over Trials and Temptations

In His Judean wilderness temptation, our Lord's first response to the devil's temptations was to reiterate the noteworthy revelation of Deuteronomy 8:3, "… man does not live by bread alone, but man lives by everything that proceeds out of the mouth of the LORD." Those ancient Israelites, having lived in their own wilderness of trials and temptations, also lived on the sustenance that His oral instructions, the very words of God, commanded to appear—their manna. Therefore, even the manna they consumed was the direct result of God's spoken word (Ex. 16:4-5). The Lord is not hereby deprecating the bountiful agronomic endeavors of man with respect to producing bread for daily sustenance. Rather, He is placing pronounced emphasis on the significance and the essentiality of depending on everything—whatever it is—that God's words declare, whether concerning manna or otherwise. We must never lose sight of this basic lesson in Successful Spiritual Living 101, which is, that all trials come from the hand of a loving heavenly Father to produce traits within us that He desires (Rom. 5:3-5; Jam. 1:2-4). He employs such adversities to teach us to constantly seek and lean upon His wisdom—a wisdom found only in His Word, a word "that proceeds out of the mouth of the Lord" (Dt. 8:3; James 1:5). The answers we seek for all of life's trials and tribulations are to be found only in the Word of God. We waste our time and His resources when we seek means of relief elsewhere. David clearly understood the relationship between extreme difficulties and God's Word when he wrote, "When I am afraid, I will put my trust in You. In God, whose **word** I praise, In God I have put my trust; I shall not be afraid. What can mere man do to me?" (Ps. 56:3-4).

The Lord's response to Satan's attack in the Judean Wilderness consisted exclusively of one thing—God's written revelation. In the Lord's first refutation, as recorded in Matthew's account, the Lord quickly pointed out that a temporal life consisting of adequate physical sustenance, still yet lacked the one essential element—the eternal words of God—for they alone provide the sustenance adequate to provide life everlasting (Mt. 4:4; Col. 1:5-6; 1 Thess. 2:13; 1 Pet. 1:23-25; James 1:18). Let's ask the obvious question—would you rather receive bread alone and live a few dozen years or would you rather have the message of the Word of God, whereby you may believe and inherit life eternal?

Every time the Lord was tempted to make His own needs and desires the primary focus, He directed Satan to focus solely on God's interests. In His first temptation, Jesus' approach to overcoming His difficulties did not consist of identifying, entertaining and satiating His own felt-needs. He also saw no need to heed any of Satan's advice concerning His medical condition and personal nutrition. Jesus pointed out that God's Word is the ultimate source of relief and satisfaction. In His second temptation, Satan took a page from our Lord's own biblical approach and sought to tempt Him through a manipulation of the Word of God. As often the case, Satan twisted the intent of the passage even though he correctly quoted it. The passage in Psalm 91:11-12 neither encouraged nor commanded anyone to perform such a brazen, foolish and presumptive act suggested by Satan, simply to demonstrate that God is faithful to His Word. God is faithful to His Word simply because God cannot lie. Jesus would not take presumptuous advantage of the Word of God and tempt the Father to intercede in what would have been a brazen act of impudence. Though being the actual and eternal Son of God, Jesus humbly submitted to *not tempting* God; He refused to enhance His own self-worth and bolster His own self-esteem by luxuriating in the instantaneous devoted concern of His angels, as they promptly discharged their duty to protect Him—God in human form. What an ego-boosting self-esteem rocket that would have been—yet, He would have none of it. In His third temptation, the Lord demonstrated His patience and perseverance. According to the Father's timing, Jesus will supremely rule all things when He returns after the Tribulation period to establish the physical throne of David in Jerusalem (Acts 1:6-7). He demonstrated that He loved the Father supremely by submitting to the Father's timing, even though Jesus Christ, as God Almighty, was supremely worthy of all the kingdoms of the world even at that very moment. Jesus Christ would never obtain His rightful place apart from the prophetic timing and biblical methods of His Father. Obedience to His Father's methods and commands is all that consumed the Lord Jesus, even during this intense time of personal temptation.

Dear Lord, even now, please ever instill within each of us, Your all-consuming devotion to the Father!

Irrational Evolutionary Influences Dominate Medicine and Psychology

Unfortunately, the modern scientific perception of the natural revelation of God, His creation, has been obscured by the willful misunderstanding, deception and perversion known as Darwinian Evolution. While many believers will enthusiastically agree with the previous statement concerning evolution's effect on the scientific perception of God's natural revelation, the following statement shall seem incredible, perhaps even ridiculous, to many of those same believers. It is this: *In many churches, Darwinian Evolution itself currently plays a very significant role in the way Christians are being taught and shaped to respond to life's difficulties.*

One usually responds to that statement by either inquiring, "What does one's view of evolution have to do with daily living?" or by stating, "I completely reject the theory of evolution and, therefore, suffer from none of its influences." This section endeavors to reveal the evolutionary background of current medical and psychological thought and expose its influence affecting the way we respond to the challenges of daily life. We need to be aware of its background in order to fully comprehend how evolutionistic thinking, even now, impacts Christians as they respond to life's difficulties. The link between modern psychiatry and Darwinian Evolution is quite significant and readily recognized and accepted by those of the psychiatric community, as is the link between modern medicine and Darwinian Evolution. Since modern medicine is a discipline of modern science, and certainly modern science is a loyal disciple of Darwinian Evolution's basic principles, no one is surprised that modern medicine explains life only in mechanistic, organic, natural terms—the same terms which Darwinian Evolution employs. Therefore, no one should be surprised when modern medicine also seeks to ameliorate the human condition using techniques exclusively developed by such an evolutionistic understanding. Even so, Christians need not disparage modern medicine in its noble endeavor to understand, explain and alleviate all that ails mankind. Yet, knowing its evolutionistic basis and bias, we must ever be vigilant to critically review all its assumptions and recommendations concerning how we are to live our lives and how we are to respond to difficulties. The study of medicine, as with any science, is indeed a lofty, Creator-honoring enterprise when it is properly understood through the lens of Scripture. As a division of modern medicine, psychiatry also receives its basic understanding of the physiological makeup of a human being from medicine's evolutionistic underpinnings.

During the development of psychology through history, as with all endeavors whose modern basis rests upon evolutionistic theories, the concepts of purpose and causality have always been contentious and perplexing subjects. The presence of purpose in nature is especially thorny for evolutionists for it introduces the teleological idea of someone who purposed, designed and caused the contents and order of the Universe. Modern science believes it was primitive man who initially developed the idea of purpose, intention and causality.[1] According to modern science, primitive man recognized purpose in the activities he performed. Primitive man saw that it was his own activities that produced or caused the desired effects based on his own intentions. When primitive man began to analyze the natural forces of his world, such as the apparent rising of the sun, he logically extrapolated from his own personal experiences to explain the natural phenomena. By the exercising of his own will, primitive man purposed to render the desired outcome of his own activities, and in recognition of this situation, he believed there then must also be a "sun-god" that did the same; for, to the primitive man *someone* had to first desire or purpose the apparent rising of the sun, and then, perform or cause that activity. This attribution of conscious life to natural objects is called animism. The natural object, called the sun, performed its activities because a conscious being called a "sun-god" animated it to do so. Science uses such illustrations to also explain how primitive man derived his original concept of a powerful, and more-or-less, personal entity that he then described as a "sun-god." Unfortunately, science's explanation does not take the truth of God's Word into account which reveals a much different and actual explanation for man's belief in deity. Romans 1:19-21 explains the truth of what actually happened this way:

> because that which is known about God is evident within them; for God made it evident to them. For since the creation of the world His invisible attributes, His eternal power and divine nature, have been clearly seen, being understood through what has been made, so that they are without excuse. For even though they knew God, they did not honor Him as God or give thanks, but they became futile in their speculations, and their foolish heart was darkened.

Science teaches that disciplines such as medicine could not progress from man's earlier history to the modern medicine we know today until it freed itself of such animistic theories and primitive ideas of causality based on

---

[1] Franz G. Alexander and Sheldon T. Selesnick, *The History of Psychiatry*, (New York: Harper & Row, 1966), 10.

purpose. Science also believes that it could not develop and mature fully (*i.e.*, evolve) until man replaced his primitive understanding of purpose and causality with a causality described strictly in terms of physics and chemistry, based on the regularity and consistency of impersonal natural laws. Science views favorably the Greek rationalistic philosophers of seventh and sixth centuries B.C. as foundational to scientific thought, but views the Middle Ages as filled with a bias they describe as being religious, magical and demonological. Science teaches that it has only been in the last three hundred years or so that the emphasis and understanding of impersonal natural laws have began to dominate over the religious, magical and demonological influences concerning our understanding of us and our universe. Their rejection of all things religious is truly unfortunate because so many of the early key scientific contributions were made possible by scientists who believed the record of the Bible concerning history and science.[2] Their belief in the veracity of Scripture was intrinsic to their understanding of science and the work such an understanding produced. In contrast, secular natural science views all occurrences in nature as having a cause but not a purpose, for the concept of randomness is at the core of their understanding and randomness embodies the antithesis of purpose.[3] Early, concentrated, medical research seemed to confirm the mechanistic understanding of the human body as an intensely-complicated physical-chemical entity that exclusively functioned by converting chemical energy into mechanical energy, thus explaining the *cause* of how man operates in his environment. But, much to the dismay of many, that same early medical research also appeared to equally assert the "abhorrent and dreaded" concept of *purpose*. Remember, purpose implies design and design implies the inclinations of ... the dreaded Designer who, like any and every inventor, places "unreasonable" and "constricted" expectations upon His design. If there is a Designer, it is incumbent upon those things designed to dutifully respond to the intentions of their proper design. But, if there is no purpose, then there is no design and no dreaded, expectation-laden Designer. Then, all things are a result of randomness which places no expectations upon its progeny, for nothing can be certain if all things are random. Randomness

---

[2] Henry M. Morris, *Men of Science Men of God*, (El Cajon, CA: Master Books, 1988), 8.

[3] That randomness should reside at the core of modern scientific understanding is ironic, at best, and sophomoric, at worst. Both pure and applied scientists today must rigorously and methodically study and apply rules of empiricism, logic and mathematics, none of which exist when randomized. The consistent, verifiable, confirming and repeatable empirical method called, "the Scientific Method," is the bedrock and essence of scientific experimentation. *Randomness* finds, with complete *certainty*, no place, no solace and no intelligent basis, for explaining life.

certainly bodes well for the rebel at heart; conversely, purpose and design bode poorly for those who wish to live strictly as they please, unconstrained by the fetters of Another's expectations.

Nonetheless, early medical research did notice the parts and functions of the human body cooperated sensibly, as if animated by an ultimate objective or purpose—and that purpose was *survival*. Of course, this notice also raised the uncomfortable teleological analogy of the human body with that of man-made machines, which were obviously and intelligently constructed for a purpose. The purpose of the human body was seen to be survival, yet *who* or *what* endowed it with such purpose? Natural science could observe the causes of what happened in nature, but it could not explain mechanistically what or who was purposefully behind those causes. Therefore, medical research itself, in the early 1800's, raised again the detestable specter of *purpose*, a previous threat that science felt it had already faced and defeated, so as to emerge victoriously after the pre-scientific era that was dominated by animism. Science now believes the predicament of purpose, which early medical research unintentionally re-introduced, has been thoroughly eliminated by the timely arrival of the contributions of Charles Darwin (1809-1882) and by an understanding of the concept of stability. Darwin is credited with facilitating the salvation of the biological sciences from a decline toward animism, and its teleological undertones, by his concept of "natural selection by the survival of the fittest." Darwin said survival occurred because of the existence of accidental (*i.e.*, random) changes in a species that are then perpetuated by heredity.[4] Therefore, *no one* was necessary to intelligently guide the process for it was all so very accidental. But alas, *survival* seemed to once again imply the dilemma of *purpose*. However, there was no real need for trepidation within the ranks of evolutionists because science responded to its new dilemma with the concept of stability.

Science believes the concept of stability resolves this quandary, for the principle of stability, or homeostasis, describes how an organism tends to automatically maintain constant conditions necessary for life. Science explains that just as in Newton's first law of motion, where bodies tend to continue stationary or in motion through inertia, the concept of stability thus allows an organism to remain stable within a range of conditions necessary to sustain life. Science says that just as inertia displays no purpose, likewise stability also manifests no purpose. Based on these suppositions, science believes it has forever removed the teleological implications of purpose by

---

[4] Ironically, heredity is governed by statistically-consistent non-random laws.

eliminating purpose altogether, having replaced it with Darwinian evolution and the concept of stability. There—discussion over. Science has spoken with a profound sense of finality, so that forever settles the issue. But, simply saying it is so, does not make it so. The Bible comments on such vacuous suppositions by saying, "For even though they knew God, they did not honor Him as God or give thanks, but they became futile in their speculations, and their foolish heart was darkened. Professing to be wise, they became fools" (Rom. 1:21-22). What extraordinary irony that many men of science today, so blessed with a high degree of intelligence, so highly motivated and so very capable, are seeking knowledge concerning their existence, yet will not be able to fully realize it because they will not honor the Lord as Creator and express their gratitude for His great wisdom. Yet, we must never forget that it is only by the grace of a merciful God that you and I, beloved, have had our hearts enlightened, for once we too were unthankful rebels such as them.

Dear Lord, even now, open the eyes of these men who study the wonders of Your creation, but refuse to perceive Your marvelous wisdom in its rational design!

Falling Prey to Irrational Evolutionistic Thinking- Swallowing the Gap and Day-Age Theories: Hook, Time-Line and Sinker

Within just twenty-five years of Darwinian Evolution's acceptance by the American academic community, virtually every major seminary surrendered to liberalism which denies everything supernatural.[5] Woefully, there is a significant segment of the modern conservative church that has permitted the inclusion of heresy, such as Darwinian Evolution, to be not only tolerated, but enthusiastically taught and embraced. It is all-too-often taught as fact, if not in its entirety then certainly in part, by church pastors and seminarians. There are, no doubt, some within that segment who deeply love the Lord with great sincerity. But to be certain, we should not allow someone's sincerity and devotion to be the basis for determining truth. The truth we seek concerning cosmogony, the origin of the Universe, and of man's current condition is derived only when such information is confirmed and reconciled with divine written revelation.

So far, we have observed the conclusions which science and modern medicine have developed concerning man's origin and condition based on their evolutionistic thinking. Is it possible that we Dispensationalists could ever find ourselves agreeing with their unbiblical conclusions? Being the

---

[5] James D. Owen, *Christian Psychology's War on God's Word: The Victimization of the Believer*, (Santa Barbara, CA: EastGate Publishers, 1993), 12.

literal, objective, level-headed, right-thinking, fundamental people that we are, surely we would never find ourselves wedded to any such inane evolutionistic beliefs, right? After all, we need only take simply and literally the Bible's record of man's origin and condition and then we should avoid finding ourselves coming to any of their evolutionistic conclusions, right? Actually, the answer is ... yes. However, that would be true only if we would constantly interpret the Bible both literally and consistently without fail. "Constantly" is the limiting factor, for though we make such claims, part of our history yet belies our inconsistent confession. Every time we relinquish any position of divine truth taught in the Word of God, we should expect the adversary of God to capitalize upon such high treason. Dispensational history reveals that we are indeed susceptible to aberrant forms of subtle evolutionistic thinking. Two examples will reveal how easily, yet sincerely, we as believers, fall prey to the satanic influence of evolutionistic thinking.

Our first example where well-meaning earlier and current Dispensationalists evince a propensity to relinquish literal truth is observed in those who teach and believe what is called the Gap Theory.[6] This theory was first introduced around 1814 by non-Dispensational Scottish theologian, Thomas Chalmers (1780-1874).[7] Whereas belief in the Gap Theory by some Dispensationalists today does not necessarily make them a card-carrying Darwinian Evolutionist, it does set a dangerous precedence of allowing the scientific community to define and set the level of the "bar of facts," with which theology is now expected to reconcile and mold its understanding of the Bible. It should be the other way around. In the early 1800's, the latest, leading, so-called "scientific conclusion" of that day, known as uniformitarianism,[8] stated the Earth was very, very old, having undergone gradual change over millions of years. Today the "scientific" number of the Earth's age has somehow grown from "millions" to almost five billion years.[9]

---

[6] In its simplest form, the Gap Theory states there is an undetermined amount of time existing between Gen. 1:1 and 1:2. God initially created the world in verse one. Between verses one and two, there existed an earth inhabited by angelic creatures, dinosaurs and a race of pre-Adamite men. Lucifer, one of the angelic creatures, fell into sin so God destroyed that "first" earth with a flood. Verse two is a description of the results of God's judgment on the "first" earth. The balance of the first chapter is the literal six-day "re-creation" of the world we know today.

[7] Kent Hovind and Stephen Lawwell, *The Gap Theory*, (Pensacola, FL: Creation Science Evangelism), 4.

[8] Uniformitarianism is the theory that all geological processes, strata and topography can be explained from observing current geologic forces and that such forces operate uniformly and gradually over the entire time of the Earth's existence. It can be summed up in the phrase, "The present is the key to the past."

[9] (For full effect, the reading of this footnote must be preceded by a flurry of majestic trumpet blasts, then followed by a reading in an authoritative and dignified voice): As of October 9, 1997, the official United States Geological Survey reported the current age of the Earth and our Solar System to be 4.54 billion

How is that number able to spontaneously increase or generate? Spontaneous generation was originally an ancient and evolutionistic explanation concerning the origin of microbiological life. The error of spontaneous generation was soundly debunked by a Bible-believing scientist, Louis Pasteur. Perhaps, its use is now plausible in describing the age of the Earth. After all, the evolutionistic age of the Earth, as assessed numerically by the scientific community, is increasing so rapidly that perhaps even the numbers themselves are appearing spontaneously as if by spontaneous generation. And apparently nothing, including the upward spiraling age of the Earth, is secure from the ravaging influences of inflation.

Sadly, in the church's rush to assuage the sharp attacks of science upon Scripture, some had accommodated and harmonized this latest and greatest theory of geology by proposing the Gap Theory and the Day-Age Theory. The Day-Age Theory states that the six days of creation in Genesis chapter 1 are not literal twenty-four-hour days, but are instead, vast expanses of time.[10] This theory possesses only one reason for its existence—making vast quantities of time available to evolutionists. It is an attempt to account for immense quantities of time to account for and explain Earth's geologic features and to accommodate the vast quantities of time the biological evolutionists claim is necessary for biological evolution to occur. These theories were presented by well-meaning, sincere Bible teachers so that, perhaps, fellow biblical literalists would not be perceived as pre-scientific, unsophisticated, country bumpkins who were completely out of step with the refined, cutting-edge contemplations of evolutionistic men. The irony is that some of the evolutionists these Bible teachers relied upon for "scientific truth" actually hated God and relished the thought of refuting His holy record with their theory of evolutionary origins, thereby tarnishing the reliability of God's Word.[11] If God's Word was proven to be unreliable according to its scientific content, might its revelation concerning the moral condition, divine expectations and the fate of man also be unreliable? This undermining of the Bible's authority eventually resulted in the removal of its practical expository teachings from mainline churches in Europe and the American Northeast only one half-dozen decades later. Most Dispensationalists, including myself, have found themselves to be unwitting students of the Gap Theory and Day-Age Theory, through the teachings of

---

years with an uncertainty of less than 1 percent. (Should we thank our lucky stars for such accuracy?) The age of our Milky Way Galaxy is from 11 to 13 billion years and the age of the Universe is 10 to 15 billion years. I suppose 5 billion years is apparently only an inconsequential spread of time.

[10] Weston W. Fields, *Unformed and Unfilled*, ((Collinsville, IL: Burgener Enterprises, 1994), 165-166.

[11] Henry M. Morris, *The Long War Against God*, (Grand Rapids: Baker Book House Company, 1989), 99.

the prominent Dispensational teacher, C. I. Scofield, as a result of studying his very profitable work, *The Scofield Reference Bible*.[12] Another prominent teacher of these theories was Clarence Larkin through his work entitled, *Dispensational Truth*. Lewis Sperry Chafer also promoted the Gap Theory in his various volumes of *Systematic Theology*.[13] I take no comfort in pointing out the theological shortcomings of men who would, by comparison of spiritual maturity, Christ-like devotion and biblical acumen, simply prove me to be little more than a *rank Philistine*. However, one hundred and fifty years ago, a theological crossroad placed Christianity's belief in the literal teachings of the Creation account at loggerheads with the latest darlings of the scientific world—uniformitarianism and Darwinian Evolution. Christianity yielded valuable ground to the cause of evolution by not vigorously opposing it with tough, meticulous, exegetical exposition. Christians must now resolve to never again be intimidated by the gleaming white coats of the science laboratory, by the lofty titles, by the impressive addresses or by the ivy-covered walls of secular or sacred academia when it comes to exposing and confronting error. We Dispensationalists bear certain responsibility for the part we played in promoting an evolutionistic theory that was unscriptural, unscientific, unnecessary and that resulted in a dangerous compromise of what God's Word clearly teaches.

Dear Lord, even now, we thank You for those men, yet imperfect like us, who went before us and endeavored to guard the treasure that is Your Word. Keep us ever humble and enamored only by the truth expressed in Your Word, for it speaks of You and Your great majesty and wisdom!

Falling Prey to Irrational Evolutionistic Thinking, Again! - Psychology and the Abuse of Psychotropic Drugs

The second example that reveals how easily we continue to fall prey to the satanic influence of evolutionistic thinking is exhibited by our uncritical embrace of the conclusions medical research has reached concerning the appropriateness and efficacy of psychotropic drug use to solve mental and emotional issues such as fear, anxiety and despair. A psychotropic drug[14] is any drug that influences the thinking ability of the mind. It is also called a "mind-altering" drug. It can be legal or illegal, prescribed or non-prescribed,

---

[12] C. I. Scofield, ed., *The Scofield Reference Bible*, (New York: Oxford University Press, 1945), 3-4, 776.

[13] Lewis Sperry Chafer, *Systematic Theology*, 4-volume edition, (Grand Rapids: Kregel Publications, 1976), II:39; VI:67.

[14] The following trademark brand names are only a few examples of prescribed psychotropic drugs: Abilify, Adderall, Clozaril, Cymbalta, Effexor, Lexapro, Luvox, Paxil, Prozac, Remeron, Risperdal, Ritalin, Serzone, Thorazine, Valium, Wellbutrin, Xanax, Zoloft and Zyprexa. There are many, many more.

for such considerations are really only political distinctions. The one abiding characteristic of a psychotropic, or mind-altering, drug is that it has the capacity to change the way we think and process reality.

By the end of the nineteenth century, science had proven to itself that all phenomena of life could now be understood in mechanistic natural processes described strictly in terms of physics and chemistry, based on the regularity and consistency of impersonal natural laws. The great existential chasm between inanimate mineral and the animate organism was now considered sufficiently bridged through those same physical and chemical processes governed by such consistent, impersonal, natural laws. Science's *certain* belief that highly-evolved *random* atoms somehow *randomly* evolved into inanimate *random* rocks, and that highly-evolved *random* inanimate rocks somehow *randomly* evolved into animate *random* man, naturally (or is it, *randomly?)* leads science, and modern medicine, to their *certain* conclusion that the driving influence which directs man must be his chemical composition—which is, by the way, ironically recognized to be consistent and orderly—*not at all random*. It would also lead to the modern medical conclusion, one which is thoroughly evolutionistic at its core, that *since* man is the sum of his chemicals, it must be the presence of an imbalance of his chemicals that produces emotional dysfunction. Now, brain chemistry, not personal choices and responsibilities, becomes the focus of solving all of man's "mental health" challenges ranging from boredom, fear, anxiety, depression and Lottery Stress to addictions and disorders of shopping, stealing, gambling, the Stock Market, Star Trek, the Internet, over-eating and under-eating. (With respect to the last malady mentioned, and from all outward appearances, perhaps our society has very few of those victims actually within its ranks). Medical science believes man is not and should not—no rather, man *cannot* now be responsible for a condition caused by a chemical imbalance, a condition now considered a certified and therefore insurance-billable medical disease, because man is only a hapless victim of miscreant neuro-chemicals.

The materialistic, mechanistic theory of evolution has left us with an American culture that accepts little to no personal responsibility for the way it thinks and acts. Our society places few expectations on personal thinking and its corresponding behavior and places even fewer consequences when such prove aberrant or egregious; therefore, little incentive exists to accept personal responsibility. Evolution teaches we are nothing more than a highly-evolved group of amoral, random atoms that somehow chemically interact to produce thoughts of consciousness. Materialistic evolution does not believe the immaterial part of man—the mind, the soul—even exists for it has to be material, hence chemical, to exist. According to the definition of the two Greek root-words that combine to yield our word, "psychology," we may state their combined meaning as the, "study of the soul." Again, one of the greatest ironies perhaps, is that modern psychologists do not actually believe at all, in the soul of man.[15] Their scientific academic is evolutionistic at its root, teaching them that man is the sum of mechanistic natural processes described strictly in terms of physics and chemistry, based on the regularity and consistency of impersonal natural laws. Because, in fact, of that very reason, the study of consciousness, for many years, was not considered important:

> Since consciousness is such a defining feature of human life, one might expect the study of conscious awareness to lie at the heart of psychology. However, this is not the case. The topic was a prominent issue for the first psychologists, but it did not retain its prominence for long because it is difficult to study and is difficult to reconcile with materialistic views of human nature. Materialists deny the existence of a spiritual realm or human spirits, assert that all life came into being by chance through evolution, depict humans as highly evolved animals, and believe that all human capacities arise solely from the physical operations of the brain. Attributes like self-awareness, human choice, and conscious agency are difficult to explain with a reductionistic model of this type. For these reasons the study of consciousness was largely neglected until the late 1960s.[16]

The human brain is a very complex physical organ—but it is not the mind, the soul, the spirit or the essence that makes a person, a person. It is estimated that the human brain is composed of 100,000,000,000 (100 billion) nerve cells called neurons; 500,000,000,000 to 1,000,000,000,000 (500 billion to 1 trillion) support cells called neuroglia; and an estimated 100,000,000,000,000 (100 trillion) connections between them, called synapses.[17] I have chosen to express these values numerically, as well as textually, because such large numbers are much too easily expressed by simple words, without sufficient comprehension of their enormity. Such extraordinary complexity at the microscopic, cellular level should give one pause, *at this very moment*, to reflect upon and worship the great God that created such an organ for the sheer benefit of man. Yet, it is the very same man who abuses such a magnificent organ and dishonors his Creator by

---

[15] Henry M. Morris, 33.
[16] *Baker Encyclopedia of Psychology and Counseling*, 2nd ed., ed. David G. Benner and Peter C. Hill, s.v. "Consciousness," by Elizabeth L. Hillstrom, (Grand Rapids: Baker Books, 1999), 255.
[17] Grace E. Jackson, *Rethinking Psychiatric Drugs*, (Bloomington, IN: AuthorHouse, 2005), 44.

claiming only a serendipitous, impersonal, and indiscriminate accident brought his brain to fruition.

The human mind God created is immaterial. It is a created thing, yet we are not able to empirically assess and study it in the same way we do other created objects that are composed of physical and chemical substance. We understand very little how the brain and the mind interrelate precisely, but one thing is certain, many of the same physical and chemical things that effect the brain also have a profound effect upon the mind. I am herein speaking of the mind's ability to function as a source of the intellect, the will and the emotions. Physical and chemical influences that impact the brain, such as pain, sleep deprivation or alcoholic beverages, commonly affect one or more of the mind's functions at the same time. Physical injury to the brain will exert a profound negative effect on our mind's memory and psychotropic, mind-altering drugs will affect the way we think and process reality. Thinking is critical, for as a man, "thinks within himself, so he is" (Prov. 23:7). The "real me" is how I think; I can say anything to anyone I want and deceive them for a while, but should one be able to read my thoughts, they would be able to truly assess the "real me." The believer relies on his mind to assist in understanding doctrine so as to overcome sin in his life. Paul writes, "... So then, on the one hand I myself with my mind am serving the law of God, ..." (Rom. 7:25). David writes, "Your word I have treasured in my heart, That I may not sin against You" (Ps. 119:11). Anything, whether it is someone's teachings or a medically-prescribed drug, that has the potential to affect how a Christian thinks, must first be critically analyzed through the lens of Scripture. A given technique may certainly be legal; a certain technique may even be effective to some degree; but, neither advantage necessarily means that such a technique is appropriate for Christians who are seeking to honor the Lord's methods. Naturally, the use of illegal drugs is an obvious "no-brainer," (*i.e.*, no-go in-brain).

There are some things about the existence of human beings that are only revealed in Scripture, and the immaterial aspect of man is one example. The ideas of good and evil, of sin and righteousness, and of eternity are *concepts* of immateriality just as the mind, the soul and the spirit of man are created *things* of immateriality. Science can tell us nothing about the concepts of good and evil, of sin and righteousness, and of eternity; science can also tell us nothing about the created immaterial entities we call the mind, the soul or the spirit of man. We should not be surprised that God has bound up such knowledge exclusively in His Word. It is God's Word alone that reveals the true origin of man, of his past, present and future problems and predicaments, of his obligation to His Creator God and any remedial adjustments that man requires should he fail in those obligations. God has reserved for Himself the dispensing of truth concerning immaterial entities, whether they are concepts or created things, for He alone can reveal the truth of such for they cannot be empirically or experimentally assessed; they must be spiritually assessed and Biblically revealed.

The Holy Spirit has graciously entered man's existence and has revealed God to man through revelation, inspiration and illumination (1 Cor. 2:10-16). In the first and second chapters of First Corinthians, the Apostle Paul informs us that immaterial or spiritual concepts such as foolishness, justification, shame, wisdom, righteousness, sanctification, redemption, predestination, glory, and that spiritual entities such as the mind of Christ cannot be sensibly or empirically assessed or measured (1st Cor. 2:9-13). Again, God has reserved for Himself the dispensing of truth concerning immaterial concepts such as sin. Sin is known because of the special revelation that only God provides (Rom. 7:7b). Since immaterial concepts and entities are revealed by God in His Word, only He can accurately assess the cause, the condition and then the cure, when they go awry.

Dispensationalism again stands at a new theological crossroad with the science of our culture. This time the science at hand does not specifically concern geological or biological origins—but it does concern their evolutionistic influence upon other disciplines, such as psychology and medicine. I fear the church's former proclivity to promptly capitulate to the pressures and intimidation of the scientific community, as represented by our former and even current support of the evolutionistic Gap Theory, only demonstrates that we are still yet susceptible to further compromise with evolutionistic issues. Such compromise occurs because we refuse to think biblically as we critically analyze our life condition, assuming of course, that we will at all shoulder the personal and corporate responsibility to critically analyze our life condition in the first place. I fear the siren song of our preoccupation and enamorment of all things scientific and academic will predispose us to reject again the simple truth found in the Word of God and seek solutions from "broken cisterns that can hold no water" (Jer. 2.13).

This time, the compromise at hand involves solutions proposed by the psychological and medical profession and it concerns how we are to respond to life's difficulties. Knowing that we are indeed capable of embracing and promoting unintended heresy, will we now renew our commitment to honor the literal teachings of the Word of God and trust wholly in its revelation concerning man's condition and its solution to man's problems? Will we eschew "oppositions of science falsely so called" (KJV), and endeavor to boldly seek and speak the truth that honors the Lord in its methods? One would certainly hope for that encouraging response, but, Dispensationalists have all-too-often considered this second example of evolutionistic thinking in an uncritical and indiscriminating way because it is considered "medical" and therefore considered to be beyond the scope of theology. Such dereliction of spiritual duty and unfounded capitulation, *once again*, of literal, objective truth to appease subjective, hypothetical, theoretical, evolutionistic musings has indeed occurred with respect to modern medicine's favorite solution to maintaining "mental health" and correcting any perceived malfunctions. Their favorite solution is the ubiquitous, at least in Western culture, and ever-profitable chemical pill which, of course, must be prescribed by medical doctors who rely heavily on the advice of the inherently unselfish and unbiased pharmaceutical industry.

Some would say that Scripture does not address the use of modern mind-altering drugs and therefore it cannot pass judgment upon the tools of modern medicine. At one time, blood-letting by leeches was considered state-of-the-art by what was then considered modern medicine. Yet, the "scientifically out-dated" and "medically irrelevant" Bible simply stated the "life was in the blood." Perhaps they should have kept more of the life-sustaining blood in the veins of their patients? As to the charge that the Scripture has nothing to say concerning mind-altering, psychotropic drugs, we will have much to say later. Others have said that medical doctors represent another class of authority to which believers are expected to biblically submit, therefore, we must utilize these drugs as our doctors advise. Fortunately, the Bible is very clear to whom we owe submission, and medical personnel, though very helpful and appreciated, are not on that list. Just because much of the advice we receive from them may be expedient does not mean that all of it is appropriate. When it comes to critically evaluating the mental, emotional and psychological difficulties we face, Christians are expected to seek the wisdom of the Lord found in His Word to explain and mitigate such difficulties. Because modern medicine derives its understanding of the composition of human beings from its evolutionistic education, it views most cures in a physical-chemical methodology.

To be quite candid, the universal image projected by the medical profession is quite impressive, quite compelling and quite confidence-instilling. Medical professionals certainly possess a long legacy laden with much-deserved goodwill. Their beneficent legacy continues today; but, its many accomplishments tend to lull the culture into believing everything it does must certainly be appropriate, therefore, there is no need to question it. Today's drugs are administered in an antiseptic and clinical environment. They are efficiently formulated in a compact, concentrated pill or caplet design; they are professionally packaged and marketed with meticulous care. Highly educated and respected men prescribe them, and as a result, very few Christians biblically analyze the ramifications of this issue. Whereas, because of many former and current triumphs over man's pathological disease problems using drugs, appropriate gratitude and honor is indeed given to the noble causes of medicine and pharmacy—disciplines that exist to alleviate the physical problems and diseases of beings created in the image of God. However, Christians must not assume that the relevance of medicine and pharmacy necessarily applies to *every* human condition or that their current expertise in problem-solving necessarily transcends *every* field of endeavor they choose to pursue. It just might be that when it comes to effectively solving the mental problems of man, they possess no actual solution for they are already hamstrung by their evolutionistic understanding of a problem that cannot be truly solved through natural, mechanistic, chemical means. For instance, concerning the use of psychotropic drugs and the "diseases" that supposedly exist for such drugs to treat, Fred A. Baughman, M.D., had this to say in the dedication section of his excellent book entitled, *The ADHD Fraud: How Psychiatry Makes "Patients" of Normal Children*:

> This book is dedicated to parents and children everywhere—all of them told the "chemical imbalance" lie and drugged. None can imagine a betrayal so deceitful, so complete, by educators, psychologists, psychiatrists, pediatricians, neurologists, family practitioners, the pharmaceutical industry, the White House, the Senate, the House of Representatives and all agents and agencies of government. When a child has been killed or maimed by a drug, made a drug addict, a crazed killer, or a suicide, or when a parent sees custody of their child—their flesh and blood—given the parent who plays psychiatry's game, or to the court itself—which always does—they awake, too late, to the fact that the betrayal has been complete, that there was never a disease to treat, never a "chemical imbalance" to balance—that ADHD and all psychiatric "diseases" were a total, 100% fraud all along.[18]

Just in case what Dr. Baughman said was not sufficiently clear, and should there be any doubt, the following excerpt is from his testimony given on June 2, 2004 to the Education and Health Standing Committee of the Parliament of Western Australia:

---

[18] Fred A. Baughman, Jr., *The ADHD Fraud*, (Victoria, BC: Trafford Publishing, 2006), iii.

By now there should be no doubt that my message is simple: that no child or adult said to have a psychiatric "disorder"/ "illness"/ "syndrome"/ "disease"/ "chemical imbalance" has an abnormality/disease in a true medical sense. Instead, all of them are physically/mentally normal. Further, it is this lie/perversion of science and medicine, invented and exported by US psychiatry in collusion with the pharmaceutical industry, that is the linchpin of the still-burgeoning, world-wide epidemic of psychiatric drugging/poisoning. Nor is this a matter of belief, consensus, or opinion, rather it has to do with the fact that nowhere in the scientific/medical literature of the world does replicated proof exist that ADHD or any psychiatric disorder is a physical abnormality/disease.[19]

Consider now the following excerpt from *Church Leaders Intelligence Report* that was entitled, *The World's Most Depressed Nation*:

It's hard to believe, but Americans are the unhappiest people on earth. That is the conclusion of a new study by the World Health Organization and the Harvard Medical School, which found that 9.6 percent of Americans suffer from depression or bipolar disorder? the highest rate of the 14 nations surveyed. Our "Prozac nation" has a greater percentage of depressed people than war-torn Lebanon (6.6 percent); job-starved Mexico (4.8 percent); carefree, hedonistic Italy (3.8 percent); and overworked, socially rigid Japan (3.1 percent). And how's this for a paradox: Nigeria, a land of desperate poverty, rampant corruption and violent tribal conflict, had the lowest depression rate of all? just 0.8 percent. How can this be? One possibility is that when your life is a struggle for clean water and adequate food, you don't have time to indulge in existential despair. In New York, on the other hand, a lawyer making $200,000 a year may find himself "depressed" if he doesn't make partner in his mid-30s. It may also be that in less modern societies, people find comfort and meaning in their families, their religion and their cultural traditions.[20]

This should raise the question, "Why is Western culture in general, and American culture specifically, so susceptible to depression?" After all, all humans share the same genetic code and are composed of the same organic compounds. Is American molecular and genetic makeup really different from that of other humans that inhabit this planet? The answer is no—we are, after all, human beings every one. But, Americans have ready access to all the things that make life necessary, even pleasurable, in excess. Of all people on earth, we should be the most carefree, for our struggle to survive pales in comparison to the rest of the world's inhabitants. If we are all made of the same chemicals, if through the "concept of stability" we studied earlier we all tend "to automatically maintain constant conditions necessary

---

[19] Ibid., 218.
[20] Excerpt from an email newsletter from Gary D. Foster, ed., *Church Leaders Intelligence Report* (Vista, CA: Church Leaders, 10-31-2007) referencing an article by Vince Siciliano in *Wall Street's Journal's The Week Magazine*, 3-03-2007.

for life" as an essential condition of existence, then why do we Americans respond so poorly to our veritable and comparative Shangri-La, our Paradise, our virtual utopian state of Nirvana? After all, we already have all the conditions necessary for survival, for existence, for life. Why can't we get our elements to behave? Which element deserves the spanking this time? Is it that noxious Sulfur? Irritating Chlorine? Air-headed, indolent Oxygen? Excessively-liberal and permissive Californium? (OK, delete the last element—it is not naturally found in the human body, though you can certainly see it has the potential to be a real problem, so, please be vigilant.)

That author's assessment is accurate. It is difficult to be too wrapped up in yourself and focused on your own petty problems when your daily life is simply filled with trying to make provision for the survival of you and your family, and when some discretionary time is available, it is spent with others still. Part of the answer to our culture's depression lies in (1) a thankless heart that has been conditioned to expect more and ever more, and (2) a heart full of its own desires due to a view of self that stems from an over-inflated self-esteem ("you are so very special!"), and an exaggerated self-potential ("you can be anything you want!"). Well, I have disappointing news for you: You're not and you can't. I suspect the reason other parts of Western culture have not approached America's self-imposed levels of depression, may be because they have not been sufficiently conditioned (brainwashed) by media exposure and the medical profession to alter their thinking concerning the function of personal responsibility in this matter. However, once additional media advertising from pharmaceutical companies and changes in clinical practice from medical peer pressure are placed upon others of Western culture, they will eventually succumb to America's weak-minded example of shirk-a-'sponsibility.

This particular psychiatric dilemma of where to properly place responsibility was foreseen over four decades ago by psychiatrist Franz Alexander, M.D.:

> Whatever the cause of faulty brain chemistry may be, the new conviction is that the disturbed mind can now be cured by drugs and that the patient himself as a person no longer needs to try to understand the source of his troubles and master them by improved self-knowledge.[21]

Not only does that person need no longer try to understand the source of his troubles and master them, now he need no longer endure the stigma of

---

[21] Franz G. Alexander and Sheldon T. Selesnick, 14.

having a "psychological disorder." Apparently, most patients and families prefer to consider the problem to be physical rather than psychological.[22] The reason given is that a "psychological problem" implies the individual is weak, uninitiated, and unmotivated to solve his own problems. It may also imply that the associated family was equally unwilling to behave properly to avoid, perhaps, the development of the problem in the first place. Additionally, when a problem is described as biochemical, there is no need to divulge any selfish personal details to the therapist and so it is easier to believe the problem can be solved by the impersonal pill.

Dear Lord, we praise Your great wisdom for creating us, for we are indeed fearfully and wonderfully made by You and You alone.

Alcohol- The Original Psychotropic Drug

When discussing the scriptural propriety of administering mind-altering drugs to another for improving their behavior or for enhancing one's ability to cope with the exigencies and vicissitudes of life, the passage of Proverbs 31:1-9 must be addressed. It is my contention, that the legally-prescribed mind-altering drugs that proliferate within our society are nothing really new to mankind. It is just that now, in convenient pill form, prescribed by professionals, popped by the willing and paid for by a third party, it is so much more, well, ... chic. The use of today's psychotropic drugs is really only a variation of the world's oldest mind-altering drug—alcohol.[23] Eventually, someone will make the connection between the former use of alcohol and the current use of today's psychotropic drugs and will attempt to make a Biblical justification for the "moderate and appropriate" use of today's psychotropic, mind-altering drugs. We will see that such interpretation is really only eisegesis by those intent upon justifying the use of mind-altering drugs in a culture that is already virtually devoid of personal responsibility. Their interpretation would go something like this: (1) moderate, appropriate use of alcoholic beverages is condoned and even encouraged in the Bible; (2) alcohol is a psychotropic drug; (3) therefore, the moderate, appropriate use of today's psychotropic drugs is also to be condoned, even encouraged. One major problem: *It is precisely the psychotropic effects of alcohol which the Bible forbids and seeks to avoid.*

Virtually all Christians agree the Bible forbids ordinary drunkenness and many see that ordinary daily use of wine was part of man's routine in

---

[22] Elliot S. Valenstein, *Blaming the Brain*, (New York: The Free Press, 1998), 219.

[23] Frank Minirth, Paul Meier, and Stephen Arterburn, *Miracle Drugs*, (Nashville, TN: Thomas Nelson Publishers, 1995), 245.

many parts of the world for much of man's existence. The extent of the alcoholic content of that wine is widely debated, yet, given the environmental conditions, it appears that the "fruit of the vine" was alcoholic to some extent, unless it was consumed while freshly pressed during the short harvest season. For many Christians, and certainly this is also the case for most unbelievers, the questions asked concerning the use of psychotropic drugs are usually, "Is it necessary, and if so, is it effective— will it work?" Of course, that assumes the rarity that someone will even think analytically and critically about life situations in the first place, resulting in the inquiry. Yet, the question for believers should never be, "Are psychotropic drugs truly effective in mitigating the effects of anxiety, depression and fear?" but rather, "Is their use the acceptable, God-glorifying response to life's difficulties and trials?" We have observed previously in this chapter that there are significant troubling questions being raised by the medical experts concerning the safety and efficacy of today's mind-altering drugs of choice. In fact, an ever-growing number of very concerned medical doctors dispute whether there is any genetic, organic disease actually associated whatever with most issues of "mental illness" to begin with.[24] Naturally, if this is true, and many are coming to this conclusion, the discussion of these very dangerous drugs as a cure is nothing more than time wasted. Therefore, it cannot be maintained that these modern secular treatments are truly efficacious for the purpose they intend. However, just for the sake of argument, let's assume that psychotropic drugs may be effective for the use they intend (*yet, in fact, they are not!*). (Even given this purely imaginary situation, I cannot allow even my hypothetical idea to be presented without stating again that such an idea is patently false). Does such efficacy become the basis for their use in the church, in believers? I say that even if they were effective, and they are not, they do not pass the "glory of God" test. Truly there are methods employed in the world, by those who do not love the Lord, which are effective in what they seek to accomplish. The effective outcome of such methods does not necessarily condone their use. Such methods are employed for pragmatic reasons—not scriptural, God-honoring reasons. For example, gambling may produce profits that can be used to support missions outreach, but is such a successful undertaking glorifying to the Lord? There are situations where some techniques may be effective, but not appropriate. The medical use of mind-altering drugs for the purpose of treating anxiety and depression is neither effective nor appropriate.

---

[24] Timothy Scott, *America Fooled*, (Victoria, TX: Argo Publishing, 2006), 46-49.

Rational Advice Rendered to Royalty: Proverbs 31:1-9

The context of this passage concerns the ability of a king to effectively lead his people by judging righteously and by defending the rights of the afflicted and needy. Although it speaks concerning the king's relationship to alcohol, it does not attempt to exhaust every aspect of that relationship. The specific relationship it seeks to deal with is that effect alcohol has upon the ability of a king to remember the laws of the land and to competently apply them to a juridical circumstance. Clearly the context is intimating the deleterious and derogatory effects that alcohol has on the brain in processing information. What is being discussed in this passage is the effect of intoxication on good judgment and it is not attempting to exhaust every aspect concerning the use of alcoholic beverages. It only mentions two polar opposites, two contradictory situations where intoxication occurs. Rather than giving wine to the king and allowing wine to affect his judgment, it would be far better to give it to the one who is perishing and beyond all hope; the one who has no need for his analytical mental faculty whatever; the one who has no responsibilities. The king is not to open his mouth to imbibe that which would clutter and cloud his mind, but was rather to open his mouth and use his voice to assist those who have no voice; those who are in need of his thoughtful skills in determining justice and equity. It was common for condemned criminals to be given wine prior to their execution.[25] The intoxicating drink was not given in order to help the condemned thoughtfully process his circumstances. It was given to make him thoughtless, not thoughtful. Wine appears here to be appropriately dispensed to those who are in the position of having no responsibility to think clearly. It is for those who are in no position to evaluate their circumstances and come up with real solutions based on sound, valid judgment. Intoxicating influences are best suited to those who are in a position to evaluate nothing, because their circumstance is one that will not improve. No amount of thoughtful evaluation and consideration will improve their terminal lot. This context does not include the person who is having "a bad day." It is for those who have no hope, for their position is terminal—they are dying.

In this context, when the word "poverty" is used, as in, "Let him drink and forget his poverty," it means, in effect, "let him drink and forget he has nothing left to live for; help him forget the trouble that he is now in." This person who is offered the intoxicating effects of alcohol no longer has to think through his problems. On the other hand, the king cannot afford to

---

[25] Walter C. Kaiser, Jr., Peter H. Davids, F. F. Bruce, & Manfred T. Brauch, *Hard Sayings of the Bible*, one-volume edition, (Downer's Grove, IL: InterVarsity Press, 1996), 291.

take such an approach to his circumstance for he is not dying—he is expected to think, to evaluate and to adjudicate. The poverty referred to here is not financial difficulty. This proverb is not to be used to excuse the all-to-often indiscriminate use of alcohol to forget the routine financial troubles and social perplexities we face. Its recommendation here is meant to allow the mind-altering effects be applied to those who are dying. In reality, the routine troubles, fears and anxieties of life that we face should be faced, not with intoxication, but with analyzation. They should be faced, not by a retreat into a position of not thinking and not evaluating, but by motivating us to think our way through our problem. In this context, alcohol is meant as an escape from thinking and evaluating, not a means to an answer. To suggest that a mind-altering drug will somehow improve the situations we daily face is simple and literal madness. There has never been a time when intoxication improved or ameliorated the bitterness or the financial poverty of life. The hangover that follows such a drunken bout has done nothing to help the situation. If anything, financial poverty is a common *result* stemming from the abuse of alcohol; alcoholic abuse is not a solution to cure financial poverty. You cannot cure financial poverty or bitterness by intoxication. When the hangover clears, you are still in the same, or worse, situation you were in before. Often the situation is made worse with alcohol because it does cloud our thinking and it minimizes our inhibitions to do things we otherwise would not do. Because of reduced inhibitions, we say things and do things we often regret and they often have dire consequences. None of that appears to be the answer to financial poverty. The context here is not financial poverty, but terminal trouble. It could be phrased: "Give intoxicating drink to the one whose soul is bitter and near death; allow him to drink and forget his troubled situation in which there is absolutely nothing left in which to hope."

All too often in literature explaining this and other passages in the Bible, we are told that the immoderate use of alcohol produces a favorable situation of stimulation and conviviality. Yet, in reality, the alcohol-produced euphoria is very temporary and quickly leads to a state of drunkenness where the mental faculties are diminished, not stimulated. That is one of the reasons why alcohol is designated by the medical profession, not as a stimulant, but as a depressant. Such effects only come when alcohol consumption reaches the point of abuse. Some commentaries have actually viewed this so-called beneficial, stimulative, effects of abundant drinking as favorable and convivial because the phrase "were merry" is used in the King James Version to translate the Hebrew word *shakar* (Gen. 43:34, KJV). Yet, "were merry" should rather be translated "drunken" or "drank freely," as in the New American Standard Bible. With the exception of Song of Solomon 5:1, in every other instance this Hebrew word is used in the Bible, it refers to a state of drunkenness whose effects are most undesirable.

The use of it in Song of Solomon 5:1 refers metaphorically to drinking deeply into the effects of love-making—to be abundantly drunk and under the influence of the physical act of love.[26] The idea is this, "You know how greatly influenced you are with the effects of abundant drink; in like manner, allow yourself to become abundantly influenced by the effects of making love with your wife." In this analogy it does not seek to indicate anything concerning the undesired effects of abundant drink, only the fact that abundant drink, like love, has a certain pronounced effect upon you. It assumes the fact that abundant use of alcohol will have an effect upon you. By analogy, this passage applies the certainty of one pronounced effect to another. In this case, the effect is desirable because it is not from abundantly consuming wine, where one would get physically drunk, but the effect is desirable for the thing that brings you under its complete influence is the love you have for your wife—not the wine you abundantly consumed.

Alcohol does produce a fleeting euphoria, yet, could it be, the Lord gave mankind the temporary effect of euphoria, as a kind of forewarning, a caution, so that we might, by its presence, take note that we are progressing over the line of moderation? Far too many assumptions have been made by many concerning any perceived benefits that inebriation brings. Such are often merely anecdotal and based solely upon the experience of that particular culture. Just because our culture values "coppin' a buzz" does not mean we are to live under its effects. Some say the inebriating affects of the depressant, alcohol, will make the person merry, glad or cheerful and therefore it must be viewed favorably. The following passages will help us to understand that such is not the case. In Judges 9:13 and Ps. 104:15 it is said that wine cheers man and God, yet neither passage demands that they be drunk in that attitude of gladdening. The Hebrew word *samach* that is translated "cheers" (Judg. 9:13), "glad" (Ps. 104:15; Zech. 10:7) and "merry" (Ecc. 10:19) simply "denotes being glad or joyful."[27] There is no connotation or demand of anything untoward. The heart can be gladdened and made merry from this alcoholic wine simply from the sweet refreshment that it brings to the body long before the temporary effects of euphoria occur in the

---

[26] Henry M. Morris, *The Remarkable Wisdom of Solomon*, (Green Forest, AR: Master Books, 2001), 46.

[27] R. Laird Harris, Gleason L. Archer, Jr., Bruce K. Waltke, eds., s.v. "2268, *samah*," in *Theological Wordbook of the Old Testament*, vol. 2, (Chicago: Moody Press, 1980), 879.

beginning stages of inebriation. One need not introduce the euphoria of a mind-altered state of inebriation into these passages simply because the word "cheers, glad, or merry," is present, for such cannot be proven. In our culture, there is a perception that if one is in a state of mind-altered inebriation, then that one must be glad, merry or cheerful. Yet, it is possible to drink wine and be refreshed, gladdened, cheered and made merry by its taste and its thirst-quenching effects without having to become drunk. These verses do not indicate that the beneficial effect of merriment or gladness is derived from the inebriative effect of drunkenness. However, there is a passage where one is called "merry" and that effect appears on the surface to be associated with drinking wine and then getting drunk (1 Sam. 25:36). The Hebrew word for "merry" in this passage is *towb*. It means to be "glad or joyful,"[28] and it is part of the daily greeting, "good morning." Nabal was merry, glad, joyful and in good spirits because he was feasting like a king with his friends, not because he was very drunk. The conjunction in the NASB "for" as in "for he was very drunk" could easily be primarily translated, "and he was very drunk." Being very drunk is not the cause of being merry. The fact of his feasting like a king with his friends was the reason for his merriment. It is neither helpful nor necessary to draw conclusions from a word that the text does not support. Just because we know of individuals who get very drunk and become jovial does not mean this is a good reason for all to become inebriated. A drunk who is a "merry" or "happy drunk" when he is drunken, merely and most likely exhibits the disposition of his own personality. You cannot make a case from these texts that the effects of inebriation are good just because an individual happens to be merry when he is drunk. A heart that is gladdened need not "cop a buzz" in order to be glad. It need not be in a state of inebriated, euphoric bliss in order to be happy.

However, if you do want to review the happiness that occurs to some who get drunk, then here are a few examples of the merriment, conviviality and rejoicing that occur when people become inebriated—a sort of "Fun Facts" list. Please note that these are not the consequences of the moderate, reasonable use of alcohol, but of its use in excess:[29]

(1) 25% of all college dropouts are connected to alcohol problems.
(2) From 20-36% of suicide victims are alcohol abusers.
(3) Alcohol is a factor in 80% of domestic disputes.

---

[28] Francis Brown, S. R. Driver, and Charles A. Briggs, *The Brown-Driver-Briggs Hebrew and English Lexicon*, s.v. "*towb*, 2895," (Peabody, MA: Hendrickson Publishers, 2000), 373.
[29] *Baker Encyclopedia of Psychology & Counseling*, 2nd ed, ed. David G. Benner and Peter C. Hill, s.v. "Alcohol-Induced Disorders," by John R. Cheydleur, (Grand Rapids: Baker Books, 1999), 64.

(4) Alcohol-dependent men are three times more likely to physically abuse their wives as those who are not alcohol-dependent.

(5) 40% of state prison inmates were under the influence of alcohol when they committed their crimes.

(6) 68% of manslaughter convictions and 62% of assault convictions are alcohol-related.

(7) Alcohol use is implicated in the following four leading causes of accidental death in the US: in 50% of deaths due to traffic crashes; in 24% of deaths due to falls; in 38% of deaths by drowning; in 64% of deaths due to fires and burns.

(8) Alcohol is related in 25% of medical problems leading to hospitalization.

(9) Alcohol abuse increases the risk of seizure up to twenty times and is the leading cause of liver disease.

(10) 46% of cirrhosis deaths in men and 15% in women are caused by heavy drinking.

(11) Various infectious illnesses as well as certain cancers are more common in alcohol-dependent individuals due alcohol's effect on the immune system. These include such *desirable* diseases as pneumonia, tuberculosis, diarrhea, skin and soft tissue infections, urinary tract infections, and sexually transmitted diseases. (Wow, who can deny these really are "Fun Facts?")

(12) More than 1000 infants are born mentally retarded each year due to fetal alcohol syndrome (FAS) due to the use of alcohol by pregnant women (Should one conclude from this statistic that the benefit the pregnant mother derives from the "merriment, conviviality and rejoicing" in her selfish inebriation more than compensates for the risk of this miserable consequence? Otherwise, surely she would not be so reckless!)

With such a "merry, convivial and joyful" list of "Fun Facts" like this, perhaps one can now see why getting drunk is so very appealing. No, it is simply gross inconsideration, negligence and irresponsibility. Perhaps it is exceedingly more reasonable to conclude that, contrary to the prevailing opinion of our culture and its advertising and entertainment media that shape it, the actual consequences of alcohol's inebriative effects, are a far cry from the "merriment, conviviality and rejoicing" we see in the "high life" conveyed by the media. The transient euphoria that is received through the abuse of alcohol certainly should not convince believers that inebriation produces, what the Bible calls, a "merry heart."

One misconception that frequently occurs regarding our understanding of alcohol concerns the differences between the alcoholic beverages today compared with those of long ago. People incorrectly assume that since the same word used in Biblical times is the same we use today, the products must therefore also be the exact same products. Yet, the wine and strong drink we know today does not possess the identical alcoholic properties as the wine and strong drink known previously, due to the methods used to ferment them. It is believed that the wines of ancient history did not contain as much alcohol as those produced today for the wines of the Biblical era were naturally fermented, without the use of adjuvant additives. At that time, sugar and yeast were not added to the grape juice; their absence allowed the alcoholic content to remain at a lower level.[30] In Proverbs 20:1 "strong drink" is the Hebrew word, *shekar*, which through the cognate Arabic word, *sukkar*, appears in our English word, "sugar."[31] This beverage was considered to be more potent than wine and it was fermented from fruit juices such as pomegranate and dates. It was prepared not only from barley, but other grains and fruits as well. Strong drink in the Bible is not the same alcoholic beverage we call "hard liquor," though some confuse it with that term. There is no evidence of distilled liquor in ancient Hebrew times.[32] Distillation of alcohol into the potent, hard liquor forms of today began to be developed by the Romans around A.D. 100.

People also assume that in biblical times there was pervasive poor water quality in the Middle East; therefore, these persons had nothing else available to safely drink all day except wine or strong drink, which, during most of the year was alcoholic. Due to the climate at harvest, the natural fruit juices did not remain non-alcoholic for long. Naturally, such a situation would present a serious problem in a very warm and dry climate where much thirsty labor was performed outdoor in the hot sun. Obviously, the Israelites could not drink their wine incessantly, much less our more-potent version of wine, and remain sober for long. It should be obvious that sufficient potable water was available to them in sufficient quantities to slake their thirsts and allow them to work in a sensible and sober manner. It is believed that for most personal uses, wine may have been reserved, to some degree, for special occasions such as times of celebration and feastings, weddings, and as a drink offering, rather than as the normal table beverage for every meal.[33] However, it is reasonable to believe that wine may have been served daily at the evening meal. In the Roman era, a Jewish

---

[30] Jennifer Marie Jordan, "The Wine of Israel and the Bible," *Blogcritics Magazine, Tastes,* (www.blogcritics.org/archives/2006/10/27/170144.php), October 27, 2006.
[31] Abraham Cohen, ed., *Proverbs, The Soncino Books of the Bible,* (London: The Soncino Press, 1952), 131
[32] R. Laird Harris, et. al., eds., s.v. "2388a, shekar," 926-927.
[33] Barry L. Bandstra, *The International Standard Bible Encyclopedia,* Vol. 4: Q-Z, s.v. "Wine," (Grand Rapids: William B. Eerdmans Publishing Company, 1988), 1070.

family was estimated to consume 92 gallons of wine per year.[34] However, that amount is by no means sufficient to account for the minimum daily consumption of all forms of liquid refreshment necessary to sustain life for just two adults, much less the quantity vital for the typically large family required by agrarian cultures of antiquity.

Clearly, the Bible does not support the use of alcohol in coping with life's problems. The world's oldest psychotropic drug was only to be used in quantities that prevented the psychotropic properties of that product from being expressed. Drunkenness is not appreciated in the Bible. The use of today's psychotropic drugs finds no biblical basis for support.

Dear Lord, we are ever so thankful that you teach us that the state of peaceful mental stability comes when we trust completely in You, and keep our minds steadfastly focused upon You.

Irrationality Invades the Church: Where Will We Now Go for Victorious Living?

It has been said the 13th century was considered the Age of Faith and the 18th century the Age of Reason.[35] Because of many great technological advances, the 20th century has been labeled with several titles: the Electrical Age, the Age of Aviation, the Atomic Age, and the Cyber Age. You have to admit, we are making such great progress—too bad we are often going in the wrong direction. In spite of our great accumulation of technological knowledge in our modern culture, there still remains a dearth of eternal wisdom. Perhaps the 21st century we now enjoy merits one name above all others. Accordingly, we should label this age with the ignoble moniker, the "Age of Irrationalism." Simply summed and said, this generation does not value rational reasoning stemming from objective truth. Our faith depends on objective truth, yet, what is the modern thought on faith? The following is part of an address given to the Ruling Elders' Association of Chester Presbytery:

> In exalting faith, we are not immediately putting ourselves in contradiction to modern thought. Indeed faith is being exalted very high by men of the most modern type. But, what kind of faith? There emerges the difference of opinion. Faith is being exalted so high today that men are being satisfied with any kind of faith, just so it is faith. It makes no difference what is believed, we are told, just so

---

[34] Yael Zisling Adar, "Winemaking in Israel – A Modern Industry Based on an Ancient Traditions," *Gems In Israel*, (www.gemsinisrael.com/e_article000033156.htm), August/September 2001.

[35] This section owes much of its inspiration and some of its content to John W. Robbins' addendum entitled, "The Crisis of Our Time," in Gordon H. Clark, *Thales to Dewey*, 2nd ed. (Jefferson, MD: The Trinity Foundation, 1989), 549-552.

the blessed attitude of faith is there. The undogmatic faith, it is said, is better than the dogmatic, because it is purer faith—faith less weakened by the alloy of knowledge.[36]

That modern assessment of faith was given by J. Gresham Machen on November 3, 1921, almost 90 years ago. It was quite prescient for it aptly describes still the current attitude of today.

In the past, secular philosophers considered knowledge[37] something man could attain and understand. Consequently, they expended a great deal of effort and enthusiasm explaining and justifying knowledge. Until the Enlightenment, truth was assumed to be absolute, objective, and propositional correspondence to reality.[38] It was knowable, and once known, became knowledge—part of man's vast reservoir of comprehendible knowledge. However, beginning with the 20th and continuing into the 21st century, the exuberance seen of earlier philosophers began to vanish. The philosophers of today despair of knowledge for they are no longer confident what knowledge is. John W. Robbins states, "Contemporary secular intellectuals are anti-intellectual. Contemporary philosophers are anti-philosophy. Contemporary theologians are anti-theology."[39]

In the not too distant past, the respected theologians of the church taught that knowledge and wisdom was not only possible, but also prerequisite and essential to the Christian experience. As is often and unfortunate the case, most individuals in the Church have allowed the irrational cultural views, rather than the Word of God, to impact and alter their thinking and subsequent behavior. Now it seems, many of the latest generation of theologians have discarded such necessities as the acquisition of wisdom and knowledge. Consequently, they too despair of knowledge and wisdom. Yet, if the rational, objective Word of God contains the information that dispenses "the wisdom that leads to salvation through faith which is in Christ Jesus," then how can the Church ever diminish the study of its rational, objective truth? Yet, too many seminaries have become the finishing schools of irrationalism, completing the job begun by the government schools and colleges.[40] John W. Robbins aptly describes the

---

[36] J. Gresham Machen, *Christianity and Liberalism* (Grand Rapids: William B. Eerdmans Publishing Co., 1923), 141.

[37] Knowledge, unless otherwise described, will always refer to truthful information and observations. Knowledge that is not truthful is superfluous at best and pernicious at worst.

[38] Steven L. McAvoy, *The Fundamentals for the Twenty-first Century*, ed. Mal Couch (Grand Rapids: Kregel Publications, 2000), 29.

[39] Gordon H. Clark, *Thales to Dewey*, 2nd ed. (Jefferson, MD: The Trinity Foundation, 1989), 549.

[40] Ibid., 551.

legacy left to students who will instruct the Kingdom of God in its churches and schools. He said, "the Christian in the 20th (and 21st) century is confronted with an overwhelming cultural consensus—sometimes stated explicitly, but most often implicitly: Man does not and cannot know anything truly."[41]

Why should we as Christians concern ourselves with what is considered, by many, to be epistemological minutia? Because, if we can know nothing for certain to be true, then the only certain thing we will know, is that we know nothing. Often, when discussing theological issues within conservative circles, such as ongoing revelation and the current aberrant use of tongues that only a few decades ago was considered heretical, some sincere seminary students will be heard to exclaim, "You can't be so *certain* of your position! There is no real way to truly know what God is actually saying in that biblical text. It can mean different things to different people so we must allow for such latitude when attempting to explain that passage." Yet, where do they obtain their own *"certain"* hermeneutic principles? They are taught such *certain* drivel in their seminary class on hermeneutics, of course. It is ironic that the only *certain* thing we can be *certain* of in teaching is that we *cannot be certain* of what we teach. What nonsense! What folly! If they are right though, the only ethically responsible and logically consistent action for them is to close their school for they have nothing to teach! Yet, is that the case? Of course not! Apparently, their jobs are more important to them than consistently living out their hermeneutical belief system. Naturally, they think there are some things we can still be certain of. However, as the years go by, even that reservoir of certainty is rapidly evaporating due to the drought of objective, consistent hermeneutics in their seminaries. (No doubt, another consequence of the dreaded Global Warming.)

How then will we handle life's problems victoriously? How do we respond to life when our expectations appear to be unfairly resolved? One thing is for certain, if you remove the reliability of God's Word, you eliminate the only source that provides a God-glorifying solution to handling life's problems. When the gullible, undiscerning Church begins to believe the ever-changing culture which confidently asserts the unreliable nature of the Bible, then believers of such persuasion are only left with psychoanalysis and psychotropic drugs with which to cope, yet neither is appropriate. One frustrating situation a believer occasionally finds himself is in the situation of being falsely accused. Some find they are overwhelmed by a desire to

---

[41] Ibid., 549.

angrily lash out, to strike back at their accusers; others are beleaguered by discouragement for they know they are innocent, they know God is aware of their innocence, they know God could remove this situation from them if He desired—but He does not. Another frustrating situation is where a believer does what is right, yet is punished for his good deeds.

John the Baptist knew well this situation for in spite of all his ministry and experience, he was overwhelmed by his personal expectations and hope of a political kingdom that would provide relief. John knew Christ was the Messiah and His miracles only confirmed for him Christ's true identity. But John needed a Messiah that would overturn the current political situation and obtain his release from his incarceration. His expectation was not being realized and he needed additional assurance (Mt. 11:1-6). Remember, it was John who had uttered the profound announcement of Christ's identity as "the Lamb of God who takes away the sin of the world!" yet, because of his own dire predicament, he longed for political relief instead of the redemptive relief God first intended. In view of John's unrealized expectations, Christ told him not be offended because John was faced with the uncomfortable reality of Christ's redemptive mission coming first, according to a sovereign God, before any political mission could be fulfilled. It was simply not time for the political mission of Christ's millennial reign in Jerusalem. It is not uncommon to expect one outcome and then receive another, as did the people who went out to hear John the Baptist's message (Mt. 11:7-11). So it was with John and the Messiah, for John was not to be offended that his own expectations were not fulfilled by his sovereign Lord. All of us tend to be greatly offended when our expectations of life conflict with God's sovereign purposes. It is imperative that believers know how to handle such situations because the outside world, and the inside church, indeed observes our actions and reactions.

The Apostle Peter explains how we can live victoriously and avoid despair, anxiety, and fear under such a similar situation where we receive treatment we did not deserve:

> But even if you should suffer for the sake of righteousness, you are blessed. AND DO NOT FEAR THEIR INTIMIDATION, AND DO NOT BE TROUBLED, but sanctify Christ as Lord in your hearts, always being ready to make a defense to everyone who asks you to give an account for the hope that is in you, yet with gentleness and reverence; and keep a good conscience so that in the thing in which you are slandered, those who revile your good behavior in Christ will be put to shame. (1st Pet. 3.14-16)

Due to sowing and reaping, there are certain difficulties of life we deserve due to incorrect thinking and behavior. The simple remedy for that is to repent, to change our mind about our behavior, and then act like we repented by producing the fruit appropriate to our change of mind. There are some situations, such as John the Baptist's, where believers suffer for doing the right thing. Please note the first reaction Peter expects of us in order to avoid despair, anxiety and fear, is to consider ourselves blessed. This is an act of our will based on believing the truth of God's Word. If we fail here, we will not be able to appreciate that God is sovereign and He knows what is best for us at this time and in this situation; if we fail here, we will not be able to express gratitude for receiving what the Lord thinks is best for us; if we fail here, a thankless heart or mind becomes a grumbling mouth (Isa. 29:23-24). And, God has a long, long history of, let's just say, "under-appreciating," grumblers, so "do the math"—and I must warn you about grumblers. There is much divine "subtraction" involved when God deals with grumblers. In the fourth chapter of his epistle to the Philippians, Paul also gives great insight on this subject. He counsels that in order to avoid anxiety, we should (1) dwell on God's Word; (2) make requests to the Lord; (3) be thankful in all things; (4) and finally, practice the things that Paul taught and modeled.

The next step Peter describes is an act of the will that chooses not to fear. Fear and anxiety are chosen responses, acts of the will, which can lead to despair and depression. Fear, anxiety and depression are not caused by genetic malfunction or abnormal chemical levels.[42] Proverbs 12:25 explains that, "Anxiety in the heart of man causes depression, But a good word makes it glad." Can you imagine a more appropriate good word for any situation than that from the Creator-Designer? Peter says you are to will, to resolve to express a fearless attitude concerning the terror that your situation would seek to will, or impose, upon you. That terror also seeks to intensify your fear into a level of anxiety. Now, instead of choosing to fill your mind with fear, you choose to think properly about Christ's rightful position over you and your circumstances, as sovereign Lord; you choose to have already prepared your mind by using the Word of God in providing the basis for your defense of your faith. The only reason a believer can give an account, a word of the hope that is within, is because he has studied that hope in the Word of God. Any other kind of preparation is mere conjecture stemming from unreliable emotions. God expects us to use our minds in order to reason

---

[42] David Healy, *Let Them Eat Prozac: The Unhealthy Relationship Between the Pharmaceutical Industry and Depression*, (New York: New York University Press, 2004), 12.

based on the Word of God so we may defend the faith. Mindless, emotional mysticism has no place in pleasing God for we must reason from the Scriptures to make a defense for our faith.

Verse fifteen uses the term, "sanctify", referencing our attitude about the Lord. Sanctify is *hagiazo,* and it simply means to "make holy or set apart". God is intrinsically holy; therefore, we cannot *make* Him holy so the emphasis here is that we are to set Him apart in our heart. The question then is how or why should we set the Lord God apart in our hearts? We are to regard, in the preferred sanctuary of worship—our heart, Christ as Lord. As Lord and God, He is also entitled to our obedience, reverence, worship and total submission. Live in that attitude and we will have nothing to fear according to verse 14. After all, it is Christ who is the only Lord of true significance and we must answer to Him first and foremost. All other earthly lords labor under the jurisdiction of His providential permission. Do we truly grasp that? Not only do all earthly lords labor accordingly but so do *all things*—there is no situation composed of anything or anyone that acts apart from divine permission (Rom. 8:28-39). The believer's view of Christ's authority as Lord of his life deeply impacts his ability to respond to difficulties. A shallow view of Christ's Lordship produces a life that sees no benefit in Bible study, therefore it has no basis, no foundation from which to realize it is blessed, from which it can will to act fearlessly, from which it can answer others who inquire about our Savior. When Christ is viewed in His rightful position as Lord, the heart is quieted from fear and the mind is free to reason from Scripture of the eternal hope that is within the soul. Without the removal of fear of earthly lords, it is difficult to reason in our heart because we are paralyzed with fear. We are commanded to use our mind, our intellect, to defend the hope that is within us. Without the mind we cannot articulate the careful defense the Lord expects us to offer. Even though we need not fear earthly lords, it provides no excuse for belligerence or disrespect. We must treat them with meekness and reverence according to their position. I believe Peter is saying:

> Even if you are unjustly punished for right behavior, you are and will be blessed. There is no need to fear them in any way, rather realize and meditate on the fact that Christ is the only true Lord. It is He who is in full control of the situation, so do not allow your mind to become frozen with fear. Instead, as you fully acknowledge His overall control as Lord, allow your mind to explain the reasons why you possess this eternal hope of salvation. Don't be haughty even though you realize the earthly lord before whom you stand is not truly in charge and is only a pawn of the Lord's choosing. In all things, show commensurate respect and honor. With such attitude

and actions your conscience will remain clear and it will instead be your accusers who will be shamed by their actions.

Final Thoughts

We have observed that the most effective attacks by Satan are always those that begin with questioning the very words, intentions and authority of whatever God says. Our modern culture and many theologians, because of their pandering to the intelligentsia of science, dismiss the reliability of the Word of God whenever it addresses science. But, when you question God's reliability in one area, all other disciplines become compromised as well, "for a tainted Bible, t'ain't a Bible at all." Most Dispensationalists recognize that such misunderstandings are a consequence of treating the supernatural revelation of God's Word in two disrespectful ways.

The first disrespectful way is that the Word of God is treated as inferior to, and therefore subservient to, the so-called "scientific" theories and musings of man. As such, they say we can only understand Scripture as we are informed by the natural sciences we observe, and by the conclusions we draw from such observances. Such individuals may or may not see the Bible as a supernatural revelation. Such individuals will not believe the biblical record is completely accurate in its explanation of science and history.

The second disrespectful way is that, though appreciated as God's supernatural revelation, some or much of the Bible is treated as if God did not actually intend to communicate to His creatures in a simple, straight-forward, literal way. Some in the modern Church see His supernatural revelation as simply ambiguous, as burdened with veiled meanings and purposes which only the seminary-trained can aptly perceive and explain. As a result, the diligent study that the Word of God expects from all of God's children is seen, by them, as simply not worth the effort. They believe an individual cannot accurately determine what God is essentially saying to His people.

However, if we recognize the Bible to be what God intended it to be—a supernatural, completely accurate and reasonable revelation concerning both God and our true situation in life—then we will be able to fathom the riches of its depth, as we carefully study its pages and obediently apply it to every area of our life (Jam. 1:25). Such determined study must be performed in reliance upon His Holy Spirit and in the straightforward, literal way in which any other textbook is to be understood and trusted. Dispensationalists, and others, have long honored this literal approach to Bible study and interpretation so we may understand precisely what the Lord expects of His children. The literal approach has been reasonably and consistently applied in other areas of life such as the study of history, science, and music as well as theological disciplines pertaining to the way we should live in simple obedience to the Lord.

One way of recognizing and expressing the competency and completeness of the Bible to deal with matters pertaining unto salvation, and the resultant abundant life that salvation compels us to live, is to say we believe in the authority and sufficiency of Scripture. Such belief in its supernatural origin compels us to recognize that it has unqualified authority to inform our lives and as such, it is to be obeyed without reservation. It is grossly inconsistent to recognize Scripture's supernatural origin and then casually treat it as if its demands were negotiable or elective. Was it not God Almighty who asked the question, "Why do you call Me, 'Lord, Lord,' and do not do what I say?" (Lk. 6:46)? Should we, perhaps, take Him seriously?

We know all too well the fallen state of our world and flesh; we do expect trials, temptations and difficulties in this life. Should we expect the same Lord who made the gracious, all-wise, and magnanimous remedy for the *penalty* of sin to have also prepared instructions how to overcome the *power* of sin in our daily affairs as we move forward through life? It would seem most reasonable—and we do indeed serve a reasonable God. We also do recognize that we often refuse to heed the instructions to overcome sin and its various influences in our life. The Lord knows our frame of existence (Ps. 103:13-14). We should therefore expect that when we fail, as we often do, such all-sufficient Scripture will also aid us in issuing the appropriate remedial instruction to transform our thinking and its corresponding behavior (Rom. 12:1-2; 2 Tim. 3:16-17). It should be no surprise that the *all-authoritative* Scripture asserts its claim to be the *all-sufficient* truth that we can rely upon in any area that pertains to and that affects our life and godliness (2 Pet. 1:2-11). It then would also be inconsistent and unreasonable to *treat* such authority as if it were insufficient, as if it could not assist us in *all of life's difficulties*. It is not appropriate to simply say with our tongue that the Scripture is all-sufficient; God expects us to confirm our declaration with obedient activity (1 Jo. 3:7-8). Often, we truly render honest, respectful allegiance to the Bible in many areas of our lives. Yet, for too many, even in Dispensational circles, there is an area of our life in which we somehow have begun to shift our allegiance away from the sufficient words of Scripture, to the words of the pseudo-science of psychology.

Psychology may truly be capable of observing and studying the responses of a man's soul to his environment, but it cannot draw *accurate* conclusions as to the cause of, or the solutions to, the problems of the soul. Psychology certainly provides nothing to inform the biblical record concerning the root cause and solution to man's true dilemma—sin. Where psychology's musings agree with Scripture, they prove to be superfluous reiterations; where psychology's musings disagree with Scripture, they prove to be unreliable at best and dangerously deceptive at worst. Such musings will diminish a person's ability to obtain reliable information concerning the true plight of their situation; such musings only assist in incarcerating that soul further into the bondage of error. Psychology seeks to understand the personality of man; it seeks to answer the destination of man; and it seeks to address the question concerning the meaning of life.[43] But, apart from divine revelation, psychology cannot address these issues. Yet, the modern Church would rather listen to, what is apparently considered by them, the lofty, academic rhetoric of men such as Sigmund Freud and his disciples, rather than the clear instruction of the Word of God (Jer. 2:8-13). The objective truth found in Christianity speaks of man's sinfulness. Many in the psychological field consider such objective truth as only capable of producing the unnecessary baggage that is guilt. We are told that such guilt is an extreme hindrance to personal mental health because it promotes feelings of inferiority that conflict with psychology's holy trinity of self-mage, self-esteem, and self–worth. Some of them tell us that once individuals are "self-actualized" by getting in touch with their "real self," they can finally learn to worship their "perfect selves."[44] Oh, that should be rich. Consider this:

> Psychology's best-known personality, Sigmund Freud, may have scorned Christianity—indeed, all religious belief—as a mere "illusion." But Christians these days are opening their minds and hearts to his teachings and to those of other psychologists, Freudian or otherwise .... How did this happen? Psychologists have long been a secular bunch—modern psychology itself was built upon the rejection of religion as unscientific. Because Freud and other early 20th-century psychologists were eager to establish psychology as a "real" science, they went out of their way to denigrate the truth-claims of religious belief, seeing them as a mere manifestation of personal forces (e.g., the need for a father figure) .... Psychology that embraces rather than rejects religion even has its evangelical poster-children. Take the commentator James Dobson, a Ph.D. and licensed psychologist who is also an evangelical Christian. His Focus on the Family organization is one of the most successful evangelical groups in the country. "When well-known and respected individuals like James Dobson support something like psychology," says John A. Addleman, who leads the psychology department at Messiah College in Grantham,

---

[43] Franz G. Alexander and Sheldon T. Selesnick, 5.

[44] David A. Noebel, *Understanding the Times* (Manitou Springs, CO: Summit Press, 1991), 356.

Pa., "they make choosing a career in that field a better option for those who might not have considered it before."[45]

How sad. Psychology, as a field of Christian academic endeavor, is better suited for repentance than school attendance—and incredible as it is, at a college named "Messiah," meaning Christ. I can only think of "For My people have committed two evils: They have forsaken Me, The fountain of living waters, To hew for themselves cisterns, Broken cisterns That can hold no water" (Jer. 2:13)

Some believe that Bible study may be appropriate, perhaps, for those who are happy and carefree; the Bible may be relevant to those who enjoy a measure of success; but, to those who are disenfranchised by society, who are lower on the ladder of perceived success and happiness, who are struggling with fear, anxiety and depression as a result of a life's uncertainties, to them the Bible is seen as having no real solutions. As a result, the modern Church sees the Bible—her sole source of actual compassionate truth and solutions—as simply irrelevant to daily life when it counts most—when life is most difficult. This is an example of the lofty position that Christian counselor Larry Crabb places upon God's Word when life is difficult:

> Reminders of God's love and exhortations to meditate on Jesus' care sometimes provide about as much help as handing out recipes to waiting in a food line.[46]

I have actually listened to a Sunday morning sermon given in a conservative church where a pastor expressed from the pulpit, "Sometimes, Jesus simply is not enough!" The context, you ask? It concerned how we should assist Christians who were deeply depressed and anxious. That view expressed his recommendation as to why "Christian psychology" was essential, even preferable, since only it could truly relate to people's deepest hurts. You see, "the Man of Sorrows who was acquainted with grief"—"our merciful and faithful high priest" who was "made like his brethren in all things"—well, sorry, He could not really relate or assist—yet, it is still politically correct to pray to Him even though such effort is not really effective. The Bible, then, is there to help happy Christians stay happy, that is, if only their body chemicals will cooperate. However, when the going gets tough, deeply hurting Christians must get help from trained "professionals." What does it

---

[45] Martin Bobgan, "Psych Notes," *Psychoheresy Awareness Letter*, Vol. 15, No. 5, Sept-Oct 2007, p. 4, excerpted from *The Wall Street Journal*, Editorial Page, March 30, 2007.
[46] Larry Crabb, *Inside Out*, (Colorado Springs, CO: NavPress, 1988), 194.

mean when our Redeemer-God says "Trust in Him at all times, O people; Pour out your heart before Him; God is a refuge for us." (Ps. 62:8) or ... "My grace is sufficient for you, for power is perfected in weakness." (2nd Cor. 12:9a)?

As Dispensationalists, we must highly value the written revelation the Lord has providentially preserved to instruct us for our benefit. Yet, when we choose to listen to the voice of psychology and medicine to answer our anxieties, our fears, our panics and our depressions, in effect we give mere lip-service to the Word of God. It is a *most-wicked* approach to honoring the One who lovingly provides for us "everything pertaining to life and godliness, through the knowledge of Him." Please note that we humbly and diligently seek God's revelation to provide salvation in order to mitigate the legal and eternal consequences of sin. Note that we ardently seek the revelation of His Word to avoid the damning effects of sin whereby unbelieving and unrepentant sinners face the prospects of an eternity in Hell. Note that we seek to avoid the dire, hopeless situation where we have offended the righteous sensibilities of an all-powerful God who will toss those offenders into the Lake of Fire (Rev. 20:11-15). Who, then, by their own wisdom and effort, can stay such an omnipotent hand?

Yet, when it comes to alleviating the effects of sin in our daily life, we somehow believe the Bible, a product of God the Holy Spirit, lacks sufficient power and authority to ameliorate our situation. One may well ask, "You mean to say, the Bible alone contains sufficient wisdom to keep our souls from eternal damnation, to keep our souls from the clutches of a judging omnipotent God, to vouchsafe our souls for eternity, yet that same Word of God is feeble and insufficient to allay our daily fears, needs and anxieties?" Well, judging by the treasonous response of many believers who seek the advice and comfort from psychology's broken cistern instead of their Bible, one can only assume that is precisely the conclusion many have made. Yet, to come to such a conclusion is, at best, logically preposterous and, at worst, a result of being duped by diabolical disinformation. God expects the same revelation, both Living and written, not only to save our souls eternally, but also allow us to live victoriously (Eph. 4:11-16; Titus 2:11-15). Satan cannot prevent a believer from making heaven his eternal residence, so he is perhaps content to make the believer's temporary residence meaningless, powerless and ineffective in his witness to mankind (Mt. 5:16) and in his witness to the spiritual world (Eph. 3:10). It is nothing less than tragic that believers willingly choose to trust in a Bible-less psychology rather than the sufficiency of God's word.

Dear Lord, Your gracious Holy Spirit gave us Your Word for our benefit to display Your great glory. Please make us ever the willing and obedient students of Your Most Holy Word, so we may become acceptable servants of You, the Most High God.

COMES NOW THE OBLIGATORY MEDICAL DISCLAIMER:
Neither the author nor the publisher is dispensing medical advice. The readers must assume full responsibility, in consultation with their medical professional, for their own medical decisions, even though the medical information herein is derived from highly respected medical doctors. You alone are responsible for your attitudes and actions. The author and publisher specifically reject any and all responsibility for any harm, risk, loss or liability which is incurred personally or otherwise as a result of reading, consulting or making inferences from any of the medical contents of this chapter. Abruptly ending the use of psychotropic drugs can result in withdrawal symptoms that can range from mild to severe. Consult your medical professional when choosing to cease the use of these drugs.

Helpful and Recommended Books

Almy, Gary L., M.D., *How Christian is Christian Counseling? The Dangerous Secular Influences That Keep Us from Caring for Souls.*

---------- and Carol Tharp Almy, M.D., *Addicted to Recovery: Exposing the False Gospel of Psychotherapy; Escaping the Trap of Victim Mentality.*

Baughman, Fred A., Jr., M.D. and Craig Hovey, *The ADHD Fraud: How Psychiatry Makes "Patients" of Normal Children.*

Bobgan, Martin, DEdPsy, and Deidre Bobgan, *Competent to Minister: The Biblical Care of Souls.*

----------, *The End of "Christian Psychology."*

----------, *Four Temperaments, Astrology & Personality Testing.*

----------, *Missions & Psychoheresy.*

----------, *Prophets of Psychoheresy I: Critiquing Gary Collins, Lawrence Crabb, Jr., Paul Meier and Frank Minirth.*

----------, *Prophets of Psychoheresy II: Critiquing James C. Dobson.*

----------, *Twelve Steps to Destruction: Codependency Recovery Heresies.*

Breggin, Peter R., M.D., *Toxic Psychiatry*

----------, *Talking Back to Prozac: What Doctors Aren't Telling You about Today's Most Controversial Drug.*

----------, *Talking Back to Ritalin: What Doctors Aren't Telling You about Stimulants for Children.*

---------- and David Cohen, Ph.D., *Your Drug May Be Your Problem: How and Why to Stop Taking Psychiatric Medications.*

----------, *The Anti-Depressant Fact Book: What Your Doctor Won't Tell You about Prozac, Zoloft, Paxil, Celexa and Luvox.*

----------, *The Ritalin Fact Book: What Your Doctor Won't Tell You about ADHD and Stimulant Drugs.*

Bulkley, Ed, Ph.D., *Only God Can Heal the Wounded Heart.*

Dineen, Tana, Ph.D., *Manufacturing Victims: What the Psychology Industry is Doing to People.*

Ganz, Richard, D. ClinPsy, *PsychoBabble: The Failure of Modern Psychology and the Biblical Alternative.*

Gumprecht, Jane, M.D., *Abusing Memory: The Healing Theology of Agnes Sanford.*

Healy, David, M.D., *Let Them Eat Prozac: The Unhealthy Relationship between the Pharmaceutical Industry and Depression.*

Jackson, Grace E., M.D., *Rethinking Psychiatric Drugs: A Guide for Informed Consent.*

MacArthur, John F., Jr., D.D., *Anxiety Attacked: Applying Scripture to the Cares of the Soul.*

----------, *Our Sufficiency in Christ.*

----------, *The Vanishing Conscience: Drawing the Line in a No-Fault, Guilt-Free World.*

Owen, James D., Christian *Psychology's War on God's Word: The Victimization of the Believer.*

Ross, Colin A., M.D. and Alvin Pam, Ph.D., *Pseudoscience in Biological Psychiatry: Blaming the Body.*

Scott, Timothy, Ph.D., *America Fooled: The Truth about Antidepressants, Antipsychotics and How We've Been Deceived.*

Valenstein, Elliot S., Ph.D., *Blaming the Brain: The Truth about Drugs and Mental Health.*

"If by two "ways" of salvation is meant different content of faith, then dispensationalism does teach various ways because the Scriptures reveal differing contents for faith in the progressive nature of God's revelation to mankind. But if by "ways" is meant more than one basis or means of salvation, then dispensationalism most emphatically does not teach more than one way, for salvation has been, is, and always will be based on the substitutionary death of Jesus Christ."

- Charles C. Ryrie
Dispensationalism, 1995, page 121

11

Content, Object & Message of Saving Faith
S Jeff Heslop

Introduction

Is what must be believed for salvation the same throughout the Bible? Does what must be believed change between the Old and New Testaments? Does it change with each different dispensation? Non-dispensationalists stress the sameness of what must be believed while dispensationalists have been accused of teaching that this changes with the progress of revelation. For example, Walvoord states,

> It is clear that Old Testament saints did not believe in Christ in the same way and with the same comprehension that believers with the New Testament do. In the nature of the case the issue of faith is to believe in the revelation given. On the other hand there are not two ways of salvation. All salvation of God stems from the Savior, the Son of God, and His work on the cross...The two great essentials of salvation remain the same from the salvation of Adam to the last soul which God takes to Himself in the future. Faith is the condition and the death of Christ is the basis.[1]

Here Walvoord taught that the two unchanging essentials of salvation throughout both testaments are that the condition is faith and the basis is the death of Christ. He also taught that the issue of faith is to believe in the revelation given. The revelation given then is not always the same since he understood revelation to progress. Revelation about God expands and accumulates throughout the Bible. Walvoord recognized that some aspects of salvation never change and others do. The terminology and definitions used by dispensationalists to describe the unchanging condition and basis of salvation and the expanding revelation have sometimes caused a tension in soteriology.

---

[1] John F. Walvoord, "Series in Christology—Part 4: The Preincarnate Son of God," *Biliotheca Sacra* 104 (October 1947):,422.

Definition of Terms

Dispensational writers of the past have described saving faith in different ways. C. I. Scofield in a note on Heb 11:39 wrote this about the essence of faith:

> The essence of faith consists in receiving what God has revealed, and may be defined as that trust in the God of the Scriptures and in Jesus Christ whom He hath sent, which receives Him as Savior and Lord, and impels to loving obedience and good works (Jn 1:12, Jas 2:14-26)...For salvation, faith is a personal trust, apart from meritorious works, in the Lord Jesus Christ, as delivered for our offences and raised again for our justification (Rom. 4:5, 23-25).[2]

There are two parts to Scofield's definition of saving faith. The first is to believe in a message or revelation containing some facts that God has revealed. These facts include Christ delivered for our offenses and raised again for our justification. The second is to believe in God Himself. So there is a message to believe and a person to believe in. The two are related because the message to be believed is a pointer to the person to believe in.

Lewis Sperry Chafer also recognizes the need to believe a message revealed by God and the need for personal belief in Him:

> The Epistle to the Hebrews opens with a reference to the messages of God which have been projected into this world, and which have widened the possible scope of man's understanding and action from the limitations of the things of this world and the conclusions of finite minds to the issues of the entire sphere of God's redemptive purposes and the verities of the Infinite...It is not enough to believe generally that God has spoken. What he has said must be carefully weighed and personally applied.[3]

Chafer recognized that it is not enough to believe messages revealed from God. The message must not only be believed but also personally applied. The personal application is to put one's belief in God. Both of these writers recognized two aspects saving faith: (1) the message that revealed something about God as Savior, and (2) God Himself. While both are essential, they are not the same.

The word *content* is sometimes used by dispensationalists to mean what God has revealed about Himself regarding what must be believed to be saved. A dictionary meaning for content is something contained, as in a receptacle or the water in a glass. It means all a thing contains. It may also

---

[2] C. I. Scofield, *The Scofield Reference Bible* (New York: Oxford University Press, 1917 ed.), 1302.
[3] Lewis Sperry Chafer, *Salvation* (Findlay, Ohio: Dunham Publishing Company, 1917), 15-16.

mean the substantive or meaningful part. Given these meanings, it is easy for one to understand the content of what must be believed to mean God.

God is also recognized as the *object* of faith by many writers. Dispensationalists often refer to God as the object of faith. A lexical meaning of *object* is a focus of attention. God surely is the focus of attention in salvation. So God is the object of faith but also its content. Content and object have meanings that are closely related. It is hard to distinguish between the two. This is cause for confusion when one states that the object of faith (God) never changes but the content of faith (the revelation or message) does since God is both object and content of saving faith. Rather than restrict the presentation of saving faith to the words *object* and *content*, a third term seems to be justified: *message*. The message acts as a pointer to God as the One in Whom must be believed. Belief about the message then is not the end, belief in God is. The content of faith is belief *in* God Himself. God is not simply the object of faith as faith is not believing about God but believing *in* Him.

Here then is a most important distinction that should be made. The content of faith is God. The message to be believed is the instrument with which God presents Himself to be believed in. The content of faith never changes. The person of God has always been and will always be what must be believed in. The message or instrument whereby God presents Himself as the One to be believed in does change. It has pleased God to reveal Himself in many ways over the ages (Heb. 1:1), but He always reveals Himself as what must be believed in. A distinction between object and content may be made but the much more helpful distinction is between the content of faith and the message. Note the following passages as they will help clarify the proposed distinction between content of faith and the message that points to Him: "The LORD said to Moses. 'How long will this people spurn Me? And how long will they not believe in Me, despite all the signs which I have performed in their midst?'"(Num. 11:14) In this passage, the message that pointed to Yahweh was the signs or miracles he had performed for them. The Israelites did not deny the miracles, they believed them, but they did not believe in the God that these miracles pointed to. They spurned God. They did not believe *in* God. Believing the miracles was not enough. They failed to believe in the content of saving faith, God Himself.

2 Kings 7:14 reads, "However, they did not listen, but stiffened their neck like their fathers, who did not believe in the LORD their God." What the Israelites did not listen to was the message that pointed to Yahweh. Just like their fathers, they did not believe in the One the message pointed to. In this

case they rejected both the message and the content of faith, God. After describing the wonders God performed when leading the Israelites out of Egypt and caring for them in the wilderness, Asaph gave the reason God's wrath was on them. "Because they did not believe in God and did not trust in His salvation" (Ps. 78:22). The message was the wonders God performed. The content of faith in which they were required to believe was Yahweh. Although they did not deny the message of the works of God, but this did not lead them to believe in Him.

This concept is also clear in the New Testament: "How then will they call on Him in whom they have not believed? How will they believe in Him whom they have not heard? And how will they hear without a preacher?" (Rom 10:14). A person must hear something in order to believe in Him. The message is what they must hear that points them to God. But they must believe in Him to be saved. The content of faith is belief in God. One more example will do: "Jesus answered them, 'I told you, and you do not believe; the works that I do in My Father's name, these testify of Me'" (Jn. 10:25). In this case the message came in two forms, Jesus' own words and His works. Because they did not believe the message of His words that pointed to Him, they did not believe *in* Him. So then the content of faith is always belief in God. It is God in Whom must be believed for salvation. As seen above, the message that points to God can be believed, but that alone is not sufficient for salvation. Belief of a message does not necessarily produce belief in God. The message is necessary. Certain facts must be believed. If the message is rejected then one will surely reject the person it points to. The message therefore is very important. But it should not be confused with the content of saving faith. Although the content of faith never changes, the message that points to God as Savior does. The evidence for a changing message will be addressed later in this chapter.

The Content of Saving Faith is Belief in God.

Genesis 15:6 is a central passage on saving faith: "Then he [Abraham] believed in the LORD; and He reckoned it to him as righteousness." Paul uses this passage as a model for justification by faith in Romans 4 the text said he believed *in God*. The preposition before Yahweh shows that Abraham believed more than simply God's testimony[4], rather he believed *in* God Himself.

---

[4] In Rom 4:3 Paul wrote that Abraham believed God rather than in God. But here and in Gal 3:6 he was quoting from the Septuagint that uses the words tw`/ qew`/ in Gen 15:6. That Paul understood Gen 15:6 to teach faith *in* God see Rom 4:23-24.

On the relationship of the message of salvation and the object, Ryrie comments, "To believe in Christ for salvation means to have confidence that He can remove the guilt of sin and give eternal life."[5] The confidence is in the person of Christ to save but the message must first be heard to know that He died for sins and offers salvation to all. God uses the message to bring about belief in Himself.

Some suggest that belief in the message itself is sufficient. For example, Hodges writes, "What faith really is, in biblical language, is receiving the testimony of God. It is the inward conviction that what God says to us in the gospel is true. That – and that alone – is saving faith."[6] Of course the message is important but it is so because it points to God Himself. But one can believe a message or proposition without fully believing in the person who gave it. Paul knew that King Agrippa understood what the prophets wrote concerning Christ. "King Agrippa, do you believe the Prophets? I know that you do" (Acts 26:27). Although the king believed the message of the prophets, he still had not believed in God. Despite his previous comment, Hodges says with some irony,

> It would be hard to find a statement in the Bible more superbly simple than the words of the Lord Jesus Christ when he said: 'Most assuredly, I say to you, he who believes in Me has everlasting life (Jn 6:47).'[7]

Jesus did not say 'he who believes Me', stressing what Jesus said, but he who believes *in* Me. Abraham believed *in* Yahweh and Jesus said that one should believe *in* Him not in what He said independent of Himself. The message is the instrument to point to the personal God.

While the Old Testament teaches belief *in* God, it does not seem to point to any one Person of the godhead. The New Testament, however, specifically on some occasions stresses belief in Christ, God the Son. There are many passages[8] that teach one must believe in or on Christ for salvation. In these passages the content of faith is belief in God the Son. On other occasions the New Testament points to belief in God the Father for salvation. Jn. 5:24 and Rom. 4:24 are two examples. "Truly, truly, I say to you, he who hears My word, and believes Him who sent Me, has eternal life, and does not come into judgment, but has passed out of death into life" (Jn. 5:24). In this verse the message was Jesus' own words which pointed to God the Father as

---

[5] Charles Ryrie, *So Great Salvation* (Victor Books, 1989) ,119.
[6] Zane Hodges, *Absolutely Free* (Grand Rapids: Academie Books, 1989), 31.
[7] Ibid., 25.
[8] E.g., Jn. 3:15, 16, 18, 36; 6:40; 7:38; Rom. 3:26; 1 Tim. 1:16; Php. 1:29; 1 Pet. 1:8; 1 Jn. 3:23; and 5:13.

the One in Whom is to be believed. The content of faith remains belief in God, and specifically here in God the Father. While considering Gen. 15:6, Paul writes in Rom. 4:23-24, "Now not for his sake only was it written that it was credited to him, but for our sake also, to whom it will be credited, as those who believe in Him who raised Jesus our Lord from the dead." The content of faith according to this verse is belief in God the Father who raised Jesus from the dead. Paul points to God the Father as the One in Whom is to be believed even though Jesus had already finished His work on Calvary. Rom. 10:9 also points to God the Father as the One in Whom is to be believed, as He raised Jesus. The passage actually points to both the Father and Son. A person is to believe that Jesus is Lord *and* that the Father raised Him from the dead.

Jesus is Yahweh

Belief in the Father and/or Son has always been the content of faith because both are called Yahweh. The New Testament writers understood this. Acts 2:36 reads, "Therefore let all the house of Israel know for certain that God has made Him [Jesus] both Lord and Christ--this Jesus whom you crucified." Christ here means *Messiah*, but Lord means *Yahweh*. The immediate context shows this to be true. In his sermon Peter quotes from Joel 2:32 in Acts 2:21 to support his claim that Jesus is Lord. "And it shall be that everyone who calls on the name of the Lord shall be saved." *Lord* is translated from the Greek word *kurios* (in the LXX) which is itself a translation of the Hebrew word *Yahweh* (in the Hebrew OT).

One may also compare Is. 45:23 to Php. 2:10. In Is. 45:23 Yahweh speaks, "I have sworn by Myself, the word has gone forth from My mouth in righteousness and will not turn back, that to Me every knee will bow, every tongue will swear *allegiance*." Php. 2:10 reads, "so that at the name of Jesus EVERY KNEE WILL BOW, of those who are in heaven and on earth and under the earth." Here Paul equates the name of Jesus with the name Yahweh.

Isaiah writes, "It is the LORD of hosts whom you should regard as holy..."(Is. 8:13). The Hebrew word translated *Lord* is *Yahweh*. "Regard as holy" means to sanctify or set apart. The Septuagint translates this as ἁγιάσατε which is the same word Peter uses in 1 Pet. 3:15. Peter writes, "but sanctify Christ as Lord in your hearts...", presenting Christ as Yahweh.

Thus when the Scripture says that Abraham believed in Yahweh and it was counted to him as righteousness, it would not be wrong to claim that He too believed in Christ (whether directly or indirectly), as Christ is Yahweh. However, Abraham may not have known specifically the depths and significance of the triunity of Yahweh. The name Yahweh belonged to both the Father and the Son (and of course the Spirit as well), but the revelation of the Son as Son was not yet clear in Abraham's day (although Abraham did have specific interaction with the preincarnate Christ – and understood that in such interaction he was dealing with God, see Jn. 8:56). Nor was Abraham presented the same gospel message pointing directly to the death of Christ as that preached later. Today Jesus is proclaimed as God who died, was buried, and rose again.

Opposing Views Described and Compared

Covenant theologians stress the sameness of the content of faith. Charles Hodge, a covenant post-millennialist, believed that the content of faith is always the same.

> As the same promise was made to those who lived before the advent is now made to us in the gospel, as the same Redeemer was revealed to them who is presented as the object of faith to us, it of necessity follows that the condition or terms of salvation, was the same then as now. It was not mere faith or trust in God, or simply piety, which was required, but faith in the promise of redemption through the Messiah.[9]

Hodge here teaches that the content of faith has always been faith in Jesus Christ and, if his use of promise is taken to mean message, the message was always the same. In referring to the promise of the seed of the woman in Gen. 3:15 he wrote,

> This promise was repeated and amplified from time to time, until the Redeemer actually came. In these additional and fuller predictions, the nature of this redemption was set forth with ever increasing clearness.[10]

Hodge seems to teach that the essential message was always the same even though it was later amplified.

Louis Berkhof is another well respected covenant theologian and amillennialist. He wrote that there is only one gospel and that the content of that gospel is the same. To him the condition of salvation is always faith and the message of that faith is always the same:

---

[9] Charles Hodge, *Systematic Theology*, Vol II (Grand Rapids: Wm B. Eerdmans Publishing Co, 1986), 371-372.
[10] Ibid., 369.

> The Bible teaches that there is but a single gospel by which men can be saved. And because the gospel is nothing but the revelation of the covenant of grace, it follows that there is also but one covenant...The way of salvation revealed in the covenant is the same. Scripture insists on identical conditions all along.[11]

One should note how Berkhof strongly connects the legitimacy of the covenant of grace with the sameness of the content of the faith required for salvation. This may explain the insistence of covenant theologians that the object and content of saving faith are unchanging.

The covenant position on the unity of the Bible seems to be stressed most strongly in its doctrine of salvation. Therefore, any suggestion that the content of saving faith might be developing over time threatens the unity of the covenant. This is why the dispensationalist is commonly accused of destroying the unity of the Bible. In this regard Ryrie writes,

> What is this unity that is supposedly destroyed? It is, in the nondispensationalist's opinion, the unity of the overall purpose of redemption. The so-called covenant of grace is the governing category by which all Scripture is to be understood. God's purpose in the world is to redeem, and men have been, are, and will always be redeemed in the same manner throughout all time.[12]

Like Hodge, Berkhof seems to teach that the essential message is unchanging even though he recognizes some progressive development of it. Later in his chapter on faith, he understood that the knowledge of that faith expands as more revelation is given from God. He writes,

> On the one hand it would be an over estimation of the knowledge of faith, if it were regarded as a complete comprehension of the objects of faith...It is impossible to determine with precision just how much knowledge is absolutely required in saving faith. [13]

Yet he still believed that the one object of saving faith is Jesus Christ, as he indicates saying, "The object of special faith, then, is Jesus Christ and the promise of salvation through Him."[14] Berkhof's knowledge of faith is what is here referenced as the message. He too recognizes that the message expands and develops over time. His object of faith is Jesus Christ and the message of the promise of salvation through Him.

---

[11] Louis Berkhof, *Systematic Theology* (Grand Rapids: Wm. B. Eerdmans Publishing Co., 1984), 279-280.

[12] Charles Ryrie, *Dispensationalism* (Chicago: Moody Publishers, 2007), 106.

[13] Berkhof, *Systematic Theology*, 503-504.

[14] Ibid., 506.

J. Barton Payne in his chapter on faith taught that believing on the Lord Jesus has always been the one condition for salvation:

> So also today, as 1900 years ago (or over 3900 years ago, in the case of Abraham), the question, 'What must I do to be saved?' is answered by the same simple but profound truth, 'Believe on the Lord Jesus, and thou shalt be saved, and thy house (Acts 16:31).'[15]

Like Berkhof, he seems to link the idea of one broad covenant to his conclusion of sameness of saving faith. He again says,

> A fundamental failure of Scofield Dispensationalism is its short sighted inability to appreciate the Sinaitic law as a part of the one gracious testament, which had been revealed immediately after man's fall.[16]

It may be seen here again how a reliance on the one covenant of grace influences one's position. It is agreed that one must believe on the Lord Jesus Christ or Yahweh but the message that points to Him is not always the same. Barton also wrote that "The fundamental requirement of the law was faith, belief in God (Deut 1:32; 9:23)."[17] The context indicates that by God he meant Yahweh. With this the dispensationalist would agree. Millard Erickson writes: "...the type of faith necessary for salvation involves both believing that and believing in, or assenting to facts and trusting in a person."[18] Agreed. The "believing that" is the message pointing to the person and this person is Yahweh.

Benjamin Warfield, also a covenant theologian, had similar views. In his chapter on faith, he taught that there is no distinction in the faith of the two covenants. In his review of the historical presentation of faith, he writes,

> Nowhere is the demand of faith treated as a novelty of the new covenant, or is there a distinction drawn between the faith of the two covenants; everywhere the sense of the continuity is prominent.[19]

---

[15] J. Barton Payne, The Theology of the Older Testament (Grand Rapids: Zondervan Publishing House, 1962), 305.

[16] Ibid., 308.

[17] Ibid., 309.

[18] Millard J. Erickson, *Christian Theology,* One Volume Edition (Grand Rapids: Baker Book House, 1985) 940

[19] Benjamin B. Warfield, *Biblical and Theological Studies* (Philadelphia: The Presbyterian and Reformed Publishing Company, 1968), 404.

But just like the above mentioned covenant theologians, he too recognized the progressive nature of the message:

> Between the faith of the two Testaments there exists, indeed, no further difference than that which the progress of the historical working out of the redemption brought with it.[20]

Warfield has much to say on this historical development of the faith. He taught that the Mosaic Law did not make a major change in the religion of Israel. It was still based on faith in the promises of God. In fact, the Law of Moses was given to a people who already had a relationship to God. He understood that the New Testament had the primary task of bringing men to believe in the Redeemer who had come and that this is why the New Testament had such a strong and clear emphasis on using the name of Christ as the content of that faith.

Warfield believed that the message did differ in the past based on historical development. In contrasting the New Testament books, which were primarily concerned with faith in the Redeemer who had come, with Old Testament books, he writes,

> ...for the rest [Old Testament books] they differ among themselves in the prominence given to it [faith] and in the aspects in which it is presented, in accordance with the place of each in the historical development of the new life.[21]

So Warfield rightly recognized the idea of a progressive revelation and its effects on the message as it pointed to belief in Yahweh. In concluding this chapter on faith, he wrote that faith's value is solely derived from its object and that object is the God of grace. He says,

> It is, accordingly, solely from its *object* [emphasis his] that faith derives its value. This object is uniformly the God of grace...This one object of saving faith never varies from the beginning to the end of the scriptural revelation, though, naturally, there is an immense difference between its earlier and later stages in the fullness of knowledge as to the nature of the redemptive work by which the salvation entrusted to God shall be accomplished; and as naturally, there occurs a very great variety of forms of statement in which trust in the God of salvation receives expression.[22]

---

[20] Ibid., 405.
[21] Ibid., 411.
[22] Ibid., 423.

Warfield taught that the object of faith is always God. It never varies. But it is not belief about the object but belief in the object that saves. His use of revelation is just what is meant by message. This message and its understanding expand in its fullness as revelation progresses. On this he says,

> Jesus Christ, God the Redeemer, is accordingly the one object of saving faith, presented to its embrace at first implicitly and in promise, and ever more and more openly until at last it is entirely explicit and we read that a man is not justified save through faith in Jesus Christ.[23]

Yes, the content of saving faith is always belief in Yahweh and the message or presentation of Yahweh expands as revelation progresses. So it seems that many who insist on the unity of saving faith throughout the Bible also recognize that the message expands or grows with additional revelation. They exhibit [commendable] zeal in defending a singular way of salvation throughout the Bible, and often those who would note any significant differences in the message are counted as teaching more than one way of salvation. But it is evident that special care must be taken in the terminology used. William Cox emphasizes,

> Every person who ever graced, or ever will grace, the portals of heaven will have one thing in common with all other citizens of heaven. Each one will have come there through a childlike faith in the shed blood of Jesus Christ. *There is only one plan of salvation.* Yea, and there has never been another plan. Nor will there *ever* be a different plan [emphasis his].[24]

Based on his emphasis, it seems he is saying that anyone who disagrees with the idea that the earliest saints were saved by personal and specific faith in the shed blood of Jesus Christ is teaching another way of salvation. While the basis of salvation has always been the death of Jesus Christ, the revelation of that fact was revealed much later in the progress of revelation.

Dispensationalists also believe that the condition of salvation has always been faith and that the basis of salvation has always been the death of Jesus Christ as the payment for the penalty of sins. But they see from the progress of revelation that the message pointing to Yahweh changes or expands.

---

[23] Ibid., 424.
[24] William E. Cox, *Amillennialism Today* (Phillipsburg, NJ: Presbyterian and Reformed Publishing Co., 1966), 29.

Walvoord, sees the problem with the sameness view as an over emphasis on unity and a failure to see or allow the progression of revelation. One should note that his concern is not primarily theological but hermeneutical. While he sees that the message does change, he insists on only one way of salvation:

> It is clear that Old Testament saints did not believe in Christ in the same way and with the same comprehension that believers with the New Testament do. In the nature of the case the issue of faith is to believe in the revelation given. On the other hand there are not two ways of salvation. All salvation of God stems from the Savior, the Son of God, and His work on the cross...The two great essentials of salvation remain the same from the salvation of Adam to the last soul which God takes to Himself in the future. Faith is the condition and the death of Christ is the basis.[25]

He taught that faith must be in what God had revealed up to that time. The message changes as a result of a cumulative revelation. The message is according to what had been revealed up to that time. Yet, as he clearly wrote, there are not two ways of salvation even though the message does change over time.

Grossman taught that the death of Christ is always the ground of salvation but the personal understanding of that work may not always be the necessary condition. So an Old Testament saint might exercise saving faith without understanding that his salvation depended on the death of the coming Messiah.

> So that the ancient believer laid hold, not so much (at least consciously) upon the redemptive *work* which was to be the ground of his salvation, nor perhaps even upon the promise objectively considered, but upon the *Promiser* Himself. Did the promised Deliverer then occupy exactly the same place in the Old Testament plan of salvation which the Lord Jesus Christ occupies in the New? As to the *ultimate ground* of salvation—Yes! But as to the conscious object of his faith—No![26]

To Grossman the object of faith was more the *Promiser* than the specific promise.

Pentecost, in a discussion on salvation during the tribulation period, taught that salvation in every age was by faith based on the shed blood of Jesus Christ and applied by the Holy Spirit:

---

[25] Walvoord, "Series in Christology—Part 4: The Preincarnate Son of God," 422.
[26] Lucius E. Smith, "Is Salvation Possible without a Knowledge of the Gospel?", *Bibliotheca Sacra* 38:626 (Oct 1881) quoted by Philip W. Grossman, "Jewish Anticipation of the Cross," *Bibliotheca Sacra* 106 (April 1949): 241.

I wish, therefore, explicitly to state my own conviction...that the salvation of all the saved at all times depends on the work of Christ, and that the Spirit is the only efficacious applier of it to any soul" (William Kelly, *Lectures on the Revelation*, p. 164, f.n). It may be asserted with confidence, then, that the salvation offered through the blood of the Lamb, to be received by faith, will be more effectual through the working of the Holy Spirit.[27]

The *Message* Changes/Expands with the Progress of Revelation

Testimony of the Old Testament Scriptures

As noted above, the concern of men like Walvoord is not first theological but hermeneutical. Sound theology depends on a sound hermeneutic. They see the message changing and growing over time thus doing justice to the idea of progressive revelation. John Feinberg describes this as a cumulative hermeneutic. He believes that the message of faith in the Old Testament is cumulative over time.[28] This is a very simple idea. Men cannot know what God has not yet revealed. For example, the Spirit of God in Mic. 5:2 revealed that the Messiah would be born in Bethlehem. No one could have known this prior to that revelation simply because God had not yet revealed it. The same reasoning here should be applied to any later revelation regardless of how much was then known. The fact that we now know that Jesus was born in Bethlehem does not cause us to believe that anyone knew this before God revealed it in Mic. 5:2. One must turn to the Bible to see if the message ever changes/expands as revelation progressed. Did the Old Testament saints always know the specifics that Christ would one day die for their sins? Gen. 3:15 gives an early promises of salvation: "And I will put enmity between you and the woman, and between your seed and her seed; he shall bruise you on the head, and you shall bruise him on the heel." One should ask what Adam and Eve would have understood from these words of Yahweh to Satan. Of course Bible students today would know that this offspring referred to the coming Son of God but how could anyone at that time possibly know that God the Son would take on flesh and die for the sins of the world?

While Christ's work on Calvary was the basis of his salvation, Abraham, for example apparently would not have known that fully. Some might reference Jn. 8:56 and Gal. 3:8 at this point to show that Abraham knew more than what was revealed at the time of his imputed righteousness. But, while it is possible that God may have given him more insight at a later time,

---

[27] Dwight L. Pentecost, "Salvation in the Tribulation," *Bibliotheca Sacra*, 115 (Jan 1958): 58.

[28] John S. Feinberg, "Salvation in the Old Testament," in John S. and Paul D. Feinberg, ed., *Tradition and Testament – Essays in Honor of Charles Lee Feinberg* (Chicago: Moody Press, 1981), 57-58.

Abraham was made righteous right then at Gen. 15:6 when he believed in Yahweh. The promise of God was the message that pointed him to Yahweh and belief in Him.

Paul teaches in Rom. 4:20-24 that the faith of Abraham is like the faith of all believers today. But Paul also makes it clear that the message is different. Rom. 4:20-24 reads,

> Yet, with respect to the promise of God, he did not waver in unbelief but grew strong in faith, giving glory to God, and being fully assured that what God had promised, He was able also to perform. Therefore IT WAS ALSO CREDITED TO HIM AS RIGHTEOUSNESS. Now not for his sake only was it written that it was credited to him, but for our sake also, to whom it will be credited, as those who believe in Him who raised Jesus our Lord from the dead, *He* who was delivered over because of our transgressions, and was raised because of our justification.

The promises of God - His message to Abraham - was that Abraham's offspring would be as numerous as the stars of the heaven and that he would have a son. Abraham's belief in Yahweh was credited to him as righteousness. But Paul taught that believers of his day believed the message that God raised Jesus from the dead after he was delivered up for our trespasses. Paul here clearly teaches what is constant, namely faith in God, and what changes, namely the message of what God has revealed.

The Bible teaches the idea of a substitutionary or vicarious death very early in its revelation: "Then Abraham raised his eyes and looked, and behold, behind *him* a ram caught in the thicket by his horns; and Abraham went and took the ram and offered him up for a burnt offering in the place of his son" (Gen. 22:13). Here Abraham understood the idea of substitution, but there is no revelation that Christ would be the substitute for his sins. "He shall lay his hand on the head of the burnt offering, that it may be accepted for him to make atonement on his behalf" (Lev 1:4). This verse also teaches the death of the sacrifice on behalf of or as a substitute for the sinner. Once again there is no revelation that Christ personally would be the ultimate sacrifice on behalf of the sinner. Of course today, it is easy to see that both of these were typical of the substitutionary atonement.

Bible students recognize that the first clear passage that teaches that the Messiah would die for the sins of Israel is in Is. 53, which reads, "All of us like sheep have gone astray, each of us has turned to his own way; but the LORD has caused the iniquity of us all to fall on Him." Even then, because of the absence of additional revelation the Israelite would not have grasped the fullness of all that this passage entailed. Later God revealed to Daniel that after the 69th week of the prophesied 70 weeks the Messiah would be cut off

(Dan 9:26). Given the context of God's intention to put an end to iniquity during this period, this too is a reference to the death of the Messiah for the forgiveness of sins. But if Isaiah and Daniel understood this as clearly as we do today, then why didn't they proclaim it perhaps more specifically? The answer seems to be that the salvation message to Israel was not the cross of Christ but the coming glory of the kingdom. It was the kingdom that was preached to the Jews. Philip Grossman estimates that the predictions of the glory of the coming Messiah in His kingdom exceeded the predictions of the Messiah's suffering eight to one.[29] After the death of Christ, God made the gospel as known today clear and then commanded that this gospel be proclaimed first to Israel and then to the whole world.

Old Testament Sacrifices
Since the animal sacrifices of the Old Testament were types of the one final sacrifice of Christ on Calvary, their effect on the understanding of Old Testament saints regarding salvation should be addressed. These blood sacrifices did not begin with the giving of the Mosaic Law. They may be found very early after the fall of Adam. Cain offered a blood sacrifice from his flock and it was accepted by God (Gen. 4:3-5). Noah built an altar for sacrifice after he went out from the ark when the flood receded and built an altar for sacrifice (Gen. 8:20). Abraham built an altar to the Lord after God had made the promises of Gen. 12:1-7 to him. And God instructed the Jews at the time of the exodus to slay a lamb and apply the blood to the doorposts so that the angle of death would pass over them (Ex. 12:1-13). So God's teaching of animal sacrifices existed before the giving of the Mosaic Law. Abel, Noah, Abraham, and those of the Exodus all knew that blood sacrifice was required by God in order to approach Him. But nowhere do these accounts indicate that these sacrifices were known to mean that Jesus Christ would one day die for their sins. God had not yet revealed this. They offered these sacrifices in faith because they believed in the One who commanded it. Like Abraham, these saints were justified by faith in God based on what He had revealed up to their time.

    John Whitcomb wrote that the purposes of Old Testament animal sacrifices were functionally distinct from the redemptive work of the cross.[30] Of course animal sacrifices could never finally take away sin (Heb. 10:4,11). But is it true that these sacrifices taught those under the Mosaic Law that

---

[29] Philip W. Grossman, "The Jewish Anticipation of the Cross" *Biliotheca Sacra*, April 1949: 248.

[30] John C. Whitcomb, "Christ's Atonement and Animal Sacrifices in Israel" *Grace Theological Journal*, Fall 1985: 201-217.

Christ would one day die for the sins of Israel or the sins of the world? Whitcomb taught that these blood sacrifices were more than just symbolic or a type of a future once for all atonement. They actually were an atonement for sins committed - not an atonement for salvation but an atonement for restoration to covenant blessings. They restored the transgressor back into a right relationship with the covenant God made with Israel. He distinguishes between a ceremonial atonement which restores covenant relationship and a spiritual atonement which brings eternal salvation. The point is that while believers today see these animal sacrifices as types of Christ's atonement, the Israelite did not necessarily understand them as types.

John Feinberg recognized that it is wrong to discard the original meaning of an Old Testament type in favor of the New Testament antitype meaning. One should keep the Old Testament meaning in its original context even though it points to its antitype in the New Testament.[31] According to the original context, the Israelite understood the animal sacrifices not as a symbol of Christ's death but as a God given means of restoration back into the covenant blessings promised to Israel. On this Whitcomb writes,

> In the covenant at Sinai, God provided a highly complex and rigid structure for his "kingdom of priests." Within that structure, national/theocratic transgressions would receive national/theocratic forgiveness when appropriate sacrifices were offered to God through legitimate priests at the tabernacle/temple altar. This "forgiveness" was promised regardless of the spiritual state of either the offerer or the priest. However, such sacrificial blood could never cleanse the conscience or save the soul (Heb 10:1–2), so God repeatedly sent prophets to call his people to love and obey their God from the heart. Apart from such genuine faith, all the ceremonially "kosher" animals in the whole world would avail nothing in the spiritual realm (Ps 50:7–15; Isa 1:12–20; Amos 4:4–5; 5:20–27 ; Hos 5:6; Mic 6:6–8; Jer 6:20; 7:21–23). It was not to be either faith or sacrifices; rather, it was to be both faith and sacrifices (cf. Ps 51:19)... *This was the unique tension within the theocracy of Israel that many Christian theologians apparently do not comprehend.* [emphasis mine][32]

One must remember that the Mosaic Law did not do away with the promises to Abraham (Gal. 3:17). The Israelite was saved by faith in God and the specific content revealed historically up until that time. The animal sacrifices restored the Israelite to the blessings of the covenant that he already possessed by birth.

---

[31] John S. Feinberg, "Salvation in the Old Testament," in John S. and Paul D. Feinberg, ed., *Tradition and Testament – Essays in Honor of Charles Lee Feinberg* (Chicago: Moody Press, 1981), 46.
[32] Ibid., 210-211.

The book of Leviticus makes it clear that these sacrifices actually made an atonement for sin. For example, Lev. 4:20 reads, "...So the priest shall make atonement for them, and they will be forgiven." See also Lev. 4:31, 35; 5:6, 10, 16, 18. But these verses could not mean forgiveness of sin for eternal salvation because they had to be repeated with each sin committed. No, these sacrifices were for restoration for one who was already in a national covenant relationship with God. The Israelite understood them primarily in terms of restoration. The Old Testament teaches that sacrifices were actually effective in the forgiveness of sins. But the New Testament teaches that sacrifices cannot remove sin, as Heb. 10:4 reads, "For it is impossible for the blood of bulls and goats to take away sins." The Bible clearly teaches both ideas. How can these two ideas both be true? Ryrie's solution is to recognize that all Israelites are related to God theocratically, spiritually, or both.[33] All Israelites are physically born into the nation of Israel and are related to God through being part of the theocracy of Israel. This relationship is true regardless of one's spiritual state. Sin, at least temporarily, broke that theocratic relationship and consequently the relationship with God. So one type of forgiveness is simply a restoration back to a right relationship with the government or theocracy.

A broken theocratic relationship may be restored and sins forgiven by sacrifice. There is no evidence that the spiritual state of the one offering the sacrifice impacts the effectiveness of his sacrifice. An Israelite could be restored theocratically whether he was eternally saved or not. Ryrie described this as a theocratic adjustment. While every Israelite was related to God theocratically, some were also related spiritually. They have eternal life. Again, the basis of this eternal life is the death of Christ. All the Israelite understood at the time was that he believed in Yahweh based on the message revealed up to that time just as Abraham had. They could not have understood that their salvation was based on the death of Christ that their sacrifices prefigured. If they had they would have stopped making the sacrifices. Heb. 10:2 reads, "For the Law, since it has *only* a shadow of the good things to come *and* not the very form of things, can never, by the same sacrifices which they offer continually year by year, make perfect those who draw near. Otherwise, would they not have ceased to be offered, because the worshipers, having once been cleansed, would no longer have had consciousness of sins?" This passage teaches that faith in the death of Christ removes the consciousness of sin in the sense that the believer no longer recognizes any more need for sacrifices.

---

[33] Ryrie, Dispensationalism, 136-139.

Two things were operating simultaneously during the time of the Mosaic Law - salvation by grace through faith based on the Abrahamic grace covenant, and restoration back into covenant blessings by animal sacrifices. No Israelite ever received eternal salvation by offering of sacrifices, but he could be restored through them. This is just the same as 1 Jn. 1:9 that teaches the Christian if he confesses his sin God is faithful and just to forgive. He knows this means restoration not that he needed to be eternally saved again. Ryrie says,

> The distinction between ceremonial and spiritual atonement is by no means a minor one, for it is at the heart of the basic difference between the theocracy of Israel and the Church, the Body and Bride of Christ.[34]

So the sacrifices had at least two major purposes. One was restoration of the Israelite back to the blessings of the theocratic nation of Israel. These sacrifices were a means to a real forgiveness of sins in a theocratic sense. Some see this restoration as sanctification as well since one's sins were cleansed. The second was to foreshadow or to prefigure the future death of Christ as the basis of their salvation. The Old Testament saint did not understand that this was the basis of his salvation because if he had, he would not have continued to offer sacrifices. He believed in the God who made the promises according to what God had revealed up to his on time.

Testimony of the New Testament Scripture
The New Testament scriptures reveal that the Jews did not understand that the death of Christ was the basis for the forgiveness of sins. They could not reconcile the promised glory of the Messiah with His suffering foretold by the prophets. Even Jesus' disciples failed to see this. Peter rebuked Jesus for teaching them that He must suffer and die (Mt. 16:21-22). Jesus told His disciples that he would be killed and be raised from the dead. They were deeply grieved even though He had told them he would be raised from the dead (Mt. 17:22-23). Luke writes, "But the disciples understood none of these things, and *the meaning of* this statement was hidden from them, and they did not comprehend the things that were said" (Lk. 18:34). The disciples had not yet come to understand the meaning of Christ's death. These same men had come to believe that Jesus was the Messiah prior to His revealing that He had to die (Jn. 1:45, 49). Luke 24:44-45 gives evidence that the death of Christ as a substitute for sins was not understand prior to

---

[34] Ibid., 211.

Calvary, saying, "Now He said to them, 'These are My words which I spoke to you while I was still with you, that all things which are written about Me in the Law of Moses and the Prophets and the Psalms must be fulfilled.' Then He opened their minds to understand the Scriptures." Jesus spoke these words to a gathering that included the eleven disciples. So they too did not understand the Scriptures. Yet it is hard to doubt that they had been justified by faith prior to witnessing his death and resurrection.

Some might take Paul's writings in Eph. 2:11-18 as evidence that both Jew and Gentile were saved in the same way in all ages. But Paul was referring to his own day, not the days of the Old Testament. It was only after the death of Christ that believing Jews and Gentiles have been reconciled in one body to God through the cross.

The New Testament writers were missionaries. They were given their commission in Mt. 28:18-20 to make disciples of all nations. After the death, burial, and resurrection of Christ, God having now made the gospel clear, they truly had a message for the entire world.

Changing Message no Support for Inclusivism
Some may conclude that a changing message gives support for the inclusivist doctrine that not everyone today needs to hear the gospel to be saved, but even though the message changes, each age has its own message to believe – pointing to the unchanging object and content. Today the message is that God sent His Son to die for the sins of the world. Rom. 10:9-15 makes it clear that to be saved in this age one must hear the gospel that Christ died for sinners, was buried, and rose again and then believe in Him.

Conclusion
It is here suggested that a clear distinction between *object* and *content* of faith is very difficult to make. Therefore, it is most helpful to introduce a third term, *message*. The message is the specific revelation of God that points to Himself as the one in Whom to believe. A strong distinction must be made between content/object of faith and the message. God is the object of faith but, more importantly, the content of saving faith is always Yahweh. The message that points to Yahweh, however, expands with the progress of revelation. This distinction provides an understanding of Biblical soteriology with proper focus on progressive revelation while avoiding even the appearance of introducing more than one way of salvation.

"I am a premillennialist because I think it unwise to take the words of the Bible in a nonliteral sense when the literal meaning is plain. These promises to Abraham and David concern the physical descendants of Abraham. Why expect them to be fulfilled by the church, unless *Israel* no longer means *Israel* but means the *church*? Since the New Testament continues to distinguish the Jews from the church, it appears that we should expect these promises to be fulfilled through the Jews rather than the church (1 Cor. 10:32; Rom. 11:26)."

- Charles C. Ryrie
The Final Countdown, 1982, page 52-53

12

The Times of the Gentiles
David Criswell

Introduction

Replacement theology teaches that the church has replaced Israel. In eschatological passages "Israel" is interpreted to mean the predominantly Gentile church. In this regard there has been much debate between replacement theology and dispensational theology, with each side scoring points along the way, yet there remain a number of issues which covenant theology, replacement theology, and realized eschatology have not adequately answered, perhaps none so problematic (from the non-dispensational perspective) as the following: *if Israel, as a nation and people, have been replaced by the church, then what is the "time of the Gentiles" to which Jesus refers, and what does its end mean?*
Jesus said:

> But when you see Jerusalem surrounded by armies, then recognize that her desolation is at hand. Then let those who are in Judea flee to the mountains, and let those who are in the midst of the city depart, and let not those who are in the country enter the city; because these are days of vengeance, in order that all things which are written may be fulfilled. Woe to those who are with child and to those who nurse babes in those days; for there will be great distress upon the land, and wrath to this people, and they will fall by the edge of the sword, and will be led captive into all the nations; and Jerusalem will be trampled under foot by the Gentiles until the times of the Gentiles be fulfilled. (Luke 21:20-24)

Some believe that Jesus was prophesying here about the invasion of Jerusalem which took place in 70 A.D. while others believe that this is an invasion in the Last Days before the second coming. However, for the purpose of our discussion here, the timing of the invasion is not the issue, but rather the central point of discussion is the fulfillment of the times of the Gentiles (21:24). It should be noted here that a discussion of preterism is irrelevant, as the reader will see, for regardless of when the invasion of Jerusalem took place (or will take place), the passage itself makes clear that "the times of the Gentiles" has *not* yet been fulfilled. Three essential ingredients are apparent in this passage.

Jerusalem Trampled Under Foot

The first key ingredient in Jesus' prophecy is that "Jerusalem will be trampled under foot by the Gentiles until the times of the Gentiles be fulfilled" (Luke 21:24). As long as the times of the Gentiles exist Jerusalem will be trampled under foot. Once the times of the Gentiles are fulfilled Jerusalem will be at peace. Preterism ignores this fact, choosing to emphasize the destruction of Jerusalem in 70 A.D., but Jerusalem did not cease to be trampled after the Roman armies ended their siege, nor did the Gentiles cede their power.

The year 70 A.D. brought not the end of Gentile trampling, but the beginning. In the early second century a certain Bar Kochba claimed to be the Messiah and started a new revolt against Rome.[1] By 135 A.D. Hadrian had defeated the rebellion and in 138 A.D. he renamed Jerusalem "*Colonia Aelia Capitolina.*"[2] Historian Philip Schaff, himself a preterist, records that Jerusalem was "again destroyed"[3] during that Bar Kochba rebellion when "more than a half million of Jews were slaughtered after desperate resistance."[4] Some even believe that Bar Kochba had rebuilt the Holy Temple of Jerusalem only to see it destroyed again, on the 9th day of Av, as with the previous temples.[5] Following this the Jews were expelled from Jerusalem and the city became dedicated to the pagan god Jupiter.[6]

The expulsion of Jews and the permanent occupation of Jerusalem by Romans could hardly bee seen as the end of Jerusalem's woes. Even before the Arabs swept across the middle east, Jerusalem remained a prize to be won. In 614 A.D. the Persian general Shahr-Baraz conquered Jerusalem and slaughtered most of its inhabitants.[7] In 629 A.D. the emperor Heraclius reclaimed Jerusalem for the Roman empire,[8] but just three years later a certain "prophet" named Mohammed died. His followers were destined to conquer the Mideast and Jerusalem along with it. By 637 Omar had conquered Jerusalem and the Dome of the Rock was eventually built where the Holy Temple of Solomon once stood.[9] To this very day that Dome stands as a stumbling block to Jews who seek to rebuild the temple and is a thorn in the politics of Arab-Jewish relations.

---

[1] Cf. Martin Gilbert, *Altas of Jewish Civilization* (New York, NY: MacMillian Publishing, 1990), 50-51.

[2] Ibid., 51.

[3] Philip Schaff, *History of the Christian Church Vol. 2* (Peabody, MA: Hendrickson Publishers,1858), 873

[4] Ibid., 37.

[5] Randall Price, *The Coming Last Days Temple* (Eugene, OR: Harvest House, 1999), 89-96.

[6] Chaim Potok, *Wanderings* (New York: Fawcett Crest, 1978), 303.

[7] John Julius Norwich, *A Short History of Byzanium* (New York: Random House, 1999), 90.

[8] Ibid., 95.

[9] J.J. Saunders, *A History of Medieval Islam* (London, England: Routledge Press, 1965), 48-49.

Eventually the Byzantine empire (eastern Roman empire) and the Muslim Omayyid dynasty reached an agreement that would allow Christians to make pilgrimages to Jerusalem unmolested, but this came to an end with the Muslims themselves were divided.[10] The Seljuk Turks honored no treaty and were so brutal that many Muslims themselves despised their cruelty and atrocities which included pulling living person's intestines out and tying them to a pole like a rope. Then they would make the person walk around the pole until his intestines fell out.[11]

Soon the Byzantines were so desperate that they turned to the Holy Roman Empire for help and the age of the Crusades began during which Jerusalem would again be trampled. The first Crusade ended with the conquest of Jerusalem in 1099, but with it came many atrocities. The knight Sir Tancred had placed the Jews of Jerusalem under his protection and placed them in a synagogue, but the Tafur mercenaries defied Tancred and burned the synagogue to the ground, killing its inhabitants.[12] With this conquest the kingdom of Jerusalem was founded, but it was destined to last less than a hundred years as the Muslim warrior Saladin, slaughtering many villages en route, came and surrounded Jerusalem, forcing its surrender in 1187.[13] Although the Crusades would continue for some time the Muslims continued to hold Jerusalem, desecrating its sacred spots, until World War I when the Ottoman empire finally fell.

During World War I the Ottoman Empire had chosen to ally itself with Germany. General Allenby of Great Britain was given the task of capturing Palestine from the Turks. His job was assisted by the famed Lawrence of Arabia who stirred up an Arab revolt against the Ottoman Turks and on December 9, 1917 Jerusalem surrendered to General Allenby.[14] The capture of Jerusalem, however, did not solve the problems of Palestine. Many Jewish settlements had already existed, and in many places Jews outnumbered Arabs, but there was an immediate debate as to what to do with the land claimed by so many. The British were put in charge of Jerusalem during this "mandate" period in which the eventual fate of Jerusalem would be decided.[15] This fate, however, would not be decided

---

[10] Steven Runciman, *A History of the Crusades* (Cambridge, England: Cambridge University Press, 1951), 42-50.

[11] Robert Payne, *The Dream and the Tomb* (New York: Cooper Square Press, 2000), 34.

[12] David Criswell, *Rise and Fall of the Holy Roman Empire* (Baltimore, MD: Publish America, 2005), 169-170.

[13] Ibid., 232.

[14] S. L. A. Marshall, *World War I* (Boston, MA: Houghton-Mifflin, 1964), 309-311.

[15] Cf. Randall Price, *Fast Facts on the Middle East Conflict* (Eugene, OR: Harvest House, 2000), 22-25.

until after World War II and many decades of Islamic terrorism within the Holy City.[16]

In 1936 an Arab revolt began.[17] Even before World War II Muslim extremist were intent on starting a new "holy war" and driving the infidel from Jerusalem. When the Second World War finally broke out Hitler promised the Arab nations that they could have Palestine and remove all the Jews from the land. The Mufti of Jerusalem went to Berlin where he met with the leaders of the Third Reich and promised to create an Arab-Islamic army to conquer Palestine and Jerusalem.[18] By the end of World War II millions of Jews were displaced and the Palestinian situation was still not resolved. Most countries did want to accept Jewish immigration[19] and there were already nearly two million Jews in Palestine by 1946.[20]

In 1947 the United Nations created a partition plan which would divide Palestine between the Jews and Arabs.[21] The Arabs, however, refused to accept the partition declaring the whole of Palestine belonged to them. They promised to "throw the Jews into the sea,"[22] and further declared, "we will strangle Jerusalem."[23] Seven nations, counting Palestine, invaded Israel[24] but God was with Israel and by the end of the war, Israel had won its independence, but Jerusalem was still divided. A wall ran down the middle of Jerusalem. It was still a city "trampled" by Gentiles. In 1967 Egypt again prepared to invade Israel and the Six-day war began, but again Israel prevailed. This time Jerusalem was in Jewish hands, except for the temple mount itself.[25] The city's most Holy site to Jews remained in Muslim hands, and has to this day.

Terrorism has become common place in Jerusalem; a city which remains populated by Palestinians in the western half. Jerusalem has been, and continues to be, trampled by Gentiles. It seems that even since Nebuchadnezzar invaded Jerusalem over 2600 years ago Jerusalem has been "trampled under foot by the Gentiles" (Luke 21:24). The destruction of Jerusalem by Titus was hardly the end of trampling, but one in a series of

---

[16] Howard Sacher, *A History of Israel from the Rise of Zionism to Our Time* (New York: Alfred Knopf, 2003), 135-200.

[17] Ibid., 203.

[18] Martin Gilbert, *Israel A History* (Toronto, ON: Turner Books, 1998), 117.

[19] Cf. David S. Wyman, *The Abandonment of the Jews* (New York: New Press, 1998).

[20] Price, *Fast Facts* op. cit., 39.

[21] Mitchell Bard, *Myths and Facts* (Chevy Chase, NY: American-Israeli Cooperative Enterprise, 2001), 54.

[22] Larry Collins & Dominique Lapierre, *O Jerusalem* (New York: Pocket Books, 1972), 75.

[23] Ibid., 94.

[24] Thomas Friedman, *Beirut to Jerusalem* (New York: Anchor Books, 1989), 15.

[25] Martin Gilbert, *Jerusalem in the Twentieth Century* (New York: John Wiley & Sons, 1996), 272-321.

tramplings which continue to this very day. To this day Jerusalem is still not at peace, a fact which prompts the question, "if Jerusalem is still trampled then how could the times of the Gentiles be said to be fulfilled?" Obviously that time has not yet come, for the trampling must continue "until the times of the Gentiles be fulfilled." The next question to be answered then is, "what is the time of the Gentiles?"

Gentiles vs. Jews

The word Gentile references one who is not a physical descendant of Jacob. The church is made up predominantly of Gentiles. The world at large is predominantly Gentile. If the "times of the Gentiles" must come to a close one day what can this mean but that the *Jews* time will come?

Covenant theology, replacement theology, and realized eschatology all struggle with the issue as related to Romans 11. Here is what Paul said:

> If the root be holy, the branches are too. But if some of the branches were broken off, and you, being a wild olive, were grafted in among them and became partaker with them of the rich root of the olive tree, do not be arrogant toward the branches; but if you are arrogant, *remember that* it is not you who supports the root, but the root *supports* you. You will say then, 'Branches were broken off so that I might be grafted in.' Quite right, they were broken off for their unbelief, but you stand by your faith. Do not be conceited, but fear; for if God did not spare the natural branches, neither will He spare you. Behold then the kindness and severity of God; to those who fell, severity, but to you, God's kindness, if you continue in His kindness; otherwise you also will be cut off. And they also, if they do not continue in their unbelief, will be grafted in; for God is able to graft them in again. For if you were cut off from what is by nature a wild olive tree, and were grafted contrary to nature into a cultivated olive tree, how much more shall these who are the natural *branches* be grafted into their own olive tree? (Romans 11:16-24)

The church is not Israel. One may be an Israeli and a member of the church and one may be a member of the church and be a part of Israel, but that no more means that the church is Israel than Israel is the church. To confuse the church and Israel is a significant error. Moreover, one who makes such an error finds himself at odds with the warning of Paul: "do not be conceited, but fear; for if God did not spare the natural branches, neither will He spare you" (11:20-21).

The equation of Israel and the church, if legitimate, would do be of no benefit to covenant theology for purposes of resolving this issue, for the "the time of the Gentiles" clearly comes to *an end* at some point in time. No covenant theologian believes that the church age will ever end, so the question still remains, "what is the time of the Gentiles?" Obviously, the "time of the Gentiles" refers to the time during which the Gentile nations of the world will reign over the earth. This is clearly taking place now. The majority of governments of the earth are neither God fearing nor could they be called "new Israel." Believers are generally agreed that their time will come and the world powers will one day fall, but this begs the very question. Shall the "times of the Gentiles" be replaced with "Gentiles"? If the "times of the Gentiles" ends, then the time for *Israel* must begin. To this the critic can only discard the natural meaning and suggest that it is "new Israel" which will rule, but the term "new Israel" is not to be found in the Bible. The typical misquote is to refer to Galatians 6:16 but it says "peace and mercy *be* upon them, **and** upon the Israel of God." It does not say "peace and mercy *be* upon them, **for they are** the Israel of God" but rather it *contrasts* the uncircumcised believers with "the Israel of God." Both are believers, both are a part of the church, each are distinguished.

Progressive dispensationalism affirms that the Church has not replaced Israel but "superseded Israel."[26] It will argue that "Israel has been 'incorporated' or 'reconstituted' into the church as the 'new Israel.'"[27] In fact, the opposite is more accurate. Believers within Israel may become incorporated into the church, but Israel is nowhere shown to cease its distinction and if it did, then "the times of the Gentiles" could not be distinguished from any other time.

It is not logical to assume that Christ would contrast Gentiles with Gentiles. The world at large is Gentile. The church is predominantly Gentile. Christ did not say the "times of the pagan," nor the "times of the unbelievers," nor even the "times of the unchurched," but the "times of the *Gentiles*".

Fulfilled : Completed or Begun?

One answer sometimes offered is that the word "fulfilled" has multiple meanings. The Greek word *plarothosin* can be defined as "fulfilled, make full, bring to completion, complete, or accomplish."[28] In each case the meaning involves the completion or end of a thing, not its beginning. The covenant theologian sees the church age as eternal. He must, therefore, see the "fulfillment" as the *beginning* of the church age. I have already shown, however, that the "times of the Gentiles" ends when Jerusalem is no longer

---

[26] J. Lanier Burns, "Israel and the Church of a Progressive Dispensationalist," *Contemporary Dispensationalism* op. cit., 274.

[27] Ibid., 271.

[28] Barclay Newman Jr., ed., *A Complete Greek-English Dictionary of the New Testament* (Stuttgart, Germany: United Bible Societies, 1971), 144.

trampled under foot. That day has not yet come, so there is only one other alternative offered.

Tertullian's views often reflect evangelical doctrine, however, Tertullian himself seemed confused as to the "times of the Gentiles." He says in one breath that the "times of the Gentiles" means "those which were to be chosen of God, and gathered in with the remnant of Israel – He then goes on to proclaim, against this world and dispensation"[29] which will pass away. So he defines "times of the Gentiles" with the chosen of God and the remnant of Israel but he admits that this dispensation (and such is the word he uses) *will pass away*. The careful reader will note that Tertullian, like the apostle Paul, distinguishes here between Gentile and Jewish believers, so even though he appears to equate the "times of the Gentiles" with the church he distinguishes between Jewish and Gentile believers and then argues that this dispensation shall pass! This makes for an interesting view and it is a shame that Tertullian didn't elaborate further on this point, but it is clear from this and other passages that Tertullian leaves the door open for a future Israel, which he believed was prophesied in Scripture. We cannot read too much into Tertullian's thesis here, however, for he is perhaps not clear enough at this juncture, and yet his view illustrates a significant problem with covenant theology. No matter how we read or interpret the "times of the Gentiles" it is a certainty that this time period will pass away. If the "times of the Gentiles" refers to the earthly rulers of the world, then their time will pass away. If the "times of the Gentiles" refers to the church age, then it will pass away.

A Jewish Millennial Kingdom?

If the "times of the Gentiles" will pass away, does this mean that Gentiles shall no longer inhabit the earth? No such argument is made. The issue is not Gentile population but domination. While the governments of the world today are primarily Gentile, the Millennial kingdom is primarily Jewish. This has created a flurry of controversy among many Christians. Some even argue that to accept a literal interpretation of Jewish-Messianic prophecies of the Millennial kingdom is nothing short of blasphemy! They suggest, for example, that taking Ezekiel's temple (Ezekiel 40-43) literally would negate the gospel itself. Says one critic, "Jesus Christ is the only Mediator, His blood the final sacrifice. There can be no going back. If there is a way back to the ceremonial law, to the type and shadows of what has now become the

---

[29] Tertullian, "On the Resurrection of the Flesh," *Ante-Nicene Fathers* Vol. 3 Alexander Roberts & James Danaldson, eds. (Peabody, MA: Hendrickson Publishers, 1999 ed.), 560.

bondage of legalism, then Paul labored and ran in vain – more than that, Christ died in vain."[30] Of course, the statement, although true, assumes much that is false. Namely, that a literal Jewish kingdom would be a return "to the type and shadows of what has now become the bondage of legalism."[31] Let us examine the prophecies of the Messianic kingdom to see if these arguments are valid.

The prophecies of Ezekiel's temple are surely among "the most difficult portions of Scripture in all the book of God"[32] and traditionally the Jews would not allow any to read the passages until they reached thirty years of age![33] The problem is not the existence of a grand Millennial temple but that Ezekiel describes ritual sacrifices which most Christians believe were negated by the blood of Christ. Does not Hebrews says that the ancient sacrifices are but shadows and types of the coming sacrifice of Christ? Would not a return to sacrifices be a return "to the type and shadows of what has now become the bondage of legalism"?[34] These criticism seem valid save that the critic forgets a very vital point. Hebrews also states that "it is impossible for the blood of bulls and goats to take away sins" (Hebrews 10:4). This is *not* new to the New Testament. The Hebrew Old Testament itself is clear that sacrifices were **never** valid or sufficient for the remission of sins (cf. Isaiah 1:11, 34:6; Jeremiah 11:15). *Nowhere* does the Bible teach that animal sacrifices were sufficient to atone for man's sins. That is exactly the point of the author of Hebrews. He does not presume to argue with the prophets of old but to explain them. He does not invalidate the law but explains its fulfillment through Christ (see also Matthew 5:17).

Ezekiel 40-43 actually differs substantially from the Mosaic sacrifices of old. Ezekiel does not describe a return to Mosaic sacrifices, but something new. Nathaniel West has demonstrates many of the differences between the two:

> There is no Ark of the Covenant, no Pot of Manna, no Aaron's rod to bud, no Tables of the Law, no Cherubim, no Mercy-Seat, no Golden Candlestick, no Shew-bread, no Veil, no unapproachable Holy of Holies where the High-Priest alone might enter, nor

---

[30] Edmund Clowney, "The Final Temple," Carl Henry, ed., *Prophecy in the Making* (Carol Stream, IL: Creation House, 1971), 85.

[31] Ibid.

[32] Matthew Henry, *Matthew Henry's Commentary on the Whole Bible : Vol. 4* (Peabody, MA: Hendrickson Publishers, 1991), 770.

[33] Ibid.

[34] Ibid.

is there any High-Priest to offer atonement to take away sin, or to make intercession for the people.[35]

Instead, the Prince will be present during the sacrifices (Ezekiel 45:16). It is has been debated whether or not this prince is Jesus, David, or a representative of the Lord. Since the prince is said to present a sin offering in Ezekiel 45:22, it is probably best to take the prince as a subordinate, whether David or another. In either case, there is *no sacrifice offered for the remission of sins in the Millennial temple.* Christ's sacrifice was sufficient once for all. No Christian denies this.

Why then have sacrifices at all? Dwight Pentecost suggest that *"the sacrifices will be memorial in character."*[36] *This would in no way negate the cross of Christ.* As Charles Feinberg remarks, "the celebration of the Lord's Supper through the Christian centuries has added not one infinitesimal particle to the efficacy of the work of Christ on the cross."[37] It is of interest to note that many Catholics believe that Christ is literally re-sacrificed at the Eucharist, yet we know this to be heresy. Does that negate a valid act of Eucharist? Of course not. "Just as the Old Testament sacrifices could have value in pointing forward to the death of Christ, why may they not have equal value in pointing back to the death of Christ"?[38] Yet critics say that such a memorial would be a "retrogression." To this is the response, "if the system is planned by God as a memorial of Jesus Christ, it can no more be said to be a retrogression to the 'weak and beggarly elements' than the bread and wine can be said to be weak and beggarly memorials of the broken body and shed blood of Christ."[39] In fact, the memorial sacrifices will better illustrate the sacrifice of Christ, for we live in a day and age in which the bloody and cruel nature of Christ's sacrifice is forgotten. The movie *Passion of the Christ* created much controversy, not only from secular critics but from godly Christians who felt that the emphasis on the cross somehow diminished the resurrection. Nevertheless, the movie did remind most of us the harsh reality of what Christ did for us and what we deserved. The bloody animal sacrifices of the Millennial Temple will also remind us in a cogent manner of Christ's sacrifice. Since Christ Himself will be present in the Millennium it is natural to assume that a memorial to Him will also be more

---

[35] Nathaniel West, *The Thousand Year Reign of Christ* (Grand Rapids, MI: Kregel Publications, 1993 [orig. 1899]), 430.

[36] J. Dwight Pentecost, *Things to Come* (Grand Rapids, MI: Zondervan Publishing House, 1958), 525.

[37] Charles Feinberg, *The Prophecy of Ezekiel* (Chicago, IL: Moody Press, 1969), 234.

[38] Ibid.

[39] Ibid., 530.

real. When the blood of an animal is poured out, the realness of the blood will emphasize all the more the realness of His sacrifice; far more than wine and bread.

Another criticism is that the priesthood depicted in Old Testament prophecies of the kingdom would negate the priesthood of the believer (1 Peter 2:3-5, 8-10; Revelation 1:6). This, however, hinges upon unspoken assumptions. The critic is assuming that our dispensation is the last and final dispensation. As Feinberg states, "the opposition, with a false view of what God is accomplishing in time, wrongly makes our age the last one before the eternal age."[40] The critic assumes that the Millennial Kingdom is a continuation of the church age, when it is, in fact, a new dispensation for the restoration and purification of the nation of Israel. Each dispensation looks for the same result, but they do not require the same system. Each acknowledges that Christ's blood alone was given as a sacrifice of atonement, but each memorializes it in its own way. Moreover, to say that a priesthood of Israelites contradicts the priesthood of believers is false. Many Christian churches have priests. Even those of us who do not have priest, have the equivalent of priests, for pastors, deacons, bishops, and others fill the same basic role. This is semantics. It is a game of rhetoric. The fact that we are all priest before God does not imply that we must all perform the duties of the Israel priesthood anymore than equality before God (Galatians 3:28) proves that we must all be the same and perform the same tasks (1 Corinthians 12:19-24). So the existence of a priesthood in the Millennial kingdom no more invalidates the priesthood of the believer than does the existence of the pastor who is in charge of the Eucharist.

How then can the critic dismiss the numerous passages from the Old Testament which clearly describe a Jewish character to the Messianic age? Invariably if a literal interpretation is rejected then an allegorical one is preferred. Even great men of God like John Lightfoot and Charles Spurgeon argued that "a new Jerusalem, bigger than all the land of Canaan" proves "by these very dimensions showing, that these things cannot literally, but must be spiritually, be understood."[41] Of course, Lightfoot failed to explain exactly what that spiritual understanding was. He, like Spurgeon, can only make the ambiguous claims that "the house of which Ezekiel speaks is typical of the Church of the living God."[42] Yet neither offers any proof. John Gill argues

---

[40] Feinberg, *Ezekiel* op. cit., 234.

[41] John Lightfoot, *The Whole Works of the Rev. John Lightfoot* (London, England: J. F. Dove, 1822), 305.

[42] C. H. Spurgeon, *The Treasury of the Old Testament Vol. 4* (Grand Rapids, MI: Zondervan, 1951), 336.

that the Temple should be applied to the "Church-state"[43] while calling the anticipation of a literal third temple "vainly-expected."[44] It is interesting that Matthew Henry, after noting the comparisons to the temple in Revelation 20, turns around 180 degrees and says that this is a mere symbol of the "gospel-church."[45] This view was even accepted by dispensationalist H. A. Ironside who argues that both Ezekiel and Revelation both provide "a symbolic picture of the future of the Church of this dispensation."[46] He argues that the Cherubim symbolize divine government[47] and calls the alter, not a literal altar, but none other than Jesus.[48]

The problem with these spiritualized interpretations of Ezekiel (as with other passages) is that, to quote Jon Levenson, "the highly specific nature of the description of the Temple, its liturgy and community bespeaks a practical program, not a vision of pure grace."[49] We must take into consideration *all* the portions of Ezekiel 40-43 and not merely a handful. This is the fundamental problem with the allegorical views. They pick and choose rather than seeking to explain everything within the passage. Randall Price asks, "How would one go about building a symbol?"[50] He also points out that there is strong "architectural language"[51] in Ezekiel that does not fit well with symbolism. So much so that John Bloore, an architect, notes that every specification and measurement "can be reproduced according to scale in such a way that any architect or master-builder could follow every detail of it on a blueprint."[52] Measurement are given, specifications cited, geography is outlined, and design specs are detailed. In symbolism one thing represents another. Each and every thing. X = Y or A = B. If this is to be a symbol then everything in the vision must represent something; not just part of the vision. If we say that Christ is the altar then we must say what the incense represents.[53] If we say that the temple represents the "church-state"[54] then we must say that the measurements represent. Thus the

---

[43] Ibid.

[44] Ibid.

[45] Henry, *Vol. 4* op. cit., 770.

[46] H. A. Ironside, *Expository Notes on Ezekiel the Prophet* (New York: Loizeaux Brothers, 1949), 281.

[47] Ibid., 294.

[48] Ibid., 295.

[49] Jon Levenson, *Theology of the Program of Restoring of Ezekiel 40-48* (Missoula, MT: Scholars Press 1976), 45.

[50] Randall Price, *The Coming Last Days Temple* (Eugene, OR: Harvest House, 1999), 514.

[51] Ibid.

[52] These words are Ironside's but describe Bloore's opinions (Ironside *Ezekiel* op. cit., 284).

[53] Ironside, *Ezekiel* op. cit., 295.

[54] John Gill, *Expositions of the Old Testament* Vol. 4 (London, England: William Hill Collinridge, 1852, 437.

allegorical view is, as Arno Gaebelein says, "the weakest of all and yet the most accepted."[55]

What of the literal view? Is it not also plagued with problems? Critics argue that the size of the Temple described in Ezekiel could not fit upon Mount Moriah and must, therefore, be symbolic. Ezekiel goes into great detail as to the size and dimensions of the new city and state (c.f Ezekiel 45 & 48). Isaiah 26:15 also attests to the enlarged boundaries of Israel's national borders. According to Merrill Unger the dimensions Ezekiel records for the "holy oblation," a sacred portion of Jerusalem, would encompass over a thousand square miles for itself.[56] Randall Price has similar calculations which would enlarge the "Prince's portion" of Jerusalem to over 2500 square miles![57] The New Jerusalem, which will not exist until the Millennial age is passed, will actually be nearly as large as the entire continent of Europe (cf. Revelation 21:16). This Jerusalem of the Millennial age will not be as large, but it will far exceed the limits that it has ever known in this age. Does this not prove the Temple and city are symbolic? On the contrary, the Bible also describes drastic geographical changes in the Millennium. These major geographical change include the raising of land and the lowering of valleys. In both Revelation and Zechariah Jerusalem is divided by a massive earthquake (cf. Revelation 11:3, 19; 16:8; and Zechariah 14:4-10) and the Mount of Olives is split asunder. The Temple mount is itself explicitly mentioned in Isaiah when the prophet says, "the mountain of the house of the LORD will be established as the chief of the mountains, and will be raised above the hills" (2:3). Thus the Bible appears to teach that the geography of the earth will be altered and the "mountain of the house of the Lord" (the Temple Mount) will be greatly enlarged, as will the Temple itself.

The purpose for the Millennial Temple is obviously not to replace Christ, who will be present at the Temple, nor does anyone teach that this is so. Ralph Alexander suggests that "Ezekiel sets forth two major purposes for the millennial temple. First, the temple will provide a throne for God among his people (43:6-7), the residency of his glory (43:1-12) from which he will rule over his people. Second, the temple complex will reflect God's holiness."[58] A Church altar does not replace Christ; why should the Temple? The argument is frivolous.

---

[55] Arno Gaebelein, *The Prophet Ezekiel* (New York: Our Hope Press, 1918), 272.

[56] Merrill Unger, "The Temple Vision of Ezekiel," *Bibliotheca Sacra* 105 (October, 1948), 427-428.

[57] Price, *Coming Temple* op. cit., 528.

[58] Ralph Alexander, "Ezekiel," *The Expositor's Bible Commentary* Vol. 6 Frank Gaebelein, ed., (Grand Rapids, MI: Zondervan Publishers, 1986), 947.

Those who argue that a literal interpretation of the Millennial kingdom in the Old Testament is a denial of grace or a return to legalism are not standing on solid ground. The promises that the Lord made to the nation of Israel - and there were many - were not all conditional and the Lord will not break His word. Most of God's promises have always been unconditional. We cannot argue for the sovereign grace of God while denying that grace will be given to the nation of Israel.

The Millennial Kingdom and Gentiles

What role then, if any, do Gentiles have in the Millennial kingdom? If the "times of the Gentiles" have passed, will there be no church in the Millennial kingdom? First, the Bible is clear that the Gentile nations will still exist. At the end of the Millennium it is the Gentiles nations that revolt against God (Revelation 20:8). However, there is a question as to the exact identification of these Gentile tribes for they are clearly different in identification from those of the current and past dispensations. Since the Millennial Kingdom will be predominantly Israeli, and since the geography of the earth will change dramatically, Gog and Magog of Revelation 20:8 may be different from the Russian tribes spoken of elsewhere in the Bible. There will certainly be Gentiles in the Millennium, and some will be from the stock of Gog and Magog. It is therefore their descendants to whom this passage refers. This means that the Gentile tribes will lead the revolt. This is both ironic and just, for even as Jews have traditionally rejected Christ as Messiah in the church age, Gentiles will reject Jesus the Messiah in the Millennial age where Israel is given prominence.

Of course the question still remains, what of the Church and the Gentiles during the Millennial age? Interestingly enough, the church may have a place, but not in the manner that replacement theology envisions. We know that Christ promised that we would reign with Him (Revelation 20:6; cf. 2 Timothy 2:12). Therefore, we who are resurrected at the Rapture and return with Him at the Second Coming, will reign on earth with Him. But if this is so, then this means that the government of the Millennium will be made up of mortal Jews and immortal believers (mostly from the church age). How then do mortals interact with immortal administrators? George Peters, in discussing the risen saints role in the Millennium, states, the Theocratic king will also have His associated rulers assuring the most perfect administration of the laws, and securing the most perfect government, productive of peace, prosperity, and happiness, such as the world has never yet witnessed.[59]

We shall then be the governors, judges, magistrates, and administrators, as well as other important positions in a just government. Some of us will be teachers, and some have suggested that we will also occupy the role of priests. Peters, for example, believes that if the saints are to be "kings and priests" (cf. Revelation 1:6) then both must be literal in the Millennium.[60] However, others believe that the Levite Priesthood, made up of mortal Jews, must continue in the Millennium. Randall Price maintains that "the ancient promises to the Levitical priesthood cannot have a literal fulfillment unless Ezekiel's prophecy is eschatological."[61] In other words, the Levitical priesthood must be restored in the Millennial Kingdom itself. Of this, there seems little doubt.

It is not hard to see that the covenant and replacement theologians, in trying to deny Israel its promises in the kingdom, is actually denying the church our promises as well. By replacing Israel with the church, our role would actually be diminished and God made out to be a liar whose transfers Him promises from one group (the Jews) to another (the church) in the same way a lawyer manipulates a contract for his own selfish gains. We must, as Paul warned, not be arrogant (Romans 11:20) but fear the Lord. "If God did not spare the natural branches, neither will He spare you" (11:20-21).

Conclusion

Jesus said, "many *who are* first will be last; and *the* last, first" (Matthew 19:30; Mark 10:31). The Jews were the first group to whom God made covenant promises. Gentiles were but pagans who practiced human sacrifice, cannibalism, barbarity, and cruelties beyond imagination. It was God's pleasure to show His grace by transforming the barbaric cultures of the Gentiles. If, however, he forgets the *first*, who were the Jews, then how can we expect God to keep His promises to us; the *last*. We accepted Jesus first, though we were last. The Jews, who are first (Romans 1:16; 2:10), will be the last to accept the Messiah, but they, as a nation, will accept Him.

In Acts 1:6 the disciples asked Jesus, "Lord, is it at this time that You will restore the kingdom to Israel?" It should be important for covenant theologians and amillennialists to note that Jesus *did not* say that he would

---

[59] George Peters, *The Theocratic Kingdom Vol. II* (Grand Rapids, MI: Kregel, 1884 op. cit., 570.

[60] Ibid., 604.

[61] Price, *Coming Temple* op. cit., 524.

not restore the kingdom to Israel, but that "it is not for you to know times or epochs which the Father has fixed by His own authority" (1:8). Nowhere in the Bible does the Lord deny that the promises made to *the nation* of Israel will be fulfilled. Covenant theologians, and amillennialists, have argued that the church has replaced Israel, but the reader will be reminded that Romans 11:25-26 states that "a partial hardening has happened to Israel until the fullness of the Gentiles has come in; and thus all Israel will be saved." Indeed, *all* surviving Israel will literally be saved. This does not imply that Israel is not Israel, but that at the Second Coming all Jews who have survived to the end will be saved. When the Millennial Kingdom is ushered in, it will be to Jews, because the "the gifts and the calling of God *are irrevocable!*" (Romans 11:29). The idea that God's covenants to the Jews have been revoked is not Biblical. It is true that some covenants were conditional, but many of the covenants were *unconditional*. The God of Abraham does not lie. He is not a lawyer who tries to find loopholes or manipulate the meaning of a contract. Dwight Pentecost has written extensively upon each of the covenants God made to the Jews. He has shown that most of these covenants are indeed unconditional.[62] James Brookes also insisted that the fact that these promises were unconditional meant that these covenants *will* be fulfilled in the future.[63] Those who argue that the church will be the recipients of these promises are allowing their pride to fool themselves, even as the pride of the Jews once denied them eyes to recognize the Messiah. When the Millennial Kingdom begins, the "times of the Gentiles" will have passed. No theologian can dismiss the importance of the passing of the "times of the Gentiles." If the Gentiles' time passes, then the Jews' shall begin and God's grace and His promises will be revealed to all men; not merely to the Gentile.

---

[62] Pentecost, *Things to Come* op. cit., 65-115.
[63] James Brookes, *Maranatha* (New York: Fleming Revell Co., 1889), 396.

"But concerning the Rapture there is no Old Testament revelation. This omission from over a hundred passages seems hard to understand if the Rapture is the first event of the Day of the Lord, as posttribulationalism teaches. But if the Rapture is a mystery, unrevealed in the Old Testament, and if it precedes the actual beginning of the Day of the Lord, as pretribulationalism teaches, then it is not strange that Paul had to inform them about the Rapture but needed only to remind them what they already knew about the Day of the Lord...The question of the beginning of the Day of the Lord is a watershed between pre- and posttribulationalism."

- Charles C. Ryrie

Basic Theology 1982, page 485-486

13

The Pre-Day of the Lord Rapture
David E. Olander

Introduction
The day of the Lord is a major doctrine of the Old Testament and an extremely important teaching in *all* Scripture. It describes an unparalleled time when the Lord Himself will directly bring about defined judgments and desolations on the entire planet. Nothing and no one will be spared in all His creation including the heavens and the angelic world during the day of the Lord. The day of the Lord is so central that a thorough understanding is essential for any proper interpretation of eschatology.

While Scripture clearly teaches the premillennial pretribulational rapture of the church, the terminology pretribulational rapture might be better phrased and more biblical using the term 'pre-day-of-the-Lord rapture.' This would be nothing novel as Paul taught clearly that it is not possible for the church to go into the day of the Lord (1 Thes. 4:13-18; 5:1-11; 2 Thes. 2:1-12). Paul's second epistle to the Thessalonians speaks primarily of the relation of the church to the day of the Lord. The Thessalonians believed they had entered the day of the Lord because of some false teachings (2:1-3). Paul is not ambiguous in his refutation of that misguided idea. Scripture clearly and precisely teaches the pre-day-of-the-Lord rapture.

The day of the Lord, the tribulation, and the great tribulation, each individually has a biblically defined beginning as given in Scripture. As the tribulation and the great tribulation are part of the day of the Lord, what will be of most concern is the rapture of the church in relation to the day of the Lord. Certain exegetes also hold that the second coming and millennial kingdom are also included in the day of the Lord. Again, what is of most concern here is the pre-day-of-the-Lord rapture, and it will be considered here in three stages: (1) the rapture and the day of the Lord, (2) the day of the Lord, and (3) the rapture.

The Rapture and the Day of the Lord
The day of the Lord is a major theme of the Old Testament (the day of the Lord, section B). It is a time of God's unprecedented wrath, His coming

wrath, the wrath of the Lamb, the Lord's burning anger, etc. (Zeph. 2:1; 1 Thes. 1:10; Rev. 6:16-17) when *all* the earth will be devoured (Zeph. 1:18). These biblically defined coming judgments precede Christ's second coming and the millennial kingdom. It must be noted that once the day of the Lord begins, no one will be safe or escape. At first, many will think they are in a time of peace and safety but they are deceived. They will believe the lie and they will not escape (1 Thes. 5:1-9; 2 Thes. 2:10-12), for sudden destruction is imminent.

The day of the Lord begins with His wrath but this does not mean severe judgments are being poured out immediately. The church, the body of Christ, has been waiting for the One Who delivers from the coming wrath as the church has not been appointed to wrath (1 Thes. 1:10; 5:9).[1] The church has been waiting for the Bridegroom Who comes from heaven to take His bride to the Father's house to be with Him forever. The church has had an appointment to meet Him in rapture for almost 2,000 years (1 Thes. 1:10; 4:17; 5:9; Rev. 3:10). The church has been commanded to be watching for Him continually for this is the true blessed hope (1 Thes. 4:18; Titus 2:13; Phil. 3:20). But, the day of the Lord is coming upon an unbelieving world from which no one will escape His wrath[2] (1 Thes. 5:3; Rev. 6:16-17). *It is critical to understand that the day of the Lord cannot begin until the church has been raptured or removed from the planet* (the rapture, section C).

The Rapture Then the Day of the Lord
In First Thessalonians, Paul made it perfectly clear that the day of the Lord cannot begin until the church has been removed from earth. This is essential to understand for the church's glorious appointment is to meet Him in the air as He comes from heaven. This is not the second coming as He is meeting the

---

[1] 1 Thessalonians 1:10 'and to wait for His Son from heaven, whom He raised from the dead, *that is* Jesus, who rescues us from the wrath to come' καὶ ἀναμένειν τὸν υἱὸν αὐτοῦ ἐκ τῶν οὐρανῶν, ὃν ἤγειρεν ἐκ [τῶν] νεκρῶν, Ἰησοῦν τὸν ῥυόμενον ἡμᾶς ἐκ τῆς ὀργῆς τῆς ἐρχομένης. Note the tenses used and the construction. The church is actually commanded to be waiting (a continuous state of expectation; note also Phil. 3:20) for His Son from heaven, Who is the Deliverer from the coming wrath (note the articulation with the present participle in a periphrasis with restrictive attributive; this is highly emphatic). The contrast is essential here as the church's appointment is to be waiting for Him, not the coming wrath of the day of the Lord. Paul develops this throughout 1st Thessalonians. The contrast is highly emphatic. The church is not waiting in any sense for the day of the Lord's wrath, but for Him from heaven.

[2] The day of the Lord has not been appointed for the body of Christ, as the day of the Lord is completely an Old Testament doctrine having to do with Israel, the nations, even angels. The church's appointment is to meet Him in the air with joy and blessing not in wrath pertaining to the day of the Lord and the second coming. The day of the Lord begins with His wrath. The rapture begins the eternal blessing of being with Him forever as He is (1 Thes. 4:17). This is to be continually taught in the church age for this is our great hope and blessing not the day of the Lord.

church in the air (1 Thes. 4:17; more technically 'in air'). He will come to the earth in wrath during the day of the Lord. The church is commanded to be waiting for Him expectantly[3] (Phil. 3:20; 1 Thes. 4:18; Titus 2:13), as the imminency of the rapture was to have a continual purifying effect on the church (1 John 3:2-3). Yet it is critical to understand that the day of the Lord cannot possibly begin until the church has been removed from the earth. Paul consistently taught the rapture of the church must take place first, and only then can the day of the Lord begin.

1. The rapture of the church (1 Thes. 4:13-18)
2. (*then*) The day of the Lord (1 Thes. 5:1-11)

The Lord never gave signs and appointed times to the church (1 Thes. 5:1), yet there are certain things the church was to understand. The church has one appointment i.e. to be waiting in anticipation for His coming from heaven. All the things concerning Israel, the Gentiles, judgments of the nations, the second coming of Christ, His kingdom, His throne, etc., all have very specific appointed times. Everything else concerning end times the Thessalonians understood, and the church was to be continually taught, encouraged, and exhorted in all these things primarily the rapture and living with that glorious and joyful expectation (1 Thes. 2:19-20; 3:13; 4:18; 5:11).

The rapture has been the blessed hope of many believers (including the Apostles) in the church for almost two millennia, while living in a sin-ridden world. The rapture is also the deliverance promised from the coming wrath of the day of the Lord (1:10; Rev. 3:10). There would not be much hope in waiting expectantly for the day of the Lord and His wrath and complete destruction. That would be anything but hope. The day of the Lord comes as a thief in the night when Christ will return in His wrath (1 Thes. 5:2, 4; 2 Pet. 3:10). Jesus Christ will not come for His bride as a thief in the night especially in wrath. The rapture of the church and the day of the Lord are two completely separate and contrasting events yet one in effect triggers the other. One is an imminent hope and blessing (Titus 2:13), the

---

[3] '*looking* for the blessed hope and the appearing of the glory of our great God and Savior, Christ Jesus' (Titus 2:13); προσδεχόμενοι τὴν μακαρίαν ἐλπίδα καὶ ἐπιφάνειαν τῆς δόξης τοῦ μεγάλου θεοῦ καὶ σωτῆρος ἡμῶν Ἰησοῦ Χριστοῦ, the word looking (*prosdecomaii*) has the meaning of wait for, expect; receive; welcome; accept, or hold. The teaching here is to be waiting for this blessed hope or expecting His glorious appearing continually. This had the meaning of expecting with great anticipation. Note also the one article connecting hope and appearing. These two most definitely go together especially in the rapture of the church as she has been waiting for His appearing for almost 2,000 years. At least the faithful have who believe have been waiting.

other is coming with wrath, judgments, and complete destruction (1 Thes. 5:2-3).

After the rapture of the church, everyone who is left alive on the earth will go into the day of the Lord and His coming wrath. However, this does not mean the day of the Lord begins immediately. Many will believe they are in a time of peace and safety (1 Thes. 5:3). Satan and his coming man of lawlessness (Antichrist) will completely deceive the world, and the world will believe the lie (2 Thes. 2:11). Yet the enemy will be gathering Israel and the world together to prove that he is god and to be worshipped as God for this is his ultimate goal and deception (Is. 14:12-14; Rev. 13:8). He is attempting to capture everything in creation for his doxological purposes. As everything was created to bring glory to God even angels, Satan wants this glory for himself (2 Thes. 2:3-4). Satan is deceived and is a deceiver and from that nature, all he does is a deception. Once the restraint has been taken away, Satan will be free to finalize his deceptive work and bring on his man of lawlessness (2 Thes. 2:6-8).

All this and much more will take place in the day of the Lord, but to be much more technical the day of the Lord cannot begin until very specific events occur. One very specific event is the rapture of the church.

Paul had dealt with the timing of the day of the Lord in First Thessalonians. It is most essential to understand that the rapture of the church must take place prior to the beginning of the day of the Lord (1 Thes. 4:13-18; 5:1-11).[4]

1. The rapture (1 Thes. 4:13-18)
2. (then) the day of the Lord (1 Thes. 5:1-11)

Paul did not go into specific details of the exact beginning of the day of the Lord in First Thessalonians for this was not an issue with the church at Thessalonica at that time. The Thessalonians knew they had not been appointed to the day of the Lord and His wrath but a joyful meeting with Him in the air. They knew from Paul's teachings they were not to go into the day of the Lord. The Thessalonians were not in darkness as the unsaved, but were to be living in the light of His salvation and waiting for the completion of this great salvation. They were not of the night but of the day (1 Thes. 5:1-11). They were not waiting for a thief in the night (2 Thes. 5:2, 4; 2 Pet. 3:10), but for the One Who loves them most and Whom they love and would

---

[4] This section of 4:13-18 and 5:1-11 appears together and seems to be one paragraph in the GNT. This would take the whole topic of the rapture and the day of the Lord together in context.

be with forever. They were not to be conducting their lives as those living in darkness, for they were always to be ready to meet Him at any moment.

Paul had not spent much time in Thessalonica (at least several Sabbaths, Acts 17:1-3), yet he had taught great eschatological truths. Not too long after Paul's departure from Thessalonica, rumors, letters, or messengers arrived falsely teaching that the day of the Lord had already begun (2 Thes. 2:1-2). Had they missed the rapture and His coming for them? Certain believers in Thessalonica were confused that the day of the Lord had already started and perhaps they were in it. They had understood from Paul's teaching that they could not possibly go into the day of the Lord which includes the tribulation and the great tribulation. They believed they were to be raptured first and then the day of the Lord would begin. Paul had written clearly that it is not possible that the church could go into the day of the Lord or none of this would be significant or mean anything. Paul wrote Second Thessalonians to calm and encourage the Thessalonians theologically and primarily eschatologically.

First and Second Thessalonians are completely eschatological, and there can be no proper understanding of these epistles without a correct view of the rapture of the church and the day of the Lord. While there is no sign, event, or precursor to the rapture, there are very detailed events prior to the beginning of the day of the Lord. No other book of Scripture details the *exact beginning* of the day of the Lord except Second Thessalonians. It is not possible for the day of the Lord to begin until 'the apostasy occurs first, and then the man of lawlessness be revealed' (2 Thes. 2:1-3).[5] This should be expected as the church is not a doctrine of the Old Testament and is a completely new work defined in the New Testament. However, the day of the Lord cannot begin until the church is removed and then the man of lawlessness is revealed. Only after these two events can the day of the Lord begin.

1. The apostasy (2 Thes. 2:3a)
2. The man of lawlessness revealed (2 Thes. 2:3b)

---

[5] 2 Thessalonians 2:3 'Let no one in any way deceive you, for *it will not come* unless the apostasy comes first, and the man of lawlessness is revealed, the son of destruction' Μή τις ὑμᾶς ἐξαπατήση κατὰ μηδένα τρόπον. ὅτι ἐὰν μὴ ἔλθη ἡ ἀποστασία πρῶτον καὶ ἀποκαλυφθῇ ὁ ἄνθρωπος τῆς ἀνομίας, ὁ υἱὸς τῆς ἀπωλείας, the apostasy must come first. This is essential in this passage with the emphasis upon it. Then and only then the man of lawlessness be revealed. After the apostasy then the man of lawlessness is revealed, the day of the Lord has begun.

The Day of the Lord Begins

There needs to be a correct understanding of the apostasy, and the revelation of the man of sin. For only then will the day of the Lord begin.

The Apostasy (2 Thes 2:3)

Apostasy has a root meaning of departure from, or standing apart from. The question is departure from what and context is normally the key for understanding the Text. The church has gone through forms of apostasy concerning biblical truth throughout its history even from the beginning. Paul marveled that the Galatians had moved away from the grace of Christ (Galatians 1:1-10). The Lord rebuked at least five of His seven churches for departing from various truths (Rev. 2-3). Christ is found standing outside of one of them (Rev. 3:20). Paul warned of continued apostasy in the latter days of the church age (1 Tim. 4:1-2; 2 Tim. 3:1-9), and there are many other examples.

Paul had written to the Thessalonians about another departure of the church (1 Thes 4:13-18) and her gathering together unto Him (2 Thes. 2:1). This is the rapture and a legitimate use of the word for departure, stand apart, or apostasy. Historically the word can easily mean this.[6] Once the church has departed (been raptured) there is not one believer left on the planet. This would be total or complete apostasy in at least several ways. In essence, one departure or apostasy causes the other and Paul could easily use the word he did certainly referring to the secondary part in total. The word apostasy is used with articulation (2:3) giving it a structured identity the Thessalonians would have understood as previous reference for uniqueness, i.e. par excellence.

Therefore after the rapture of the church (1 Thes. 4:13-18), Paul had discussed the condition of the world of unbelievers (unbelief) on earth (1 Thes. 5:1-11). The Thessalonians fully comprehended this apostasy, for they were believers. Paul reminded them that he had been continually discussing and teaching all these things while he had been with them (2 Thes. 2:5). The fact is that the Thessalonians were to be waiting for the Lord to meet Him in the air and not be living as those who were continually in darkness and would be going into the day of the Lord. Paul wrote nothing cryptic or difficult for them to understand concerning this matter. In fact he expressed it in such a way as that they fully did understand exactly to what he referred.

---

[6] ἀποστασία, ας, ἡ … *rebellion, abandonment* in a religious sense especially against God;... *departure, disappearance*... *Liddell & Scott Greek English Lexicon* (New York: Oxford University Press, 1985), 218.

1. The church raptured, i.e. the departure (1 Thes. 4:13:-18)
2. The complete embodiment of the faith has departed (1 Thes. 5:1-11)
3. Faith in general has departed
4. Concerning all the above – the apostasy (complete)

Any of the above and certainly all the above is included in the apostasy. Once the church has departed, there is no 'faith' as an embodiment of biblical truth on earth. This would completely support Christ's discussion concerning His second coming in the day of the Lord (Luke 18:8).[7] Christ was not referring to faith in general, as context and grammar would not support this. The fact there will not be 'the faith' on earth has never happened since Adam's departure from God.[8] There is most definitely a connection between the rapture (apostasy) and the departure of faith (apostasy). This is completely related to the Lord saying 'when the Lord comes will He find faith on the earth.' If the church were still on the earth, He would find some faith. This also argues for a separate coming (the second coming during the day of the Lord) and definitely not for His body on the planet which is primarily characterized by faith or the faith as a total embodiment of truth.

In essence, the apostasy (2 Thes. 2:3) has never happened, and it will not happen until the rapture of the church. The fact that there is not one believer on the planet the moment after the rapture has to be the apostasy to which Paul referred and that which the Thessalonians fully understood (2 Thes. 2:5).[9]

The Man of Lawlessness Revealed
It seems strange that while there is much discussion on the apostasy and exactly what that means (1 Thes. 2:3), there is little or no emphasis on the man of lawlessness (man of sin i.e. the Antichrist) being revealed. This is

---

[7] Luke 18:8 "I tell you that He will bring about justice for them quickly. However, when the Son of Man comes, will He find <u>faith</u> on the earth?" λέγω ὑμῖν ὅτι ποιήσει τὴν ἐκδίκησιν αὐτῶν ἐν τάχει. πλὴν ὁ υἱὸς τοῦ ἀνθρώπου ἐλθὼν ἆρα εὑρήσει <u>τὴν πίστιν</u> ἐπὶ τῆς γῆς; will He find faith on the earth? Notice this has to do with His second coming and not the rapture. Notice the articulation before the word faith. He will find the faith on the earth when He comes for the church and meets her in the air. But, this verse is addressed to that after the rapture and the second coming where the body of truth is not there. There are believers on the planet but very little will be discussed on that planet during the tribulation except trusting Him and survival.

[8] What is most interesting in all this discussion on the apostasy (2 Thes. 2:3), is that once the church departs or is raptured, the literal faith as an embodiment of truth is gone plus there is literally no 'faith' in general on earth either. When Adam sinned, man literally turned from God.

[9] The Thessalonians fully understood the rapture (1 Thes. 4:13-18) and the apostasy (1 Thes. 5:1-11; 2 Thes. 2:3) were connected, or better one and the same. No matter what, Paul made it clear that the rapture of the church must take place before the day of the Lord.

actually the key to the beginning of the day of the Lord not the rapture. Because once the rapture occurs this does not mean the day of the Lord begins immediately the same hour or day. While Paul did not discuss this particular issue in his first epistle (4:13-5:11), he thought it necessary now as there was clearly some confusion among the Thessalonians (2 Thes. 2:1-3). He clearly defines the beginning of the day of the Lord in much more detail. As the apostasy or rapture must happen first, the more focused issue Paul dealt with is the man of sin and the restraint that is on him (2 Thes. 2:1-12). Paul even said the Thessalonians knew what was restraining him (2:6). The man of lawlessness is Satan's masterpiece coming and confirmed with all false signs, miracles, and wonders (2:9-10). He will take his seat in the temple of God in Jerusalem, displaying himself as God (2:4). The only question is *when* is the revelation of the man of sin?

Daniel spoke of the coming prince who will make or confirm a seven-year covenant with Israel and break it in the middle of the seven years (Dan. 9:27). The man of sin could easily be revealed in the middle of the seven years but more likely, he could be revealed when he makes this covenant specifically with Israel.[10] One thing to note is that once he has been revealed, the day of the Lord begins.

However, for him to be that powerful enough to guarantee a treaty with the nation Israel giving them liberty with the land even to rebuild the temple, he would have risen to power and most likely have been revealed before this (the 70th week of Daniel i.e. the tribulation). Daniel has more to say in relation to this, as the vision of the ten toes and the ten horns are very significant (Dan. 2; 7:7-28). Satan's man will rise through the ranks of the ten toes or horns and he will gain power and prominence gradually (Dan. 2:42-44; 7:7-8).[11] This is part of the satanic deception as he will come on the scene as a little horn and rise through the ranks quickly. He is most likely the little horn that puts Rome back together (the eighth from the seven, Rev. 17:11) and finally claims rule of the kings of the west or the fourth of the four world empires (Dan. 11). His ascendency will be meteoric and supernatural. Anyone living at that time who becomes a believer would be able to interpret what is happening. The rise of the little horn appears to be the man of sin's primary or first manifestation i.e. when he is revealed.

---

[10] The man of sin, lawlessness, i.e. the Antichrist could certainly be revealed then , and many commentators accept this timing as when he is revealed.

[11] As Daniel was contemplating the 10 horns (same as 10 toes) i.e. the final form of the Roman Empire, the little horn was noted and quite identifiable. This is most significant. The little horn was just as identifiable as the beast and the 10 horns . Seemingly insignificant but yet very powerful at its rise to power.

However, this is still not the whole picture, for Paul adds some information in Second Thessalonians that is most significant. He describes the man of sin as the one who will take his seat in the temple of God, claiming to be God. This would be a final revelation of the man of sin with all satanic power to do this. The entire world will worship this satanic figure (Rev. 13:8). Nevertheless, Paul said '*you know what restrains now, so that in his time he may be revealed*' (2 Thes. 2:6). There is restraint at this time so that he cannot be revealed. Note that Paul used this expression several times in Second Thessalonians (2:6-7). The only Person Who could possibly restrain him now is God the Holy Spirit, and the Thessalonians knew this. He is doing His work now of restraining evil especially the man of sin. The Restrainer will not be removed but the restraint will be removed. Even though times are getting more difficult as Scripture said it would, evil is mostly restrained at this time. A time is coming when the restraint, literally the brakes are taken off the evil one so he may present his man. However, the rise will be gradual and yet completely deceptive. This is a masterpiece of evil, and in today's jargon 'a real piece of work.' The interesting thing is that the rapture must take place first then the man of sin is revealed. The day of the Lord cannot begin until these two events happen first.

1.   The rapture (2 Thes. 2:2-3) and
2.   The man of sin revealed *then* the day of the Lord.

The Day of the Lord, the Tribulation, the Great Tribulation, the Man of Sin
The day of the Lord has a beginning or starting point as well as the seven year tribulation (70th week of Daniel, Dan. 9:27), and the great tribulation defined by Christ Himself (Mat. 24:15-22).

1.   the day of the Lord (2 Thes. 2:3)
2.   the tribulation (Dan. 9:27; 70th week of Daniel)
3.   the great tribulation (Dan. 9:27; Mat. 24:15-21; the middle of Daniel's 70th week)

If the man of sin is revealed at the guaranteeing of a decree with Israel then the day of the Lord has begun at the tribulation (Dan. 9:27).[12] If

---

[12] There are many associate the revelation of the man of sin with Dan. 9:27 when he signs or confirms a treaty with Daniel's holy people, Israel. This in itself would preclude any idea that the church goes into the tribulation period (usually the seven years) or even the great tribulation which is technically the last three and one years. Each of these has a different beginning point.

the man of sin is revealed at the breaking of the treaty triggering the great tribulation, then the day of the Lord has begun (Dan. 9:27; Mat. 24:15-21). However, the church must be raptured previously for any of this to have occurred. Any believer during this time would recognize Satan's man, for Scripture is referring to believers. Unbelievers believe the lie. Again, it is extremely difficult to believe that the man of sin has not been revealed before this. He could not just come along with no discernable recognition at all and claim such authority and power. Again, it would be better to understand his revelation or manifestation as the little horn of Daniel and the eighth horn of Revelation (Rev. 17:11-13) rising through the ranks of the ten horns and finally the ten horns (kings and kingdoms) giving him their power, kingdoms, and authority. He would then have tremendous authority such as to confirm a Mideast covenant (Dan. 9:27). In addition, he will have supernatural power to rise and this is part of satanic deception. Any believer would know Satan's man way before he makes the treaty with Israel, breaks the treaty with Israel, or claims to be God (2 Thes. 2:4). Yet all these are biblical manifestations or revelations of the working of Satan through him.

Shortly after this restraint has been taken away, Satan's masterpiece will be revealed. It is most likely that this is associated directly with the rapture of the church. This can be shown in context as well as in direct association with Paul's teaching on the day of the Lord (2 Thes. 2:1-12). Again, once the rapture happens this does not mean the day of the Lord begins. This is not possible as the man of sin has not been revealed and cannot be revealed prior to the rapture. When the restraint has been removed it is just a matter of time (2:6-8).

The major issue in Daniel as to the revelation of the man of sin is in direct connection with the rise of the latter form of the Roman Empire. This is where he begins his base of power, and from here, he is catapulted into an attempted world rule. The beast (man of sin, lawlessness, the Antichrist) is completely associated with this empire and the latter part of this empire plays a huge part in satanic strategy. It is interesting that two of the final bowl judgments are poured out on beast worshippers and his kingdom directly (Rev. 16:2, 10). Probably, the man of sin is the one who solidifies the final form of the Roman Empire, rises quickly through the horns as the little horn, and gains continual power through deception. Satan is limited in power and it is not known how much he will be granted in his final days. He is never completely unstrained and uncontrolled (although during the tribulation most restraint is removed), yet this is a great period of deception so that the world will believe the lie.

It is absolutely impossible for the church to go into the day of the Lord, both parts of the tribulation, i.e. the tribulation itself, or the great tribulation. The day of the Lord is the greater issue for Scripture speaks clearly on this subject, both Old and New Testaments (see section B). As the tribulation includes the great tribulation, the day of the Lord includes both these and much more. Several commentators believe that the day of the Lord includes the millennial kingdom and extends into eternity. The most important thing to know is that each of these periods (the day of the Lord, the tribulation, and the great tribulation) have different starting points, yet they all have one thing in common, a particular revealing of the man of sin. Moreover, the man of sin cannot be revealed prior to the rapture of the church. Only after the rapture of the church can the man of sin, the Antichrist, be revealed.

1. The day of the Lord begins only after the rapture and after the man of sin is revealed
2. The tribulation period of 7 years begins with the man of sin, the prince making or confirming a covenant with Israel (Dan. 9:27) (*the rapture must have taken place*)
3. The great tribulation begins with the man of sin breaking of the covenant after 3.5 years (Dan. 9:27)(*the rapture must have taken place*)

The revelation of the man of sin is really the key for understanding the beginning of these time periods (the day of the Lord, the tribulation, the great tribulation), not the rapture. However, the man of sin cannot be revealed until after the rapture. This makes great sense as the church has nothing at all to do with these eschatological , Old Testament, and day of the Lord events - especially the man of sin. Throughout the church age attempts have been made to ascertain just who might be this man of sin, but such efforts will remain futile as the church must be raptured for the man of sin to be revealed. The church will not go into any one of these periods. And actually, the greater issue is the day of the Lord, for this time includes the tribulation and the great tribulation and much more.

The Day of the Lord
The day of the Lord is a major teaching of Scripture developed especially in the Old Testament. It is most definitely a day of the Lord's wrath and vengeance against a God rejecting world. Zephaniah spells out the true meaning of this time of His wrath.

Be silent before the Lord God! For the day of the Lord is near, For the Lord has prepared a sacrifice, He has consecrated His guests" (Zephaniah 1:7). "Near is the great day of the Lord, Near and coming very quickly; Listen, the day of the Lord! In it the warrior cries out bitterly. A day of wrath is that day, A day of trouble and distress, A day of destruction and desolation, A day of darkness and gloom, A day of clouds and thick darkness, A day of trumpet and battle cry, Against the fortified cities And the high corner towers" (Zephaniah 1:14-16). "Neither their silver nor their gold Will be able to deliver them On the day of the Lord's wrath; And all the earth will be devoured In the fire of His jealousy, For He will make a complete end, Indeed a terrifying one, Of all the inhabitants of the earth." (Zephaniah 1:18). *"Gather yourselves together, yes, gather, O nation without shame, Before the decree takes effect— The day passes like the chaff— Before the burning anger of the Lord comes upon you, Before the day of the Lord's anger comes upon you. Seek the Lord, All you humble of the earth Who have carried out His ordinances; Seek righteousness, seek humility. Perhaps you will be hidden In the day of the Lord's anger* (Zephaniah 2:1-3).

There are many other references in Scripture to the day of the Lord, and each follow some basic parameters of definition, referring to the day when His wrath will be released on an unbelieving world.   Enns has this to say about the coming day of the Lord.

> Peter describes the suddenness of the coming of the day of the Lord (2 Pet. 3:10). The day of the Lord is used in several ways in Scripture, but as a general term it views the entire period beginning with the rapture and terminating at the end of the millennium; thus, the day of the Lord involves judgment upon unbelievers but blessing for believers. From 2 Peter 3:10*b*–12 Peter describes the eternal state. At the end of the millennium the heavens will pass away with a great noise and the earth will be burned up. This is the sphere where sin took place; it is renovated in anticipation of eternity. Peter concludes his study on last things with a practical exhortation (2 Pet. 3:11)[13] ...A term that can be used: (1) of any judgment of God in history; (2) of God's judgment in the Tribulation period; (3) of the blessings in the millennial kingdom; (4) of the entire period from the beginning of the Tribulation to the end of the millennium.[14]

What is of primary concern is the entire period from the beginning of the day of the Lord (2 Thes. 2:3) to His second coming (but the day of the Lord may include the millennial kingdom).   One of the reasons for His coming is to preserve what ever is left after the tribulation or His wrath (Rev. 6:16-17) for the sake of the elect (Mat. 24:21-22).   Had He not come at this time none would be left. Therefore, the second coming has several purposes.   This will

---

[13] Paul Enns, *The Moody Handbook of Theology* (Chicago, IL.: Moody Press, 1989), 129.
[14] Ibid., 633.

end His wrath and He will claim His covenanted Davidic throne over Israel, the Jews (Mat. 25:31).

References to the Day of the Lord
1. Isa. 13:6 Wail, for *the day of the Lord* is near! It will come as destruction from the Almighty.
2. Isa. 13:9 Behold, *the day of the Lord* is coming, Cruel, with fury and burning anger, To make the land a desolation; And He will exterminate its sinners from it.
3. Isa. 58:13 "If because of the sabbath, you turn your foot From doing your own pleasure on My holy day, And call the sabbath a delight, the holy *day of the Lord* honorable, And shall honor it, desisting from your own ways, From seeking your own pleasure, And speaking your own word,
4. Ezek. 13:5 "You have not gone up into the breaches, nor did you build the wall around the house of Israel to stand in the battle on *the day of the Lord*.
5. Ezek. 30:3 "For the day is near, Even *the day of the Lord* is near; It will be a day of clouds, A time of doom for the nations.
6. Joel 1:15 Alas for the day! For *the day of the Lord* is near, And it will come as destruction from the Almighty.
7. Joel 2:1 Blow a trumpet in Zion, And sound an alarm on My holy mountain! Let all the inhabitants of the land tremble, For *the day of the Lord* is coming; Surely it is near,
8. Joel 2:11 And the Lord utters His voice before His army; Surely His camp is very great, For strong is he who carries out His word. *The day of the Lord* is indeed great and very awesome, And who can endure it?
9. Joel 2:31 "The sun will be turned into darkness, And the moon into blood, Before the great and awesome *day of the Lord comes.*
10. Joel 3:14 Multitudes, multitudes in the valley of decision! For *the day of the Lord* is near in the valley of decision.
11. Amos 5:18 Alas, you who are longing for *the day of the Lord*, For what purpose will the day of the Lord be to you? It will be darkness and not light;
12. Amos 5:20 Will not *the day of the Lord* be darkness instead of light, Even gloom with no brightness in it?
13. Obadiah 15 "For *the day of the Lord* draws near on all the nations. As you have done, it will be done to you. Your dealings will return on your own head.

14. Zeph. 1:7 Be silent before the Lord God! For *the day of the Lord* is near, For the Lord has prepared a sacrifice, He has consecrated His guests.
15. Zeph. 1:14-16 Near is the great *day of the Lord*, Near and coming very quickly; Listen, the *day of the Lord*! In it the warrior cries out bitterly. A day of wrath is that day, A day of trouble and distress, A day of destruction and desolation, A day of darkness and gloom, A day of clouds and thick darkness, A day of trumpet and battle cry, Against the fortified cities And the high corner towers.
16. Zeph. 1:18 Neither their silver nor their gold Will be able to deliver them On *the day of the Lord's wrath*; And all the earth will be devoured In the fire of His jealousy, For He will make a complete end, Indeed a terrifying one, Of all the inhabitants of the earth.
17. Mal. 4:5 Behold, I am going to send you Elijah the prophet before the coming of the great and terrible *day of the Lord*.
18. Acts 2:20 The sun shall be turned into darkness, And the moon into blood, Before the great and glorious *day of the Lord* shall come.
19. 1 Cor. 5:5 I have decided to deliver such a one to Satan for the destruction of his flesh, that his spirit may be saved in *the day of the Lord Jesus*.
20. 1 Thes. 5:2 For you yourselves know full well that the day of the Lord will come just like a thief in the night.
21. 2 Thes. 2:2 That you may not be quickly shaken from your composure or be disturbed either by a spirit or a message or a letter as if from us, to the effect that *the day of the Lord* has come.
22. 2 Pet. 3:10 But *the day of the Lord* will come like a thief, in which the heavens will pass away with a roar and the elements will be destroyed with intense heat, and the earth and its works will be burned up.

The majority of these verses refer to the tribulation period and the time of His coming wrath. Is it no wonder that the Thessalonians were terrified that they might be in that day (2 Thes. 2:1-3). Paul made it clear they cold not possibly go into the day of the Lord. All the verses referring to the time of His coming wrath are more than enough to support the position of an unprecedented time of the Lord's judgment coming upon the entire world (Mat. 24:21; Rev. 6:16-17). Of all these verses, Zephaniah 1:18 spells out well this terrible time coming on all mankind: *"Neither their silver nor their gold Will be able to deliver them On the day of the Lord's wrath; And all the earth will be devoured In the fire of His jealousy, For He will make a complete end, Indeed a terrifying one, Of all the inhabitants of the earth."*

John Hannah comments on this context,

> They would have no hope of deliverance; their wealth (silver [cf. "silver" in v. 11] and gold) would not be able to buy off their attackers (cf. Ezek. 7:19). Zephaniah then returned to the theme of universal judgment (cf. Zeph. 1:2-3). The whole world will be destroyed and all its inhabitants will quickly (He will make a sudden end) be subjected to the wrath of God. All this will stem from His jealousy, His consuming passion and concern that His own people follow Him, not false gods... Having described the awful day of God's wrath on Judah, the prophet at last brought his readers to his purpose. His goal was not to bring the people to despair, but to repentance and obedience. As Matthew Henry so appropriately stated, Zephaniah intended "not to frighten them out of their wits, but to frighten them out of their sins."[15]

No one will be spared His wrath during the day of the Lord. Amazingly some will make it through the tribulation both Jews and Gentiles (Dan. 12:1; Mat 25:31-46). Only after the second coming will the King receive the Davidic throne and kingdom over Israel (the Jews) as David's Son and Heir apparent to the throne. Only after the King takes His literal earthly royal throne (biblical covenants define one throne), will the King judge the sheep and goats (Mat. 25:31). The sheep will enter His kingdom prepared for them before the foundation of the world (25:34). These will enter with Him into His literal earthly reign. This blessed kingdom has been the main subject of biblical prayer for almost 2000 years (6:10 'let Your Kingdom come'). However, before this time of blessing and His millennial reign, His wrath will be poured out in the day of the Lord (24:4-51).

Is it no wonder that the Thessalonian believers were distressed (2 Thes. 2:1-3). Believers in the church age were never appointed to the time of His wrath in the day of the Lord (1 Thes. 1:10). Scripture teaches clearly the pre-day-of-the-Lord rapture.

The Rapture

There are many warnings and cautions in life. Sometimes these warnings relate to health, finances, life in general, and even to eternal things. Paul wrote to believers in Thessalonica making it very clear that the rapture of the church was imminent. He was reminding them to remain pure in all conduct (1 Thes. 4:1-8), walk in love of the brethren (4:9-10), and live an orderly life (4:11-12). By doing this, they would avoid spiritual slothfulness and remain faithfully alert waiting to meet Lord in the air (4:13-18), that is the rapture of

---

[15] Walvoord, John F., and Zuck, Roy B., *The Bible Knowledge Commentary, Old Testament Edition* (Wheaton, IL: Scripture Press Publications, Inc., 1987), 1528.

the Church. The Thessalonians were to be continually exhorted in these things especially the rapture of the church (4:18). The rapture was imminent and should be expected and anticipated in this age at any moment. There can be nothing more clearly taught in the Text. The church will be raptured prior to the day of the Lord and His wrath and this is perfectly clear.

The imperatival exhortation for believers was to be living for Him as the rapture was impending (4:18). On the other hand the day of the Lord was clearly for unbelievers and completely unexpected by unbelievers (5:1-11). Scripture is clear and consistent on these specific issues. However, the Thessalonians had been confused even deceived by conflicting information that the day of the Lord had already come (2 Thes. 2:2).[16] They knew they could and would not go into the day of the Lord. Paul wrote his second letter to the Thessalonians concerning this foremost issue.[17] No matter what, the rapture is obviously taught in the Text.

The Rapture of the Church is Biblical Truth

The rapture of the church is a glorious event, clearly taught in Scripture. The rapture of the church is not only assured by the word of the Lord, but also as certain as the death and resurrection of Christ (1 Thes. 4:13-18; 14-15). Those who say nothing about the rapture or believe it is not in Scripture, the burden is on them to prove it is not. For it is undoubtedly a doctrine of the Text. There are passages, chapters, and almost whole books such as First and Second Thessalonians supporting and teaching the rapture of the church. To proclaim that Scripture does not teach the rapture or the catching up of the church has to be more than unintentional. "The teaching of the Bible is so clear on this subject that nearly all evangelical believers, whether Pre- or Post-Millennialists, believe in 'the translation of the saints' as described in 1 Thes. 4:16; 1 Cor. 15:23, 50-52, giving to it their own interpretation."[18] Whatever position one may hold on this subject, the church will be caught up to meet Him. The church, His body will meet Him in the air, and this is biblical fact.

---

[16] They had been going through some great trials and suffering. They thought perhaps they were in or had entered the day of the Lord. If they had any thought that they would enter the day of the Lord based on Paul's teachings and missed the rapture of the church, none of this would be significant.

[17] While there was continual exhortation to be ready to meet Him in the air, there was no way the church could go into the day of the Lord, for the rapture *must* happen first. Both First and Second Thessalonians teach clearly the relation of the rapture of the church to the day of the Lord. The rapture must occur first then the day of the Lord. Second Thessalonians deals more specifically with rapture of the church by defining the very beginning of the day of the Lord. The rapture of the church, the day of the Lord, and the relation of the church to the day of the Lord are fundamental to understand.

[18] Francis Asa Wight, *The Rapture or The Translation of the Saints* (Harrisburg: Evangelical Press, 1929), 5.

The rapture of the church, is a most glorious and magnificent event ending the entire dispensation of the church age. Just as the church had a definite beginning, so it will end with a magnificent meeting of all believers from the very beginning. From the very first person Spirit baptized on the day of Pentecost unto the very last person or Gentile to believe (Rom. 11:25), all these saints who are literally in Christ will be gloriously translated to meet the Head of the church to be with Him as He is forever (1 Thes. 4:17). The words and teaching of the rapture are to be great encouragement and continually taught (4:18). Again, the magnitude of this event should at least trigger some consideration about this one time grand occurrence. This is why there are so many passages referring to His coming for His own. This is why believers are to be prepared continually looking for His coming.

What is usually lacking in any of these truths concerning the rapture is a thorough understanding of God's program for the church and His covenanted kingdom program with the nation Israel. Jesus Christ is building His church (Mat. 16:18) and He must first finish this program. Then He will return to earth and finish His covenanted program with the nation Israel, but only after His wrath is poured out on the earth. This does not mean God is through with Israel in any sense or He has been not working with this elect nation over these centuries. As there are no signs for the rapture, the church gathering in the air is no secret to believers. The truth is the rapture is anything but a secret. While unbelievers in Christ will have no part in the rapture, to them it may be secret or something that will have an earthly explanation. However, one thing is sure, when the rapture happens, there will be a noticeable absence of some from the planet. The restraint on the evil one will be removed, then all the events spoken of so long ago will begin to unfold (see section B on the day of the Lord). The rapture must take place first. This is mandatory, for none of the end time events of the day of the Lord will occur until the church is removed from the earth.

The Rapture was Comfort to the Church

Exactly what position one holds on the rapture of the church, the teaching and words concerning the rapture were written to comfort and to be a comfort. "Therefore comfort one another with these words" (1 Thes. 4:18). This is the only place in Scripture where there is a command to continually comfort with these exact words. Contextually the comfort refers to the rapture and meeting the Lord. The fact that the passage says that these words are to be used for comfort should not even be disputed, for this is just what it says. This is exactly what the Thessalonian believers needed was some comfort in their trials, and Paul most certainly knew this. They needed encouragement for several reasons.

They had suffered at the hands of their own countrymen (1 Thes. 2:13-20). "The Thessalonians were not alone in their suffering; they had abundant and worthy company. Their persecutors had killed the Lord Jesus Himself and the Old Testament prophets. They drove out their father in the faith, the Apostle Paul, and his fellow missionaries."[19] They may have been under heavy persecution because they were such a great testimony of how mightily God's Word was working among them as believers (1:6-9).

It seems that many of the Thessalonians were new believers, and they needed some encouragement especially with all the trials they were enduring. It appeared that Paul was not able to stay there very long on his second missionary journey because of the persecutions and those who were undoubtedly seeking his life (Acts 17:1-10). While the Thessalonians were very concerned about Paul and his welfare, Paul was very concerned about the Thessalonians and their condition. This shows a genuine concern of Paul for the churches, especially those who were enduring hardships because of their testimony and their new faith in Christ Jesus (1 Thes. 3:1-8). Also during this time, some of those living in Thessalonica had died and this may have added much more sadness and distress among those who were still living. Paul did not want the Thessalonians to have no hope and grieve as the world especially about those whom they loved who had died.

All believers in the church age have a most wonderful and blessed hope which is not of the world. Not only will all believers in Christ meet the Lord in the air with all their loved ones, but also all believers for the entire church age or dispensation will meet every believer in Christ for all this entire age. Therefore every one else in this church age in the rapture will meet those Thessalonians who had departed or died as well as all the others who have gone home to be with the Lord. This was a great hope for those living in Thessalonica, and Paul wanted them to have this great and blessed hope. This meeting or rapture of believers in Christ was imminent so there was no prophecy or any sign that needed any kind of fulfillment. This was a true blessed hope and joy.

> Paul wanted the Thessalonians to be neither ignorant nor grieving like the rest of men, that is, like unbelievers, over the death of fellow believers. Christians do grieve over the loss of loved ones; this is a normal human experience which even Jesus shared (John 11:35). But the grief of Christians differs from that of unbelievers, for

---

[19] BKCNT, 696.

the latter have no hope of bodily resurrection to glory with Christ (1 Thes. 4:16)... Two reasons why Christians should not grieve like unbelievers are that Christians have a revelation from God that gives them hope and they have a glorious future with Christ. Just as certainly as Jesus died and was resurrected by the Father, so God will unite the resurrected dead in Christ with their Savior at His coming. The death and resurrection of Jesus Christ are among the best-attested facts of history. Since Christians know these events took place, they can be equally certain, Paul said, that the souls of believers who have died will return with Christ when He comes for His living saints. The prophecy of the Rapture is as sure to be fulfilled as the prophecies of Christ's death and resurrection.[20]

Paul was encouraging the Thessalonians in the midst of all their sufferings. They needed this encouragement and comfort in their trials especially concerning those who had fallen asleep or died.

Believers are in Jesus by Spirit Baptism
Paul goes back to the original statement about those who are asleep in Jesus. *"For if we believe that Jesus died and rose again, even so God will bring with Him those who have fallen asleep in Jesus"* (1 Thessalonians 4:14). These are the ones who are defined as the dead in Christ (4:16). The expressions "in Jesus," "in Jesus Christ," "in Christ Jesus" are all similar expressions. These are those persons either living or departed who are in Christ. They are in Christ by Holy Spirit baptism,[21] through faith in Christ.

This is very significant as the baptizing work of the Holy Spirit is distinctively in the church age or this dispensation. This is what truly marks a traditional or classic dispensationalist. This distinction of the church and the

---

[20] BKCNT, 703-704

[21] Spirit Baptism -It is most important to observe the major passages that have to do with Spirit baptism. These passages are Mat. 3:11; Mark 1:8; Luke 3:16; John 1:32-33; Acts 1:5; 11:15-16; and 1 Cor. 12:13. From general observations several conclusions can be drawn from these passages. All these passages are highly significant as the church is the body of Christ being formed by Spirit baptism. When one believes or trusts Christ, he or she is placed into Christ's body or the church by the means of Spirit baptism. It is essential to note that these expressions are identical in the gospel passages as well as Acts and Corinthians. This is most definitely New Testament teaching and revelation. Note that the expression 'by the Holy Spirit' is actually used identically by the various writers of the New Testament. The preposition ejn can mean *in, by, with* or perhaps several other meanings. Even though certain translations may change the meaning of ejn, the original uses the identical expressions ejn pneuvmati aJgivw. There is only one Spirit baptism. Spirit baptism places *all*, anyone who believes into the body of Christ at the moment of belief. He, referring to Christ, is the one who baptizes, yet by means of the Holy Spirit. So by one Spirit *all* are baptized into one body (1 Cor. 12:13). Note the emphasis on 'by one spirit' at the beginning of Paul's explanation and 'we _all_' which refers to every believer. There is no distinction or distinctions made in this passage as well as the others at all. That would not be possible. This is most significant as there is only one body, one Spirit and one baptism by the Spirit (Eph. 4:4-6). This truly identifies the church or those in Christ in this dispensation. Paul also makes it very clear that 'all' whether Jews or Greeks (this is inclusive of everyone who believes) were made to partake or drink of one Spirit.

church age by literal definition separates traditional dispensationalism from other forms of dispensationalism such as progressive dispensationalism.[22] There is a *complete* biblical distinction between Israel and the church.[23]

Those who have fallen asleep in Jesus will be raise first at the rapture of the church. The rapture actually begins with this particular group defined as those who have fallen asleep in Jesus, or the dead in Christ. The term *in Christ* is a technical term which effectively defines only the saints of the church age or this dispensation.

The Rapture of the Church in Three Stages
The rapture of the church occurs in three distinct, yet virtually instantaneous stages. It begins with the Lord Jesus descending from heaven to meet His bride in the air. Then the rapture itself (taking or catching up of the saints) begins with a resurrection of those who have died in Christ. Actually, the rapture begins with this very particular resurrection of those who were asleep, or who have died in Christ.[24] Therefore, those who have died in Christ *must* be raised first. *"For the Lord Himself will descend from heaven with a shout, with the voice of the archangel, and with the trumpet of God; and the dead in Christ shall rise first"* (1 Thessalonians 4:16). The rapture begins with the dead in Christ being raised. If this resurrection does not take place first, then there is no rapture of the church biblically. The dead in Christ are raised first, translated into the Lord's presence and then they are reunited with their now glorified bodies. These are only saints of the church age, those who are in Christ, or in Jesus (the same expressions). This group

---

[22] It is not that they do not believe this, but there is not the systematic and consistent use of this part in their hermeneutic. That is the church began at Pentecost and will end at the rapture. The church is defined exactly in this way. Israel is the ethnic race of Jews descended from Abraham, Isaac, and Jacob. God has a separate program for Israel and for the church. Progressive dispensationalism does not believe there are these two separate and definitive peoples and programs. There is a complete distinction between Israel and the church. Scripture is very clear on this teaching.

[23] Article XIII—THE CHURCH, A UNITY OF BELIEVERS We believe that all who are united to the risen and ascended Son of God are members of the church which is the body and bride of Christ, **which began at Pentecost and is completely distinct from Israel.** Its members are constituted as such regardless of membership or nonmembership in the organized churches of earth. We believe that by the same Spirit all believers in this age are baptized into, and thus become, one body that is Christ's, whether Jews or Gentiles, and having become members one of another, are under solemn duty to keep the unity of the Spirit in the bond of peace, rising above all sectarian differences, and loving one another with a pure heart fervently (Matt. 16:16–18; Acts 2:42–47; Rom. 12:5; 1 Cor. 12:12–27; Eph. 1:20–23; 4:3–10; Col. 3:14–15). This is Article 13 of the doctrinal position of Dallas Seminary. A classic or traditional dispensationalist holds to the above teaching esp. that there is a *complete* distinction between Israel and the church. Scripture is absolutely clear on this issue.

[24] Paul also discusses some of these same issues in First Corinthians chapter fifteen. As this whole chapter speaks of resurrection, there is the concern about the body, a resurrection body made for heaven which will be given all believers for eternity (1 Cor. 15:35-50).

must be raised, then translated into the air to meet Him first, that is before the translation of the living saints.

Paul had emphasized this point. *"For this we say to you by the word of the Lord, that we who are alive, and remain until the coming of the Lord, shall not precede those who have fallen asleep"* (1 Thessalonians 4:15). Paul mentioned those who were asleep or dead in Christ four times (4:13-16). He makes an explicit point with an emphatic negation. Those who were left alive, still living, or remaining when the Lord comes to meet them (the entire church) in the air, will not precede those who have fallen asleep. The living and remaining will not go first.

The construction of "shall not precede" οὐ μὴ φθάσωμεν[25] is emphatic negation. The living will not precede those who have died to meet Him. This includes 2,000 years of church saints whose tombs will probably be opened, they don't need to be, but this may be a witness to others who are left behind. There was something similar in the past (Mat. 27:50-52).[26]

No matter what the argument on the rapture might be, there is a most definite sequence which must take place by the Word of the Lord (1 Thes. 4:15). *"For this we say to you by the word of the Lord, that we who are alive, and remain until the coming of the Lord, shall not precede those who have fallen asleep"* (1 Thessalonians 4:15).

1. we who are alive, and remain until the coming of the Lord (those living)
2. shall not precede   those who have fallen asleep (those asleep i.e. deceased)

The revelation of this resurrection came from Jesus Christ Himself. How it came to Paul is not known, but perhaps it was a direct revelation. Not only will the souls of

---

[25] "For this we say to you by the word of the Lord, that we who are alive, and remain until the coming of the Lord, shall not precede those who have fallen asleep" (1 Thessalonians 4:15). Τοῦτο γὰρ ὑμῖν λέγομεν ἐν λόγῳ κυρίου, ὅτι ἡμεῖς οἱ ζῶντες οἱ περιλειπόμενοι εἰς τὴν παρουσίαν τοῦ κυρίου οὐ μὴ φθάσωμεν τοὺς κοιμηθέντας." (1 Thessalonians 4:15). Note the οὐ μὴ with an aorist φθάσωμεν. This is an emphatic negation. It is not possible that those who are alive will precede those who are dead in Christ.

[26] "And Jesus cried out again with a loud voice, and yielded up His spirit. And behold, the veil of the temple was torn in two from top to bottom, and the earth shook; and the rocks were split, and the tombs were opened; and many bodies of the saints who had fallen asleep were raised; and coming out of the tombs after His resurrection they entered the holy city and appeared to many" (Matthew 27:50-53). It is hard to know exactly who these departed saints were but very it is very interesting that their tombs were opened. These tombs did not need to be opened very much like Christ's tomb did not need to be opened. A suggestion here is that possibly at the resurrection of the church saints prior to the translation of the living saints, all their tombs might be opened as a testimony to those who are truly left behind. God is not without witness. It must be remembered that at the rapture, at that moment, there is not one living saint left on the planet. This may be the first of several witnesses God leaves after the rapture. The open tombs of many departed saints.

the dead in Christ return with Him (v.. 14), but their bodies will also be resurrected at His coming. The bodies of dead Christians will be resurrected immediately before living Christians are conveyed upward. Clearly Paul believed that he and his Thessalonian readers might well be alive when the Lord returned. He believed that the Rapture was imminent, that it could take place at any moment (cf. 1:10; 1 Cor. 7:29, "the time is short"; Phil. 4:5, "The Lord is near"). And this truth of imminency brought comfort (1 Thes. 4:18).[27]

"Then we who are alive and remain shall be caught up together with them in the clouds to meet the Lord in the air, and thus we shall always be with the Lord" (1 Thessalonians 4:17). Paul includes himself in the 'we' who are alive, still living and are remaining on this earth are then caught up or raptured. Technically, it is the 'living' who are translated or raptured. The living are literally caught up and changed in a moment. The living (in Christ) are the ones who are translated immediately in life into His presence (1 Cor. 15:51-55).

There is an interesting construction with the word 'then' ἔπειτα [28] *"Then we who are alive and remain shall be caught up together with them"* (17). The normal meaning of the word is then or thereupon. However, it denotes a definite succession when used with πρῶτον or "first" such as in 4:16-17.[29] Paul is saying that when this happens then it will occur in this exact sequence. The rapture of the church begins with His descent, the dead in Christ are raised first (by the Word of the Lord), then the catching up or rapture of the living saints. These three events must take place: (1) the descent of the Lord from heaven in the air (1 Thes. 4:16a), (2) all the dead in

---

[27] BKCNT, 704.

[28] **ἔπειτα** ἡμεῖς οἱ ζῶντες οἱ περιλειπόμενοι ἅμα σὺν αὐτοῖς ἁρπαγησόμεθα ἐν νεφέλαις εἰς ἀπάντησιν τοῦ κυρίου εἰς ἀέρα· καὶ οὕτως πάντοτε σὺν κυρίῳ ἐσόμεθα" (1 Thessalonians 4:17). Note the use of the adverb ἔπειτα... marks sequence, thereupon,. Liddell, H., A *lexicon : Abridged from Liddell and Scott's Greek-English lexicon* (Oak Harbor, WA: Logos, 1996), 283. ἔπειτα adv...then, thereupon. 1. of time Lk 16:7; Gal 1:21; Js 4:14; ...2. to denote succession in enumerations—a. together with indications of chronological sequence πρῶτον... ἔ. *first*. . . *then* ...1 Cor 15:46; 1 Th 4:17...b. of succession alone: πρῶτον. BAGD, 284. There is no doubt there is a succession of events using this word according to the major lexicons. First there will be the dead in Christ who must be raised, then after that there will be the translation of the living saints.

[29] "For the Lord Himself will descend from heaven with a shout, with the voice of the archangel, and with the trumpet of God; and the dead in Christ shall rise **first. Then** we who are alive and remain shall be caught up together with them in the clouds to meet the Lord in the air, and thus we shall always be with the Lord" (1 Thessalonians 4:16-17). ὅτι αὐτὸς ὁ κύριος ἐν κελεύσματι, ἐν φωνῇ ἀρχαγγέλου καὶ ἐν σάλπιγγι θεοῦ, καταβήσεται ἀπ' οὐρανοῦ καὶ οἱ νεκροὶ ἐν Χριστῷ ἀναστήσονται **πρῶτον, ἔπειτα** ἡμεῖς οἱ ζῶντες οἱ περιλειπόμενοι ἅμα σὺν αὐτοῖς ἁρπαγησόμεθα ἐν νεφέλαις εἰς ἀπάντησιν τοῦ κυρίου εἰς ἀέρα· καὶ οὕτως πάντοτε σὺν κυρίῳ ἐσόμεθα The construction of **πρῶτον, ἔπειτα first. Then** is very significant. This falls into the normal use of the definition of **ἔπειτα** ἔπειτα adv...then, thereupon. 1. of time Lk 16:7; Gal 1:21; Js 4:14; ...2. to denote succession in enumerations—a. together with indications of chronological sequence πρῶτον. . . ἔ. *first*. . . *then* ...1 Cor 15:46; 1 Th 4:17...b. of succession alone: πρῶτον. BAGD, 284.

Christ are raised and translated (1 Thes. 4:16b), (3) then those who are alive will be caught up to meet them (1 Thes. 4:17).

Conclusion

The Word of God gives significant attention to the rapture of the church as the culmination and completion of the church age. The words and teachings on the rapture are to be a continual encouragement and exhortation in the church throughout the church age - this is a Scriptural command (1 Thes. 4:18). How many believers and churches are truly obedient in this?

The Word of God also makes it clear that the church has an appointment to meet the Lord in the air, and not in the wrath of the day of the Lord. The day of the Lord is indeed a central teaching but it does not pertain to the church or the church age. The church will be raptured prior to the day of the Lord. Scripture teaches clearly the pre-day-of-the-Lord rapture.

"The minimizing of a clear and consistent distinction between Israel and the church results in ignoring the great prophecy of the seventy weeks in Daniel 9:24-27."

- Charles C. Ryrie
Dispensationalism, 1969, page 176

14

Daniel 9:24-27 Considered, Part I

Charles H. Ray

Introduction

Regardless of one's theological persuasion, Daniel 9:24-27 is one of the most difficult passages to interpret. Challenges arise both in the area of linguistics and in theology, specifically eschatology. Some of the verbs are somewhat obscure, the chronological framework is not particularly easy to establish, and a dash of symbolism is thrown in the mix for good measure. The effort to unravel these four verses is worth it, however. Eschatological details are packed in them like sardines. A proper understanding of this highly scrutinized pericope will make end-time events less confusing. An overview of the passage reveals that v. 24 summarizes all four verses, v. 25 concerns the 69 "sevens," and v. 27 describes the 70th "seven."[1]

In addition to being an amazing revelation, it is one of the most wonderful answers to prayer in Scripture. Daniel read in Jeremiah that the Jews' captivity would last only 70 years, so "...it would be only natural for Daniel to inquire of God as to which of the three deportations marked the beginning of the seventy years of exile"[2] (605, 597, or 586 BC). Daniel asks the Lord about ending the exile, but His response looks to the future instead.[3] That is not to say the answer had nothing to do with his petitions. For example, the first triad of phrases (v. 24) addresses the wording of Daniel 9:5, and the last three his request of 9:7.[4] The verses will be discussed one by one, yet their teachings will be brought together at the end of the chapter.

Daniel 9:24

Enigmatic statements are discovered in the first two words of the passage. The phrase "seventy 'sevens'" (*shabi* is a heptad, a group of seven of something)[5] has generated numerous (and humorous) interpretations.

---

[1] John Walvoord, *Daniel: The Key to Prophetic Revelation*, 216.
[2] John S. and Paul D. Feinberg, *Tradition & Testament*, 191.
[3] Leon Wood, *A Commentary on Daniel*, 243.
[4] *Pre-Trib Perspectives*, Feb 2001, 6.
[5] John Goldingay, *Daniel* (WBC), 228, 229.

The Liberal Viewpoint Refuted

Many liberals advocate Daniel was penned in the second century BC, and it has nothing to do with Jesus. All of the prophecy therein, if any, was fulfilled by the time of Antiochus Epiphanes, and thus is actually just a history. The author (certainly not the real Daniel) confuses the seventy years of captivity with the 70 "sevens" announced by Gabriel.

Refutation of this liberal position has to do with Daniel's prayer and its relation to other ancient literature. A number of apocryphal books were written between 200 BC and AD 100. The prayers contained in those writings "are wordy and self-serving...Daniel's prayer is neither of these."[6] The plain reading of the book yields the idea that this great prophet lived in sixth century Mesopotamia, and thus was an eyewitness to the people and events enumerated in the story. There is absolutely no indication the author lived 400 hundred years later, as some scholars assert.

Other critics comment that the text does say "sevens" and not "years" or "months," and that "sevens" is a masculine plural instead of the expected feminine plural. Hence, they reason that no clear interpretation can be made because of these oddities.[7] Archer concisely and correctly assesses the issue, "...the term 'weeks' (rendered in NIV as 'sevens') is *shabim*, from *shabi*, which always takes a feminine plural, *shabot* when it means a seven of days, namely, a 'week.' The masculine plural here probably indicates that the word is meant as a heptad (so BDB, pp. 988-89) of years."[8]

The Meaning of 'Seventy Sevens'

Before other interpretations are discussed, it is necessary to deal with the numbers themselves and what time units are involved. Almost everyone agrees the seventy "sevens" means 490, but Bible students disagree as to the units; 490 what? The four most likely candidates are days, weeks, months, and years. The evidence will show "years" is the best answer.

"Days" is almost universally discarded. That proposition would bring the total to less than a year and a half, which is simply not enough time for all the actions of vv. 24-27 to take place. Further, if Daniel intended "days" here, he would have written that word down as he did at 10:2, 3.[9] There, he said he mourned and fasted for three weeks (so NIV; "three entire weeks," NASB) but the Hebrew is literally, "three sevens of days." Why did Daniel specify

---

[6] *Tradition & Testament*, 197.
[7] Walvoord, 217.
[8] Gleason Archer, "Daniel" in *The Expositor's Bible Commentary*, 26.
[9] J. Dwight Pentecost, "Daniel" in *The Bible Knowledge Commentary*, 1361.

"days"? Wouldn't people know he certainly didn't fast for 21 years? He put "days" because he did not want to give the impression he was still thinking in terms of "years" as in chapter nine.[10] Inserting "weeks" as the time unit creates the same difficulty. The span of time is not long enough, adding up to only nine and a half years.

A variation of this interpretation takes the verse in a straight-forward way; that is, the phrase means 70 weeks (as opposed to the 490 weeks as above). Barnes believes that explanation is not consistent with the character of the nature of the answer to the prayer. "The angel comes to bring him Daniel consolation...But what consolation would it be to be told that the city would indeed be rebuilt, and that it would continue seventy ordinary weeks - that is, a little more than a year, before a new destruction would come upon it?"[11]

In all probability "months" can be thrown out as well. In Daniel's mind there is no association between the number "seven" and the word "months." Seventy weeks of months was no significant duration of time in the Jewish culture. Gabriel would have to have been more exact in his wording if "months" was the intended time unit.

The final (and logical) selection is "years." Both BDB and Gesenius affirm this selection. Only Koehler and Baumgartner's *Lexicon in Veteris Testamenti libros* adheres to "period of seven days," and probably they come to this conclusion because they take the numbers figuratively and not literally.[12]

Daniel *would* have had "years" in his thoughts because he had just read the passage that invoked his prayer, Jeremiah 25:11, 12 (cf. Dan. 9:1, 2).[13] In painful detail, those verses declare Judah will be exiled for seventy *years* to make up for the sabbatical years they ignored (cf. 2 Chron. 36:21). God commanded the Jews to let their land lie fallow every seven years (Lev. 25:1-7), not only to honor the Lord, but also to allow the soil to replenish itself. They were in exile one year for every sabbatical year they had ignored. Calculating backwards, that would mean they had disobeyed that law for a total of about 490 years. Now God is telling them what will happen in the *next* 490 years.

Other factors support this selection (of "years"). After the *seventh* consecutive sabbatical *year* (that is, 50 years), the Jews celebrated the Year

[10] Harold Hoehner, *Chronological Aspects of the Life of Christ*, 118.
[11] Albert Barnes, *Notes on the Old Testament*, 140.
[12] Archer, 119.
[13] Ibid.

of Jubilee (Lev. 25:8-12). Lastly, the children of Abraham were to work six days but rest on the seventh. The point is, "seven" often came up in conversations in their daily lives as well as in their religious and civic duties. It would be natural for Daniel to think of these "sevens" as years.

Help from Other Passages

Further affirmation of this concept may be gleaned from a study of other passages.[14] *(1)* Dan. 4:16 speaks to Nebuchadnezzar's punishment, predicting it will last "seven periods," most likely meaning seven years. *(2)* Three verses in Dan. 12 are significant. Verse 7 mentions "time, times, and half a time." The definition of "times" (plural) must be "two," otherwise it would be impossible to discern the meaning of the expression. But does that really prove a "time" is a year? No, but the other two verses in chapter 12 point in that direction. Verse 11 speaks of 1,290 days. Verse 12 talks about 1,335 days. Both of those designations are just over three and a half years. Because all three verses have to do with the second half of the Tribulation, it would be foolish to not take them to all be approximately the same length of time. *(3)* Consider Daniel 7:25 also. It announces that the antichrist's evil events will endure "for time, times, and half a time." Holding that verse up to the corresponding passages in Revelation (as well as to the verses from Daniel just mentioned) confirms that three and a half years is the intended meaning. Rev. 11:2 laments Jerusalem will be trampled for 42 months (three and a half years). A parallel verse, Rev. 13:5, describes the same aspect of the end-time atrocities. There, the beast's (the antichrist's) power will last 42 months. A comparison of Rev. 12:6 with 12:14 yields the same result. Even though the term *shabi* ("seven") does not refer to years elsewhere in the Bible, it does carry that meaning in the Mishnah.[15] The conclusion is inescapable: in his message, Gabriel had "years" in mind.

Four Major Interpretations of the 'Seventy Sevens'

To some degree or another, all opinions as to how the "seventy sevens" played out in history (or will play out) can be placed into four major categories.[16]

(1) The "seventy sevens" are consecutive years and they end at the time of Antiochus Epiphanes (about 163 BC). In order for this theory to be true, a few unusual assumptions have to be made. The 490 years would have to start as

---

[14] This paragraph is based on Stephen R. Miller's *Daniel* (NAC), 215.

[15] Hoehner, 119.

[16] Unless otherwise noted, the explanation of the 4 theories come from Miller, 253-262.

far back as 586 BC, the date of Jerusalem's fall, and the decree of v. 25 would have to be Jeremiah's prophecy of 70 years of exile. J. A. Montgomery, a liberal, admits the position is precarious.

In the text, the 490 years are divided into three stages of 49, 434, and 7 years respectively. This viewpoint, then, plays out as follows. The first stage begins in 586 BC and ends in 538 BC, the year Babylon fell. The Anointed One (v. 25) now appears and he is one of the following men: Cyrus, Zerubbabel, Joshua (the postexilic high priest), Nebuchadnezzar, Alexander, or Seleucus Philopater.[17] The Bible says the Anointed One comes on the scene *after* the second stage, not preceding it, however. Montgomery (p. 379) appeals to the punctuation of the MT, but those marks are the Masoretes' interpretation. An *athnach* is not inspired. Keil (p. 356) recognizes an *athnach* may indicate a rest in a clause, and not always the end of a sentence. Acceptance of the MT pointing makes the message almost unintelligible, for it would be saying it will take 434 years to build the plaza and moat.[18] Too, there is no indication the stages are contemporaneous. That the seven years and 62 years are to be consecutive is confirmed by the Septuagint, Theodotion, the Syriac, and the Vulgate.[19]

Stage two starts at the death of Joshua (the most popular choice from the above list) and terminates with the passing of another "Messiah." An array of names has been put forth as to who this "Messiah" is, yet the favorite selection is the high priest Onias III (170 BC). Some believe Onias is also the "prince of the covenant" in Dan. 11:22. According to intertestamental history, he was murdered in 170 BC, and the explanation given for "and have nothing" (v. 26) is Jerusalem and its oversight were no longer his.[20] Antiochus' persecution encompasses the final seven years (170-163). There are not a few reasons why Antiochus does not meet the qualifications demanded by this passage. This menace did stop the sacrifices, but only for about three years, not the three and a half required by v. 27, nor did he destroy the Temple, as v. 26 announces, nor did he make a "firm covenant" with the Jews (v. 27).[21] A variation of this interpretation sees the 69 "sevens" as literal years but the 70th "seven" is seen as indefinite,[22] an inconsistent hermeneutic.

---

[17] *Tradition & Testament*, 218.
[18] Ibid, 212.
[19] Hoehner, 130.
[20] *Tradition & Testament*, 196.
[21] Ibid., 197, 198.
[22] Walvoord, 218.

At least five other defects can be found in this first proposal, rendering it untenable. Jeremiah did not issue a "decree;" those edicts are sent out by kings. Additionally, the prophet's message said nothing about rebuilding Jerusalem (v. 25). (This "rebuilding" aspect of the passage is a stumbling block for the first three interpretations. It will be examined in some detail below.) Second, the text says the 490 years begin with the decree, not with Jerusalem's devastation. The third defect is obvious; the kingdom did not come in 163 BC. Fourth, very few of these terms are taken literally, opening them up to a multitude of interpretations.[23] Finally, from 586 to 163 BC is not 490 years. The critics excuse this as a miscalculation on the part of Daniel's author. As noted before, most who hold to this theory are liberal and claim Daniel was penned in the second century BC, hence, after the fact. If true, why would so many mathematical mistakes be in the text?[24] Regardless, this suggestion does not harmonize with the natural reading of Daniel 9:24-27.

(2) The "seventy sevens" are symbolic, and end in the first century AD. E. J. Young favors this idea and explains it as follows. The first stage (49 yrs) commences with Cyrus' decree (538 BC) and is completed by the time of Ezra-Nehemiah (440-400). The 62 "sevens" stretch from 400 BC to the time of Christ. The last "seven" is from the first advent to an undesignated date after the resurrection but before AD 70. Rushdoony (*Thy Kingdom Come*) and Boutflower (*In and Around the Book of Daniel*) are in Young's camp but with some variation. Orthodox Jews, holding to a non-Christological view, believe these 70 "sevens" concluded in AD 70 with the destruction of the Temple.[25]

This second hypothesis has several serious errors. Each "seven" is not taken in its plain sense, but as an indefinite period of time. It is illogical to take numbers that are stated more than once, and are definite in their nature, as symbols.[26] Many scholars do the same thing with the "one thousand" in Rev. 20. Second, each "seven" is not calculated consistently in each stage. In the first portion each is about 20 years in length. For the second, six years, and in the final one the span is unknown. Even if the "sevens" were symbolic, the literal truth behind it should not change within the same context. Third, this theory places the downfall of Jerusalem after the 70 "sevens," yet it actually happens right at the end of the 69th "seven."

---

[23] Wood, 243.
[24] *Tradition & Testament*, 197.
[25] Walvoord, 218.
[26] Wood, 247.

Archer notes, "As for the purely symbolic use of 'seventy sevens,' there is not the slightest analogy for such usage in all Scripture."[27] Daniel certainly understood *Jeremiah's* seventy years to be literal.[28] Finally, to claim v. 24 was fulfilled in Christ's first coming is a flagrant distortion of that verse.

(3) Another symbolic interpretation declares the "sevens" are unspecified eras beginning in 538 BC and ending at Jesus' return at the end of the age. Keil and Leupold, two proponents of this interpretation, teach this passage is a prophecy of Church history. Obviously they are assuming the church is in the OT. According to them, just the seven "sevens" *alone* extend from 538 BC until the first century AD, roughly 550 years. The 62 "sevens" span the period from Christ until the persecution by the antichrist. During this time (at least two thousand years), the city (spiritual Jerusalem, the Church) will be built even in "times of trouble." The events of vv. 26, 27 occupy the last "seven." To be "cut off" does not mean death, but predicts (1) the persecution of the Church, and (2) Christ will have lost His place and function. The "ruler" (vv. 26, 27) is the antichrist. Organized religion will be destroyed until Jesus comes to judge the antichrist.

To the literalist, an array of red flags has popped up. First, this speculation fails to distinguish between Israel and the Church. Second, it is beyond credulity; too much subjectivity is involved. Third, in v. 25, the building of the city is taken literally, yet at the end of the verse it is understood figuratively. Fourth, to state Christ and His Church will fail is heresy. Jesus said even the gates of hell cannot conquer His Church (Matt. 16:18).There will always be witnesses (Matt. 24:14; Rev. 11). Fifth, as with the other symbolic interpretation, the time frame for each "seven" varies wildly. In fact, the duration of the last "seven" is completely obscure. Lastly, the Anointed One comes after the 69 "sevens," not after the first stage.

(4) This fourth and final proposal makes the most sense. It has the fewest difficulties and fits with the natural reading of Dan. 9:24-27. *The basic assumptions are: (1) the years are actual, and (2) the end of the 70th "seven" is at Christ's return.* The activities in each of the three stages are detailed like this.

The 49 years begin with the order to rebuild Jerusalem (possibly the edict to Ezra in 458 BC, but more likely the one to Nehemiah in 444 BC; more will be said on this issue later) and terminate with the completion of their

---

[27] Archer, 119.
[28] Lewis Sperry Chafer, *Systematic Theology*, 4:337, 338.

work (either 409 or 395). The next term (434 years) starts from Ezra and Nehemiah's ministry and goes to Christ's first advent (either His baptism in AD 26, or His presentation of Himself to the people on Palm Sunday in AD 32).

When Israel rejected her Messiah, the times of the Gentiles commenced, which are not part of the "seventy sevens." Because these two items (rejection of Messiah and times of the Gentiles) are not specifically mentioned in this passage, it is not too far fetched to believe there is a time gap between the 69th and 70th "weeks." No delay is detected in Isaiah 9:6, 7 either, yet one is there, as the ages have shown.

The last "seven" is the 7-year Tribulation when the Lord will again turn His attention to the Israel. In those days many will come to faith. It will be finished when Jesus returns to set up His 1000-year kingdom on earth. Young claims (p. 206), "The burden of proof rests with those who insist that sevens of years are intended. Of this I am not convinced. If the sevens be regarded merely as a symbolic number, the difficulty disappears." On the contrary, it is magnified. By not taking the numbers at face value, one can assign any value to them. The burden of proof rests on those who want to impute a special or unusual meaning to a phrase.[29]

History has confirmed that the traditional dispensational teachings are correct. This generation has the privilege of looking back and noticing the "sevens" are years and God did not intend for the 70th "week" to come about right on the heels of the 69th. "In this time the 490 years all prophecy concerning Israel is to be fulfilled, even to the finishing of Israel's transgression (cf. Rom. 11:26-27) and the anointing of the most Holy."[30] All other approaches are either "built on the premise that Daniel is a forgery and prophecy is impossible" or they spiritualize the passage.[31]

What God has Decreed

Now that "seventy 'sevens'" is understood, it is time to examine the balance of v. 24. It states that Jerusalem was in ruins, yet obviously the Lord still had a love for it (Dan. 9:20, 24).[32] Gabriel announced that these actions are determined ("decreed", NASB, NIV), implying He *wants* the city rebuilt. *Nehatan* (Niphal perfect; "decreed") is found only here in the OT. After comparing it with the corresponding Aramaic verb, scholars concluded the

---

[29] Archer, 121.
[30] Chafer, 4:337, 338.
[31] Walvoord, 232.
[32] Ibid, 220.

best translation is "to cut off, decide." The Lord has purposely and precisely cut these seventy "weeks" from history as special to Israel.[33] (The "decreed" of v. 27 *nehra'h* Niphal participle has a similar meaning but a different root.) At this point another mystery interrupts the chain of thought. The subject is plural ("seventy sevens") yet the verb is singular (smoothed out as "have been" in the NASB; NIV has "are"). One solution is to see it as a signal to Daniel to take these 490 years as one continuous period,[34] or, in other words, as a unit. Even though the final seven years have not happened yet, all 490 are a time when the Lord is concentrating His attention on the Jews. The preposition "for" (*ʻl*) can be rendered "against" (so Montgomery; 569 times in the OT), but since the message is one of hope for Israel, it is best to translate it as "for" (so NASB, NIV) or "concerning."[35] Yahweh is in complete command of all happenings, even the future. Fate is not in control because He has a plan.[36]

Who Benefits from God's Decree?

Much debate has focused on other expressions in 9:24.[37] Men such as Keil, Leupold, and Young believe "your people" refers to "spiritual Israel," and "your holy city" is the heavenly Jerusalem. Both are modified by "your" because Daniel was praying for both and because he belonged to both.[38] Again, some logic-defying mistakes are made. The text does not lend itself to such a speculation. This passage (9:24-27) is the answer to Daniel's prayer, a prayer in which he was petitioning Yahweh about the Jews and Jerusalem, not some entities unknown to him. In Dan. 10:14, "your people" clearly means Abraham's descendants; nothing else would make sense in that verse. The same reasoning applies to 11:14.[39] Indeed, how could a people destroy the heavenly Jerusalem (v. 26)? The term "holy city" denotes literal Jerusalem in Neh. 11:1, 18; Isa. 48:2, 52:11; Matt. 4:5, 27:53, and possibly Rev. 11:2.

The Specifics of the Decree

The remainder of v. 24 lists six items that will not be in full bloom until the end of the "seventy sevens." Even amillennarians like Keil and Baldwin

---

[33] Wood, 248.
[34] Barnes, 141.
[35] Goldingay, 229.
[36] Walvoord, 220.
[37] Unless otherwise noted, this paragraph is taken from Miller, 259.
[38] Wood, 248.
[39] Pentecost, 1361.

confess this time-table is correct. Pentecost summarizes the verse well: "The basis for the first three was provided in the work of Christ on the cross, but all six will be realized by Israel at the Second Advent of Christ."[40] However, the items are not as easy to comprehend as a brief reading would suggest, and thus some explanation is necessary.[41] They are primarily directed at Israel yet the whole world will be affected by them.

#1: 'to finish the transgression'
The first phrase is, "to finish the transgression" (NASB). Scholars disagree with each other as to which verb "finish" is rooted. If the verb is *kel'* (Piel infinitive construct, "to restrain"), which is the Kethiv reading, then this would be the only place it is found in the Piel in the OT, and it would be rendered "to restrain firmly."[42] The idea could be that transgression is only lessened, or that it is totally stopped but for only a season. Indeed, some Bible students propose Christ's work on the cross merely buffeted transgressions' influence on society.

That *kel'* is not seen in the Piel (except here possibly) is one reason most scholars look to another root to determine the definition of this infinitive. That other root is the Qere reading, *kaloh* ("to finish, to bring a process to completion").[43] Goldingay and BDB prefer this choice. *Kaloh* (like *nethitan*) has a parallel in v. 27, where it is rendered "complete destruction" (NASB) or "the end" (NIV). *Kaloh* is present in Dan. 11:16, 36; 12:7, too.[44] Miller believes the two verbs have merged, and refers the reader to Koehler and Baumgartner's *Lexicon in Veteris Testamenti libros*, page 437. The better selection is *kaloh* because Christ's work on the cross didn't just restrain sin, it paved the way for it to be completely removed.

The word "transgression" (*pash'*, a singular masculine noun) is articulated, perhaps specifying Israel's rebellion. This conclusion is supported by the fact that this passage is an answer to prayer, and Daniel prays about Israel's rebellion in particular (9:5). "Since the emphasis in this phrase is upon the finishing of Israel's transgression, then this leads to the conclusion that it will occur at the second coming of Jesus."[45] Wood holds the opposite opinion, believing it is just a general term, more so than "sin" below.[46]

---

[40] Ibid.
[41] Much of this information is derived from Miller, 259-262.
[42] Wood, 248.
[43] *Theological Wordbook of the Old Testament* (abbrv. *TWOT*), 439.
[44] Goldingay, 229.
[45] *Pre-Trib Perspectives*, Feb 2001, 6.
[46] Wood, 248.

#2: 'to make an end of sin'

The second expression is, "to make an end of sin." Again there is uncertainty as to the original meaning of the verb stem. The Qere has *lohatem*, the Hiphil infinitive of *tamam* ("to finish, complete"). The Kethiv is *lohatem*, the Qal infinitive of *hatam* ("to seal up"). Both choices will be discussed, beginning with the Qere. All but one ancient version (Theodotion) has the Qere rendering, as do the Syriac and Vulgate.[47] The Kethiv can be explained as an accidental copying of *lohatem* from the next line, where "to seal up" is the proper rendering. Wood adds (p. 249), "'to seal up' is out of place here because whenever it is used with 'sin' in other passages it indicates a sealing up for judgment." One example often given for this usage is Deut. 32:34. (Those who prefer the Kethiv could argue Jesus "judged" sin at the crucifixion.) Miller, in agreement with Archer, Goldingay, and Walvoord, declares "to finish" fits the context better,[48] for then this phrase would parallel the previous one.

Those in favor of the Kethiv cannot be readily dismissed nevertheless. Barnes is persuaded "to seal up" is the better choice, claiming the Masoretes inserted "to finish" because it made better sense to them than "to seal up" did.[49] Keil and Pentecost also take their stand for the Kethiv reading. The strongest argument in favor of the Kethiv is that BDB lists the root as *htm* (p. 367). The decision is difficult but "to finish" gets the victory by a slim margin.

There are text-critical problems with the noun, too. The Kethiv has "sins," whereas the Qere has "sin." The singular (*hot't*, meaning "to miss the mark" or "a revolt against authority") is the preferred reading because it connotes the concept of sin as well as the sins themselves. Thus, some scholars like it because it is a more encompassing term than "transgression" is (previous clause). Other scholars consider "sins" to be the better fit, believing *hot'at* refers only to our daily sins.[50] "Since this Hebrew word does not have the definite article as did 'transgression' in the previous phrase, and since 'sin' is plural, it seems to refer to the sins in general of the nation" (cf. Dan. 9:20).[51] Miller (p. 260) comments, "Sin will be controlled during the millennium and cease completely during the eternal state. The future kingdom of God includes both periods." Other scholars promote this same

---

[47] Ibid, 249.
[48] Miller, 260.
[49] Barnes, 142.
[50] Wood, 249.
[51] *Pre-Trib Perspectives*, Feb 2001, 7.

concept: that there will be traces of iniquity during the Millennium because Satan is "merely" bound; he is not yet in the Lake of Fire.

In light of all the considerations, "sin" appears to be the better suggestion for the following reasons. The expressions on either side of this one have singular nouns. Too, Jesus' sacrifice did away with the concept of sin (for the eternal state if not for the Millennial Kingdom also), which in turn eliminates the possibility of a sin being committed.

#3: 'to make atonement for iniquity'

The third item on the list is, "to make atonement for iniquity." A person who is guilty of wickedness ("perverse action")[52] has committed iniquity.[53] The verb is *kaper*, "to cover, wipe out,"[54] and being in the Piel gives it the connotation of expiation.[55] Goldingay affirms this implication by stating the verb may be more closely related to Akkadian ("to cleanse") than it is to Arabic ("to cover").[56] In addition, those passages where God is a Judge, *kaper* is usually rendered "to pardon."[57]

The words would bring back memories of the blood being sprinkled on the mercy seat, depicting the people's sins being covered (Lev. 16:15, 16), but that ritual on the Day of Atonement was only a temporary appeasement (Rom. 3:25). The Redeemer's death is a permanent removal, and the Lord is justified in expiating the iniquities of the faithful because the Son's blood was shed. Therefore, "to atone" adequately captures the sense of the clause.

Is there a progression here?

Based on his alternatives for the various verb roots and meanings, Wood sees a progression of the first three accomplishments thus: Sin is first restrained; to what degree? It is put to an end; how is this done? By Christ's atonement.[58] Perhaps Wood was thinking of 2 Thess. 2:7, which speaks of a restrainer holding back sin for the time being. Barnes' progression is: "Sin would be restrained, sealed up, covered up."[59] He continues,

> These expressions, though not of the nature of a climax, are intensive, and show that the great work referred to pertained to sin, and would be designed to remove

---

[52] Wood, 249.
[53] Miller, 260.
[54] Walvoord, 221.
[55] Wood, 249.
[56] Goldingay, 229.
[57] Wood, 249.
[58] Ibid.
[59] Barnes, 144.

it. Its bearing would be on human transgression; on the way by which it might be pardoned; on the methods by which it would be removed from the view, and be kept from rising up to condemn and destroy.[60]

Goldingay weighs in by proposing there is deliberate variety in the way the phrases are written. He translates them "the rebellion," "failures," and "waywardness," which is an articulated singular noun, then an anarthrous plural, followed by an anarthrous singular.[61]

#4: 'to bring in everlasting righteousness'

At the cross, iniquity was ended in principle, yet only at the second coming will "everlasting righteousness" (the fourth expression) be made possible.[62] Israel as a whole will finally have a right and permanent relationship with their Messiah. *'lamym* denotes "long duration, futurity," and because it is a plural intensive noun, it connotes "everlasting."[63] The kingdom will be characterized by justice forever (Isa. 60:21; Jer. 23:5, 6).[64] Justice will always be perfectly executed, and people will be made righteous perpetually (Isa. 51:6-8).[65]

"To bring in" (*haby'*) is a Hiphil infinitive construct, resulting in "to cause to come in."[66] People cannot make themselves righteous or establish the kingdom; that is God's doing. Indeed, Daniel had earlier prayed, "Righteousness belongs to Thee, O Lord..." (9:7).[67] "The essential idea in the language is, that this would be *introduced* by the Messiah from v. 25 ; that is, that he would be its author."[68]

#5: 'to seal up vision and prophecy'

The next accomplishment will be "to seal up vision and prophecy." As noted before, the root is *hetom* (Qal infinitive construct, "to seal, seal up"), not *tamam*. In the ancient world, a seal, usually of wax, kept a scroll closed, and signified ownership, authenticity, and security. Much like a letter today, it was unlawful for anyone to open it (break the seal) except the person to

---

[60] Ibid.

[61] Goldingay, 229.

[62] Wood, 250.

[63] BDB, 761, 762.

[64] Pentecost, 1361.

[65] Barnes, 144.

[66] Wood, 249.

[67] *Pre-Trib Perspectives*, March 2001, 6.

[68] Barnes, p. 144 (emphasis in original).

whom it was addressed. However, the nuances of this term cannot be captured in a simple sentence for it is a multifaceted gem.

The implications of this phrase may include all of the following: (1) God will put His seal of authentication on all true revelations, (2) These forms of revelation will cease, (3) Prophecies will be fulfilled, and (4) Nothing else is to be added to His plans and revelations (as implied by the seal).[69] When Christ comes back, there will be no more need for visions and prophecies. Feinberg elaborates, "the thought was to seal up the prophecy and make a permanent record of it, so that when it is fulfilled the event can be compared to the prophecy to show how completely the one corresponds to the other."[70] As a side note, since this sealing up won't come to pass until the kingdom is established, Daniel 9:24-27 by necessity involves both advents.[71] Wood remarks,

> The premillennial view...sees the relation between the response of God to Daniel's prayer as follows: that, whereas Daniel had been concerned regarding an early return of the Jews from their captivity to Babylon, God was interested in, first, their deliverance from a far more serious bondage to sin (which had caused their Babylonian captivity) through Christ's work at His first coming and, second, their final release from earthly oppression through the power of Christ at His second coming.[72]

The Hebrew word for "vision" comes from the root *hazah* and has a range of meanings including "look," "see" (both literal and metaphysical), and even "prophesy" (Isa. 30:10 is an example).[73] It is clear, then, that this is a revelatory term. Sometimes it is translated as "burden" or "oracle" (Nahum 1:1, NASB, NIV). These would not be just Daniel's visions, but all visions the Lord has granted.[74]

The usual word for "prophecy" (*n-bu'h*, found only three times in the OT) is not used here, but the term used comes from the same root (*niby'*), and it actually means "prophet." Again, the suggestion is that no more revelation is needed once Christ comes back. Young points out "vision" and "prophet" are OT terms and therefore they were "sealed" at Jesus' first advent, a doctrine of preterism. That proposition cannot be correct, for visions and prophecies were presented in the NT and because many prophecies are yet to be

---

[69] Walvoord, 222.
[70] Charles Feinberg, *A Commentary on Daniel*, 128.
[71] Miller, 261.
[72] Wood, 244.
[73] *TWOT*, 630, 634.
[74] Barnes, 145.

fulfilled.[75] For instance, very little in the book of Revelation has yet to come about.

#6: 'to anoint the most holy'
The last achievement is the anointing of "the most holy" (*qedosh qadashym*, a singular noun followed by its plural, literally "holy of holies"). The word "anoint" (*m-shah*, Qal infinitive construct, from which we get the word "Messiah") is defined as "to smear,"[76] especially in the sense of pouring oil on a king or priest for consecration. This term can be used for any ceremony that sets aside a person or a place for sacred use, regardless of whether or not oil is utilized.[77]

Is "a most holy" (there is no definite article in the Hebrew) a thing or a person? Some teach this statement alludes to Jesus being anointed as King of kings and Lord of lords (most amillennarians hold this view; the Vulgate also understands it to be a person), or to the New Jerusalem of Revelation 21. Preterists claim this prediction was fulfilled at Jesus' baptism, whereas another theory states the Temple was sanctified when Jesus entered it.[78] However, nowhere in Holy Writ is *qedosh qadashym* ("a most holy") applied to the Church or to a person.[79] "Holy" can also be found in v. 26, where most translations render it "sanctuary" (so NASB, NIV).[80]

Each of the 39 occurrences of *qedosh qadashym* pertains to the Tabernacle, Temple (specifically the Holy of Holies), or the things in the Temple. Those things include the altar (Exod. 29:37), holy incense (Exod. 30:36), the showbread (Lev. 24:9), and even a sin offering (Lev. 6:18).[81] A reasonable deduction from that fact is "a most holy" is the Temple. The allusion is not likely to be the Holy of Holies proper because that term almost always has the article with it.[82] The question then becomes, which Temple?

If the seventy "sevens" concluded before Christ (as some liberals espouse), then the anointing was the dedication of Zerubbabel's Temple, or its rededication after Antiochus Epiphanes desecrated it (I Macc. 4:52-56).[83] However, tradition refutes those claims. First, the proper oil could not be found at the time of Zerubbabel, and second, there is no proof Solomon's

---

[75] Cited by Wood, 250.
[76] BDB, 602.
[77] Barnes, 146.
[78] Ibid.
[79] Ibid., 147.
[80] Miller, 262.
[81] Wood, 250; Archer, 119.
[82] Wood, 250.
[83] Walvoord, 223.

Temple was literally anointed either.[84] (In Exod. 33 the things inside the Tabernacle had anointing oil poured on them.[85])

Since the passage encompasses both advents, the Temple in question must be the one minutely described in Ezekiel 40-48. In what sense will it be anointed? Probably by the presence of the Messiah (Hag. 2:7-9). In the OT, only God's Shekinah Glory is said to fill the Temple.[86] The Messiah's presence gives the Temple "a sacredness to that edifice which nothing else did give or could give, and, therefore, as meeting all the proper force of the language used here."[87] A point to ponder is, just as Acts 2 was a "preview" of the events of Joel 2, perhaps these other major Temple ceremonies (involving Zerubbabel's Temple) were just a sampling of what is yet to take place. Namely, the consecration of the Millennial Temple at the beginning of the 1000-year reign of Christ.

Two final observations about verse 24 are in order. First, Jesus' sacrifice made these six tasks possible but the benefits will not be applied until He returns and Israel repents. Second, when these six items are evident, all doubters will have to acknowledge that Yahweh never did forget Israel, for all of His covenant promises (Gen. 15; II Sam. 7; Jer. 31:31-34, *etc.*) will be "sealed up" in the kingdom.[88]

Daniel 9:25

The NASB renders v. 25a, "So you are to know and discern..." ("Know and understand this:"...NIV). The words are a follow-up to verse 23 ("so give heed to the message and gain understanding of the vision").[89] These verbs are not imperatives, but if Daniel pays close attention to Gabriel's message, then he will be able to grasp its meaning.[90] Hengstenberg and Theodotion translate it using a future tense ("will know..."). God's messenger came with the express purpose of giving Daniel "insight with understanding" (v. 22). The prophet most likely did not understand all of it, but he grasped enough to receive comfort and reassurance.[91]

---

[84] Barnes, 147.
[85] Ibid.
[86] F. Duane Lindsey, "Haggai" in *The Bible Knowledge Commentary*, 1542.
[87] Barnes, 148.
[88] Pentecost, 1362.
[89] Goldingay, 260.
[90] Barnes, 148.
[91] Walvoord, 223, 224.

The Meaning of 'know' and 'discern'

The word for "know" is *teda'* (Qal imperfect, 2ms) and can mean "know," "perceive," or "see."[92] "Discern" is a translation of *tas-kel* (Hiphil imperfect, 2ms) and can be rendered "consider," "ponder," "understand," or "be prudent."[93] "While *nab* a synonym for *tas-kel* indicates 'distinguishing between,' *lakam* relates to an intelligent knowledge of the reason. There is the process of thinking through a complex arrangement of thoughts resulting in a wise dealing and use of good practical common sense."[94]

Although they are imperfects, they function like jussives, connoting a sense of urgent obligation.[95] Gill paraphrases the verse as, "Take notice and observe, for the clearer understanding of these seventy weeks, and the events to be fulfilled in them..."[96] Since *tas-kel* is in the Hiphil, Gabriel may be saying Daniel will be caused to know these matters, or at least he will be "forced" to ponder them. Lastly, it could just be "know" and "discern" are synonyms;[97] *NIDOTTE* puts them in the same semantic field.[98]

Which Decree is in View?

One item Daniel is to know is the *terminus a quo* (beginning point) of the seventy "sevens." It is the opinion of many that *the* key to comprehending this entire passage is to determine which decree (*dabar*, "thing, matter, word," or even "commandment") is alluded to here. (The usual word for "commandment," though, is *mats-vah*).[99] The text declares the 69 "weeks" (483 years) will encompass the time from the giving of this edict until the Messiah appears. Some critics argue there is no indication the subject has changed[100] and that since the *dabar* of v. 23 ("command," NASB; "answer," NIV) was sent by God, this one is, too. That line of reasoning does not harmonize with the natural sense of the pericope, and "since the issuance of this directive would mark the definite starting point of the seventy weeks, it follows that it should be an edict known generally, thus one set forth by an

---

[92] BDB, 393.

[93] Ibid., 968.

[94] *TWOT*, 877.

[95] Wood, 251.

[96] John Gill, *Commentary on Daniel*, 206.

[97] Miller, 262.

[98] Willem VanGemeren, *New International Dictionary of Old Testament Theology & Exegesis* (*NIDOTTE*), 2:414.

[99] *Tradition & Testament*, 191.

[100] Walvoord, 224.

earthly monarch such as the Persian king."[101] Too, *mats-vah* is far more commonly used for one of Jehovah's edicts than *dabar* is.[102]

Even though *dabar* is found in both verses, the tone of v. 23 makes it apparent the message is from the Lord, yet v.25 is not that obvious as to the source. Indeed, Paul uses the same word ("head") in two consecutive verses in 1 Corinthians 11:3, 4 yet with different meanings. Lastly, this interpretation is far too subjective; it would be nearly impossible to know exactly *when* God gave the decree.

Daniel's 70 'Weeks' are not Jeremiah's 70 Years

A modified version proposes Gabriel was really talking about Jeremiah's seventy years of captivity, but that confuses two entirely different prophecies. Jeremiah said nothing about rebuilding Jerusalem, and he made this prediction about 605 BC,[103] way too early to be the *terminus a quo*.

To suggest there is here an extension of the exile is ridiculous. Porteous, for example, intimates the seventy years had passed and Daniel was asking the Lord to end the exile. Instead of doing so, Yahweh declares the Jews must remain in exile another 490 years. This interpretation is borderline blasphemy, for God cannot go back on His word (Jer. 25:11, 12). Besides, it is an historical fact that Cyrus permitted the Jews to return to Jerusalem.[104]

The Four Possible Persian Decrees

There were four major decrees concerning the Jews issued by Persian rulers that can be considered possibilities with reference to this verse. Wood contends all four could qualify because each deals with the re-establishment of Jerusalem.[105]

The first was in 538 BC by Cyrus (II Chron. 36:22, 23; Ezra 1:1-4, 5:13). The second was by Darius I (Darius Hystaspes) in 512 BC (Ezra 6:1, 6-12), yet it was mostly a confirmation of the first one. This "decree grows out of the question of Tattenai, governor of Judah, regarding the right of the returned exiles to rebuild the Temple (Ezra 5:3-17). In response to this request, Darius made a search for Cyrus's decree, and then issued one of his own (Ezra 6:1-12)."[106] These two decrees gave permission to rebuild the Temple, but said nothing about restoring Jerusalem.

---

[101] Wood, 251.
[102] *Tradition & Testament*, 191.
[103] Walvoord, 224.
[104] *Tradition & Testament*, 190.
[105] Wood, 252.
[106] *Tradition & Testament*, 193.

Artaxerxes Longimanus sent forth the third edict in 457 BC. "Temple worship was established and civil leaders were appointed (Ezra 7:11-26),"[107] but again it said nothing about the city.[108] Wood's reply is that Ezra built up Jerusalem morally and spiritually.[109] If the verse is not speaking of a physical rebuilding, then what does "with plaza and moat" (v. 25) mean?[110] According to Sir Robert Anderson (whose calculations are still highly regarded), the fourth decree was issued on March 5, 444 BC, also by Artaxerxes Longimanus. (Scholars are willing to fudge a year or two on all these dates, ergo some assert the third edict came out in 458 BC, and this one in 445 BC.)

This document was given to Nehemiah (Neh. 2:1-8) and it specifically designated Jerusalem's walls -- that they were to be reconstructed. A possible stumbling block to this theory is the "seven weeks" of v. 25. A number of scholars understand this expression to mean 49 years would be required to put the walls back up. True, it took just 52 days for Nehemiah and the people to finish the walls, but many years (in the days of no construction equipment) were required to clean up the city after decades of desolation. It would have been very difficult to construct the streets and moat (not to mention houses) if debris were in the way.[111]

More Arguments Against the 444 BC Date Given and Refuted
Those facts would seem to clear things up, but that is not the case with some scholars. Young, Leupold, Keil, and Calvin back the idea that the 490 years begin with the decree of 538 BC. One obstacle to that suggestion is Jerusalem was not rebuilt until long after Cyrus died.[112] In addition, if the 69 "weeks" are added to 538 BC, then they would terminate in 55 BC, a year in which no crucial event took place.[113] Archer, Payne, Wood, and Miller are of the opinion the starting point was 458 BC (despite Wood's admission that the 444 BC decree comes closest to the idea of rebuilding the city).[114] Miller comments about the 444 BC issuance,

> A second decree of Artaxerxes I issued to Nehemiah (445 BC) is a popular view (e.g., Walvoord, Whitcomb, Sir Robert Anderson, Hoehner). Actually, this does not seem to have been a formal decree but involved permission for Nehemiah to visit

---

[107] Ibid.
[108] Pentecost, 1362, 1363.
[109] Wood, 254.
[110] Goldingay, 261.
[111] Pentecost, 1363.
[112] Miller, 262.
[113] Walvoord, 227.
[114] Wood, 253.

Palestine (Neh. 2:5-8). Nevertheless, Artaxerxes' words to Nehemiah probably meet the criteria of the *dabar*, which may mean "decree, message, or word." This decree to Nehemiah specifically mentions the rebuilding of Jerusalem (Neh. 2:5), which is the strongest argument in favor of it.[115]

Miller makes the same mistake all the others of this persuasion make. They defend their position by *assuming* that the rebuilding of the city is *implied* in the previous decrees. That is a rather unstable foundation on which to erect one's theology.

Does Ezra Suggest the Walls Were Already Being Built?

Two passages in Ezra (4:12-23 and 9:9) are thrown into relief to shore up the viewpoint of Miller, *et al*. Those verses apparently prove some building on the city walls took place about 457 BC, and thus before Nehemiah came on the scene, but further study shows that this conclusion is not necessary.

First, the 4:12-23 passage is a letter written by Ezra's enemies back to King Artaxerxes to inform him he must take action because the Jews were fortifying Jerusalem. However, one cannot look to the words of one's foes to prove a point; they may have been lying (4:19) suggests they were telling the truth) just to get the king to do something about the rebuilding of the Temple. If they were telling the truth, and (thus) Artaxerxes already knew they were constructing walls (because that is *implied* in the other decrees), then the letter wouldn't provoke him at all. He would think everything was moving along as expected.

His reply to the letter offers no substantial clue toward solving this puzzle of whether or not the walls were being fortified (Ezra 4:17-24). Ezra reports (v. 24) work on the "house of God' has ceased but no mention of the city/walls. Artaxerxes does command the city to not be rebuilt until he issues a decree to do so (v. 21), which does not prove the case either way. It seems best, however, to understand the situation thus: the Jews were constructing walls but they were not supposed to, and so Artaxerxes was alarmed. A Persian monarch is unlikely to permit a people to return home and build their city walls, for that would amount to a military threat. On the other hand, just erecting a Temple is of no concern. Lastly, if Ezra already had the materials, or at least had permission to gather them, then why would Nehemiah have to ask for permission to do so (Neh. 2:8)?

The other verse is 9:9. It talks about the many things God has provided the exiles, including "a wall in Judah and Jerusalem." A number of commentators

---

[115] Miller, 263.

(Yamauchi, Williamson, Ackroyd, Bright) believe this turn of a phrase is metaphorical or figurative. Now that the Temple is rebuilt (at least mostly), His presence and glory may return, giving protection to His children. In observing the context, Ezra is in prayer confessing the iniquities of the people, thanking God for bringing them back from captivity, and for allowing them "to raise up the house of our God." This and the previous verse (v. 8) are speaking of the Temple, not the city.[116]

Williamson further remarks Ezra may view the king of Persia (under God's supervision) as this "wall" of protection.[117] If Ezra were speaking about a literal barricade around the city, it would be unusual to describe it as "a wall of Judah..."

It is noteworthy that the word for wall here (*nadir*) is not the usual one (*chomah*). *Nadir* normally refers to a low wall or fence, such as around a vineyard, sheepfold (Num. 32:16), or along a road (Num. 22:24). It is possible, but not probable, its occurrence in Micah 7:11 means "city wall."[118] *Nadir* is the better term for this context anyway because Israel is often pictured as Jehovah's vineyard (Ps. 80:8-14; Isa. 5:1-5).[119] Finally, when Nehemiah saw the walls twelve years later they were in ruins.[120] On the other hand, Nehemiah must have expected Ezra to start erecting walls, otherwise he would not have been so disappointed when he heard the report from Hanani (Neh. 1).[121]

Again, as noted above, it is likely the Jews did begin to reconstruct the walls but actually did not have permission to do so. Therefore, the edict of v. 25 has to be the one to Nehemiah since it alone specifies the walls.

Two verses in Ezra 7 also seem to suggest the walls were constructed early in the scribe's tenure. He was given permission to do whatever he wanted with the leftover silver and gold (Ezra 7:18). He was to appoint civil authorities too (7:25), who naturally would desire to construct defense walls. But that is mere speculation. No passage directly declares those treasures were used for such a purpose, and the appointed authorities served only as judges.[122]

---

[116] H. G. M. Williamson, *Ezra, Nehemiah* (WBC), 136, 137.
[117] Ibid.
[118] Ibid.
[119] Ibid.
[120] Walvoord, 225.
[121] Archer, 114.
[122] Ibid, 125.

What About Isaiah 44:28 and 45:1 - 4, 13?

Isaiah 44:28 and 45:1-4, 13 are two other passages critics (especially amillennarians) emphasize to confirm that Cyrus did order the walls' reconstruction.[123] Isaiah 45:13 has the Lord declaring that Cyrus "will build My city." This idea is beset with the same problems as the "Ezra passages" theory is. There is no evidence the walls were restored until Nehemiah's efforts. The Isaiah passages simply announce this king will open the door for Persian favoritism toward the Jews, who will later on raise the city walls. Again, granting permission in 538 BC would eventually evolve into a military menace for Cyrus.

Other Passages

Haggai 1:2-4 is a third piece of evidence that allegedly attests to this speculation. The people were chided for living in nice homes while the Temple still looked bad. However, Nehemiah 11:1 affirms most of the Jews lived *outside* the city.[124] The passages that speak to Cyrus' edict (II Chron. 36:22, 23 and Ezra 1:1-4) mention only the Temple, not the city[125] (as noted above). Finally, the outcomes of the other three suggested decrees do not meet the requirements demanded by the phrases "restore and rebuild" and "with plaza and moat," that is, a complete restoration. Only after Nehemiah's ministry did Jerusalem start to resemble its former splendor.[126]

Did Daniel use 365-day or 360-day Years?

Miller lists some obstacles to the 444 BC theory, pointing to Sir Robert Anderson's computations in particular. His numbers place Jesus' death in AD 32, a date that Miller says contradicts the AD 30 date held by most scholars.[127] Miller is too picky. Our knowledge of Persia and of Jesus' ministry is insufficient to accurately discern a date any closer than one or two years.

To Miller, Anderson's biggest error was assuming a 360-day year for the Jews. Archer has convinced Miller they went by a 365-day year. (For ease of designation, a 360-day year will be called a lunar year, and a 365-day year will be labeled a solar year.) Miller admits some solar (also called "prophetic") years in Daniel and Revelation were rounded to 360 days, but by and large that was not the system used.[128] More details are needed to

---

[123] Walvoord, 225.
[124] Ibid, 226 (emphasis mine).
[125] Ibid.
[126] Hoehner, 123.
[127] Miller, 265; Wood, 253.
[128] Ibid.

resolve this issue. Archer's main point is this: Most, if not all, of Israel's ancient neighbors were familiar with the lunar year but they never used it exclusively. Those civilizations would sometimes appropriate the solar year, and most would make adjustments to correct one or both of their calendars (such as a "leap year" in modern times).[129] Archer seems to primarily rely on a book called *Chronology of Ancient Western Asia and Egypt* by Van Der Meer, whereas Hoehner finds support in the *Encyclopedia Britannica* and in the *Journal of Near Eastern Studies* (especially XIII, 5).[130]

Hoehner and Archer agree lunar years were known in the ancient East, and that a "prophetic" year in Scripture often consists of 360 days. But Hoehner asserts the lunar year is found outside of prophetic literature. The time measurements encountered in Genesis chapters 7 and 8 are the result of a lunar calendar. Genesis 7:11 states the flood began on the seventeenth day of the second month, and it ended on the seventeenth day of the seventh month (8:4), exactly five months. Both 7:24 and 8:3 declare the waters were upon the earth 150 days. Assuming each month is the same length, they would have 30 days apiece.[131] Skeptics say that is a big assumption because the story does not cover an entire year, and thus doesn't take into account any days the ancients may have added on to their year.[132] Nevertheless, that the years in Daniel are lunar is not out of the ordinary.

More Historical Considerations

Archer, Payne, and Wood all teach the *terminus a quo* is 458/457 BC. R. J. M. Gurney concurs but is also of the opinion all *70* "weeks" were fulfilled by AD 33. Payne agrees, adding AD 33 was the year Paul converted.[133] Daniel 9:27 makes it clear a man will make a "firm covenant" with the Jews, yet Gurney and Payne do not account for that event.

Miller confesses that a hurdle in the 458 BC proposition is that the edict does not address the restoring of Jerusalem. He tries to circumvent this problem by declaring that since Nehemiah's and Ezra's decrees were by the same king just thirteen years apart, the second is merely an extension of the first[134] (much like Cyrus' and Darius I's; see above). Thus, the fourth decree is

---

[129] Archer, 114, 115 where more information is given.
[130] Hoehner, 135.
[131] Ibid., 136, 137.
[132] *Tradition & Testament*, 215.
[133] Miller, 266.
[134] Ibid.

not a major one.[135] This reasoning is not sound, for Artaxerxes would have asked Nehemiah why he needed permission to construct the walls if Ezra were already doing it.

Miller crowns this theory by espousing these details: 49 years after 458 BC would be 409, and that is about the time Ezra and Nehemiah terminated their ministry. "In the Elephantine Papyri another man is stated to be governor of Judah in 407 BC, indicating that Nehemiah had passed from the scene at that time."[136]

Wood's variation on this matter is the significant event of 409 must have to do with the city since the next phrase discusses the plaza and moat.[137] He also cites an "outstanding" 18th century historian named Prideaux who claims Nehemiah's work continued until the fifteenth year of Darius Nothus (423-404 BC) which would be about 409 BC.[138] "The significance of the forty-nine-year grouping may have been, then, a setting off of the period of Ezra and Nehemiah and their efforts toward the reestablishment of the Judean capital."[139] Sixty-two "weeks" after that brings one to AD 26, the "accepted"[140] date of Jesus' baptism and anointing (cf. Acts 10:38).[141]

The Double Interval View

A resolution proposed by Allan MacRae is a combination of some of these theories, and in that sense is unique.[142] He perceives two intervals, not just one, in this passage, and thus his suggestion is commonly referred to as the double interval view. The decree in question is actually God's command to rebuild Jerusalem given in 587 BC (Jer. 32:44). At the end of the first stage (49 years) the one anointed is Cyrus. This fulfillment of prophecy would boost Daniel's confidence in the trustworthiness of Gabriel's message. MacRae does toy with the idea of placing the *terminus a quo* in 538 BC (Cyrus' edict) because, for two vital reasons, he sees it as having much biblical significance. First, he claims it is the only decree of which we have historical evidence. Second, the Lord found it crucial enough to twice speak of it in Holy Writ (Ezra 1 and 6).

---

[135] *Tradition & Testament*, 195.
[136] Miller, 266.
[137] Wood, 254.
[138] Ibid.
[139] Ibid.
[140] Ibid., 253.
[141] Pentecost contends (1362, 1363) the anointing of v. 25 applies to Christ only when He returns as King.
[142] *Tradition & Testament*, 210, 211.

About a century later (437 BC), the second (62-week) stage would begin with no particular event to mark it. During this period Jerusalem is rebuilt, and at the end of it the Messiah is cut off. Another interval of several centuries would commence and it would last until the appearance of the antichrist.

MacRae offers further reasons for his position. Since prophecies are general anyway, his theory is as literal as it needs to be. This proposal also has the advantage of being in harmony with the Masoretic pointing, which creates the need for two anointed rulers. Dozens of times *mashiach* (messiah) does *not* refer to the Christ, and thus Cyrus could fill the bill here.

Despite these factors, the suggestion must be thrown out. It is most unusual for a *terminus ad quo* of a prophecy to be placed chronologically before the prediction is given. Too, prophecies are not general. In almost every case they are quite specific. To assert two intervals are intended is not easily defensible. An era for the Church Age can be demonstrated, but no solid reasons exist for inserting another one.

In summary, holding to a 444/445 BC *terminus a quo* for the seventy "sevens" is confirmed by the following considerations. (1) The most severe "times of distress" took place during Nehemiah's day. (2) No decrees were later issued by Persian monarchs concerning the rebuilding of Jerusalem.[143] (3) It is not probable the parties involved in the first three decrees would assume rebuilding Jerusalem was part of the deal. (4) This interpretation comes closest to the literal method since it alone specifies the restoration of Jerusalem as delineated in v. 25. (5) All three stages are readily harmonized with known historical incidents. (6) The 4th decree best explains Luke 19:42. As He enters Jerusalem for the last week of His earthly ministry, Jesus says, "If you had known in *this day*, even you, the things which make for peace!"[144] (7) Therefore, a final factor favoring this position is that the math works out *to the day*. The Messiah is "cut off" after the 483 lunar years, which is 173,880 days. From March 5, 444 BC to March 30, AD 33 on the Gregorian/Julian calendar is likewise 173,880 days.

This author is bothered, however, by one as yet unmentioned snag. Most would agree Jesus was born about 5 BC, and He was baptized at age 30 (Luke 3:23), which would be about AD 25. If His ministry lasted about three and one-half years, then He would have been crucified about AD 28/29. How can a date of AD 32/33 be reached? Nevertheless, the decree of 444/445 BC is the suggestion with the fewest difficulties.

---

[143] Hoehner, 126.
[144] Chafer, 4:338.

"to restore and rebuild"

Some attention will now be given to a few other linguistic matters. The phrase "to restore and rebuild" (so NASB, NIV) is from *v-lib-nit l-hashyb*, and "is a rich and suggestive phrase that combines reference to the restoring of the community and the rebuilding of the city."[145] *L-hashyb* (Hiph. inf. constr.) primarily means "to turn back, return," but it is translated into numerous other English words, including "bring back," "again," "recovered," and "restore." In the Hiphil, it is literally "to cause to return." Barnes elaborates on the significance of this matter by saying Jerusalem is to be reinstated to "its former condition as a holy city - the city where the worship of God would be celebrated..." Other occurrences of this same nuance are found in Psalm 80:3, 7, 19 and Isaiah 1:26.[146] The most common rendering of *v-lib-nit* (Qal inf. constr.) is "to build," appearing some 298 times as either "build," "builds," or "built." Idiomatically it can also refer to having children, as in Gen. 16:2.[147] There is some dissension as to whether or not it can be given as "rebuild." Goldingay thinks not, and thus the expression should read, "to build a restored Jerusalem."[148] He claims (p. 229) that to obtain "to rebuild" one has to emend *lahashyb* to *lashib*. For the other side, BDB (p. 124; and others) affirms "to rebuild" is proper. Whatever the precise English wording should be, the point is the city will be renovated to its full former glory.

"Until Messiah the Prince"

"Until Messiah the Prince" is the *terminus ad quem* of the sixty-nine "weeks." Not a few scholars pinpoint this phrase to the day of the Triumphal Entry, because on that day He officially presented Himself to the Jews as their Messiah, in fulfillment of Zech. 9:9. As mentioned before, Luke 19 seems to confirm this theory, stating, "And when He approached, He saw the city and wept over it, saying, 'If you had known in this day, even you, the things which make for peace! But now they have been hidden from your eyes'" (vv.41, 42).[149] The Hebrew will not allow *nigiyd mashiyach* (two masculine singular nouns) to be translated "anointed prince" (so Archer, BDB, Keil, and Young). To obtain such an expression the Hebrew would have to be *nigiyd mashiyach*.[150]

---

[145] Quoted from Lacocque by John Goldingay, *Daniel* (WBC), 260.

[146] Barnes, 149, 150.

[147] *TWOT*, 116.

[148] Goldingay, 226.

[149] Pentecost, 1363.

[150] Archer, 120.

This grammatical reality implies this person must be both a ruler and an anointed one (NASB, "Messiah the Prince"; NIV, "the Anointed One, the ruler"). "Prince" comes from the root *ngd* and denotes "to be conspicuous, out front" (BDB, p. 617). Similarly, because "messiah" could designate a king or a priest, this leader must be one or both.[151] Those terms rarely speak about a non-Israelite leader, so this person is most probably an Israelite. In Daniel, a non-Israelite prince is usually referred to as *malek'*.[152] Again, Jesus obviously meets all these qualifications, for He is the "Anointed One" (*i.e.*, Christ), and He is called a priest (Heb. 4:14,15) and a king (Matt. 27:11).[153] Wood concurs this passage must be anticipating Jesus. He writes,

> Both terms are applied to various leaders of the Old Testament, but here they clearly refer to Christ. He is the supreme Messiah and Prince; no one else fits the chronology developed in the text; this One is said in the next verse to be "cut off," which fits for the crucifixion of Christ; and by far the majority of expositors agree on this point.[154]

The Vulgate, the Syriac, and Theodotion actually insert the word "Christ" in this verse.[155] Amillennialists seek to deny this assertion by reasoning as follows:

> "Messiah" is epithet of king, of priest (*cf.* 2 Mac 1:10), of prophet; and in a spiritual sense of patriarch (Ps. 105:15), and even of Cyrus, who is "My Anointed," Is. 45:1...The second term "prince," qualifying the first, is used of various officers of rank: as a chief among officials, esp. in the temple *personnel*, *e.g.* 11:22 of the high priest, *q.v.*; of nobles or princes, *e.g.*, Job 29:10, 31:37; then of royalty, appearing as an early title for the king in Israel, *e.g.*, 1 Sa. 9:16, and also of foreign kings. Hence both terms are ambiguous, and their combination does not assist identification, for which three candidates have been proposed: Cyrus, the "Anointed" of Is. 45:1; Zerubbabel, the acclaimed Messiah of the Restoration; and his contemporary, the high priest Joshua b. Josedek.[156]

In Hebrew, proper names do not take the definite article, and neither do titles that have become virtual proper names by usage. A few examples are: *shadai* ("the Almighty"), *satan* ("the Adversary"), *tebel* ("the world"), and *'el-yin* ("the Most High"). Therefore the words are not so vague. Daniel intended

---

[151] Miller, 264.
[152] Goldingay, 261.
[153] Miller, 264.
[154] Wood, 251.
[155] Barnes, 151.
[156] Quoted by John Walvoord, *Daniel: The Key to Prophetic Revelation* (p. 229) from Montgomery (ICC; 378, 379), italics in original.

them to be understood as "Messiah the Ruler."[157] Since there is no definite article used here, the "reference is not to *the* anointed one, as of one who was already known or looked forward to as such - for then the article would have been used; but to someone who, when he appeared, would have such marked characteristics that there would be no difficulty in determining that he was the one intended."[158]

"plaza and moat"

When Jerusalem is rebuilt, it is to have a plaza and moat. The word *r-chib* comes from the root *rhb* and can be rendered "street" (NIV), "open place," or "square."[159] Virtually every city had a plaza (NASB translation) for town meetings or markets.[160] "Moat" (*charots*), also translated "trench" (so NIV), comes from a verb that means "to cut, sharpen."[161] The idea of "trench" comes from its Aramaic usage, and "city moat" finds its origins in the Akkadian language.[162] That the word "determined" (v.26) comes from the same root invokes some expositors to render this phrase as: "the street will certainly be rebuilt."[163]

It seems unlikely Jerusalem would have a moat since it is in a dry area. This feature may allude to a trench around the walls to make them even higher. This term has been found in the Dead Sea Copper Scroll with the meaning "conduit" and would refer to the water system of Jerusalem.[164] Perhaps the whole expression has to do with the internal layout of the city and its external defenses.[165]

"in times of distress"

The book of Nehemiah leaves no doubt the city was restored "in times of distress" (NASB). *Tsik* ("distress"; masc. sing. noun in constr.) is nowhere else in the OT in this form, and includes the idea of constraint.[166] *Ha'tiym* is actually "the times" (masc. plural noun). That the rebuilding would take longer than expected is likewise implied by this phrase.[167]

---

[157] Archer, 120.
[158] Barnes, 151 (italics original).
[159] *TWOT*, 840, 841.
[160] Miller, 266.
[161] BDB, 358.
[162] Hoehner, 120.
[163] so Hengstenberg, Barnes, 153.
[164] Taken from Porteous' commentary (p. 142) by Miller, 267.
[165] As quoted from Hartman by Goldingay, 261.
[166] *TWOT*, 760.
[167] Barnes, 153.

"These different scenarios turn on one's view of how plainly we should understand the prophecies of the Bible."

- Charles C. Ryrie

Countdown to Armageddon, 1999, page 8

15

Daniel 9:24-27 Considered, Part II
Charles H. Ray

Daniel 9:26

So far the news has been good. Jerusalem is to be rejuvenated, and the Jews (through Daniel) are assured the Messiah is coming. Now, the prophecy turns sour. Some time after the second stage (the 62 "weeks") this long-anticipated Messiah will die, and a foreign power will invade the city, destroying both it and the Temple. It is reasonable to assume He will be "cut off" shortly after the 69th "seven," but the time lapse is not specified.[1]

"cut off"

The Hebrew verb here is *yikaret* (Niphal imperfect) has a basic meaning of "to cut," but it can also indicate death.[2] It is the word used for execution in Lev. 7:20, Ps. 37:9, and Prov. 2:22.[3] Miller gives more details,

> The verb translated "cut off" is the common verb for "cut" [*taraki*]. It can be used literally (Exod 4:25; 1 Sam 5:4; 1 Kgs 5:6; Job 14:7) or figuratively. The word is used figuratively of eliminating, removing, or destroying something (e.g., Deut 12:29; Josh 7:9; Ps 37:38), often specifically referring to being "cut off" in death (e.g., Gen 9:11; Exod 31:14; Jer 9:21; 11:19). Here it is found in one of the Old Testament prophecies of the crucifixion of Christ.[4]

A synonym for *yikar-t, nag-zar* is found in Isaiah 53:8, where the death of the Suffering Servant is also described as "cut off."[5]

"have nothing"

The term "have nothing" (*v-'iyn li*) can be literally rendered "and (or "but") not to (or "for") him."[6] Furthermore, *'yn* can have the meaning "no one."[7] With such a multitude of choices it is no wonder there has been much

---

[1] Miller, 267.
[2] *TWOT*, 456.
[3] Wood, 255.
[4] Miller, 267.
[5] Ibid.
[6] Ibid.
[7] Archer, 113.

speculation as to what it means. The KJV has "but not for himself" which implies substitutionary atonement but that truth is not taught in this verse. The Vulgate has "they shall not be his people."[8] The phrase is a Hebrew idiom for "not have" (Gen. 11:30, Isa. 27:4).[9] Goldingay places the next clause with this one and comes up with "and will have neither the city nor the sanctuary." Not only does that arrangement not make sense, it also forces him to render the next few phrases as: "A leader to come will devastate a people, and its end will come with a flood." "People" is in construct (*m*) and yet Goldingay doesn't connect it with anything.[10] Additionally, since he teaches the one "cut off" is Onias III, the words "...have neither the city..." must refer to Onias' exile to Daphne.[11]

The significance here may evince Christ's ministry appeared to be all for naught when He died. He had not accomplished what He had set out to do.[12] Wood (p. 255) adds He died without friends or honor. He was rejected, and treated like a criminal. "In the realm of things attractive and desirable, His portion was equivalent to 'nothingness'." His people had rejected Him and the kingdom could not now be set up (cf. John 1:11). The judgment for rejecting the Messiah would fall in the form of the leveling of the holy city (Matt. 24:2).[13] Walvoord observes (p. 230), "Nothing that rightly belonged to Him as Messiah the Prince was given to Him at that time...Outwardly it appeared that evil had triumphed." A few scholars direct attention to Matthew 27:46, "My God, My God, why have You forsaken Me?" The verse in no way negates vicarious atonement.[14]

"people of a prince, the one coming"

The next few words can be read, "people of a prince, the one coming" (*haba'*).[15] It was Josephus' opinion (among many others) the Roman invasion of AD 70 fulfilled this verse,[16] and thus eschatologically speaking this prince is a leader of the last phase of the Roman Empire, the antichrist. Some intimate the "people" are the Israelites, but it is ridiculous to believe the Jews would

---

[8] Gill, 209.
[9] Miller, 267.
[10] Goldingay, 226.
[11] Ibid., 262.
[12] Miller, 267.
[13] Pentecost, 1364.
[14] Walvoord, 230.
[15] Wood, 255.
[16] Miller, 268.

tear down their own city. This prophecy is for "your people" (Dan. 9:24), so "the coming people" must be some other ethnic group.[17]

No doubt this verse would have been enigmatic to the Jews, for it did not fit their concept of the Messiah. They envisioned Him saving their country, but here He dies and Gentiles overrun the city. The reason the devastation of the Tribulation is not primarily in view here is the fact that this one occurs before the 70th "week."[18] The word for "prince" is the same one found in v. 25 (*nigiyd*). That fact on top of the unidentified "he" of v. 27 compounds the confusion this passage can cause.

So, who is the prince of v. 26? In the near term he is the Roman General Titus who wiped out Jerusalem in AD 70. In the long run he is a foreshadowing of the antichrist. (This conclusion will be more thoroughly discussed under Dan. 9:27.) Other factors cause Bible students to see a distinction between the two "princes" of vv. 25 and 26. The one of v. 25 is the Messiah, Who is later killed. The two men do not live at the same time, for the natural reading of v. 26 has "the one coming" on the scene after the Christ is "cut off." Lastly, the Messiah would not raze the holy city.

"its end will come with a flood"
Concerning Jerusalem, "its end will come with a flood." More literally translated, *bashet v-kitsi* is "its end with the flood." Grammatically, *ki'i* can mean "its" or "his," and hence the antecedent can be Jerusalem, the coming prince, or the prophecy.[19] The most logical choice is Jerusalem. "As the principal and immediate subject of the prophecy, however, is the city, it is more natural to refer it to that."[20] "Flood" (*shete*), "torrent, overflowing") speaks to the degree of ruination meted out, not to the method.[21] The Roman army quickly and thoroughly leveled Jerusalem.

The historians of the day vividly lament the horrific scene. "On the 105th day of the siege ...the temple and the lower city were burnt, and the last day found the whole city in flames. Only the three great towers of Herod, Hippicus, Pharsael, and Mariamne, with the western walls, were spared to protect the camp of the Xth Legion which was left to guard the site...The rest of the city was dug up to its foundations."[22] *Shete* "denotes the

---

[17] John Whitcomb, *Daniel,* 133.
[18] Wood, 256.
[19] Barnes, 180.
[20] Ibid.
[21] Wood, 256.
[22] *The International Standard Bible Encyclopedia,* 1619 (from Josephus).

number, power, and irresistible force of the enemy."[23] Daniel utilizes this "flood" imagery for describing war in 11:10, 22, 26, and 40 as well (cf. Psalm 32:6).[24]

What is it That Has Been Determined?
It is easy to bungle the end of v. 26 because the grammar allows more than one acceptable interpretation. What has been determined (*necheretset*, Niph. participle, "to decide, decree;" also used in v. 27): the war or the desolations? The student must dig deeper to find the correct answer. "War" (*mil-chamah*), "determined," and "desolations" (*shomemiot*) are all feminine. Does "the end" look to the culmination of the city's woes, or the completion of the Church Age? If the emphasis is on desolations, then the punctuation would be "until the end of the war desolations are determined." If it's war that is to be highlighted, then it would be written "until the end will be war; desolations are determined."[25] Miller's view (p. 269) is that it is war that has been decreed, and it will continue until Jerusalem is totally ruined ("the end"). Archer recommends, "And the end of it will be in the overflowing, and unto the end there will be war, a strict determination of desolations," or "the determined amount of desolations."[26]

In accordance with the fact that "end" is written twice in this verse, one can assume two terminal points are in view. The general sense is Jerusalem will be wiped out as if a flood had hit it, yet troubles will haunt the region until the Messiah comes again. These thoughts harmonize well with Christ's words in Matt. 24:7-22 where He talks about continuous hardships throughout this present age.[27] However the Lord intended the grammar to be read, it is true that Israel has been at war for most of the 2500 years since the prophecy was revealed to Daniel. "Jerusalem will be trampled under foot by the Gentiles until the times of the Gentiles be fulfilled" (Luke 21:24).[28]

Archer lays stress on the truth that all these events take place before the 70th "week," which is not brought up until v. 27 (p. 116), affirming the need for an era between the 69th and 70th "weeks." Even Pusey, an amillennialist, agrees the death of the Messiah comes about not in the 69

---

[23] Gill, 210.
[24] Walvoord, 231.
[25] Wood, 256.
[26] Archer, 116.
[27] Ibid.
[28] Whitcomb, 133.

"weeks" but after them.[29] Finally, it is important to notice Zech. 14:1-3. That passage indicates Jerusalem will not be *totally* demolished in the end times, in contrast to the details given in 9:26. That observation not only solidifies the AD 70 date for v. 26, but it also implies virtually all of v. 26 has been fulfilled.[30]

Daniel 9:27

Who is this "he"?

It has been noted several times in this chapter that the two salient beings in this prophecy are the Messiah and the antichrist. Obviously, then, one of them is the "he" of this verse. It is highly improbable the Messiah is the referent; the weight of the evidence favors the identification of the "he" as the antichrist. Critics who contend that Christ is the "he" look to four reasons. First, this entire prophecy is about Him. Second, Titus did not make a covenant with the Jews. Third, nowhere else in Scripture is this covenant-making prince found. Lastly, the word used for "firm" (or "prevail") is the same one used in Isaiah 9:6 for "mighty God."[31] This reasoning is unconvincing, if for no other reason than nowhere else is this seventy "weeks" addressed in this manner either.

That no consensus can be reached as to which covenant is in view is another weakness of this theory. Some believe it is the New Covenant, whereas others assert it is an already existing covenant. Goldingay draws attention to the covenant found in Dan. 9:4 and 11:28, 30, 32. It is very unlikely, however, the same compact is referred to here. The reader comes away with the impression the covenant of 9:27 will not be signed until the latter days. Daniel 9:4 has the definite article (9:27 does not), "the covenant," indicating the Mosaic Covenant. Daniel is confessing the people's violations of that agreement.

The three verses in Daniel 11 seem to be figurative uses of "covenant" (no definite article). In context, *b-riyt* symbolizes "the entire Mosaic system."[32] "The term 'holy covenant' appears to have the same basic meaning that it has in 1 Maccabees 1:15, where it is used in general terms to refer to all things religious in Israel."[33] This statement also refutes the

---

[29] E. B. Pusey, *Daniel the Prophet*, (Minneapolis: Klock & Klock, 1978, 1885), 192, as pointed out by Tommy Ice, *Pre-Trib Perspectives*, August 2001, 7.
[30] Walvoord, 231.
[31] *Tradition & Testament*, 203.
[32] Pentecost, 1369.
[33] Wood, 299.

proposal favored by Goldingay: 9:27 "refers to the covenant between reformist Jews and Gentiles reported in 1 Macc 1:11" (p. 262).

In deciding between the Messiah or the "prince to come" as the antecedent, Barnes contends "it is not reasonable to suppose that the latter is referred to, because it is said (ver. 26) that the effect and the purpose of his coming would be to 'destroy the city and the sanctuary.'"[34] In other words Barnes is saying the prince is coming to make peace. He is wrong on two accounts. Verse 26 says it is the *people* of the prince, not the prince himself, who execute the destruction. Too, he is implying it *is* reasonable to suppose the Messiah would bring about the devastation. To assume v. 27 deals with Christ is presumptuous, for that is the very question for which interpreters are seeking an answer. Lastly, it is not unthinkable a future leader would bring about such an agreement with Israel;[35] people will do almost anything to have peace in the Middle East.

This "he" is the Antichrist

Verse 27 has a negative tone to it that is out of character with the Messiah. If the "he" were Christ, the wording would have been more direct...and positive. *Haba'* (v. 26) is a Qal active participle with the definite article modifying "prince." That he is *the* prince may be a hint he is referred to earlier in the book, and indeed that is the case. Many conservative scholars regard him as the "little horn" of chap. 7, and the "little horn" is generally understood to be the antichrist. A question to consider is: about which person is the reader expecting more information in v. 27? Since the Messiah was "cut off" and *the* prince didn't do anything in v. 26 (the people are the focus), it is safe to assume the latter is in mind (or a future ruler who is typified by this one.)[36] Wood's remarks are noteworthy.

> The use of the term "prince" for this coming one, the term used in reference to Christ in verse twenty-five, signifies him as one who would in some sense parallel Christ in the role he would play - something uniquely true of the Antichrist, who will be Satan's counterfeit for Christ...Since the Antichrist has been presented in Daniel's two earlier occasions of revelation (7:8, 23, 24; 8:23-25) and will be again in the last (11:36-45), one might expect that he would be brought into this third location as well.
>
> ...The descriptions in the remainder of this verse fit all that is revealed elsewhere regarding the Antichrist. Amillennarians frequently identify this one with Titus Vespasian, who led the Roman legions against Jerusalem, but Titus simply was not of

---

[34] Barnes, 181.
[35] Walvoord, 233.
[36] Wood, 257.

sufficient importance to biblical history to warrant such a mention. Actually, since the interest of the text taken alone was only to tell of Jerusalem's destruction and not the identity of the destroyer, there was no reason to mention either "people" or "prince" unless both carried biblical significance, which one could expect to be shown elsewhere. Daniel's first vision presented this significance, using the figures of the "fourth beast" (people) and the "little horn" (prince).[37]

Leupold and Keil are some of the few non-premillennarians who admit the "he" is the antichrist. In doing so, they are driven to the conclusion at least part of this pericope is still future.[38] In order to get around this inference, Keil (p. 365) translates the initial part, "One week shall confirm the covenant to many," leaving out the "he" altogether. Goldingay defends this alternative because the subject is otherwise too vague.[39] However, most expositors would consider Keil's rendering grammatically untenable.[40] His translation has a feminine subject with a masculine verb. "It is not usual to represent *time* as an agent in accomplishing work."[41] Furthermore, if more testimony emerges that supports the concept of a time gap after the 69th "seven," then one would be forced to admit this "he" is a heretofore undisclosed character. That evidence will now be rehearsed.

Reasons to Believe a Time Gap Exists

(1)Verse 26 declares the *people* will level the city, whereas verse 27 states the *prince* is the instigator of evil. The best solution sees the antichrist in v. 27, and v. 26 as evidence he comes from the regions of the ancient Roman Empire.[42] The unusual wording of v. 26 causes one to disassociate the people from the prince in some way. It says "the people of the prince who is to come" when it could have simply said "a coming Roman prince."[43] Chapter seven confirms this wicked being is of the fourth empire, Rome.[44] (2) The text does not say Jesus was executed *in* the 70th "week;" it asserts it happened *after* the 69th "week." (3) Christ anticipated this time interval by His statement of building His Church (Matt. 16:18).[45] He also predicted the temporary setting aside of Israel (Matt. 21:42, 43). The reasonable conclusion is the Church would fill that time interval because, unlike Daniel

---

[37] Ibid., 258.
[38] Walvoord, 233.
[39] Goldingay, 230.
[40] Walvoord, 234.
[41] Barnes, 181.
[42] Miller, 268.
[43] *Pre-Trib Perspectives*, August 2001, 7.
[44] Ibid.
[45] Pentecost, 1363.

9:24-27, it concerns the Gentiles. (4) In Luke 4:18-19, Jesus quotes Isaiah 61:1, 2 while teaching in his hometown synagogue. He does not read the entire passage, however. He mentions "the favorable year of the Lord" (the theme of His first advent), but does not continue to the next portion that proclaims God's judgment (the purpose of His second coming). (5) In v. 26 the Temple was taken down, yet in v. 27 the normal rituals are being carried out. (6) The predictions of v. 27 have not come about yet.

"Amillennarians teach that Christ's First Advent ministry was in the 70th 'seven,' that there was no interval between the 69th and 70th 'sevens,' and that the six actions predicted in Daniel 9:24 are being fulfilled today in the church."[46] Others of this persuasion, such as Young, believe Jesus' death caused the sacrifices to cease since He was the perfect sacrifice, which likewise means the 70th "week" was immediately subsequent to the 69th. Barnes comments,

> The literal signification of "cause to cease" here would be met by the supposition that an end would be made of these sacrifices, and this would occur either by their being made wholly to cease to be offered at that time, or by the fact that the object of their appointment was accomplished, and that henceforward they would be useless and would die away. As a matter of fact, so far as the Divine intention in the appointment of these sacrifices and offerings was concerned, they ceased at the death of Christ - in the middle of the 'week.'[47]

A number of factors make this eschatological explanation unlikely. Verse 27 is a strange place to bring up the atonement, for the Messiah died in v. 26.[48] The offerings did not stop for forty more years, and even then it was by the hand of the Romans, not by the dissolution of a contract.[49] The crucifixion certainly ended the *need* for subsequent sacrifices, but Young's proposal cannot satisfactorily explain when the 7-year period terminates.

Another flaw is this: Christ dies after the 69 "weeks," but not in the 70th "seven." The sacrifices do not cease until the middle of the 70th "week." Barnes declares the prophecy finishes about three and one-half years after the crucifixion, for that is when the apostles turned their attention from the Hebrew people (for whom this prophecy is intended) and began evangelizing the Gentiles. This belief raises more questions than it answers (what covenant is this?, how does turning to the Gentiles stop the sacrifices?). He

---

[46] Ibid., 1364.
[47] Barnes, 186.
[48] Wood, 257.
[49] Walvoord, 235.

goes on to claim the leveling of the Holy city was not immediate but gradual.[50] Young is forced to conclude the endpoint is not vital to this prophecy,[51] a stark contrast to the truth: it is Christ's second coming!

It must be recalled that "unseen" gaps are found in other pericopes, too, even within this book (Dan. 7; 8; and 11). (Isa. 9:6 is perhaps the best known one.) Other portions of Scripture affirm the conclusion that the antichrist is not active until the seventieth "seven" (Dan. 7:26,27; 8:25; 11:45; Zech. 14:1-4; Rev. 19:11-21).[52] Since the major aspects of Daniel 9:24-27 concern the descendants of Abraham and the two advents of the Messiah, it is no surprise these 490 years are not consecutive. Many Bible students rightly contend that because Israel (the recipient of these promises) is not experiencing "everlasting righteousness" nor have its sins been removed, those blessings await the second coming.[53] The righteousness people experience in this age is buffeted and temporal.

Therefore, the promise of v. 24 implies there is a time gap, contrary to the amillennialists who teach righteousness is gradually increasing as the Church conducts its ministry.[54] Other arguments refuting these claims were presented above, with the strongest refutation being the Messiah would not wipe out Jerusalem, not to mention the fact that it didn't occur until forty years after the crucifixion. If some scholars are willing to put a forty-year interval in this prophecy in order to bring it to a climax in the first century, then it is not much of a leap to claim an era of some duration is intended between the 69th and 70th "sevens."[55]

To summarize, the "he" is the antichrist, and he will (1) be the leader of the final phase of the Roman Empire, (2) establish a seven-year covenant with Israel, (3) break his agreement after three and a half years, (4) force the Jews to cease their sacrificial system, and (5) demand they worship him only, likely setting up a statue of himself in the Temple. Lastly, he is depicted in chapter two by the ten toes and, in chapter seven as the ten-horned beast.[56] Other scholars agree there are epochs of time in those passages (Isa. 9:6, *etc.*) but none of those other predictions involve numbers as 9:24-27 does. While true, the uniqueness of this prophecy places it in a category for which no other passage qualifies. That uniqueness is the fact that the number 490

---

[50] Barnes, 182-184.
[51] Miller, 270.
[52] Wood, 261.
[53] Hoehner, 131.
[54] Wood, 260.
[55] Ibid.
[56] Archer, 116, 117.

is broken down into seven, sixty-two, and one. Thus, attempts to discredit the interval theory are futile from this perspective.[57]

The Details of Verse 27
The first two Hebrew words are literally, "shall cause a covenant to be strong."[58] *Hog-biyr* is a Hiphil perfect 3ms whose root can mean "prevail, have strength, be great,[59] have stability, make firm."[60] The potency of this wording may imply the Jews are forced to accept the agreement because of the antichrist's superior power.[61] Young advances the idea that this covenant is the Covenant of Grace, and Jesus has come to commission it. The agreement in question is not a new one but one that already exists because *hog-biyr* is not the common way to express the making of a new covenant.[62] Thus Young espouses: "shall cause to prevail a covenant." If his conclusion is true, then this is an awkward way to express it. One would be more likely to see "shall fulfill the terms of the covenant."[63]

A number of other obstacles emerge here as well. In what sense is it just for "one week"? How could Christ break the Covenant of Grace (if it exists at all), or any other commitment on His part? The amillennialists might have a stronger case if the Hebrew had "the covenant" and not "a covenant."[64] Lastly, the antichrist's administration will be marked by major changes, as spelled out by Daniel 7:25, "he will intend to make alterations in times and in law; and they will be given into his hand for a time, times, and half a time."[65]

Other amillennarians claim this is the Abrahamic Covenant, and Jesus has come to confirm and fulfill it.[66] However, there is no evidence in the Gospels He purposed to do such a thing. Barnes agrees, stating this is the covenant "which God not the antichrist is said to establish with his people - so often referred to in the Scriptures as expressing the relation between Him and them."[67] To believe the interpretation this verse speaks to a compact between the antichrist and the Israelites is much more reasonable. The NIV

---

[57] *Tradition & Testament*, 214, 215.
[58] Wood, 258.
[59] *TWOT*, 148.
[60] Barnes, 181.
[61] Miller, 271.
[62] *Tradition & Testament*, 205.
[63] Wood, 259.
[64] Ibid.
[65] John Whitcomb, *Daniel*, 133, 134.
[66] Pentecost, 1365.
[67] Barnes, 181.

("he will confirm a covenant") does not capture the nuance of these words as well as the NASB does ("he will make a firm covenant").

It is interesting to speculate on the details of this agreement. One can make educated guesses as to what some of the clauses in the contract stipulated. The antichrist may promise to protect Israel in exchange for money.[68] First Thessalonians 5:3 makes it clear people will be content with the peace and safety just before the judgment. That the second half of the "seven" is a time of horror likewise indicates it is a peace treaty of some sort.[69] Another possible clause may have permitted the Jews to resume their Temple rituals, for later the antichrist has to force them to stop. In other words, the Levitical system didn't just start up again but it was by the consent of the antichrist.[70]

These events precipitate other implications. Since the Jews are looking for a "Prince of Peace" (Isa. 9:6), they will be that more easily taken in by the antichrist. They will quickly discover, however, he is their destroyer, not their deliverer.[71] It will be fascinating to see how the Dome of the Rock will be removed so the Temple can be reconstructed.

Who are "the many"?

The text shows the antichrist's commitment is with "the many" (literal rendering). These "many" are the Jews (specifically unbelieving Jews),[72] for this passage bears upon "your people" (v. 24). The fact that the children of Abraham have to be involved in such an alliance suggests they are totally helpless.[73] Based on Isaiah 53:11, 12, Archer and Young assert "the many" are true believers.[74] They point out that "the many" of 53:11 (*larabiym*, an articulated masc. plural adjective) are the ones for whom the Servant gave up His life. Thus, they are the elect, the true believers. An identical role is played by *rabiym* in 53:12. Additional support is found in a Qumran parchment called *Rule of the Congregation,* where *larabiym* "often occurs in reference to the sectarian community of 'true believers.'"[75]

If the second party consists of believing Jews as Archer espouses, then why would they have any interest in the Levitical system? He responds:

[68] Miller, 271.
[69] Pentecost, 1364.
[70] Wood, 261.
[71] Ibid.
[72] Walvoord, 234.
[73] Pentecost, 1364.
[74] Miller, 271.
[75] Archer, 117.

"Since these Jewish believers trust in Jesus as their Messiah, it may well be that the sacrifices will be conducted as memorial services like the Lord's Supper, rather than for atonement purposes as in OT times. This will certainly be the case during the Millennium - if indeed Ezek 43 pertains to that age..."[76] Such a claim raises at least three problems. First, it does not make sense true believers would want to unite with the devil. Second, all true believers went up in the rapture before the Tribulation began. Third, Archer and Young are mixing two different events. Isaiah 53 concerns Jesus' earthly ministry, and "the many" are the ones for whom Christ died. Daniel 9:27 has to do with the Tribulation, and "the many" are the ones who align themselves with the devil.

"In the middle"

Chatsy (a masculine singular noun in construct) can mean "half, half part" (Exod. 24:6, Num. 12:12), or "the middle, the midst" (Judg. 16:3).[77] The sense would then be either something of importance happened in the middle of the seven years, or it took three and one-half years for something to come to completion. Dispensationalists hold to the former sense and maintain this section of the verse predicts the breaking of the covenant by the antichrist in the middle of the Tribulation. "All pretense of religious toleration will be dropped, for the *nogidi* ('ruler') will aspire to absolute authority and complete control over the life and thought of all mankind."[78] Archer provides this modern parallel to the beast's sly methods.

In many ways this step-by-step progression of tyranny here described bears a remarkable resemblance to the development of the Nazi tyranny in Germany; those of strong religious convictions were at first lulled into a false sense of security till Hitler had consolidated his power through the whole security system of the German Reich.[79]

Sacrifices will Cease

The words "put a stop to" (NASB; "put an end to," NIV) are a translation of *ysh-biyt* (Hiphil imperfect 3ms) that properly means "to rest," hence the word "Sabbath." The Hiphil leads to "cause to cease."[80] "Sacrifice" (*zebach*, masc. sing. noun) primarily means "sacrifice, slaughter" and thus pertains to bloody sacrifices. By contrast, *min-chah* (fem. sing. noun) speaks to grain, oil,

---

[76] Ibid.
[77] Barnes, 185.
[78] Archer, 117.
[79] Ibid.
[80] Barnes, 186.

and wine offerings. Other definitions include "gifts" and "oblation."[81] "The word *min-chah* is used in secular contexts of gifts to superior persons, particularly kings, to convey the attitude of homage and submission to that person."[82] This nuance is brought out to some degree by the NASB ("sacrifice and grain offering;" "sacrifice and offering," NIV). Second Thessalonians 2:4 elaborates on these transactions, predicting the antichrist will "take his seat in the temple of God, displaying himself as being God."

The Meaning of "wing of abominations"
V-'al k-na shiqvtsiym can be directly translated "and upon the wing of abominations," for which an array of interpretations have been proposed. The NASB is rather literal as above, but the NIV has "And on a wing of the temple he will set up an abomination..." placing brackets around "of the temple" because the expression is not in the Hebrew. Like the NIV, the NRSV is patterned after the Greek versions (*Boelugma*) and has it as "abomination" (singular), apparently in an attempt to harmonize it with 11:31 and 12:11[83] (cf. Rev. 11:2). Walvoord agrees, adding this summation, "The Hebrew is rendered 'abomination of desolation' in 1 Maccabees 1:54; Matthew 24:15; Mark 13:14 and is supported by the most ancient translations including the Septuagint, Theodotion, and the Vulgate" (p. 235). The Syriac reads, "And upon the extremities of the abomination shall rest desolation."[84] Leupold (p. 431) recommends, "upon the wing of abominable idols." Goldingay stresses the concept that the idol will be on the *altar* and not on the *Temple*. Additionally, "the altar had 'winglike' top corners, usually described as horns. Perhaps Gabriel speaks of wings rather than horns because 'winged one' (*B'l k-nap*, 'lord of wing' or 'winged one') is a title of Baal."[85]

The knottiest conundrum is figuring out the legitimate root meaning of *kn*. Wood (p. 261) sides with Gesenius over BDB and alleges the base definition is "to cover over." BDB does acknowledge the meaning is in doubt, but asserts the word originated from the Arabic verb "to fence in, enclose" and the Aramaic verb "to collect, assemble."[86] However, both BDB ("wing, extremity") and Owens[87] parse it as a noun. One can readily perceive why confusion arises, for an "overspreading wing" is related to the idea of

---

[81] *TWOT*, 233-235, 514-515.
[82] Ibid., 514.
[83] Miller, 272.
[84] Barnes, 186.
[85] John Goldingay, *Daniel* (WBC), 263.
[86] BDB, 489.
[87] John Joseph Owens, *Analytical Key to the Old Testament*, 744.

"enclosing." *TWOT* (pp. 446, 447) lists "wing, winged, border, corner, and shirt" as acceptable translations, and concurs with BDB that the only occurrence of this root in a verbal form is Isaiah 30:20 ("hide Himself"). Some examples of the noun are "the edge of Saul's robe" (I Sam. 24:4) and "the ends of the earth" (Isa. 24:16).

What is not in dispute is that the vast majority of its OT usages are figurative and a few are in a context of judgment. Some examples are Isaiah 8:8, Jeremiah 48:40, and Ezekiel 17:3, 7. At Jeremiah 49:22, the NASB reads "Behold, He will mount up and swoop like an eagle, and spread out His wings against Bozrah; and the hearts of the mighty men of Edom in that day will be like the heart of a woman in labor." It may be that the expression "on the wing" refers to some symbol the antichrist designates for himself, or perhaps the royal insignias of ancient Egypt, Assyria, or Rome.[88]

The word "abomination" is often associated with idol worship (Jer. 16:18; Ezk. 5:11). The NASB translates the noun as "detestable" (Hos. 9:10) and as "filth" (Nah. 3:6).[89] Keil (p. 372) states the wing represents the power of idolatry that conveys the desolator over the whole world to bring about ruination. "Wing" is used in a similar way by Matthew (4:5) and Luke (4:9) in their accounts of the temptation. Jesus is taken to "the pinnacle (*pterugion*, "wing") of the Temple." Hence, the drift here in Daniel 9:27 is the Temple has become thoroughly saturated by the filth of idolatry.

Jesus' discourse on the Mount of Olives sheds some light on this issue. The halting of the Levitical system marks the beginning of the Great Tribulation (Matt. 24:15-26). He reiterates that the mid-point of the Tribulation "week" will be determined by a distinct action, "the abomination of desolation...for then there will be a great tribulation..." (Matt. 24:21). Walvoord understands the last part of Daniel 9:27 to be describing that destruction. This desolation "will continue until the consummation pictured dramatically in Revelation 19 when the beast and the false prophet are cast into the lake of fire. This will be the *terminus ad quem* of the seventy sevens of Daniel and coincides with the second advent of Jesus Christ to the earth."[90]

---

[88] Archer, 118.
[89] Miller, 273.
[90] Walvoord, 235.

Parallel Passages to "wing of abominations"
Meshmem ("to be desolated, appalled") is a Poel participle and can be converted into English as "something desolated," "something desolating,"[91] or "things that are to be held in abhorrence."[92] A noun derivative (*shamah*) can mean "waste," or even "horror" (Dan. 8:13).[93] The correct understanding of this verse is aided by an examination of Daniel 11:31 and 12:11, where a nearly identical syntax is employed. In all three verses (9:27, 11:31, and 12:11) a noun is followed by a participle. Daniel 11:31 has *m-shimem hashquts*, a singular noun with the definite article followed by a Poel participle (as in 9:27). One could render it "the abomination that makes desolate" or "the abomination of desolation" (so NASB; cf. Rev. 13:14, 15). This occurrence alone has the definite article. Another commonality between 9:27 and 11:31 is both have to do with the cessation of the Levitical system.[94] Daniel 12:11 is slightly different: *shiquts shomem*, an anarthrous single noun followed by a Qal active participle. However, the same translations apply.

As a result of these factors, one would think "abomination of desolation" is what was intended for 9:27, but there is enough difference in the syntax (among 9:27, 11:31, and 12:11) for scholars to rethink this position. The present verse is distinct in that it is the only one of the three that has a word in construct directly influencing the identification of this abomination. True, there is a construct in Daniel 12:11 but that one has to do with the *fact* of the abomination being set-up. For Daniel 9:27, the construct deals with *how* it is established. Lastly, what is actually present here is a periphrastic construction of imminence ("he is about to commit abominations") rather than a noun of agency ("because of abominations").[95] Wood defends the "abomination of desolation" resolution for 9:27 by claiming the plural ("abominations") is a plural of importance since the antichrist's desolation is more significant than was Antiochus' in 168 BC. The "wing" stands for the widespread evil influence of the antichrist's actions.[96] God will pour out the desolation He has decreed during the Great Tribulation and thus the "end" speaks about the end of the "week."[97] "The Antichrist will cause sacrifice and offering to cease and, in their place, erect, even unto the end of causing an overspreading influence, a detestable statue (or altar) in

---

[91] Wood, 261.
[92] Barnes, 187.
[93] *TWOT*, 936.
[94] Wood, 262.
[95] Archer, 118.
[96] Wood, 262, 263.
[97] Ibid, 263.

the Temple, desolating in effect" is Wood's paraphrase of 9:27 (p. 263). Some commentators see the natural reading of the text as alluding to some idol on top of a building, probably the Temple.[98]

Some of those who hold that this verse has been entirely fulfilled draw attention to the Roman invasion of AD 66-70. They claim it is not impossible this "idol" is some kind of banner or standard of the Romans conspicuously placed on the Temple that would be offensive to the Jews.[99] However, Miller (p. 272), along with Leupold, asserts "wing" is never used for a part of a building in the OT. Too, the MT has no word for "set up" here, nor is the word "Temple" found (as pointed out above).

The Septuagint is of little help. The Greek of 11:31 has no article, and 9:27 has the plural "desolations." Jesus' statement in Matthew 24:15 has the singular "abomination," which is no surprise because the verse is a direct quote of Daniel 12:11 of the LXX.[100] One would not expect Matthew to quote Daniel 11:31 because that verse was fulfilled by Antiochus.

This verse continues by saying the Lord has "decreed" the following: (1) the atrocities will not go on forever (cf. Luke 21:24) but will have an end, and (2) "the desolating one" (*shomem*, a Qal active participle alluding to the antichrist) will be judged. "The desolating one" or "one who makes desolate" is preferred to "make something desolate" because *shomem* is intransitive.[101] The choice of "is poured out" (*titak*, a Qal imperfect) as the verb reminds the reader of "flood" in v. 26.[102] It can be used figuratively (Job 10:10) or literally (Exod. 9:33). Students of prophecy also look to Revelation 16 where bowls of God's wrath are poured out during the end times.

If the Masoretic pointing is ignored, the last portion of v. 27 could be paraphrased, "He shall cause the sacrifice and the offering to cease. And - upon the wing - the porch of the temple - abominations! And a desolator!"[103] It is now necessary to tie together all this information in order to explain this entire verse as succinctly yet thoroughly as possible. In the last days, the antichrist will sign an accord with Israel promising to protect them for seven years. However, after only three and one-half years he will turn on them. The Jews will no longer be allowed to carry out their Temple rituals, and the beast will swiftly ("on a wing") make Jerusalem detestable. It seems he will do that by setting up an idol of himself in the Temple, but that likely scenario

---

[98] so Barnes, 187.
[99] so Ibid, 188.
[100] Donald Hagner, *Matthew* (WBC), 699.
[101] Goldingay, 231.
[102] Miller, 273.
[103] Barnes, 188.

is not explicit in 9:27. By this time, the beast will have obtained worldwide authority, and now he will style himself as the earth's religious leader. God has assured His people though that the enemy will be judged at an appointed moment in history.

Conclusion

Despite its veiled prophetic statements, Daniel 9:24-27 presents a broad, powerful, and of course accurate description of future events. The Jews are informed as to what is in store for them as a nation for a total time frame of 490 years.

Yahweh graciously replied to Daniel's prayer by assuring the prophet that sin will be dealt with. One day all iniquity will be gone. But the Lord doesn't stop there. He goes on to tell of some specific events, people, and time frames. Daniel was thus further comforted with the reminder that the Messiah was indeed coming, and that his beloved city would be restored. On the other hand, the great prophet must have been perplexed by verse 27. How and why were these things going to take place? Nevertheless, he certainly had a great deal of prophetic history made known to him during his lifetime. Goldingay is quite off-base when he declares,

> In Jewish and Christian tradition, Gabriel's promise has been applied to rather later events: the birth of the messiah, Jesus' death and resurrection, the fall of Jerusalem, various subsequent historical events, and the still-future manifesting of the messiah. Exegetically such views are mistaken. The detail of vv 24-27 fits the second-century B.C. crisis and agrees with allusions to this crisis elsewhere in Daniel. The verses do not indicate that they are looking centuries or millennia beyond the period to which chaps. 8 and 10-12 refer.[104]

The details of this apocalyptic piece of literature are, by and large, clearly understood when viewed through the lens of dispensationalism. This theological perspective has two advantages. It seeks an interpretation based on an historical-grammatical hermeneutic, from which the natural sense of the passage can arise, and it alone harmonizes well with other related prophecies. An objective study of the book of Revelation affirms the idea that a literal approach to these verses is the only acceptable one.[105]

---

[104] Goldingay, 267.
[105] Walvoord, 234.

A Summary for All of Daniel 9:24-27

Daniel 9:24-27 can be summarized as follows. A decree to rebuild Jerusalem will be granted, and that reconstruction will endure for 49 years. The phrase "with plaza and moat" strongly suggests the restoration will not be partial but total. Four hundred and thirty-four years later the Messiah will appear. Some time later He will be executed, followed by an overwhelming invasion by a foreign people. The atrocities of AD 70 make it plain those people are Romans. Their leader, or better, a type of this leader, must somehow be vital to the whole picture. Otherwise, the Bible would not draw attention to him.

A mysterious lapse of time, not revealed until the New Testament, is subsequent to the desolation. This age is unforeseen here because 9:24-27 primarily concerns the Jews. At some point in history, a dynamic ruler will emerge who will woo the Israelites, even to the degree they will entrust their well-being to him. His biblical title is appropriate, for the people will think he is their long-awaited deliverer. That infamous title is antichrist. Although he will betray the children of Abraham, the Lord will take vengeance. The finale will be as a fairy tale, but in this case it will be reality. Transgressions will never again be a problem, for they will be replaced by everlasting righteousness.

A handful of theologically significant themes can be rather easily traced throughout this relatively short passage. All of them bring glory to God the Father. One theme woven into these verses is the sovereignty of the Lord. His incalculable power is thrown into relief by noting He is able to control the affairs of men. His might, though, is not used haphazardly. He always has good reason for wielding it, and it is tempered by His grace and love. A similar theme speaks to another of His attributes. The fact that He is willing to reveal this information through one person to His chosen people demonstrates Jehovah is also a personal God. He is not only involved on a national level but on an individual one as well. Lastly, He is a God of justice. This paragraph contains good news and bad news. When the Lord's plan has been completely played out, those who are the objects of His wrath will receive their proper penalty.

Bibliography

Anderson, Robert *The Coming Prince*. Grand Rapids: Kregel, 1967

Archer, Gleason L. "Daniel" in *The Expositor's Bible Commentary*. Grand Rapids: Regency, 1985

_____, R. Laird Harris, and Bruce Waltke *Theological Wordbook of the Old Testament*. Chicago: Moody Press, 1980

Baldwin, Joyce *Daniel: An Introduction and Commentary* (TOTC). Wheaton: InterVarsity Press, 1978

Barnes, Albert "Daniel" in *Notes on the Old Testament*. Grand Rapids: Baker, 1998 (reprint of 1853 edition)

Brown, Francis, S. R. Driver, and Charles A. Briggs (eds.) *A Hebrew and English Lexicon of the Old Testament*. Oxford: Clarendon Press, 1955

Chafer, Lewis S. *Systematic Theology*. (8 vols. in 4). Grand Rapids: Kregel, 1993

The Collected Writings of John Gill on CD-ROM. Rio, WI: AGES Software, Inc., 2000

Feinberg, Charles Lee *A Commentary on Daniel*. Winona Lake, IN: BMH Books, 1981

Feinberg, John S. and Paul D. (eds.) *Tradition & Testament: Essays in Honor of Charles Lee Feinberg*. Chicago: Moody Press, 1981

Goldingay, John E. *Daniel*. (WBC). Dallas: Word, 1989

Hagner, Donald A. *Matthew*. (WBC, 2 vols). Dallas: Word, 1995

Hengstenberg, E. W. *Christology of the Old Testament*. Edinburgh: 1872-1878

Hoehner, Harold W. *Chronological Aspects of the Life of Christ*. Grand Rapids: Zondervan, 1977

Ice, Thomas D. "Pre-Trib Perspectives" newsletter, Vol. V, No. 10, February 2001

_____. "Pre-Trib Perspectives" newsletter, Vol. V, No. 11, March 2001

Keil, C. F. *Biblical Commentary on the Book of Daniel*. Grand Rapids: Eerdmans, 1973

Leupold, Herbert C. *Exposition of Daniel*. Minneapolis: Augsburg, 1949

Lindsey, F. Duane "Haggai" in *The Bible Knowledge Commentary*. Wheaton: Victor Books, 1985

Miller, Stephen R. *Daniel* (NAC). Nashville: Broadman & Holman, 1994

Montgomery, J. A. *A Critical and Exegetical Commentary on the Book of Daniel* (ICC). Edinburgh: T & T Clark, 1979

Orr, James *The International Standard Bible Encyclopedia*. Grand Rapids: Eerdmans, 1956

Owens, John J. *Analytical Key to the Old Testament*. (4 vols) Grand Rapids: Baker, 1989

Pentecost, J. Dwight "Daniel" in *The Bible Knowledge Commentary*. Wheaton: Victor Books, 1985

Porteous, Norman W. *Daniel: A Commentary*. Philadelphia: Westminster Press, 1965

Pusey, E. B. *Daniel the Prophet*. Minneapolis: Klock & Klock, 1978 1885

Quinn, Jerome D. and William C. Wacker *The First and Second Letters to Timothy* (ECC). Grand Rapids: Eerdmans, 2000

VanGemeren, Willem A. (ed.) *New International Dictionary of Old Testament Theology & Exegesis*. Grand Rapids: Zondervan, 1997

Walvoord, John F. *Daniel: The Key to Prophetic Revelation*. Chicago: Moody Press, 1971

Whitcomb, John C. *Daniel* (EvBC). Chicago: Moody Press, 1985

Williamson, H. G. M. *Ezra, Nehemiah* (WBC). Waco, TX: Word Publishers, 1985

Wood, Leon *A Commentary on Daniel*. Grand Rapids: Zondervan, 1973

Yamauchi, Edwin "Ezra-Nehemiah" in *The Expositor's Bible Commentary*. Grand Rapids: Regency, 1988

Young, Edward J. *The Prophecy of Daniel*. Grand Rapids: Eerdmans, 1949

"First and foremost, however, have a correct definition of the word(s) on which the doctrine is based. Do not necessarily be satisfied with the meaning translators choose to translate, but look up definitions in Greek, Hebrew, and English dictionaries. "

- Charles C. Ryrie

Ryrie's Practical Guide to Communicating Bible Doctrine, 2005, page 41

16

Metaphor & the Rapture
Kevin D. Zuber

Introduction

In his nearly classic work *Exegetical Fallacies*, D. A. Carson exposes, among other word study fallacies, the fallacy of "false assumptions about technical meaning." "In this fallacy, an interpreter falsely assumes that a word always or nearly always has a certain technical meaning."[1] Carson, of course, is dealing with instances where a term may or may not have a technical meaning and the fallacy is "importing" the technical meaning into a context where it is inappropriate. In a number of books and commentaries on 1 Thessalonians the interpretation of *apantesis* in 1 Thessalonians 4:17 in the phrase "to meet (*apantesis*) the Lord in the air" may qualify as an instance of this fallacy. As will be demonstrated below, the view that *apantesis* has a very specific technical meaning, one that would prevent us from interpreting Paul as teaching a pre-tribulational rapture, is very widely espoused in the literature on 1 Thessalonians. This view suggests that 1 Thessalonians 4:13-18 is not describing "Christ coming for His Church" but "His church coming for Him!" This view contends, on the basis of this specific technical meaning of *apantesis* that Paul is describing, not "The Bridegroom Coming for His Bride," but rather the "Subjects of the King going out to greet and welcome the King to His Kingdom." However, the question in this case would be, can this be an instance of the *terminus technicus* fallacy if the word *apantesis* is not actually a "technical term" at all?

Structure

I will argue that 1) *apantesis* is not such a technical term, that is to say, it does not have the "full technical meaning" confidently asserted by many. I will examine what I will call the "full technical meaning" proposed for *apantesis* and show that a) it is weakly attested, b) is actually contested by many scholars (which makes any confident assertion that 1 Thessalonians 4:17 is undoubtedly an instance of such a technical meaning a bit more than a little suspect) and c) that such a technical meaning claims too much for the word standing by itself, particularly in the light of its other uses in the New

---

[1] D. A. Carson, *Exegetical Fallacies*, (Grand Rapids: Baker, 1996, second edition), 45-46.

Testament. In other words, *apantesis* on its own, apart from particular contexts, does not have a technical meaning such that one can determine the nature of the "meeting" indicated, much less the direction the parties take after the meeting. I will suggest a "limited technical meaning" of the term, that fits virtually all the uses of *apantesis* both outside and inside the New Testament but does not prevent us from seeing a pre-tribulational rapture in 1 Thessalonians 4:17. Furthermore, I will argue that 2) even if there were such a technical term, the context of 1 Thessalonians 4:17, renders the imposition of any presumed "full technical meaning" here impossible. In other words, this *would be* an instance of the *terminus technicus* fallacy if in fact the term *apantesis* were such a specific technical term. I will also argue that 3) the supposed metaphor or picture drawn by those who understand *apantesis* in the "full technical" way does not do justice to this and the other texts which describe the prophetic event(s) in view. My argument here is that the interpretive picture drawn by the advocates of the "full technical meaning" of *apantesis* a) confuses the Rapture of the Saints with the Second Coming (a very typical mistake of advocates of non-pre-tribulational views) and b) leaves the several texts that do speak of the Rapture, as well as the Lord's relationship to His church rather disconnected. In short, I want to ask which picture brings more texts together and which draws a more biblically consistent picture—the view of those who imagine a technical meaning for *apantesis*, a formal reception for a dignitary or those who understand 1 Thessalonians 4 as teaching the Rapture, the coming of Christ, the Bridegroom, for His bride, the church?

Summary of the View That *apantesis* is a Technical Term.

Let me begin with a brief synopsis of the view that *apantesis* is a technical term and then I will briefly suggest what it means for the interpretation of 1 Thessalonians 4:13-18. In the simplest terms the view of those who take *apantesis* as a technical term (in what I call the "full technical sense") is the view that this term itself indicates a particular type, "meeting" ("meeting" is the basic lexical meaning of *apantesis*. This is a "meeting" that would entail some the rather specific proceedings such as: it would take place between a delegation of citizens or officials and a visiting dignitary; it would take place just prior to the visiting dignitary's arrival, just outside a city; there would often be certain formal preparations for this visit; the "greeting party" so to speak would take the initiative to go out from the city to receive the dignitary; and then they would escort him back into the city. It is this last detail that is most significant for advocates of this view, for they would contend that this technical meaning precludes any view that understands Paul in 1 Thessalonians 4:17 to be describing a pre-tribulational rapture, for, if the technical meaning is granted, the procedure would be for the dignitary to continue (with the delegation) into (back into) the city. In no case where this technical meaning applies, it is argued, did the delegation return with the dignitary back to his point of origin.

Evaluation and Analysis

What should we think of this technical meaning of *apantesis*? A little background on the origin of this view will help us to evaluate it. Virtually all advocates of this view reference (as if a "proof text") an article written by Erik Peterson in 1929-30-- Erik Peterson, "Die Einholung Des Kyrios", *Zeitschrift fur systematische Theologie* 7, 1929-30 [682-702]. Peterson also wrote the brief article on *apantesis* in the *Theological Dictionary of the New Testament*.[2] Michael R. Crosby notes that Peterson's article drew on "citations from material from ancient Greek papyri, inscriptions and literature" to describe the custom(s) of "Hellenistic formal reception(s)."[3] These studies led to Peterson's conclusion that in 1 Thessalonians 4:15-17 Paul has these custom(s) of Hellenistic formal reception(s) in view in describing the return of Christ. The list of books and commentaries that reference Peterson's articles (more or less directly) is impressively large[4] and those that merely assert the "technical meaning" of *apantesis* as describing the formal welcome of a visiting dignitary, is equally large.[5] Often there is only the confident assertion, as for instance, this from Anthony Hoekema,

---

[2] Erik Peterson, "apantesis," *Theological Dictionary of the New Testament*, Vol 1, ed. by G. Kittel, trans by G. W. Bromiley, (Grand Rapids: Eerdmans, English ed. 1964), 380-81.

[3] Michael R. Crosby, "Hellenistic Formal Receptions and Paul's use of *APANTSIS* in 1 Thessalonians 4:17," *Bulletin for Biblical Research* 4:1994,17 [15-34].

[4] A mere representative sample of the list here includes: Ernest Best, *The First and Second Epistles to the Thessalonians*, (London: Hendriksen Publishers, 1986), 199; D. Michael Martin, *1, 2 Thessalonians*, (Nashville: Broadman & Holman, 1995), 153n86; Abraham J. Malherbe, *The Letters to the Thessalonians*, (New York: Doubleday, 2000); Gene L. Green, *The Letters to the Thessalonians*, (Grand Rapids: Eerdmans, 2002), 226; Anthony A. Hoekema, "Amillennialism," *The Meaning of the Millennium: Four Views*, ed. by (Robert G. Clouse, Downers Grove, Illinois: IVP, 1977), 183, 216n19; Wilhelm Mundle, "*katantao*," in *New International Dictionary of New Testament Theology*, Vol 1, ed. by Colin Brown, (Grand Rapids: Zondervan, 1967, English ed., 1975), 325.

[5] E.g. Robert H. Gundry, *The Church and the Tribulation*, (Grand Rapids: Zondervan, 1973), 104; F. F. Bruce, *1 & 2 Thessalonians*, (Waco, TX: Word, 1982), 102-03; I. H. Marshall, *1 and 2 Thessalonians*, (Grand Rapids, MI: Eerdmans, 1983), 131; John Stott, *The Message of Thessalonians*, (Downers Grove, IL: IVP, 1991), 104; Earl J. Richard, *First and Second Thessalonians*, (Colleville, MN: Liturgical Press, 1995), 246; G. K. Beale, *1-2 Thessalonians*, (Downers Grove, IL: IVP, 2003), 140-41n; Barbara R. Rossing, *The Rapture Exposed*, (Boulder, CO: Westview Press, 2004), 176; Ben Witherington, *The Problem with Evangelical Theology*, (Waco, TX: Baylor University Press, 2005), 119-20.

that "The word translated 'to meet' in 1 Thessalonians 4:17 (*apantesis*) is a technical term used in the days of the New Testament to describe a public welcome given by a city to a visiting dignitary. People would ordinarily leave the city to meet the distinguished visitor and then go back with him into the city."[6] Likewise Barbara Rossing asserts, "Paul's description of 'meeting' the Lord in the air employs a very specific Greek word for greeting a visiting dignitary in ancient times: *apantesis*, a practice by which people went outside the city to greet the dignitary and then accompanied him into their city."[7] Taking those who directly reference Peterson's work, the argument for the "technical meaning" of *apantesis* is most often bolstered by citing instances from ancient sources such as Cicero's description of Rome's welcome of Julius Caesar in 49 B.C.[8] or Josephus's description of Vespasian's welcome as the new emperor in Rome after putting down the Jewish rebellion.[9]

No "Technical Meaning" for the Term *apantesis* in and of Itself

Limitations of space prohibit a detailed analysis of these and the other instances of the so called "technical use" of *apantesis* to describe these events but it can be simply observed that the events themselves seem to dictate the "formal elements" and not the term *apantesis* by itself. In other words, we may simply ask if there are other uses of *apantesis* in settings other than these formal receptions that indicate a non-technical sense to the term. Indeed, Crosby notes,

> A computer search of the literature written during the several centuries surrounding Paul's era using the *Thesaurus Linguae Graecae* (*TLG*) produced 91 pages of citations of passages that employ forms of *apantesis apantano*, *hupantesis*, and *hupantano*. Yet only a minority of the uses of these terms describes formal receptions. For example, Philo Judaeus uses these words 27 times, but not once to describe the meeting of a dignitary. Similarly, Josephus employs them 92 times but only ten times in descriptions of formal receptions. In the LXX the noun *apantesis* is used frequently. . . Often it designates the hostile meeting of armies, although it also describes virtually any kind of meeting.[10]

In short, "Word use alone . . . does not decide the issue of whether or not people of Paul's day considered *apantesis* to be a technical term for the

---

[6] Hoekema, "Amillennialism," 183.

[7] Rossing, *The Rapture Exposed*, 176.

[8] See Crosby, "Hellenistic Formal Receptions," 19.

[9] See, Green, "Thessalonians," 227.

[10] Crosby, ""Hellenistic Formal Receptions," 20-21, Greek has been transliterated.

Hellenistic formal reception."[11] Clearly, *apantesis* was used in the description of the formal meeting and greeting of a dignitary, but often it was used in contexts when such a formal meeting was *not* being indicated. Simply put, the word considered apart from a context, considered in and by itself, was not a *terminus technicus*. *Context*, not the term alone, determined whether the "meeting" carried any significance beyond a meeting between a group and an individual. (Actually, if there is a more "limited technical meaning" that would be it; that is, if the term *apantesis* has anything like a "technical meaning" it seems to be used whenever a group met individual; but even that might be questioned.) Attaching any further connotations to the term, *in and of itself*, by virtue of its use in contexts describing those formal receptions, is simply unwarranted.

The "Technical Meaning" Does Not Apply in 1 Thessalonians 4:17

Indeed, there are several scholars who have questioned this "full technical meaning." That is, they simply deny that considered on its own *apantesis* has the specific technical connotations asserted for it by some, particularly in its use in 1 Thessalonians 4:17. Interestingly, both Witherington[12] and Stott[13] cite F. F. Bruce in their explanation of the meaning of *apantesis* in 1 Thessalonians 4:17; Bruce writes, "When a dignitary paid an official visit (*parousia*) to a city in Hellenistic times, the action of the leading citizens in going out to meet him and escort him on the final stage of his journey was called the *apantesis*."[14]) However, neither of these authors references this, also from Bruce, "But there is nothing in the word *apantesis* or in this context (in 1 Thessalonians 4) that demands this interpretation."[15] Thus, although Green confidently asserts, "there remains little doubt that this custom {i.e. of formal receptions} formed the background of this teaching"[16] (in 1 Thessalonians 4) we must agree with Malherbe that to understand Paul's use of *apantesis* as an allusion to the formal reception of a visiting dignitary is "improbable" on "a number of counts."[17] Crosby is clear, "Peterson . . . was incorrect in reading Hellenistic formal reception *into* 1 Thessalonians 4:13-17. The text does not support his assertion that Paul's

---

[11] Crosby, ""Hellenistic Formal Receptions," 20.

[12] Witherington, *The Problem with Evangelical Theology*, 120.

[13] Stott, *The Message of Thessalonians*, 104.

[14] Bruce, *1 & 2 Thessalonians*, 102.

[15] Ibid., 103.

[16] Green, "Thessalonians," 228.

[17] Malherbe, *The Letters to the Thessalonians*, 277. The reader should not miss the point here: the juxtaposition of Bruce's two comments and Malherbe's comment belies Green's assertion—in fact, there is very much doubt!

use of *apantesis* in 4:17 brings with it the entire baggage of the custom of greeting dignitaries."[18] Likewise, Joseph Plevnik argues that Peterson's argument "is weak, since the expression *apantesis* or *eis apantesis* is neither limited to Hellenistic parousias nor does it always suggest a bringing in."[19]

So the term *apantesis*, considered on its own apart from a context of formal receptions, is *not* well attested as a technical term (at least in the full technical sense) and it *is* a matter of some sharp disagreement, to say the least, as to whether that presumed full technical meaning (even if it does exist) should be understood here in 1 Thessalonians 4:17.

The Other Uses of *apantesis* in the New Testament

Now, some of the advocates of the full technical meaning of *apantesis* have appealed to the other instances of *apantesis* in the New Testament to support their conclusions. There are only two such contexts: Matthew 25:6, 10 in the Parable of the Ten Virgins and in Acts 28:15 describing Paul's reception by the Christians in Rome. However, even a quick glance at these uses, and the arguments used to defend the technical meaning of *apantesis*, will reveal that the advocates of the technical meaning are engaging in some "special pleading." Neither the meeting in Acts 28:15 nor that of the bridesmaids and bridegroom in Matthew 25 have any of the "formal features" of the Hellenistic formal reception of a visiting dignitary.[20] These uses again emphasize that it is context that determines the features of the meeting and whether or not one sees in that meeting the features of the so called "Hellenistic formal receptions." So while it is true that the Christians greeting Paul did not "change directions" and return to where Paul came from,[21] (he was after all on the way to Rome!) that in no way is a matter to be determined by the meaning of *apantesis*! It is clearly the context and the historical circumstances of the situation being described that determined the "direction" the parties traveled after their meeting. With respect to the use in Matthew 25, Rossing suggests that the term "meet" indicates the "bridegroom goes with the bridesmaids into the house from where they came, where everyone is waiting for him."[22] But there is nothing in the text that indicates this. In fact, following the pattern of ancient wedding customs,

---

[18] Crosby, "Hellenistic Formal Receptions," 31.

[19] Joseoph Plevnik, "1 Thessalonians 4:17: The Bringing in of the Lord or the Bringing in of the Faithful?," *Biblica* 80:4, 1999, 543 [537-46].

[20] See below where I discuss the features of the Hellenistic formal reception compared to the context of 1 Thessalonians 4:17.

[21] Rossing, *The Rapture Exposed*, 177.

[22] Ibid., 176-77.

the event pictured would probably be that of the bridegroom, returning to his father's house, with his bride.[23] Far from describing the "formal reception of a dignitary" the "meeting" indicated in Matthew 25 is rather unique, even for the setting indicated by the parable—namely the pattern of wedding customs. In other words, the meeting between the bridegroom and the bridesmaids has some "odd features" that would not be regular or expected features of the typical wedding party meeting of the day. It happened at midnight, it was delayed for unspecified reasons and it happened suddenly, taking the bridesmaids by surprise when it did come. None of the features of the supposed "technical meaning" of *apantesis* fit this context; and it would be equally in error to suppose that any of these "odd features" of this meeting can be attached to the meaning of *apantesis*. In short, when *apantesis* is used in *any* context it is the description of the meeting itself, in these texts where the term appears, that tells us more about the meeting than the term *apantesis*, does by itself. It is clear that the use of the term in contexts such as Acts 28 and Matthew 25 tells us way more about the nature of those meetings than any supposed technical uses or associations the term may or may not have had; and so far from supporting the idea that the technical meaning of *apantesis* helps us understand the nature of these meeting, these examples tell us to pay close attention to the context.

But perhaps in examining the context of 1 Thessalonians we should be discovering that Paul is using instances of supposedly "imperial cult language," "anti-imperial rhetoric" as Witherington suggests. I frankly find this sort of "scholarship" tiresome. If accepted it would mean that only those who are able to penetrate into the "deeper nuances" of the "deeper meaning" of Paul's "loaded language" so as to pick up the "associations" (political, social, etc) of the terms, would be able to really know what he meant and/or what the Thessalonians would or would not have understood by the "deep, loaded," nearly "coded" terms. After a close reading of the context in 1 Thessalonians 4 I find it a very dubious assertion to say, as Witherington does, that in his answer to the Thessalonians regarding "the fate of the Thessalonian Christian dead" (surely this *is the point of 1 Thessalonians 4:13-17!*) Paul is really, on some deeper level which only Witherington, N.T. Wright, and other "scholars" will see, actually "busily deconstructing the extant pagan value system" and expressing his "opposition to Caesar" in an effort to subvert Caesar's empire." Witherignton wants to see this "imperial cult language," "anti-imperial rhetoric" because it would support the idea that *apantesis* is also actually

---

[23] See J. Julius Scott, Jr., *Jewish Backgrounds of the New Testament*, (Grand Rapids, MI: Baker, 1995), 250.

one of those "loaded" terms (loaded with the technical meaning of visiting dignitary—[Ha! Take that Caesar! Jesus is Our Coming Lord!]) which the Thessalonians would have instantly understood as "subversive." I may be mistaken here but I really think I have drawn out Witherington's point fairly, if simply—and I find it, again, dubious! I honestly do not see Paul trying to make "deep points" about "subverting the empire" by the use of "anti-imperial rhetoric," in this context at least, nor is he busy "coopting imperial rhetoric and applying it to Jesus."[24] He's just trying to comfort the believers concerning the one's who have died—will they miss the "catching away" at the "coming of the Lord?" Paul says, "No, they will not miss it, be comforted." He doesn't need—and I for one do not find—"deeply nuanced anti-imperial rhetoric" to say that!

We may conclude, therefore, since the term *apantesis* on its own, does *not* automatically indicate that Paul had the formal reception of a dignitary in mind we may *not* "as Green suggests "assume that the Thessalonians would have understood [on the basis of some purported technical meaning of *apantesis*] that the Lord would continue his *parousia* until he arrived at the final destination of the city or the earth."[25]

The Context of 1 Thessalonians 4 and Hellenistic Formal Receptions

In fact, as we turn our attention specifically to the context of 1 Thessalonians 4:15-17 it will become clear that, even if there were a well recognized technical meaning of *apantesis* that included even the slightest indication of which direction the parties took after the meeting, that technical meaning simply would not fit the context. In his article on *Hellenistic Formal Receptions*, Michael R. Crosby[26] examines the features of the so-called Hellenistic Formal Receptions as these were identified by Peterson in the article previously cited. Some of these features are: decrees to make elaborate preparations; preparations for wearing festive clothing, garlands and wreaths; sacrifices were often prepared on offered as a part of the

---

[24] All of this can be found in Witherington, *The Problem with Evangelical Theology*, 120-22.

[25] Green, "Thessalonians," 228.

[26] It should be noted that Crosby clearly has no sympathy for Dispensational Pre-tribulationism. He regards such teaching as "discredited," "naïve," "misguided," and "fanciful"—a doctrine he "detests"; Crosby, ""Hellenistic Formal Receptions," 32. He says he undertook the study of Peterson's aforementioned article to secure information to "steer Christians away from the escapist theology" of the rapture. However, to his credit, his studies indicated that any interpretation of 1 Thessalonians 4:17 which suggests that *apantesis* has this technical sense indicating a "formal reception of a dignitary" was simply not tenable, not true to the text.

[26] Crosby, "Hellenistic Formal Receptions," 29.

reception; loud acclamations would be a prominent part of the receiving crowd's behavior. Crosby describes these features with quotes from primary sources recounting these receptions. And then he summarizes the point I want to emphasize here: "All of the main elements of Hellenistic receptions found in ancient papyri, inscriptions and literature are missing from 1 Thess 4:15-17."[27] The context in 1 Thessalonians describes an event that is "sudden and unexpected"; certainly none of the elaborate preparations are indicated. The Thessalonians are not told be prepared with special garments or garlands. It is not the Thessalonians who take the initiative for the meeting. It is not the Thessalonians who are making noise but the shout, the voice of the archangel and the trumpet of God. Crosby is dead on! There is no evidence of a formal reception in this context so there is no way to determine the direction the parties take after the meeting based on such notions. Even if there were a technical meaning of *apantesis*, it would be, as noted earlier, a classic example of Carson's fallacy of the "false assumptions about technical meaning" wherein, interpreters see the technical meaning of a term where it clearly (and the context here says it clearly) does not pertain.

On the other hand there are several features in the context which indicate that the "direction" the parties take after the "meeting" is *not* back into the city or to earth. For one thing, even Green notes (against his view of *apantesis*) that the term "caught up" (the term is *harpagasometha* from *harpadzo*) "means to take someone away by force . . .or to catch away to a celestial place."[28] To go on to suggest that "no other explanation is offered of the events after the meeting" as Green does[29] and to suggest that we assume the parties continued on into the city (on the basis, again, of the technical meaning of *apantesis*) is simply faulty interpretation. As Plavnik argues, Peterson's explanation of *apantesis* does not fit with "the being snatched up" nor does it fit with "the cloud motif" in the 1 Thessalonians 4 context: "In Petersons's interpretation, the people's going up on a cloud is equivalent to the citizen's going out of the city, which is rather strained."[30] The term *harpagasometha* just does not fit the picture of a group of excited celebrants who take the initiative to go out to greet the "royal-dignitary arriving" but it does indicate a sudden, unexpected removal of the believers away from the earth. Furthermore, the meeting is left, literally, up in the air with only this to indicate what happens, what direction is next—"and so we

---

[27] See Crosby's comment in text above at footnote 18; see also Plevnik, "1 Thessalonians 4:17: The Bringing in of the Lord," 543-44.
[28] Green, "Thessalonians," 226.
[29] Ibid., 228.
[30] Plevnik, "1 Thessalonians 4:17: The Bringing in of the Lord," 543.

shall always be with the Lord." One can hardly miss the allusion to another instance of "cloudy removal from the earth"—I am thinking of Acts 1. In Acts 1:9, at the ascension of the Risen Christ, a "cloud" (the Shekinah perhaps) "received Him out of their sight" and in 1:11 the disciples are informed that He went to "heaven." Admittedly, Paul does not *specify* that the destination is heaven, but he is explicit in 1 Thessalonians 4:17 that we shall "always be with the Lord" and the Lord went to heaven. Paul Benware offers this summary:

> Clouds are also used figuratively in the Bible to refer to the presence and glory of God (e.g., Ex. 14:19-24; 16:10; 19:9, 16; 20:21; 40:34-38). It is best in this rapture passage to understand the clouds as referring to the visible presence and glory of the Lord. At the rapture, it is the glorious Lord Jesus who appears and brings the saints into the presence of His glory.[31]

One other point needs to be made regarding the context. It must be obvious that Paul's main concern is to answer the question of the Thessalonians concerning believers who have "fallen asleep." They were concerned about those who had died—would they miss the promise of the Blessed Hope? Paul makes it clear in verse 14; No! They will not miss out, for "God will bring with Him those who have fallen asleep." Those who advocate the "formal reception of a dignitary view" will acknowledge that resurrection is a part of Paul's answer here, but it seems they ignore this detail—which clearly does *not* fit the pattern of the so called Hellenistic Formal Receptions. Yet, again, this, the answer to the question concerning the destiny of those who have "fallen asleep" in the Lord, is in many ways Paul's main reason for directing the Thessalonians to the truth of this prophetic event! The union of the living / translated saints with those whose souls are finally reunited with glorious resurrected bodies *is the main point* here (cf. 1 Corinthians 15:51-53) and Paul teaches it to produce comfort and hope; and that is the rapture!

Which Metaphor?

Finally, I would like to deal with a somewhat wider issue. One of the ways we can test the credibility of any particular interpretation of a text is to ask how this interpretation "fits" with respect to the interpretation of other related texts. Simply put we may ask, how does this interpretation of 1 Thessalonians 4:15-17 which pictures Christ as the returning King, fit with

---

[31] Paul N. Benware, *Understanding End Times Prophecy*, (Chicago, IL: Moody, 2006), 212.

other prophetic texts? Similarly, we may ask how does this text fit with other texts if one adopts the pre-tribulational interpretation?

Those who take the view that *apantesis* is a technical term that points to the custom of the formal reception of a visiting dignitary assume, of course, that Jesus Christ is that dignitary and thus that the coming indicated in 1 Thessalonians 4:17 is therefore His "Second Coming."[32] In this view the term *parousia* has reference to one coming ("since Paul did not predict two parousias") and that "one event must encompass both the gathering of the church and final judgment."[33] From here the advocates of this view contend that Paul goes directly in 1 Thessalonians 5:1-11 to speak of the same event, here designated "the Day of the Lord" and they often add to this argument by drawing supposed parallels between 1 Thessalonians 4:15-5:11 and Matthew 24:29-44, which clearly describes the post-tribulational *return* of Christ.

In response it may be pointed out that the term *parousia* is used in a number of passages in the New Testament: in a "general and not technical" way to describe simply someone "coming"—1 Cor 16:17 of "Stephanas and Fortunatus"; 2 Cor. 7:6, 7 of "Titus"; with reference to specific end times events such as the rapture—1 Cor. 15:23; 1 Thess. 2:19, and the bodily return of Christ to the earth—Matt. 24:3, 27, 37, 39.[34] A study of the New Testament uses of this term reveals that "*parousia*, lit. 'a presence' . . . denotes both the 'arrival' and the consequent 'presence with.'" "In some passages the word gives prominence to the beginning of that period, the course of the period being implied, 1 Cor. 15:23; 1 Thess. 4:15; 5:23; 2 Thess. 2:1; Jas 5:7-8; 2 Pet. 3:4. In some, the course is prominent, Matt. 24:3, 37; 1 Thess. 3:13; 1 John 2:28; in others the conclusion of the period, Matt.24:27; 2 Thess. 2:8."[35] In other words, the term can be used to describe the entire period of the Lord's appearing or particular features or events that occur in the course of that appearing. So there is *one parousia* but it is not *one* dimensional and it does not occur all at *once*. Thus, while 1 Thessalonians 5:1-11 certainly continues the general theme of the *parousia* it is also quite clear that Paul has begun an new topic. He even uses the typical transitional phrase *peri de*, which indicates a new subject. Here in 5:1-11 Paul is stepping back and looking over not just the immediate occasion of the "catching up," the "meeting in the air" but the wider picture of "the day of the Lord." This

---

[32] See Martin, *1, 2 Thessalonians*, 154-55; Witherington, *The Problem with Evangelical Theology*, 123-24.

[33] Martin, *1, 2 Thessalonians*, 154.

[34] J. Dwight Pentecost, *Things to Come*, (Grand Rapids, MI: Zondervan, 1958), 156-57.

[35] W. E. Vine, *Expository Dictionary of Biblical Words*, (Nashville, TN: Nelson, 1985), 111.

phrase designates "the whole program of events, including the tribulation period, the second advent program and the entire millennial age."[36] Paul is simply moving from the specific to the general, from a focus on one part of the whole end times program (the rapture) to the broader picture of "the times and the epochs." There is no reason to think that 1 Thessalonians 4:13-18 and 5:1-11 must be speaking of "precisely the same event"[37] or that taking 1 Thessalonians 5:1-11 as referring to events after the catching up of 4:17 is an instance "special pleading."[38]

However, there are some very strong reasons to think that what Paul is describing in 1 Thessalonians 4 and what, for instance, Jesus is referring to in Matthew 24 are very different events. As noted the advocates of the view that *apantesis* is a technical term that points to the custom of the formal reception of a visiting dignitary often assume that 1 Thessalonians 4:15-17 is a description of the "Second Coming." This is a fairly common error. Paul Benware has analyzed the main passages dealing with the rapture (1 Thess. 4:13-17; 1 Cor. 15:51-53; John 14:1-3) and those dealing with the second coming (Joel 2:12-16; Zech. 14:1-5; Matt. 24:29-31; Rev. 19:11-21) and identified several contrasts that indicate the two events are indeed different.[39] This chart conveys the key points:

	The Rapture	**The Second Coming**
Place	The Lord comes in the air; returns to the Father's house.	The Lord descends to the Mount of Olives; remains on earth.
Purpose	The Lord comes to gather, unite and bless His church; glorified bodies.	The Lord comes to judge unbelievers, wrath; no glorified bodies.
Result	No mention of establishing a Kingdom; believers removed from earth.	The Lord comes to establish the kingdom; believers remain on earth.
Time	Imminent, any time!	After the Tribulation

---

[36] Pentecost, *Things to Come*, 174.

[37] For a more thorough discussion of the connection between 1 Thess. 4:13-18 and 5:1-11 see Robert L. Thomas, "1 Thessalonians," *Expositor's Bible Commentary*, Vol. 11, ed. by F. C. Gaebelein, (Grand Rapids, MI: Zondervan, 1978), 280-82.

[38] Witherington (*The Problem with Evangelical Theology*, 123) argues that it is "special pleading"; but it is far from clear as to why. He himself concedes that the two passages describe "the rescue of believers" on the one hand, the "judgment of unbelievers" on the other (124). Unless he wants to suggest that some act of judgment occurred in connection with the "Hellenistic formal reception" (he would not, of course) then he must concede that the events of 5:1-11 come after those of 4:13-18. Again, Witherington's problem here stems from not understanding the meaning of *parousia* which he takes in a rather flat "it's all a one time event" sort of way.

[39] Benware, *Understanding End Times Prophecy*, 230-31.

So Benware concludes, these differences "do suggest we are looking at two separate events."[40]

On the other hand, those who take Paul as teaching the Pre-tribulational Rapture in 1 Thessalonians 4 can tie this understanding to an impressive, wider (than the formal reception of a dignitary view), biblical New Testament metaphor that places it on a firmer footing when, as suggested earlier, one considers how the interpretation "fits" with other passages. That metaphor is that of the Church as the Bride of Christ, the Bridegroom. Robert L. Saucy writes, "One of the most beautiful images of the church is that of the bride of Christ."[41] The metaphor appears prominently in Ephesians 5 where Paul "uses the union of Christ and His church to illustrate the relation of husband and wife (Eph 5:22-23)."[42] Understanding key aspects of this metaphor requires a knowledge of the ancient wedding customs with which the disciples and the early church would have been assuredly acquainted. Saucy describes the main features of these customs that are pertinent to understanding the main metaphor: he writes, "the Oriental practice of marriage . . . consisted of three stages. First came the betrothal, which was more than a promise of marriage. It was the very initiation of marriage, for the bride was legally considered a married woman from the time of betrothal." After the betrothal, there would follow an indefinite time of preparation. This time was devoted to, on the man's part, preparation of the future home and on the woman's part, preparation of herself for the new role she was intended to fulfill. At an undesignated time, would come "the retrieval" when "the actual marriage took place. On that day the bridegroom and his friends went to the home of the bride and then, in company with the bride and her friends, the festal company proceeded to their future home."[43] When the couple arrived at their future home there would be a more formal ceremony of presentation and often "it was a friend of the bridegroom who made the presentation" of the bride to the groom.[44] Then would follow a marriage supper and time of celebration.

It is that simple outline, I suggest, that forms the background to understand the significance of the several passages that teach the rapture of the church, including 1 Thessalonians 4. The first passage in the New Testament revealing the rapture of the church is found in John 14:1-3

---

[40] Benware, *Understanding End Times Prophecy*, 231.
[41] Robert L. Saucy, *The Church in God's Program*, (Chicago, IL: Moody, 1972), 44.
[42] Saucy, *The Church in God's Program*, 45.
[43] Saucy, *The Church in God's Program*, 45; See J. Julius Scott, Jr., *Jewish Backgrounds of the New Testament*, Grand Rapids: Baker, 1995, 250.
[44] Saucy, *The Church in God's Program*, 48.

recorded in the very words of the Bridegroom Himself, is a promise to fulfill the tasks of the bridegroom in *preparation*, and a promise in anticipation of the time of *retrieval*. "The church is presently the betrothed bride of Christ (2 Cor 11:2)."[45] The text noted earlier, Ephesians 5, indicates that the Bride, the church is to be active as well, fulfilling her part in the period of *preparation* (cf. Revelation 19:7b). Then follows of course the actual *retrieval* and this is obviously what 1 Thessalonians 4:15-17 is all about. "Following the analogy of the Oriental practice, the church as the bride now awaits the coming of Christ to take her to Himself (again alluding to John 14:3). The Apostle Paul speaks of this day" in 1 Thessalonians 4:16-17.[46] Finally, the *retrieval* leads to the *presentation*; only in this case "Christ presents His own bride to Himself. (cf. Eph 5:27) He and no other presents the bride, and He and no other receives her to Himself."[47] After the *presentation,* there follows the *marriage supper*, which is of course indicated in Revelation 19:7-9.

The fact that we can "fit" 1 Thessalonians 4 into this wider, biblical metaphor of Christ and His Bride does not prove the pre-tribulational rapture, but it does offer a more satisfying and biblically consistent picture of the prophetic event in view in 1 Thessalonians 4:17 than the dubious opinion of the formal reception of a dignitary view.

---

[45] Saucy, *The Church in God's Program*, 48.
[46] Ibid.
[47] Ibid.

"Never for a moment doubt the truth and accuracy of the prophecies of the Word of God. There are many details about which we can't be dogmatic, but the outline of things to come is perfectly clear in the Scriptures. Don't worry about what you can't understand, but be concerned about what you *do* understand about the future. The routine and normalcy of life can easily lull you into the sleep of disbelieving that these things will come to pass in our world."

- Charles C. Ryrie
The Final Countdown, 1982, page 120

17

The Two Witnesses[1]
John C. Whitcomb

The Time of Their Ministry

Most dispensational commentators agree that the holy city, Jerusalem, will be "trodden down" by the Gentiles for 42 months *during the last half of the 70th Week of Daniel* (Rev. 11:2; cf. Luke 21:24)). This time period is identical to the 42 months of Rev. 13:5, which is the time God assigns to the Beast, the Antichrist, to blaspheme His name and to persecute His people.

This will be the fulfillment of Daniel's prophecy in Dan. 7:21, that "the little horn" will make war against the saints and will prevail against them until "the Ancient of Days" finally comes. Daniel is also told that "the saints will be given into his hand for a time and times and half a time" (7:25), and that after these three-and-one-half years, "when the power of the holy people has been completely shattered, all these things shall be finished" (12:7).

What, then, are the "one thousand two hundred and sixty days" during which "My two witnesses" will receive authority to "prophesy...clothed in sackcloth" (Rev. 11:3)? Time indicators, such as "1,260 days" are to be understood literally. John F. Walvoord explains: "Very prominent in the book of Revelation is the use of numbers, namely, 2, 3, 3 1/2, 4, 5, 6, 7, 10, 12, 24, 42, 144, 666, 1,000, 1,260, 1,600, 7,000, 12,000, 144,000, 100,000,000, 200,000,000 . . .The general rule should be followed to interpret numbers literally unless there is clear evidence to the contrary."[2]

For several reasons, I suggest that *this is the first half of the Seventieth Week. First*, there seems to be an intentional distinction between the time of the Gentile occupation of the Temple's outer court and the city, and the time of the two witnesses, by means of the different time-units used: 42 months for the Gentile domination and 1,260 days for the two witnesses. If the same time period is intended for both groups, why is not the 42-month time-block sufficient to cover both?

---

[1] Scripture taken from the New King James Version®. Copyright © 1982 by Thomas Nelson, Inc. Used by permission. All rights reserved.
[2] John F. Walvoord, *The Revelation Of Jesus Christ* (Chicago, IL: Moody Press, 1966), 28; cf., 175; and Robert L. Thomas, *Evangelical Hermeneutics* (Grand Rapids, MI: Kregel, 2002),232-233.

Second, and more important, in the very next verse (Rev. 11:4), the ministry of the two witnesses is compared to the ministry of the two olive trees of Zech. 4:3, namely, *Joshua* the high priest and *Zerubbabel* the governor of the Jewish remnant, who returned from Babylon to re-establish legitimate worship in Jerusalem (Zech. 3:1 and 4:6). *These leaders did not have to wait for the Temple to be rebuilt to begin sacrificing on the altar which they erected on the ruins of Solomon's Temple* (cf. Ezra 3:2-3). *By the same token, the two witnesses will not have to wait for the third temple to be built in order to begin sacrificing on a divinely legitimate altar on the present ruins of the second temple.* What they *will* need is supernatural protection to re-institute the sacrifices (cf. Dan. 9:27) in the presence of enormous, even global, opposition (cf. Rev. 11:10).

The reason why this will happen during the first half of the seventieth week is that "in the middle of the week He [the Antichrist] shall bring an end to sacrifice [*zevach* = bloody sacrifices] and offering [*minchah* = non-bloody sacrifices]" (Dan. 9:27). As J. Dwight Pentecost explains, "This expression refers to the entire Levitical system, which suggests that Israel will have restored that system in the first half of the 70th 'seven.'"[3] Antichrist will replace the legitimate, God-honoring Jewish worship system, which only the two witnesses can inaugurate, with his own system, namely, *the abomination of desolation* (cf. Dan. 9:27b, 12:11; Matt. 24:15; 2 Thess. 2:4; Rev. 13:14-15). *But the Antichrist cannot do this until the 1,260 days of ministry allotted by God to the two witnesses has been completed* (cf. Rev. 11:7).

Third, the Lord Jesus issued this command to Jews of the tribulation period: "when you see the 'abomination of desolation,' spoken of by Daniel the prophet, standing in the holy place . . . then let those who are in Judea flee to the mountains . . . For then there will be great tribulation such as has not been since the beginning of the world until this time, no, nor ever shall be" (Matt. 24:15-21). Here an obvious question arises: Would the two Jewish witnesses remain in Jerusalem during the 42 months of Antichrist's dominion if the Lord Jesus, their Messiah, told them to flee to the mountains?

Fourth, if the 1,260 days occur during the last half of the Week, then the entire world would be celebrating the death of the two witnesses for three-and-a-half days after the Battle of Armageddon and the destruction of the Antichrist! This is very difficult to imagine. As Gary G. Cohen explains, "at the end of the second three-and-a-half year period, the Beast followers are lamenting over Babylon and the vials, [are] gathered for the great battle at

---

[3] "Daniel," in *The Bible Knowledge Commentary*, (Wheaton, IL: Victor Books, 1985), 1365.

Armegeddon, and [are] finally slain by Christ, whose coming is surrounded with the powers of the heavens being shaken (Rev. 16-18; 19:11-21; Matt. 24:29-30). This picture does not harmonize well with the three-and-a-half days of rejoicing and gift-giving in which the earth-dwellers participate following the murder of the witnesses. This discordance between the end of the second three-and-a-half year period and the three-and-a-half days <u>following the end</u> of the three-and-a-half year ministry of the witnesses makes it most unlikely that the prophesying of God's two servants takes place during the latter half of the week."[4]

Fifth, putting the two witnesses into the last half of the Week compromises the totality of Antichrist's dominion during that same period. How can he bring fire from heaven upon *his* enemies (through the False Prophet, Rev. 13:13) if the two witnesses are simultaneously bringing fire from heaven upon *their* enemies (Rev. 11:5)? We are clearly dealing with two different time periods: the first half of the Week with the overwhelming power of the two witnesses, and the last half of the Week with the overwhelming power of the Beast and the False Prophet. When the world asks the rhetorical question, "Who is able to make war with [the Beast]?" (Rev. 13:4), it seems obvious that no one can answer, "The two witnesses are able to make war with him," for their 1,260 days of ministry will have ended, and they will be gone.

Sixth, our Lord stated that "Elijah is coming first *and will restore all things* (italics added)" (Matt. 17:11). Whoever "Elijah" turns out to be (see below, The Identity of the Two Witnesses), his spectacular success (under God) in bringing Israel back to her Messiah *must be during the first half of the seventieth week*, for Isaiah prophesied that Israel will have given birth "to her children" as soon as her time of tribulation begins (Isa. 66:8).

Furthermore, the basically regenerated nation, called "the woman" in Rev. 12, will flee into the wilderness and be nourished by God for 1,260 days (Rev. 12:6, 14; cf. Isaiah 26:20-21), namely, the last half of the week. "The dragon," Satan, will then "make war with the rest of her offspring, who keep the commandments of God and have the testimony of Jesus Christ" (12:17), presumably the 144,000 witnesses from the 12 tribes of Israel and multitudes of their Gentile converts.

The crucial question, then, is this: by whose testimony is the nation of Israel brought into the blessings of the New Covenant of Jeremiah 31:31-34 (cf. Jer. 32:37-41; Ezek. 36:25-28)? And by whose witness are 12,000 from

---

[4] Gary G. Cohen, *The Chronology of the Book of Revelation* (TH.D. Diss., Grace Theological Seminary, May 1966), 251.

each of the twelve tribes led to the Lord, in order that, as our Savior promised, "this gospel of the Kingdom will be preached in all the world [during the last half of the Week] as a witness to all the nations, and then the end will come" (Matt. 24:14)?

The prophet Malachi provides the answer: "Behold, I will send you Elijah the prophet *before* (italics added) the coming of the great and dreadful day of the LORD [i.e., the final 42 months of the 70th week], and he will turn the hearts of the fathers to the children, and the hearts of the children to their fathers" (Mal. 4:5-6). Our Lord, of course, was referring to this final statement of the Old Testament when He assured Peter, James and John that, "indeed, Elijah is coming first and will restore all things" (Matt. 17:11).

Some have mistakenly assumed that Israel as a nation cannot be converted until "they will look on Me whom they pierced" (Zech. 12:10), namely, at Christ's second coming in glory. But our Lord insisted: "Blessed are those who have not seen, and yet have believed" (John 20:29). These words were spoken to Thomas who refused to believe until he could "see in His hands the print of the nails" (vs. 25). Was Thomas converted when he did see the marks of his Lord's crucifixion? No, for he, like the other ten apostles, was already a born-again believer (cf. John 13:10-11). Likewise, Israel will be filled with contrition when they finally see the Savior whom they had crucified, and "will mourn for Him, as one mourns for his only son," with "all the families that remain, every family by itself, and their wives by themselves" (Zech. 12:14). Doubtless, this will also be the occasion when they will cry out, "Surely He has borne our griefs ...yet we esteemed Him stricken, smitten by God and afflicted" (Isa. 53:4-5). Thus, there will be at least a 42-month gap between Israel's conversion and the overwhelming sight of their pierced Savior.

Immediately following the rapture of the church, there will be no believers left on this planet. Assuming that God never leaves Himself without a witness in the world, the two witnesses will suddenly appear in Jerusalem to begin their powerful work. In the words of Alva J. McClain, founder and president of Grace Theological Seminary, "The effect of their testimony is very impressive, appearing very early in the book of Revelation and probably accounting for the martyrs seen under the fifth seal (6:9). In chapter 7 the effect greatly expands, including 144,000 Israelites (vss.3-8), and also a great multitude, which no man can number, of all nations" (vss. 9-14).[5] His colleague and successor, Herman A. Hoyt, agreed that "The importance of their testimony cannot be overestimated (Rev. 11:4)...By their testimony, it is

---

[5] Alva J. McClain, *The Greatness of the Kingdom* (Winona Lake, IN: BMH Books, 1959), 458 .

my opinion, they bring about the conversion of the 144,000 who will become the witnesses during the final half of the tribulation period."[6] In addition to my personal mentors, Alva J. McClain and Herman A. Hoyt, several others have concluded that the two witnesses will proclaim the gospel of the Kingdom (i.e., the true Gospel of the saving work of Christ as a prerequisite for entering the Kingdom) during *the first half* of the 70th week.[7]

An interesting parallel to the amazing effects of the preaching of the two witnesses may be found in the ministry of the Apostle Paul at the school of Tyrannus in Ephesus: "And this continued for two years, so that all who dwelt in Asia heard the word of the Lord Jesus, both Jews and Greeks" (Acts 19:10).

The Identity of the Two Witnesses[8]

For 2,400 years Jews have anticipated the literal return of Elijah as the forerunner of Messiah. At the Passover meal (*the Seder*), "there is an extra place setting and a special cup on the Seder table designated just for

[6] Herman A. Hoyt, *Studies in Revelation* (Winona Lake, IN: BMH Books, 1977), 74.

[7] James L. Boyer, "Notes on the Book of Revelation" (Syllabi, Christian Workman Schools of Theology), 22. See www.whitcombministries.org for more details; Gary G. Cohen, *The Chronology of the Book of Revelation*, (TH.D. Diss., Grace Theological Seminary, May 1966), 251-254 and *Understanding Revelation* (Chicago, IL: Moody Press, 1978), 46, 133-135; Tom Davis, *The Revelation of Jesus Christ* (Schroon Lake, NY: Word of Life Bible Institute, 2005), 30; Theodore Epp, *Practical Studies in Revelation* (Back to the Bible, 1970), p. 144; Arno Froese, *119 Most Frequently Asked Questions About Prophecy* (Columbia, SC: The Olive Press, 2003), 152-153; Arnold G. Fruchtenbaum, *The Footsteps of the Messiah*, rev. ed. (Tustin, CA: Ariel Ministries, 2003), 240, 250; Robert Gromacki, *Revelation* (Schaumburg, IL: Regular Baptist Press, 2000), 65-66; I.M. Haldeman, *Synopsis of the Book of Revelation*, 13 (a pamphlet series, n.d., listed in Walvoord, p. 178); Hippolytus, in *The Ante-Nicene Fathers* 5:248, col. B, nd fragment 39, 184 (documented by J.B. Smith, *A Revelation of Jesus Christ*, pp. 170-171); Thomas Ice and Timothy Demy, *Prophecy Watch* (Eugene, OR: Harvest House Pub., 1998), 160, 164; Thomas Ice, "Why Futurism?" in Tim LaHaye and Thomas Ice, *The End Times Controversy* (Eugene, OR: Harvest House, 2003), 414; Harry A. Ironside, *Revelation* (Loizeaux Bros., 1930), 191; Alan Johnson, "Revelation" in K.L. Barker and J. Kohlenburger III, eds. *The NIV Bible Commentary* (Winona Lake, IN: BMH Books, 1994), 1178; Tim LaHaye, "Twelve Reasons Why This Could Be The Terminal Generation," in *When the Trumpet Sounds,* eds. Thomas Ice and Timothy Demy, (Eugene, OR: Harvest House, 1995), 441; David Larsen, *Jews, Gentiles and the Church* (Grand Rapids, MI: Discovery House, 1995), 274, 293; David M. Levy, *Revelation: Hearing the Last Word* (Bellmawr, NJ: Friends of Israel, 1995), chart following p. 287; Robert Lightner, *Last Days Handbook* (Nashville, TN: Thomas Nelson Pub., 1997), 16; William R Newell, *The Book of Revelation* (Chicago: Moody Press, 1935), 158-160; Charles C. Ryrie, *Revelation* (Chicago: Moody Press, 1996), 84; J.B. Smith, *A Revelation of Jesus Christ* (Scottsdale, PA: Herald Press, 1961), 170-171; Wilbur M. Smith, "Revelation" in *Wycliffe Bible Commentary,* edited by C. Pfeiffer and E. Harrison, (Chicago: Moody Press, 1962), 1510; Gerald Stanton, *Kept From the Hour* (Miami Springs, FL: Schoettle Pub. Co., 1992), 187-188; Lehman Strauss, *The Book of Revelation* (Loizeaux Bros., 1964), 218; H.L. Wilmington, *The King Is Coming* (Wheaton, IL: Tyndale House Pub., 1981), 166.

[8] John C. Whitcomb, Adapted from "Elijah is Coming" in *Conservative Grace Brethren Publications* (Warsaw, IN: Lakeland Conservative Grace Brethren Church, June, 1999), 24-34. Used by permission. Cf.Timothy Demy and John C. Whitcomb, "Witnesses, Two," in Tim LaHaye and Ed Hindson, eds., *The Popular Encyclopedia of Bible Prophecy* (Eugene, OR: Harvest House, 2004), 401-403.

Elijah...The meal is followed by a prayer, and a member of the family is then asked to go to the door, open it, and see if Elijah the prophet is coming."[9] This expectation, of course, is based on the final words of the prophet Malachi at the very end of our Old Testament: "Behold, I will send you Elijah the prophet before the coming of the great and dreadful day of the LORD. And he will turn the hearts of the fathers to the children, and the hearts of the children to their fathers, lest I come and strike the earth with a curse" (Mal. 4:5-6).

When Peter, James and John beheld *Elijah* on the Mount of Transfiguration, they were astounded. Could it really be true that Elijah would personally, physically, and visibly appear as the forerunner of Christ at the inauguration of His Kingdom? A week before they climbed this mountain, the Lord Jesus had told them: "Assuredly, I say to you, there are some standing here who shall not taste death until they see the Son of Man coming in His kingdom" (Matt. 16:28). So this was a foretaste, a powerful visual aid, of the manner in which the Son of Man would return to the earth: personally, physically and visibly, in glory (cf. Acts 1:11).

But why did this foreview also include the visible presence of Elijah? Peter, James and John were very concerned about this. Coming down from the mountain, they asked the Lord: "'Why then do the scribes say that Elijah must come first?' And He answered and said, 'Indeed Elijah is coming first and will restore all things'" (Matt. 17:10-11). Thus, the Lord Jesus was agreeing with the scribes that the prophecy of Malachi should be interpreted literally, just as the chief priests and scribes had interpreted Micah 5:2 literally when they were asked concerning the birthplace of the Messiah (Matt. 2:3-6).[10]

---

[9] Scott Bruce, *The Feasts of Israel* (Bellmawr, NJ: Friends of Israel, 1997), 44, 47, 54. cf. Alfred Edersheim, *The Life and Times of Jesus the Messiah* (New York: Longman, Green, and Co., 1896), Vol. I, pp. 142, 43; Vol. II, pp. 706-09.

[10] The ultimate tragedy, of course, was the refusal of the Jews to worship Jesus when they understood perfectly His claim to be God's Son and saw His undeniable Messianic sign-miracles (John 5:18-47). Many orthodox Jews today are still waiting for a personal Messiah; but they do not believe He will have a divine nature. Peter himself, while on the Mount, was confused as to the absolute uniqueness of the Lord Jesus in contrast to Elijah and Moses (Matt. 17:4), even though God the Father had illumined him on this matter a week earlier (Matt. 16:17; cf. 2 Pet. 1: 16-18)! God's explanation for human suppression of biblical Christology is that "no one can say, 'Jesus is Lord,' except by the Holy Spirit" (1 Cor. 12:3). For a helpful study of the deity of Messiah, see Ron Rhodes, *Christ Before the Manger: The Life and Times of the Preincarnate Christ* (Grand Rapids: Baker Book House, 1992). Cf. John N. Oswalt, *The Book of Isaiah: Chapters 40-66* (Grand Rapids: Wm. B. Eerdmans Pub. Co., 1988), 328, 336.

The Greatness of John the Baptist
Now this created a great dilemma for the disciples. If Elijah was to prepare Israel for the Kingdom (which they expected to happen at any moment), when and how would he appear, and how did John the Baptist, their former (and now dead) mentor (John 1:35-40) fit into this scenario? Was not the Baptizer "the burning and shining lamp," in whose "light" the disciples "were willing to rejoice" because "he has borne witness to the truth" (John 5:33-35)? Was he not "more than a prophet" (Matt. 11:9)? Was he not the fulfillment of Isaiah 40:3 ("The voice of one crying in the wilderness: 'Prepare the way of the LORD'" cf. Matt. 3:3)? Was he not "My messenger" whom God would send "to prepare the way before Me" (Mal. 3:1; cf. Matt. 11:10)? In fact the Lord Jesus asserted that "among those born of women there has not risen one greater than John the Baptist" (Matt. 11:11). Thus, in the mind of our Lord, John was personally and prophetically at least as great as Enoch, Noah, Abraham, Isaac, Jacob, Joseph, Moses, Joshua, David, Solomon, Isaiah, Jeremiah, Ezekiel, Daniel, -- and even Elijah!

Israel's Responsibility
It is perfectly clear, then, that it was not because of some lack of dedication or wisdom that John the Baptizer failed to bring Israel to the place of spiritual readiness to acknowledge Jesus of Nazareth as the long-awaited Messiah. The national rejection of Jesus was entirely the fault of the people and their leaders! With respect to John, therefore, our Lord explained: "If you are willing to receive it, he is Elijah, who is to come" (Matt. 11:14). Then, amazingly, He added: "'Elijah has come already, and they did not know him, but did to him whatever they wished'…Then the disciples understood that He spoke to them of John the Baptist" (Matt. 17:12-13).

Thus, *John could have been Elijah if Israel had accepted his message.* This is a theme that dominates the entire Bible – *men are responsible moral agents before God*, and can never reject this accountability by arguing that since *God is the sovereign LORD of history* they cannot make genuine choices (cf. Rom. 9:18-24). Judas Iscariot could have reasoned: "Since my betrayal of the Messiah has been predestined [e.g., Luke 22:22a – "truly, the Son of Man goes as it has been determined…"], I have been deprived of my freedom of choice, and am therefore innocent!" But our Lord, anticipating such depraved thinking, added: "but woe to that man by whom He is betrayed!" (Luke 22:22b; cf. Acts 2:23 concerning the entire nation). Thus, Joseph could say to his murderous brothers: "As for you, you meant evil against me, but God meant it for good, in order to…save many people alive" (Gen. 50:20).

There are at least three reasons for concluding that John was *not* Elijah. First, the angel Gabriel announced to Zacharias the priest concerning his son John: "He will also go before Him *in the spirit and power of Elijah*" (Luke 1:17). Therefore, he was not literally Elijah. Second, our Lord stated, soon after the death of John, "Elijah is coming first and will restore all things" (Matt. 17:11). Thus, the Lord Jesus interpreted Malachi's prophecy literally: "Behold, I am going to send you Elijah the prophet..." (Mal. 4:5). Third, the leaders of Israel confronted John with a direct question: "Are you Elijah?" His answer was unequivocal: "I am not" (John 1:21).

However, in spite of the fact that John was not Elijah, *his offer of the Kingdom to Israel was absolutely genuine*: "Repent, for the kingdom of heaven is at hand" (Matt. 3:2). This identical appeal was made by our Lord, and by the Twelve and the Seventy. Therefore, no Jew could say, "We never heard a clear and genuine offer of the Kingdom!"

The Theological Antinomy

But here we must face a great theological antinomy, namely, an apparent contradiction of logic that mere human intelligence cannot resolve: first, *the offer* of the Kingdom was absolutely genuine. *The contingency* was this: *the coming of the Kingdom was dependent upon the believing response of the nation of Israel.* Without national repentance on the part of God's chosen people, there can be no Messianic kingdom on this earth (see Romans 11:12, 15, 25-29, and many Old Testament prophecies). Also for individuals, whether Jew or Gentile, there can be no salvation without genuine faith in God and His Word. This is a fundamental reality in all human history under God.

Second, at the same time, God had planned from all eternity that the Kingdom offer would be rejected at Christ's first coming, and would be accepted at His second coming. [11] Yes, we always need to be reminded of Deut. 29:29, "The secret things belong to the LORD our God, but those things which are revealed belong to us and to our children forever," and Isaiah 55:8-9, "'For My thoughts are not your thoughts, nor are your ways My ways,' says the LORD. 'For as the heavens are higher than the earth, so are My ways higher than your ways, and My thoughts than your thoughts.'"

No Jew could escape the ultimate urgency of the Baptizer's message by reasoning: "John himself admits that he is not Elijah. Therefore, since the

---

[11] Arnold G. Fruchtenbaum has pointed out, in light of Mark 9:9-13, that "if Elijah had come before the first coming of Christ and restored all things, then the prophecies of the sufferings of the first coming would remain unfulfilled" (*The Footsteps of the Messiah* [Tustin, CA: Ariel Press, 1982], p. 90.).

Kingdom cannot come until Elijah appears, we have no need to humble ourselves before this non-Elijah!" To excuse themselves, the Jewish leaders finally concluded that John had a demon! (cf. Matt. 11:18).

A similar urgent responsibility rests upon people today. No one, however exalted (in political, social, economic, educational, or scientific realms), may dismiss the urgency of the Gospel message because of the personality traits of the messenger. Like the Corinthians long ago, people in our day sometimes make a great issue of who won them to the Lord and/or baptized them. Paul's response to the Corinthians was pointed: "Who then is Paul, and who is Apollos, but ministers through whom you believed, as the Lord gave to each one" (1 Cor. 3:5; cf. 1:12-17; 3:21-23; 4:6).

John's appearance and life-style (like Elijah's – 2 Kings 1:8; cf. Zech. 13:4) were not impressive to sophisticated Jews: a garment of camel's hair and a diet of locusts and wild honey (Matt. 3:4). Who among the leaders would want to be identified with such a strange-looking character? But God intended for his appearance to be a rebuke to the luxurious materialism of the royal family and the Pharisees and the priests (Matt. 11:8). Many of the common people, however, did respond to his powerful preaching (Matt. 3:5-6; 11:12; 21:26).

Thus, to summarize the antinomy: God assures us, on the basis of His unchangeable foreknowledge, that Elijah – not John – will bring the nation to repentance. But human responsibility required that John's message be received with genuine repentance and faith, just as fervently as if Elijah himself had been God's messenger.

Has Elijah Been Glorified?

Elijah is coming back as a messenger to Israel. But how can he come back to the earth in a physical, mortal body? Was he not last seen being swept "to heaven" by a whirlwind (2 Kings 2:11)? This is a major reason why many evangelical theologians deny that Elijah can literally return to the earth and be killed (Rev. 11:7). If Elijah was glorified without dying, how can he return to the earth and die?

A very important factor in solving this problem may be found in our Lord's statement: "No one has ascended to heaven, but...the Son of Man" (John 3:13). In the immediate context, our Lord was explaining to Nicodemus that He alone could testify concerning things in heaven, because He alone had been there. While this statement sheds significant light on our Lord's unique authority to speak of "heavenly things," His statement also seems to exclude the possibility that anyone, including Enoch and Elijah, could ever have ascended to the third heaven.

Furthermore, the Lord Jesus was "the first fruits of those who have fallen asleep," in the sense of receiving a glorified body; and no one else will receive such a body until "those who are Christ's" have that inconceivably marvelous experience "at His coming" (1 Cor. 15:20-23). Technically, of course, it could be argued that our Lord was referring only to a resurrection from the dead, and that neither Enoch nor Elijah had died. But, in the light of the "first fruits" statement of 1 Corinthians 15:20, 23, it is very difficult to believe that two men could have been physically glorified before the Savior was glorified.

Renald E. Showers agrees that "Enoch and Elijah did not receive glorified bodies when God took them from the earth." But he also finds strong evidence in Hebrews 11:5 that Enoch did not "see" (=experience; cf. Luke 2:26) death. The text states that the very purpose for God's taking Enoch was so that he should not experience death.[12] So we are left with the question of Enoch's condition after he was "taken up." A similar question may be asked concerning Korah, Dathan and Abiram who "went down alive into the pit [Sheol]" (Num. 16:33). My understanding would be that they *did* die after disappearing from the sight of men.

After the glorification of Christ, the apostle Paul "was caught up to the third heaven...into Paradise" (2 Cor. 12:2, 4). But he was not glorified, for the experience was temporary, and he returned to the earth with a mortal body (complete with a sin nature) and finally died. The truly amazing statement, however, is that he didn't know whether his brief visit in heaven was "in the body or apart from the body" (12:2-3). Renald Showers sees 2 Corinthians 12:2-4, therefore, as indicating that Paul "believed in the possibility of a human being in a mortal body being caught up to and existing in God's heaven for some period of time."[13]

This brings us again to the fascinating statement of Hebrews 11:5 – "By faith Enoch was taken away so that he did not see death." The termination of his life on earth was totally different from that of any before him – he simply disappeared! Now it should be noted that two other God-honored men in the Old Testament shared the distinction of leaving this world with no one seeing them dying or dead – *Moses* (Deut. 32:48-52; 34:1-6) and *Elijah* (2 Kings 2:11-14). The author of Hebrews stated: "...it is appointed for men to die once" (9:27). However, the "mystery" (divine truth

---

[12] Personal correspondence, Nov. 4, 1998.
[13] Ibid.

once hidden but now revealed) of the rapture of the Body and Bride of Christ without dying (1 Cor. 15:51-52; 1 Thess. 4:15-17) is the glorious exception to this "die-once" rule. But is it really legitimate to stretch this exception to include Enoch or Elijah? Old Testament saints were not members of the Body and Bride of Christ to whom this "blessed hope" was exclusively given (cf. Eph. 3:4-10). That Enoch entered the realm of the righteous dead[14] without dying seems to be the teaching of Hebrews 11:5. That he was physically glorified is highly unlikely.

Enoch did not "see death." But the Scriptures do *not* say this of Elijah. In fact, there seems to be some support for the concept that Elijah finally did die after he was caught up by a whirlwind. Nearly 900 years after that event, three of our Lord's disciples saw *Moses* (who had died 1,400 years earlier) and *Elijah* together (Matt. 17:1-8). Since Moses could not have had a glorified body (cf. 1 Cor. 15:20, 23), the implication is quite strong that Elijah did not either. Like Samuel 1,000 years earlier (1 Sam. 28:15), they were temporarily "brought up" from their place of rest in the "Paradise" of pre-resurrection-of-Christ history (cf. Luke 23:43 with 2 Cor. 12:2-4 and Eph. 4:8-10), which our Lord also described as "Abraham's bosom" (Luke 16:22), and which was located at that time in "the heart of the earth" (Matt. 12:40 cf. 1 Pet. 3:19).

Moses and Elijah appeared briefly to Peter, James and John, but had nothing to say to them. Instead, they were conversing with their Lord. As they "talked with Him" (Luke 9:30), they "spoke of His decease [Gk. *exodus* = a euphemism for His death] which He was about to accomplish at Jerusalem" (Luke 9:31). They were presumably concerned about the fact that not until their great King/Priest/Messiah shed His blood upon the Cross could they be fully redeemed. However, in the meantime, they had been redeemed, like Abraham (Gen. 15:6), as it were "on credit," because the blood payment of the Lamb of God for pre-Calvary believers was already accomplished in the mind of God (cf. Rom. 3:25-26; Eph. 1:3-11). If Elijah was concerned about the "decease" which his Lord was soon to accomplish in Jerusalem, the implication is that he (like Moses) had not yet been physically glorified. Thus, the fact that they appeared "in glory" on the mount was merely a temporary foretaste of their ultimate glorification at the time of Christ's Second Coming. A significant analogy to this experience may be seen in the face of Moses which glowed brightly after he communed with God on Mount Sinai (Exodus 34:29-35).

---

[14] Our Lord described this place as "Abraham's bosom" (Lk. 16:22), "Paradise" (Lk 23:43) and a special realm within Sheol/Hades before His resurrection (Lk. 16:23).

On the basis of these theological inferences, then, we understand that Elijah will be brought back from the dead (like Lazarus and several others) to mortal life, and to die again three-and-one-half years later (Rev. 11:3-13). In Bible times God raised some people from the dead *after only a few hours,* and Lazarus *after four days* (when it was evident to everyone that his body was decomposing [John 11:39]). The main point at issue here, however, is that God is not limited by time or by the availability of any part of a person's physical body in order to perform the miracle of glorious resurrection, or even the miracle of resuscitation/restoration to mortal life.

We read in 1 Corinthians 15:38 that God gives "to each seed its own body," and "that which you sow [in death and burial], you do not sow that body that shall be." This is the basic reality of all resurrections. On the human level, we might describe it this way: God knows the unique "blueprint" or "DNA information code" of every human being, and is perfectly capable of giving a person a glorified body, and even another mortal body (complete with the original sin nature) after thousands of years.

Elijah and Moses

Yes, Elijah is coming back to this earth again, and he will not come alone as he did at the beginning of his first ministry. Rarely does God send a servant into a significant ministry without a coworker. Robert L. Thomas has observed: "The OT required two witnesses as competent legal testimony to secure a conviction (Deut. 17:6; 19:15; Num. 35:30; cf. Heb. 10:28). Jesus also made the number two a minimum to confirm a point of discipline (Matt. 18:16) or verify truth (John 8:17). Paul too alluded to the need of a plurality of witnesses to validate a judgment (2 Cor. 13:1; 1 Tim. 5:19)."[15]

But who will be Elijah's companion witness? Many have suggested *Enoch;* but this great antediluvian saint and prophet would not be an appropriate fellow-witness with Elijah in *a prophetic ministry directed exclusively to Israel.* Far more appropriate for such a unique function would be *Moses.* For future apostate Israel, after the rapture of the Church, no man in her entire history would have greater respect and appreciation than Moses. In fact, Moses is named *80* times in the New Testament (compared to Abraham, 73 times, David 59 times and Elijah *29* times)! God raised up these men *to confront Israel in times of deep apostasy.* Moses was God's great deliverer and lawgiver for Israel, of whom He said: "There has not arisen in Israel a prophet like Moses, whom the LORD knew face to face, in all the signs and wonders which the LORD sent him to do in the land of Egypt…and

---

[15] Robert L. Thomas, *Revelation 8-22: An Exegetical Commentary* (Chicago, IL: Moody Press, 1995), 87.

by all that mighty power and all the great terror which Moses performed in the sight of all Israel" (Deut. 34:10-12). By the time our Lord appeared in Israel, the Jews actually thought that *Moses* had given them the bread in the wilderness (John 6:32).

As for *Elijah*, surely one of the greatest of the prophets, God answered his humble prayer (cf. 1 Kings 18:36-37) by sending *fire from heaven* to consume his sacrifice on Mount Carmel and thus to defeat the 450 prophets of Baal; and finally to vindicate him by means of "a chariot of fire and horses of fire" to escort him out of Satan's world (2 Kings 2:11).[16] When he was almost overwhelmed by the spiritual darkness of Israel under the demonic Jezebel, Elijah identified himself with Moses by fleeing to "*the* cave" (Heb: *ha-m* ^{e} ' *ārâ*) where Moses 600 years earlier was hidden by God as His glory passed by (1 Kings 19:9; Exod. 33:21-23). So highly did the Jews of Jesus' day think of Elijah, that when they saw His miracles, some concluded that Elijah had returned (Matt. 16:14). Also when our Savior cried out from the cross, "Eli, Eli…," they believed He was "calling for Elijah" to save Him! (Matt. 27:47-49; Mark 15:35-36).[17]

When the two witnesses appear in Jerusalem at the beginning of the Seventieth Week, "they immediately begin their prophetic ministry. Just prior to this (hours, days, weeks?) the rapture will have removed all believers from the earth. Therefore, there will be no one to train these two witnesses, and no time to train them. They must be men already possessing full knowledge of the Scriptures and well seasoned for such a demanding ministry. Moses was the lawgiver; Elijah was the law-enforcer. Both will be men of experience. They will be perfectly equipped for a ministry to Israel before a world-wide audience."[18]

Neither Moses nor Elijah ever entered Jerusalem, though Moses might have seen it from a distance (Deut. 34:2), and Elijah wrote a letter of judgment to one of the worst kings Jerusalem ever knew (2 Chron. 21:12-15). And, as we have seen, both Moses and Elijah, emerging temporarily from "Paradise" to appear on the Mount of Transfiguration, were very concerned about something soon to happen in Jerusalem. (cf. Luke 9:31)

---

[16] "The mystery surrounding Moses' death (Jude 9) and the translation of Elijah offer some corroborations of these as the two witnesses" – Robert L. Thomas, op. cit., p. 88.

[17] See the high praise of Elijah, who will "restore the tribes of Jacob," in *Ecclesiasticus* (Sirach) 48:10. Cf. H. Bietenhard, "Elijah," in Colin Brown, ed., *Dictionary of New Testament Theology* (Grand Rapids: Zondervan, 1975) I, pp. 543-45.

[18] Personal communication from Scott M. Libby, Pastor of the Grace Brethren Church, Coventry, VT, September 20, 1998.

The Lord Jesus said that "it cannot be that a prophet should perish outside of Jerusalem" (Luke 13:33)! In the light of this statement, it is noteworthy that these two great Israelite prophets will not only enter Jerusalem, but will experience their second and final physical death in its streets at the hands of "the beast that ascends out of the bottomless pit" at the mid-point of the Seventieth Week (Rev. 11:7-10; cf. Dan. 9:27).

One of the most convincing evidences that *Elijah* and *Moses* will be the two witnesses in Revelation 11 is the nature of the judgment-miracles these men will perform. "If anyone wants to harm them, fire proceeds from their mouth and devours their enemies...These have power to shut heaven, so that no rain falls in the days of their prophecy; and they have power over waters to turn them to blood, and to strike the earth with all plagues, as often as they desire" (Rev. 11:5-6). The first two types of judgments listed were those which *Elijah* inflicted upon Israel (three-and-one-half years of drought — 1 Kings 17:1; cf. Luke 4:25; James 5:17; and fire from heaven upon two military detachments sent by King Ahaziah to capture Elijah — 2 Kings 1:10, 12); and the second two types of judgments (blood from water and a variety of plagues) were those which *Moses* inflicted upon Egypt (Ex. 7-12).

Why are Elijah and Moses not named as the two witnesses in Revelation 11? Perhaps the Old Testament and the Gospels are so clear on this point that the Holy Spirit deemed it unnecessary to identify them by name. Would not the final words God addressed to Israel in the Old Testament have been sufficient?[19] "Remember the Law of *Moses*, My servant, which I commanded him in Horeb for all Israel with the statutes and judgments [cf. Matt. 24:20]. Behold, I will send you *Elijah* (italics added) the prophet..." (Mal. 4:4-5).[20]

---

[19] It must be emphasized that the book of Revelation stands solidly upon the Old Testament, like the capstone of a pyramid upon all the levels of stone beneath it. "Of the 404 verses of the Apocalypse, there are 278 which contain references to the Jewish scriptures" (cited by Walvoord, op. cit., p. 31).

[20] Among those who identify one of the two witnesses as Elijah are: William Barclay, *The Revelation of John*, Vol 2, rev. ed. (Philadelphia: Westminster Press, 1976): "much more likely the witnesses are Elijah and Moses," 70; James L. Boyer, *op. cit.*: "one would be Elijah...the other would probably be Moses," *21;* M.R. DeHaan, *Revelation* (Grand Rapids, MI: Zondervan, 1946): "Elijah and Moses," 159; H.W. Frost, *Matthew 24 and the Revelation* (New York & Oxford, 1924): "Moses and Elijah," 144. (cited by C. Keener, p. 290); Herman A. Hoyt, *Studies in Revelation* (Winona Lake, IN: BMH Books, 1977): "Without a doubt, one of these witnesses is Elijah...Moses may be the other," 75; Robert Govett, *The Apocalypse* (London: C. J. Thynne, 1920): "Elijah and Enoch", 225-250. Cited by Walvoord, op. cit., 179; Craig S. Keener, *The NIV Application Commentary* (Grand Rapids, MI: Zondervan, 2000): "Hippolytus, Tertullian, and Jerome believed Enoch and Elijah remained alive and would return as witnesses...such a view is not impossible. See SIR 48:10; SIFRE DEUT 41:4:3; 342; 5:2; 4 Ezra 6:26," 290-91; David Larsen, *Jews, Gentiles and the Church* (Grand Rapids, MI: Discovery House, 1995): "Probably Moses and Elijah," 293; Hal Lindsey, *New World Coming*: "Elijah and Moses" 162-63 (cited by C. Keener, p. 290); John MacArthur, *Revelation 1-11* (Chicago, IL: Moody Press, 1999): "They may be Moses and Elijah," 300; Alva J McClain, *The Greatness of*

Conclusion

The true Church is not destined to see the Antichrist or the two witnesses in Jerusalem. Our "blessed hope" is to see Christ our Bridegroom and our Head (Titus 2:13; 2 Cor. 11:2). Nevertheless, our covenant-keeping God also has a special appointment for His Chosen People Israel (Rom. 11:25-32); and that appointment includes national repentance through the prophetic ministry of Elijah (and Moses). Even before "the great and terrible day of the LORD" (the second half of the Seventieth Week) begins, Zion will "give birth to her children" (Isa. 66:8), and through them (presumably disciples of the two witnesses), "this gospel of the kingdom will be preached in all the world as a witness to all the nations" (Matt. 24:14). When contemplating the destiny of ethnic Israel in the light of the unconditional and thus unbreakable Abrahamic Covenant promises[21], we can only say with Paul, "Oh, the depth of the riches both of the wisdom and knowledge of God! How unsearchable are His judgments and His ways past finding out!" (Rom. 11:33).[22]

---

the Kingdom (Winona Lake, IN: BMH Books, 1959): "As to their identity, one is most certainly Elijah," 457; Henry M. Morris, The Revelation Record (Wheaton, IL: Tyndale House, 1983): "it does seem quite probable that [Enoch and Elijah] will be Christ's two witnesses," 194-95; Walter K. Price, The Coming Antichrist (Chicago, IL: Moody Press, 1974): "Moses and Elijah," 194; Walter Scott, Exposition of the Revelation of Jesus Christ (London, England: Pickering & Inglis Ltd., n.d.): "Probably Elijah and Moses," 230; J.A. Seiss, The Apocalypse (Grand Rapids, MI: Zondervan, n.d.): "Elijah and Enoch" (a very detailed discussion), 244-54; J.B. Smith, A Revelation of Jesus Christ (Scottsdale, PA: Herald Press, 1961): "Moses and Elijah," 169; The Targums (Aramaic Translation/Interpretation of the Hebrew Bible, cited by H. Dietenhard, op. cit., p. 544): God will "gather the diaspora through Elijah and Moses;" Merrill Tenney, Earth's Coming King: Revelation (Wheaton, IL: Scripture Press, 1977): "Elijah and Moses," 55; Robert Thomas, op. cit.: "the balance of the evidence is for an expectation of the actual return of [Moses and Elijah]," 89.

[21] For a masterful refutation of "replacement theology," namely, that the Church has permanently replaced Israel, see Ronald E. Diprose, Israel and the Church: the Origin and Effects of Replacement Theology (Johnson City, TN: STL Distribution, 2004).

[22] For more information on this subject, listen to Dr. Whitcomb's recording, "Background to 'The Two Witnesses of Revelation 11,'" at www.sermonaudio.com/whitcomb.

"If the yet unfulfilled prophecies of the Old Testament made in the Abrahamic, Davidic, and new covenants are to be literally fulfilled, there must be a future period, the Millennium, in which they can be fulfilled, for the church is not now fulfilling them. "

- Charles C. Ryrie

Dispensationalism, 1995, page 147

18

The Realization of Ezekiel's Temple

Jerry Hullinger

Introduction

The remarkable content of Ezekiel 40-48[1] has been viewed by many as the Achilles' heel of dispensationalism. In this passage Ezekiel[2] pictured a temple in which sacrificial ritual was taking place. It is asserted that restoration of a sacrificial system during the millennium (as claimed by most dispensationalists)

---

[1] The unity and authenticity of Ezekiel, including 40-48, has been targeted for over fifty years (for a detailed history, see S. R. Driver, *Introduction to the literature of the Old Testament, xix-xxiii*). Many see 40-48 as non-genuine based on style and content (G. A Cooke, "Some Considerations on the Text and Teaching of Ezekiel 40-48." *Zeitschrift fur die alttestamentliche Wissenschaft* 42 [1924]: 105-115; Walther Eichrodt *Ezekiel: A Commentary*, [Philadelphia: Westminster, 1970]: 550-551; Walther Zimmerli, *Ezekiel* [Philadelphia: Fortress, 1979]: 2:549). Consequently, 40-48 is viewed as an appendage to the work as a whole. Summarily, there are at least eight reasons for the complete unity of the book: 1) the former view assumes the documentary hypothesis, 2) the book has a balanced and perspicacious structure, 3) the book as an inner consistency with the center being the destruction of Jerusalem (John Taylor, *Ezekiel* Tyndale Old Testament Commentary [Downers Grove: InterVarsity, 1969], 15-16), 4) the book does evince a uniformity in style and language. Though this has been called into question, see Greenberg's comparison of Ezekiel with the Qumran Temple Scroll, the Sefire Treaties, and the Hittite Instructions for Temple Officials (Greenberg, "The Design and Themes of Ezekiel's Program of Restoration," *Interpretation* 38 [1984]: 185-189), 5) a clear, chronological sequence of the work, 6) an autobiographical flavor throughout, 7) the person of Ezekiel is consistent throughout (R. K. Harrison. *Introduction to the Old Testament* [Grand Rapids: Eerdmans, 1977]: 838), and 8) the lack of unanimity as to which portions of 40-48 are genuine (cf. Zimmerili. 2:547//Eichrodt. 530). This shows the unreliability of reconstructing an accurate redactionist history (see also, Ralph Klein, *Ezekiel: The Prophet and His Message* [Columbia: University of South Carolina Press, 1988]: 170; and, Niditch's argument for unity based on the parallels between Ezekiel 40-48 with the victories and enthronements of Marduk and Baal (Susan Niditch, "Ezekiel 40-48 in a Visionary Context," *Catholic Biblical Quarterly* 48 [1986]: 221).

[2] In answer to the charge that Ezekiel was mentally unstable (W. F. Albright, *From the Stone Age to Christianity* 325: Edwin Broome, "Ezekiel's Abnormal Personality," *Journal of Biblical Literature* 65 (1946): 291), see Harrison, *Introduction to the Old Testament*, 850: Klein, *Ezekiel: The Prophet and His Message*, 8; Timothy Polk, "Paradigms, Parables, and Mesalim: On Reading the Masal in Scripture," *Catholic Biblical Quarterly* 45 (1983): 564-83; David Fishelov. "The Prophet as Satirist," *Prooftexts*, 9 (1989): 195-211; Stephen Garfinkel. "Another Model for Ezekiel's Abnormalities," *Journal of the Ancient Near Eastern Society* 19 (1989): 39-50; Daniel Tropper, "Ezekiel's Role: An Unconscious Dimension in Prophecy," *Tradition* 12 (1971): 44-54.

cannot be reconciled with the finished work of Christ. Snowden likened this to returning to a "withered and empty husk."[3] Hamilton wrote that this idea is a "dishonor to the sacrifice of Christ."[4] And Hughes averred that this is "apostasy" and the "saddest feature of the millennial scheme."[5]

While the issue of millennial sacrifices has been dealt with elsewhere,[6] there is another question which is prologue to the entire discussion that must be answered by all sides. When will Ezekiel's temple vision be realized? If the temple envisioned was fulfilled in the past, or spiritually in the church instead of during the millennium, the query into animal sacrifice is moot. It is the proposition of this section that the temple will be realized during the kingdom[7] age. If this can be demonstrated to be the best explanation of the text, then this strengthens the dispensational view of a renewed sacrificial system in the future as well as buttressing its *sine qua non*. On the other hand, there is also a burden of proof on those who deny a future sacrificial system. They must first prove that the temple is *not* future before their position can have validity.

---

[3] James Snowden, *The Coming of the Lord* (New York: The MacMillan Co., 1919), 207.

[4] Floyd Hamilton, *The Basis of the Millennial Faith* (Grand Rapids: Eerdmans, 1942), 40, 42.

[5] Archibald Hughes, *A New Heaven and a New Earth* (Philadelphia: The Presbyterian and Reformed Publishing Co., 1958), 157. See also Curtis Crenshaw, *Dispensationalism Today, Yesterday, and Tomorrow* (Memphis: Footstool Publications, 1985), 238; Loraine Boettner, *The Millennium* (Philadelphia: The Presbyterian and Reformed Publishing Co., 1959), 93, 95, 96; Oswald Allis, *Prophecy and the Church* (Philadelphia: The Presbyterian and Reformed Publishing Co., 1973), 243, 246-247; Patrick Fairbairn, *An Exposition of Ezekiel*, reprint ed., (Grand Rapids: Zondervan, 1969), 441; Taylor, *Ezekiel*, 252-253. Referring to dispensationalism's layout of other eschata, Reymond asserts: "With such eschatological confusion running rampant today in scholarly circles, never has the need been greater to return to Scripture and to see what God's Word says concerning this vital, all-important, capstoning locus of theology" (Robert Reymond, *A New Systematic Theology of the Christian Faith* [Nashville: Thomas Nelson, 1998]: 986); Gary DeMar, *Last Days Madness: Obsession of the Modern Church* (Atlanta: American Vision, Inc., 1997), vii, ix; Keith Mathison, *Dispensationalism: Rightly Dividing the People of God?* (Phillipsburg, NJ: P & R Publishing, 1995), 7.

[6] For an alternative to the memorial view, see Jerry Hullinger, "The Problem of Animal Sacrifices in Ezekiel 40-48," *Bibliotheca Sacra* 152 (1995): 279-89; "The Divine Presence, Uncleanness, and Ezekiel's Millennial Sacrifices," *Bibliotheca Sacra* 163 (2006): 405-422; "Two Atonement Realms: Reconciling Sacrifice in Ezekiel and Hebrews, *Journal of Dispensational Theology* 32 (2007): 33-64; John Whitcomb, "Christ's Atonement and Animal Sacrifices in Israel, *Grace Theological Journal* 6 (1985): 201-217.

[7] The writer is using the term "kingdom" in this context as synonymous with "millennium." However, the mediatorial idea of the kingdom is traceable as far back as Eden and developed throughout the Old Testament by means of the covenants. This kingdom will be instituted at the Second Advent.

The Time of Realization for the Temple

The Ideal View

There have been several proposals as to when the temple of Ezekiel is to be, or was, realized. Some have taken the temple vision of Ezekiel as an apocalyptic dream or ideal in which God gave to Ezekiel an ethereal vision of what God would do for His people. Craigie wrote:

> Only in the vision did this marvelous temple exist; it was a sign to him that God would not always be absent from His people...but the prophet is not prophesying a physical and geographical transformation; rather, in the symbolism of the vision, he is anticipating the extraordinary transformation that would overcome the people of Israel, when once again the temple in their midst was the residence of God.[8]

Taylor suggested in a similar fashion that "the vision of the temple was in fact a kind of incarnation of all that God stood for and all that He required and all that He could do for His people in the age that was about to dawn."[9] Allen concurred when he suggested that "memories blend with hopes and create a condition of trance in which what was active in his waking moments now takes shape before him in symbolic forms."[10] This, Allen felt, came on Ezekiel because he was musing on recollections of the Solomonic temple which were blended in his mind with the possibility of a fresh beginning in the life of his people. And finally, Abba stated that "Ezekiel's vision of a new temple...is a symbolic representation of Yahweh dwelling in holiness in the midst of His people."[11]

---

[8] Peter Craigie, *Ezekiel* (Philadelphia: Westminster, 1983), 281, 313. Another part of this view which creates problems is the characteristic statement by Craigie that "the writing is apocalyptic in style expressing in a profoundly symbolic manner the nature of the restored Israel that God would establish in the future" (275). There seems to be no textual basis to corroborate his statement of the "profoundly symbolic manner" of the passage. The text seems to militate against this understanding. Further, granting the fact of a "restored Israel that God would establish in the future" is the issue of what form this would take. Assuming for sake of argument that a futuristic view of 40-48 is correct, how much clearer could this have been set forth by God through the prophet?

[9] Taylor, *Ezekiel*, 253.

[10] E. L. Allen, "Lamentations, Ezekiel, Daniel, Twelve Prophets," in *The Interpreter's Bible*, ed. George Buttrick, vol. 6 (Nashville: Abingdon Press, 1956), 283.

[11] Raymond Abba, "Priests and Levites in Ezekiel," *Vetus Testamentum* 28 (1978): 2. Another apparent proponent of this view is Levenson: "In sum, the order defined by the vision is still a goal to be effected through human striving and was understood as such by the tradition....It is only because Ezekiel fell into an ecstasy that he or his school presents the program of restoration as an eschatological vision....It is purely ideal....The service of man in his ideal condition can and must render to God" (Jon Levenson, *The Theology of the Program of Restoration of Ezekiel 40—48* [Missoula, MO: Scholars Press, 1976], 46, 116, 129). Other adherents to this view are Moshe Greenberg, "The Design and Themes of Ezekiel's Program of Restoration," *Interpretation* 38 (1984): 181-208; John Wevers, *Ezekiel*, reprint ed., (Grand Rapids:

This view grasps the spirit of what God wanted to do for His people; however, it fails in that it is unable to do justice to the details given by Ezekiel. If the point of the vision were simply to present the symbolic truth that God would one day dwell in the midst of His people, why would Ezekiel give nine chapters of specific measurements and regulations? A possible answer to this question is that Ezekiel was presenting a truth in a way that was familiar to his audience. While it is valid to assume that he was presenting a truth in a familiar way, this point becomes invalid when it is realized that Ezekiel's picture of the temple is contradictory in many ways to the temple with which he was familiar, as well as to the priestly regulations set forth in the Pentateuch.

It is easily demonstrable that there are glaring dissimilarities between Moses' and Ezekiel's schemes.[12] Concerning the subtractions from the Mosaic system, Haran observed that

> There is neither ark nor cherubim in the inner sanctum of Ezekiel's temple, neither table for the showbread, no lampstand in its outer sanctum, no anointing oil within the temple or in the court.... Ezekiel's code and P agree on the principle that the

---

Eerdmans, 1982), 343; Walther Eichrodt, *Ezekiel*, 542; George Berry, "The Composition of the Book of Ezekiel," *Journal of Biblical Literature* 58 (1939): 172. And Moeller stated that "the whole is an ideal scheme" (Wilhelm Moeller, "Ezekiel," in *The International Standard Bible Encyclopedia*, ed. James Orr, vol. 2 [Grand Rapids: Eerdmans, 1980], 1078). See also, Keith Carley, *The Book of the Prophet Ezekiel* (Cambridge: University Press, 1974), 267; Crawford Toy, *The Book of Ezekiel* (New York: Dodd, Mead, & Co., 1899), 177; G. C. M. Douglas, "Ezekiel's Temple," *ET* 9 (1897/98): 517; F. W. Farrar, "The Last Nine Chapters of Ezekiel," *The Expositor* 9 (1899): 7-9; Toni Craven, *Ezekiel, Daniel* (Collegeville, MN: Liturgical Press, 1986), 83. Daniel Block also seems to fall under this view in his fine commentary when he writes that "it seems best to interpret chs. 40-48 ideationally....Ezekiel's final vision presents a lofty spiritual ideal: Where God is, there is Zion" (Daniel Block, *The Book of Ezekiel: Chapters 25-48* [Grand Rapids: Eerdmans, 1998], 505, 506). Some even argue that perhaps we have measurements which are "units in a complex numerological system" (Joseph Blenkinsopp, *Interpretation—A Bible Commentary for Teaching and Preaching—Ezekiel* [Louisville: John Knox Press, 1990], 199). Even those who take a literal view of the temple will toy with this idea: "The eight steps that lead to the inner court of the sanctuary (40:31, 34, 37) will be eight literal steps, but they are also a symbol of the Messiah, who is 'the way' of access to fellowship with God (John 14:6)....Why not seven or five or fifteen? Eight seems to have symbolized the Messiah" (Lamar Cooper, *Ezekiel*, The New American Commentary [Nashville: Broadman & Holman, 1994], 353, 373).

[12] It could be objected that these subtractions are arguments from silence. While arguments from silence are not normally weighty, this instance seems to be different. Ezekiel was a priest who was obviously concerned about meticulous detail. It would seem strange for him to omit some of the key elements found in the Mosaic system with this in mind. In addition, Ezekiel introduces changes from the Mosaic scheme. This suggests that these were purposeful omissions because he was describing a semi-new arrangement.

priesthood is the exclusive right of a certain part of the tribe of Levi, but they differ as concerns the identity and extent of that part.[13]

Regarding additions to the Mosaic system, West pointed out:

> The entrance of the glory into Ezekiel's temple to dwell there forever; the living waters that flow, enlarging from beneath the altar; the suburbs, the wonderful trees of healing, the new distribution of the land according to the 12 tribes, the Prince's portion, and the city's new name, "Jehovah-Shammah" all go to prove that New Israel is a converted people worshipping God in spirit and in truth.[14]

Hence, if Ezekiel were simply presenting a spiritual truth in an apocalyptic dream in language with which he was familiar, it is very strange that he would diverge from the temple he knew as well as standard cultic practices laid down in the Levitical law.

A further difficulty with this position is that 40-48 really gives no textual clues that it is to be interpreted symbolically. This is in stark contrast to other visions in the book where unrealistic characters are present (e.g. ch. 1).[15]

The Historical View
The historical view of Ezekiel's temple realizes the weaknesses of the first view and therefore attempts to find a historical fulfillment for chapters 40-48. The historical referents for this realization are said to be either the

---

[13] Menahem Haran, "The Law-Code of Ezekiel 40-48 and its Relation to the Priestly School," *Hebrew Union College Annual* 50 (1979): 61. Other omissions include: the ark of the covenant, manna, Aaron's rod, mercy seat, etc. Greenberg observed: "Very strange is the absence of a wall around the inner court.... No equivalent to the lavers or to the bronze sea appears in the outer court....All of these concerns and adjustments to later institutions are beyond the horizon of the priestly legislation of the Pentateuch" (Greenberg, "The Design and Themes of Ezekiel's Program of Restoration," 206). And Douglas made this startling contrast: "This leaving the entrance to the most holy place wide open is the more remarkable, when we contrast with it the arrangement by which the outer east gate of the house was kept shut, because Jehovah had entered by it in his glory....The restriction of Leviticus 16:2 was at an end. Every priest at any time might go within the veil, or rather where the veil had been; for Ezekiel's temple had no veil" (George Douglas, "Ezekiel's Temple," 366. See also, Cooke, *A Critical and Exegetical Commentary on the Book of Ezekiel*, reprint ed., [Edinburgh: T & T Clark, 1967], 466; George Berry, "The Composition of the Book of Ezekiel," 173ff.; John Skinner, "The Book of Ezekiel," in *The Expositor's Bible*, ed. W. Robertson Nicoll, vol. 4 [New York: Wilbur Ketcham Publishers, n.d.], 338; Hals, *Ezekiel*, 311; Ralph Alexander, "Ezekiel," in *The Expositor's Bible Commentary*, ed. Frank Gaebelein, vol. 6 [Grand Rapids: Zondervan, 1986], 946-47).

[14] Nathaniel West, *The Thousand Years in Both Testaments* (New York: Fleming H. Revell, 1889), 430. For other differences, see Leslie Allen, *Ezekiel 40-48* (Dallas: Word Book Publishers, 1990), 259.

[15] This raises significant hermeneutical questions which will be addressed later in this section. However, it is at this point that all non-literal views break down, for they are unable to give reasonable correspondence between the details of the passage and what is being taught.

Solomonic temple or Zerubbabel's post-exilic temple. In this view, Ezekiel was looking at a literal return which would result in a literal temple in Jerusalem in the sixth century. The underlying rationale for this position was stated by Terry. "All Jewish-carnal theories of a literal restoration of Jerusalem and the Jewish state....The notion... that at Christ's second coming Jerusalem and the temple will be rebuilt and become the throne center of the kingdom of the Messiah is inconsistent with a rational interpretation of the prophets and the spiritual nature of the kingdom."[16]

One of the primary proponents of this view is Hengstenberg who dogmatically asserted that "with the exception of the Messianic section in 47:1-12, the fulfillment of all the rest of the prophecy belongs to the times immediately after the return from the Chaldean exile."[17] He elaborates on this position:

> The return of the people to the old home, the restoration of the temple, of the priestly service to be performed by the sons of Zadok, of the sacrifices in the Old Testament form—these are obvious realities; and nothing leads us to suppose that they are to be regarded as figures belonging to the action of the prophetic scene of the future. If so interpreted, the prophecy would be altogether vain.[18]

The strength of the historical view lies in the recognition that the details of this section must be given some concrete, literal interpretation. However, this view is beset by many difficulties. The first problem is the assertion by Hengstenberg that the prophecy is vain if it is relegated to the eschaton. This assertion would be tantamount to saying that no prophecy has relevance during any age other than the period of its historical utterance.

Speaking from the vantage point of Zechariah's post-exilic prophecies, Harrelson has suggested six purposes for future visions which made them meaningful to the post-exilic community: 1) coming judgment should lead to present holiness of life, 2) hope, 3) the promises draw the community to the eschatological ideal, 4) the certainty of the promises change the present, 5) it presents a world of beauty which the people would

---

[16] Milton Terry, *Biblical Hermeneutics*, 131-32. Terry's comment also implies the common false dichotomy between a "spiritual" kingdom and a "literal, earthly" kingdom. The Scripture does not present one in opposition with the other. Rather, the mediatorial kingdom always had and will always have a spiritual base. This was seen in the Edenic theocracy where God made requirements of the first couple; it is seen in Israel's theocracy in the Mosaic commandments; and, it will be seen during the future kingdom age in which the kingdom is characterized by "holiness unto the Lord" (Zech. 14:20).

[17] E. W. Hengstenberg, *The Prophecies of the Prophet Ezekiel Elucidated* (Edinburgh: T. & T. Clark, 1869), 348.

[18] Ibid., 352. See also Adam Clarke, "Ezekiel," in *Clarke's Commentary* (New York: Phillips & Hunt, n.d.), 535.

seek to emulate, and 6) it shows that the world to come is the only perfect one.[19]

The second problem with the historical view is that the temple described by Ezekiel has never existed. The Scriptures give the specifications of both temples (1 Kings 6:2-7:51; 2 Chron. 3:3-4:44; Ezra 6:3-4), and a comparison of these with the Ezekiel passage shows that Ezekiel's temple was never built. Furthermore, there is no evidence that Zerubbabel or the exiles ever sought to implement Ezekiel's temple plan. Hals has noted that one is forced to the conclusion "that the temple of 40-48 is, for unspecified reasons, new and different from its predecessor.... No real connections of a significant sort can be established between 40-48 and Zerubbabel's temple."[20]

A third problem with the historical view relates to the fact that there are many elements in Ezekiel 40-48 which never occurred at the time of Solomon or Zerubbabel. Bullock noted: "To view his new temple and community as limited to the historical restoration from the exile is to ignore the supernatural elements in the account....The restoration under Zerubbabel no more exhausted the requirements of the prophecy than the return depleted the meaning of Isaiah's program of restoration."[21]

Some of the things which were never fulfilled historically include the flowing river of healing waters, the glory of the Lord, topographical changes, the temple on a very high mountain (40:2), and the unreality of the boundaries of the tribes which could never be worked out geographically on hilly Israel.[22] While Zerubbabel did experience divine intervention (Zech. 4:1-7), he did not experience the manifestations of divine intervention described by Ezekiel.

Fourth, if Ezekiel were thinking of the former temple, one wonders what hope this would have provided his poor and oppressed brethren. More likely, this would have discouraged them if they were reminded of the glory of Solomon's temple which now lay in ruin. In addition, the books of Kings and Chronicles already had descriptions of Solomon's temple, and another would not be needed.

---

[19] Harrelson, "Messianic Expectations at the Time of Jesus" *St. Luke's Journal of Theology* 32 (1988): 28-42.

[20] Hals, *Ezekiel*, 301.

[21] Hassell Bullock, "Ezekiel, Bridge Between the Testaments," *Journal of the Evangelical Theological Society* 25 (1982): 29-30. Bullock also presented the caveat, however, that one must not assume that the prophecy was without relevance in the post-exilic period, for the temple represented the continuation of the hope and life of Israel.

[22] See Taylor, *Ezekiel*, 251-53; Moeller, "Ezekiel," 1078; Hobart Freeman, *An Introduction to the Old Testament Prophets* (Chicago: Moody Press, 1968), 312; John Mitchell, "The Question of Millennial Sacrifices," *Bibliotheca Sacra* 110 (1953): 251.

The Church/Christ View

Others have seen the Ezekiel passage fulfilled either in Christ or the Christian Church. This was the position of many of the Reformers and was stated by Fairbairn:

> The whole representation was not intended to find in either Jewish or Christian times an express and formal realization, but was a grand complicated symbol of the good God had in reserve for his Church, especially under the coming dispensation of the Gospel.[23]

Those who link the prophecy with Christ rely heavily on: a) the symbolism of the river in Ezekiel and its connection with John 7, and b) the temple and its connection with the person of Christ. Grigsby is representative of this understanding when he stated that "the resurrected Christ fulfills the role of the new temple in Ezekiel 47:1-12 and dispenses living water to a barren world with John 7:37-39."[24] Klein noted on John 7:37-39:

> The stream of Ezekiel 47 may even provide a new level of meaning to an incident at the crucifixion of   Jesus, when a soldier pierced his side with a spear and at once there came out blood and water (John 19:24). If God's presence in his temple means new life for his people, John's symbolism would suggest that the body of Jesus is now that temple, and that God was nevermore "with" his people than when Jesus hung on a cross.[25]

While the above view is very sermonic, its validity is doubtful on several counts. First, if the vision were a reference to the Church or to Christ, it would have had absolutely no meaning for the reader's of Ezekiel's day.[26]

---

[23] Patrick Fairbairn, *An Exposition of Ezekiel*, reprint ed., (Grand Rapids: Zondervan, 1960), 434-35. Luther wrote that "this building of Ezekiel is not to be understood to mean a physical building, but like the chariot at the beginning so this building at the end (40-48) is nothing else than the kingdom of Christ, the holy church or Christendom here on earth until the last day" (Martin Luther, *Luther's Works,* E. Theodore Bachmann, ed., [Philadelphia: Muhlenberg Press, 1960]: 35:293). However, Luther also relates the Ezekiel vision to the heavenly Jerusalem (*Works*, 35:283).

[24] Bruce Grigsby, "Gematria and John 21:11—Another Look at Ezekiel 47:10," *Expository Times* 95 (1984): 177.

[25] Klein, *Ezekiel: The Prophet and His Message*, 182. See also for Jesus as the temple, David Holwerda, *Jesus & Israel: One Covenant or Two?* (Grand Rapids: Eerdmans, 1995), 74-75.

[26] Hengstenberg argued for a historical fulfillment on the basis that a future fulfillment of the prophecy would be irrelevant to Ezekiel's readers. The six points made by Harrelson showed this not to be true (footnote 19). With this in mind, there is no contradiction in opposing the "Christ/Christian Church view" on the basis that a prophecy relating to the church would have had no relevance to Ezekiel's audience. The difference is that in this instance the people would have had no connection with the prophecy if it were speaking of the church, while in the other instance, a renewed nation with a renewed place of worship was a constant hope for the nation, and one which they held dearly based on the covenanted promises made to their fathers.

Second, it resorts to heavy allegorical interpretation which is very tenuous in light of the large number of details in the prophecy. If this were a legitimate method, it would be a small step to allegorize the details given by Moses concerning the tabernacle. As Mitchell warned, this view "passes by the text with no exposition whatsoever and finds itself abounding in fanciful speculations, with the greater part of the vision being left unexplained."[27] Dyer noted this subjectivity to be shown in the fact that the ones who hold this view "interpret Ezekiel's earlier, now-fulfilled prophecies literally, yet interpret his yet unfulfilled prophecies symbolically."[28] Third, this view would be subject to the same criticisms as the "apocalyptic dream" ideal view. Fourth, Jesus was speaking in light of Herod's temple and not the one mentioned by Ezekiel. And fifth, as Swanson asks, "could any readers then or even in the NT era, possibly have read the text and concluded that its 'import' was the perpetuity of the Church?"[29]

The Eternal State View
The next view identifies the vision of 40-48 with the eternal state. Keil represents this view and suggested that the vision "is partly to be regarded as the Old Testament outline of the New Testament picture of the heavenly Jerusalem in Revelation 21 and 22."[30] Likewise, Hoekema wrote:

> The details about the temple and sacrifices are to be understood not literally but figuratively. The closing chapters of the book of Revelation, in fact, echo Ezekiel's vision. In Revelation 22, we read about the counterpart of the river which Ezekiel saw….What we have in Ezekiel 40-48, therefore, is not a description of the millennium, but a picture of the final estate on the earth, in terms of the religious

---

[27] John Mitchell, "The Question of Millennial Sacrifices," 251; Moeller, "Ezekiel," 1078. See also Beasley-Murray who noted that "it need hardly be said that Ezekiel has here advanced plans which he expected to be carried out to the letter. To make them a deliberately symbolic description of the worship of the Christian Church is out of the question" ("Ezekiel," in *The New Bible Commentary* [Grand Rapids: Eerdmans, 1953], 663). This view could also be discounted by the following descriptions of allegory: "[In it] the details of the story represent in obvious fashion a corresponding set of concepts or allegorical meanings" (Leland Ryken, *The Literature of the Bible* [Grand Rapids: Zondervan, 1974], 301). "Allegory is always stated in the past tense, and never in the future. Allegory is thus distinguished from prophecy. The allegory brings other teaching out of past events, while the prophecy tells us events that are yet to come" (E. W. Bullinger, *Figures of Speech Used in the Bible*, reprint ed., [Grand Rapids: Baker, 1968], 749).

[28] Charles Dyer, "Ezekiel," in *The Bible Knowledge Commentary* eds., John Walvoord and Roy Zuck, vol. 1 (Wheaton: Victor, 1985), 1313; C. F. Keil and F. Delitzsch, *The Prophecies of Ezekiel*, reprint ed., (Grand Rapids: Eerdmans, 1949), 417.

[29] Dennis Swanson, "Expansion of Jerusalem in Jer 31:38-40: Never, Already, or Not Yet?" *The Master's Seminary Journal* 17:1 (2006): 28.

[30] F. Keil, *Ezekiel*, 417.

symbolism with which Ezekiel and his readers were familiar.... All that was foreshadowed in such visions John sees fulfilled.[31]

While this appears to be a formidable argument upon first glance, there are a number of details which argue against it. It is true that Ezekiel and John are similar,[32] but it is also true that there are some major discrepancies between the two accounts. First, the most obvious difference is that Ezekiel uses four chapters in explaining the temple (making a clear distinction between the temple and the city [48:8, 15]) while John states in his vision that there is no longer a temple (21:22).

Second, the river which Ezekiel sees flows from the threshold of the temple eastward (47:1), while the river seen by John proceeds out of the throne of God for there is no temple (22:1). Third, Ezekiel sees the presence of sin (e.g., 45:20), while John states that there will be no more curse (22:3).[33] In response to these discrepancies, Keil simply says that Ezekiel's vision "could not rise to such an eminence of vision" as did John.[34] A final argument against the eternal state view is the hermeneutical method. Geisler explains:

> The premillennialists rejoices that at least some amillennialists have taken the promises as literal, as yet unfulfilled, and as finding their fulfillment in the new earth (as premillennialists have upheld all along). However, their skipping over the Millennium as the beginning point in this fulfillment is inconsistent; the same

---

[31] Anthony Hoekema, *The Bible and the Future* (Grand Rapids: Eerdmans, 1979), 205-6.

[32] The parallels between Ezekiel and John have been brought out well by Trimaille who noted the comparison in the facts that both Ezekiel and John were in exile, and both were concerned with what God would do for His people in the midst of persecution. He suggested that there are eighty-one citations of Ezekiel in the Apocalypse, while citations from all the other prophets combined account for only a third of that number. He further draws a parallel between Ezekiel 1-3 and Revelation 4-5; Ezekiel's oracles against Israel and the nations 4-24 and 25-32 with the seals, trumpets, and bowls of John (M. Trimaille, "Ezechiel et l'Apocalypse de Jean," *Le Monde de la Bible* 40 [1985]: 40-41). Even though there may be similarities, neither the position of the amillennialist nor the dispensationalist is strengthened since both schools would approach the Apocalypse with their distinctive hermeneutical viewpoint (idealistic and futuristic respectively).

[33] Hoekema contradicted himself at this point. He argued against the millennial view in that the typical "memorial" position does not give full weight to the use of "atonement" in its expiatory and propitiatory senses in Ezekiel. And yet, if Ezekiel is picturing the eternal state where there is no sin, as he argued, giving "atonement" its full weight would negate his own position.

[34] Keil, *Ezekiel*, 418. One other view is that presented by Susan Niditch. She compared Ezekiel 40-48 to a Tibetan Buddhist mandala (a symbolic representation of the sacred realm or cosmos) in which the cosmos is a building or city ("Ezekiel 40-48 in a Visionary Context," 212-13). No other writers examined have followed Niditch on this point.

hermeneutic that yields a literal future fulfillment of these promises also yields a literal thousand-year messianic reign and a clear difference from the eternal state.[35]

The Kingdom View

A final view holds that Ezekiel 40-48 will be realized during the future kingdom period. This position holds that the descriptions given by Ezekiel in 40-48 will be literally implemented on earth during the visible reign of Christ in His millennial kingdom. This includes the building of the glorious temple, the restoration of animal sacrifices, the presence of God with His people, and the various topographical phenomena which are mentioned. This subsection will present arguments in favor of this interpretation and will attempt to deal with the two major objections.

Arguments in Favor of the View

The first strength of the kingdom view is that it is able to deal with the supernatural elements of the passage. As noted previously, there are elements in the prophecy that did not occur historically and must therefore have a future fulfillment. Allen specifically pointed out regarding the Dead Sea, circumstances that have never taken place. "The healing effect of the river upon the Dead Sea is described in 8-10. It was to become a freshwater lake, able to sustain an enormous abundance of fish. The upper half of the west shore of the Dead Sea is portrayed as a fisherman's paradise. In its backwaters, however, would be left salt water to provide salt for cultic and human needs."[36] Another statement of this point is provided by Davidson.

> The fact that the subject of the passage is the final blessedness of the people accounts for the supernatural elements in the picture. But both the natural and the supernatural features of the peoples' condition are to be understood literally. The temple, the services, and the like are meant in a real sense, and no less literally meant is the supernatural presence of Jehovah in His house, the transfiguration of nature, the turning of the desert into a garden, and the sweetening of the waters of the Dead Sea.[37]

---

[35] Norman Geisler, *Systematic Theology, Volume Four: Church, Last Things,* (Minneapolis: Bethany House, 2005), 580.

[36] Leslie Allen, *Ezekiel 20-48,* 279. It is interesting to point out that in the Ancient Near East the home or temple of a god was often situated on a river or a stream. El's home, for example, in the Ugaritic texts is located by two rivers (Klein, *Ezekiel: The Prophet and His Message,* 181; Coogan, *Studies from Ancient Canaan* [Philadelphia: Westminster Press, 1978], 95; Richard Clifford, *The Cosmic Mountain in Canaan and the Old Testament* [Cambridge: Harvard University Press, 1972], 158).

[37] A. B. Davidson, *Ezekiel,* xvi.

The other views of the passage do not account well for these supernatural elements. If a historical view is taken, then these supernatural issues are stripped of any reality. If a Christian Church view is adopted, then the language of the text is reduced to the whim of the interpreter. And finally, if the passage is placed into the eternal state, then the contradictions between Ezekiel and John must be reconciled, as well as the inconsistent methodology.

It can also be pointed out that the returnees to Jerusalem did not compare their rebuilt temple with Ezekiel but rather with the temple of Solomon (Haggai 2:3). And concerning the altar, Stalker has observed that there is no evidence that it was modeled on the description given by Ezekiel.[38]

A second support for this view is the seemingly clear meaning of the text.[39] Beasley-Murray cogently explained that "to tackle the vision verse by

---

[38] D. M. G. Stalker, *Ezekiel* (London: SCM Press Ltd., 1971), 291; Roland de Vaux, *Ancient Israel* (New York: McGraw-Hill, 1961), 412.

[39] One could object to this statement in that, if the text is so clear, why does so much disagreement exist? This leads to the important hermeneutical debate between premillennialists and amillennialists (i.e., "literal" versus "symbolic" tendencies in interpreting prophecies). Of course, the question is really not an issue of a strictly literal versus a strictly symbolic approach, because even the most extreme literalist takes some things as symbolic. Conversely, even the most stringent symbolist interprets some things as literal. Frequently, dispensational literalism is made to look inconsistent by producing a passage which clearly has to be interpreted symbolically. While a number of responses could be made, one important point is that literal interpretation is more than deciding whether a text should be taken figuratively or literally, for this is a question with which all interpreters wrestle. Rather, literal is a framework brought to the text from which the literal vs. figurative is decided (Mike Stallard, "Literal Interpretation: The Key to Understanding the Bible," *The Journal of Ministry and Theology* 4 [2000]: 27). Therefore, it is a red herring to point to an isolated passage which could be taken figuratively as arguing against dispensational literalism. For a discussion of this issue and clarification of the meaning of "literal" in today's discussion, see the following: Thomas Ice, "Dispensational Hermeneutics," in *Issues in Dispensationalism* (Chicago: Moody Press, 1994), 29-49; Elliott Johnson, "Premillennialism Introduced: Hermeneutics," in *The Coming Millennial Kingdom* (Grand Rapids: Kregel, 1997), 15-34; "A Traditional Dispensational Hermeneutic," in *Three Central Issues in Contemporary Dispensationalism* (Grand Rapids: Kregel, 1999), 65, 67, 76; "What I Mean by Historical-Grammatical Interpretation and How That Differs from Spiritual Interpretation," *Grace Theological Journal* 11 [1990]: 157-158; "Literal Interpretation: A Plea for Consensus," *When the Trumpet Sounds*, (Eugene, OR: Harvest House, 1995), 213, 216, 217; Robert L. Thomas, "A Critique of Progressive Dispensational Hermeneutics," in *When the Trumpet Sounds* (Eugene, OR: Harvest House, 1995), 413-425); Bernard Ramm, *Protestant Biblical Interpretation* (Boston: W. A. Wilde, 1950), 64; Geisler, *Systematic Theology*, 415-21, 423-26, 441-48; Mike Stallard, "The Rediscovery of the Jewish Perspective of the Bible," in *The Gathering Storm* (Springfield, MO: 21st Century Press, 2005): 57-71. There are basically three definitions of "literal": 1) a letterism which excludes figures of speech, 2) a normal reading of the text that allows for figures, historical, contextual, and progressiveness, and 3) a normal approach which takes most prophetic material as symbolic and figurative, most of which is applied to the Church (Alexander, "Ezekiel," 905-6). But as evinced by Hoekema's comments in the text, there is a trend among some amillennialists to move slightly away from this (and possibly a trend among progressive dispensationalists to move toward it, at least methodologically). This article falls into the camp described as #2 above, with the well-known caveat of Lange: "The literalist is not one who denies figurative language, that symbols are used in prophecy, nor

verse and try to take symbolically 'thirteen cubits,' 'hooks a handbreath long,' 'the sixth part of an ephah,' place names like Berothat and Hauran, is out of the question, to contradict all reason."[40] If God or Ezekiel did not intend the language to be taken in their normal, sense, then they were being blatantly deceptive.[41]

---

does he deny that spiritual truths are set forth therein; his position is, simply, that the prophecies are to be normally interpreted (i.e. according to revealed laws of language) as any other utterances are interpreted—that is manifestly figurative being so regarded" (J. P. Lange, "The Revelation of St. John," in *Lange's Commentary on the Holy Scriptures*, ed. Philip Schaff, vol. 12, reprint ed., [Grand Rapids: Zondervan, 1980, 98]. Ramm continues to provide six defenses for this approach: 1) it is the normal approach in all language, 2) secondary meanings parables, types, etc., depend on a literal meaning of terms, 3) most of the Bible makes sense this way, 4) it does not rule out symbols and figures, 5) it is the only safe check on interpretation, and 6) it is consistent with plenary inspiration (Ibid., 54ff.). Having examined the interpretive approaches to the realization of Ezekiel's temple, it is seen why this issue is important and how the other views do not treat the text in this manner. As Terry observed: "Its (allegorism's) habit is to disregard the common signification of words and give wing to all manner of fanciful speculation. It does not draw out the legitimate meaning of an author's language, but foists onto it whatever whim or fancy of an interpreter may desire" (Milton Terry, *Biblical Hermeneutics*, 224). Again, Ramm noted that "spiritualizing is an open door to almost uncontrolled speculation and imagination. For this reason we have insisted that the control in interpretation is the literal method" (Ramm, *Protestant Biblical Interpretation*, 65). Even Allis agreed that if the allegorical or symbolic method is "used to empty words of their plain and obvious meaning, to read out of them what is clearly intended by them, then allegorizing or spiritualizing is a term of reproach which is well merited" (Allis, *Prophecy and the Church*, 18). There are visions in Ezekiel that merit a symbolic interpretation due to their presentation, such as wheels within wheels, dry bones coming to life, etc. However, to spiritualize 40-48, which does not employ such symbolism, seems to belie the prejudice of the interpreter. The text speaks of historical places, solid buildings, exact measurements, and precise cultic sacrificial language as found in the legislative portions of the Pentateuch, and therefore seems to demand a normal and literal interpretation. For interpreting prophetic portions of Scripture see, C. C. Ryrie, *The Basis of the Premillennial Faith*, 40-46; J. Randolph Jaeggli, "The Interpretation of Old Testament Prophecy," *Detroit Baptist Seminary Journal* 2 (1997): 3-17. One final noteworthy observation has been made by John Walton, "Inspired Subjectivity and Hermeneutical Objectivity," *The Master's Seminary Journal* 13 (2002). He points out that there are two distinct methods of interpretation. "One is defined by hermeneutical guidelines and is objective in nature. The other is subjective in nature but finds its authority not in the science that drives it, but in its source—inspiration from God. If you have inspiration, you do not need historical-grammatical hermeneutics. If you do not have inspiration, you must proceed by the acknowledged guidelines of hermeneutics. The credibility of any interpretation is based on the verifiability of either one's inspiration or one's hermeneutics" (70). "We must push on in our question to preserve the objectivity of our hermeneutics, for it provides the foundation for our commitment to biblical authority....For an interpretation of the text to claim credibly that it represents the authoritative teaching of the text, it must depend on either hermeneutical objectivity or inspired subjectivity" (77). Since we are not writing Scripture today, we cannot rely on the subjective (as perhaps the apostles did), but we need to lean as heavily as possible on what is objective. In the writer's view, this is best done by taking Ezekiel at face value.

[40] Beasley-Murray, *Ezekiel*, 663; Cameron MacKay, "Why Study Ezekiel 40-48," *Evangelical Quarterly* 37 (1965): 155.

[41] For a good description of the temple as Ezekiel described it, see T. Chary, "Le Temple d'Ezechiel," 34-38. In this article, Chary conducts a tour through the temple beginning from the exterior through the main gate into the court and its various annexes. This is followed by the temple proper (interior). He describes the details with great precision. Interestingly, Ezekiel had a profound influence on the Qumran community (E. Cothenet, "Influence d'Ezechiel sur la spiritualite de Qumran," *Revue de Qumran* 13 [1988]:

A third argument in favor of the kingdom view is the emphasis in the passage on the distribution of the land[42] which is reminiscent of the promises made to the Patriarchs. It is clear that Israel has never dwelt in the land with the divisions presented by Ezekiel. Therefore, if 40-48 is to be taken seriously, a fulfillment of this aspect of Ezekiel's vision must be proleptic.[43] Allen observed:

> This passage functions as an introduction to 48:1-29 where the allocation of the land is described. Verse 14 lays down a theological premise, the revival of the theme of the land promised to the Patriarchs, which runs through the Pentateuchal

---

431-39). For example, in the Qumran text "Description of the New Jerusalem," the author says that he had a vision in which he was shown buildings and streets with their measurements. In this vision, he was shown a city which had the last chapters of Ezekiel as its model. Particularly notable are the enormous streets and massive city (Jacob Licht, "An Ideal Town Plan from Qumran—The Description of the New Jerusalem," *Israel Exploration Journal* 29 [1979]: 45-59).

[42] The importance of the land cannot be overstated. Consider the following statement: "In the Old Testament few issues are as important as that of the promise of the land to the patriarchs and the nation Israel. In fact, Jr#a 'land' is the fourth most frequent substantive in the Hebrew Bible. Were it not for the larger and more comprehensive theme of the total promise with all its multifaceted provisions, the theme of Israel and her land could well serve as the central idea or the organizing rubric for the entire canon.... The land of Israel cannot be reduced to a sort of mystical land defined as a new spiritual reality.... the Bible is most insistent on the fact that the land was promised to the patriarchs as a gift where their descendants would reside and rule as a nation" (Walter Kaiser, "The Promised Land: A Biblical-Historical View," *Bibliotheca Sacra* 138 [1981]: 302. Later postexilic prophets continue to pledge to Israel their restoration to the land. As Kaiser notes, "the sheer multiplicity of texts...is staggering" (309); see also Jeffrey Townsend, "Fulfillment of the Land Promise in the Old Testament," *Bibliotheca Sacra* 142 [1985]: 321-332). Moreover, in Ezekiel's discussion of the New Covenant, he not only describes spiritual blessings which will occur, but physical blessings also. He states that towns and ruins will be rebuilt (36:33, 35) and desolate land will be cultivated (36:34). The fact that the New Covenant presents spiritual *and* physical blessings provides support that the temple Ezekiel envisions is consistent with his physical concerns.

[43] Some have argued that the fulfillment of the land promise was fulfilled historically either during the time of Joshua or during the reign of David and Solomon. Yet premillennialists have maintained that the promise will find its ultimate fulfillment during the kingdom period. Amillennialists have contended that the promise is spiritualized in the church (older), was conditional, and therefore forfeited during the Conquest, or will be realized during the eternal state (some newer). The problem faced by premillennialists is that the text states that the promise was fulfilled (Josh. 21:43-45; 23:14-15; Neh. 9:8). With this in mind, there are several points to remember. First, the historical allocations of land were never made according to Ezekiel's plan, nor accompanied with the concomitants he presents. Second, the Abrahamic Covenant and its land extension in the Palestinian Covenant are unconditional. Third, the covenant was made with the physical seed of Abraham. Fourth, Israel never completely removed the Canaanites from the whole land so as to possess all of it (Josh. 11:16-17; 12:7; 13:2-6; Judges 3:3). Fifth, the Lord was faithful to give Israel the land (Josh. 21:43), but Israel was still responsible to obey the directives of the Mosaic Covenant in order to maintain possession.

Thus the land was given to the nation by Yahweh and was theirs to take, but they forfeited the full blessings of the land through disobedience. This demonstrated the truth of Leviticus 26 and Deuteronomy 28-30 that the enjoyment of the blessings of the unconditional Abrahamic Covenant was obedience. So, while historically Israel enjoyed a partial taste of this fulfillment, it will not be until the enactment of the New Covenant (Ezekiel 36), by a gracious God, that they will permanently enjoy the full blessings of the Covenant during the kingdom age as they are restored to the land.

sources....There is a tradition deeply embedded in Israel's faith that inextricably linked together are the fortunes of the temple and the land. To worship in the temple carried with it the privileges of dwelling in the land and enjoying God's blessings there.[44]

Another indication which supports the kingdom interpretation is the emphasis in 40-48 on the glory of Yahweh. The passage stresses the fact that the new sanctuary will again be His dwelling place. Thus Ezekiel records the divine initiative in Ezekiel 37:26b, "I will put my sanctuary among them." In fact, the glory of God is one of the unifying themes of the entire book. Ezekiel sees a vision of the glory of God in chapter 1, sees the departure of the glory of God in 8-11, and then sees the return of God's glory in 40-48. Clearly, this return of God's glory has never been experienced by the nation as evinced from their present condition. Alexander commented that "the return of God's glory...is the climax of the book. The context implies that this could only occur after Israel has been restored to her promised land and cleansed....When God's glory returns, it will remain in Israel's midst forever. The development of this unifying factor in Ezekiel would argue strongly for a future fulfillment of 40-48."[45]

A fifth consideration in favor of the kingdom view revolves around the fact that the features presented by Ezekiel are different than those of the programs of Moses, Solomon, or Zerubbabel. Surely if Ezekiel were looking at these as models, there would have been a great deal of similarity, but in fact there are a great number of dissimilarities (see footnotes 12 and 13). This strongly suggests that he is looking into the future. In addition, economically speaking, the returnees to the land were bankrupt and in no condition even to attempt what Ezekiel was suggesting. This leads to the conclusion suggested by Eichrodt: "It becomes evident that the prophet is especially interested in something far wider than the familiar features of the old future hope, for he names new miracles by the covenant of God through which the

---

[44] Allen, *Ezekiel 20-48*, 280, 285.

[45] Alexander, *Ezekiel*, 944. Another argument related to the glory of God is to note Ezekiel's strong concern for God's name in his book. This is seen by the recurrent phrase "they will know that I am Yahweh." Zimmerli has observed that of the 947 verbal occurrences of the stem "to know" "not less than 99 are found in Ezekiel, with virtually all of them making significant theological statements" (Walther Zimmerli, *I Am Yahweh* [Atlanta: John Knox Press, 1982], 29-30). He further defined this knowledge as a "form of self-revelation of a person in his name" (Walther Zimmerli, *Ezekiel: A Commentary on the Book of the Prophet Ezekiel*, vol. 2 [Philadelphia: Fortress Press, 1979], 38). The result of this concern for the divine name is an indirect assurance of salvation to Israel. This is absolutely necessary if God's name is to be vindicated because of Israel's sin. Ezekiel 40-48 convincingly argues for a restored Jewish temple and land with the resultant phrase "the house of Israel will never again defile my holy name" (43:7). If the events of 40-48 are not fulfilled as laid out by the prophet, then God's plans and covenants with the nation have been frustrated, and His preeminence as God will not be established.

fulfillment takes on a tone all of its own (e.g., Spirit is imparted, rebuilding, obedience, united kingdom, etc.)."[46]

The provenance of Ezekiel 40-48 presents another support for this view. It is quite possible that 40-48 is continuing the message of 34-39, and belongs to them as an extended oracle of salvation. In particular, it would be a direct outworking of the New Covenant in chapter 37. Thus, "the four motifs of new temple, covenant, king and land find here a practical grounding and a detailed development."[47] Therefore, since Israel has never experienced the full blessings of the New Covenant, their future fulfillment would be placed into the eschaton along with the realization of Ezekiel's temple.

A final strength of the position adopted here is the parallel that exists between Ezekiel's ideas and those of other prophets. Some commentators dismiss the idea of a literal, future fulfillment of Ezekiel 40-48 by simply referring to it as an apocalyptic dream or spiritualizing it into oblivion. However, it needs to be observed that several other prophets foresaw the same future for Israel when sacrifices in a temple would again be instituted (e.g., Isaiah 56:7; 66:20-23; Jer. 33:18; Zech. 14:16-21; Mal. 3:3-4). Isaiah saw a temple in the holy land (Isa. 2:2-3; 56:3; 60:13) where animal sacrifices would be offered on its altar by the Egyptians (19:21) and the Arabians (60:7). Of these sacrifices, Yahweh says, "even these I will bring to my holy mountain and make them joyful in my house of prayer. Their burnt offerings and their sacrifices will be acceptable on my altar" (56:6-7; cf. 66:19-20). Hosea also speaks of sacrifices to be resumed in the last days (3:4-5). Jeremiah says the same thing (33:17-22), as does Amos (9:11), and Zechariah (14:21). And even more significant is the fact that Jeremiah spoke of these sacrifices after noting the demise of the Old Covenant and its replacement by the New Covenant.[48]

---

[46] Eichrodt, *Ezekiel: A Commentary*, 37.

[47] Allen, *Ezekiel 20-48*, 213. Regarding the New Covenant context of Jeremiah 31, it is striking that one of the provisions of the New Covenant regards the very city that Jeremiah was before long to see destroyed by the Chaldeans. As noted by Swanson, the city of Jerusalem "will be rebuilt and enlarged, sanctified, and immune from future devastation" ("Expansion of Jerusalem in Jer 31:38-40," 20).

[48] See also for the kingdom view: Alexander, "Ezekiel," 945; Lamar Cooper, Sr., The New American Commentary, *Ezekiel* (Nashville: Broadman & Holman, 1994), 353, 381; Dyer, *Ezekiel*, 1302-04; Paul Enns, *Ezekiel* (Grand Rapids: Zondervan, 1986), 180; Charles Feinberg, *The Prophecy of Ezekiel* (Chicago: Moody, 1969): 233-39; Hobart Freeman, *An Introduction to the Old Testament Prophets* (Chicago: Moody, 1968), 312.

Arguments against the view

There are, of course, objections to the kingdom position. The two primary objections involve envisioned topography and the renewal of animal sacrifices.[49] Concerning the first, Taylor remarked: "There are elements which are so impracticable that a completely literal interpretation of the vision must be ruled out (e.g. the setting of the temple on a very high mountain, 40:2; the impossible source and course of the river of life, 47:1-13; the unreality of the boundaries of the tribes which could never be worked out geographically in hilly Israel)."[50] Martyn Lloyd-Jones added the same complaint:

> Let us turn for instance, to the prophecy of Ezekiel from chapters 40 to the end....Read those chapters and try to interpret them literally. If you work out all those measurements about the restored Temple, you will find that you have measurements which cannot be fitted into a literal Palestine. If you work out what you are told there about the river, you will find that river will have to rise and flow up over mountains—impossible if you take it literally! But if you understand Ezekiel's words pictorially and spiritually there is no difficulty. A literal interpretation of these chapters involves us in believing that a day is coming when the Jews will again occupy the whole of the land of Palestine with a literal Temple again built in Jerusalem. Not only that, but burnt offerings and sacrifices for sins will again be offered.[51]

---

[49] A third objection sometimes made by those opposed to the dispensational premillennial scheme is that this reduces the kingdom into a carnal hope. However, two points should be kept in mind. First, the so-called "carnal" (physical) aspects of the kingdom were instituted in creation and have merely been marred by sin. It is only fitting that God should undo these effects. Curiously, those who are not dispensational have produced some of the best work arguing for the goodness of creation (see for example, Michael Horton's excellent and enjoyable volumes, *Where in the World is the Church* [Chicago: Moody, 1995]; *Putting Amazing Back into Grace* [Grand Rapids: Baker, 1995], 38-40, 42, 199-200). Second, as mentioned previously, the kingdom always has a spiritual base as is seen by the glory of God, cleansing, the work of the Spirit, the regenerate nature of those who enter, etc. The "carnal" objection attempts to force one into an either/or decision which does not exist. For further rebuttal to this objection, see John Walvoord, "Spiritual Life in the Millennium," *Bibliotheca Sacra* 115 (1958): 97-108.

[50] Taylor, *Ezekiel*, 252.

[51] Martyn Lloyd-Jones, *The Church and the Last Things* (Wheaton, IL: Crossway, 1998), 108-09. Likewise, Keil stated: "It is upset by the fact that not only are its supporters unable to make anything of the description of the spring which issues from the threshold of the temple, flows through the land, and makes the waters of the Dead Sea sound, but they are also unable to explain the separation of the temple from the city of Jerusalem; as it would never have occurred to any Jewish patriot" (Keil, *Ezekiel*, 385). Also, O. Palmer Robertson, *The Christ of the Prophets*, (Phillipsburg, NJ: Presbyterian & Reformed, 2004), 298-99. And what can rival Luther's way of putting it: "The blind Jews do not see the absurdity. This cannot be any physical building; still less can it be at the place where Jerusalem was situated, as they falsely hope. There shall also be a great flow of water out of the temple into the Dead Sea (Ezek. 47:1-12) (which the papists—fools that they are!—take to be their holy water); but this in no way squares with the topography of Israel" (*Works*, 35:292).

Three responses are in order here. First, it has always been maintained by premillennialists that the kingdom will be one in which changes in topography and in the course of nature will occur. This will be accomplished by the power of God and is anticipated in all of the prophets (e.g. Isa. 11:6-9; Joel 3:18-21; Amos 9:13-15; Obad. 19-21; Zech. 14).[52] It should be no more difficult to accept this than it should be to accept the changes regarding the eternal state.

The second response deals with the issue of miracles. Geisler defines a miracle as "a divine intervention into, or an interruption of, the regular course of the world that produces a purposeful but unusual event that would not (or could not) have occurred otherwise. The natural world is the world of regular, observable, and predictable events. Hence, a miracle by definition cannot be predicted by natural means."[53] Unless one denies all of the miraculous throughout the biblical history, this is a bogus objection. Why would this be any different?

A third response deals with dispensationalism's philosophy of history. Showers correctly notes that several consequences resulted from Adam's rebellion.[54] These included the theocracy being lost from planet earth, Satan usurping the "rule" of the world, and nature being subjected to the curse. In response to these consequences, the "ultimate purpose of history is the demonstration of God's sovereignty."[55] To accomplish this purpose, God must undo all of the above consequences. This means that God must restore the theocracy, crush Satan, and remove the curse from nature. All of these will occur during the Kingdom age. This is the goal toward which history is moving, and if paradise lost is not paradise regained then God has lost the war.[56] Eugene Merrill writes in his *magum opus*:

> The creation account is thus the beginning of the sacred narrative, and it is there that the central theological theme is introduced. The fall and its tragic consequences become the sotto voce of everything that subsequently follows in the narrative; but the notes of divine redemption, growing ever more audible and clear, eventually

---

[52] Alva McClain, *The Greatness of the Kingdom* (Winona Lake, IN: BMH Books), 230.

[53] Norman Geisler, *Miracles and Modern Thought* (Grand Rapids: Zondervan, 1982), 13.

[54] Renald Showers, *What on Earth is God Doing?* (Neptune, NJ: Loizeaux Brothers, 1973), 14-16. These consequences relate mostly to dispensationalism's goal of history. For a development of the anthropological consequences see Augustine's seven-fold list cited by Philip Schaff, *History of the Christian Church* (Grand Rapids: Eerdmans, 1981), 3:825-829.

[55] Showers, *What on Earth is God Doing?* 18. For an expanded definition see Renald Showers, *There Really is a Difference! A Comparison of Covenant and Dispensational Theology* (Bellmawr, NJ: The Friends of Israel, 1990), 1-6.

[56] Geisler, *Systematic Theology*, 565.

drown out the despair of the human dilemma and point to the triumphant day of full restoration of God's eternal and glorious designs.[57]

The second argument against the kingdom view is the anticipation of the renewal of animal sacrifices. The logic also includes the claim of literal interpretation and goes as follows: one of the major sine qua non of dispensationalism is the insistence on a normal, literal interpretation of the prophets. If the literal interpretation of the prophets is abandoned when it comes to Ezekiel 40-48, then dispensationalism is undercut for the logic of the entire system is weakened. If, however, literal interpretation is maintained, then the dispensationalist is left with a renewal of animal sacrifices which appears to demean the cross of Christ and is contradicted by the Book of Hebrews. Adherents of other eschatological schemes are quick to note this apparent discrepancy. Snowden remarked:

> It is a cardinal principle of premillennarianism that the prophecies of the Messianic kingdom in the Old Testament apply, not to the first, but to the second coming of Christ and to the millennial kingdom he will inaugurate.... It is a further principle of this system that these prophecies must be interpreted in a literal sense.... Premillennialism is therefore required by its own logic to take the prophecy of Ezekiel 40-48 literally.... If any premillenarians pause at this or say that they do not hold it, we must repeat that we are not dealing with individuals but with the logic and literature of the system.[58]

Concerning the same matter and the return to animal sacrifices, Hamilton concurred, "If the literal method of interpretation of all Old Testament prophecies is to be followed, this is exactly what will be necessary.... This is a picture upon which premillennialists do not like to dwell."[59] And more recently, Hoekema has said: "These words [that sacrifices are not literal] convey a far-reaching concession on the part of the dispensationalists. If the sacrifices are not to be taken literally, why should we take the temple literally? It would seem that the dispensational principle of literal interpretation of Old Testament prophecy is here abandoned, and

---

[57] Eugene Merrill, *Everlasting Dominion: A Theology of the Old Testament* (Nashville: Broadman & Holman, 2006), 647. Ross adds: "It is important to note that contrary to popular opinion the ultimate destiny of God's people is an earthly destiny. The Bible places the redeemed on the new earth and not only in a heavenly realm; they will reign with Christ on earth (Rev. 5:10)" (Allen Ross, *Recalling the Hope of Glory* [Grand Rapids: Kregel, 2006], 495).
[58] James Snowden, *The Coming of the Lord*, 207-9, 217.
[59] Floyd Hamilton, *The Basis of the Millennial Faith*, 41.

that a crucial foundation stone for the entire dispensational system has here been set aside."[60]

These objections are valid in that they insist on hermeneutical consistency. If one is committed to the truth of dispensational theology, he must interpret Ezekiel literally with whatever apparent difficulties that may entail. However, one additional observation is appropriate. The impression from the above quotations is that these authors feel that they have dispensationalists in a no-win situation. Yet, it is equally clear, that the postmillennialist and amillennialist have no basis on which to allegorize Ezekiel 40-48. While it is granted that there could be "problems" associated with these sacrifices, these problems are not diminished by unwarranted license with the text. There are as many problems if one accepts a non-literal view of the passage as when one accepts a literal view of it. As suggested by Alexander, "The figurative or 'spiritualizing' interpretive approach does not seem to solve any of the problems of Ezekiel 40-48; it tends to create new ones."[61] There is no reasonable explanation concerning the numerous details of the temple service, worship, and re-allotment of the land which can be given by advocates of a symbolic view. The spiritualization of this prophecy in applying it to the church or the eternal state is unsound hermeneutically and results in confusion when the immense number of details is examined. The allegorists' interpretations of these chapters border on exegetical license and subjective theories.[62]

Summary

The sacrificial system envisioned in Ezekiel 40-48 has been considered to be a major weakness of normative dispensationalism. However, before this issue is even discussed, it must be determined when Ezekiel's temple will be

---

[60]Hoekema, *The Bible and the Future*, 204. Similar statements are made by LaSor: "This would appear contrary to the prophetic emphasis on the spiritual nature of the cult and of Yahweh as the God who does not delight in blood offerings. It is certainly contrary to the New Testament view" (William LaSor, *Old Testament Survey* [Grand Rapids: Eerdmans, 1982], 477; see also Keil, *Ezekiel*, 388; Stalker, *Ezekiel*, 42).

[61] Ralph Alexander, "Ezekiel," 4:943. Or Feinberg: "The non-literal approach has no system of its own; it dwells on negation and offers no positive exposition of the revelatory material" (Charles Feinberg, "The Rebuilding of the Temple," in *Prophecy in the Making*, Carl F. H. Henry, ed. [Carol Stream, IL: Creation House, 1971], 109).

[62] Hobart Freeman, *An Introduction to the Old Testament Prophets*, 310-11. Sauer likewise commented that "Ezekiel pictures a future temple with so very many particulars and measurements that it will be simply impossible to declare that all this is only figurative and must therefore be spiritualized...how can this be spiritualized" (Erich Sauer, *The Triumph of the Crucified* [Grand Rapids: Eerdmans, 1952], 179-80)? For a discussion of the tension of interpretation between millennial systems, see David Turner, "The Continuity of Scripture and Eschatology: Key Hermeneutical Issues," *Grace Theological Journal* 6 (1985): 275-87. Ironically, some of those opposed to interpreting Ezekiel 40-48 literally provide a series of maps of the various details in the vision.

realized. If one is going to bring a dispensational grid to Ezekiel 40-48 and argue for a renewed sacrificial system, then he must be able to demonstrate first that the temple will be realized during the kingdom period. Similarly (though not as often pressed), if one is going to argue against a renewed sacrificial system in the millennium, then one must demonstrate that the temple is *not* meant for the future. This, in the writer's opinion, has not been done. When the various views are considered as to when Ezekiel's temple will be realized, it is felt that the Kingdom interpretation best fits the data. Therefore, we anticipate with Ezekiel a temple during the glorious reign of the Messiah.

"At the very outset, let's clarify some things about law and grace. For one thing, they are antithetical concepts, and that antithesis is vitally related to the Christian life. When Paul answers the question of why sin shall not have dominion over the believer, it is with the statement that we are not under law but under grace (Rom. 6:14). "

- Charles C. Ryrie
Balancing the Christian Life, 1969, page151

19

Released From the Law for Sanctification:
A Dispensational Perspective on Romans 7:6

John F. Hart

Introduction

Christians have regularly and historically debated the role of the law in sanctification and Christian living. For theologians, it is common to speak of the "third use" of the law.[1] The law has as its first purpose to convict man of sin, and as its second purpose to act as a "schoolmaster" (Gal. 3:24–25 KJV; "tutor," NASV, NKJV; "guardian," ESV) in leading people to Christ.[2] But the third use of the law is its so-called purpose as a rule of life for Christian sanctification and godliness. But if the Christian is obligated to the Mosaic law for sanctification, verses such as Romans 6:14–15 and 7:6 become a quandary. How can the New Testament believer be "released from the law" (Rom. 7:6) and no longer be "under law" (Rom. 6:14) while at the same time being under the Mosaic law for sanctification?[3] A dispensational approach has long insisted that the new covenant believer is not under the Mosaic law

---

[1] Although it is disputed, Luther seems to be alone among the Reformers in speaking against the third use of the law. For example, Luther writes, "The scholastics think that the judicial and ceremonial laws of Moses were abolished by the coming of Christ, but not the moral law. They are blind. When Paul declares that we are delivered from the curse of the Law he means the whole Law, particularly the moral law which more than the other laws accuses, curses, and condemns the conscience. The Ten Commandments have no right to condemn that conscience in which Jesus dwells, for Jesus has taken from the Ten Commandments the right and power to curse us." Martin Luther, *A Commentary on St. Paul's Epistle to the Galatians,* transl. Theodore Graebner, 2nd ed. (Grand Rapids: Zondervan, n.d.), 187. After Luther, however, Lutheranism adopted the threefold use of the law. See F. F. Bruce, *Paul, Apostle of the Heart Set Free* (Grand Rapids: Eerdmans, 1977), 191.

[2] This purpose of the law may be questioned. While several versions translate *eis christon,* "(to lead us) to Christ" (NIV, NASV), others render the phrase temporally ("the law was our guardian/custodian until Christ came") as do the ESV, NET, NRSV, and REB. The surrounding verses ("before faith came," v. 23; "now that faith has come, v. 25) are clearly temporal. Additionally, the word *paidagōgos* ("custodian, guardian") "does not suggest the notion of instruction that leads to Christ....The ancient 'pedagogue' was not a teacher but a babysitter." Douglas J. Moo, "The Law of Christ as the Fulfillment of the Law of Moses: A Modified Lutheran View," *Five Views on Law and Gospel,* ed. Wayne G. Strickland (Grand Rapids: Zondervan, 1999), 338. Thielman writes, "Those under the pedagogue's charge sometimes remembered their caretaker fondly; but frequently in satire and in artwork he is depicted as a harsh figure, rod in hand, ready to punish any disobedience. As Galatians 3:23 shows, Paul's purpose for comparing the Sinaitic covenant to a pedagogue in this passage is twofold: to emphasize its purpose of identifying and punishing sin and, at the same time, *to highlight its temporary nature*" (italics added). Frank Thielman, "Law," *Dictionary of Paul and His Letters* (Downers Grove, IL: InterVarsity, 1993), 539.

[3] English translations are taken from the NASV 1995 unless noted otherwise.

for justification or for sanctification. It may be even argued that the role of the Mosaic law to the New Testament believer is foundational to dispensationalism.[4] This article briefly supports this theology from Romans 7:6 in its context, and answers some objections to the abrogation of the entire Mosaic law in the New Testament economy.

Released From the Mosaic Law in Romans 7:1–6

Romans 6:14–15 as the Context to Romans 7:6

The need in Romans for an explanation about our release from the Mosaic law in Romans 7:6 arises from the apostle's announcement in Roman 6:14, "For sin shall not be master over you, for you are not under law but under grace." Paul repeats the thought in 6:15: "Shall we sin because we are not under law but under grace?"[5] The text is straightforward and should be taken at face value. No one should fail to see that Paul sets in diametrical opposition being "under law" (*hypo nomon*) and being "under grace." Therefore, one cannot be under grace and under law at the same time. To be under grace for sanctification precludes being under the law of Moses for sanctification and vice versa. This contrast is marked out by Paul's use of *hote gar ēmen...nuni de* ("For while we were...but now") in Romans 7:5–6, signaling the arrival of a new age of God's working with believers (cf. Rom 3:21; 6:22; 11:30).[6]

Galatians 5:18 also sets in polar opposition being led by the Spirit and being "under law" (*hypo nomon*): "But if you are led by the Spirit, you are not under the Law." Moo is correct in stating that to be "under law" for Paul in Romans 6:14 is to be "under the Mosaic economy," not merely to be under moral obligations and commands from God.[7] Paul does not use the word "law" in a broad sense of demands that one is to obey. In that sense, every person in every age of history can be said to be under law. "What is crucial to recognize is that this is *not* the way in which Paul usually uses the term *nomos*" (italics original).[8]

---

[4] Cf. Wayne G. Strickland, "The Inauguration of the Law of Christ with the Gospel of Christ: A Dispensational View," *Five Views on Law and Gospel,* 230.

[5] The interconnection of 6:14 and 7:1 can be established by the following: 1) the last use of *kurieuoœ* ("to have power over, rule over") preceding 7:1 is found in 6:14. The law, much like sin, "lords it over" a person; 2) the last use of *nomos* ("law") before 7:1 is found in 6:14.

[6] Cf. Don N. Howell Jr., "Pauline Eschatological Dualism and Its Resulting Tensions," *Trinity Journal* 14 (spring 1993): 15.

[7] Douglas J. Moo, "'Law,' 'Works of the Law,' and Legalism in Paul," *Westminster Theological Journal* 45 (1983): 82.

[8] Ibid., 88.

Moo also notes, "Traditional Reformed (and especially Puritan) exegesis has emphasized that the contrast here [in Rom. 6:14] is between justification and condemnation."[9] In the Reformed view, the believer's new status under grace has delivered them from a "covenant of works." But Paul does not imply that the Christian has been set free from the law for justification but not for sanctification. Romans 6 concerns deliverance from the power of sin rather than deliverance from the penalty of sin. "If sin is not to rule believers (6:14a), more than forgiveness (i.e. freedom from the law's curse) is necessary."[10] Moo supports this with two arguments. First, Romans 5:20a, the last mention of law before 6:14, states that "the Law came in so that the transgression would increase." Therefore, when Paul states, "sin shall not be your master, because you are not under law, but under grace" (Rom. 6:14), the thought likely includes a release from the sin-inciting power of the law stressed in 5:20. Second, if Paul intended to say that believers were only released from the Mosaic law for justification but not sanctification, he certainly would have needed to add a proviso to avoid being seriously misunderstood. But no proviso is offered. The best answer to this missing caveat is to interpret Paul as meaning the believer in this age is not under the law as a rule of life.[11]

An examination of the phrase "under law" (*hypo nomon*) bears out the interpretation that the New Testament believer's freedom from being "under law" means to be released from the entire law of Moses. The exact Greek phrase is used eleven times (Rom. 6:14–15; 1 Cor. 9:20; Gal. 3:23; 4:4–5, 21; 5:18). In every context, the entire Mosaic law is under consideration. When Paul described Christ being born "under the law" (Gal. 4:4), there is no suggestion that Paul means Jesus was born under only a certain portion of the law (the civil law versus the moral law, or the ceremonial law versus the civil law). Nor does Paul intend us to think that Jesus was born under legalism or the misuse of the law (as some interpret the word "law" in sections of Galatians and Romans). Galatians 4:4 is decisive in denying this approach.[12] Paul also adds that Christ was born under law so as to redeem those who were "under law" (4:5), i.e., under the whole Mosaic system. Those who were "under law" were required to be in submission to the entire Mosaic code, not just part of it. If being "under law" means obligation to the entire Mosaic code (1 Cor. 9:20; Gal 3:23; 4:4–5, 21), then not being "under

---

[9] Douglas J. Moo, "A Modified Lutheran View," *Five Views on Law and Gospel*, 365.

[10] Ibid.

[11] Ibid., 366.

[12] Gerald W. Peterman, "Paul and the Law in Romans 7:1–6" (master's thesis, Trinity Evangelical Divinity School, 1988), 21n57.

law" (Rom. 6:14; Gal. 5:18) means release from obligations to the entire Mosaic code. Galatians 3:23 clearly sets being "under law" in contrast to the New Testament era ("...we were kept in custody under the law, being shut up to the faith which was later to be revealed").

Does Theology or Exegesis Determine the Christian's Relationship to the Law? Romans 7:6 fits into the well-recognized unit of Romans 5–8. But contextually, Paul is not discussing justification in chapters 5–8 but sanctification. Romans 6:14 and 7:6 cannot be adjusted to imply that not being "under law" (or being released from the law) means not being under the law of Moses for justification. The very wording of Romans 7:1–6 (as will be demonstrated more fully below) demands the interpretation that believers in the New Testament economy are not obligated to the Mosaic law as their rule of life, i.e., for sanctification. F. F. Bruce writes,

> In the Reformed tradition derived from Geneva, it has frequently been said that, while the man in Christ is not under the law as a means of salvation, he remains under it as a rule of life. In its own right this distinction may be cogently maintained as a principle of Christian theology and ethics, but it should not be imagined that it has Pauline authority. According to Paul, the believer is *not* [italics original] under law as a rule of life—unless one thinks of the law of love, and that is a completely different kind of law, fulfilled not by obedience to a code but by the outworking of an inward power. When Paul says, "Sin will have no dominion over you, since you are not under law but under grace" (Romans 6:14), it is the on-going course of Christian life that he has in view, not simply the initial justification by faith—as is plain from the point of the antinomian retort which Paul immediately quotes, "What then? Are we to sin because we are not under law but under grace?" (Romans 6:15).[13]

Despite the statements by Paul to the effect that Christians are no longer under the Mosaic code for sanctification, theologians and evangelical leaders find ways of explaining away these passages. In the final analysis, believers become obligated to keep some aspects or parts of the Mosaic law (e.g., the Ten Commandments) for sanctification. Stott argues, "We are set free from the law as a way of acceptance, but obliged to keep it as a way of holiness. It is as a ground of justification that the law no longer binds us (for our acceptance we are 'not under law but under grace'). But as a standard of conduct the law is still binding, and we seek to fulfill it, as we walk according

---

[13] Bruce, *Paul*, 192. Perhaps Bruce makes the statement that "this distinction may be cogently maintained as a principle of Christian theology and ethics" to avoid offending Reformed theologians. But since he admits that Paul does not teach this theology, his statement is confusing.

to the Spirit."[14] Stott is certainly not alone in affirming the role of the law in sanctification. Reformed theology is especially concerned that New Testament Christians develop holiness by means of the law.[15] Rushdoony comments, "From beginning to end, the Scripture makes clear that…justification is by the grace of God through faith, and that sanctification is by law, God's law."[16] Such declarations can only be accomplished by explaining away the clear statements of Romans 6:14, 15, and 7:6. As can be seen by the quotations above, this is done by delimiting the phrase "not under law" to a release from the moral law for justification. Hoekema reasons, "'Not under law' here [Rom. 6:14] means that we are no longer under condemnation because of our failure to keep the law." A few sentences later, he reasons, "In the sense that believers no longer need to keep the law as a way of earning their salvation, they indeed have been delivered from it. In another sense, however, believers are not free from the law. They should be deeply concerned about keeping God's law as a way of expressing their gratitude to Him for the gift of salvation."[17]

Can Hoekema's interpretation be correct? He holds that "believers no longer need to keep the law as a way of earning their salvation." If this is the meaning of "under law" in Romans 6:14, then Old Testament believers (since they were all "under law") needed "to keep the law as a way of earning their salvation." Such an interpretation contradicts all revelation on the nature of Old Testament justification (e.g., Rom. 4:1–10). Even Old Testament believers were never "under law" as a means of justification. But they were "under law" as an obligation as a rule of life (sanctification). Additionally, gratitude is not an adequate apologetic for keeping the law, as Hoekema suggests. Were Old Testament saints permitted to keep the food laws, the sacrifices, and other ceremonial laws with an ungrateful heart? Most likely not. Should New Testament believers "be deeply concerned about keeping" the ceremonial laws "as a way of expressing their gratitude to Him for the gift of salvation"? Certainly not. Nor are New Testament

---

[14] John R. W. Stott, *Men Made New. An Exposition of Romans 5–8* (Downers Grove, IL: InterVarsity, 1966), 82–83.

[15] Willem A. VanGemeren, "The Law Is the Perfection of the Righteousness in Jesus Christ: A Reformed Perspective," in *Five Views on Law and Gospel*, 52–54; Greg L. Bahnsen, "The Theonomic Reformed Approach to Law and Gospel," *Five Views on Law and Gospel*, 109–15. But in the same volume, a non-Reformed scholar holds the same viewpoint. See Walter C. Kaiser Jr., "The Law as God's Gracious Guidance for the Promotion of Holiness," 177–99.

[16] Rousas John Rushdoony, *The Institutes of Biblical Law* (Phillipsburg, NJ: Presbyterian and Reformed, 1973), 549.

[17] Anthony A. Hoekema, "The Reformed Perspective," in Melvin E. Dieter et. al., *Five Views of Sanctification* (Grand Rapids: Zondervan, 1987), 85.

believers obligated, even by gratitude, to keep the "moral" commands of the Mosaic code. By keeping the commands of Christ, the Christian indirectly keeps the universal, moral laws of God. But if the church is obligated to keep the Ten Commandments, then it is also obligated to keep the imposed penalties for violating the Ten Commandments. Death was the penalty for violating the first four commandments, and for overt disobedience of all the other commandments. Is this to be obeyed by the church today?[18]

Bruce is worthy of citing a second time here. "Again, it is said that Christ is the end of the ceremonial law (including not only the sacrificial cultus but circumcision and the sacred calendar) but not of the moral law. Once more, this is perfectly valid, and to some extent an obvious theological and ethical distinction; but it has no place in Pauline exegesis. It has to be read into Paul, for it is not a distinction that Paul himself makes."[19] On the other hand, it is the exegesis of such passages as Romans 6:14–15 and 7:6, not primarily a theological system, that generates a dispensational viewpoint on the role of the law for the New Testament believer.

The Immediate Context of Romans 7:6

In Romans 7:1–6, the apostle illustrates our release from the law with an analogy from marriage (vv. 2–3). A woman is released from obligations to her husband if her husband dies. She is then free to marry another. So believers have died to the law and now have been married to Christ.[20] Their former marriage to the law (the old husband) is no longer in force. Paul may imply by this analogy that to return to one's former husband (the law) is to commit spiritual adultery against Christ. We have been released from the law and now have been married to Christ (7:4, 6). To place oneself again under the Mosaic law as a New Testament code for living is to join oneself again to the law as a woman joined again to her ex-husband (cf. Deut. 24:1–4). Theologians who advocate sanctification by adherence to the Mosaic law should consider the possibility that "lawism" (legalism) for sanctification is a form of spiritual adultery. The wife (the believer) cannot have both Christ

---

[18] In arguing against a division of the Mosaic code into moral, civil, and ceremonial instructions, Williamson writes, "the law made no such distinction *when assigning penalties for violators*" (italics original). Joel T. Williamson Jr., "The Sabbath and Dispensationalism," *Journal of Dispensational Theology* 11 (March 2007): 84.

[19] Bruce, *Paul*, 192–93.

[20] In Paul's following discussion, the believer has died to the law, but it is implied that the law (the former husband) is very much alive. Paul has been circumspect in his wording to imply that the law is still "alive" as the ex-husband. It is the believer who has died to the law. Rather than the careful articulation of reality, some see this as an unfortunate problem in the illustration. William Manson, *Jesus and the Christian* (Grand Rapids: Eerdmans, 1967), 145.

and the law of Moses as her husband.[21] Neither is there any thought that the husband can be divided so that part of the marriage to the former husband continues into the new marriage. The husband is an indivisible entity and illustrates the single entity of the Mosaic code.

This perspective is enhanced by the close association between the analogy of the slave master in Romans 6 and the analogy of the married woman in Romans 7.[22] Death has brought about a release from the former slave master (sin) so that the commands of the old slave master are no longer an obligation. Similarly, the woman has undergone a death that releases her from obligations to her former husband. No one would suggest that Paul wishes to teach that the believer is released from certain kinds of sins, but not from others. Neither are we to conclude that the believer is released from certain kinds of Mosaic laws (ceremonial, civil), but not from others (moral).

Are Believers Released from a Part of the Law or from the Whole Law?
One patent response to the teaching that Christians are released from the Mosaic law is to suggest that this is a freedom only from the ceremonial aspect, or the ceremonial and civil aspects of the law.[23] While it is convenient to categorize the law of Moses by the traditional tripartite division—the civil, ceremonial, and moral law—this cataloging cannot be found in the Old Testament or the New Testament.[24] Neither the law of Moses itself (cf. Deut. 27:26) or the subsequent prophets that describe its violations among the nation reveal a division.[25] Even the Jews themselves did not recognize this division[26] or at least did not insist on it.[27] To hint at the inadequacy of any

---

[21] Some commentators argue that the woman does not represent an individual who has become a Christian but Israel. Cf. John E. Toews, *Romans,* Believers Church Bible Commentary (Scottsdale, PA: Herald Press, 2004), 182.

[22] Bruce, *Paul,* 193–94.

[23] The New Perspective of Paul also approaches the difficulties of Paul's view of the law in this manner. Thielman writes, "It is precisely these highly prized, and ethnically specific, aspects of the Law that Paul considers no longer valid." Later, he remarks, "When Paul speaks of the 'old covenant' as 'made obsolete in Christ' (2 Cor. 3:14), he may have in focus not everything the Law contained....If this perspective is correct, then Paul does not say in these passages that every aspect of the Mosaic legislation was abolished...." Again, he says, "Some of the content of the Mosaic Law emerges unscathed from Paul's critique [of the negatives of the law in Gal]...." Thielman, "Law," 539.

[24] Contra Bahnsen, "Theonomic Reformed Approach," *Five Views of Law and Gospel,* 104.

[25] Arnold G. Fruchtenbaum, "Israelology: Part 1 of 6," *Chafer Theological Seminary Journal* 5 (April 1999): 43.

[26] Cf. 4 Mac. 5:19–21 (NRSV): "Therefore do not suppose that it would be a petty sin if we were to eat defiling food; to transgress the law in matters either small or great is of equal seriousness, for in either case the law is equally despised." See further references to the unity of the law in Jewish thinking in Peter H. Davids, *The Epistle of James: A Commentary on the Greek Text* (Grand Rapids: Eerdmans, 1982), 116.

exegetical or theological division, Radmacher says that the Mosaic law included "moral law, ceremonial laws, civil laws, criminal laws, sanitary laws, and governmental laws."[28] The New Testament treats the law as a unit (James 2:10; Gal. 3:10; 5:3) that cannot easily be divided into lesser and greater parts.[29] Moo comments, "As has often been pointed out, the threefold distinction of moral, ceremonial, and civil law as separate categories with varying degrees of applicability is simply unknown in the Judaism of the first century, and there is little evidence that Jesus or Paul introduced such a distinction."[30]

The threefold division of the civil, ceremonial, and moral aspects of the Mosaic law may be a helpful tool for superficially summarizing the law. Nevertheless, for understanding the relevance to the Jews of the Old Testament or for interpreting the continuity/discontinuity of the law, such divisions are rather artificial.[31] On what basis are we to obey the fifth commandment to honor father and mother (Ex. 20:12a), but cannot claim the promise attached to it, "that your days may be prolonged in the land [of Israel] which the LORD your God gives you" (Ex. 20:12b)?[32] Into what division should we place the Sabbath, the fourth of the Ten Commandments?[33] Is it a moral, ceremonial, or civil law? The Sabbath was inextricably tied to the ceremonial system since sacrifices were required of Israel every Sabbath day (Num. 28:9–10). The Sabbath observance was also linked to many of Israel's feasts (Hos. 2:11). For example, the Feast of Tabernacles began and ended on a Sabbath (Lev. 23:39). By what logic can we eliminate the celebration of

---

Dorsey comments, "The scheme of a tripartite division is unknown both in the Bible and in early rabbinic literature. Its formulation appears rather to be traceable to modern Christian theology." David A. Dorsey, "The Law of Moses and the Christian: A Compromise," *Journal of the Evangelical Theological Society* 34 (September 1991): 329.

[27] Charles C. Ryrie, "The End of the Law," *Vital New Testament Issues,* ed. Roy B. Zuck (Grand Rapids: Kregel, 1996), 79.

[28] Earl D. Radmacher, *Salvation* (Nashville: Word, 2000), 64.

[29] Aldrich quotes from numerous scholars that argue for the unity of the law, such as H. A. W. Meyer, F. Godet, J. Denney, G. B. Stevens, A. S. Peake, E. Sauer, and H. C. Thiessen. Roy L. Aldrich, "Has the Mosaic Law Been Abolished?" *Bibliotheca Sacra* 116 (October 1959): 322–29. Cf. also Robert Lightner, "Perspectives on Theonomy. Part 3: A Dispensational Response to Theonomy," *Bibliotheca Sacra* 143 (July 1986): 236.

[30] Moo, "'Law,' and Legalism in Paul," 85. Cf. also, Moo, "Modified Lutheran View," 336–37.

[31] "The arbitrariness of classification is a major problem with the division of the law." Williamson, "Sabbath and Dispensationalism," 84n27.

[32] Moo observes that Paul appreciably changes the promise attached to the fifth commandment when he obligates Christians to obey its directive. By this means, it is evident that Paul incorporates within the law of Christ some of the teachings of the law of Moses. Moo, "Modified Lutheran View," 337, 370.

[33] Interestingly, Calvin taught that Sunday was not a continuation of the Jewish Sabbath, but that the Sabbath was abrogated (*Institutes,* 2.8.32–34). However, the Westminster Confession of Faith held sway for the Reformed tradition, calling Sunday the "Christian Sabbath" (21.7).

Israel's feasts from the New Testament church, yet still require the Sabbath? Can the Sabbath *day* remain for the church but not the sabbatical *year* (Lev. 24:4–5)?

Despite evangelical sophistry, it must be admitted that working on Saturday but worshiping on Sunday does not fulfill the command regarding the Sabbath revealed to Moses.[34] Even for gathering wood on the Sabbath, the penalty was death (Num. 15:32–36)—the very same penalty for adultery (Lev. 20:10), incest (Lev. 20:11–12), and idolatry (Ex. 22:20; Deut. 13:10). God considered a disregard for any part of the Mosaic law as a highly moral (or immoral) act (cf. Isa. 56:2–4). So, "If the Sabbath—one of the Ten Commandments—is no longer binding, how can any part of the law still be in effect?"[35]

Kaiser rejects the indivisible unity of the Mosaic law based on two premises. First, the law contains the promises made to the patriarchs. If the law is abrogated as a unit, these promises must also be set aside. Second, according to Jeremiah 31:33, the law is to be placed in the heart of the believer as part of the new covenant. This suggests the ongoing validity of the moral aspects of the law.[36] Strickland's response is quite satisfactory. The promises contained in the Mosaic code are reiterations and expansions of the Abrahamic covenant. The promises came before the law and were added to the law. The law can be set aside without invalidating the promise (Gal. 3:17–19). Regarding the Jeremiah 31 passage, Strickland reasons that in context the new covenant law placed in the heart of the believer is contrasted with the old covenant. From the perspective of the New Testament, the law that Jeremiah predicts will be placed in the believer's heart can be easily understood to be the law of Christ (Gal. 6:2).[37]

In the immediately following verses to Romans 7:6, Paul unmistakably identifies the moral regulations of the law as the subject of his concern since he speaks of coveting (7:7–8), the tenth commandment.[38] The

---

[34] For similar ideas to those offered here and a more complete presentation of the role of the Sabbath for the Christian, see the entire article by Williamson, "Sabbath and Dispensationalism," 77–95.

[35] Ibid., 85.

[36] Kaiser, "The Law as God's Gracious Guidance," *Five Views on Law and Gospel*, 189.

[37] Wayne G. Strickland, "Response to Walter C. Kaiser," in *Five Views on Law and Gospel*, 211–13. Strickland points out that the distinction of the moral law from the civil and/or ceremonial laws is essential to the arguments of the two Reformed positions (VanGemeren and Bahnsen) and Kaiser's approach in *Five Views on Law and Gospel*, but only that of Kaiser (a non-Reformed position) offers any defense. Strickland, "Response to Walter C. Kaiser," 223.

[38] Donald M. Davies, "Free from the Law: An Exposition of the Seventh Chapter of Romans," *Interpretation* 7 (April 1953): 157. Segal thinks Paul is coveting the easier life of law-keeping and ceremonial observance—a life easier than a faith alone relationship with Christ. Segal, *Paul the Convert*, 245. But this is a gratuitous limitation of the context and the word "covet" to ceremonial law.

civil and ceremonial regulations are not mentioned or implied in the entire chapter but a perspicuously moral obligation is. Therefore, the release from law that Paul specifically addresses in 7:6 implies a release from the Ten Commandments as the focus for sanctification in the New Testament. Fee points out the life in Christ "for Paul is decidedly *not under Torah*" (italics original).[39] He comments further, "And it will do no good, as is so often attempted, to bring Torah through the back door in some theological way that lies beyond Paul's concerns—as though for Paul Torah is still about, even though we may not be under it. That may work for some theologically, but it is decidedly not an issue raised by Paul either here or anywhere else in Romans. Thus Fung ('Impotence,' 40) suggests that Paul's purpose is 'to show that the law is powerless to sanctify the Christian'...."[40]

As Aldrich concludes, "The unity of the Mosaic law leaves only two alternatives—either complete deliverance from or complete subjection to the entire system."[41] Schreiner also makes a similar statement, "The law was a single fabric for Paul, and the acceptance of part of the law necessarily and logically implied that one had to obey the rest of the law as well."[42] Ryrie agrees, "Unless the New Testament expressly says so, part of the law cannot be ended without doing away with all of it."[43]

Misunderstanding:
Being Released From the Law for Sanctification

Misunderstanding #1: Release from the Law for Sanctification Results in Lawlessness?

Those who insist that a New Testament Christian is not under any form of the Mosaic law for sanctification will be radically misunderstood.[44] As mentioned above, the false assumption will be made that such teachings

---

[39] Gordon D. Fee, *God's Empowering Presence: The Holy Spirit in the Letters of Paul* (Peabody, MA: Hendrickson, 1994), 511.

[40] Ibid., 511n115. Fee, however, disregards Fung's exegesis of Rom. 7:14–25, which in this author's opinion is one of the best treatments of the passage. See footnote 82 below.

[41] Aldrich, "Has the Mosaic Law Been Abolished?" 325.

[42] Schreiner, however, is speaking of justification, not sanctification. Thomas R. Schreiner, "Paul and Perfect Obedience to the Law: An Evaluation of the View of E. P. Sanders," *Westminster Theological Journal* (fall 1985): 265. Nevertheless, his comment can and should be equally applied to sanctification.

[43] Ryrie, "End of the Law," 81.

[44] A strong grace-oriented approach to salvation (i.e., those who insist that eternal life is a free gift apart from *any* form of works) is especially charged with antinomianism. It is interesting to observe the definition given by the Anchor Bible Dictionary for antinomianism: "The conviction that believers are freed from the demands of God's law by depending upon God's grace for their salvation (thus *anti* 'against' + *nomos* 'law')." Robert W. Wall, "Antinomianism," *Anchor Bible Dictionary*, ed. D. N. Freedman (New York: Doubleday, 1992), 1:263.

lead to antinomianism and lawlessness.[45] Even Calvin misunderstood the teaching that Christians are freed from all the law of Moses.

> Some unskillful persons, from not attending to this, boldly discard the whole law of Moses, and do away with both its Tables, imagining it unchristian to adhere to a doctrine which contains the ministration of death. Far from our thoughts be this profane notion. Moses has admirably shown that the Law, which can produce nothing but death in sinners, ought to have a better and more excellent effect upon the righteous....If it cannot be denied that it contains a perfect pattern of righteousness, then, *unless we ought not to have any proper rule of life*, it must be impious to discard it [italics added].[46]

But to say that the New Testament believer is not under the law of Moses does not mean that he or she is without *all* forms of law.[47] Sanctification is not possible apart from obedience to some moral law. But this moral law does not have to be the law of Moses. On the contrary, it can be maintained that the New Testament believer is under the law of Christ instead of the law of Moses. Moo remarks, "The fallacy of castigating someone as an 'antinomian' because he argues that believers are not under the Mosaic law should at least be obvious. Such a charge would 'stick' only if it were demonstrated that the Mosaic law contains the *complete* and *sole* revelation of God's will for man (italics original)."[48]

In 1 Corinthians 9:20–21, Paul presents the relevance of the law of Christ for the believer over against the law of Moses: "...to those who are under the law, [I became][49] as under the law, that I might win those who are under the law; to those who are without law, [I became] as without law (not being without law toward God, but under law toward Christ)..." (NKJV).[50]

---

[45] "This is the so-called *tertius usus legis,* the third use of the law. The law is a rule of life for believers, reminding them of their duties and leading them in the way of life and salvation. This third use of the law is denied by the Antinomians." Louis Berkhof, *Systematic Theology* (Grand Rapids: Eerdmans, 1957), 615. Cf. also John H. Gerstner, *Wrongly Dividing the Word of Truth: A Critique of Dispensationalism* (Brentwood, TN: Wolgemuth & Hyatt, 1991), 217, 249.

[46] John Calvin, *Institutes* 2.7.13.

[47] Radmacher, *Salvation*, 64.

[48] Moo, "'Law,' and Legalism in Paul," 90. Cf. also Ryrie, "End of the Law," 84–85, where he points out that God gave several codes of ethics throughout history, such as the ones to Adam, to Noah, and to Abraham. "In the law of Christ are hundreds of commandments of the New Testament epistles, and together these form a new and distinct code of ethics" (85).

[49] The aor. middle indicative of *ginomai* is supplied from the preceding clause in the verse, "and to the Jews *I became* as a Jew" (italics added).

[50] Paul appears to purposefully avoid any parallel to the harsh authority the Mosaic law had for the Jew. This relationship he referred to as being simply "under law" (*hupo nomos*). Paul used this Greek phrase four times in 1 Corinthians 9:20 alone, and elsewhere only in Romans and Galatians (Rom. 6:14–15; Gal. 3:23; 4:4–5, 21; 5:18). However, in 1 Corinthians 9:21, when considering his obligations to Christ, he used

What is the sense of the words, "I became as *under the law*"? Would Paul "become as under the law" for justification to win the Jews? Certainly not! This would be contradictory to the very gospel to which he was trying to win them. So then, "not being under law" cannot be restricted or limited to release from a justification by law. But if believers are indeed under the Mosaic law for sanctification, it is equally troublesome to explain how Paul "became" as under the law. According to covenant theology, Paul the apostle (as a model for all Christians) was always "under the law" for sanctification. But to the contrary, the text can only mean that the leading apostle for the church age was not under law for justification or sanctification but "became as under the law [*egenomēn... hōs hypo nomon*]."

One additional observation is to be gleaned from 1 Corinthians 9:20–21. The apostle contends that to those who were without law, he became "as without law." Yet he qualifies his pronouncement. At no time was he without *all* moral law toward God, i.e., he was never lawless. Theologians should carefully note that although Paul had a perfect opportunity to do so, he did not assert his obligation to the law of Moses. Instead, he asserted his obligation to the law of Christ. A fundamental flaw in a discussion of the role of the Mosaic law for New Testament sanctification is to regard the law of Christ as essentially identical to the law of Moses.[51] The law of Moses and the law of Christ must be distinguished. Just as there are two distinct covenants (the old covenant and the new), so there are two distinctive laws: the law of Moses and the law of Christ. It is obvious that the law of Christ did not exist before Christ's teachings on earth. The greatest commandment that Jesus put forward does not appear in any of the Ten Commandments.[52] "The Ten Commandments have a prominent place in the law [of Moses] but Christ taught that the greatest commandment was not one of the ten (Matt. 22:36–

---

the Greek word *ennomos*, roughly translated "in law to Christ" as opposed to the more severe phrase, "under law to Christ."

[51] Hoekema blurs this distinction when discussing the third use of the law. Hoekema, "Reformed Perspective," 87.

[52] Covenant theology finds the Ten Commandments in the covenant of works given to Adam. Therefore they are the very essence of the eternal moral law of God. "In its discussion of the moral law, the [*Westminster*] *Confession* [*of Faith*] (Chapter 19, 'Of the Law of God') stated that God offered Adam a law, as a covenant of works, which bound him and all his posterity to perfect and exact obedience. After the fall, this law remained a perfect rule of righteousness, and as such was delivered by God to Moses in the form of the Ten Commandments. The moral law binds all humans forever to obedience, including believers." Curtis J. Evans, "The Role of the Moral Law in Thomas Shepard's Doctrine of the Sabbath," *Westminster Theological Journal* 63 (fall 2001): 309. One might ask why the law of love was not given to Adam since it is the pinnacle of God's moral law. Also, Paul makes it clear that the law of Moses did not exist from Adam to Moses (Rom. 5:13 NIV, ESV, "before the law was given"). Covenant theology does not give proper weight to progressive revelation.

37)."[53] In fact, under the law of Christ, the standard of holiness is increased in comparison to the law of Moses. "As would be expected the infinitely high demands of the moral law of God are more clearly and emphatically presented in the New Testament than in the Old. There is no need to return to Moses for deliverance from license and antinomianism."[54] Chafer has written,

> It is unfortunate that the theological discussion which has proceeded on the supposition that a Christian must either be under the law of Moses, or else be absolutely lawless and ungoverned, could not have made place for the fact that there is a third ground of relationship to God which is neither the law of Moses, nor the ungoverned lawlessness of the world. To be "inlawed to Christ" is to be under the teachings of grace as a rule of life. These teachings include the "commandments" of Christ which are addressed to Christians as such in the upper room, and these "commandments" of Christ have been taken up, enlarged, and advanced, under the guidance of the Spirit in the book of the Acts and the Epistles of the New Testament. They constitute a separate and sufficient rule of life for the believer which is divinely adapted to his position in grace....[55]

Misunderstanding #2: Release from the Law for Sanctification Means There Is No Longer a Function for the Law

Second, the false assumption is often made that freedom from the Mosaic law for sanctification must mean that there is no function for the Mosaic law in the New Testament era. Kaiser illustrates this misunderstanding: "Some describe the relationship between Law and Gospel as one in which the law is no longer obligatory....Accordingly, we are delivered both from the law's *usefulness*, now that the promise came (cf. Rom. 7:6; Gal. 3:19–25; 4:1–5), and from its dominion (cf. Rom. 6:14; 7:4)..." (italics added).[56] Perhaps dispensationalists have been at fault for creating this impression about the role of the law. To the contrary, Paul taught in 1 Timothy 1:8–9, "But we know that the Law is good, if one uses it lawfully, realizing the fact that law is not made for a righteous person, but for those who are lawless and rebellious, for the ungodly and sinners...." The Mosaic law (and all of the Old Testament Scriptures) continues in the New Testament era to reveal sin and the righteous character of God (Rom. 3:20).[57] This also establishes or upholds

---

[53] Aldrich, "Has the Mosaic Law Been Abolished?" 322.

[54] Ibid., 333.

[55] Lewis Sperry Chafer, *Grace: The Glorious Theme* (Grand Rapids: Zondervan, 1922), 100–101.

[56] Kaiser, "The Law as God's Gracious Guidance," 177.

[57] It should be clearly noted that conviction of sin and a revelation of the character of God is not restricted to the Mosaic law. The teachings of Christ and the New Testament as a whole are equally powerful to bring conviction and reveal the moral character of God. What evangelical preacher or teacher will refer to

the ongoing validity of the law's usefulness (cf. Rom. 3:31; cf. 2 Tim. 3:16).[58] But if a person can become righteous (sanctified) apart from the Mosaic law (and he can), then the law has no "lawful" use for such a person.[59] This is the logical implication of the apostle's remark that the "law is not made for a righteous person." Since sanctifying righteousness can be attained—and must be attained—through the Spirit without the assistance of the Mosaic law, the Mosaic law must not be made a rule of life for the New Testament believer. Any teaching that the law is to be used to aid in sanctification is to violate the lawful (rightful) use of the law. Paul insists elsewhere that "the law gives sin its power" (1 Cor. 15:56 NLT) rather than "the law gives sanctification its power." The law is not given to decrease sin, but "the Law came in so that the transgression would increase" (Rom. 5:20). The apostle also clearly teaches that the law does not bring godliness. In Romans 7:8 Paul writes, "But sin, taking opportunity through the commandment, produced in me coveting of every kind; for apart from the Law sin is dead."[60] According to opponents of the complete abrogation of the law for the Christian, Paul should have written, "under the Law, sin is dead," not "apart from the law, sin is dead." Earlier in his epistle, the apostle wrote, "the Law brings about wrath, but where there is no law, there also is no violation" (Rom. 4:15). Here Paul gives an early hint to a theme he will develop in chapters 7–8, namely, release from the law ("where there is no [Mosaic] law") together with a life dependent on the Spirit will lead to victory over sin ("there also is no violation").

---

the commandment against adultery and not also mention Jesus' teaching that lust in the heart also constitutes adultery (Matt. 5:27–28)?

[58] Strickland believes that according to 1 Tim. 1, Paul is addressing this ongoing applicability of the law to the unbeliever, not the believer. Strickland, "A Dispensational View," 242. Moo also interprets these verses to mean that the law is not binding on those made righteous by faith in Christ. Moo, "A Modified Lutheran View," 367. But Bahnsen believes 1 Tim. 1 is applicable to the believer as well. Greg L. Bahnsen, "Response to Wayne C. Strickland," in *Five Views of Law and Gospel,* 300–301. If 1 Tim. 1:9–10 is applied to believers, then the law has abiding effect to convict sin in disobedient Christians. Two observations can be made about this interpretation. First, the ongoing convicting power of the law cannot be extended to mean that the church saint is under its authority for sanctification. The disobedient believer corrects his unrighteousness, not by obeying the law but by walking in the Spirit (Gal. 5:16) and in this way producing the fruit of the Spirit (Gal. 5:22–23). There is *no law* (the law of Moses or the law of Christ) against the fruit of the Spirit (Gal. 5:23b). Second, Reformed theologians like Bahnsen, who believe in the perseverance of the saints, would have to admit that Paul applies to true believers all the sins in the 1 Tim. 1:9–10 lists. For the apostle says the law was designed for "lawbreakers and rebels, the ungodly and sinful, the unholy and irreligious; for those who kill their fathers or mothers, murderers, for adulterers and perverts, for slave traders and liars and perjurers" (1 Tim. 1:9–10a).

[59] The apostle employs a powerful word play in 1 Tim. 1:8 with the word, "lawfully" (*nomimōs*).

[60] In 7:8b, the NLT has, "If there were no law, sin would not have that power."

It should come as no surprise that Paul himself models how to use the law to reveal sin in the book of Romans itself. In Romans 7:7, Paul declares of his own experience, "I would not have come to know sin except through the Law." A good summary of the rightful New Testament use of the law is found in Romans 3:19, "Now we know that whatever the Law says, it speaks to those who are under the Law, so that every mouth may be closed and all the world may become accountable to God."[61]

Mounce specifically connects Romans 7:6 with the new wineskin parable of the Lord (Matt. 9:16–17). "In context, the new cloth and fresh wine represent the joyous spirit of the new age. Old garments and hardened wineskins are the restrictive forms of previous worship. In Romans 7:6 the same two Greek words are used to compare the 'old [palaiotēti] way of a written code' and the 'new [kainotēti] way of the Spirit.'"[62] Consequently, New Testament believers must refuse to put new wine in old wineskins (Matt. 9:17; Mark 2:22; Luke 5:37–38). They must resist placing the ministry of the new covenant and the Spirit into the wineskin of the old covenant (the law).[63]

The ministry of the Holy Spirit mentioned in Romans 7:6 certainly coincides with the new covenant,[64] not with the old covenant. Paul proclaims, "But now we have been released [katērgēthēmen] from the Law...so that we serve in newness of the Spirit and not in oldness of the letter." The Spirit-letter antithesis also appears in 2 Corinthians 3:6 where Paul discusses the contrast between the old covenant and the new covenant: "[God] who also made us adequate as servants of a new covenant, not of the

---

[61]In Rom. 3:19, "law" in the phrase "whatever the law says" probably means the entire Old Testament since Paul has just quoted several times from the Psalms and Isaiah. Cf. John F. Walvoord, "Law in the Epistle to the Romans: Part 1," *Bibliotheca Sacra* 94 (January–March 1937): 22–23. However, "law" in the phrase "under the Law" has reference to the Mosaic code.

[62] Robert H. Mounce, *Matthew*, New International Biblical Commentary, ed. W. Ward Gasque (Peabody, MA: Hendrickson, 1991), 1:85. These Greek words are also the ones used of the new (*kainos*) covenant and old (*palaios*) covenant in 1 Cor. 3:6 and 14 respectively.

[63] Carson wishes to dismiss what he thinks are extremes of the dispensational view. D. A. Carson, "Matthew," *Expositor's Bible Commentary*, ed. Frank E. Gaebelein (Grand Rapids: Zondervan, 1984), 8:227–28. But the old(ness)/new(ness) wording shared by Rom. 7:6 and Matt. 9:16–17 better supports the dispensational perspective.

[64] The same Greek word (*katargeō*) is used in 2 Corinthians 3:7 to describe the passing away of the law (the old covenant) and its glory. The Ten Commandments are clearly in view when Paul speaks in the same verse of the old covenant as "in letters engraved on stones." Cf. also Fee, *God's Empowering Presence*, 508. Therefore, Paul places the Ten Commandments at the forefront of that aspect of the law that was passing away. The old covenant has been brought to an end (*katargeō*), especially the Ten Commandments. Wright states, "the echoes of 2 Corinthians 3 in Romans 7.6 indicate clearly enough that what Paul is talking about here is indeed the inauguration of the new covenant..." N. T. Wright, *The Climax of the Covenant. Christ and the Law in Pauline Theology* (Minneapolis: Fortress Press, 1991), 196.

letter but of the Spirit; for the letter kills, but the Spirit gives life." Here the Greek word for "letter" (*gramma*) refers to the Decalogue since in the next verse Paul uses the same word in the phrase, "letters [*gramma*] engraved on stones." It was the Decalogue that was written on the stone tablets on Mount Sinai.[65] Therefore, to be released from the law in Romans 7:6 is to be released from the "letter," including the Ten Commandments. Following Paul's statement that we do not serve any longer in the "oldness of the letter," the word "command" (*entolē*) appears six times (Rom. 7:8–13), demonstrating the *gramma* ("letter") for Paul carries with it the strict demands of the law without the new covenant provision of the indwelling Spirit.

Instead of the law and the Ten Commandments cooperating with the Spirit to bring holiness, Paul categorically sets in opposition the law and the Spirit in 7:6. Christians do not serve in newness of the letter (law) and Spirit but "in newness of the Spirit and not in oldness of the letter." The law is repetitively linked to sin, flesh, and death, not sanctification.[66] As Paul remarks in Romans 7:6, "we serve in newness of the Spirit and not in oldness of the letter."[67]

Misunderstanding #3: Continuity Between the Mosaic Law and the Law of Christ Means New Testament Believers Continue to Be Under the Moral Aspects of the Law of Moses

It is true that nine of the Ten Commandments are repeated in the New Testament (the Sabbath commandment is not repeated), demanding their obedience.[68] Dispensationalism is not opposed to continuity where continuity exists. However, the presence of nine of the Ten Commandments in New Testament teaching, not their presence in the law of Moses, establishes them as an obligation for the church. Leviticus 19:18 ("you shall love your neighbor as yourself") is also in the law, but the New Testament

---

[65] Peterman, "Paul and the Law in Romans 7:1–6," 90.

[66] Cf. Fee, *God's Empowering Presence*, 504.

[67] Rom. 10:4 needs to be interpreted in this light. It is certainly true that Christ is the "goal" (*telos*) of the law. But if the themes of Romans and the thrust of chapter 7 as a whole are considered, it is more appropriate to interpret *telos* as meaning that Christ is the "end" of the law for any and every form of righteousness among those who believe. Harrison argues, "However, the decisive factor that favors 'termination' rather than 'purpose' as the main idea is the contrast in 9:30ff. between the law and God's righteousness. Though the law is righteous in its requirements, it fails as an instrument of justification (cf. 8:3, 4)." Everett F. Harrison, "Romans," *Expositor's Bible Commentary*, ed. Frank E. Gaebelein (Grand Rapids: Zondervan, 1995), 111. But it should be added that it also fails as an instrument of sanctification.

[68] Radmacher, *Salvation*, 66.

believer now has, by virtue of the instructions of Christ and the apostles, new revelation on the importance and the centrality of love for one's neighbor.

Many of the moral principles underlying the laws of the United States are derived from English law. A legitimate continuity exists between numerous English laws and early American legislation. But when the newly founded government of the United States broke away from Great Britain and formed an independent nation, citizens of the American colonies did not remain under ten of the best laws of Britain. The fact that some of the laws of the new nation were quite similar to some of the laws of Great Britain did not confuse or compromise the new exclusive responsibility of a citizen of the United States. No one regards the continuity to form a responsibility to the old nation.[69] In the same way, the believing Jew of the first century moved entirely from an obligation to the Mosaic law into the new economy of grace instituted by the Lord Jesus (John 1:17).[70] Dispensationalists correctly emphasize discontinuity over any continuity between the Mosaic law and the law of Christ.[71]

Practical Benefits of Being Released From the Entire Law

If it is true that nine of the Ten Commandments are repeated in the New Testament, aren't dispensationalists playing a semantic game? After all, under the law of Christ the believer is still (at least indirectly) called on to obey the moral requirements found in the Ten Commandments. But to the

---

[69] While not committing himself to dispensationalism, Dorsey arrives at the same truth. He uses a labor contract to illustrate the point. "When a new treaty or contract replaces an older one, as in modern labor contracts, the terms of the older contract are normally nonbinding upon the parties. Granted, parties might be interested in the terms of a former contract for various reasons. But as far as legal applicability is concerned, it is the terms of the new contract, not the old, that are binding." Dorsey, "The Law of Moses and the Christian: A Compromise," 325.

[70] This illustration is an adaptation of one given by Aldrich, "Has the Mosaic Law Been Abolished?" 326. Aldrich carefully implies that "the moral principles" underlying the Mosaic law and the law of Christ are the same. Some prefer to express the unity of the Mosaic law and the law of Christ by suggesting that several OT laws pass over into the law of Christ. "Parts of the Old Testament are included under the law of Christ. Fulfilling the Law of Christ, therefore, is the ability under the filling of the Spirit to live in the spirit of all God-given laws that are neither modified nor abrogated by the New Testament. The believer then produces the righteousness of not just the Mosaic Law (Romans 8:4), but of the whole of God's eternal law." Paul R. Schmidtbleicher, "Law in the New Testament," *Chafer Theological Journal* 9 (fall 2003): 69.

[71] Lightner points to the distinction between the church and Israel as a primary reason that the Mosiac law is not a rule of life for the church. "The fact that God gave the Law to the people of Israel and not to the church is the beginning point for dispensationalism's difference with theonomy [on the role of the law of Moses]. All other points of disagreement stem from this one. In fact the same difference exists between dispensationalism and Reformed theology....Nowhere in Scripture is the Law of Moses ever said to have been given to the church. Only when the church's program is not seen as distinct from Israel's can it be said that the Law was given to the church." Lightner, "A Dispensational Response to Theonomy," 236–37.

contrary, it is of utmost importance to maintain a distinction between the law of Moses and the law of Christ, and to insist that the believer is freed from the entire law. The following practical considerations highlight the importance of the dispensational perspective.

First, the Mosaic law emphasizes negative commands (i.e., "you shall not" commands),[72] whereas the law of Christ stresses the positive commands such as the command to love. Leviticus 19:18 alone ("Love your neighbor as yourself") is cited in the New Testament by Jesus (Matt. 5:43; 19:19; 22:39; Mark 12:31), by Paul (Rom. 13:9; Gal. 5:14), and by James (James 2:8) a total of ten times. The law (and the Old Testament in general) does not give prominence to love for others; the New Testament and the law of Christ do. This law is a "new commandment" (John 13:34; 1 John 2:8–10; 2 John 5) and cannot be read back into the Old Testament as a characteristic trait of the Mosaic economy. Like the Pharisees, a Christian could fulfill externally or outwardly most of the Ten Commandments without being characterized by genuine love. The New Testament believer is to be known by what he does (i.e., love, John 13:35; cf. John 15:12, 17)), not by what he does not do. Also under a law orientation, one may place a greater stress on the separation from "sinners" than on compassion to reach them. Israel was primarily to come out and be separate, demonstrating God's holiness; the church is primarily to go out and be witnesses, demonstrating and proclaiming God's love (2 Cor. 5:18–19).

Second, wherever the law is stressed for sanctification, there is often a conscious or unconscious neglect of the ministry of the Holy Spirit for daily Christian living. Nearly all Christians are well aware of the Ten Commandments, but few Christians understand the ministry of the Spirit in producing Christlikeness in the believer (Rom. 8:2–13; Gal. 5:16, 22–23).[73] The only other use of the letter-Spirit contrast in Romans besides 7:6 is found in 2:28–29 where the inner person and the heart are contrasted with the outer person and the law: "For he is not a Jew who is one outwardly, nor is circumcision that which is outward in the flesh. But he is a Jew who is one

---

[72] All but the fifth commandment ("honor your father and mother") of the ten contain a negative command, mostly (in English), "You shall not...."

[73] Ryrie writes, "Now a rule of life involves at least three aspects: the specific laws, the enabling power, and the motivation. Thus when we speak of law and grace as rules of life we include not only the specific command but also the power and motivation which are part of the rule of life. And in this sense law and grace are antithetical opposites, for the laws, the power and the motivation were different under law from what they are under grace." Charles C. Ryrie, *Balancing the Christian Life* (Chicago: Moody, 1969), 152.

inwardly; and circumcision is that which is of the heart, by the Spirit, not by the letter...."

Third, and closely related to the second point above, when it is maintained that the believer must obey the Ten Commandments, a greater stress may be placed on the outward expressions of faith than on inner character. Law often results in legalism and self-righteousness just as it did among the Pharisees, with an accompanying spirit of exclusiveness and superiority. Frequently, distinctions are made between various kinds of sins, with certain sins viewed as heinous (adultery, homosexuality), while other sins are subtly accepted (e.g., gossip, gluttony).

Finally, in Romans 7:7–25 or 7:14–25, the immediately following passage to Romans 7:6, Paul describes his experience with the law. Reformed theology has traditionally argued that Paul is speaking from the vantage point of his maturity as he reflects on his inability to keep the law perfectly.[74] If Romans 7:6 is interpreted to mean that the believer is released from the civil and ceremonial law but not the moral law, Romans 7:7–25 or 7:14–25 should describe how the moral law assists Paul in sanctification to reach his joyful and successful Christian maturity. Clearly, the function of the law is not depicted in Romans 7 with such an optimistic outcome. Instead, Paul portrays the law as weak and powerless to bring righteousness for sanctification (Rom. 8:3). The severe descriptions of Paul's own defeat and oppression by sin cannot describe straightforwardly Paul in his maturity after numerous years of ministry.[75] Under this perspective of Romans 7, only a minor interconnection is inferred between the release from the law affirmed in 7:6 and the interpretation of 7:7–25.

Because the language of verses 14–25 appears to be too strong to apply to the Christian experience, modern scholars have continued to

---

[74] J. I. Packer, "The 'Wretched Man' of Romans 7," *Studia Evangelica* 2 (1964): 621–27; reprinted in *Keeping in Step with the Spirit* (Old Tappan, NJ: Revell, 1984), 127–29, 263–70; ibid., "The 'Wretched Man' Revisited: Another Look at Romans 7:14–25," *Romans and the People of God*, ed. Sven K. Soderlund and N. T. Wright (Grand Rapids: Eerdmans, 1999), 70–81; John Murray, *The Epistle to the Romans,* The New International Commentary on the New Testament (1968; repr. Grand Rapids: Eerdmans, 1977); 256–59; Charles Hodge, *Commentary on the Epistle to the Romans* (1886; repr. Grand Rapids: Eerdmans, 1977), 227–28, 246–47. Dispensationalists have sometimes chosen this view as well. John A. Witmer, "Romans," *Bible Knowledge Commentary, New Testament* (Wheaton: Victor Books, 1983), 467–69; Robert L. Saucy, "'Sinners' Who Are Forgiven or 'Saints' Who Sin," *Bibliotheca Sacra* 152 (October 1995): 409–11.

[75] These descriptions include "but I am of flesh, sold into bondage to sin" (v. 14); "I am doing the very thing I hate" (v. 15); "the good that I want, I do not do, but I practice the very evil that I do not want" (v. 19); "but I see a different law...making me a prisoner of the law of sin" (v. 23); "I myself...with my flesh [am serving] the law of sin" (v. 25).

interpret Romans 7:14–25 as a description of the unregenerate Paul[76] or as a representative of all Jews under the law.[77] In this way, Romans 7:6 can speak of a release from the entire law, but primarily for justification. Romans 7:7–25 outlines how the law convicted Paul but could not justify. However, several statements of Paul are impossible to explain in any other way than that the apostle is speaking of his regenerate state.[78]While each of these views attempts (and succeeds in varying degrees) to reveal something of Paul's theology, none ultimately harmonizes both the statements that give evidence to Paul's regeneration and the statements that demonstrate a repeated, unsuccessful conquest of sin. Neither do these approaches attempt to find in Romans 7 an interpretation that fully considers the audience and the occasion of the book, particularly the issues related to the weak in faith and strong in faith (Rom. 14:1–15:6).[79]

While it would take a full-length article itself to defend, the proposal made here is that Paul is addressing the weak in faith who as Christian Jews have remained under law (Rom. 14:1–6, 14–14, 20, 22–23; 15:1). While instructing the strong in faith to accept their weaker brothers, Paul does not want the weak in faith to remain weak.[80] By using his own past experience put into a vivid present tense, Paul is able to encourage the weak in faith—a state of Christian immaturity and unwilling failure—to become strong in faith through walking in the power of the Spirit (Rom. 8:1–4).[81] If this is the correct

---

[76] Anthony A. Hoekema, *The Christian Looks at Himself* (Grand Rapids: Eerdmans, 1977), 61–67; Robert H. Gundry, "The Moral Frustration of Paul Before His Conversion: Sexual Lust in Romans 7, 7–25," in *Pauline Studies*, ed. David A. Hagner and Murray J. Harris (Grand Rapids: Eerdmans, 1980), 228–45; Gordon D. Fee, *Paul, the Spirit, and the People of God* (Peabody, MA: Hendrickson, 1966), 133–35.

[77] Douglas J. Moo, *The Epistle to the Romans* (Grand Rapids: Eerdmans, 1996), 447–51.

[78] Rom. 7:22 ("I joyfully concur with the law of God in the inner man") and 7:25b ("I myself with my mind am serving the law of God..."). These comments cannot be harmonized with Paul's description of the nonbeliever in Rom. 1–3 or such statements as in Rom. 8:7, "the mind set on the flesh is hostile toward God; for it does not subject itself to the law of God, for it is not even able to do so."

[79] As is well known, the occasion and audience of the book of Romans has been the subject of much discussion. See Karl P. Donfried, ed. *The Romans Debate*, rev. and expanded (Peabody, MA: Hendricksen, 1991).

[80] This is evident in a number of ways. 1) Paul labels himself as strong in faith (Rom. 15:1); 2) the term "weak in faith" as opposed to "strong in faith" implies an unfavorable condition; 3) Paul sets before his readers Abraham as a prototype of the faith he wants in his readers. With precise terminology that clearly prepares for Rom. 14, Paul declares that Abraham did not become weak in faith but grew strong in faith (Rom. 4:19–20). "Paul took good care to dissociate Abraham from the weak in faith...." Paul S. Minear, *The Obedience of Faith: The Purposes of Paul in the Epistle to the Romans*, Studies in Biblical Theology, Second Series 18 (Naperville, IL: Alec R. Allenson, 1971), 54.

[81] The very terms Paul connects to the law in Rom. 8:3 are linked to the weak in faith in Rom. 15:1. ("For what the law was *powerless* [adunatos] to do in that it was *weakened* [astheneō] by the sinful nature," Rom. 8:3 NIV, italics added). These are the only places in the epistle where both *adunatos* and *astheneō/asthenēma* come together.

interpretation of Romans 7:14–25, those who teach that the Mosaic law is still in effect for sanctification are setting up the believer for the continuing immaturity, weakness, and defeat described in Romans 7:7–25 or 7:14–25.[82]

Conclusion

The great struggle for theologians and Christians in general is the seemingly contradictory Pauline statements about the Mosaic law. On the one hand, "the law is holy, and the commandment is holy, righteous and good" (Rom. 7:12). But on the other hand, "...the letter [Mosaic covenant] kills, but the Spirit gives life" (2 Cor. 3:6). Additionally, "...and this commandment, which was to result in life, proved to result in death for me" (Rom. 7:10). How can that which is holy, righteous, and good kill rather than give life? This is one of the primary stumbling blocks in setting aside the law of Moses for sanctification. Paul makes it clear that the law is not at fault (7:13). Nevertheless, sin uses the law; therefore, the Mosaic law must be set aside if sin is to cease. If the believer walks by the power and strength of the Spirit, he will actually fulfill "the requirement of the Law" (Rom. 8:4) while not being "under the law."[83]

To promote obedience to the Mosaic law—even the Ten Commandments (the old covenant)—is to promote sin and defeat in the Christian. It also promotes the spiritual adultery described by Paul in Romans 7:4–6. Legalism for sanctification must be replaced by an inflexible emphasis on the New Testament freedom found in living by the Spirit. Living by the Spirit (Gal. 5:22–23) will not produce anything less than Christlikeness in the believer. Biblically speaking, then, a consistent theology of grace must not only be concerned about the role of grace as opposed to obedience to the law for justification. It must also be concerned about the role of grace over against obedience to the law for sanctification.

---

[82] The most recently scholarly approach that treats Romans 7:14–25 in a broadly similar manner (but without any reference to the occasion of the epistle), see Ronald Y. K. Fung, "The Impotence of the Law: Toward a Fresh Understanding of Romans 7:14–25," in *Scripture, Tradition, and Interpretation*, ed. W. W. Gasque and W. S. LaSor (Grand Rapids: Eerdmans, 1978), 34–48.

[83] In Rom. 8:4, Paul is careful *not* to say that the New Testament believer fulfills the law but that the believer fulfills "the requirement [*dikaiōma*] of the law." Moo points out that the noun, *dikaiōma*, is singular but is unfortunately translated as a plural in the NIV. As the singular, it may refer to love that fulfills the entire law (Rom. 13:8, 10). Moo, "A Modified Lutheran View," *Five Views on Law and Gospel*, 371. There is nothing more righteous than love. Love remains the eternal principle behind all of the Ten Commandments.

"If rapprochement refers to "a state of having cordial relations", then I, for one (and there are many others) have always had such a relationship with believers I have known who have held to differing theological viewpoints (including covenant amillennialists, errantists, Pentecostals, Roman Catholics, Arminians, and Lordship Salvationists). But if rapprochement means "conformity" or "accord" applied to theology, then there simply will not be rapprochement between various theological viewpoints as long as we are here on earth."

- Charles C. Ryrie

Issues in Dispensationalism, 1994, page 24 (Willis & Master, eds.)

20

The Kingdom of Emergent Theology

Gary E. Gilley

It has been claimed that Sigmund Freud enjoyed telling his followers a story of a pastor who visited an atheist insurance agent who was on his death bed. The family had asked the pastor to share the gospel with their dying loved one as they waited in another room. As the conversation continued longer than expected there was hope that the pastor was being successful in his mission. When the pastor finally emerged from the bedroom it was discovered that the agent had not converted to Christ but he had been able to sell the pastor an insurance policy. While Freud used the illustration to warn his fellow psychoanalysts to stay true to their beliefs, Richard Mouw, president of Fuller Seminary, from whom I obtained this account, has another application to offer. While a most unlikely source (in my opinion) to offer the following warning, Mouw writes,

> In rejecting the very real defects of fundamentalism during the past few decades, evangelicals have begun to take very seriously their responsibilities to the larger culture – and with some obvious signs of success. The questions we must face honestly are these: *Have we sold a new policy to the culture – or has the culture sold us a policy* (emphasis mine).[1]

This is a most thought-worthy question in light of the emergent church movement's recent inroads into evangelicalism, and in some cases even fundamentalism. The emergent church is a movement deeply concerned with impacting the culture. But evidence is mounting to the effect that culture is having more impact on the emergent movement than the other way around. As a matter of fact emergent seems to be chasing culture, even imitating culture, rather than changing it. The reason this is true has to do with its understanding of the kingdom of God.

Mark Driscoll defines the emerging church as

---

[1] Richard J. Mouw, *The Smell of Sawdust* (Grand Rapids: Zondervan, 2000), 64.

> a growing, loosely-connected movement of primarily young pastors who are glad to see the end of modernity and are seeking to function as missionaries who bring the gospel of Jesus Christ to emerging and postmodern cultures.[2]

Thus defined, the emergent church sounds like a welcome addition to the Christian community. However, all is not as it seems. Whatever the intentions of the original founders of the movement (or conversation, as they call it), it has rapidly morphed into a serious threat to the faith. Today, while the emergent community is barely a decade old it has permeated churches, Bible colleges, seminaries, and parachurch organizations throughout the world. It is a movement that is difficult to define because it is not monolithic or static. However, at least two basic wings have become discernable. One wing calls itself "emerging," claiming to have solid theological credentials, having only adopted methods more in tune with postmodern mindsets. The other wing is termed "emergent" and is composed of those who not only are adopting new methodologies but who also challenge the most sacred of doctrines. This wing is obviously the most concerning to us and is even under fire from the emerging wing. For example, Driscoll, who was one of the originators of the conversation, but has since distanced himself from emergent leaders such as Brian McLaren, writes,

> The emergent church is part of the Emerging Church Movement but does not embrace the dominant ideology of the movement. Rather the emergent church is the latest version of liberalism. The only difference is that the old liberalism accommodated modernity and the new liberalism accommodates postmodernity.[3]

I have written extensively on the emergent church movement in other venues and will not rehash that information here.[4] I would mention that, while the "emergent" movement is far more disturbing, the "emerging" element is not without its doctrinal and philosophical problems. Both, for instance, embrace errant views of the kingdom of God which in turn lead to a misunderstanding of the role of the church (a role emerging leaders call missional), which in turn has a distorting affect on the gospel message. Since both emerging and emergent camps have the same view of the kingdom, I will be using the term "emergent" throughout this discussion to refer to both wings.

---

[2] Mark Driscoll, *Confessions of a Reformission Rev.* (Grand Rapids: Zondervan, 2006), 22.
[3] Ibid., 21.
[4] See Gary E. Gilley, *This Little Church Stayed Home* (Darlington, England: Evangelical Press, 2006).

Emergent Eschatology

Emergent and emerging leaders may differ over any number of issues but they present a united front when it comes to the kingdom of God—and the kingdom of God plays the pivotal role in their theology and purpose. At a recent conference in Baltimore – The Big Event 2007, Imagine a World…a New Vision for God's Kingdom on Earth – the PowerPoint presentation assures us "the kingdom of God is here now."[5]

The idea that the kingdom is here now is the one doctrinally unifying factor in emergent theology, yet some in the "conversation" have been honest enough to admit that even they are not always sure what is meant by the term. Mark Scandrette confesses,

> A central and reoccurring theme of conversation has been a renewed fascination with the present availability of the kingdom of God… [Yet] the term *kingdom of God* has become so popular, and its usage so varied, that it is difficult to know if we are even talking about the same thing… There is a tendency to see the kingdom of God as whatever is progressive, exotic, foreign, and obscure (emphasis in the original).[6]

Nevertheless a consensus by both emerging and emergent leaders is expressed by Sherry and Geoff Maddock: "Our principle (sic) desire is to see God's kingdom come on earth as it is in heaven. We believe this happens when God's people are renewed around God's mission of love and justice in the world."[7] The conversation apparently views the kingdom as being on earth now but progressively becoming like the kingdom in heaven as Christians live missionally on earth.

Such an understanding of the kingdom of God is obviously at odds with premillennialism, yet the Maddocks' view is reflected by many in or on the fringes of the movement. Tony Campolo represents many emergent thinkers as he contrasts dispensationalism with emergent theology,

> This is a theology that – with its implicit threat of being left behind, of time running out – is used by Dispensational preachers to great evangelistic effect. It has been a very effective goad to conversion… To the contrary, the history of the world is infused with the presence of God, who is guiding the world toward becoming the

---

[5] www.baltimorepresbytery.org/TheBigEvent2007ImagineaWorld.htm.
[6] Mark Scandrette, "Growing Pains" in *An Emergent Manifesto of Hope,* ed. Doug Pagitt and Tony Jones (Grand Rapids: Baker Books, 2007) , 26, 29.
[7] Sherry Maddock and Geoff Maddock, "An Ever-Renewed Adventure of Faith, *An Emergent Manifesto of Hope,* 80.

kind of world God willed for it to be when it was created. Human history is going somewhere wonderful.[8]

N. T. Wright, the primary link between the "New Perspective on Paul" (which claims we have misunderstood Paul and, in turn, the gospel, since the foundation of the church) and evangelicalism, has the same eschatological underpinnings,

> [Paul] was to declare to the pagan world that YHWH, the God of Israel, was the one true God of the whole world, and that in Jesus of Nazareth he had overcome evil and was creating a new world in which justice and peace would reign supreme.[9]

Jim Henderson, co-author of *Jim and Casper Go to Church*, is also interested in bringing the kingdom of God to earth.

> I want to make this world a better place. I want to see Jesus' prayer answered that his Kingdom would come on Earth as it is in heaven. I want to see kingdoms of this world become the kingdoms of our God and his Christ.[10]

To Brian McLaren, the most prolific emergent writer, the ultimate goal of Jesus (and God) is the kingdom of God, brought to earth.[11] Just how is the kingdom brought to earth? Through our good works. McLaren states,

> I hope that they [his neighbors] and I will become better people, transformed by God's Spirit, more pleasing to God, more of a blessing to the world **so that God's kingdom** (which I seek, but cannot manipulate) **comes on earth as in heaven** (emphasis mine).[12]

What does this kingdom that we are to bring through our good works look like? Rob Bell has some thoughts:

> Salvation is the entire universe being brought back into harmony with its maker. This has huge implications for how people present the message of Jesus. Yes, Jesus can come into our hearts. But we can join a movement that is as wide and as big as the universe itself. Rocks and trees and birds and swamps and ecosystems. God's desire is to restore all of it.[13]

---

[8] Tony Campolo, in Brian McLaren and Tony Campolo, *Adventures in Missing the Point* (El Cajon, Calif,: Youth Specialties, 2003), 59.

[9] N. T. Wright, *What Saint Paul Really Said*, (Grand Rapids: Wm. B. Eerdmans, 1997), 37.

[10] Jim Henderson and Matt Casper, *Jim and Casper Go to Church* (2007), 168.

[11] Brian McLaren, *A Generous Orthodoxy*,(Cajon, CA: Youth Specialties Books, 2004), 267.

[12] Ibid., 263.

[13] Rob Bell, *Velvet Elvis* (Grand Rapids: Zondervan, 2005), 109-110.

And

> For Jesus, the question wasn't how do I get into Heaven? but how do I bring heaven here?... The goal isn't escaping this world but making this world the kind of place God can come to. And God is remaking us into the kind of people who can do this kind of work.[14]

Emergent theology sees the kingdom of God as present now with future culmination as we (the subjects of the kingdom) restore justice, eliminate poverty, clean up the ecosystem, tame global warming and the like. Of course the issue is not whether Christians ought to be involved in finding solutions to these earth-related concerns (we should be and have been and are), but whether this is the mission of the church and whether doing so will more quickly bring in the kingdom.

I do not believe Scripture teaches either, but Robert Webber, in his very influential book *Ancient-Future Faith,* differs, "[The] result of the cosmic work of Christ is that the kingdom of God, God's rule over all things, is now manifest."[15] By Christ's "cosmic work" Webber means, among other things, that "Christ has bound Satan and all demonic powers."[16] While Webber admits to a future in which a more complete binding of demonic forces will prevail, demons are limited enough at this time to allow for a "secular salvation" (that is the salvation of the planet and culture) within society. Webber is confident that due to the present binding of demonic forces, and God's kingdom rule now, believers can and should expedite massive social and cultural changes. As a matter of fact it is the mandate of the followers of Christ to be focused on this "secular salvation." He writes,

> Faith in Jesus Christ, who is the ultimate ruler over all of life, can break the twisting of political, economic, social, and moral structures into secular salvation. Because those structures that promise secular salvation are disarmed, they can no longer exercise ultimate power in our lives. The powers have been dethroned by the power of the cross.[17]

The church, given this paradigm, becomes the change agent in society. "The church," writes Webber, "as a transforming presence in the world stands in the tradition of those Scripture passages that emphasize the power of the

---

[14] Ibid., 147,150.
[15] Robert Webber, *Ancient-Future Faith*, (Grand Rapids: Baker Books, 2004) 53.
[16] Ibid., 49.
[17] Ibid., 51.

gospel to change not only the life of an individual but also the life of culture."[18]

It is thought within emergent circles that when the church operates as this type of change agent the world can't help but get better. Carla Barnhill, former editor of *Christian Parenting Today* magazine, assures us that emergent style parenting, a style in which it is more important to teach creativity than obedience, "is about celebrating the goodness of life with God, a life that looks more like the kingdom with every generation."[19] Prominent emergent leader Tony Jones, in the process of poking fun at the dispensational understanding of this age and the one to come, states, "But those of us represented in this book take the contrary view. God's promised future is good, and it awaits us, beckoning us forward."[20] To both Barnhill and Jones the world is becoming a better place to live as time goes by, and it is our job to hasten its rejuvenation.

If there is one thing the emergent conversation has closed ranks around it is that the kingdom of God is on earth now, but it will progressively resemble God's kingdom in heaven as Christians understand their true mission, which is to make this world a better place for all. The emerging movement sees itself as a wakeup call to those who would follow Jesus. It is our task to bring the kingdom of God on earth as it is in heaven by aggressively challenging injustice, fighting poverty, aiding the sick, working on ecological concerns and, in general, saving this planet and everything on it. Emergent leaders believe that people are catching on to this new vision of the kingdom, and as a result, are optimistic about the future. No doomsday tribulation period is on their radar screen nor is Jesus coming in judgment upon the wicked. The kingdom, while already here, will progressively become like heaven as we attend to the social ills and needs around us. Tomorrow looks bright and the day after that looks brighter still.

We Have Heard This Before

All of this stirs hope within our hearts. Maybe the emergent leaders are right, maybe the world is getting better and better and, if we Christians would just get more involved, eventually earth will be like heaven. Sounds great, but is it biblical?

It is helpful to know that the Christian community has been down this trail before. Emergent eschatology is by-and-large identical to liberal

---

[18] Ibid., 169.

[19] Carla Barnhill, "The Postmodern Parent," *An Emergent Manifesto of Hope*, 58.

[20] Tony Jones, "A Hopeful Faith," *An Emergent Manifesto of Hope*, 130.

postmillennialism which flourished prior to the mid-twentieth century. In general postmillennialism is the view that Christ will return after the millennium, or the kingdom age, which is presently on earth. Conservative postmillennialists believe that "through the proclamation of the gospel in the present age, an unprecedented number of people in the world – in fact, the vast majority – will turn to Christ and be saved."[21] The focus of God's people in this kingdom age then is to expand the kingdom through the preaching of the gospel. As the world is increasingly evangelized it will become a place of "spiritual prosperity, universal peace and righteousness, and economic well-being."[22] In conjunction with the spread of the gospel is the progressive binding of Satan. As the world is Christianized Satan will gradually lose his hold over its inhabitants. Loraine Boettner, a postmillennial theologian, summarizes,

> Postmillennialism is that view of the last things which holds that the kingdom of God is now being extended in the world through the preaching of the gospel and the saving work of the Holy Spirit in the hearts of individuals, that the world eventually is to be Christianized and that the return of Christ is to occur at the close of a long period of righteousness and peace commonly called the millennium.[23]

Theological liberal postmillennialism shares some of the same optimism as its conservative counterparts but directs its attention to social enhancement of the planet.

> Liberal postmillennialism focuses on societal transformation rather than personal conversion. Their "social gospel" sees the saving of society from social evil as the great purpose of the church. The mission of the church is not to preach the gospel to sinners in need of God's great salvation, but rather, to liberate mankind from poverty, racism, disease, war and all kinds of injustice.[24]

The similarity between liberal postmillennialism and emergent philosophy is striking. It is worth noting that the postmillennial system, which was nonexistent in the early days of church history, was originally systematized by liberal Unitarian minister Daniel Whitby (1638-1726). His system grew legs due partly to the optimism of the age, but lost steam when the two world wars of the twentieth century shattered dreams of the world

---

[21] Matthew Waymeyer, *Revelation 20 and the Millennial Debate* (TheWoodlands, TX: Kress Christian Publications, 2004), 3.

[22] Ibid., 4.

[23] Loraine Boettner, "Postmillennialism," in *The Meaning of the Millennium: Four Views*, ed. R. Clouse (Downers Grove, Il: InterVarsity, 1977), 117.

[24] Paul N. Benware, *Understanding End Times Prophecy* (Chicago: Moody Publishers, 2006), 144.

progressively improving. Since that time a more realistic understanding of human development has set in and most recognize that the earth is not only not moving toward utopia but is more likely closer to annihilation.

Emergent kingdom theology, like its postmillennial predecessor, is based not so much on the observation of an improving world but on feelings of desperation. McLaren admits that many might see his kingdom views as a mere pipe dream, but if that is so, "what do [we] have to look forward to if they are right? Simply more of the same in human history..."[25]

But truth does not emerge from groundless optimism or "what if" desperation; it emerges from the Scriptures. What God says about life now, the future and the kingdom is what matters. In answer to McLaren's question, we have much to look forward to, for Christ will one day bring His kingdom to earth, at which time the very social and earthly issues that concern emergent people will be corrected and made right. But this kingdom will come through the power of Christ, not the good deeds of men. It will come when He returns, not as a prelude to it. It will not only remedy societal wrongs it will usher in the world-wide righteousness and justice of Christ. We have much to look forward to when the kingdom comes, but it will come about because of God's actions, not ours.

The Effect on the Gospel

It is not surprising with this understanding of the kingdom of God that David Gushee in a recent *Christianity Today* article asks, "Is it permissible to reopen the question of salvation?" While Gushee follows up his question with some things worth pondering, he states that when

> Jesus was asked about the criteria for admission to eternity, he offered a fourfold answer: love God with all that you are, love your neighbor (like the Samaritan loved his neighbor), do God's will by obeying his moral commands, and be willing, if he asks, to drop everything and leave it behind in order to follow him.[26]

While Gushee is confusing salvation with sanctification – the free gift of righteousness with its effects on our lives – at least he is still talking about salvation. Brian McLaren, on the other hand, is not concerned about these matters. In reply to his own question about who is in heaven and hell, he neatly sidesteps the whole issue by asking another series of questions,

---

[25] Brian McLaren, *The Secret Message of Jesus,* 128.
[26] David P. Gushee, *Christianity Today,* March 2007, 72.

Isn't it clear that I do not believe this is the right question for a missional Christian to ask? Can't we talk for a while about God's will being done on earth as in heaven instead of jumping to how to escape earth and get to heaven as quickly as possible? Can't we talk for a while about overthrowing and undermining every hellish stronghold in our lives and in our world?[27]

It would be hard to imagine a more arrogant statement. McLaren speaks as if Christianity began yesterday and we are just now getting around to asking basic questions pertaining to life and eternity. But this is no problem for McLaren who boldly states that we do not have even the gospel right yet. "What does it mean to be saved?... None of us have arrived at orthodoxy."[28] More than that, we have virtually no truth nailed down.

> Ask me if Christianity (my version of it, yours, the Pope's, whoever's) is orthodox, meaning true and here's my honest answer: a little, but not yet. Assuming by Christianity you mean the Christian understanding of the world and God, Christian opinions on soul, text, and culture... I'd have to say that we probably have a couple of things right, but a lot of things wrong, and even more spreads before us unseen and unimagined. But at least our eyes are open! To be a Christian in a generously orthodox way is not to claim to have the truth captured, stuffed, and mounted on the wall.[29]

Samir Selmanovic, in *An Emergent Manifesto of Hope*, goes so far as to totally distinguish Christianity from the kingdom of God. "The emerging church movement," Selmanovic states, "has come to believe that the ultimate context of the spiritual aspirations of the follower of Jesus Christ is not Christianity but rather the kingdom of God."[30] What is Selmanovic's point? Simply that the message of Christ and salvation as found in the biblical record is incomplete. God "place[s] his truth in others [religions] too."[31] Therefore salvation is obtainable without a relationship with Christ,

> If a relationship with a specific person, namely Christ, is the whole substance of a relationship with the God of the Bible, then the vast majority of people in world history are excluded from the possibility of a relationship with the God of the Bible, along with the Hebrews of the Old Testament who were without a knowledge of Jesus Christ—the person. The question begs to be asked: would God who gives enough revelation for people to be judged but not enough revelation to be saved be a God worth worshiping. Never![32]

---

[27] Brian McLaren, *A Generous Orthodoxy*, 112.
[28] Quoted in Andy Crouch, "The Emergent Mystique", *Christianity Today*, November, 2004, 40.
[29] Ibid., 293.
[30] Samir Selmanovic, "The Sweet Problem of Inclusiveness, "*An Emergent Manifesto of Hope*, 192.
[31] Ibid., 194.
[32] Ibid., 194-195.

As a result of this type of thinking the emergent church has become a champion of inclusivism, the idea that while salvation (whatever that means to the emergent crowd) may be based on the person and work of Christ, people who may have never heard of Christ can be saved by responding to God on the basis of the revelation they have received. With this understanding a Hindu, Muslim or animist, while not a follower of Christ, could nevertheless be in the kingdom of God because they have followed the light they have been given in nature and in their religious system. These individuals would not be Christians as such, but they would occupy a place in the kingdom every bit as much as Christians, perhaps more so because citizenship in the kingdom is predicated more on what we do rather than on what we believe. So, theoretically a kind-hearted spirit worshipper from New Guinea would occupy a greater place in the kingdom than the dreaded fundamentalist, foundationalist, dispensationalist who, according to emergent thinking, has in his exclusivism declared those of other religions lost and bound for hell.

It is because people from all religions and all walks of life (people who are in the kingdom now) are working together to bring the kingdom of heaven to earth through their efforts of love and missional living that Rob Bell can say, "The gospel is good news, especially for those who don't believe it.... [As a matter of fact] if the gospel isn't good news for everybody, then it isn't good news for anybody."[33]

According to McLaren, our concern should not be about who is saved but how to be blessings. "...My missional calling: blessed in this life to be a blessing to everyone on earth... My mission isn't to figure out who is already blessed, or not blessed, or unblessable. My calling is to be blessed so I can bless everyone."[34] All of this blessing is for the purpose of helping "our world get back on the road to being truly and wholly good again, the way God created it to be."[35] In other words, by our good deeds to mankind and the planet we will usher in the final stage of the kingdom, "I hope that both they and I," McLaren continues, "will become better people, transformed by God's Spirit, more pleasing to God, more of a blessing to the world so that God's kingdom (which I seek, but cannot manipulate) comes on earth as in heaven."[36]

---

[33] Rob Bell, 166-167.
[34] Brian McLaren, *A Generous Orthodoxy*, 113.
[35] Ibid., 223.
[36] Ibid., 263.

A positive response to the emergent message concerning the kingdom would result in the "new world...promised by the prophets. Jesus' secret message tells us, then, that this new world is so possible it is at hand, within reach... We can be part of God's dreams for planet Earth coming true"[37]

The emphasis on this world is partly because of the belief that this world will not be destroyed but transformed, not replaced but fulfilled. McLaren dreams of this world becoming "a place God is at home in, a place God takes pride and pleasure in, a place where God's dreams come true."[38]

As can be deduced by now, many within the emergent movement equate "eternal life" or salvation with the kingdom of God. To be in the kingdom is "a life that is full and overflowing, a higher life that is centered in an interactive relationship with God and with Jesus. Let's render it simply 'an extraordinary life to the full centered in a relationship with God.'"[39] While this is a truncated understanding of the kingdom and of eternal life at best, it gets more complicated when we are informed that the kingdom is really within us. McLaren writes,

> The secret message, the mystery of the kingdom of God: that Christ the King indwells you, which means that his kingdom is within and among you here and now.[40]

In the emergent gospel, salvation, in the sense of forgiveness of sin, redemption, and being given God's righteousness because of the finished work of Christ, plays a minor, often nonexistent, role. McLaren believes that most planet dwellers are in fact already in the kingdom:

> *Maybe God's plan is an opt-out plan, not an opt-in one. If you want to stay out of the party, you can... But it's hard for me to imagine somebody being more stubbornly ornery than God is gracious"* (emphasis mine).[41]

If McLaren's understanding of the citizens of the kingdom is on target we should not be surprised to find that people from all religions are in the kingdom and possibly more advanced in that kingdom than many Christians.[42]

---

[37] Brian McLaren, *The Secret Message of Jesus* (Nashville: W Publishing Group, 2006), 181, 183.

[38] Ibid., 203.

[39] Ibid., 37.

[40] Ibid., 100-101.

[41] Brian McLaren, *The Last Word, and the Word After That* (San Francisco: Jossey-Bass, 2005), 138.

[42] See Brian McLaren, *The Secret Message of Jesus* , 86-89.

No wonder Heather Kirk-Davidoff echoes McLaren's idea of evangelism by asking, "What would evangelism look like if we...counted conversations rather than conversion?"[43] Such an evangelistic transformation is predicated on the perceived purpose of the gospel. Kirk-Davidoff goes on the explain,

> It is a change in the reason we engage in evangelism, shifting the focus from recruitment to the cultivating of relationships that are an end in themselves, indispensable to our spiritual journey... We want to build relationships with other human beings. Because of that, we're willing to give up just about everything we've ever learned about how to grow a church or spread the gospel.[44]

Sherry and Geoff Maddock flesh out this understanding of salvation:

> Through practices such as caring for AIDS sufferers, feeding the homeless, protesting the wanton destruction of the environment, or welcoming newly arrived refugees, we find salvation that is closer to the *shalom* of Scripture (emphasis in the original).[45]

True to its liberal postmillennial roots the emergent gospel has been reduced to social betterment of culture and physical improvement of the planet. There is little discussion or interest in the true spiritual needs of mankind; instead the focus is on physical and perhaps emotional needs. If we can relieve suffering, care for the ozone layer, correct injustice and racism we can save the planet and make this a better place to live for all. This is the same agenda used by old liberalism which thrived under modernity. All that has changed is making adjustments for the same theology under postmodernity.

If we would protest that none of this is biblical, the emergent leaders have a retort: God is doing a new thing, something not revealed in Scripture.

> It would not be the first time God has broken out of religion, which carries his message, and made something new. If God found it good for his followers to break out of the confines of a religion two millennia ago, why should we expect God not to do such a thing in our time? Maybe Christianity should be thinned out and broken up, spent like Christ who gave himself for this world.[46]

Of course, in response Hebrews 1:1-2 comes quickly to mind, "God, after He spoke long ago to the fathers in the prophets in many portions and in many

---

[43] Heather Kirk-Davidoff, "Meeting Jesus at the Bar," *An Emergent Manifesto of Hope*, 35.
[44] Ibid., 36, 37.
[45] Sherry Moddock and Geoff Maddock, *An Emergent Manifesto of Hope*, 82.
[46] Samir Selmanovi, *An Emergent Manifesto of Hope*, 199.

ways, in these last days has spoken to us in His Son..." (NASB). When God chose to replace the dispensation of Law with that of the church age that change was communicated to us through His Son and those who wrote the New Testament (Hebrews 2:1-4). Why should we not expect God to dump the Christian faith and give us something new? Because God "in these last days has spoken to us in His Son." The final revelation to mankind has been given. There is no further revelation forthcoming; no new era to be started by the actions of men; rather the next era will be initiated by the return of Jesus Christ.

A Dispensational Understanding of the Kingdom

Acts 1:3 informs us that during the 40 days in which Jesus was making appearances following the resurrection He spoke to the apostles concerning the kingdom of God. We are uncertain about exactly what He said but we know the kingdom was at the heart of His discussions with them during that time. In verse six Jesus is preparing to depart the earth and they have one question for Him, "Lord, is it at this time You are restoring the kingdom to Israel?"

While we do not know precisely what Jesus had told them about the kingdom we do pick up on a couple of important pieces of information.

- The kingdom was still coming. Whatever Jesus told the apostles about the kingdom it had not dampened their expectation that it would be eventually "restored to Israel." This of course implied that the kingdom had not yet come. If the kingdom was on earth at that moment, whether in their hearts or in another form, they would not have asked such a question. The only thing they did not know was the timing. In Jesus' reply he does not deny that the kingdom is coming. The disciples were on target and Jesus did not deny this in any way. This is important to observe for, as John MacArthur states, "If they are mistaken about this, Jesus' failure to correct them is mystifying and deceptive."[47] Jesus had promised earlier that the kingdom would come in the future (Luke 21:25-31; 22:18, 30) and all the apostles wanted to know was when.

---

[47] John MacArthur, *The MacArthur New Testament Commentary, Acts 1-12*, (Chicago: Moody Press, 1994), 20.

- The kingdom would take form as promised. Throughout the Gospels it was obvious that the Jewish people were expecting the Messianic kingdom as foretold in the Old Testament prophecies. Jesus never contradicted their basic understanding of that kingdom, and as a matter of fact repeatedly told them in the early years of His public ministry that the "kingdom was at hand" (Matt 4:17). That is, Jesus made a legitimate offer to establish the kingdom at that time, but to do so they would have to accept Him as their King, something they ultimately refused to do. The kingdom therefore was postponed until Christ would return, but it was never withdrawn altogether. This is the obvious understanding of the apostles as Jesus prepares to ascend. The promised kingdom was still on the agenda – but when?

What tends to confuse the interpreter of Scripture at this point is that the term "kingdom of God" does not always refer to the same kingdom.[48] To get a handle on this we first must recognize three essential elements of any kingdom:

- There must be a ruler.
- There must be a realm to rule.
- There must be the exercising of authority.

With these elements in mind we turn to the Scriptures and there we can identify five or six unique kingdoms as related to God:

- The universal kingdom of God. This is God's rule over the entire universe. He is the eternal, sovereign ruler over all creation.

- The spiritual kingdom of God. This is God's rule over all believers. Anyone who is born again is part of this kingdom (Col. 1:13). Therefore during this dispensation the church could be called the spiritual kingdom of God in the sense that God has a special ruling relationship over the church, His subjects.

---

[48] This outline is a summary of the excellent presentation found in Paul N. Benware's book, *Understanding End Time Prophecies* pp. 185-195. See also John Walvoord, "Biblical Kingdom Compared and Contrasted," *Issues in Dispensationalism*, (Chicago: Moody Press, 1994), 75-91.

- The theocratic kingdom. This was God's rule over Israel in the OT, which was to be ruled directly by God not by kings. It is for this reason that when Israel demanded a king they were in rebellion against the monarchy of God. This kingdom ceased in practice with the set up of earthly kings, and in totality with the rejection of Christ.

- Many (Pentecost, Walvoord, Ryrie, Fruchtenbaum, etc.) suggest a mystery form of the kingdom. Appealing to Matthew 13 and offering by way of explanation that when Israel rejected its King it also rejected the promised Messianic kingdom. As a result it was temporarily replaced by a mystery form in which both good and evil are present. It is what we might call today "Christendom;" that is, all who would claim to be Christians are in this mystery form of the kingdom but not all are regenerated. Therefore it is not equivalent to the church. Toussaint[49] however, suggests the kingdom here alluded to is not a mystery form but rather the mystery elements of Matthew 13 reference the same kingdom as previously offered while simply presenting new revelation regarding an intercalation or delay in its arrival.

- The Messianic kingdom. This was the kingdom promised to Israel in the Old Testament. It was to be an earthly kingdom with Christ (the Messiah) sitting on David's throne ruling the earth in righteousness. It was postponed due to Israel's rejection of Christ but will come at the end of the church age and, according to Revelation 20, will last for 1000 years.

- The eternal kingdom. This is God's rule throughout eternity following the Millennial kingdom.

It was the Messianic kingdom about which the apostles were inquiring in the first chapter of Acts. They specifically wanted to know when the Lord would restore the "kingdom to Israel." If the Lord was not intending to restore the kingdom, with all of its physical and land promises, to Israel, would not this have been a great time to say so? If the Lord intended to take the promises of Israel away from it and roll them over into the church why did He not tell

---

[49] Stanley Toussaint, *Behold the King*, (Portland, OR: Multnomah Press, 1980), 171-172

the disciples? Instead He clearly implies that the kingdom will be restored to the people of Israel but the timing is not for them to know.

Alva McClain makes a compelling argument in his *The Greatness of the Kingdom* that the kingdom is actually offered again to the Jews in Acts 3:19-21. But as it was rejected when Jesus was on earth, so it is rejected under the ministry of the apostles and therefore it is postponed until a later date.[50]

It is interesting to note that the kingdom is prominent in the Gospels but begins to fade in the Acts and the epistles. The word "kingdom" is found only five more times in Acts (8:12; 19:8; 20:25; 28:23, 31). Each of these passages references the kingdom but none gives us any more details about the kingdom than we already processed from the Old Testament and the Gospels.

Of the 18 references to a kingdom in the epistles, most are referring to a future kingdom (either the Messianic or the eternal). However a few passages (only 4 clearly) such as Romans 14:17 and Colossians 1:13 show that God's kingdom is what McClain calls a mediatorial kingdom. That is, a kingdom already chartered but which will have its manifestation in the Millennium when Messiah comes and literally restores the kingdom to Israel and sits on David's throne.

Conclusion

The emergent church has badly misunderstood the biblical teaching on the kingdom of God. Actually, it has chosen to ignore what the Scriptures teach and has chosen to impose its own understanding of the kingdom in order to set forth its own agenda for the church and the world. One is reminded of Jesus' warning to the Pharisees in Matthew 15:3, 6, "Why do you yourselves transgress the commandment of God for the sake of your tradition?" Then he said, "By this you invalidated the word of God for the sake of your traditions." Without question the emergent church is doing something very similar today. In fact, the Messianic kingdom of God is not on the earth today but awaits the return of Christ. People's good deeds toward one another and the planet are welcomed, but they do not form the kingdom, advance the kingdom or hasten the kingdom. The church's mandate is not to clean up the planet, wipe out illness, eradicate poverty and injustice and call for peace treaties, as worthy as these actions are in their place. Our mandate is to make disciples of all nations (Matthew 28:19-20). We are not to set up

---

[50] Alva McClain, *The Greatness of the Kingdom*, (Winona Lake: BMH Books, 1987), 403-406.

Christ's kingdom on earth, that is His job. We are instead to call sinners to Christ that they might join us in proclaiming "the excellencies of Him who has called you out of darkness into His marvelous light" (1 Peter 2:9). By rejecting the biblical teaching on the kingdom, a teaching dispensationalist have long championed, the emergent thinkers are leading their followers down a path Christ does not choose to take us. In so doing they have wrapped the emergent movement around a superimposed doctrine of the kingdom that agrees neither with Scripture nor reality.

"God's hope for this world surely does not lie in social regeneration, but in regeneration of individual hearts through faith in the substitutionary death of the Son of God. A child of God thus regenerated is expected to live in the world in certain relations which are specifically defined in the Bible."

- Charles C. Ryrie

Neoorthodoxy, 1956, page 33

21

The Church & Social Responsibility
Ron J. Bigalke, Jr.

Although he would agree that his essentialist approach to the definition of dispensationalism was not "inspired," this author is grateful for Dr. Charles C. Ryrie's articulation of the crucial issues of defense in regards to dispensationalism. Dr. Ryrie's *sine qua non* of dispensationalism included: (1) belief in a distinction between Israel and the church; (2) distinction between Israel and the church as the necessary corollary of a consistent system of hermeneutics that is usually called literal (plain) interpretation; and, (3) the principal purpose of God in the world is His own glory.[1] Dr. John S. Feinberg likewise sought to articulate elements essential to all dispensational systems. He delineated six essentials of dispensationalism.[2] Both Ryrie and Feinberg agreed concerning three distinctive characteristics of dispensationalism. First, they affirmed the uniqueness of the church, which began at Pentecost (in distinction with Israel), in the current dispensation (as opposed to supersessionism). Second, both men affirmed belief in a future national Israel. Third, they referenced the issue of hermeneutics; the main difference between dispensational and nondispensational hermeneutics is an understanding of Testament priority (dispensationalists affirm more discontinuity between the Testaments and systematize eschatological doctrines from the priority of the Old Testament, as opposed to the New Testament changing the original meaning; nondispensationalists formulate eschatology from the priority of the New Testament which allows change and reinterpretation of the Old Testament). Consequently, it is not the concept and term of "dispensation" that is the essence of dispensationalism. The essence of dispensationalism is hermeneutical, that is, the relationship between the Old and New Testaments.[3]

Nondispensationalists believe the New Testament spiritualizes, or reinterprets, Old Testament texts. They view the church as the application of Old Testament promises made to ethnic believing Israel. Opposed to discontinuity between the Testaments, nondispensationalists would view the

---

[1] Charles C. Ryrie, *Dispensationalism*, rev. ed. (Chicago: Moody Publishers, 2007), 45-48.
[2] John S. Feinberg, "Systems of Discontinuity," in *Continuity and Discontinuity: Perspectives on the Relationship Between the Old and New Testaments*, gen. ed. idem (Wheaton: Crossway, 1988), 67-86.
[3] Ibid., 74.

death and resurrection of Jesus Christ as the culminating event for believers of all ages, as it unites them without distinction for a common purpose into the kingdom of God. The covenantal promises with Israel by God in the Old Testament find fulfillment in the church. Consequently, dispensationalists and nondispensationalists significantly differ in regards to God's purposes with history.

> For nondispensationalists history is seen primarily as salvation history. In other words, the emphasis is on God's ongoing plan in saving men. For dispensationalists history is the gradual implementation and outworking of the kingdom of God. A major part of that implementation involves saving people, but the soteriological and spiritual elements are not the only aspects of the kingdom. . . . For example, nondispensational treatments of the nature of the covenants and of Israel's future invariably emphasize soteriological and spiritual issues, whereas dispensational treatments emphasize both the spiritual/soteriological and the social, economic, and political aspects of things.[4]

Nondispensationalists primarily emphasize salvation history as fulfillment of God's covenantal promises. Both systems would emphasize a doxological purpose to history, but the dispensationalist approach is much broader. Dispensationalism emphasizes both spiritual and physical blessings within the doxological purpose of history. Continuity issues are important to address when considering the relationship between the church and social action because the more one understands the Bible to teach discontinuity, it will be understood that "God does not always work with and through the same peoples, nor does he have the same social and political program for each group."[5]

The Church and Social Action

Foundational to an emphasis upon social action as essential to the mission of the church is an "already, not yet" view of the kingdom. For instance, Carl F. H. Henry was adamant that to seek justice was "a mandate based on the lordship of Christ, the stewardship of creation, and the servanthood of believers."[6] The social imperative to seek justice was developed from the principal message of Christ concerning the kingdom of God.[7] If there is an

---

[4] Ibid., 85.

[5] Ibid.

[6] David Weeks, "Carl F.H. Henry," in *Encyclopedia of Religion in American Politics*, ed. Jeffrey D. Schultz, John G. West Jr., and Iain Maclean (Phoenix: Oryx Press, 1999), 118.

[7] Carl F. H. Henry, *The Uneasy Conscience of Modern Fundamentalism* (Grand Rapids: Eerdmans, 1947), 27-52. On page 47, Henry noted the necessity "to think of the church age in terms of divine continuity

"already" aspect of the kingdom, there are widespread social implications for the current dispensation.[8] Henry's burden was "not to press a personal kingdom viewpoint, but rather to promote an evangelical conviction that nothing is so essential among Fundamentalist essentials as a world-relevance for the Gospel." He concluded, "Whatever in our kingdom views undercuts that relevance destroys the essential character of Christianity as such."[9] An emphasis upon social action, as a consequence of a realized form of the kingdom, is the "world-relevance for the Gospel." Therefore, any theological system that does not emphasize continuity between the Testaments and would teach that the current age is a parenthesis (or, intercalation) would be viewed as a "revolt against the Christian social imperative."[10] Although his stated convictions were "broadly premillennial,"[11] Henry thoroughly rejected dispensational premillennialism that affirms the biblical teaching of the messianic (Davidic) kingdom being established after the second coming of Jesus Christ. It is essential to affirm the Christian social imperative on the basis of any already form of the messianic kingdom.

Stone affirmed correctly, "The profound significance that the March 1956 *Christian Life* article "Is Evangelical Theology Changing?" had on the future of American evangelicalism cannot be overstated.[12]" One of the stated emphases of that article,[13] which became a major statement of the neoevangelical movement, was the changing of theology to "a more definite recognition of social responsibility" through greater relevance "to the political and sociological realities" of the time. George Zeller noted,

> Contrarily, traditional dispensationalists have long recognized that present society bears no resemblance to the righteousness and justice that will characterize the kingdom, and that man, by his own efforts, will never produce kingdom conditions.

---

rather than of parenthesis, in terms of the amazing unity of the redemptive plan rather than in terms of an amazing interlude."

[8] It is best to understand that Christ announced the nearness of the kingdom as opposed to the arrival of the kingdom [Ron J. Bigalke Jr. and George Gunn, "Contingency of the Davidic Reign," in *Progressive Dispensationalism: An Analysis of the Movement and Defense of Traditional Dispensationalism* (Lanham, MD: University Press of America, 2005), 181-185].

[9] Henry, *Uneasy Conscience*, 48.

[10] Ibid., 22.

[11] Ibid., 46.

[12] Jon R. Stone, *On the Boundaries of American Evangelicalism: The Postwar Evangelical Coalition* (New York: St. Martin's Press, 1997), 100.

[13] Carl F. H. Henry, "Is Evangelical Theology Changing?" *Christian Life* 17 (March 1956): 16-19. It is interesting to note (another subject for another time) that *Christianity Today* began its first publication in this year. One response to the article was the concern that the editors of *Christian Life* would move "away from objective matters of Christian faith toward matters of subjective experience" [Alva J. McClain, "Is Theology Changing in the Conservative Camp?" *The Brethren Missionary Herald* (23 February 1957): 123].

> Only the omnipotent Messiah will accomplish that. . . . Traditional dispensationalists have long maintained that while believers are the salt of the earth and will influence society by godly living, the main mission of the church is to preach the gospel to every creature and fulfill our Lord's great commission. . . .[14]

Forcing the Christian social imperative is developed from George Ladd's covenant premillennialism. Carpenter noted that Ladd's view sought to replace dispensationalism "with an evangelical view of the kingdom of God and the end-times that was more conversant with classic Christian beliefs and more able to sustain evangelical social engagement."[15]

> By placing the kingdom of God beyond the second coming of Christ, dispensationalists had cut the nerve of evangelical social and cultural witness, [Henry] believed. Evangelicals had to recover a theology of the kingdom that would enable them to be its advance agents and effect significant social transformation before Christ's return to establish the kingdom in its fullness. One of the central themes of the new evangelicalism, then, would be a movement from dispensationalism and the sectarian, culturally alienated position that it suggested.[16]

When one considers its history, it is understandable why neoevangelicalism is so biased against dispensationalism (often to the point of refusal to understand and represent the system with charity and integrity). Of course, it is understandable why theological liberals are opposed to dispensationalism. Ryrie wrote, "Whatever else dispensationalists are, they are conservative in their view of the fundamental doctrines of the Bible, an approach unsavory to the liberal."[17] Nevertheless, dispensationalism was logical to many Calvinists who were pessimistic about individual human nature as totally depraved, and consequently society as a whole was in the same condition. Just as individual salvation requires a supernatural work, so would society if it were to be changed. Kraus noted that dispensationalism emerged from within the womb "of orthodox Calvinism."[18] Sandeen asked, "To what kind of Christians did dispensationalism appeal?—particularly the Calvinists. Most of the converts seem to be Presbyterians or Calvinistic

---

[14] George Zeller, "Development or Departure?" in *Progressive Dispensationalism*, 173.
[15] Joel A. Carpenter, *Revive Us Again: The Reawakening of American Fundamentalism* (New York: Oxford University Press, 1997), 195.
[16] Ibid., 203.
[17] Ryrie, *Dispensationalism*, 14.
[18] Norman C. Kraus, *Dispensationalism in America* (Richmond: John Knox Press, 1958), 60.

Baptists...few Methodists . . . [and not] many U. S. Episcopalians, although many British and Canadian Anglicans became [dispensationalists]."[19]

> Thus a doctrine of the Church emerged from a philosophy of history: The church was made up of God's elect who were always only a handful, seldom if ever the possessors of power. The true church could not possibly be identified with any of the large denominations, which were riddled with heresy, but could only be formed by individual Christians who could expect to be saved from the impending destruction.[20]

Christians are certainly obliged to demonstrate justice on both personal and societal levels. However, neoevangelicals distort biblical teaching on justice by attempting to make it justify emphases for the current age that are not found in Scripture. One example is liberation theology which gives a modern meaning to the word "justice" and ignores the fundamental Old Testament concept of justice as righteousness.[21] Furthermore, liberation theology endeavors to consider modern ideas of distributive justice in the same manner as biblical assertions regarding justice. Former missionary and president of CAM International, Dr. J. Ronald Blue wrote,

> The liberationists' concern for the injustices in society is admirable, but to contend that society can be transformed solely through naturalistic forces is at best misguided if not naive. Social sin is, after all, simply a conglomerate of personal sin. Society does not commit acts of torture, murder, and rape. People do. Therefore society can only be changed when people are changed. . . .
>
> The good news of the Lord Jesus Christ, who came to suffer the ultimate injustice of death on the cross to pay the penalty for man's sin and to thereby offer new life, eternal life, is still the best news of all. Through supernaturally redeemed individuals perhaps society can be relieved from so much injustice.[22]

Clearly, some in the church have misunderstood biblical teaching concerning justice. As already stated, the fundamental Old Testament concept of justice is righteousness. To interpret justice according to modern ideas of distributive justice is clearly misguided. One should not understand Jesus' earthly ministry as providing salvation wholly for the impoverished.

---

[19] Ernest R. Sandeen, "Toward a Historical Interpretation of the Origins of Fundamentalism," *Church History* 36 (March 1967): 71.

[20] Ibid., 69.

[21] Paul K. Jewett, "Justice of God," in *Wycliffe Bible Dictionary* [formerly titled *The Wycliffe Bible Encyclopedia*], eds. Charles F. Pfeiffer, Howard F. Vos, and John Rea (Chicago: Moody Press, 1975; reprint, Peabody, MA: Hendrickson Publishers, 1998), 981.

[22] J. Ronald Blue, "Major Flaws in Liberation Theology," in *Vital Contemporary Issues*, ed. Roy B. Zuck (Grand Rapids: Kregel, 1994), 132-133.

Nevertheless, the notion of an upward socioeconomic mobility is a crucial dimension of the neoevangelical social imperative.

> It is revealing that some of the most prominent details of Henry's memoirs concerning the late 1940s were his purchases. The young family that struggled along in faculty housing and with second hand cars in Chicago came to Pasadena in a new Buick, and they were able to purchase a home. This too was an important dimension of the neo-evangelical impulse. Bound up with doctrinal revisions and the recovery of social concern was the determination to stake a fresh claim on middle-class respectability.[23]

Jesus did not come to earth for the sake of liberating the penurious; He came "to seek and to save that which was lost" (Luke 19:10), namely, the "poor in spirit" (Matt 5:3). It is because man is totally depraved, hence he is poor spiritually, that "the Son of Man has come." Faithfulness to the Great Commission is not engaging in political activism and emphasizing social action. Jesus' earthly ministry was to provide salvation for those who were without the righteousness of God and to liberate the spiritually impoverished. As a result of "the progressive reformers' work and the message of the Social Gospel, middle class Americans readily applied private moral standards to such socioeconomic and political problems as monopolies, urban housing, industrial wages, and political corruption. Christian progressives saw character in this light. The calculation was quite simple: good character put the law of love into practice and issued forth in service, which in turn would overcome all the social evils stemming from selfishness."[24]

According to early adherents of the "Social Gospel" movement, it was imperative to apply Christian principles to the changing social and industrial conditions in the United States, and the church was castigated for not doing all that she should. Charles Sheldon's *In His Steps* (1897) was one of the most popular and prominent books for the Social Gospel movement. According to Sheldon, the church should base her public and private actions as an answer to the question "What Would Jesus Do?" and then American society would experience a notable social revolution. In his book *Christianity and the Social Crisis* (1907), Walter Rauschenbusch excoriated the church for not taking more seriously the need to restore social order. Rauschenbusch's book was quite influential since it explained the nature and purpose of the

---

[23] Carpenter, *Revive Us Again*, 203.

[24] Heather A. Warren, "The Shift from Character to Personality in Mainline Protestant Thought, 1935-1945," *Church History* 67 (September 1998): 539.

Social Gospel. For instance, he praised *gemeinschaft*, a society which is not individualistic but extols the importance of community as opposed to self interest, and criticized the idea of *gesellschaft*, a social or civil society which is anonymous, atomistic, and individualistic wherein people are motivated by materialism and self interest.

The Social Gospel movement is wrong to excoriate the church for failure to meet the needs of society, since this is not the responsibility of the church. Certainly private charity could help the poor and unemployed; however, the church is not commissioned to be a welfare organization but to make disciples and teach them (Matt 28:18-20). Furthermore, Scripture is quite specific about who the church should or should not help. For example, 1 Timothy 5:9-10 reads, "Let a widow be put on the list only if she is not less than sixty years old, *having been* the wife of one man, having a reputation for good works." Private charities can be beneficial, but people must understand this is not the responsibility of the church. Without a saving relationship with Jesus Christ, the welfare state is a relatively empty achievement for those who are not *looking for the city which has foundations, whose architect and builder is God* (Heb 11:10), and have become completely passive and reliant to the absolute planning of a more progressively structured society.

The Development of the Social Gospel

Walter Rauschenbusch (1861-1918) was born in Rochester, New York. His father was a German pastor who was commissioned as a Lutheran missionary to the United States. Karl August Rauschenbusch taught for thirty-two years at Rochester Theological Seminary. The younger Rauschenbusch was reared in conservative German Baptist piety, and his father converted to such views from Lutheran pietism. Rauschenbusch studied in Germany and the United States. In 1879, he had "a conversion experience which led to his baptism on confession of faith."[25] His conversion experience in 1879 was a major impetus in his endeavors to merge "the evangelical gospel with the social gospel."[26]

In 1884, he served briefly as a pastor of German Baptist Church in Louisville, Kentucky. It was during that pastorate that he said, "It is now no longer my found hope to be a learned theologian and write big books; I want to be a pastor, powerful with men, preaching to them Christ as the man in

---

[25] Robert T. Handy, "Walter Rauschenbusch," in *A Handbook of Christian Theologians*, eds. Dean G. Peerman and Martin E. Marty (Nashville: Abingdon Press, 1984), 192.
[26] Ibid., 209.

whom their affections and energies can find the satisfaction for which mankind is groaning."[27] Although he pastored a small congregation, it had a profound affect upon his Christian thought and life. He said, "I wanted to do hard work for God. Indeed, one of the great thoughts that came upon me was that I ought to follow Jesus Christ in my personal life, and die over again his death. I felt that every Christian ought to participate in the dying of the Lord Jesus Christ, and in that way help to redeem humanity, and it was that thought that gave my life it's fundamental direction in the doing of Christian work."[28] It was during the summer pastorate in Louisville that he felt a call to ministry.

He had a turbulent relationship with his father regarding theology.[29] His ideas of the kingdom of God as a community-oriented religion were a marked change from those of his father. Rauschenbusch is known for his radical reorientation of theology in America as the "Father of the Social Gospel."[30] He was not popular in his own lifetime mainly because he opposed American participation in World War I. After his death, he was known for radically changing the church's theology. The Northern Baptist Convention referred to him as "the most potent personality in America in the modern revival of the idea of the Kingdom of God."[31]

In 1886, he accepted his second pastorate in a poor and dangerous area of New York City known as "Hell's Kitchen." He was terribly grieved by the dire economic and social conditions of the people. As pastor in Hell's Kitchen, he thought "how ineffectual was pious [conservative], individualistic philanthropy in solving major social problems"[32] and he began developing "his own understanding of Christian discipleship to reach out in love to help the victims of social misfortune and injustice."[33] Rauschenbusch regarded his individualistic conservatism as ineffective for addressing the economic and social conditions of his ministry. He believed capitalism was an enemy, and began reading numerous liberal and social writings in contrast to evangelical

---

[27] Robert T. Handy, ed., *The Social Gospel in America: 1870-1920* (New York: Oxford University Press, 1966), 254.

[28] Dores Robinson Sharpe, *Walter Rauschenbusch* (New York: Macmillan, 1942), 57.

[29] Handy, *Social Gospel*, 253; Sharpe, *Rauschenbusch*, 41.

[30] H. Leon McBeth, *The Baptist Heritage: Four Centuries of Baptist Witness* (Nashville: Broadman Press, 1987), 598.

[31] Donald K. Gorrell, *The Age of Social Responsibility* (Macon, GA: Mercer University Press, 1988), 323.

[32] James C. Livingston, *Modern Christian Thought: From the Enlightenment to Vatican II* (New York: Macmillan Company, 1971), 262.

[33] Handy, "Walter Rauschenbusch," 194.

writers.[34] He "became convinced that the message of Jesus applies to society as well as to individuals."[35]

Rauschenbusch believed the church would remedy societal ills as the temporal kingdom of God. In 1892, he formed the non-denominational Brotherhood of the Kingdom for the purpose of applying the Gospel to social needs.[36] In 1893, he published criterions for membership in his Spirit and Aims of the Brotherhood of the Kingdom. Members in the Brotherhood were those who gave a social priority to Christianity and desired a religious influence among secular reformists. The Brotherhood worked together to communicate the social gospel to the conditions of the working class and the whole of society.[37]

The most influential books written by Rauschenbusch were *Christianity and the Social Crisis* (1907) and *A Theology for the Social Gospel* (1917). The latter work claimed that the Kingdom of God is "the necessary background for the Christian idea of God."[38] According to Rauschenbusch, the central message of Jesus was the kingdom of God. The kingdom of God was not entirely future, therefore, there had to be realization in modern society. He pleaded with both church and society to work toward the realization of the ideals of the kingdom of God. Although Rauschenbusch did not abandon conservative views entirely, the modern "trend of Northern Baptists to emphasize social action owes much" to his legacy. Shailer Matthews (1863-1941) and Harry Emerson Fosdick (1878-1969) also influenced Northern Baptists with a social gospel. The latter, for instance, believed modernism could help people to have faith in God (as opposed to traditional creeds).[39]

According to the theology of Rauschenbusch, the priority of the church is to take the best elements of socialism for building the kingdom of God in modern society. He rejected the communist belief of revolution for creating change; he believed the kingdom of God would be progressive in its realization. Rauschenbusch did not believe there was any inconsistency between the social and religious since both balance and reciprocate in building the kingdom of God. Therefore, the relationship between the social and the religious is what motivated Rauschenbusch to "link the evangelical

---

[34] Handy, *Social Gospel*, 254-255; Sharpe, *Rauschenbusch*, 60-61, 64-65.

[35] McBeth, *Baptist Heritage*, 598.

[36] Handy, *Social Gospel*, 257; Sharpe, *Rauschenbusch*, 119-120.

[37] Sharpe, *Rauschenbusch*, 119-122.

[38] Walter Rauschenbusch, *A Theology for the Social Gospel* (New York: Abingdon Press, 1917; reprint, Louisville, KY: Westminster John Knox Press, 1997), 178.

[39] McBeth, *Baptist Heritage*, 598-599.

gospel with the social gospel, to add the latter to the former, and thus to create a public opinion that would bring about renewal of both church and society."[40]

Rauschenbusch's Teachings

A major feature of Rauschenbusch's teachings is his distinction between the priests and the prophets. He was intent to prove that the prophets protested the priestly religion.

> Under the influence of non-Christian customs and conceptions Christianity early developed its own ceremonial system. It is, of course, far more refined. Our places of worship have no stench of blood and entrails; our priests are not expert butchers. But the immense majority of people in Christendom have holy places, where they recite a sacred ritual, and go through sacred motions. They receive holy food and submit to washings that cleanse from sin. They have a priesthood with magic powers which offers a bloodless sacrifice. This Christian ritual grew up, not as the appropriate and aesthetic expression of spiritual emotions, but as the indispensable means of pleasing and appeasing God, and of securing His favors, temporal and eternal, for those who put their heart into these processes. This Christian ceremonial system does not differ essentially from that against which the prophets protested; with a few verbal changes their invectives would still apply. But the point that here concerns us is that a very large part of the fervor of willing devotion which religion always generates in human hearts has spent itself on these religious acts. The force that would have been competent to "seek justice and relieve the oppressed" has been consumed in weaving the tinsel fringes for the garment of religion.[41]

According to Rauschenbusch, prophets are preferable to priests since the former "have no stench of blood and entrails." The comparison was made between the priesthood "against which the prophets protested," and the customs and conceptions of a priestly Christendom. The social gospel, therefore, is likened to the prophets. Rauschenbusch explained, "The prophets were public men and their interest was in public affairs. Some of them were statesmen of the highest type. All of them interpreted past history, shaped present history, and foretold future history on the basis of the conviction that God rules with righteousness in the affairs of nations, and that only what is just, and not what is expedient and profitable, shall endure."[42] The false dichotomy between priests and prophets is a

---

[40] Handy, "Walter Rauschenbusch," 209.
[41] Walter Rauschenbusch, *Christianity and the Social Crisis* (London: Macmillan, 1908), 7.
[42] Ibid., 9.

fundamental tenet of the social gospel. For instance, although "Ezekiel was a prophet by calling," he was disparaged as "a priest by birth and training."

> His ideal city was no longer a city of justice so much as a city of the true worship. The older prophets had condemned the sins of man against man, especially injustice and oppression. Ezekiel dwelt on the sins of man against God, especially idolatry. Not justice but holiness had become the fundamental requirement, and holiness meant chiefly ceremonial correctness. The righteous nation was turned into a holy church. Ezekiel was a prophet by calling, but he was a priest by birth and training, and in comparing his literary style, his outlook on life, and his spiritual power with that of the older prophets, it is impossible to avoid a sense of religious decadence.[43]

Rauschenbusch believed the ministry of the older prophets, which "condemned the sins of man against man," was more important than Ezekiel's ministry that "dwelt on the sins of man against God." Social justice and liberation should be sought as opposed to "a city of the true worship." By focusing on sins against God and holiness of life before Him (in contrast to a primary emphasis upon "sins of man against man"), "it is impossible to avoid a sense of religious decadence." In praising the prophets in contrast to the blood-stenched priests, Rauschenbusch did not affirm all the biblical prophecies.

> When religion was driven from national interests into the refuge of private life, it lost its grasp of larger affairs, and the old clear outlook into contemporary history gave way to an artificial scheme. Instead of reading present facts to discern God's purposes, men began to pore over the sacred books, and to piece the unfulfilled prophecies of the dead prophets into a mosaic picture of the future. The sunlight of the prophetic hope gave way to the limelight of the apocalyptic visions of later Judaism.
>
> It is profoundly pathetic to see how a people, paralyzed, broken on the rack, and almost destroyed, still clung to its national existence and believed in its political future. Even the crudest dreams of apocalypticism have a tragic dignity and a lingering touch of vital force. In those dreams the Jewish people kept alive both their memories and their hopes, much as an impoverished aristocratic family will preserve the tarnished swords and the faded uniforms worn by illustrious ancestors, and nurse the hope in its sons that they may some day regain the old position. But it is a mistake to look for political wisdom in a people that had no politics. Bands of foreign political refugees gathered in England have often dreamed intensely of the liberation of their fatherland, but they have rarely planned wisely, and usually fail to take account of changes since they left their home. Yet the unhistorical and artificial schemes of apocalypticism have been and are now more influential in shaping the imagination of men about the future course of history than the inspired thoughts of the great prophets. Men still rival the rabbis in learned calculations that somehow

---

[43] Ibid., 30.

> never turn out correct, and follow wandering lights which have thus far disappointed and led astray all that have ever followed them.[44]

According to Rauschenbusch, "the old clear outlook into contemporary history gave way . . . to apocalyptic visions." Such visions are "the crudest dreams." As opposed to "the unhistorical and artificial schemes of apocalypticism," Christianity should direct attention "with passionate enthusiasm to moral righteousness as the true domain of religion," that is, "the social and political life of their nation."[45] The Book of Daniel, consequently, was criticized for its "boldest hope" in a "catastrophe that would break this [i.e. oppressive world forces] power [that] was conceived as a supernatural cataclysm out of all relation to human activity."[46] Rauschenbusch asked, "How wise is it for the Christian leaders of a democratic nation to take their interpretation of God's purposes in history and their theories about the coming of the kingdom of God from the feeblest and most decadent age of Hebrew thought?" By contrast, he believed "the true prophets" would oppose "the complacent optimism of the people and of their particular spokesman." Therefore he inquired, "If they lived among the present symptoms of social and moral decay, would they sing a lullaby or sound the reveille?"[47] The wisest of Christian leaders will work together for a "harmonious development of a true social life."[48] The "prophetic hope" is the accomplishment of this great social task. The social gospel is perceived as "sunlight" since it is more important to resolve the sins of man against man. The "limelight of the apocalyptic visions" is a false hope because it anticipates a cataclysmic turning of events by God as opposed to man effecting the change. Evidently, the "hope" of the social gospel is man, which helps one understand the relationship to liberal postmillennialism.

The focus of the social gospel is not upon a spiritual Gospel. Rauschenbusch wrote, "The kingdom of God is still a collective conception, involving the whole social life of man. It is not a matter of saving human atoms, but of saving the social organism. It is not a matter of getting individuals to heaven, but of transforming the life on earth into the harmony of heaven."[49] Realization of the kingdom of God is the essence of the teaching of Christ and the mission of the church. The social gospel is more

---

[44] Ibid., 35-36.
[45] Ibid., 41.
[46] Ibid., 35.
[47] Ibid., 42.
[48] Ibid., 422.
[49] Ibid., 65.

concerned with the salvation of the social organism, not the salvation of souls. Rauschenbusch explained, "To us, salvation means victory over sin rather than escape from hell. This change in attitude dignifies the present life. It is not, then, too paltry for earnest effort. The hope of personal salvation after death no longer monopolizes the Christian hope. There is now room beside it for the social hope."[50] Transformation of life on earth, in response to the industrialization and modernity of the new world, is primary as opposed to individual salvation. Christianity, according to Rauschenbusch, must turn from individual salvation and personal holiness to social salvation. Therefore, he was able to conclude, "The swiftness of evolution in our own country proves the immense latent perfectibility in human nature."[51]

The social gospel disparages apocalypticism because the hope is not in God, but in humanity. It is an interesting historical fact that most Americans rejection postmillennial optimism of "a latent perfectibility in human nature" as they witnessed the Civil War, two world wars, the development of immigration, large commercial organizations, rising crime, slums, and other social conditions as the result of the industrialization of the new world. Dispensationalism was certainly consistent with Calvinists[52] who were already pessimistic due to the biblical teaching of the total depravity of individual human nature and consequently the whole of society experienced the same condition. The depravity of sinful humanity necessitated individual salvation to be a monergistic work of God; therefore, it is an understandable corollary that the transformation of society will require a cataclysmic work of God. Due to the injustice of his time, Rauschenbusch concluded, "When I began to apply my previous religious ideas to the conditions I found, I discovered that they didn't fit."[53] He actually believed that individual salvation was unjust.[54] Social reform should be the commitment of the church, which would eliminate sins of man against man and prepare the world for the coming of God.

Do the Differences Matter?

One's theological position impacts his view of God's ultimate purpose for history and how future events in Scripture will unfold. Doctrine determines attitudes and practice. Therefore, the system of doctrine to which a person is committed does make a difference. Os Guinness has been one critic of

---

[50] Ibid., 204.
[51] Ibid., 422.
[52] Kraus, *Dispensationalism in America*, 59-60.
[53] Walter Rauschenbusch, *The Righteousness of the Kingdom* (Nashville: Abingdon Press, 1968), 16.
[54] Handy, *Social Gospel*, 255.

premillennial dispensationalism stating that it "has had unfortunate consequences on the Christian mind."[55] He accused dispensationalism as being anti-intellectual "by its general indifference to serious engagement with culture" and associates it with a "careless crossover between the Bible and historical events of its day."[56] The problem with such a statement is that all conservative evangelicals, regardless of being dispensational or not, reacted to the liberal social gospel of the nineteenth century and early twentieth century so that many were indifferent toward "serious engagement with culture" due to the issues of that time.

Neoevangelicals have accused dispensationalism as undercutting the "world-relevance for the Gospel." In light of such criticisms, it is interesting to read how Richard J. Mouw, president and professor of Christian philosophy at Fuller Theological Seminary, responded to his Reformed colleagues.

> Dispensationalists were supposed to downplay the relevance of the Old Testament for the Christian life; but some of the best preaching I have ever heard on the Psalms was from dispensationalists. Dispensationalist theology drew strict theoretical boundaries between Jesus as Israel's messiah and Jesus as the Lord of the church; but the Jesus I learned about from dispensationalists was a heaven-sent Savior who showed a matchless love for both Gentile and Jew. The dispensationalist perspective undercut Christian social concerns; but long before I had ever heard of Mother Teresa, I saw dispensationalists lovingly embrace the homeless in rescue missions. Whatever the defects of the older dispensationalism as a theological perspective, it embodied a spirituality that produced some of the most Christlike human beings I have ever known.
>
> One hundred years ago, as dispensationalists anticipated the beginning of a new century, they were not optimistic. They expected wars and rumors of wars. They feared the coming of Antichrist. In contrast, mainline Protestantism and liberal theologians expressed a deep faith in historical progress. They saw the kingdom of God expending in its influence. The twentieth century was to be "the Christian century": war and poverty and famine would be virtually eliminated.
>
> Now, I ask, who had a better sense of what was going to happen in the twentieth century? It seems obvious that Protestant liberalism was simply wrong in its predictions, whereas much of the dispensationalist scenario was vindicated. Why have we not given the dispensationalists more credit for their insights? Who was better equipped to prepare their children for the now much-heralded demise of Enlightenment optimism—the dispensationalists or their cultured despisers?[57]

---

[55] Os Guinness, *Fit Bodies, Fat Minds* (Grand Rapids: Baker Book House, 1994), 64.
[56] Ibid., 65.
[57] Richard Mouw, "What the Old Dispensationalists Taught Me," *Christianity Today* 39 (6 March 1995): 34.

John M. Frame, professor of systematic theology at Reformed Theological Seminary, wrote similarly concerning the godly influence of Donald B. Fullerton at Princeton. Fullerton was a graduate of Princeton and led a campus ministry called Princeton Evangelical Fellowship (PEF). Remembering the influence of Fullerton, he wrote:

> My Reformed friends often disparage and ridicule the "broad evangelical," "fundamentalist," and "dispensationalist" traditions. It is typical for these friends to say something like this: "When I was in a fundamentalist church, they taught the Bible superficially, assumed Arminianism, disparaged the Lordship of Christ, saw the Christian life as a series of legalistic prohibitions on trivial issues. But when I heard Reformed teaching, it was the first time for me that the Bible made sense. It was the first time that the Lordship of Christ and the Sovereignty of God made a real impression on me." I heard testimonies like this over and over again among Westminster students and others in the Reformed movement. Such people often concluded by saying that Reformed people should radically reject anything connected with American evangelicalism and live by the Reformed traditions alone.
>
> Because of PEF, my evaluation of "broad evangelicalism" was very different. I did not think Fullerton's teaching was superficial at all. There was a great depth to it, underscored by the powerful, godly example of his life. His teaching on the sovereignty of God and the Lordship of Christ were powerful and deeply biblical. He showed a passion for holiness that I rarely saw in Reformed circles, including a passion for prayer and evangelism. Reformed people talked about evangelism and missions, but frankly they did not do it nearly to the extent I had seen in the PEF. Fullerton and PEF cared deeply about people, spending hours in mutual prayer, exhortation, counseling, gospel witness. I never experienced that depth of fellowship in any Reformed church or institution. In fact, the Reformed consensus often seemed to be that such mutual commitment, such perseverance in prayer, such passion for the Lord, should be deprecated as "Pietism." (Reformed people have a knack for condemning others with the use of historical labels.)[58]

Concerning the life of John Nelson Darby, Bethel Seminary Professor of Theology Emeritus Clarence B. Bass wrote,

> The single motivation of Darby's entire life was his love for Christ. If any principle is sufficient to explain the multiple facets of his personality, most probably it is this love. Because of it he has been called "a saint of the highest and purest stamp. . . ." He preferred being with the poor, for he was essentially humble in spirit. This characteristic endeared him to the folk of humble status, and was perhaps one of the secrets of his success with the poor Romanists of Ireland and the peasants of France and Switzerland. . . . It is not surprising that such self-abandonment should result in a life of humble service. Trained as a scholar among the intellectuals, he

---

[58] John M. Frame, "Remembering Donald B. Fullerton" [online] (The Works of John Frame and Vern Poythress, accessed 31 August 2007) available from http://www.frame-poythress.org/frame_articles/Remembering_fullerton.htm.

found peace in laboring among the poor and ignorant. His unchallenged consistency, sincerity, and unwearied service to the faith commanded the reverence and admiration of those who recognized in him a spiritual guide. . . . Nor was this place of supremacy confined to his relation with the poor, for he was held in high regard by men of scholarly attainment.[59]

Historically, dispensationalists have shown a passion for evangelism and missions that makes biased assertions of social disengagement challenging to uphold. Nevertheless, the fundamental imperative of the Great Commission is to make disciples. The Greek word *matheteusate* is an imperative of command, which means literally "to make a disciple of, teach." Matthew 28:19 in the KJV reads "Go ye therefore, and teach all nations." The word teach means literally to "make disciples" as in the NASB. The Greek word meaning "to make a disciple of, teach" is the only verb in the commission; therefore, it emphasizes the most important detail of the passage. The words *go* and *baptize* in verse 19 and the word *teaching* in verse 20 are all participles, which means they inform how one is to make disciples, how one is to teach. Before one can become a disciple, he or she must first understand the Gospel, which is the need for evangelism and is certainly implied in the word *go*.

On a basic level, *matheteuo*, which is translated to become a "disciple" means to believe another's doctrine. However, there is a more significant meaning, which is not only to learn but also to commit oneself as the teacher's follower in both doctrine and lifestyle. Furthermore, the word *matheten* ("disciple, adherent") refers to the disciple as an adherent who receives the teaching communicated to them and makes it their standard of conduct. What is the curriculum then for this teaching? Second Timothy 3:16 states that the result of the inspiration of Scripture is to make it "profitable for teaching, for reproof, for correction, for training in righteousness." The word "teaching" is *didaskontes* from *didasko*. Teaching is a synonym for doctrine. It is undoubtedly mentioned first because understanding (doctrine) chronologically and logically precedes practice of the Christian life. Doctrine without practice is dangerous. However, practice without doctrine is deadly. It is impossible to isolate doctrine from the practical, which would cause both to suffer. Sound doctrine is essential. The remaining three ("reproof, correction, and training in righteousness") of the four profitable uses of the inspired Scripture are the corollary (i.e. the effect, the result) of sound doctrine. The desired result (3:17) is "that the man of God may be adequate,

---

[59] Clarence B. Bass, *Backgrounds to Dispensationalism* (Grand Rapids: Eerdmans, 1960), 52-53.

equipped for every good work." Paul commended Timothy because he continued in the things he learned, and internalized the learning (i.e. the learning became a part of his life). Timothy was committed to the sound doctrine he had learned from childhood.

A disturbing trend that is influencing American Christianity is a growing opposition against God's chosen methods for fulfilling the Great Commission. No Christian can claim obedience to the Great Commission until he has "made disciples" through preaching the Gospel, "baptized" converts in the Name of the Father, Son, and Holy Spirit, and "taught" converts in the whole counsel of God's Word. There is a tendency on the part of Christians to ignore the truth that Christ and the early church gave utmost emphasis upon teaching of converts in "the whole counsel of God's Word." For instance, in the New Testament, one reads that the apostles won converts, baptized them, and organized them into local churches for the purpose of doctrinal and practical edification and observance of all biblical commands. Although evangelism and communicating to a lost person the reality of salvation by grace through faith in Christ alone are vitally important components of the total responsibility of the local church, one must be continually reminded that the New Testament places the utmost emphasis upon the feeding (teaching) of those who are already Christians! Indeed, it may be said that the teaching of converts in the whole counsel of God's Word is the basic New Testament pattern for world evangelization. Apart from this emphasis, Christian evangelism will soon become ineffective and superficial.

A Theology of Ministry

It is essential that ministry involve trust in God in obedience to His commands. As Christians are obedient to God's commands through earthly ministry, they are preparing themselves for eternal ministry in the life to come. Ephesians 1—3 may cause one to speculate that heaven may involve a wholly unknown spectrum of ministries to the most intelligent, unfallen creatures whose glories of the eternal God may surpass anything imagined. Nevertheless, these unfallen and glorified creatures would not have experienced the sundry wisdom of God through the redemptive work of the Lord Jesus Christ as the glorified saints. Living with an eternal perspective means, among so many others, that new opportunities for art, music, poetry, and teaching will be the divine privilege of the saints of God when time itself is amalgamated with eternity, with reverential and righteous desire.[60] Nevertheless, the church is not currently who she will be fully in eternity, therefore it is necessary to think biblically concerning ministry in the present time.

The Sanctity of Work

Ministry occurs within every aspect of life. From the beginning of human history (Gen 1:26), God mandated mankind to work and be accountable for their work. Work was an aspect of creation, continues today as God's mandate, and will be restored in the millennium. The present reality of sin in this world means the work is often less than the initial aims and objectives. Nevertheless, Christians are reminded to be "abounding in the work of the Lord, knowing that your toil is not *in* vain in the Lord" (1 Cor 15:58). As God purposed it, work encompasses the community, the church, the factory, the home, the office, etc. The church is to influence all spheres of society both geographically and occupationally. The Christian life is to add flavor to this world, and to shine light in the midst of darkness (Matt 5:13-16). Christians are commanded by Christ to penetrate a dark and fallen world. The church is not an oligarchy in which holy service is performed sacerdotally. Every member of the church is a priest with full privileges and rights. All who are believers bear equal weight of responsibility to minister wherever they find themselves. There are Christians who are called to fulltime church or parachurch ministry, but this certainly does not restrict Christian ministry to "professionals.

Jesus promised that the Holy Spirit "will convict the world concerning sin and righteousness and judgment" when He comes (John 16:8). Since the Holy Spirit permanently indwells every Christian and accomplishes His work through the church, then the church is the necessary means by which the Holy Spirit convicts. Since it will always be challenging for Christians being a minister-priest in an ungodly world, Jesus prayed, "They are not of the world, even as I am not of the world. Sanctify them in the truth; Your word is truth. As You sent Me into the world, I also have sent them into the world" (17:16-18). Christians are not of the world, they are to be sanctified by Scripture in and from the world, and then sent into the world for the glory of God.

The desire of all Christians should be to reproduce their faith in every sphere of society whether deemed sacred or secular (by conventional terms). By living in such a manner, the church will be fulfilling her God-given

---

[60] G. Campbell Morgan, *Discipleship* (New York: Fleming H. Revell, 1897).

role in society as salt and light in obedience to the cultural mandate, as Christians work for the restoration of the world from the damning effects of sin. Jesus said, "My food is to do the will of Him who sent Me and to accomplish His work" (4:34). The words of Jesus apply to all believers for His ministry is continued through His disciples (Matt 28:18-20). The Gospel should be proclaimed in all human endeavors. Christians are to find themselves engaged in sanctifying work in the midst of ordinary situations of their work, and of their church, family, and social relationships. The church is not called to a "double life" that separates the sacred and the secular. There is just one life, which is to be lived for the glory of God (1 Cor 10:31). It is sin that does not do everything for the glory of God; indeed, sin is distinguishing and separating God from the ordinary situations of life.

In the ancient world, the Greeks viewed manual work as a curse. The Romans viewed work as something vulgar. Work was something for the lower classes and slaves. Christianity, however, changed such views. There is sanctity to work as ministry, as opposed to regarding it as mere drudgery. Even the often bitter and mocking Voltaire famously stated: "Work spares us from three great evils: boredom, vice, and greed." Historically, the church regarded work as a synergistic calling of God to develop the full potential of His creation.[61] By medieval times, for instance, the church developed many of the craft and merchant guilds.[62] The standard of good workmanship was the result of workers taking satisfaction in their labors. Martin Luther preached that all work—whether preaching the Gospel or plowing a field—should be done to the glory of God because any honest work is pleasing to the Lord. The Protestant work ethic (commendable character and will to work diligently) is generally attributed to the great Reformer, John Calvin. Of course, some historians view the connection negatively and others positively. Not only was the Christian influence felt in Western Europe, but also in the New World colonies. The Protestant work ethic was deeply ingrained in the minds of Americans during the great age of free enterprise capitalism in America (i.e. the latter half of the nineteenth century). Most Americans viewed work as a blessing from God; they believed their labor had great dignity since it fulfilled their responsibility as good stewards of creation (thereby glorifying God). In the words of Nehemiah, "the people had a mind to work" (Neh 4:6).

---

[61] Randall Dattoli and Robert E. Shackelford, class notes from ED 120, Survey of Christian Ministry, Moody Bible Institute, 1996.
[62] Eamon Duffy, *The Stripping of the Altars: Traditional Religion in England 1400—1580* (New Haven: Yale University Press, 1992).

Of course, the Protestant work ethic is not to be confused with the self-centered modern consumer society. The work ethic is not solely concerned with hard work, but also serves God by being other-centered in its formation and function. Honest work is a labor of love. Work is often the basis for obedience to the great commandment. It demonstrates love of God and loving service to one's neighbor (cf. Matt 22:36-40). God leads individuals to a variety of callings, including businesses, ministries, schools, and services in society. The believer's work is given for faithful responsibility in accordance with the gifts that God bestows. The calling upon the believer is always to serve God and others. Through the gift of work, man can better explore and subdue God's creation for His eternal glory. God calls His people to be good stewards with His creation and to be responsible with energy, resources, talents, and time. Being a good steward creates the opportunity for greater service to God and others. In the present time, it should be the goal of each believer to seek appropriate work in response to God's Word.

Conclusion

In 1 Corinthians 15:1-8, the Gospel is identified with the death, burial, and resurrection of Jesus Christ. The resurrection of Christ is the central truth of the Gospel: it is central to conversion (15:1-2), the Gospel message itself (15:3-4), the believer's resurrection (15:12-13, 16, 19), the apostolic preaching (15:14-15), and the remission of sins (15:14-17). The resurrection of Christ guarantees the believer's resurrection, and is the foundation for the believer's practice, in addition to the reason for living and suffering (15:20-34). Romans 1:4 states that Jesus Christ "was declared the Son of God with power by the resurrection from the dead," an essential fact of the Gospel. The grace of God is received through the Lord Jesus Christ, and empowers believers in the proclamation of the Gospel message (1:5-9). Second Timothy 2:8 also confirms the centrality of the resurrection to Gospel proclamation: "Remember Jesus Christ, risen from the dead, descendant of David, according to my gospel." As Ephesians 1:3-14 declares, this Gospel of grace for those chosen and blessed of God is personal.[63] Trust in the Lord Jesus results in the sealing of the Holy Spirit, who is the "earnest" (3:14) of more

---

[63] God acts and His act is that of election. 'Exelevxato translated "chose" comes from two Greek words, ejk and levgw, meaning "to speak out," which means literally "to call forth" or "to select out." The aorist tense indicates a given point in past time that God chose those who will exercise faith in Christ. The middle voice indicates God's sovereign purpose of selecting His elect. God is the subject of the verb. The direct object of the verb ejxelevxato is hJma'", the second person plural pronoun. Paul used a personal direct object, making the choice personal and distinct. God "chose" believers, not a nameless group, that is, hJma'".

promises to come.[64] The benefits which are brought to believers by the Lord Jesus Christ and of which the church is made partakers of the Gospel are primarily in the age to come, that is, the "pledge of our inheritance, with a view to the redemption of God's own possession, to the praise of His glory" (1:14).

The benefits of the Gospel, which are brought to believers, are so extensive that it would surely be a lack of gratitude to live the present life as the unregenerate who are never contented or peaceful. Furthermore, 2 Corinthians 5:17 states, "Therefore if anyone is in Christ, he is a new creature; the old things passed away; behold, new things have come." Accurately did slave preacher and pastor John Jasper say, "if you is, what you was, you ain't." Scripture does not teach that obedience in the Christian life is optional because saving faith will manifest itself. The doctrines of grace are not adaptable to man's sin and lack of repentance, as if sanctification was not a necessary corollary of justification. If a professed Christian distinctly and deliberately declares to know God's will and is not obedient to it, Scripture will not pamper his presumption. The Gospel is not magnified or God glorified by telling the world they may be saved by simply accepting Christ as Savior, and their hearts may still remain in love with sin. To teach that the Gospel does not change lives is to distort the Gospel, insult Christ, and turns the grace of God into lasciviousness.[65] Scripture affirms that the regenerative work of God makes the entire being of the believer new; not some things, not one's attitude merely, but all things are become new. The change is not merely in the destiny of the soul, but it is the one in sin, who is made alive in Christ Jesus, and now is becoming one like Christ. The changed life of the regenerate individual is at the core of Christianity and confirmed throughout the New Testament. The believer, who is growing in the grace and knowledge of the Lord Jesus Christ by the empowering of the Holy Spirit will seek to obey the teachings and commandments of Scripture (John 14:15-24; Acts 1:8; 2 Pet 3:15-18).

Obedience to the Lord's teachings and commandments has personal and social implications. True regeneration is a cultural event. Scripture presents two means of influencing society with God's Word, each of which is necessary: holy lives and verbal proclamation. As God's Word influences society, there should be a marked difference in society as a whole, and it

---

[64] As the eschatological gift, the Holy Spirit is operative in the present. "Every spiritual blessing" (1:3) is another way of declaring the reality of promises already commenced but that will be consummated in the future (i.e. eschatological pneumatology).

[65] Charles H. Spurgeon, *The Soul-Winner: How to Lead Sinners to the Saviour* (reprint, Grand Rapids: Eerdmans, 1963), 38.

should be a difference that even the unbeliever will notice, for light will not go unnoticed by darkness (cf. Matt 5:13-16). Social benefits are often the result of holy lives and verbal proclamation of God's Word, but societal improvement is not the gospel the church is charged to proclaim. Social action apart from the biblical Gospel often prioritizes the conversion of social structures, as opposed to personal salvation in Christ alone, which supposedly reaches its climax in the complete inauguration of the kingdom of God. God does have a purpose for all creation, but it awaits the redemption of the body for the saints according to the will of God (Rom 8:18-23; Phil 3:20-21). Before the foundation of the world, God chose those "to be saved through the sanctifying work of the Spirit and through belief in the truth . . . to share in the glory of [the] Lord Jesus Christ." Therefore, the church is to "stand firm and hold to the teachings" of the Gospel and to do so "in every good deed and word" (2 Thess 2:13-17). When the church stands firm, God will be glorified and society will be better for it!

"Here is the secret of peace on earth – a ruler who can enforce peace righteously."

- Charles C. Ryrie

The Final Countdown, 1982, page 114

22

Is Dispensationalism Hurting American Political Policies in the Middle East?[1]
Michael Stallard

"It's hard to believe, but the Bush administration's foreign policy and the invasions of Afghanistan and Iraq are influenced by the writings of a cave-dwelling hermit who had apocalyptic visions some 2000 years ago."[2] Such a claim, in spite of its clear overstatement, nonetheless echoes a belief that is held by religious and political liberals and many conservative evangelicals. Another concerned writer notes that "it is somewhat alarming that swathes of the evangelical community...naively accept a potted version of biblical eschatology in relation to the Middle East which puts them firmly on the side of injustice and post-colonial oppression, as far as most inhabitants of the region are concerned."[3]

In a similar vein, a recent edition of *Christianity Today* highlights the analysis of Kevin Phillips, a former Republican strategist, who is apparently quite unaware of the many varieties of evangelicals in America. Phillips, in a stark criticism of dispensationalism (perhaps without knowing the term), complains, "The rapture, end-times, and Armageddon hucksters in the United States rank with any Shiite ayatollahs, and the last two presidential elections mark the transformation of the GOP into the first religious party in U.S. history."[4] Collin Hansen's *CT* review summarizes Phillips' massive tome with a test to discover if any individual is contributing to the downfall of the United States—Are you now, or have you ever: (a) attended a megachurch; (b) driven an SUV; (c) read any of the Left Behind books; (d) voted for President Bush; (e) lived in the South. Hansen asserts that the tone of

---

[1] Reprinted with permission from Michael Stallard, Is Dispensationalism Hurting American Political Policies in the Middle East?, in the *Journal of Dispensational Theology*, Vol. 10, No. 31, December 2006

[2] Chip Berlet & Nikhil Aziz, "Culture, Religion, Apocalypse, and Middle East Foreign Policy" *Right Web* 5 December 2003, <http://rightweb.irc-online.org/rw/848> (accessed 27 September 2006). Berlet and Aziz work at Political Research Associates (www.publiceye.org) which is a self-labeled progressive Boston think tank. The cave-dwelling hermit is, of course, the Apostle John who gave us the book of Revelation. What is being criticized is the dispensational understanding of that New Testament book.

[3] Peter Wilkinson, "Eschatology and the Middle East" *Open Source Theology* 3 June 2006, <http://www.opensource.theology.net/node/924> (accessed 21 September 2006).

[4] Kevin P. Phillips, *American Theocracy: The Peril and Politics of Radical Religion, Oil, and Borrowed Money in the 21st Century* (New York: Viking, 2006), vii.

Phillips' book is that a "yes" answer for two or more of these questions means that you as an individual American are causing America's downfall.[5] This means deep trouble for this author. I have in my life been a member of a church of almost 20,000 members. I have read *all* of the Left Behind books in the original series. I voted for Bush *twice* (and his father *twice*). I was born and raised in the southern part of the United States. To add insult to injury I recently bought my first SUV. To those like Phillips I am a hyper-demon responsible for the coming destruction of a once-great country.

The reference above to the Left Behind series of novels by Tim LaHaye and Jerry Jenkins highlights the concern of dispensational theology, which they attempt to portray. The concern of Phillips and other critics of dispensationalism point to its undue influence in American politics especially as it relates to foreign policy related to Israel. This common complaint in our day is somewhat of an enigma. Dispensationalism is viewed as having too much power while at the same time other historians and theologians are telling us that dispensationalism is in serious decline as a theological option within evangelicalism.[6]

Dispensationalism and Neoconservatism

It is no wonder then that there exists within the politico-religious debates in America a parallel between shrill criticism of dispensational theology and harsh aversion to neoconservatism. The latter is considered to be a movement starting earlier in the twentieth century with once-liberal activists who vigorously opposed communism and have morphed in recent times into a new wing of conservative politics. This group has been intensely pro-Israel in Middle Eastern policies. Many Jews are part of this movement although historically the term does not limit itself to Jewish proponents of the political philosophy. The Bush administration is considered to have too many of this persuasion in critical foreign policy positions. One name that often surfaces is that of Paul Wolfowitz, current President of the World Bank, but formerly the Deputy Secretary of Defense under Donald Rumsfeld from 2001-2005, a time when the Bush Administration was formulating its planned response in the War on Terror.

Dispensationalism has been perhaps the most caricatured and misrepresented theological position within evangelicalism since its rise in the

---

[5] Collin Hansen, "Logic Left Behind," *Christianity Today* (September 2006): 126. Hansen's critique of Phillips is largely and appropriately negative.

[6] For example, see Ronald M. Henzel, *Darby, Dualism and the Decline of Dispensationalism* (Tuscon, AZ: Fenestra Books, 2003).

early nineteenth century. Committed to a literal (grammatical-historical) interpretation of the Bible including prophecy, it has always affirmed some form of significant and institutional distinction between Israel and the Church. Dispensationalism has strongly rejected any form of replacement theology in which Israel has been done away with in God's plan for history and thus superseded by the Church. The Church has typically not been defined as simply the collection of all the elect of all ages. Consequently, dispensationalists accept the promises of the Old Testament relative to an ultimate restoration of Israel to its land before and after the return of the Messiah (Jesus Christ) to planet earth.[7]

Usually dispensationalists and political neoconservatives, who disagree perhaps on many social issues, share one fundamental aspect of their world view: Israel has a right to its land in present-day Palestine. Another way to voice this shared belief is to say that most dispensationalists and neoconservatives are Zionists. Dispensationalists would be called *Christian* Zionists although not all Christian Zionists could be labeled as *dispensationalist*. Dispensationalists believe in Israel's right to the land by embracing the biblical prophecies about Israel's land in a straight-forward way. Neoconservatives would come to it from the vantage point of modern geo-politics. Therefore, as a result of the existence of neoconservatives in the present administration coupled with the fact of supposedly easy access for dispensationalists to a self-proclaimed evangelical president, the Bush administration is perceived as favoring Israel over against the Islamic Arabs in Middle-Eastern policies. Over-generalizations of this kind need to be avoided by all parties since Bush's so-called "Roadmap to Peace" includes the establishment of a Palestinian state, something that is not welcomed easily by those with a pro-Israel bent.

The Charge of Racism

In a misrepresentation of dispensationalism, there is the charge that the dispensational view of the Bible, Israel, and the end-times leads to blatant racism and prejudice. One Baptist minister incredibly argues that

> Dispensationalists, who are found in many fundamentalist and evangelical denominations, follow the theological beliefs of John Nelson Darby, C. I. Scofield and Hal Lindsey, who taught that ethnic Jews constitute a superior race who are destined to take over Palestine, then the entire Middle East and finally the world.

---

[7] By "before and after" I mean the biblical fact that Israel must be in the land in unbelief during the seven-year tribulation period (70th week of Daniel) and will be part of God's coming kingdom under Christ as a believing nation after He returns at the end of that tribulation period.

> This naturally leads to resentment of Palestinian Arabs, and all other Middle Eastern nations that sympathize with the Palestinians in their resistance to the program of pushing them out of their historic homelands. Dispensationalism, taken to its logical conclusion, leads to racism.[8]

It is hard to take such a paragraph seriously. The writer shows evidence of having never actually read and studied in detail any dispensational writings, including works by the men he names—Darby, Scofield, and Lindsey. Instead, his words come across as a rant that raises the moniker of racism over the heads of those with whom he disagrees.

To parse the charge of racism, one must begin with the claim that dispensationalists teach that "ethnic Jews constitute a *superior* race." Such a statement is acutely misleading in its use of terms. Dispensationalism teaches that the Jewish people are a *chosen* race, not a *superior* race.[9] While dispensationalists certainly hold that the Jewish people are *special* in God's eyes this does not logically imply superiority to other people groups. The Bible is clear on the reason that God chose the Hebrews:

> For you (Israel) are a holy people to the LORD your God; the LORD your God has chosen you to be a people for His own possession out of all the peoples[10] who are on the face of the earth. The Lord did not set His love on you nor choose you because you were more in number than any of the peoples, for you were the fewest of all the peoples, but because the LORD loved you and kept the oath which He swore to your forefathers, the LORD brought you out by a mighty hand, and redeemed you from the house of slavery, from the hand of Pharaoh king of Egypt (Deut. 7:6-8; NASB).

> Do not say in your heart when the LORD your God has driven them out before you, 'Because of my righteousness the LORD has brought me in to possess this land,' but it is because of the wickedness of these nations that the LORD is dispossessing them before you. It is not your righteousness or for the uprightness of your heart that you are going to possess their land, but it is because of the wickedness of these nations that the LORD your God is driving them out before you, in order to confirm the oath which the LORD swore to you fathers, to Abraham, Isaac and Jacob. Know, then, it is not because of your righteousness that the LORD your God is giving you this good land to possess, for you are a stubborn people (Deut. 9:4-6; NASB).

---

[8] Thomas Williamson, "Dispensationalism and Racism," *Media Monitors Network 4 June 2001,* <http://www.mediamonitors.net/williamson3.html> (accessed 27 September 2006). At the time of this writing, Williamson serves as the Assistant Pastor at Metropolitan Baptist Tabernacle in Melrose Park, Illinois. The church is associated with the Baptist Missionary Association of American which split off from the landmark American Baptist Association in 1950.

[9] Throughout this paper I will make no distinction between the terms *Jews, Hebrews,* or *Israelites.*

[10] It is probably worth noting that the King James Version (and NKJV) translates the words which NASB gives as "out of all the peoples" as "above all peoples." This is an unfortunate translation which could be read to indicate the divine establishment of superiority for Israel above all other nations.

These passages clearly show that God's attitude toward the Israelites was not that they were a cut above the other people groups they were displacing following the exodus from Egypt. God's faithfulness to his covenant pledge to Abraham is highlighted as well as the necessary judgment in light of the wickedness of the other nations. Dispensationalists have consistently, on my reading, been faithful in pointing out these details.[11]

The charge of racism cited above also lends itself to the incitement of unjustified fear on the part of those who are anti-Zionists. Recall that the writer said that dispensationalists teach that the superior Jewish people are the ones "who are destined to take over Palestine, then the entire Middle East and finally the world." The brevity of the remark, without any context of Messiah's coming or without the happy kingdom sharing of all nations or people groups as taught in Scripture and by dispensationalists (Dan. 7:13-14), misses the mark horribly. It reads as if dispensationalists along with other Zionists are engaging in a kind of Israeli imperialism. This, of course, is exactly how modern-day Islamic terrorists seek to portray the nation of Israel. The modern nation of Israel, far from being established in 1948 out of the horror of the Holocaust of World War II and in keeping with its ancient homeland boundaries, is considered an oppressive occupier of territory that belongs to someone else, i.e., the Palestinians.

American Zionists, including dispensationalists, are seen as supporting the imperial bent of the founding of Israel and its continued possession of its land and nationhood. Since hostile statements against the nation of Israel are so numerous, it is hard to choose a starting place for discussion. Perhaps it is best to begin with the well-known United Nations General Assembly Resolution 3379 (November 10, 1975) which links South African racism and Zionism while using the expression "unholy alliance." It further quotes from an earlier Mexican declaration: "international cooperation and peace require the achievement of national liberation and independence, the elimination of colonialism and neo-colonialism, foreign

---

[11] John Nelson Darby noted, "Nor did God set His love upon them [Israel] on account of their own importance, but because of the election and love of God" (*Synopsis of the Books of the Bible* [Reprint ed.: Addison, IL: Bible Truth Publishers, 1979], 1:291). I reviewed Hal Lindsey's *The Late Great Planet Earth* and found no hint of "superiority" language relative to the Jews and Israel. To my knowledge there is no note in the *Scofield Reference Bible* that clearly teaches the superiority of the Jews over all other peoples. Finally, Arnold Fruchtenbaum, a typical present-day dispensationalist, speaks clearly of God's election of the nation of Israel to carry out His purposes without tying it to any superiority theme relative to the Jews (*Israelology: The Missing Link in Systematic Theology* [Revised ed., Tustin, CA: Ariel Ministries, 1992], 567-70).

occupation, Zionism, apartheid and racial discrimination in all its forms..."[12] Clearly, the United Nations sentiment officially expressed in an approved resolution is that Zionism, which primarily consists of Israel's right to its land, is racism. The Palestinian Rabee' Sahyoun describes Zionism with the harshest of terms. Israel should not be described in a positive way due to its alleged democracy because to "do so is to miss the normal atrocities that occur in Israel daily, the millions who are under curfew and blockade, starving and brutalized, in the Middle East's only colonized state. To do so is to feign the reality of zionism, a racist and irredeemable movement, that survived the twentieth centuries' other genocidal and seemingly passing revolutions such as Bolshevism, Nazism, and Apartheid."[13]

Within such a mindset it is not difficult to see President Bush and current United States foreign policy as advancing a neo-colonialist agenda that marginalizes the Palestinians as a people. Added to this is the President's refusal, two weeks before 9-11, to send U. S. representatives to a U. N. conference on racism if the conference insisted on calling Zionism a form of racism.[14] Since dispensationalism has more often than not supported the nation of Israel, it is easy to see the connection between the influential evangelical world and Bush administration policies as leading to racist imperialism and oppression if one accepts the premise of a pre-1948 Palestinian homeland of some sort.

In response, one must point out that belief that Zionism is racism can not be rationally maintained on such a shaky historical foundation. In the 1800s the land of Palestine was a largely uninhabited and deteriorating region.[15] Even Arabic leaders in those days welcomed the Jews to the land, believing them able to build it up and bring life to the region.[16] Thus, in the beginning the Jewish return to the land was not viewed as anti-Arab. Furthermore, if Zionism is a form of racism, how can one understand the fact that there are one million Muslim and Christian Arabs as well as other ethnic groups who live in Israel (some even holding seats in the Knesset and all

---

[12] *Jewish Virtual Library*, <http://www.jewishvirtuallibrary.org/jsource/UN/unga3379.html> (accessed 6 October 2006).

[13] Rabee' Sahyoun, "Why Zionism is Racism," *Albalagh*, <http:www.albalagh.net/current_affairs /zionism_racism.shtml> (accessed 6 October 2006).

[14] Office of International Information Programs, U.S. Department of State, "Bush Says U. N. Conference on Racism Must Not Target Israel," 24 August 2001, <http://www.usembassy-israel.org.il/publish/peace/ archives/2001/ august/0824a.html> (accessed 6 October 2006). This posting comes largely from a Bush news conference on August 24, 2001.

[15] Mitchell G. Bard, *Myth and Facts: A Guide to the Arab-Israeli Conflict* (Chevy Chase, MD: American-Israeli Cooperative Enterprise, 2001), 29-30.

[16] Ibid., 30.

having voting rights)?[17] In addition, Israelis can point to the great financial and time expense to which they have gone to bring Ethiopian (black) Jews into the country.[18] On the other side, the absence of Jews from Arab nations is telling: "By contrast, the Arab states define citizenship strictly by native parentage. It is almost impossible to become a naturalized citizen in many Arab states…Jordan, on the other hand, instituted its own 'law of return' in 1954, according citizenship to all former residents in Palestine, except for Jews."[19] In light of the many statements down through the years coming out of the Arab and Persian lands, which call for the extermination of the Jews and eradication of the state of Israel, the dispensationalist must be forgiven for wondering out loud if the racism is not on the other side.

Dispensational Theology and National Ethics

Related to the specific issue of racism and oppression is the larger question of God's dealings with nations generally. Some critics of dispensationalism have posited a theological deficiency as the basis for mistreatment of the Arabs in the Arab-Israeli conflict. These critics would argue that dispensationalism with its influence on American policy makers leads, probably unintentionally, to a diminishing of attention for the Arabs which, in turn, causes mistreatment at various levels.

The actual vehicle for alleged mistreatment of Arabs by dispensationalism is its undue and uncaring influence on the United States government. For example, David Brog, a Jewish friend of Christian Zionists (mostly dispensationalists), describes one actual scenario that no doubt bothers those who are not dispensationalists:

> Israel has sent troops into the West Bank to seek and destroy terrorist cells responsible for a wave of suicide bombings that have killed hundreds of Israeli civilians. While sympathetic to Israel's need to fight terrorism, President George W. Bush wants to stop Israel from conducting too long and deep a raid. A few days after the incursion begins, Bush starts pressuring Israel to pull its soldiers out of the West Bank.
>
> This time, protest comes not only from the Jewish community but also from the evangelical Christian community. The White House is flooded with hundreds of thousands of e-mails and phone calls from the heartland in support of Israel. Evangelical Christians organize a nationwide day of prayer for Israel with the participation of an estimated sixteen thousand churches and five million

---

[17] Ibid., 230.
[18] Ibid., 31.
[19] Ibid.

parishioners. The Christian Coalition holds a large rally in Washington to demonstrate its solidarity with Israel.

While George W. Bush received no more Jewish support than did his father, evangelical Christians formed the core of his political base. This time, the administration could not afford to ignore the protests. And this time, due to his own evangelical leanings, President Bush was, by all accounts, predisposed to listen. When Israel kept its tanks in the West Bank for many months thereafter, the U. S. administration was silent.[20]

Consequently, the beliefs of dispensationalism concerning Israel dominate the evangelical conversation with the current administration so as to affect the outcome of major geo-political decisions in the Middle Eastern conflict.

One writer from a nondispensational perspective summarizes well a negative response: "Perhaps the most glaring weakness in the Christian Zionist program is its failure to relate to or defend Palestinian Christians, who are fleeing their homeland in record numbers not due to Islamic extremism, but because of Israel's brutal occupation policies, including economic closures, theft of land and settlement construction, and military aggression."[21] Such a statement gives an indictment of dispensationalists and other Christian Zionists on the basis of ethics. In the minds of these interpreters of the Middle Eastern situation, Zionists are turning a blind eye to the needs of others in violation of Scripture just like the priest and Levite in the Good Samaritan story (Luke 10:30-37). In light of this particular passage, one critic argues that dispensationalism has an unbiblical "bias in favor of Israelis above Palestinians" which is not in harmony with the teaching of Jesus. Therefore, the conclusion is drawn that dispensationalism is doctrinally "anti-Christ."[22] Another author words the ethical challenge in a slightly different direction, when he skeptically wonders when dispensationalists will finally be obedient to Christ's exhortation to be peacemakers instead of holding to their pro-Israel posture.[23]

A dispensational reaction to such a viewpoint begins by questioning the claims of brutality and military aggression by the Israeli military. Without arguing for the perfection of the nation of Israel and its large military

---

[20] David Brog, *Standing with Israel: Why Christians Support the Jewish State* (Lake Mary, FL: FrontLine, 2006), 133-34. Brog is a lawyer who worked on the staff of Senator Arlen Specter of Pennsylvania.

[21] Donald E. Wagner, "Short Fuse to Apocalypse?" *Sojourners Magazine* (July/August 2003), <http://www.findarticles.com/p/articles/mi_qa4010/is_200307/ai_n9284400/print > (accessed 9 September 2006).

[22]Steve Wohlberg, "Is Dispensationalism 'Antichrist,'" *White Horse Media*, <http://whitehorsemedia.com/articles/ artDetails.cfm?artID=43> (accessed 11 October 2006).

[23] Timothy P. Weber, *On the Road to Armageddon: How Evangelicals Became Israel's Best Friend* (Grand Rapids: Baker, 2004), 267.

machine, it is quite easy to show that the reverse is generally true. One can ask a few simple questions to highlight the quandary for those who favor the Arab side of the debate. When did Israel ever attack another nation without provocation? In 1948 on the day after the announcement of its statehood, was not Israel attacked by Egypt, Syria, Jordan, Iraq, Saudi Arabia, and Lebanon?[24] The only provocation from Israel's side was its existence. In the 1956 Suez War, did not Egypt blockade the Straits of Tiran? Even in the 1967 Six-Day War when Israel made a pre-emptive strike against Egypt, Egypt had massed troops on the border and had again blockaded the Straits of Tiran, Israel's major outlet for shipping—an act that could be construed as an act of war. Did not Egypt and Syria invade Israel in 1973 on the high, holy day of Yom Kippur? If Arab nations were attacked in surprise on any day of Ramadan, what would be the outcry? In 1982, was not Israel's incursion into Lebanon caused by the heavy use of katusha rockets coming from the PLO located in safe havens in southern Lebanon? Did we not recently witness a similar event this year when Israel entered Lebanon because of rocket attacks from Hezbollah? Let's make sure to get the details right. Has Israel ever declared its desire to exterminate Arabs or eliminate any particular Arab nation from the face of the earth? No, it is quite the other way. Have we ever had to worry about Jews hijacking airliners for political reasons? Who was it that murdered Olympic athletes in Munich in 1972? Has any Arab nation had to rescue its people as Israel was forced to do at Entebbe in 1976? One must confess a certain amount of consternation when confronting those who want dispensationalists to join Israelis as sweet peacemakers when it is the other side that has consistently demonstrated a lack of desire for peace apart from the annihilation of national Israel. In light of such a litany of facts, it is quite bizarre for faculty representatives from a significant evangelical school to charge that the bad theology of dispensationalism "is attributing to secular Israel a divine mandate to conquer and hold Palestine, with the consequence that the Palestinian people are marginalized and regarded as virtual 'Canaanites.'"[25]

The same approach can also be held relative to economic and humane treatment of Palestinian Arabs. It is not the Israelis who are on the short end of the evaluation. Arab stinginess with respect to Palestinian

---

[24] For a good summary of the Arab-Israeli conflict from 1948 to 1982, see Chaim Herzog, *The Arab-Israeli Wars: War and Peace in the Middle East from the War of Independence through Lebanon* (New York: Vintage Books, 1984).

[25] "An Open Letter to Evangelicals and Other Interested Parties: The People of God, the Land of Israel, and the Impartiality of the Gospel," *Knox Seminary* (2002),
<http://www.knoxseminary.org/Prospective/Faculty/WittenbergDoor> (accessed 21 September 2006).

refugees is a well-known fact. Little effort has been put forward by Arab and other Moslem nations to assist them financially, when oil revenues make such an undertaking easy to do if only there were the will to do so.[26] In fact, the maintaining of a Palestinian refugee problem serves as a political necessity for Israel's enemies as they attempt to win the propaganda war in international discourse. Millions of Palestinians remain in refugee camps while the Arab nations refuse to assimilate them for political reasons.[27]

Now what can be made of such discussions? First, one must point out that the debate over the ethical treatment of Arabs in Palestine by Israelis supported by the United States, which in turn is heavily influenced by pro-Israel dispensational theology, involves primarily an interpretation of *history* and not theology. For example, differences as those discussed above do not involve one's interpretation of the story of the Good Samaritan. Dispensationalists heartily concur with Jesus' given teaching and believe it to be universally applicable to Arabs in the Middle East as well as Jews in Israel. What divides dispensationalists from their critics at this juncture is an analysis of the facts on the ground, so to speak. How does one interpret the history of the rise of modern Zionism and the happenings in the Middle East leading up to the present time? Enough details have been cited above to suggest why dispensationalists enjoy the upper hand.

Second, the issue that has emerged and is alluded to in the critiques of dispensationalism's powerful influence in Middle Eastern political affairs is that pro-Israel theology leads dispensationalists to overlook treatment of the other side. In other words, the theological bent serves as a presuppositional grid which does not allow dispensationalists to consider the misdeeds of Israel or have a fair and balanced treatment of issues in the region. To be sure, the dispensationalist must be true to the facts of history, accurate in understanding current events, and exact in his exegesis of Scripture. This means that no genuine Israeli oppression of the Arabs can be justified and must be opposed even by dispensational Christian Zionists. The dispensationalist would also hasten to say that the correct interpretation of alleged Israeli oppression is not to be determined by any anti-Israeli American press coverage on CNN or by the imaginations found at Al Jazeera. An honest attempt must be made toward full objectivity.

In addition to these basic thoughts, the dispensationalist needs to remind his critics that they too must be equally leery of a potential bias on

---

[26] Mitchell G. Bard, *Myth and Facts: A Guide to the Arab-Israeli Conflict* (Chevy Chase, MD: American-Israeli Cooperative Enterprise, 2001), 182-85.

[27] Ibid., 185-87.

their part. For example, the position of preterism which, among other theological positions, has no future for national Israel, might be prone to lead to a presuppositional grid leaning unfairly toward the Arabs and against Israel. In fact, the existence of Israel in the land since 1948 could potentially turn out to be the precursor to God's final plan for that nation in the judgment of the tribulation period followed by its national and spiritual restoration to kingdom glory at the return of Christ. This potential alone has kept some (perhaps many) evangelicals from taking seriously the preterist proposal that most or all prophecies relative to the Second Coming have already been fulfilled. Such a circumstance could provide a strong motive for holding a pro-Arab or an anti-Israel position. After all, the preterist's ability to defend his views within the evangelical community would probably be enhanced if Israel was simply not in the land. This example shows that bias on the other side is equally plausible. Both sides need to examine their presuppositions and let the Bible arbitrate final decisions, not current events or status. Dispensationalists no doubt take great satisfaction in knowing that the earliest dispensationalists in modern times taught the same interpretation of the Bible without Israel being in the land. In the end, there will probably be no fruitful dialog in the debate between dispensationalists and their critics if the avenue of discussion is damage caused by presuppositions.

Dispensationalism, War-Mongering, and Self-Fulfilling Prophecy

There is no question that some dispensationalists have acted in ways attempting to help prophecy along. For example, William E. Blackstone (1841-1935), who founded the Chicago Hebrew Mission in 1887, wrote a stirring summary of Bible prophecy entitled *Jesus is Coming* (1878), a fairly accurate work that is still in print. In addition to social and evangelistic outreach to Jews, he had a heart to see the Jews return to their homeland in Palestine. This was not merely a theological wish on his part nor did he leave it up to the rest of history to bring about. Instead, Blackstone, whom Brog calls the "Father of American Zionism," made specific efforts to bring about the national homeland of the Jews.[28] Concerned about the horrible plight of Russian Jews, Blackstone organized a petition with the signature of 413 prominent Americans, which was sent with a letter to President Benjamin Harrison in 1891.[29] The petition, which later came to be called the

---

[28] Brog, *Standing with Israel*, 97.
[29] The activities of Blackstone on behalf of Zionism have been well covered by both pro-Zionists and critics. See Brog, *Standing with Israel*, 98-118 and Weber, *On the Road to Armageddon*, 102-07.

Blackstone Memorial, called for the support of the American government for the return of the Jews to their own nation, which had been taken from them by the Romans in 70 A.D. Although action was not taken by President Harrison, the petition was revived and presented to President Woodrow Wilson on June 30, 1917. In October of that year, Wilson sent word to the British government that he was sympathetic with the idea of a homeland for Israel. The next month the British government authorized the idea of statehood for the Jews in Palestine in the famous Balfour Declaration. What makes the statement viable at that time is that the British were soon expected to capture Jerusalem from the Ottomans, which they did in December 1917.

All in all, Blackstone's desire to help oppressed Russian Jews, something that foreshadowed the world's response to the Holocaust after World War II, was a noble one. If his desire to help them also coincided with his belief in Bible prophecy about the end-times, so much the better. However, in more recent times, the charge has been leveled at dispensationalism that portrays such involvement as an evil in its own right. For example, David Carlson, one detractor, regrets the notion that the book of Revelation is taken in a literal fashion and that Bible prophecy is taken to support present-day Israel. Notice the strong wording: "In this view, not only are Palestinians of no value, but the sole reason for Jews to return to Israel is to hasten the slaughter that triggers the return of Christ."[30] This disturbing rant against dispensationalists sees them as anti-Arab and anti-Israeli simultaneously. The goal in mind for dispensationalists is the Second Coming of Christ. They desire to see, in Carlson's view, the awful tribulation period with its wars and judgments killing millions upon millions of people. Supporting Israel speeds this process up so we can get to the Second Coming. In this scheme dispensationalists are presented as not caring about any individuals along the way. No wonder that the same author elsewhere describes dispensationalism as the view where "Israeli displacement of Palestinian villages...is celebrated as a necessary part of God's plan."[31] Furthermore, Carlson notes, "An upside-down Christianity emerges with premillennial dispensationalism. It creates a skewed view of the Christian faith that welcomes war and disaster, while dismissing peace efforts in the

---

[30] David Carlson, "'Left Behind' and the Corruption of Biblical Interpretation," *OrthodoxyToday.org* (2003), <http://www.orthodoxytoday.org/articles/CarlsonPremillenial.php> (accessed 11 October 2006). Carlson is Professor of Religious Studies at Franklin College, Franklin, Indiana. According to this posted article he is also Greek Orthodox.
[31] Ibid.

Middle East and elsewhere—all in the name of Christ."[32] One can easily visualize such critics correlating the so-called dark side of dispensationalism here with the "cowboy diplomacy" of President Bush and his relatively harder line toward the Arabs, the War on Terror, and the war in Iraq.

On the face of it, such a harsh analysis comes across as mere emotionalism with nothing that is logically compelling. First of all, is it really fair to say that dispensationalists *welcome* war? Even if one assumes the most die-hard dispensationalist possible, to say that one is *expecting* war is not the same thing as affirming that one *wants* war. There is no glee or emotional satisfaction that dispensationalists get out of knowing that war is on the horizon in light of the Bible's predictions. The Bible has predicted many things, some of which have been fulfilled in the past, which were not positive experiences. For example, the text of the Bible predicts the death of Ahab and Jezebel in grizzly detail (1 Kings 21:17-24), the political intrigues and murders during the Greek period (Dan. 11:3-35), and war during the reign of David (2 Sam. 12:10ff). There are countless examples of these kinds throughout the pages of the Bible. To affirm the truth of the Bible in its predictions of war with past or future fulfillment does not turn the interpreter into a war-monger. Perhaps some of the reluctance on the part of many dispensationalists to support various peace initiatives in the Arab-Israeli conflict is founded on the track record of the Arabs which has been described earlier. At this point in history, the anti-Zionist actions of many Arabs speak louder than any peace treaty proposals. The recycling of peace proposals that are then broken may be a better explanation for the dispensational reluctance, especially when the stated goal of so many Arabs is the elimination of the nation of Israel. If all of the Arab peoples would live in peaceful harmony with Israel at this present moment in history, dispensationalists would rise up and rejoice.

Secondly, the claim that dispensationalists want to help prophecy along by influencing American policy to lead to war and conflict in the Middle East falls to the ground due to a lack of detailed information about what the dispensational position actually entails. Dispensationalists believe in a pre-tribulational rapture of the Church. True Church-Age believers will be taken to be with the Lord before the dreadful day of the Lord (tribulation period of seven years) happens on the earth. As individuals, Christians will have no direct involvement or personal stake in what goes on during that time since they will not be here. Moreover, war is not a necessary pre-condition for the rapture of the Church to take place. A critic could respond by noting that a

---

[32] Ibid.

speeding up of the events that could lead to the tribulation will of necessity move the possibility of the rapture closer to our own time. In reply, it must be noted that the only biblical prerequisites for the tribulation to take place are the existence of Israel in the land and the rise of Antichrist—these two parties sign a *peace* treaty that begins the seven-year tribulation (Dan. 9:27). In light of these prophetic realities and the love for Israel that dispensationalists possess for God's chosen people, dispensationalists should be viewed as seeking the security of Israel and not happily pursuing war.

One final comment must be made in this regard. The book of Revelation, whose literal interpretation Carlson disdained in the quote above, teaches clearly that God's ways are true and just (Rev. 19:2). These ways, on any interpretive scheme of the book, include judgment upon people for sin. Therefore, to impugn the details of the book taken at face value may also, in the end, impugn the character of God. Most dispensationalists have a healthy regard for God's bigger role in all of this, including those like William Blackstone. It is God's prerogative to bring the rapture, tribulation, Second Coming of Christ to earth, and the kingdom in His own timing and His own way in keeping with His revealed Word. Dispensationalists understand that there is a bigger player on the field who gets to bat more often.

Conclusion

Moslems have no doubt read the book of Genesis, taking special notice of the land boundaries promised to Abraham and his children: "To your descendents I have given this land, from the river of Egypt as far as the great river, the river Euphrates" (Gen. 15:18; NASB). Most dispensationalists understand this text in harmony with the Moslem reading—the boundaries are from the Nile River in Egypt to the Euphrates in modern day Iraq. Both dispensationalists and Moslems have noticed that the land boundaries have never been realized for Israel. Mitchell Bard notes, "In Iran, a map purporting to show Israel's 'dream' boundaries – an empire including Saudi Arabia, Iraq, Kuwait, and parts of Turkey and Iran – was included in a 1985 reprint of the *Protocols of the Elders of Zion*, the notorious Czarist forgery."[33] Similarly, there is a myth commonly believed in the Islamic world that a large map hanging in the Israeli parliament documents the Israeli hunger to obtain the entire empire indicated by the land boundaries.[34] This myth is maintained tenaciously even though there is not one documented soul,

---

[33] Bard, *Myths and Facts*, 113.
[34] Ibid.

including a Moslem, who has seen the map. To counter the claim that Israel is clandestinely planning the conquest of those lands through war one only has to look once again at the history of modern Israel. When it has been attacked, it has put down its enemies and generally given back the land obtained, some of it more than once (Sinai). Of course, there is the question of the West Bank, the disputed "occupied" territory. However, even on the wildest imagination, one can not turn Israel's reluctance to give it up into a campaign to march to the Euphrates. Dispensationalists know that Messiah will one day give the entire land promised to Abraham to Israel at the beginning of His coming kingdom. Therefore, there is no need to posit some theological need to pursue conquest in the present hour. Current dispensationalists, no doubt in harmony with President Bush, only wish for the Arabs and other Moslems to leave Israel alone.[35]

---

[35] One related subject that is beyond the scope of this paper is the theological issue of the Jewish possession of the land while in unbelief from a Christian point of view. I have responded to this question to some degree in Mike Stallard, "A Dispensational Response to the Knox Seminary Open Letter to Evangelicals," *The Journal of Ministry and Theology* 7 (Fall 2003): 5-41. See also John Piper, "Land Divine?" *World Magazine* (May 11, 2002). A corollary of this line of thought would be the question, from a dispensational point of view, of whether Israel can be removed from the land in the course of present human affairs with the dispensational theological perspective still intact. My answer is "yes" in terms of biblical reasoning, but the dispensational tradition needs to wrestle with this question a bit more than it normally does.

"The success of your study will be measured by the godliness of your life. May you always be an "A" student of prophecy."

- Charles C. Ryrie

The Final Countdown, 1982, page 120

23

Biblical Prophecy: An Essential Element in Living a Genuine & Useful Christian Life[1]

Paul N. Benware

Some years ago a woman approached this author at the beginning of a prophecy conference where the author was ministering and informed him that she was not a fan of messages on Bible prophecy. This author was, of course, intrigued as to why this was the case. Her reason was that she was tired of the speculation and the sensationalism that seemed to always surround prophetic preaching. What she wanted was a Bible message that helped her to live her Christian life in a more authentic way. She felt that when Jesus returns, then He will return and there is nothing that can be done to hinder or hasten His return. Meanwhile, she had to live her Christian life in the "real" world. Bible prophecy to her lacked substance and was simply not relevant with "real life." What she failed to recognize was that "real life" can only be lived to its fullest when prophetic truth is known and embraced by the believer.

At another prophecy conference where the author was participating, the pastor of the church said he was very glad that this author was there, since he knew very little about Bible prophecy and felt his people should have some exposure to the subject. It seems that at the seminary he attended, the consensus was that eschatology was so unclear and controversial that time was better spent on matters of greater significance. The pastor did not seem to be convinced of this but nevertheless was a product of that school which helped shape his approach to preaching and teaching. What he failed to appreciate was that prophecy was a key ingredient in bringing his people into a genuine walk with the Lord, the very thing he wanted to witness in his church.

The woman and the pastor seem to represent a significant part of the church today. Unfortunately it is true that prophecy has been abused by too many preachers and, of course, by non-preachers such as those on the History Channel. However, the church must not ignore biblical prophecy or marginalize it to the periphery of the unimportant. Pastors who do not

---

[1] Reprinted with permission from Paul N. Benware, Biblical Prophecy: An Essential Element in Living a Genuine and Useful Christian Life, in the *Journal of Dispensational Theology*, Vol. 11, No. 32, March 2007

regularly include the truths of the prophetic Word in their preaching and teaching deprive their people of one of the most significant elements in living godly, authentic Christian lives in today's world. In doing so, they really do a terrible disservice to their people.

Those who fail to inform their flock of things to come do not follow the example of Christ and the Apostles whose teachings were peppered through and through with truths about future things. Even New Testament writings that are not normally considered eschatological are filled with exhortations and instructions based on future events. For example, James made eight such references in his letter and Peter referred to prophetic events almost thirty times in his two epistles. Jude, Hebrews, and Paul's writings are simply packed with statements about future events. The Gospels record dozens and dozens of statements about future things in the teachings of the Lord Jesus. Why is there such an emphasis on prophetic events in the ministries of Christ and the Apostles? It is because they knew that these truths about the future are essential in living a life that is wise, holy, and godly. These truths give the believer needed strength to "press on toward the goal for the prize of the upward call of God" while at the same time cultivating the much needed "two world view" in the mind and heart of the believer.

The Biblical "Two World View"

A "two world view" can be described as *living well for Jesus Christ in this world because there is a clear focus on the world to come.* When believers do have this clear focus on and understanding of the world to come, their lives will be lived with greater authenticity and with greater consistency. This is *the* biblical approach to life found in the Scriptures whether it be the Old Testament saint who "died in faith, without receiving the promises, but having seen them and having welcomed them from a distance, and having confessed that they were strangers and exiles on the earth" (Heb 11:13) or the New Testament saint who understood that "the sufferings of this present time are not worthy to be compared with the glory that is to be revealed to us" (Rom 8:18).[2] Furthermore, it has been the thinking of serious Christians over the centuries. Years ago, C. S. Lewis observed the need for this "two world view."

> Hope is one of the theological virtues. This means that a continual looking forward to the eternal world is not (as some modern people think) a form of escapism or

---

[2] Scripture quotations are from the *New American Standard Bible*.

wishful thinking, but one of the things that a Christians is meant to do. It does not mean that we are to leave the present world as it is. If you read history you will find that the Christians who did the most for the present world were just those who thought most of the next. The Apostles themselves, who set on foot the conversion of the Roman Empire, the great men who built up the Middle Ages, the English Evangelicals who abolished the Slave Trade, all left their mark on Earth precisely because their minds were occupied with Heaven. It is since Christians have largely ceased to think of the other world that they have become so ineffective in this world. Aim at heaven and you will get earth "thrown in": aim at earth and you will get neither.[3]

One can only wonder what he might write today as he analyzed the North American church in this new millennium.

Over the last few decades, it seems that the vision of the world to come has become badly blurred in the American church. Evidence seems to indicate that many have steadily embraced more of a "one world view" which focuses instead on improving one's lot in the present world. Much of the emphases of contemporary preaching and writing have been on how one can "succeed" and enjoy life here and now. However, while many have been hard at work trying to recreate Eden now, many have strayed from the path walked by the saints of old. These understood that while God has granted many good things to enjoy in this world (1 Tim 4:4-5), this world must not be the focus since believers are strangers and aliens (Heb 11:9, 13; 1 Pet 2:11).

The one world view that is prevailing in the church has resulted in scandalous behavior that is destroying the vitality and impact of the evangelical church in North America. According to a recent article based on current studies by Gallup and Barna, American Christians "are as likely to embrace lifestyles every bit as hedonistic, materialistic, self-centered, and sexually immoral as the world in general."[4] This situation is not the product of a biblical "two world view."

Understanding and embracing biblical prophecy will have significant, positive results in the believer's life. The following realities are set forth in the Scriptures and are worthy of thoughtful consideration.

---

[3] C. S. Lewis, *Mere Christianity* (New York: Macmillan, 1952), 118.

[4] Ronald J. Sider, "The Scandal of the Evangelical Conscience" (accessed 28 February 2007) available from http://www.christianitytoday.com/bc/2005/001/3.8.html.

Biblical Prophecy Understood and Embraced Gives Needed Help in the Struggle against Personal Sin

Serious believers are very aware of the "sin which so easily entangles us" (Heb 12:1) and sincerely desire that their flesh was not so powerful. However, these also understand that focusing on the Lord's return and appearance before Him, which could be at any moment, is a great help in dealing with personal sin. One can say "no" to many sinful and suspect things in this world when looking towards heaven waiting "for a Savior, the Lord Jesus Christ" (Phil 3:20).

Imagine for a moment that the angel Gabriel appeared at your bedside tonight and provided the knowledge that Jesus was going to return sometime this month. Assuming it truly was Gabriel, does the reader think he would have a serious problem with sin from that moment onward? Would pornography on the Internet be a successful seduction? Would angry, hateful statements flow from the reader's lips? Would the reader involve himself in power struggles or politicking? Would the reader find himself coveting and envying? It is seriously doubted. Would the reader want to be as spotless as possible when the Savior appeared and any sin that wiggled its way into his life would immediately be shunned? This is the Apostle John's point when he wrote to believers to remain in vital fellowship with Christ so that at His return no one would be embarrassed by ongoing sinful behavior.

> And now little children, abide in Him, so that when He appears, we may have confidence and not shrink away from Him in shame at His coming. If you know that He is righteous, you know that every one also who practices righteousness is born of Him. . . . Every one who has this hope fixed on Him purifies himself, just as He is pure (1 John 2:28-29; 3:3).

It is obvious that John placed active responsibility on the believer himself to keep sin from his life. While it is, of course, the powerful blood of Christ that cleanses the believer from sin, he nevertheless is responsible to deal with sin by keeping it as far from his life as possible. According to John, the coming of Christ will either be a time of "confidence" or "shame" for the believer and this reality is to energize him in his efforts to be pure. The Apostle Peter had the same emphasis.

> Since all these things are to be destroyed in this way, what sort of people ought you to be in holy conduct and godliness. . . . Therefore, beloved, since you look for these things, be diligent to be found by Him in peace, spotless and blameless (2 Pet 3:11, 14).

Therefore, if Christians are not anticipating the Lord's return and of their subsequent appearance before Him, are they not deprived of one great spiritual reality in fighting against the flesh and sin? And is that not the very thing that is reflected today? "Scandalous behavior is rapidly destroying American Christianity. By their daily activity, most 'Christians' regularly commit treason. With their mouths they claim that Jesus is Lord, but with their actions they demonstrate allegiance to money, sex and self-fulfillment."[5]

Sider's article, "The Scandal of the Evangelical Conscience," documented that the rate of divorce, involvement in pornography, attitudes towards money, cohabitation with a member of the opposite sex, racism, and a number of other vital issues reveal almost no difference between believers and the non-Christian. Apparently these believers are giving little serious thought to seeing Christ and living in light of that event. Biblical prophecy understood and embraced can provide needed resolve and empowerment in dealing with sin and the flesh.

Biblical Prophecy Reminds the Believer that He Will Give an Account of His Life and Will Gain or Lose Reward as a Result of How He Lives

Believers, along with all other creatures, must give an account to the Lord God. Salvation does not remove the believer from being accountable to the Lord. Many in the church correctly place emphasis on the believer's secure position when they place their faith in Christ alone, but then fail to balance this with the truth that our faithful works for Christ are significant in determining the kind of life the Christian will experience in the coming Kingdom.

The Scriptures inform the church that believers will be judged first and then unbelievers (cf. 1 Pet 4:17; Luke 19:15-27). The salvation of the believer is not the issue at this Judgment Seat of Christ, but rather it is the believer's works that will be evaluated. And this evaluation by the Lord Jesus will result in the receiving of rewards or the losing of them.

> . . . it is still possible for them to feel shame in the presence of Christ, and particularly at His Judgment Seat. There is nothing strange about this. Even though eternal salvation is an entirely free gift which can never be lost, the New Testament makes plain that the believer must give an account of his or her Christian life in the presence of Christ . . . this judgment is not merely a review of our good deeds, but a comprehensive review that embraces both "good and bad". . . .[6]

---

[5] Ibid.
[6] Zane C. Hodges, *The Epistles of John* (Irving: GTS, 1999), 125.

For we must all appear before the judgment seat of Christ, that each one may be recompensed for his deeds in the body, according to what he has done, whether good or bad" (2 Cor 5:10).

If any man's work which he has built upon it remains, he shall receive a reward. If any man's work is burned up, he shall suffer loss, but he himself shall be saved, yet so through fire (1 Cor 3:14-15).

Do you not know that those who run in a race all run, but only one receives the prize. Run in such a way that you may win. And everyone who   competes   in the games exercises self-control in all things. They then do it to receive a perishable wreath, but we an imperishable (9:24).

The idea that all believers will be the same in the future is simply false and contrary to the consistent teachings of the Bible.[7] Such a view does not deal adequately with the many warnings given to unfaithful believers about negatives they face when appearing before Christ.

No wise parent treats rebellion and obedience in the same way. Suppose that Dad and Mom left for a weekend retreat and gave careful instructions to their two teenage sons. Each was given three specific tasks that were to be finished by the time their parents returned on Sunday afternoon. Now, the younger son woke at a reasonable time on Saturday morning and finished all his work by early afternoon, doing a very good job. The older son slept late and did not complete any work, choosing instead to go and have fun with his friends. By Sunday afternoon he had completed none of his three tasks. When their parents returned home, Dad correctly appraised the situation. He called for his two boys and congratulated the younger son for a job well done, and then reached into his wallet and unexpectedly gave him a $50 bill. The older son now regretted his disobedience and poor use of time. The father looked unhappily at his older boy, rebuked him for his disobedience but then reached into his wallet and gave his older son $50 also. How unreal! No good father would ever do that, rewarding good behavior and bad behavior in the same way. And yet that seems to be the prevailing opinion in the church regarding the way in which the Heavenly Father will deal with His children.

The Word of God teaches that there are rewards that will be received because of faithful service of Christ and there are rewards that can be lost by unfaithfulness (cf. 1 Cor 3:15; 2 John 8; Col 3:23-25). The faithful believer will be given "crowns" (e.g. 1 Cor 9:24-27; 1 Pet 5:3); receive that

---

[7] Paul Benware, *The Believer's Payday* (Chattanooga: AMG Publishers, 2002), 21-56.

desired commendation of "well done" by the Lord (Luke 19:17; Matt 25:21, 23) and, be granted a place of ruling alongside Messiah (e.g. 2 Tim 2:11-13; Luke 19:17, 19). The believer who is unfaithful to the Lord Jesus will not receive crowns, may well be addressed by Christ as a "worthless slave" (cf. Luke 19:22), and will not reign with Him (cf. 2 Tim 2:11-13; Luke 19:24-26). Their salvation is secure, but their rewards are not. Believers have a secure inheritance because they are children of God, but there is another aspect of inheritance that depends on being a faithful child of God. This inheritance (not salvation) can be lost. "Simple faith brings assurance of heaven. Persistent faith brings inheritance."[8] What believers do in this life will have a very real effect on life in the coming kingdom of God. After exhorting believers to be holy as their Heavenly Father is holy, the Apostle Peter stated, "And if you address as Father the One who impartially judges according to each man's work, conduct yourselves in fear during the time of your stay upon earth" (1 Pet 1:17).

One wonders why Peter would exhort the church to "fear" if it really does not actually matter what believers accomplish or do not accomplish in this life. However, according to the New Testament, the works done by believers are important and do have consequences beyond this life. This author doubts that Peter and the other New Testament writers would subscribe to the teaching that all will be the same in the future kingdom of God. The knowledge of a coming time of accountability and rewarding can have a profound impact on the way believers live today. However, without such truth the "one world" view will prevail in the thinking and in the living of Christians.

Biblical Prophecy Provides a Valuable Mindset in Times of Trial and Temptation

The fact that believers are faced with some burdensome and painful trials in this life is not a new revelation. The church knows that God has not exempted believers from the sudden death of a loved one, or the arrival of a debilitating disease, or the appearance of great financial loss. Moreover,

---

[8] Michael Eaton, *No Condemnation: A New Theology of Assurance* (Downers Grove: Intervarsity, 1995), 181. In a thought provoking study, Eaton believes that both Calvinism and Arminianism are too rigid in their concept of "inheritance." He observed that in both the Old and New Testament, inheritance is seen as a reward for obedience and that inheritance does not come by initial faith alone but by persistence in faith. This author would agree with much that Eaton wrote and argue that passages like Galatians 5:21, Ephesians 5:5, and 1 Corinthians 6:9 which speak of the loss of an inheritance in God's kingdom is written to believers, yet the reference is not the loss of salvation but rather the loss of reward. While many would say this is a warning to the "professed believer," the passages themselves were written to believers and there is not a professed believer in sight. See also, Benware, *The Believer's Payday*, 22-40.

even if such "major tragedies" do not enter the believer's life, the child of God still experiences scores of "minor" pressure, grief, disappointment, and setback.

James, and others, observed that believers can respond well or they can respond poorly to the painful times in life. In order for trials to be successfully endured, James said that the believer must possess God's wisdom, which is seeing life from God's perspective. An integral part of God's perspective is the future. This is how Jesus faced the trial of His crucifixion. The writer of Hebrews said that Jesus "for the joy set before Him endured the cross, despising the shame, and has sat down at the right hand of the throne of God" (12:2). Jesus looked beyond those six hours on the cross to that time in His glorious kingdom when He would be with those that He would redeem and restore.

The believer who is focused on this world will likely not do well in trials when things go terribly wrong in this world. Without a working knowledge of things to come, he will have to fall back on the "stiff upper lip" approach or to wishful thinking. However, the believer who anticipates the glorious age to come will be better positioned to deal well with the pain and disappointment that accompany trials in this world.

After speaking about the universality of trials and the need for God's wisdom, James referenced the future (Jas 1:12). The "crown of life", also mentioned in Revelation 2:10, does seem to focus on the future reward given to the believer who loves the Lord so much that he does not resent what the Lord has allowed into his life. An incentive for enduring in trials is the understanding that there is future reward for the enduring believer. "Blessed is the man who perseveres under trial; for once he has been approved, he will receive the crown of life, which the Lord has promised to those who love Him" (Jas 1:12).

As James' letter came to a close, the author returned to the matter of the trials of life and the need to patiently endure like Job and the prophets of old. And here, James again appealed to the future to give strength to his friends.

> Be patient, therefore, brethren, until the coming of the Lord. . . . You too be patient; strengthen your hearts, for the coming of the Lord is at hand. Do not complain, brethren, against one another, that you yourselves may not be judged; behold, the Judge is standing right at the door (5:7-9).

Peter gave the same kind of encouragement.

> In this you greatly rejoice, even though now for a little while, if necessary, you have been distressed by various trials, that the proof of your faith, being more precious than gold which is perishable, even though tested by fire, may be found to result in praise and glory and honor at the revelation of Jesus Christ (1 Pet 1:6-7).

What believers need in times of trial is not positive thinking, but prophetic thinking.

Biblical Prophecy Gives Protection to Believers from False Teachers and their False Teaching

Sometimes when believers view certain religious teachers on television, they wonder what attracts people to them and their teachings. Their messages are devoid of any real biblical substance and yet their followers seem to hang on every superficial word uttered. This religious "happy hour" seems to draw many sane and sensible people, but nevertheless they appear mesmerized by such nonsense. What is the magnet that draws people to these teachers?

False teaching characteristically has a "one world" focus and a person who is not indoctrinated with a "two world" perspective will easily fall prey to this kind of false teaching. The Apostles warned the church that the basic element in much of false teaching is "lust." Lust (ejpiqumiva) does not, as some think, simply refer to immorality. While immorality is included, the word rather refers to wrong desires of any kind.[9] God, of course, has given mankind many desires that are legitimate and normal. However, these desires are elevated by false teachers to *a place of lordship* in peoples' lives. Subsequently, health, personal comfort, wealth, enjoyment in life, good kids and a good marriage, positions of prominence, material possessions, and a host of other desires become the focus of life. These all can have legitimacy in their rightful place (cf. 1 Tim 4:4-5) but in false teaching they become the "lords of life."

This focus on the "good life" in this present world is the reason for the immense popularity of false teachers. They appeal to the natural desires that people have and inform their followers that God is quite happy when they pursue these things in this world. This "one world view" teaches that the most important life is right now. According to the Apostles, "lust" is the common element in the teachings of these teachers who themselves love money, pleasure, and personal comfort (2 Tim 3:2-4).

---

[9] Johannes P. Louw and Eugene A. Nida, *Greek-English Lexicon of the New Testament* (New York: United Bible Societies, 1989), 1:290-291; F. Wilbur Arndt and William F. Gingrich, *A Greek-English Lexicon of the New Testament and Other Early Christian Literature* (Chicago: University of Chicago Press, 1952), 293.

For the time will come when they will not endure sound doctrine; but wanting to have their ears tickled, they will accumulate for themselves teachers in accordance to their own desires ("lust,"); and will turn away their ears from the truth, and will turn aside to myths (4:3-4).

And many will follow their sensuality, and because of them the way of the truth will be maligned. . . . For speaking out arrogant words of vanity they entice by fleshly desires ("lust,"), by sensuality. . . . Knowing this first of all, that in the last days mockers will come with their mocking, following after their own lusts (2 Pet 2:2, 18; 3:3)

These are grumblers, finding fault, following after their own lusts; they speak arrogantly, flattering people for the sake of gaining an advantage (Jude 1:18).

When the Apostles spoke against these teachings that promote and encourage "lust" (wrong desire), they at the same time looked ahead to future events. Peter spoke of the coming day of the Lord, of the certainty of future judgment, and of the wonderful world to come (2 Pet 2:9, 17; 3:7, 10-13). Jude also spoke of the sure judgment to come, using examples of past judgments (Jude 1:4-7, 15). Paul reminded Timothy that God will judge these false teachers at Christ's return and will also reward those who have been faithful to the Word and stayed away from false teaching (2 Tim 4:1, 8).

It seems clear that if a believer consciously lives day by day reflecting on the Lord's return, the Judgment Seat of Christ, and the glorious coming Kingdom that this believer will not be drawn into the one world view and the "lusts" of false teaching. However, if the believer is not informed by these truths of the future, then he will be far more susceptible to such things. It is much easier to say "no" to self when looking for something that is far superior. Is that not what Hebrews 11 is promoting?

Biblical Prophecy Provides a Framework for a Believer to Prioritize Life Better and Make Better Decisions

Everyone knows that if a person had knowledge of future events, then better decisions would be made. For example, would Fred take a job next week with the ABC Company if he knew that in four months the ABC Company would be going bankrupt? Would the Jones family buy that house down by the river if they knew that next spring the "flood of the century" would wash away all dwellings by that river? Or would the remodeling of an old home be the priority in the lives of Bill and Sue if they knew that it would burn to the ground as soon as it was completed? Knowledge of the future would, in these cases, undoubtedly reshape decisions and priorities.

Bible prophecy can play such a life-changing role today. When believers become convinced of the truthfulness of these prophetic portions dealing with accountability and reward, they will prioritize life differently, make better decisions, and order their lives in a much more biblical way. The reality of future things sheds significant light on the important issues of life and provides a framework for evaluating what is most important. Those who live with an awareness of what lies ahead in the plan of God think differently regarding the use of their time, money, and resources. The goals and purposes of life are altered by a conviction about future realities. Again, note the Apostle Peter's exhortation when he said, "what sort of people ought you to be in holy conduct and godliness" in view of future events (2 Pet 3:11).

After Jesus gave His powerful prophetic discourse on the Mount of Olives (cf. Matt 24—25), He then gave six parables which emphasized three things. He said that in light of these coming events, His followers were to: (1) be watching expectantly for His return, (2) be prepared spiritually for His arrival, and (3) be faithfully serving Him until He returned. What His servants do is of great importance to Him and He advised them to order their lives according to the prophetic truths He had just revealed. And these three attitudes are exactly what biblical prophecy is designed to produce in the day by day living of God's people.

Biblical Prophecy Reveals the End of Evil and of the Unbeliever

The problem of the presence and apparent success of evil has been a thorny theological and philosophical problem for all of man's history. Biblical prophecy does not deal with the origin of evil but it does deal with the end of evil. Wickedness will not prevail and evil people will be punished and will not "get away with murder." It is clear that evil and evildoers will be removed from life that will be experienced forever in God's eternal kingdom.

> But according to His promise we are looking for new heavens and a new earth, in which righteousness dwells (2 Pet 3:13)

> . . . and nothing unclean and no one who practices abomination and lying, shall ever come into it, but only those who names are written in the Lamb's book of life (Rev 21:27).

> And the devil who deceived them was thrown into the lake of fire and brimstone, where the beast and the false prophet are also; and they will be tormented day and night forever and ever (20:11)

As the Scriptures describe the fate of the unbeliever, it is a terrible fate that they face. As one contemplates the eternal end of the unbeliever, it is not good to become satisfied with wonderful futures, but to be motivated by biblical prophecy to share the good news with those who futures are horrible.

> Then He will also say to those on His left, "Depart from Me, accursed ones, into the eternal fire which has been prepared for the devil and his angels. . . . and these will go away into eternal punishment. . . . (Matt 25:41, 48).

The Apostle Paul added graphically to this statement by Jesus.

> . . . when the Lord Jesus shall be revealed from heaven with His mighty angels in flaming fire, dealing out retribution to those who do not know God and to those who do not obey the gospel of our Lord Jesus. And these will pay the penalty of eternal destruction, away from the presence of the Lord and from the glory of His power (2 Thess 1:7-9).

Paul's prophetic word on the fate of unbelievers is terrifying. They not only will be sent into eternal fire, but their lives will be ruined eternally ("eternal destruction"). It is the opposite of that quality of life known commonly as "eternal life." This eliminates anyone having a good time partying in hell, or any other such nonsense. That which God designed life to be and have by way of meaning and purpose will be gone. Hiebert wrote, "This banishment from the presence of 'the Lord', the glorified Jesus, will be the very essence of eternal punishment. The result will be a negative vacuum for them, depriving them of the Lord's favor and all which gives meaning and blessedness to life."[10]

The banishment will be similar to eternal depression, where life has no meaning to it forever. Furthermore, they will be "away from the presence of the Lord." Today even the wicked are recipients of God's common grace and are therefore blessed. However, in the Lake of Fire there appears to be a complete separation from any of God's grace and mercy. Can anything be more terrible than what Paul described in these verses? These forceful statements about the fate of the unbeliever ought to resonate in the hearts of believers causing the church to be more active in proclaiming the good news that there is a powerful Savior who can deliver from the wrath of God to come. Believers who are armed with this prophetic knowledge will be encouraged by the demise of evil even though, according to what is heard

---

[10] D. Edmond Hiebert, *The Thessalonian Epistles* (Chicago: Moody Press, 1971), 292.

daily on the news, evil appears to be winning the day. In the world to come, it is righteousness that reigns supreme.

Biblical Prophecy Provides Hope Which is a Key Element in Establishing a Biblical Worldview

If there is anyone who ought to live in this world with confidence, it is the child of God (cf. Tit 2:13). If there is anyone who ought not live under the load of defeat, fear, and depression, it is the child of God. While none of the church is exempt from painful situations in life, believers should not live hopeless, negative, defeated lives because they understand where all of life is headed and that they have an amazing future as the children of God. "Let us rejoice and be glad" (Rev 19:7) will be the prevailing sentiment for the redeemed.

This attitude of hope is not wishful thinking because it is grounded in the commitment of God to restore what was lost in the Garden of Eden. Man's willful disobedience resulted in the loss of paradise, fellowship with God, and the privileged position of ruling the earth. At that moment in time, God could have destroyed everything and started over again (after all, what would He have lost but two people and six days of work). However, He promised instead that there would be restoration and reconciliation through the "seed of the woman." And, at that time, He embarked on the path that would accomplish the restoration of all things that had been lost. He chose to do this through the nation of Israel with whom He would later enter into a binding covenant agreement.

When the reader turns to Revelation 20—22, he will discover that those three things that were lost will be fully regained because of the Cross, and the powerful working of the Creator God. Unhindered fellowship with God, a wonderful paradise, and the opportunity of ruling with Messiah will again be the experience of people. Biblical prophecy make believers aware of this marvelous ending and gives them the confident expectation which assists the church in living well for Christ right now. Biblical prophecy provides the church with a clear, comprehensive worldview which in turn generates biblical hope because believers are in fellowship with a God who is faithful to His promises.

Some Concluding Thoughts

When the church thoughtfully considers the way in which biblical prophecy was used by Jesus Christ and His apostles, it is apparent that this was not a peripheral area of theology to them. They saw that these truths are powerful helps and motivators, which provide needed wisdom and strength to live godly in Christ Jesus. The woman who did not like prophetic messages because they did not help her live her Christian life simply had it all wrong. The pastor who did not preach the prophecies of the Bible because they tended to be obscure and controversial deprived his flock of the very truths needed to run this marathon known as the Christian life.

Does this doctrine of eschatology make any practical difference to believers today? If biblical prophecy is expounded clearly and correctly, and is embraced as true by believers, it will have profound effects on the way believers live their lives. Moreover, it will go a long way in correcting the damaging "one world" view that is entrenched in many churches.

.

"Like all doctrines, dispensational teaching has undergone systematization and development. In more recent times it has come under attack from a growing number of Christian leaders. Present-day dispensationalists feel strongly that their teaching is often misrepresented, and that if this were not so, many of the criticisms of dispensationalism would disappear."

- Charles C. Ryrie
Dispensationalism Today, 1965, page 9

Made in the USA
Middletown, DE
19 October 2017